TRIAL TECHNIQUES AND TRIALS

ASPEN COURSEBOOK SERIES

TRIAL TECHNIQUES AND TRIALS

ELEVENTH EDITION

THOMAS A. MAUET

Director of Trial Advocacy, Retired
and Milton O. Riepe Professor of Law, Emeritus
University of Arizona

STEPHEN D. EASTON

President
Dickinson State University
Former Dean and William T. Schwartz Professor of Law
University of Wyoming

 Wolters Kluwer

Published by Wolters Kluwer in New York.

Wolters Kluwer Legal & Regulatory U.S. serves customers worldwide with CCH, Aspen Publishers, and Kluwer Law International products. (www.WKLegaledu.com)

Cover image: iStock.com/ftwitty

Video icon: Icon made by Kiranshastry from www.flaticon.com.

To contact Customer Service, e-mail customer.service@wolterskluwer.com, call 1-800-234-1660, fax 1-800-901-9075, or mail correspondence to:

Wolters Kluwer
Attn: Order Department
PO Box 990
Frederick, MD 21705

Printed in the United States of America

1 2 3 4 5 6 7 8 9 0

ISBN 978-1-5438-2531-2

Library of Congress Cataloging-in-Publication Data

Names: Mauet, Thomas A., author. | Easton, Stephen D., 1958- author.
Title: Trial techniques and trials / Thomas A. Mauet, Trial Advocacy,
   Retired and Milton O. Riepe Professor of Law, Emeritus, University of Arizona;
   Stephen D. Easton, President, Dickinson State University, Former Dean and William T.
   Schwartz Professor of Law, University of Wyoming.
Description: Eleventh edition. | New York : Wolters Kluwer, [2021] |
Series: Aspen coursebook series | Includes bibliographical references
   and index. | Summary: "A coursebook for law students enrolled in a Trial
   Techniques course. Also useful for practicing lawyers"—Provided by publisher.
Identifiers: LCCN 2020044650 | ISBN 9781543825312 (paperback) |
   ISBN 9781543825329 (ebook)
Subjects: LCSH: Trial practice—United States. | LCGFT: Casebooks (Law)
Classification: LCC KF8915 .M38 2021 | DDC 347.73/75—dc23
LC record available at https://lccn.loc.gov/2020044650

About Wolters Kluwer Legal & Regulatory U.S.

Wolters Kluwer Legal & Regulatory U.S. delivers expert content and solutions in the areas of law, corporate compliance, health compliance, reimbursement, and legal education. Its practical solutions help customers successfully navigate the demands of a changing environment to drive their daily activities, enhance decision quality and inspire confident outcomes.

Serving customers worldwide, its legal and regulatory portfolio includes products under the Aspen Publishers, CCH Incorporated, Kluwer Law International, ftwilliam. com and MediRegs names. They are regarded as exceptional and trusted resources for general legal and practice-specific knowledge, compliance and risk management, dynamic workflow solutions, and expert commentary.

SUMMARY OF CONTENTS

CONTENTS

CHAPTER 5

DIRECT EXAMINATIONS

CHAPTER 6

CROSS-EXAMINATIONS

CHAPTER 8

EXPERTS

CHAPTER 9

CLOSING ARGUMENTS   435

CHAPTER 11

TRIAL PREPARATION AND STRATEGY

PREFACE TO THE ELEVENTH EDITION

For the Eleventh Edition of this industry-leading text, legendary Professor Thomas A. Mauet has decided to add a co-author. He has bestowed the considerable honor of co-authorship on yours truly. As the newcomer to this project (but not to the book, as I have assigned it as required reading to my Trial Practice students for over two decades at two different law schools), I have a perspective that differs from Professor Mauet's vantage point. Permit me to make a few observations about this book that reflect that perspective.

First, it is difficult for me to imagine the teaching of trial advocacy without this book. Newcomers to the simultaneously terrifying and exhilarating world of the courtroom need a guide to the many situations they will face as student lawyers and real-world practitioners. For decades, they have turned to Professor Mauet's guidance about how to conduct a direct examination, how to get an exhibit introduced, how (and when) to object, and on and on. This book gives them that crucial starting point.

Indeed, in a sense there really was no teaching of trial advocacy before this book. A few law schools offered trial advocacy courses in the 1960s and 1970s, but only a few. Professor Mauet's first edition of *Fundamentals of Trial Techniques* appeared in 1980. This book made it possible for law schools to add trial advocacy training for their students.

The movement toward trial advocacy courses had picked up steam by the time the ABA formed the Task Force on Law Schools and the Profession in the late 1980s. The Task Force's 1992 work product, widely referred to as the MacCrate Report, criticized American law schools for their dearth of practical training. This report pumped considerable energy into the movement to teach trial advocacy, prompting many law schools to add courses in this discipline. This book was the backbone of most of those courses. It has also been used widely outside the United States.

Though Professor Mauet has now added a co-author, not much has changed. The book is still at least 98 percent Professor Mauet's work. My rather modest contributions consist largely of revising the relatively few sections that needed updating to reflect new law, making the occasionally minor editorial change, and adding a few (but only a few) short discussions of previously uncovered matters — usually about aspects of trial that seem to confound newcomers (based upon my trial advocacy teaching experience). Law students and new trial lawyers will continue to turn to the guidance and samples that Professor Mauet has provided.

This gets us squarely to the point of this book and how it should be used. Any new trial attorney, in or beyond law school, would be well served by first reviewing this book in total. (Indeed, I now require my trial advocacy students to read the entire book before the first class for my concentrated Trial Practice class.) This review will provide new trial attorneys with an impressively comprehensive overview of situations they will soon face in the courtroom.

When you face one of these situations, like the aforementioned attempt to get an exhibit introduced, go back to the relevant section of the book. First, review Professor Mauet's advice about how to best accomplish your goal. (Please do not make the mistake of turning directly to the second step.) After you have done this, but only after, turn to the specific examples in the book that most resemble the situation you face. When you do so, though, remember that these are examples, not straightjackets.

This is not a cookbook. It is, instead, a book chock full of valuable advice about how to "cook" in court, with examples that will help you get a feel for your upcoming task. Your actual time in court will almost never track the example. That, of course, is the great fun, but also the great challenge, of trial advocacy: Things happen differently than you expect. Come with a plan, to be sure, but be prepared to adjust.

That reality leads to another fundamental principle of trial advocacy that must be kept in mind when reviewing this book and its timeless advice. I call this the "default" principle. As a newcomer to trial work, you need to learn the default way to conduct a direct examination, introduce an exhibit, skewer a witness on cross, etc. In your first trials, you should endeavor to follow the default. You need to retrain your brain by jamming the default methods into it via repetition.

Defaults, though, are not "universals." For every principle of trial advocacy, even the timeworn advice that you should use leading questions on cross-examination (*see* section 6.5(1)), there are exceptions or, at least, possible exceptions. It is a major mistake to focus on or even think about the exceptions when you are in those first trials. Instead, during those first trials, you should be zealously following the defaults until they are indeed jammed into your brain. Until they become second nature, you need to force them in. Thus, for your first trials, you should only use leading questions during cross.

Once the principle has indeed become second nature, you can sometimes open yourself up to the possibility of not following the default methods. If you are a newcomer to trial advocacy, as even the most experienced of us once were, you should ignore the possibility of not following the defaults. If you think there might be an exception to the default before that default is second nature, you won't really learn the default.

Though there are a few exceptions, this book is mostly about the default tactics you need to learn well to become an effective trial attorney. Frankly, there isn't enough space in the book (or enough time in an introductory Trial Practice course) to deal with the exceptions to the default. But even more fundamentally, newcomers should be focusing exclusively on the defaults, not the exceptions.

Sometimes there is room for reasonable disagreement about the default tactics. Different trial lawyers have different experiences that lead them to different views, even about the default tactics. Even though I have tremendous respect and admiration for Professor Mauet, on a few—but only a few—occasions, I have disagreements, often minor, about the best default approaches. When I believe my views contrary to Professor Mauet's views are worthy of your consideration, I have noted them in the footnotes.

Please note, though, that there are not very many footnotes of this nature. On a huge percentage of trial tactics issues, I agree with Professor Mauet. His advice is, indeed, timely and comprehensive.

One more quick suggestion before I end this preface: Keep this book. If there is any chance you will be entering the courtroom after you graduate from law school, you will want to have this book in your office during your trial preparation and then in the briefcase you take to court. When something comes up that you have not previously experienced, you will find yourself turning to this book, as I have done many times with previous editions. In this way, Professor Mauet has sat in co-counsel's chair in thousands, if not tens of thousands, of trials. You will be glad to have him in that role in your trials.

Indeed, this book likely will be even more valuable to you than to those of us who are collecting grey hair toward the end of our trial careers. We had the good fortune of starting our practices when there were more trials. The growth of the alternative dispute resolution movement and budgetary pressures on state and federal courts have resulted in substantially fewer trials in recent decades. Thus, it probably will take you a bit longer to drill the defaults into your head, as your first trials might be spread over several years. Keep this book with you. It will help you through those first trials and then comfort and help you in later ones.

There are relatively few gems in legal writing. You are currently reading one. Congratulations on your purchase of the book and on your decision to pursue trial work!

Stephen D. Easton

Dickinson, North Dakota
November, 2020

PREFACE TO THE TENTH EDITION

Why this new text? And why now? Because both jurors and trials have changed, so trial lawyers must change as well to be successful in the new millennium.

In 1980, when *Fundamentals of Trial Techniques* was first published, psychological research on the jury trial process was in its infancy, and teaching trial skills through the learn-by-doing method was in its early stages. At that time, young lawyers learned trial skills by observing, then emulating, experienced, successful trial lawyers. *Trial Techniques* reflected this reality, by showing how experienced lawyers performed the various tasks involved in jury trials, and that became the blueprint for young lawyers.

By 2005, when *Trials—Strategy, Skills, and the New Powers of Persuasion* was first published, much had changed. Jury research showed how juror attitudes about lawsuits, courts, and lawyers have all changed. Jury research also extensively studied how juror clusters—seniors, Baby Boomers, Gen X, Gen Y—have different preferences in how they learn, how they think, and how they make decisions. *Trials* focused on the psychology of juror learning and decision making, and how these preferences have changed the way trial lawyers now perform the various tasks involved in jury trials.

In this new text I have combined *Trial Techniques* and *Trials* by taking the best from each book. From *Trial Techniques* I have kept the overall structure of the book and the chapters that discuss the trial process, the psychology of persuasion, trial preparation and strategy, and bench trials. From *Trials* I have incorporated the chapters that discuss jury selection, opening statements and closing arguments, and direct and cross-examinations. The remaining chapters take significantly from both books. The examples throughout the text now reflect the three principal kinds of trials—tort, criminal, and commercial—so that readers can either read all the examples or can focus immediately on the plaintiff's and defendant's side of a particular kind of case. The text's format has also been modernized, and the difference between text and examples has been made clearer.

In addition, the website that accompanies the text contains an edited video of a trial so that students and lawyers can see a complete jury trial in 80 minutes. The website also contains the structure and contents of a completed trial notebook that students and lawyers can use as a blueprint to customize their own trial notebooks and forms as well as all the exhibits in full color and motion from the exhibits chapter. And the website contains additional examples of opening statements, direct examinations, and closing arguments.

For the Tenth Edition, I have added dozens of video lectures and demonstrations covering key components of trial. Professor Steve Easton and I are featured in several of these lectures, as is the late Professor Irving Younger. Other lectures are presented by the skilled trial attorneys, judges, and court reporters who served as the volunteer guest faculty for the 2013 University of Wyoming Summer Trial Institute at the University of Wyoming College of Law. Thanks to Steve Easton for his skillful integration of the videos with the text.

Boxes like this one, which contain the movie camera icon, draw attention to video resources.

Finally, the teacher's manual, available to instructors, contains my suggestions on how to organize a law school trial advocacy program and how to teach trial advocacy skills effectively.

Our understanding of jury trials has changed since 1980 in several significant ways. First, we now know that juror beliefs and attitudes heavily influence whether jurors will be receptive to particular themes, messages, and evidence. Second, we know that trials must be visual, because most jurors today have been raised largely on television and computers and expect evidence during trials to be presented the same way. Third, we know that opening statements are a critical stage of the trial process where trial themes and people stories are first presented and juror impressions are first formed. Finally, trials today must be conducted efficiently, as juror attention spans have shortened. These changes have fundamentally altered how successful trial lawyers conduct themselves in all stages of a jury trial and are discussed and illustrated throughout the text.

Some things have not changed. Successful trial lawyers know that organization and preparation before trial remain essential. They know that they need effective trial skills to implement a realistic trial strategy. And they know that to get favorable verdicts they need to reach the jurors' hearts and minds. These concepts are also emphasized throughout the text.

It is the combination of understanding jury psychology, pretrial preparation, and executing a realistic trial strategy with persuasive courtroom skills that produces effective trial advocacy. *Trial Techniques and Trials* is the result of over 40 years I have spent as a trial lawyer and trial advocacy teacher. I hope you are pleased with the result.

Thomas A. Mauet

Tucson, Arizona
January 2017

Website Information

This text contains references to a website where certain additional materials can be accessed. Using the access code found inside your book, visit **www.CasebookConnect.com/Resources** for more information.

> 🌐 Website references will be called out in a website box like this.

The website contains the following:

Videos and Transcripts

Chapter 1—video of jury trial (*Gable v. Cannon*)

Chapter 4—additional opening statements in criminal case (*State v. Rausch*) and commercial case (*Thompson v. Thermorad*)

Chapter 8—additional direct examinations of experts (pathologist in criminal case; accountant in commercial case; and engineer in products case) and direct and cross-examination of an economist in a wrongful death case)

Chapter 9—additional closing arguments in criminal case (*State v. Rausch*) and commercial case (*Thompson v. Thermorad*)

Exhibits

Chapter 7—all exhibits in full color that are contained in the exhibits chapter

Trial Notebook

Chapter 11—example of a trial notebook and forms

Video Lectures and Demonstrations

You will find references to relevant lectures and demonstrations throughout the text.

> 🎥 Videos will be called out with a video text box that looks like this.

THE TRIAL PROCESS

1.1 Introduction

You have just been called into the office of a partner of the litigation firm that recently hired you. The partner tells you he has a case scheduled for trial soon that seems "just right" for you. Discovery has been completed. Pretrial motions have all been ruled on. Witnesses have been interviewed. Trial memoranda have been prepared. Settlement negotiations have just collapsed. The case now needs to be tried, and you're the person who will try it. With a smile, the partner hands you the file. Apprehensively, you walk out of his office, thinking: "My God. What do I do now?"

Jury trials are the principal method by which we resolve legal disputes parties cannot settle themselves through less formal methods. Although alternative dispute resolution methods, such as arbitration, mediation, summary trials, private trials, and the like, are becoming increasingly important, jury trials in the federal and state courts remain the most important dispute-resolving method in the United States.

In our jury trial system, the jury determines the facts, the judge determines the law, and the lawyers act as advocates for the litigants. Our adversary system is premised on the belief that pitting two adversaries against each other, with each interested in presenting her version of the truth, is the best way for the jury to determine the probable truth. The tools the litigants have, and must understand, are fourfold: substantive law, procedural law, evidence law, and persuasion "law." The first three, being principally legal, can be learned in a few years. The last, the psychology of persuasion, is what fascinates true trial lawyers, and they spend a lifetime learning about, and learning how to apply, psychology in the courtroom.

Integrating substantive law, procedural law, evidence law, and persuasion "law" and applying the result to our jury trial system is what this book is all about. Chapter 1 is an overview of the trial process. Chapter 2 discusses the psychology of persuasion. Chapters 3 through 10 cover all the specific stages of a jury trial, from jury selection through closing arguments and evidentiary objections. Chapter 11 provides a comprehensive approach to trial preparation and strategy. Chapter 12 covers bench trials and discusses how the psychology of persuasion applicable to jury trials also applies, with modifications, to bench trials.

> ■◢ For an introduction to trial advocacy, please watch Video A.1, "Wyo STI: Introduction to Trial Practice."

1.2 Local Practices and Procedures

Jurisdictions differ in how they conduct trials. First, the applicable substantive law may differ. Second, the applicable civil and criminal procedural rules may differ. Although many jurisdictions follow the Federal Rules of Civil Procedure, many do not. Criminal procedural rules vary widely. Third, the applicable evidence law may differ. Although most jurisdictions have adopted the Federal Rules of Evidence, some states, including some of the more populous ones, have not. Fourth, court rules and local rules implementing procedural statutes can vary widely. Indeed, trial procedures and customs differ from county to county and judge to judge. Judges, particularly in federal court, may impose additional limitations on the parties, such as how voir dire will be conducted, how many experts each side may call, how much time each side will have to present its case, and how much time can be used during opening statements and closing arguments.

Small wonder, then, that a trial lawyer's first job is to learn and understand all the "rules" that will be applied to the upcoming trial. Accordingly, the outline of the jury trial process in this chapter must be taken as an overview of that process. While common variations in practices and procedures will be pointed out, not all can be.

1.3 Trial Date Assignment

Cases are set for trial in two basic ways: individual calendars and central assignment systems. With individual calendars, each trial judge is responsible for the overall handling of every case assigned to that judge's docket, including setting the trial date and trying the case. In civil cases, after discovery is completed and the parties state that the case is ready to be tried, the judge will set a trial date. That date will vary, but frequently the trial date in civil cases is at least three to six months after the case is ready to be tried. Criminal cases, because of speedy trial requirements, usually get trial dates within three to four months of arrest or arraignment.

Central assignment systems are found more frequently in large urban areas. Under that system, cases remain on one central calendar for trial assignment purposes. The oldest cases are at the top. New cases then creep their way from the bottom to the top of the list. Depending on the jurisdiction, this may take from perhaps one to more than five years. When the case reaches the top, it is sent to a judge for trial. Jurisdictions having a central assignment system usually publish the trial calendar in the daily legal newspaper, and it is the lawyers' responsibility to keep track of their cases as they move up the calendar. Many jurisdictions whose court records are stored electronically also allow lawyers to access the electronic database to determine the status of any case.

1.4 Jury Selection

Congratulations! It's the day of trial. You've done all the preparatory work (discussed in Chapter 11) and the case is actually going to trial. What happens now?

You and your opposing counsel arrive in the trial judge's courtroom at the designated date and time. Clients will usually be there. Sitting on the bench is the trial judge. Other courtroom personnel will include the court clerk, court reporter, and bailiff. Other lawyers and spectators may be present.

The clerk calls the case—your case—for trial. You, your client, and the other lawyer move up and stand at the lawyers' tables in the courtroom (frequently marked "Plaintiff" and "Defendant"; if not, find out ahead of time where the sides customarily sit). The judge asks whether both sides are ready for trial. You and the other lawyer both respond "ready, your honor."

The judge next "orders a jury" and directs the bailiff or other court personnel to go to the jury room and bring a panel of 15 to 50 jurors back to the courtroom. In the meantime, the judge may again explore the possibility of settling the case, try to resolve any remaining procedural and evidentiary issues, and address any questions about how the jury will be selected. This may be done in the judge's chambers.

When the jurors are first brought into the courtroom, they usually sit in the spectator rows. The judge introduces herself, the lawyers, parties, and court personnel, mentions the case on trial, and explains how jury selection will be conducted. In a few jurisdictions, lawyers make short introductory statements about facts and issues of the case (and a few judges require opening statements before jury selection). The court clerk swears in the prospective jurors to answer questions asked by the judge and lawyers. Jury selection then begins.

How a jury is selected in a particular courtroom varies greatly, probably more than any other phase of a trial. Jury selection is controlled by statutes, court rules, and individual judicial practices. These control how jurors are initially called and qualified for jury service, how many jurors will decide the case, whether alternate jurors will be selected, the bases for cause challenges (statutory grounds to dismiss, or "strike," jurors), and the number of peremptory challenges (a party's right to strike a juror for almost any reason) each party will have and how they will be exercised. These also control what jury selection system will be used (the most common are the strike system, used in most federal courts, and the panel system, used in many state courts), the permissible topics on which jurors can be questioned (will they include questions about law or be limited to questions about jurors' backgrounds and life experiences?), and who will do the actual questioning (judge, lawyer, or both). Written questionnaires for jurors are frequently used in complex cases.

How long does the jury selection process take? While most cases take between one and three hours, in a complex or highly publicized case jury selection can take much longer. When the selection process is completed, the jurors and any alternates are sworn in by the court clerk as trial jurors to decide the case.

1.5 Preliminary Instructions of Law

After jury selection and before opening statements, the judge usually gives the jury preliminary instructions on the law. This orients the jurors and lets them know what will happen during the trial. For instance, the judge will probably summarize their duties as jurors (to follow the law, determine the facts and credibility of witnesses, and apply the facts to the law), instruct them on how to conduct themselves during recesses (do not discuss the case among yourselves or with others, do not visit the scene, and do not research the case in any way including using your cellphone or computer to do Internet research), and describe how trials are conducted. In recent years, more judges also summarize the pleadings and instruct the jury on the applicable substantive law. In a few jurisdictions, jurors are told that they may discuss the evidence during the trial when recesses occur, as long as all jurors are present in the jury room when the evidence is discussed. The judge's reading of preliminary instructions usually takes several minutes.

By this time one of the lawyers might have asked the judge to order the exclusion of witnesses during the trial (sometimes called "separating witnesses" or "invoking the rule"). This prevents witnesses from sitting in the courtroom while other witnesses are testifying. The exclusion does not apply to parties, a party's representative, or someone whose presence is essential.

> ■◖ For a discussion of exclusion of witnesses, please watch Video H.4, "Wyo STI: Exclusion of Witnesses."

Many jurisdictions permit note-taking by jurors. Some jurisdictions encourage it by providing jurors with notepads and pencils. In lengthy trials, jurors are sometimes given notebooks containing admitted exhibits, photographs of each witness, and paper for note-taking.

Other jurisdictions expressly bar note-taking. If note-taking is allowed, the notes are collected and destroyed after the jury returns its verdict.

1.6 Opening Statements

Plaintiff and defendant now give their opening statements. Opening statements are the lawyers' opportunities to tell the jury what they expect the evidence will be during the trial. This helps the jury understand the evidence when it is actually presented. The opening statements should be factual, not argumentative, although jurisdictions and judges vary considerably in how much "argument" and discussion of law they allow in opening. While many jurisdictions permit opening statements to be waived, this is rarely done.

Most opening statements are based on themes and storytelling, usually giving a chronological overview of "what happened" from either the plaintiff's or defendant's viewpoint. The statement should be engaging and memorable, presenting each side's case in the best possible light and drawing a picture that will make the jury want to find in that side's favor, and anchored to memorable, emotionally based themes. Lawyers know the importance of a good opening statement. Research has shown that most jurors return verdicts that are consistent with their impressions made during the opening statements.

How much time do the opening statements take? Most last 10 to 20 minutes per side; longer statements run the risk of either boring the jurors or overloading them with details. The judge may put time limits on opening statements as well as on other phases of the trial.

Some jurisdictions require that plaintiff's opening statement make out a prima facie case because lawyers' statements are taken as admissions. If this is the case, plaintiff's lawyer (and defendant's lawyer, if affirmative defenses or counterclaims are also involved) must be sure that the opening statement is legally sufficient.

In most jurisdictions, the defendant may reserve the opening statement until after the plaintiff has rested his case-in-chief. While this is infrequently done, the defendant may sometimes not want the plaintiff to know her specific trial strategy. (This may happen in criminal cases where the discovery rules are restrictive, and the defendant plans to present an affirmative defense and doesn't want the prosecutor to know its details.)

Finally, some judges have the lawyers make their opening statements to the entire jury panel, before jury selection is conducted. The idea is that jurors will be more likely to disclose attitudes they have that might affect their suitability to be jurors if they know more about the case being tried.

1.7 Plaintiff's Case-in-Chief

Plaintiff, having the burden of proof, presents evidence first. (This is always the case, unless defendant has admitted the plaintiff's claims, so that only affirmative defenses or counterclaims, on which the defendant has the burden of proof, remain to be proved.) This means that in the plaintiff's case-in-chief, plaintiff must present sufficient proof on each element of each legal claim alleged in the complaint or indictment, using four possible sources of proof: witnesses, exhibits, judicial notice, and stipulations.

When a witness is called to testify, he is first sworn to tell the truth by the court clerk. Once the witness is seated in the witness chair, questioning begins. Direct examination is that part of the questioning done by the plaintiff's lawyer (the side calling the witness). When the direct is completed (the lawyer usually says "nothing further on direct, your honor," "pass the witness," or "your witness," depending on local custom), the defendant's lawyer begins cross-examination. In most jurisdictions, the scope of the cross-examination is limited to the subject matter of the direct. A few states, however, follow the "English rule" under which cross-examination can go into any relevant matter.

When the cross-examiner announces she is done, the direct examiner may conduct a redirect examination (limited to explaining or refuting matters brought out on cross). The cross-examiner may be permitted to conduct a recross-examination (limited to matters brought out during the redirect). (In most jurisdictions, the judge may ask the witness questions, and a few jurisdictions allow jurors, usually through written questions submitted to the judge for approval, to ask the witness questions.) The witness is then excused, and plaintiff calls another witness.

Exhibits are the other principal source of evidence. The four principal types of exhibits are real objects (guns, blood, drugs, machinery), demonstrative exhibits (diagrams, models, maps), writings (contracts, promissory notes, checks, letters), and records (private business and public records). Exhibits need "foundations" to be admitted; that is, the party seeking to introduce the exhibit in evidence must present evidence that the exhibit complies with the applicable rules of evidence. The foundation may come from witness testimony, certification, or other methods. The formalities required in establishing the appropriate foundation for a particular exhibit vary somewhat, depending on the jurisdiction. If admitted in evidence, the exhibits may be considered by jurors just like any other evidence presented during the trial.

Judicial notice is the third method of getting information to the jury. The judge can take judicial notice when the fact is either well known in the jurisdiction where the trial is being held (the Empire State Building is in Manhattan) or the fact can be easily determined and verified from a reliable source (on July 5, 2020, the moon was full).

> ■◖ For a discussion of judicial notice and stipulations, please watch Video H.3, "Wyo STI: Profs. Easton and Younger on Judicial Notice and Stipulations."

The fourth method of proof is a stipulation, an agreement between the parties that certain facts exist and are not in dispute. This makes the presentation of undisputed evidence more efficient. Stipulations are usually made in writing and are shown or read to the jury much like any written exhibit. The judge usually instructs the jury on what a stipulation is.

In what order does plaintiff present the various witnesses, exhibits, and other evidence in his case-in-chief? This is totally up to plaintiff; whatever is most persuasive (and logistically practical) is permitted. Plaintiff must have some idea how long the witnesses are likely to testify so that he will neither run out of witnesses during the day nor have witnesses wait hour after hour to testify. Most witnesses are on the stand between 15 and 90 minutes, although some, particularly parties and experts, may take substantially longer.

When plaintiff is finished presenting all his evidence, he "rests." This is done simply by standing up and announcing to the judge and jury, "Your honor, plaintiff rests." The judge tells the jury that the plaintiff has finished presenting evidence; the judge then will probably take a recess to hear defendant's motions.

1.8 Motions After Plaintiff Rests

After plaintiff rests, and the jury has been excused and has left the courtroom, defendant usually moves for a directed verdict. While the motion may have different names in different jurisdictions (in criminal cases, for example, it is commonly called a "motion for a directed judgment of acquittal"; in federal civil cases it is called a "motion for judgment as a matter of law"), its purpose is identical. The defendant asks the judge to terminate the trial in whole or part, and enter judgment for the defense, because plaintiff has failed to "prove a prima facie case." While the motion is sometimes made orally, the better and sometimes required practice is to file a written motion with the court.

If plaintiff has failed to present any credible evidence to support any element of any claim brought in the complaint or indictment, the judge should grant the motion as to that unproved claim. The standard applicable to the motion is that the judge must view the evidence "in the light least favorable to the movant." Accordingly, if there is any credible evidence, either direct or circumstantial, supporting the claim, the motion should be denied. Hence, it is up to the defendant to point out why there has been a fatal absence of proof on any required element of plaintiff's claims, or that there is only one reasonable conclusion that can be drawn from the evidence that was admitted.

The judge may grant all, deny all, or grant part of the motion. For instance, the judge may grant the motion on one count of the complaint and deny the motion as to the other counts. In a criminal case, the judge may grant the motion on the charged offense but deny it as to a lesser-included offense (e.g., grant the motion as to the murder charge but deny it as to the lesser manslaughter charge). The trial then continues.

1.9 Defendant's Case-in-Chief

Defendant's case-in-chief has two possible components: evidence to refute plaintiff's proof and evidence to prove any affirmative defenses and counterclaims (as well as cross-claims and third-party claims in multiple-party cases).

Defendant, if she elects to present evidence, proceeds in the same way that plaintiff did—by calling witnesses and introducing exhibits, judicially noticed facts, and stipulations. The procedures are identical.

When defendant is finished presenting all her evidence, she "rests" by standing up and announcing to the judge and jury, "Your honor, defendant rests." The judge tells the jury that the defendant has finished presenting evidence; the judge then will probably take a recess to hear motions.

1.10 Motions After Defendant Rests

After defendant rests, and the jury has been excused and has left the court room, the judge again hears motions. Plaintiff can move for a directed verdict on any of defendant's affirmative defenses and counterclaims. The judge must again view the evidence "in the light least favorable to the movant" in ruling on the motions. If there is a failure of proof on any required element of any affirmative defense or counterclaim, the judge should grant the motion as to that defense or counterclaim.

1.11 Plaintiff's Rebuttal and Defendant's Surrebuttal Cases

After defendant rests, and after motions have been made and ruled on, plaintiff has an opportunity to introduce evidence that rebuts defendant's evidence. This rebuttal evidence usually proves a defense to defendant's counterclaims or contradicts other specific evidence presented by the defendant.

Defendant also may have a last chance to rebut specific matters raised in the plaintiff's rebuttal case. This is called the defendant's surrebuttal case.

1.12 Motions at the Close of All Evidence

When all the evidence is in and both sides have rested, plaintiff or defendant may again move for a directed verdict at the close of all the evidence. Again, the standard remains the same: The judge must take the evidence "in the light least favorable to the movant."

In many jurisdictions, a motion for a directed verdict at the close of all the evidence is required to preserve the right to move for judgment notwithstanding the verdict after trial.

1.13 Instructions Conference

At some point during the trial the judge will need to "settle instructions." This means that the judge must rule on which jury instructions will be submitted to the jury. The judge will probably have both plaintiff's and defendant's requested instructions before or at the beginning of trial (in civil cases, the final pretrial memorandum submitted by the parties will usually contain each side's requested instructions and any objections to the other side's). Usually, however, the judge cannot reach final decisions on which instructions to submit to the jury until she has heard all the evidence. For that reason, the instructions conference is usually held after both sides rest and before closing arguments.

During the instructions conference, plaintiff and defendant argue why instructions should be given, denied, or modified. During the conference, which may be held in court (without the jury present) or in chambers, the court reporter should be present to record the objections and rulings. In most jurisdictions, the lawyers must make specific objections on the record to requested instructions before a judge's giving that instruction to the jury, or refusing to give a requested instruction, can be raised as error on appeal.

1.14 Closing Arguments

Plaintiff and defendant now give their closing arguments. The closing arguments are the lawyers' opportunities to tell the jury what the evidence has been, how it ties into the jury instructions, and why the evidence and law compel a verdict in their favor.

Effective closing arguments integrate themes, facts, and law, and argue that the credible evidence, when applied to the law, requires a favorable verdict. Lawyers can argue inferences from the facts, refer to important testimony, use admitted exhibits, tell stories, employ analogies, and use a range of other techniques to persuade the jury.

How much time do closing arguments take? Most last 30 to 60 minutes per side. If too short, they fail to use the available time persuasively. If too long, they run the danger of boring or irritating the jury. The judge may put reasonable time limits on the closing arguments.

In most jurisdictions the party having the burden of proof, usually the plaintiff, has the right to argue first and last. That is, plaintiff has the right to argue first and, after defendant has argued, make a rebuttal argument. A few jurisdictions allow only one argument per side (and in some of these, the defendant argues first, plaintiff last).

In situations where the only issue for the jury to decide is whether an affirmative defense or counterclaim has been proved, and the defendant has the burden of proof on these issues, the defendant usually will have the right to argue first and last.

1.15 Jury Instructions

The judge must instruct the jury on the law that applies to the case. Some judges instruct the jury before the lawyers make the closing arguments. Others instruct the jury after the closing arguments are completed. In most jurisdictions the judge will both read the instructions and give the jury a written set of the instructions to use during deliberations. A few jurisdictions follow the practice that instructions are only read to the jury.

The jury will also get verdict forms. There may be a number of verdict forms, since cases may have multiple parties, claims, counterclaims, and third-party claims. In some cases, the jury may also get special verdict forms asking how the jury finds on various specific issues of fact and law.

Reading and explaining the instructions in most cases take perhaps 10 to 20 minutes, although in complex cases they can take much longer.

1.16 Jury Deliberations and Verdict

The jury is then sent to the jury room to begin deliberations. Before leaving the courtroom, however, alternate jurors, if any, are usually dismissed, and the court bailiff is sworn in to safeguard the jury's privacy during its deliberations.

The bailiff usually carries the admitted exhibits and the written jury instructions back to the jury room for use during the deliberations.

Often the only guidelines the jury receives on how it should organize and conduct itself are the standard instructions that the jurors should first select a foreperson to preside over their deliberations and that the foreperson and, in some jurisdictions, the other jurors must sign the verdict forms that reflect the jury's decisions. How the jury organizes itself and conducts the deliberations is largely up to the jury.

Jurors sometimes have questions during their deliberations. These are usually written down and brought by the bailiff to the judge, who then confers with the lawyers on how to respond. After a response is prepared, the jury is brought back into the courtroom and given the response. Deliberations then continue.

When the jury reaches a verdict (either a unanimous or majority verdict, depending on the jurisdiction) and signs the appropriate verdict forms, it signals to the judge (usually through a buzzer system or a message delivered by the bailiff) that it is ready to return the verdict. The lawyers, if they are not in the courthouse, are called, and everyone reappears in the courtroom. The jury is brought in, and the judge asks if the jury has reached a verdict. When the foreperson answers "yes," the foreperson is directed to give the verdict to the bailiff, who gives it to the judge (who checks to see that all verdict forms are accounted for and have been signed properly), who usually gives it to the court clerk to be read aloud.

After the verdict has been announced, the judge will ask whether any parties want to "poll the jury." If so (and it is common that the losing side requests it), the clerk will then ask each juror if the verdict read in court is that juror's verdict. If all say "yes," that ends the jury's service. If any jurors necessary for the verdict (some jurisdictions do not require unanimous verdicts in all cases) say "no," the jury continues deliberating.

How long does the jury deliberate? Most verdicts are probably reached in one to four hours, although every trial lawyer can tell a story about getting a 15-minute verdict or having a jury deliberate more than a day, perhaps several days, in a lengthy or complicated case.

What happens when the jury cannot agree on a verdict? The judge usually asks the jury whether further deliberations might be useful or whether the jury is hopelessly deadlocked. If the former, the judge often gives the jury an "Allen charge," which encourages the jurors to listen to each other's views and attempt to reach a verdict. If the latter, the judge declares a mistrial, excuses the jury, and schedules a retrial.

The court then usually sets a date for a hearing on any post-trial motions and, in a criminal case following a guilty verdict, sentencing. This does not occur in a criminal case when the jury enters not guilty verdicts on all counts, as such a decision will result in a dismissal that ends the case.

1.17 Post-Trial Motions and Appeal

After the verdict a party usually has a specific number of days in which to file written post-trial motions. The most common are a motion for judgment notwithstanding the verdict, which asks the judge to set aside the jury's verdict and enter judgment for the other side, and a motion for a new trial, which asks the judge to order a new trial because of claimed errors made during the first trial. These motions are frequently made alternatively. Also common in some jurisdictions are motions in civil cases for additur or remittitur, which ask the court to increase or decrease the dollar amount of the jury's verdict.

The judge will usually schedule a hearing on the motions and allow the parties to argue orally. The judge will then rule on the motions and usually will prepare a written order.

When post-trial motions have been decided, the judge enters judgment in accordance with the jury verdict and post-trial motion rulings. Entering judgment is the jurisdictional act that ends the case in the trial court. A party wishing to appeal the judgment must file a timely notice of appeal with the clerk of the trial court. In civil cases, a party must usually post an appeal bond in the amount of the judgment. This act begins the appellate process.

1.18 Conclusion

There is nothing mysterious or complicated about trial procedure. The important thing to remember is that federal and state courts historically have developed different ways of conducting the various stages of a trial, and they continue to experiment with changes today. Consequently, every trial lawyer must know how his case will be tried in the court, and before the judge, where it is scheduled. If you don't know, you must find out. Ask the judge's law clerk, court clerk, and trial lawyers who have tried similar cases before that judge how cases are tried there. Whenever possible, go to the courtroom and watch a case being tried. This will give you a feel for the judge's demeanor and how she conducts a jury trial.

> See the website accompanying this text for a videotape of a jury trial that demonstrates the trial process.

THE PSYCHOLOGY OF PERSUASION

2.1 Introduction

Trials are a re-creation of reality—an event or transaction that happened in the past. In trials, there are usually three versions of reality: your side's reality, the other side's reality, and the jury's reality. Each party firmly believes that its version of reality is correct and tries to persuade the jury to accept its version. However, the only reality that ultimately matters is the jury's reality—what the jury believes actually happened—because that reality will control the jury's verdict.

Which side's version of reality will the jury accept as its own? This depends largely on which side is more persuasive in presenting its version during the course of the trial. If neither side is persuasive, the jury will construct a version of reality entirely on its own. To persuade juries, you need to understand jurors—their backgrounds, beliefs, and attitudes, how they process information, how they think, and how they make decisions. Only when you understand the psychology of persuasion can you understand how to persuade a jury to adopt your version of reality as its own. This understanding will influence everything you do during a jury trial, from voir dire through closing arguments.

This chapter reviews what behavioral science and jury research have learned about juror backgrounds, beliefs, and attitudes, how they process information, what influences them, and how they make decisions. It also discusses how trial lawyers can use this knowledge to shape how they try cases. Although for the most part this research is consistent with what effective trial lawyers have learned through experience, it has organized and explained jury behavior in a systematic way that significantly contributes to our understanding of how jurors think, how they decide, and how they can be persuaded.

2.2 Behavioral Science and Jury Research

Until perhaps 50 years ago, a common view was that jurors objectively absorbed the evidence presented by both sides during a trial, withheld making premature judgments, dispassionately reviewed that evidence during deliberations, and ultimately reached a logical decision, based on the evidence and the applicable law. Behavioral science research, beginning in the 1940s, and jury research, beginning in the 1960s, have emphatically rejected that view. "They," the jurors, do not think and decide like "us," the lawyers.

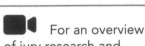 For an overview of jury research and its impact on trial advocacy, please watch Video A.2, "Mauet on the Psychology of Trial Practice."

A caveat is in order. Much of this jury research has been conducted in environments that have little to do with courtroom realities. For example, researchers frequently use written questionnaires answered by undergraduate students receiving extra credit to test the researchers' hypotheses. Researchers frequently show videotaped scenarios to volunteers, who then answer questionnaires. Whether such research yields results that can be applied with confidence to jury trials is somewhat doubtful. Fortunately, in recent years some of that research has become more realistic, by using trial lawyers to help create courtroom scenarios, and by using actual or representative jurors in real courtrooms to test the hypotheses. Such research results have more credibility in the world of trial lawyers.

What does the behavioral science and jury research tell us?

1. Affective Reasoning

People have two significantly different approaches to decision making. Most people are primarily affective ("right brain") decision makers. Affective persons have several common characteristics. First, they are usually emotional and creative, and are more interested in people than problems. They see trials as human dramas, not legal disputes. Second, they use deductive reasoning, which is primarily emotional and impulsive, in which a few premises about how life works and relatively little factual information are used to create "stories" of what probably happened, reach decisions, and attribute cause and blame quickly. Third, once they make decisions, they become committed to them, and they validate their decisions by selectively accepting, rejecting, or distorting later information to "fit" the already reached decisions. This allows them to justify their decisions and believe the decisions are logical and fair. People have an internal need to be consistent, which makes them committed to their original decisions despite the receipt of later conflicting information. Since information inconsistent with their decisions causes internal conflict and stress, they become resistant and soon hear and see only what supports their decisions.

By contrast, cognitive ("left brain") decision makers are more interested in problems than people, enjoy accumulating information, defer making decisions until they have all the available information, and, like trained scientists, use inductive reasoning to reach logical decisions. Cognitive decision makers are more likely to have higher education levels and math, hard science, or business backgrounds. After seeing a collision, affectives ask: "Was anyone hurt?" Cognitives ask: "Whose fault was it?" In short, affectives "feel"; cognitives "reason."

While most jurors are affective decision makers, most lawyers, trained in legal reasoning, are cognitive decision makers. The approach that is effective in persuading "them," the jurors, will not be the approach effective for "us," the lawyers. Lawyers must understand how jurors process information, create "stories," and make decisions before lawyers can communicate persuasively with them. This has significance at all stages of a jury trial.

2. Beliefs and Attitudes

Beliefs (what we know about something) are how we perceive life works—our value system. Attitudes (how we feel about something) are the expressions of our beliefs. Our attitudes are our convictions, biases, and prejudices about people and events, our sense of what's right and wrong, what's fair and unfair. We try to make sense of the world around us, and use stereotypes—our beliefs and attitudes—to organize our views of that world. Beliefs and attitudes are formed throughout our lives through parental training, formal education, television, news, and, most importantly, personal observations and experiences. Once developed, attitudes are usually held for life and change slowly, if at all, over time.

Attitudes subconsciously filter information about the world around us and help sort out conflicting information and fill in missing information. Attitudes are the rose-colored glasses through which we "see" information in our own unique way, accepting information that we like and rejecting, minimizing, or distorting information that we dislike, thereby achieving personal consistency and comfort.

Most jurors do not passively sit and uncritically absorb evidence. They rarely have "open minds" that are receptive to new ideas. Instead, they "test" new information by how consistent it is with their preconceived ideas of how life works and how it fits into the "story" of the case they have constructed in their minds. Jurors rapidly construct stories of what probably happened in the case, then subconsciously use their attitudes to accept, reject, or distort evidence, or supply missing information, to create a complete, plausible story. This lets jurors reach decisions they believe are consistent with the evidence, and are therefore logical and fair. The more circumstantial the evidence of liability or guilt, and the more familiar jurors are with the subject matter of the trial, the more important jurors' beliefs and attitudes become.

Juror attitudes have great significance throughout a trial. These attitudes determine if the jurors will be receptive or resistant to the parties, evidence, and themes presented during the trial. Lawyers can only persuade if jurors are willing to accept, and jurors' attitudes, not logic or reason, control whether they will accept or reject particular information or messages during a trial. Therefore, lawyers need to understand the jurors' relevant attitudes, whether these attitudes are consistent with or in conflict with each other, and how strongly those attitudes are held. This must be explored before and during the jury selection process, since it is highly unlikely that any jurors will change their attitudes about any important matters during the course of a trial.

Although juror demographic information (such as sex, race, age, marital status, family history, residence information, education, and job history) is easy to obtain, those demographics at best reflect likely general attitudes about life, and have limited use in predicting individual juror attitudes relevant to the issues in a particular trial. Single demographic characteristics, such as sex, race, and age are almost useless in predicting juror attitudes (unless, of course, the case itself involves issues of sex, race, or age).

By contrast, direct information of juror attitudes should be a better source. However, jurors are frequently inaccurate, whether intentionally or unintentionally, in describing their own attitudes about issues relevant to a particular trial. Self-disclosure of true attitudes during jury selection, particularly attitudes on sensitive issues, is notoriously unreliable, because the jurors' need to fit in and be accepted by others usually overrides the obligation to be truthful. As a result, jurors usually give socially acceptable answers to questions that probe attitudes on sensitive issues. Creating a relaxed, nonjudgmental environment for self-disclosure improves its reliability. Questioning jurors individually, out of the presence of the other jurors, improves the amount and accuracy of self-disclosure. Using written questionnaires, rather than questions in open court, may also significantly improve the candor and completeness of self-disclosure.

Lawyers usually seek to learn juror attitudes indirectly, by asking about jurors' hobbies, interests, involvement with groups and organizations, and personal experiences in life, from which attitudes can be inferred. Personal experiences similar to the case being tried are particularly important, because jurors consider these experiences to be evidence and frequently spend as much time during deliberations discussing their collective experiences as they do discussing the formally introduced evidence.

Jury selection (assuming the law and court permit such latitude) usually pursues all these approaches — getting basic demographic information, as well as direct and indirect information on attitudes — so that lawyers can make informed decisions on which jurors to accept or reject in a particular case.

3. Decision Making

A jury verdict is a product of two forces: individual decision making and group decision making. Individual juror decisions are influenced principally by affective reasoning and the jurors' beliefs and attitudes, discussed above. However, it is also important to understand that most jurors go through an emotional progression during the course of a trial, because that progression will influence how lawyers present themselves, their evidence, and their arguments. Lawyers who understand and respond to the jurors' emotional needs during the trial have a significant advantage.

At the beginning of a trial, particularly during the jury selection process, most jurors experience varying levels of anxiety. This is natural, since uncertainty creates anxiety. They are unsure of their role as jurors, unsure that they will be selected to sit as jurors, unsure of their capacity to understand what the case is all about, and unsure of their ability to reach the right verdict. For the rest of the trial those jurors are using subconscious strategies to cope with their unwanted anxiety.

As the trial begins, after they have been selected to sit as jurors, and after they have heard the opening statements, that uncertainty and anxiety, for most jurors, subsides. Their uncertainty lessens as they begin to understand courtroom procedure and their role in the trial process. They begin to come to terms with the case by constructing stories in their minds of what the case seems to be about. These stories may turn out to be accurate or inaccurate, but they are constructed just the same. The stories are the mental process by which jurors strive to make sense of the information they receive. This is not the same thing as reaching a final decision, but does have a great deal to do with how those jurors perceive the actual evidence when they receive it.

As the trial progresses, and they actually hear and see the evidence, jurors subconsciously accept, reject, or distort that evidence, depending on whether the evidence is consistent or inconsistent with the stories they have constructed in their minds. This is the filtering process, where jurors subconsciously use their attitudes and beliefs to screen the evidence as they hear and see it. For most jurors, the evidence, as filtered, serves to validate the stories they have already constructed and to "prove" that their initial impressions were right. The anxiety most jurors experienced at the beginning of the trial has subsided, as these jurors become confident of what the right outcome of the case should be.

At the end of the presentation of evidence, most jurors, now confident of and committed to their decisions, look forward to sharing their views with others during deliberations. For these jurors, the closing arguments will have little influence, since they already know what the right decision should be (although hearing arguments supporting their decision may make them stronger advocates for that decision during deliberations). Closing argument will usually influence only those jurors who are still unsure of their decision, or who do not have confidence in their decision. Closing argument may also influence those jurors who realize that their decisions are not permitted under the verdict options given in the court's instructions on the applicable law and that they must now reassess their decisions. Closing argument can also arm jurors who know what the correct decision is with arguments they can use to persuade jurors who disagree.

When the jurors retire to the jury room to deliberate, this is the time they may first realize that other jurors may not share their views and decisions, and group dynamics has a strong influence in determining whose decisions will prevail and speak for the jury as a whole.

Individual decisions are influenced by the dynamics of group decision making, since a jury is a group charged with reaching a decision—the verdict. Jury research has focused much of its attention on the dynamics of group decision making, the critical concern being the extent to which individual decisions can be overcome by group decisions.

Group dynamics do not involve an even exchange among the members of a group. Some members have more influence on the group than others. For these purposes, members are usually defined as persuaders, participants, or nonparticipants.

Persuaders are persons who make assertive statements about the evidence, freely express their opinions, and actively build coalitions supporting their views. Persuaders are the opinion leaders who have the most influence and dominate the discussion in a group. They usually have higher education levels and have positions of authority or expertise in their work. They are articulate, talk readily, and are comfortable in group settings. Many will have prior jury service. Persuaders constitute approximately 25 percent of a group. In a typical jury deliberation, three jurors do more than 50 percent of the talking, and those are the persuaders.

Participants are persons who also engage in group discussions. However, they are followers, not leaders, because they value social approval and acceptance by others. They defer to others having stronger egos, more education and higher intelligence, more experience, and greater career success. Participants readily join coalitions, since the coalition validates their decisions, but they do not lead them. They will be actively involved in the deliberations, but they are likely to state things in terms of their opinions, and do not actively try to have others accept their views. Participants constitute approximately 50 percent of a group. In a typical jury deliberation, about six jurors will be participants.

Nonparticipants are persons who rarely engage in group discussions. Jurors who are nonparticipants rarely become involved in deliberations other than to express agreement with a particular view or vote. Nonparticipants are usually followers who will go along with what the majority decides to do. (However, nonparticipants who are loners and are detached from and avoid involvement with others may exhibit independence and not be easily swayed by the majority's view.) Nonparticipants constitute approximately 25 percent of a group. In a typical jury deliberation, three jurors will be nonparticipants.

Categorization of potential jurors is, of course, particularly important at the jury selection stage of the trial, where the peremptory challenges should be used first to eliminate unfavorable persuaders. It is more important than trying to identify the potential jury foreperson, who, research has shown, is more likely to be a compromiser and consensus builder than an opinion leader or authoritarian personality.

4. What Influences the Jury

What influences jurors to accept our version of reality as their own? Communication is based on perception. It is a process involving senders (witnesses and lawyers), messages (evidence and arguments), media (testimony and exhibits), and receivers (jurors). Learning, for the receivers, is also an active process involving receiving, processing, remembering, and retrieving messages. Learning and persuasion will only occur if the messages you intend to send to the jury are the same as the messages the jury actually receives and retains.

a. Sender Credibility

The senders—witnesses and lawyers—must be credible sources of information before they can influence the jury. Influence is largely a function of credibility, and credibility is largely a function of the sender's personal attributes. People develop opinions about others quickly, often within a few minutes. Three principal characteristics of credibility are trustworthiness, expertise, and dynamism.

> ■◀ For a review of ways to increase your credibility in the eyes of the jurors, please watch Video A.4, "Wyo STI: Attorney Credibility."

First, trustworthiness refers to impartiality. Jurors obviously prefer witnesses who have no apparent bias, interest, or motive to slant testimony one way or another, or, if expert witnesses, are not hired guns willing to say anything for a fee. For lawyers, it means that the lawyers are candid in dealing with both good and bad facts, and do not try to pull the wool over the jurors' eyes.

Second, expertise refers to how knowledgeable the witnesses are about the facts and issues of the case. Knowledgeable and authoritative persons have more influence on others. With lay witnesses, it refers to how well the witnesses saw, heard, or knew about the relevant events and transactions, and how well they remember and recount the details surrounding them. With expert witnesses, it refers to the experts' education, training, and experience, and how thoroughly they did their tests and analyses. It also refers to the uniqueness of the experts' qualifications, since people put more weight on information seen to be scarce and therefore valuable.

Third, dynamism refers to the witnesses' and lawyers' ability to communicate. Jurors prefer witnesses and lawyers who are likeable and attractive, both physically and personally. They are more influenced by people they like and who appear to be much like themselves. They prefer witnesses and lawyers who project energy, enthusiasm, and confidence when they testify or argue. All the components of effective delivery—verbal content (the actual spoken words), nonverbal delivery (paralinguistics, such as speech rate, volume, pauses, and voice inflection), and body language (kinesics, such as posture, body, arm, and hand movement, facial gestures, and eye contact)—must work in a coordinated way. Boredom is the enemy of effective communication, and dynamic delivery is the best antidote. Any lawyer or witness can be taught how to be a more effective communicator.

Finally, jurors think—erroneously[1]—that they are good at detecting deception, and they use stereotypes to make such assessments. They believe that mannerisms such as lack of eye contact, nervousness, hand over mouth, hesitancy in answering, and using words like "honestly" or "believe me" indicate uncertainty or deception. These are the kinds of mannerisms that witness training and preparation can minimize.

b. Receiver Capacities

The receivers—the jurors—come with diverse interests and abilities and represent a broad spectrum of today's adult population. Many, however, have limited attention spans, limited interest in learning, and limited channels through which they are willing to learn.

First, most people's attention spans are short. The average person can only maintain a high level of concentration for about 15 to 20 minutes. After that, attention levels drop significantly. That's why half-hour television programs are more common than one-hour programs—advertisers know that viewers are likely to change channels before the hour is over. In addition, listening to others talk occupies only a small portion of the brain's capacity, allowing the rest of the brain to fade in and out and think about other things. While some jurors will pay close attention throughout a trial, most jurors will have varying levels of attention, and periodically drift off and think about other things.

Second, most people have limited interest in learning, particularly when there is no perceived self-interest involved. Learning new things takes effort. Many jurors did not like formal learning, and once their schooling was done, resist situations that repeat their school-years' experience. A trial, of course, represents in many ways the formality of classroom learning, which, for some jurors, dredges up unpleasant memories.

Third, most people have been trained, principally through television and computers, how to expect new learning. They are part of the "sound bite" generation. They now want it fast, painless, interesting, and visual. They form perceptions quickly, based on little information. Observe any television news program. Notice how each news item is short, usually less than two minutes, leads off with a few seconds' introduction from a "talking head," cuts quickly to visuals with a background voice, focuses on the human impact of the story, and wraps up before

---

1. Junior co-author Easton recognizes that simulated jury research suggests that individuals are not good at detecting deception but believes the collective group of twelve jurors can often detect deception.

boredom sets in. If this is what makes people watch television news, it speaks volumes about how lawyers in today's environment should try cases to juries.

Fourth, what people see as "evidence" is different from what lawyers understand as evidence. When people become jurors, they see as evidence any information relevant to their decision, whether it is formally introduced evidence from witnesses and exhibits, their personal experiences in life they believe, rightly or wrongly, to be relevant to the case, or their attitudes about how life works. Everything that jurors see as evidence goes into their decision making. Jurors frequently spend as much time discussing their experiences in life—such as the automobile accidents they've been involved in, their experiences with doctors and hospitals, and their experiences with the police—which they feel are as relevant to their decision as they do to the witness testimony and exhibits. It's all "evidence" to the jurors.

c. Components of Persuasive Messages

Effective communication must come from credible sources and must be attuned to the realities of today's listeners. The message itself, whether witness testimony, exhibits, or lawyer statements and arguments, must also be effectively structured. Research has contributed much to understanding the components of effective communication.

First, memory is a severe limitation on what we can effectively communicate. It makes no sense to communicate if the listeners do not retain the essence of what has been communicated. The average person forgets most of any communication within a few hours, and after two or three days retains but a small part. Trial lawyers need to understand that memory is indeed fleeting, and they must use strategies to improve jurors' retention of the key information presented during a trial.

Second, people use simplification strategies to deal with sensory overload. People are bombarded with information during a trial through testimony, exhibits, and arguments. They quickly become overloaded with information. Sensory overload is a stressful situation that people try to avoid, so they subconsciously employ simplification strategies to cope with the avalanche of information.

A key simplification strategy recognizes that people instinctively use psychological anchors, which are mnemonic devices to help them remember the gist of what they have learned. Much like we use yellow highlighters to mark key words and phrases on written material, jurors create psychological anchors to do mentally what highlighters do physically.

Psychological anchors are what trial lawyers call themes. A theme is a memorable word or short phrase—"this is a case about greed"—that summarizes and encapsulates lengthy descriptive and evaluative information. Research shows that it is human nature to condense voluminous information to an easily remembered word or phrase, so that hearing or seeing the word or phrase later will trigger some of the supporting detail. Anchoring information to a theme makes the information easier to retain and retrieve. If trial lawyers do not provide the themes during a trial, jurors will instinctively create themes themselves. An important part of trial preparation is selecting themes that are emotionally based, catchy and memorable, summarize the liability and damages positions in the case, fit the undisputed and disputed evidence, and are consistent with the jurors' beliefs and attitudes. If this is done well, and used periodically during the trial, jurors will adopt your themes during their deliberations.

Third, this is the era of visual learning. People today are part of the television age or, more recently, computer age, and are used to receiving information visually. Trials, however, largely involve witness testimony. Research has shown that, after two or three days, listeners retain only about 10 percent of aural messages, but they retain about 20 percent of visual messages. Retention is improved to about 65 percent if both aural and visual messages are used to present the same information. Trial lawyers have to focus on improving the level of retention from witness testimony and lawyer argument by using visual aids whenever possible to repeat and reinforce aural messages.

This is the era of the visual trial. Visual exhibits—photographs, diagrams, charts, models, enlarged documents, and computer simulations—that are large, clear, and vivid usually have much more immediate and lasting impact than the spoken word. They dramatically improve retention levels of the information. Whenever possible, show rather than just tell. Whenever the information is important, make it visual.

Fourth, research has shown that the impact of aural information—witness testimony and lawyer argument—can be significantly improved. Witnesses and lawyers can be trained to use "powerful language" to improve their persuasiveness and eliminate or minimize speaking styles that detract from credibility. Powerful language uses the active voice, has good speech rate and volume, uses plain English and good diction, uses present tense, and makes descriptions vivid and visceral. It avoids using tentative language, such as hollow intensifiers ("very," "really"), unnecessary hedges ("I guess," "well"), and indications of uncertainty ("it seemed like"). Witnesses and lawyers can be taught to use sensory language to make what is verbal appear to be visual by creating unique images and symbols. They can be prepared to outline details of events and transactions that enhance their credibility. They can be prepared to demonstrate what happened, rather than just tell what happened. They can be taught to create emotional messages, both positive and negative, and express confidence and certainty whenever possible.

Finally, research has shown that several concepts can be used to increase memory and persuasion. Repetition is a powerful influence. Repeating a message—such as a theme in opening statements or closing arguments—three or four times substantially improves retention. More repetition can be effective, but its form must be modified so that jurors do not turn off to seemingly endless identical repetition, and so that the repetition does not become legally objectionable. Jurors may forget the details over time, but they will retain the impressions that have been repeated effectively during the trial.

Cues are a powerful influence. A cue is simply a verbal or visual warning that something important is about to happen, so that listeners will pay particular attention. A cue can be direct—saying "this is important"—or indirect—using tone of voice, pregnant pauses, body language, rhetorical questions, and the like.

Rhetorical questions have a strong influence because they stimulate active thinking. Self-generated ideas have greater strength and retention. When jurors respond to rhetorical questions and reach the desired conclusions themselves, their conclusions will have a stronger and more lasting impact.

Order effects are also important. Where a message is placed in relation to other information has much to do with how well the message is received and retained. Because most people make up their minds quickly and become bored and tune out quickly, it is particularly important to begin with information that has impact. People remember better what they hear first—this is the concept of primacy. On the other hand, people also remember better what they hear last—this is the concept of recency. It also is important to end with information that has impact. In short, the most important information should be at the beginning and end of any message.

Order effects can sometimes be used to enhance less credible sources. Because people tend to forget the source of information over time—the sleeper effect—information from a less impressive witness can be placed in the middle of the presentation.

Order effects are important within the component parts of a trial, such as opening statements, closing arguments, and direct examinations, as well as the trial as a whole. When trials are short, primacy is the more important concept. When trials last more than a few days, recency is probably more important.

There also are specific techniques that can effectively deal with the fact that trials involve two opposing sides that are constantly bombarding the jurors with conflicting information and messages. Forewarning and inoculation are particularly important techniques for the side presenting information or arguing first. Forewarning is giving the listeners advance warning that they are going to hear contrary information and appeals from the other side. Inoculation is anticipating the other side's argument and giving the listeners information and arguments that they can use to resist the other side's arguments. Research shows that when forewarning and inoculation are used, listeners become more resistant to later contrary information and arguments.

Two-sided argumentation is also important. Research shows that when one side has a strong case and the listeners are already favorably disposed, one-sided arguments—discussing only that side's strengths—are more persuasive, since they reinforce already held views. However, where both sides have reasonably equal cases and the listeners are not disposed one way or another, two-sided arguments—including the other side's arguments and a refutation of them—are more persuasive. Because most cases actually tried have strengths and weaknesses on both sides, two-sided argumentation will usually be the more effective technique.

2.3 What Research Means for Trial Lawyers

What does this behavioral science and jury research tell us as trial lawyers about how to approach a jury trial? What are the keys we need to keep in mind throughout our trial preparation and the trial itself? Seven concepts stand out.

1. Prepare from the Jury's Point of View

The only reality that counts in the courtroom is the jury's reality. The jury's perception of reality is *the* reality. Therefore, all courtroom communication must be juror-centered—it must be planned and executed from the jury's point of view. If it's not persuasive to the jury, it's not worth doing, no matter how logical it may be to you. Always ask: What does the jury want to know? How does the jury want to learn it?

This means we must recognize that for many jurors, serving on a jury involves stress and anxiety. We must employ strategies that quickly and easily help jurors understand the trial process and what the case is all about. And it means we must understand that most jurors are affective decision makers, are emotional and people-oriented, and make decisions quickly, based mostly on their preconceived views of how life works, then resist changing their minds. It means we must recognize that jurors filter evidence through their beliefs and attitudes and subconsciously decide whether to accept, reject, or modify it. It means we must make our witnesses, and ourselves, trustworthy, knowledgeable, and dynamic. It means we must make the trial vivid and visual. And it means we must be efficient, move the story forward, and make our points quickly before boredom sets in and jurors tune out.

Jurors, like everyone else, are a product of their environment. They have been trained, primarily through television and film, to expect drama, an emphasis on personalities, and sophisticated visual effects. They expect to get everything quickly, in simple, digestible sound bites. And they want it all to be interesting and enjoyable. Anything less and you've violated the "boring rule," and jurors will quickly change channels.

After a verdict, the losing lawyer often complains: "The jury just didn't understand the case." That is a lawyer problem, not a jury problem. The lawyer didn't understand that everything you do must be from the jury's point of view.

2. Develop a Theory of the Case

A theory of the case is a clear, simple story of "what really happened" from your point of view. It is based on the law and the facts and shows why jurors should find in your favor. It must be consistent with the undisputed evidence as well as your version of the disputed evidence and the applicable substantive law. It must not only show what happened, but also explain why the people in the story acted the way they did. It should be consistent with the jury's beliefs and attitudes about life and how the world works. It must be a persuasive story that will be the basis of your evidence and arguments throughout the trial. If you cannot state your theory of the case in a minute or two, it needs more work. If you do not construct a clear, simple story that puts all the evidence together into a coherent whole—your theory of the case—the jury will construct one without you.

Start with a story that meets juror expectations and juror reactions to the facts, then frame the issues and create your story, focusing on the opposing party's misconduct, choices, and decisions. The theory of the case obviously needs to be developed as the facts of the case become known, well before trial. Consider, for example, an automobile collision case, where there is evidence that the plaintiff-driver might have been drinking before the collision with the defendant's car. Plaintiff must decide if her theory of the case is that (1) the accident was caused solely by the defendant's negligence and that no drinking occurred, (2) plaintiff had been drinking but her drinking played no part in causing the collision, or (3) plaintiff's drinking did play a part but the defendant's negligence was the primary cause of the collision. In a murder case, the defendant must decide if his theory of the case is (1) mistaken identity, (2) self-defense, or (3) accident. In a contract case, the plaintiff must decide if his theory of the case is that (1) defendant failed to perform his obligations under the contract, resulting in consequential damages, or (2) defendant intentionally breached the contract in bad faith, resulting in punitive damages. Although alternative and inconsistent theories are proper and useful at the pleading stage, by the time of trial they must be distilled down to one simple, clear story.

Trials are in large part a contest to see which party's version of "what really happened" the jury will accept as more probably true. In civil cases, the opposing sides usually have directly competing versions of reality, and each side tries to present a persuasive version that the jury will adopt as its own. In criminal cases, this is also often true (particularly when the defense is presenting an affirmative defense), but frequently the contest is whether the jury will accept the prosecution's version, when the defense is defending on the existence of reasonable doubt and is not offering a competing version of reality.

3. Select Themes and Labels

Themes and labels are the trial vocabulary that become the psychological anchors you want the jurors to accept and adopt as their own during the trial. Once you have developed your theory of the case, you have to condense it into themes and labels.

Themes are the anchors that summarize your case. They are the memorable words or phrases that encapsulate the essence of your case and your position on liability and damages and project the images you want the jury to retain about the case. A case should not have more than three or four themes, with one major theme that encapsulates your theory and drives the jury to adopt your view of the case as its own. You should repeat your themes throughout the trial, from jury selection to closing arguments. If selected properly, the jurors will adopt your themes as their own, and use your themes to argue for your side during deliberations.

A key part of trial preparation is selecting themes that arouse emotions, create memorable, moral images, state your position on liability and damages, summarize what happened (conduct), who did it (people), and why they did it (motive), and conform with the jurors' beliefs and attitudes. The best themes come from time-honored sources that contain universal moral truths about life, such as the Bible, Aesop's Fables, or Americana sayings. Single words such as love, hate, fear, trust, honor, duty, responsibility, power, greed, and revenge are powerful explanations of human motives. Phrases such as "two seconds of carelessness," "a time bomb waiting to go off," and "desperate times call for desperate measures" create powerful images of events. Phrases such as "taking responsibility for your actions," "false friends," and "profits over safety" create strong moral images.

Themes should be selected with an eye toward the central issues in the case. Trials usually revolve around three kinds of issues. First, most trials involve elements issues. Have the parties proven, to the required degree of proof, each element of the claims and defenses? Second, many trials involve inferences issues. The parties do not disagree over the basic facts, but they disagree over the inferences to be drawn from the facts. This is often the case when the issue is whether the facts circumstantially prove a mental state, such as intent or knowledge. Third, many trials involve credibility issues. When the testimony from witnesses clashes over important events, the jury must decide whose testimony to believe. Themes must be tailored to focus on the elements, inferences, and credibility issues the jurors will need to resolve to decide the case.

Labels are the tags you put on the people, events, and things involved in the case. Words convey images. Calling someone "the plaintiff" or "my client" conveys a different image than "Mrs. Johnson" or "Helen." Calling a tractor-trailer truck a "vehicle" conveys a different image than a "50,000-pound rig" or "eighteen-wheeler." Calling a death an event in which someone "died" is different from saying someone was "slaughtered." Calling an accident an "incident" or "event" is different from calling it a "collision" or "crash." In these examples, the plaintiff will want to use the emotional labels, the defendant will want to use the bland ones. You need to decide how you will label the parties, witnesses, events, and things to convey the emotional images you want the jury to see and accept and then use those labels consistently during the trial. They should be introduced in opening statements, carefully employed during witness examinations, and hammered home during closing arguments. (However, make sure your themes and labels are not objectionable. For example, some judges will sustain objections to using the term "rape" in sexual assault cases or "victim" in self-defense cases if those terms are in issue during the trial.)

4. Emphasize the People

Most jurors are people-oriented. During trials, they want to hear about the people, not the legal problems. Jurors want to know who to silently root for, i.e., who wears the white hat. Jurors want to feel good about their decisions, and they can't unless they learn enough about the key people to get a feel for them and reach a verdict that is consistent with their feelings about those people. With key people, such as parties, jurors want three-dimensional information about them.

People do things for a reason. Jurors want to know not only what they did—the conduct—but also why they did it—the motivation. Jurors always want to know who the people are, what they did, why they did it, and what effect it had on their lives. Focus on the opposing party's choices, bad decisions, and misconduct, and create a story that jurors want to believe.

Notice how television news understands and uses this knowledge. Stories of an event invariably focus on the human element. Coverage of disasters, wars, and economic events zoom in on a particular person and tell about the event through its effect on that person. This puts a human face on the news, which viewers like because they can relate to the story on a personal level. Good trial lawyers understand that trials involve the same elements.

5. Use Storytelling Techniques

Storytelling is the way people have communicated with each other since the beginning of time. Long before written language, storytelling was the way information was passed on to others, and the way oral history was preserved. People instinctively use storytelling to communicate with others, and use the story framework to organize, understand, and remember information. Jurors do the same thing during trials. If lawyers do not organize the evidence into a clear, simple story, jurors will do so on their own. It's human nature.

Good stories organize, humanize, and dramatize. They have plot, characters, and emotion. They have a narrative structure. Notice how television and film use the story framework. Someone becomes involved in an event, a conflict arises, or a crisis is reached, which culminates in a resolution. The story uses sensory language; vivid, visceral, and visual images; present tense; pace; and simplicity to give life to the story and dimensions to its characters. The story is told in a way that puts the members of the audience into the picture, engaging their hearts and minds, so that the audience cares about the people and what happens to them. The story's moral is consistent with the audience's beliefs and attitudes, so that the ending of the story is fair and justice is served. The story is highlighted with gripping visual aids. And the story is told efficiently and always moves forward, so that it never stalls or becomes boring.

Trials involve much more than merely introducing a set of facts; those facts must be organized and presented as part of a memorable story. Effective storytelling is the basis for much of what occurs during a trial, including the opening statements, direct examinations, and closing arguments. Small wonder, then, that good trial lawyers are invariably good storytellers.

6. Focus on the Key Facts and Issues

In most trials, almost all of the relevant facts are undisputed, so the few disputed facts are critical. As a trial lawyer, you need to understand what is disputed and what is not, focus on the disputed facts, deal candidly with both the favorable and unfavorable evidence, and marshal and present that evidence so that the jury accepts your version of the disputed facts.

Focus on your best facts. How can you highlight the best facts, whether testimony or exhibits? How can you make them vivid, visceral, and visual? And how can you repeat your best facts in ways that maintain juror interest? Focus also on your worst facts. How can you minimize the impact of those facts? Can you anticipate them, using the techniques of forewarning, inoculation, and two-sided argumentation? And can you rebut the worst facts with evidence that has impact? If key facts and events are disputed because witnesses remember them differently, how can you make your witnesses and exhibits more persuasive than your opponent's on these key disputed matters?

Inexperienced lawyers usually spend too much time belaboring undisputed facts, thereby boring the jury, and too little time proving their version of disputed facts, thereby failing to persuade the jury. Skilled lawyers spend a great deal of time finding witnesses and exhibits that support their version of the disputed facts, and preparing them so that they are dynamic, confident, detailed, and vivid. They understand that wars are won or lost depending on which side wins or loses a key battle. The same is true for trials.

7. Understand Your Role as an Advocate

These first six concepts are not self-executing. They require an advocate. An advocate does more than represent a client or protect a client's rights. An advocate exhibits unrelenting commitment to the client's cause, and actively seeks to influence jurors by reaching their hearts and minds. Your role as an advocate begins on the day you accept the case and ends when you close the case after trial. Always assume that the jurors (as well as judge and opposing counsel) see and hear everything you, your client, and your trial team do and say. Always assume that you are "on camera," even when the trial is not in session.

An advocate is both a director and an actor. You are a director, because a trial is much like theater. While limited to the script (what the witnesses say and exhibits show), the director uses creativity in choreographing that script (how the witnesses say it and how the exhibits are presented). You are also an actor, because you are constantly on stage. In many cases you will be the most important "witness" as you communicate with the jurors throughout the trial.

An effective advocate is always credible. This requires that you act professionally and fairly with the judge and opposing counsel. You must be trustworthy,
knowledgeable, and dynamic so that the jurors see you as the teacher, helper, and
guide. And it means that you must be yourself, so that the jurors know you are
genuine.

An advocate always conveys a sense of injustice.
Jurors must recognize it and be compelled to correct
it, so that they feel good in reaching their decision.
Jurors subconsciously ask a critical question: Are you
saying it because you've been paid to say it, or are you
saying it because you believe it? You need to project
passion and commitment to your cause and expose
the injustice to motivate the jurors to decide the case
in your favor (without crossing the line into overtly
expressing personal opinions).

For a discussion
of professionalism, ethics,
and attorney credibility,
please watch Video A.11,
"Wyo STI: Professional
Responsibility and
Attorney Credibility."

Finally, an advocate always seeks to control the atmosphere in the courtroom.
An advocate grabs and holds the jurors' attention, sets the tone for the trial, and
becomes the dominant influence as the trial progresses. Jurors should look to you
for leadership and guidance and look forward to when you do things. This means
you need to plan how you, your client, and your trial team conduct themselves
throughout the trial, not just in the courtroom, but also during recesses, during
lunch breaks, and going to and from the courthouse. Plan how you interact with
the judge, court personnel, opposing counsel, and your client whenever the jurors
are present. And plan how to organize the visuals—your attire, counsel table,
exhibits, notebooks, and files—down to the smallest detail. When you control
the atmosphere in the courtroom, through your conduct and your visuals, you
enhance your power to persuade.

In trials, good things happen when you make them happen. The true advocate understands this and acts on it.

2.4 Conclusion

These are the key concepts that trial lawyers must understand and use during
trial preparation and at every stage of a jury trial. They will influence your jury
voir dire and peremptory challenges, shape your opening statements and closing
arguments, structure your direct and cross-examinations, and design your trial
exhibits. They will influence how you, the advocate, put them together into a
persuasive whole. The key concepts are:

- Prepare from the jury's point of view
- Develop a theory of the case
- Select themes and labels
- Emphasize the people
- Use storytelling techniques
- Focus on the key facts and issues
- Understand your role as an advocate

Does this mean that, simply by using these concepts, any case can become
a winner? Of course not. The facts of most cases determine their outcomes. In

litigation, cases in which the facts strongly favor one side rarely go to trial. These usually settle. Cases where both sides have strengths and weaknesses, so that the outcome is in doubt, are most likely to go to trial. In these cases, effective trial lawyers—advocates—do make a difference.

2.5 Selected Reading List on Psychology of Persuasion

Jury Persuasion: Psychological Strategies & Trial Techniques
  by Donald E. Vinson & David S. Davis
  Thomson West, 3rd ed., 1996

Courtroom Psychology and Trial Advocacy
  by Richard C. Waites
  American Lawyer Media, 2003

Now What Makes Juries Listen
  by Sonya Hamlin
  Thomson West, 2008

Theater for Trial
  by David A. Ball & Joshua Karton
  Trial Guides, LLC, 2017

The Articulate Attorney: Public Speaking for Lawyers
  by Brian K. Johnson & Marsha Hunter
  Crown King Books, 2nd ed., 2013

Influence: The Psychology of Persuasion
  by Robert B. Cialdini
  Harper Collins, rev. ed., 2006

Influence: Science and Practice
  by Robert B. Cialdini
  Allyn and Bacon, 5th ed., 2008

Sway—The Irresistible Pull of Irrational Behavior
  by Ori Brafman and Rom Brafman
  Broadway Books, 2009

Jury Selection
  by V. Hale Starr & Mark McCormick
  Wolters Kluwer, 4th ed., 2009

Bennett's Guide to Jury Selection and Trial Dynamics in Civil and Criminal Litigation
  by Cathy E. Bennett & Robert B. Hirschhorn
  West, 1993

Mastering Voir Dire and Jury Selection: Gain an Edge in Questioning and Selecting Your Jury
by Jeffrey T. Frederick
American Bar Association, 3rd ed., 2012

Courtroom Psychology for Trial Lawyers
by Thomas Sannito & Peter J. McGovern
Aspen, 1992

Eyewitness Testimony
by Elizabeth F. Loftus
Harvard University Press, 1996

Eyewitness Testimony: Civil and Criminal
by Elizabeth F. Loftus, James M. Doyle & Jennifer E. Dysart
LexisNexis, 5th ed., 2013

Linguistic Evidence: Language, Power, and Strategy in the Courtroom
by William M. O'Barr
Academic Press, 1995

The Visual Display of Quantitative Information
by Edward R. Tufte
Graphics Press, 2d ed., 2001

Envisioning Information
by Edward R. Tufte
Graphics Press, 1990

The Wall Street Journal Guide to Information Graphics
by Dona M. Wong
W. W. Norton & Company, 2010

Inside the Jury
by Reid Hastie, Steven D. Penrod & Nancy Pennington
The Lawbook Exchange, Ltd., 2013

Inside the Juror—The Psychology of Juror Decision Making
by Reid Hastie, editor
Cambridge University Press, 1994

The Psychology of the American Jury
by Jeffrey T. Frederick
Michie, 1987

CHAPTER 3

JURY SELECTION

3.1 Introduction

In a jury trial, each side seeks to select jurors who will be receptive to its party, witnesses, evidence, and lawyer, and who will eventually return a favorable verdict. The jury selection process, also called the *voir dire*, recognizes that in an adversarial system neither side is trying to get a fair and impartial jury. That's because the lawyers are advocates and are trying to get a jury that will favor their side. A fair and impartial jury results when competent trial lawyers representing the opposing parties try to identify and eliminate those jurors most likely to favor the other party.

Jury selection is a two-way street. As the lawyers are picking the jurors, the jurors are picking the lawyer—the lawyer they like, the lawyer they trust. That lawyer is the one the jurors will prefer to listen to, the one who will be increasingly influential as the trial progresses.

To make the jury selection process effective, trial lawyers must know the applicable procedural law and the jury's perspective; how to create a comfortable environment for the jurors so that meaningful self-disclosure occurs; and what information to get. Finally, trial lawyers must know how to ask questions that produce useful information, so they can make informed decisions on how individual jurors assess the world in general and how they will react to the evidence and issues in this case. Done well, the jury selection process is reasonably effective at identifying and striking the most unfavorable jurors to each side. Done poorly, it fails to identify unfavorable jurors and succeeds only in wasting time and boring or even alienating the jurors.

3.2 The Law

The law that governs the jury selection process is jurisdiction specific. In federal court, civil cases are governed by Rules 38–39 and 47–49 of the Federal Rules of Civil Procedure; criminal cases are governed by Rules 23–24 of the Federal Rules of Criminal Procedure. In state courts, most jurisdictions have similar civil and criminal rules and statutes.

A good practice is to put a copy of the applicable federal and state rules and statutes in the jury section of your trial notebook, so it will be readily available. Note, however, that the rules and statutes frequently do not provide answers to some of the issues that arise about the jury selection process. The answers often come from case law, local practices, and the individual judge's preferences. Before you select a jury, you need to learn the following topics:

- Number of jurors and alternate jurors
- Strike and panel systems for questioning jurors
- Juror questioning methods
- Judge, lawyer, and hybrid questioning methods
- Scope of questioning
- Cause challenges
- Peremptory challenges
- *Batson* limitations on peremptory challenges

You must always know the applicable law and how the judge intends to select the jury in your case. If the rules and statutes do not provide the answers, find out. Ask other lawyers how the judge selects the jury in your type of case. Ask the judge's staff. Better yet, watch a jury selection before your judge in a similar kind of case. If you still have questions, ask the judge before your trial begins.

1. Number of Jurors and Alternate Jurors

Learn the number of jurors required in your case. Trials use between 6 and 12 regular jurors, but the specific number varies widely by jurisdiction and the type of case being tried. The number of jurors in particular civil and criminal cases is usually controlled by rule or statute. For example, federal civil jury trials use not less than 6 nor more than 12 jurors; federal criminal jury trials use 12 jurors.

Learn the number of alternate jurors required or permitted in your kind of case and, if flexible, the number your judge intends to select in your case. Alternate jurors are chosen to replace regular jurors if any of the regular jurors become unable to serve through the end of the trial, for reasons such as illness, family emergency, or other disqualification. Having alternates avoids the mistrial that would result from not having enough regular jurors to decide the case.

The number of alternate jurors is often up to the judge's discretion. For example, judges commonly allow two alternate jurors in a case that will take more than one day but less than one week to try; more alternates are selected for longer trials. As an alternative, lawyers sometimes agree not to select alternate jurors and stipulate that fewer than the usual number will be acceptable for a valid verdict. For instance, lawyers may stipulate, in a civil case, that they will not select alternates and that a verdict of not less than 10 jurors (instead of the usual 12) will be a valid verdict. (This is usually not a good idea for the defense.)

In some jurisdictions, any alternates remaining at the end of the trial are dismissed, and the regular jurors then begin their deliberations. In others, alternates remaining at the end of the trial deliberate with the regular jurors. In still others, alternates are not identified beforehand; instead, they are chosen by lot and dismissed if an excessive number of jurors remains when deliberations begin.

2. Strike and Panel Systems for Questioning Jurors

Learn which questioning system will be used. Rules and statutes rarely specify how prospective jurors are to be questioned, so the questioning system is largely left up to the judge. The two most common systems used today are the strike system and the panel system, although numerous variations of these systems exist.

The *strike system* is used extensively in federal district courts and some state trial courts. In the strike system, the prospective jurors usually sit as a group in the spectator section of the courtroom. Every juror is then questioned in the order in which their names appear on the jury list. The lawyers then make their requests for any cause challenges and exercise their available peremptory challenges. The jurors not challenged by either side are called in the same order into the jury box until the required number of jurors (and any alternates) have been seated. Those jurors become the trial jurors, and any remaining jurors are dismissed.

The *panel system* is used principally in state courts. In the panel system, the prospective jurors also sit as a group in the spectator section of the courtroom. The required number of jurors (most commonly 12), sometimes supplemented by the total number of peremptory challenges, are then called into the jury box, usually in the order in which their names appear on the jury list, and only those jurors are questioned. The lawyers then make their requests for any cause challenges and exercise their available peremptory challenges. Any jurors challenged are dismissed, and new jurors are called into the jury box to replace the dismissed jurors. These new jurors are then questioned, the lawyers again make their cause and peremptory challenges, and the challenged jurors are again dismissed and replaced by new jurors. This process is repeated until all the jurors in the jury box have been accepted by both sides. Those jurors become the trial jurors. The same process is used to select any alternative jurors. Dismissed jurors are sent back to the jury assembly room, where they may be called to another courtroom.

3. Juror Questioning Methods

Learn how jurors will be questioned. Three basic methods are used to question the prospective jurors during the jury selection process: written questionnaires, individual private questioning, and questioning in open court. As with much of the jury selection process, the method used is largely left up to the judge, and the judge may use more than one method in a particular trial.

Written questionnaires range from one or two pages to fifty pages or more. Jurors are given the questionnaires to complete either before or when they arrive in the courtroom. When the jurors have completed them, copies of the completed questionnaires are given to the judge and lawyers.

Some lawyers like written questionnaires, especially in big cases with sensitive issues, because the amount of juror self-disclosure improves significantly when written questionnaires are used instead of questioning in open court. This is because many jurors will not disclose their attitudes or personal experiences in front of other jurors, but they will disclose them in the relative privacy of a questionnaire. However, such questionnaires, often prepared with jury consultants, are expensive and time-consuming, and lawyers frequently fight over what questions should be permitted and how those questions should be worded. As a result, most judges allow written questionnaires only in trials involving substantial pretrial publicity and complex and sensitive issues, and they usually limit the number of questions asked and subjects covered. Nevertheless, if you believe your case requires a questionnaire, ask for it.

Individual private questioning is another option. With this approach, the jurors are questioned individually—sometimes in the judge's chambers, sometimes in the courtroom out of the hearing of the other jurors. The advantage is more self-disclosure by jurors; the disadvantage is that it is time-consuming.

The most common method is questioning in open court. With this approach, the jurors are questioned in the courtroom, and every juror can hear the questions asked of, and answers given by, the other jurors. Here, the advantage is efficiency, as most juries can be selected in one to three hours. The disadvantage is reduced self-disclosure, because many jurors are reluctant to disclose their attitudes and experiences in front of other jurors. If specific questions are sensitive, ask the judge to question the juror out of the hearing of the other jurors.

Because the jury questioning method is discretionary with the judge, lawyers must decide before trial which method is likely to serve them better and ask the judge to use that method. However, the judge will permit such methods only if he is convinced that a written questionnaire or individual private questioning is necessary under the particular circumstances of the case. In routine civil and criminal cases, questioning the jurors in open court is the predominant method.

4. Judge, Lawyer, and Hybrid Questioning Methods

Learn who will do the questioning. Jurors may be questioned by the judge, or lawyers, or both. Judge questioning is common in federal courts and some state courts. In some courts, the judge may do all the questioning. The lawyers' participation is limited to requesting that the judge ask the jurors particular questions or that she delve into particular subjects.

Lawyer questioning is the traditional method and is still common in some state courts. With this approach, the judge greets the jurors, introduces the lawyers and parties, and makes some introductory comments. The questioning of the jurors is then turned over to the lawyers. The usual procedure is that the plaintiff asks questions first, then the defense. The judge may put a time limit on each side.

The most common method today is a hybrid of the judge and lawyer methods. With this approach, the judge asks the preliminary questions, either of the jurors as a group or individually. The judge's questions are usually directed to matters that may trigger challenges for cause. Hence, the judge may ask questions to make sure that each juror meets the statutory requirements for jury service; has no personal problems or commitments that would interfere with jury service; has no close relationship to any of the parties, witnesses, or lawyers; and has no fixed opinion about this kind of case or what its outcome should be. The judge may also ask about the basic backgrounds of each juror, such as family, education, job, residence, and whether the juror has ever been involved in an event similar to that underlying the case being tried. After the judge rules on any cause challenges, the lawyers then have an opportunity to question the jurors. The judge may impose time limits, such as 30 minutes per side.

The hybrid method is popular because it allocates the questioning sensibly. The judge does the preliminary questioning because the judge is primarily interested in determining if the jurors are qualified to serve and have anything in their backgrounds that would trigger a challenge for cause. The lawyers do the follow up questioning, as they are interested in asking more focused questions so they can intelligently use their peremptory challenges.

Regardless of the questioning method used, when you question jurors put away any notes and checklists and communicate directly with them. Notes and checklists are a serious barrier to candid communication. Whenever possible, take someone with you for jury selection. That person must be observant, take good notes, and have common sense. That person need not be, and perhaps should not be, a lawyer.

5. Scope of Questioning

Learn what latitude the lawyers will have in questioning jurors. Most judges take the view that questioning by lawyers should be limited to learning about the jurors, their backgrounds, and their life experiences.

In a few states, however, jury questioning is more broadly permitted. There, lawyers may also ask questions that principally convey information to the jurors. When this is permitted, lawyers frequently "test" their evidence to gauge the jurors' reactions. For example, in a personal injury case involving eyewitnesses, a lawyer may ask: "Do you believe that a person can witness a terrifying crash and later accurately testify about what happened?"

Many lawyers also like to test their themes during jury selection. Most judges today permit lawyers to ask these kinds of questions. For example, in a personal injury case involving punitive damages, a lawyer may ask: "Do you think that some corporations put company profits ahead of product safety?" In an industrial accident case, a lawyer may ask: "Should workplace safety be the employer's responsibility or also the worker's responsibility?"

The line between obtaining information from and conveying information to a juror is a blurred one, however. For example, asking a juror: "Have you ever seen a person take a fast left-hand turn at an intersection trying to beat an oncoming car?" seeks information about the juror's life experiences, but it also conveys the suggestion that this is what happened in this case. Many judges do not permit questions the principal purpose of which is to test the jurors' reactions to anticipated trial evidence.

Some lawyers try to obtain the jurors' commitment to follow the law on core legal concepts such as the burden of proof, presumption of innocence, liability and damages being separate issues, and assessing the credibility of particular kinds of witnesses. Most judges allow such questions, as answers may give rise to a challenge for cause, although not all lawyers agree that such commitment questions are effective.

6. Cause Challenges

Learn the grounds for challenges for cause. A potential juror may be challenged for cause—dismissed from jury service—if the juror does not meet the statutory requirements for jury service. Common requirements are that the juror must be at least 18 years old, be a resident of the county or district in which the trial is being held, not be related to the parties, and have no felony convictions. A juror can also be challenged for cause if the juror cannot be fair and impartial, usually because the juror has a fixed opinion about the issues in the case or which side should win.

There is no limit to the number of cause challenges that can be made in any case. However, if the judge requires you to state your challenges for cause in open court, challenged jurors, as well as others on the panel, might see your challenges as attacks on the character of the jurors you challenge. Therefore, there may be a practical cost to each challenge for cause.

7. Peremptory Challenges

Learn how many peremptory challenges (also called *strikes*) each party has. Peremptory challenges generally can be used by the parties to dismiss a potential juror for almost any reason. The number of challenges is usually governed by rule or statute, but the rules frequently give the judge discretion to allow additional challenges when appropriate and to decide how to allocate the challenges if there is more than one party per side. Under 28 U.S.C. §1870, in a federal civil trial each side has three peremptory challenges; under Fed. R. Crim. P. 24, in a federal criminal trial the prosecution has six challenges and the defense has ten.

If the trial has more than one plaintiff or defendant, the rule or statute frequently permits the judge to give additional challenges to each side. The rule might permit the plaintiffs and defendants to use their challenges jointly (*pool*) or separately.

Learn if you will be allowed to reinvade the jury, also called "*back-striking.*" This means striking a juror whom you initially accepted. For example, under the panel system, the plaintiff may initially accept a panel of jurors and tender the panel to the defense. If the defense strikes any of the panel, the panel is then tendered back to the plaintiff. May the plaintiff then strike a juror from the panel that the plaintiff initially accepted? Some courts allow this, some do not. Your ability to back-strike affects your strategy in using your available strikes under the panel system.

8. *Batson* Limitations on Peremptory Challenges

The parties' general right to use their available peremptory challenges for any reason has an important limitation. In a series of cases—*Batson v. Kentucky*, 476 U.S. 79 (1986); *Powers v. Ohio*, 499 U.S. 400 (1991); *Edmonson v. Leesville Concrete Co.*, 500 U.S. 614 (1991); *Georgia v. McCollum*, 505 U.S. 42 (1992); *J.E.B. v. Alabama*, 511 U.S. 127 (1994); and *Purkett v. Elem*, 514 U.S. 765 (1995)—the Supreme Court collectively held that in civil and criminal cases, neither the plaintiff's nor the defendant's lawyers can use their peremptory challenges to eliminate potential jurors solely on the basis of the jurors' race or gender. Some lower federal courts and state courts have extended *Batson* to include ethnicity, national origin, religious affiliation, and other juror characteristics.

Under *Batson*, the procedure for questioning a peremptory challenge is a three-step inquiry. First, a party must object to the other party's use of a peremptory challenge on *Batson* grounds and make a *prima facie* showing of improper use of the challenge (e.g., a juror was struck because of race or gender). Second, the party wishing to exercise the challenge must come forward with a race- or gender-neutral explanation for using the challenge (e.g., the juror was struck because she went to the same high school as the defendant). Third, if a race- or gender-neutral explanation is made, the objecting party must then prove purposeful discrimination on race or gender grounds (e.g., the offered explanation is a pretext and the real reason for the peremptory challenge is race or gender discrimination). The trial judge determines these issues. If the judge finds discrimination, the strike is denied and the challenged juror remains on the jury.

In 2016 the Supreme Court decided *Foster v. Chatman*, 578 U.S. 399 (2016). In that case the Court reversed a conviction in a capital murder case on *Batson* grounds. Only the third part of the *Batson* test—whether the defendant had proved purposeful discrimination—was in issue. The Court, after a detailed review of the factual record of the jury selection phase of the trial, held 7-1 that the prosecution's explanations for exercising peremptory challenges against two black jurors were pretextual and demonstrated purposeful discrimination.

3.3 The Jury's Perspective

Imagine what has happened to jurors before they ever arrived in the courtroom. They received a jury summons commanding their appearance in the courthouse today. They checked in at the jury assembly room, received their juror badges, sat down, and read a pamphlet or watched a video describing their upcoming service. And then they waited. Eventually, their names were called, and a bailiff took this group of jurors to a particular courtroom and directed them to sit in the spectator section.

What are these prospective jurors feeling and thinking? What are their attitudes toward jury service, the court system, judges, lawyers, and litigants?

Many of the jurors are anxious. Many are uncertain whether they should serve at all and whether they are up to the task ahead. Some are apprehensive, fearing that embarrassing details about their private lives will be aired in the courtroom before strangers. Some feel intimidated by being in an unfamiliar environment.

Some feel uninformed, because the pamphlet or video about jury service hardly answered all their questions. Some feel alienated from the whole trial process, particularly those who resent being summoned in the first place. Some are skeptical about the motives of the litigants and lawyers who fill the courthouses.

The jurors also bring with them their personal experiences, deep-seated beliefs, and attitudes about life and how things work in the real world. They have expectations about how a trial should be conducted; how lawyers should act; how they want witness testimony, exhibits, and visual aids to be presented; and how they want to be treated during the course of the trial.

Effective trial lawyers recognize the jurors' needs, attitudes, and expectations and respond to them throughout the jury selection process.

3.4 Create a Comfortable Environment for Self-Disclosure

> ■◀ For a discussion of the psychological and social dynamics of voir dire, please watch Video B.2, "Wyo STI: Introduction to Voir Dire."

Effective jury selection requires juror self-disclosure, but that will not happen unless there is a comfortable, relaxed environment in which self-disclosure can occur. Jurors will not express their feelings, particularly on sensitive topics, unless they feel safe in doing so. How does this happen, and what should the judge and lawyers do to make it happen?

1. The Judge

First, the judge should take the lead. The judge is the authority figure in the courtroom, and sets the tone for the jury selection process. Good judges welcome the jurors to the courtroom, put them at ease by describing what is going to happen, and involve them in the process. All this should be done quickly and conversationally.

2. The Lawyers

Although the lawyers are left with the atmosphere created by the trial judge, they can also significantly influence the environment and improve juror self-disclosure. Think how you normally act when you meet someone new in a business or social setting. How do you get to know someone and connect with them?

First, establish an appropriate physical environment. Stand (unless restricted to counsel table or a podium) at a social distance, a few feet away. Keep your posture open and receptive by facing the person and avoiding crossing your arms or assuming other defensive postures. Use your voice, eye contact, facial expressions, and gestures to show genuine interest in the other person.

Second, chat. Introduce yourself, give the other person your undivided attention, and demonstrate that you are interested in getting to know the person better. Tell him something about yourself, so he reciprocates by telling you things about himself. Be candid about your worries and concerns. Search for common backgrounds, interests, and experiences. Listen and respond positively. In short order, learn about the other person and whether the two of you "connect." You can do this quickly, in two or three minutes.

Get the jurors talking! Ask them questions that require a response. For example, ask: "How many of you feel that there are too many lawsuits today?" After a few jurors raise their hands, ask one of them: "Why do you feel that way?" After the juror answers, ask the other jurors: "How many of you agree with Mr. Smith?" Ask those jurors who raise their hands to explain why they feel that way. Ask if any jurors feel differently, and ask them to explain why. These are the kinds of questions that start conversations, and let the jurors know that they can talk freely without you appearing to judge them.

Third, steer the conversation to the topics you want to talk about. Ask short, nonleading, open-ended questions that invite the other person to talk freely. Listen actively and give the person positive verbal and nonverbal feedback. Listen and respond, show understanding, and be supportive. In short, you ask (not tell), listen (not talk), and feel (not think) to get the most self-disclosure from the jurors in the shortest amount of time.

Watch a successful talk show host as she warms up a guest in front of a live audience. In a few minutes, the relationship goes from stranger to friend, and soon the guest is spontaneously talking about his life experiences. Watch the host involve the studio audience. Effective talk show hosts are experts at interpersonal and group dynamics. They understand the significance of basic psychological principles—authority, likeability, and reciprocity—and how they contribute to self-disclosure. When jurors feel comfortable in the courtroom, an environment exists in which they are willing to talk about the important things: themselves, their history, interests, experiences in life, and feelings about important issues in the case.

What things are obstacles to self-disclosure? Whenever possible, get away from the counsel table or lectern, because these are physical barriers. Put away any notes, checklists, and notepads (have someone else take any notes), because these props suggest an interrogation, not a chat. Avoid lawyer words, because a lawyer vocabulary is another barrier. Don't pry, and don't ask questions that may create anxiety or discomfort, as jurors need to feel comfortable when disclosing details of their lives. Don't be judgmental, because this will shut down further disclosure. Leave the "lawyer" out of the courtroom, and have a chat with another person whom you are genuinely interested in knowing better.

Always remember that jury selection is a two-way street. As the lawyers are picking the jury, the jury is picking the lawyer—the lawyer who is open and honest with them, the one who appears interested in them as people, the one who trusts them to reach a fair decision. That's the lawyer the jurors will listen to during the trial.

3.5 Learn Juror Attitudes

Various theories of jury selection have enjoyed popularity over the past century. In the early 1900s, jury selection frequently was ethnically based. The United States was a country of recent immigrants, and the assumption was that those immigrant groups had identifiable, commonly held beliefs that strongly influenced their jury decisions.

In the mid-1900s, jury selection frequently focused on similarity analysis. The assumption was that jurors naturally like, and therefore find more credible, persons with backgrounds similar to their own. Hence, each side preferred jurors with backgrounds similar to its party or key witness.

In the late 1900s, increasing attention was paid to jurors' body language. This trend was based on the realization that jurors are frequently less than candid in discussing their backgrounds and life experiences during the jury selection process; hence, lawyers recognized that they needed to focus more on whether the jurors' answers to questions were consistent with their intonation, facial gestures, and other body language.

In the past 40 years, research has identified a method of jury selection that has become the dominant current approach: *juror attitudes*. This method accepts the fact that most decision making is a function of a person's background and experiences in life. A person's attitudes are the expressions of his or her beliefs; those beliefs are formed throughout life, and seldom change once formed. A person's attitudes—about people, government, business, and how the real world works—operate much like a filter and cause the person to process information about other people, situations, and events in light of the person's own background and experiences. If the information is consistent with their attitudes, they accept it. If the information is inconsistent with their attitudes, they either reject it or modify the information so that it becomes acceptable. This filtering is automatic and mostly subconscious.

Attitudes rarely change radically, and they rarely change quickly. It is a mistake for lawyers to think they can change juror attitudes on core beliefs and issues during the time span of a single trial. For example, if a juror believes that executives will cheat to increase corporate profits, that attitude of distrusting corporate executives simply will not change during the course of a trial.

Where do those attitudes come from? They come from the jurors' socioeconomic backgrounds, education, and jobs and whether they have achieved their goals in life; more from their acquired hobbies and interests, reading and television habits, and other information sources; and most of all from their personal and shared life experiences. These backgrounds and experiences form the attitudes that become the colored glasses through which they view life. They are the psychological filters through which jurors assess the themes, parties, and evidence during the trial.

In short, the principal purpose of jury selection is to learn the jurors' likely attitudes on matters important to the case. This allows the lawyers to determine which jurors will be receptive and which will be resistant to each side's themes, parties, and evidence.

The more circumstantial the evidence and the more common the event on which the lawsuit is based, the more important juror attitudes become. Jurors often "fill in" missing information to make the evidence complete and consistent, and they use their attitudes about how life works to fill in "what must have happened."

How do you learn the jurors' attitudes on issues important to the case? If you are in a jurisdiction where you can get the jury list before trial, you can research the jurors and see if they are on social media. However, remember that Model Rule 3.5 allows you to research jurors on social media sites, such as seeing if the juror's name comes up in a Google search, but you may not have ex parte communications with prospective jurors in any way, in person or through social media sites.

How do you discover juror attitudes during jury selection? Jurors frequently do not disclose their true attitudes about a given subject when asked about them directly. The more personal the attitudes, the more sensitive the subject, and the more divergent the juror's attitudes are from commonly held attitudes, the less likely the juror is to reveal his true attitudes accurately when asked directly about them. The reason is emotional. Most jurors want to be accepted by and fit in with others, particularly if the others are strangers. The need to be accepted and the internal pressure to hide or distort true attitudes are strong. In addition, lawyers who directly ask jurors about their attitudes on sensitive social and personal issues are seen as prying and are quickly resented by the juror being questioned and the other jurors. In high-publicity cases, some jurors will distort their backgrounds and attitudes to get on the jury (just as some jurors will distort their attitudes to get out of jury service).

The better way to learn jurors' likely attitudes on important matters is by indirection. That is, it is usually better to ask jurors about their backgrounds, interests, and life experiences, from which their attitudes can reasonably be inferred.

The typical background information that lawyers commonly ask about includes:

- Family history
- Residence history
- Education history
- Job history

However, these provide only a general socioeconomic snapshot of the juror. In common cases, such as a personal injury, contract, or robbery case, these general demographic characteristics are usually not significant factors in learning specific juror attitudes on matters important to the case. Nonetheless, such questions get a juror talking, create rapport, and help determine whether the juror has achieved satisfaction with life, which is a good indicator that the juror believes in personal accountability and responsibility.

Other information, however, is much more significant in learning likely attitudes. These include:

- Hobbies and personal interests
- Organizations participated with and active in
- Reading interests
- Magazines and newspapers read
- Television viewing and radio listening
- Computer usage
- Bumper stickers and decals
- Social media activity

What people like to do in their free time; what organizations they actively participate in; what kinds of books, magazines, and newspapers they read; what television and radio programs they watch and listen to; if and how they use computers; and even what bumper stickers and decals they have on their cars, computers, and other objects: all these give more insight into jurors and their attitudes.

One source of information, however, is usually more important than all the rest: *experiences in life similar to the event involved in the case being tried*. We know that most persons' attitudes about common things and events in life (e.g., cars, accidents, business deals, employment relationships, personal relationships, medical treatment, consumer products) are formed by their personal experiences or those of their immediate family and close friends. These personal experiences are highly significant in determining how jurors will view similar events in the future. One of the most commonly used phrases in the jury room during deliberations is "that's just like." To jurors, their personal experiences are as much "evidence" as the formally introduced evidence from witnesses and exhibits, and they usually recount those experiences during jury deliberations. Again, though, care must be taken to avoid being too direct, because this can be seen as intrusive or assertive.

The message to lawyers conducting voir dire is clear: spend less time learning general demographic information; more time learning about hobbies, personal interests, organizations, reading habits, news and information sources, and television, radio, and computer use; and the most time learning about the jurors' personal experiences and the experiences of their immediate family members and close friends that are similar to the events on which the case being tried is based.

Listen to what the jurors say, but also listen to and watch how they say it. Most information is transmitted through nonverbal cues, such as accompanying intonation, facial gestures, and other body language. These provide the overtones that reveal the jurors' real attitudes and are frequently more revealing than the actual verbal answers.

Jurors are understandably reluctant to directly discuss their attitudes and feelings about sensitive issues, particularly if they know that their attitudes are not shared by most others. However, if the case involves sensitive issues, some lawyers prefer to tackle the issues head-on and discuss them openly and candidly with the jurors. Ask yourself: What troubles me in this case? What issues am I most worried about? What can make me lose this case? In a criminal case, it may involve attitudes on race, foreign nationality, or gun ownership. In a civil case, it may involve attitudes about too many lawsuits brought by greedy lawyers, corporations that are more interested in profits than safety, or businesses that destroy records to hide their wrongdoing. Whatever the issue, it won't go away because you ignore it. Tell the jurors your concerns and feelings. After that, you can ask the jurors to share their feelings about the issue with you and each other. For example, ask: "Who here believes that . . .?" "Why do you believe that?" "Who else feels the same way?" (That's the psychological principle of reciprocity at work.) When they do, thank those jurors who speak up for sharing their thoughts and feelings, and keep encouraging others to speak up as well. Above all, *never be judgmental*, regardless of what any juror says. Any honest disclosure by a juror—even or perhaps especially one that reveals a potentially unpopular attitude—is a gift to you!

3.6 Learn Strength of Juror Attitudes

It is not enough to identify the attitudes jurors likely hold. You must also learn the strength with which they hold those attitudes. For example, if one party in a case has police officers as key witnesses, it will be important to determine how jurors feel about the police and police officer testimony. It makes a difference if a juror has a mild distrust of police testimony because of a general attitude about the police, or if a juror has a strong distrust of the police because he was once accused of a crime based on false police testimony. If a case involves drunk driving, it makes a difference if a juror has a personal dislike of alcohol, or if the juror has a deep-seated disapproval of alcohol because a family member is afflicted with alcoholism. Learning the likely attitudes of jurors should always be coupled with determining the strength with which those attitudes are held.

How do you learn how strongly jurors hold their attitudes? Primarily, by asking open-ended questions. Three kinds of questions are important here: the what, why, and how questions.

The "what" questions get the basic facts. For example, asking: "What happened to you during the collision?" will get the basic facts. The "why" questions get the explanations; that is, asking: "Why did the collision happen?" will get the explanation from the person's point of view. But the "how" questions are the key, because they get the feelings. Asking: "How did you feel when the other car suddenly turned right in front of you?" will get the person's feelings about not only that collision, but also all other collisions that happened in a similar way. The how questions get the feelings, and the feelings usually show the strength with which jurors hold their attitudes.

3.7 Identify the Persuaders, Participants, and Nonparticipants

Even though each juror has only one vote, not all jurors are equal. Some jurors will carry more weight during the jury deliberations. A key part of the jury selection process is to identify those jurors who will have a strong influence on the other jurors. For this purpose, jury consultants usually divide jurors into three categories: persuaders, participants, and nonparticipants.

Persuaders are the leaders. They are the ones who speak up in a group, freely express their opinions and the reasons for them, readily argue why their opinions are correct, and instinctively try to recruit others to join them. In short, they express opinions and build coalitions. A persuader outside the courtroom is likely to be a persuader in the courtroom. In a typical jury, about 25 percent of jurors are persuaders.

Participants are the followers. When they speak, they express their thoughts and opinions and readily join others whose view they agree with. However, they do not argue for their views or try to persuade others. Instead, they identify the persuaders and decide which one to join in a coalition. About 50 percent of jurors are participants.

Nonparticipants take little or no part in jury deliberations. They usually hold no strong views, find little reason to contribute to the discussion, and limit their participation to voting. They are more interested in getting the deliberations over so they can get jury service behind them. About 25 percent of jurors are nonparticipants.

It is particularly important to identify the persuaders, learn their likely attitudes about issues important to the case, and learn the strength with which the persuaders hold those attitudes. In a typical jury, the persuaders do most of the talking during jury deliberations.

How do you determine whether a juror is a persuader? Persuaders are talkative and freely express their thoughts and opinions. A good way to identify persuaders is to ask group questions and see which jurors raise their hands and volunteer to speak. Note the jurors who confidently give answers and freely provide explanations. Persuaders also tend to have substantial supervisory experience in their jobs. Ask jurors about their job description, but also ask whether they supervise others. Persuaders usually have higher levels of education or training.

3.8 Identify the Punitive, Authoritarian, and Holdout Jurors

Finally, it is important to identify three other juror types: punitive, authoritarian, and holdout jurors. These jurors are dangerous in certain kinds of cases.

Punitive jurors feel a need to use their jury service to strike out against "the system." They are often loners, persons who have had recent traumatic experiences in their personal or work lives, and who feel alienated from the mainstream. They are often at the bottom of the socioeconomic order. Punitive jurors are the ones who frequently want to return large civil verdicts to punish someone or send a message to others. Such jurors are dangerous to corporations, governmental entities, and other wealthy defendants.

Authoritarian jurors believe that everything should be done "by the book" and that "rules are rules." They feel that laws are there for a reason and must be obeyed and that the way to succeed in life is to follow the rules. Authoritarian jurors are usually strongly prosecution-oriented in criminal cases.

Holdout jurors are independent enough to resist the common instinct to compromise and reach a consensus. They are often the free spirits, the nonconformists who relish living outside society's norms. They do not mind holding unorthodox views and are not easily persuaded by arguments just because they come from the majority. Holdouts are dangerous to the prosecution in criminal cases, where almost all jurisdictions require unanimous verdicts; and to plaintiffs in civil cases, if the jurisdiction also requires unanimous verdicts.

How do you learn if a juror is likely to be a punitive, authoritarian, or holdout juror? Punitive jurors are outside the mainstream, either temporarily or chronically. Find out if any jurors have had recent traumatic experiences, such as a divorce, being fired from a job, or other personal disappointments or family tragedies. Erratic employment history with many different jobs, none held for a long period, and low socioeconomic status are other cues. Punitive jurors often are angry and alienated from the mainstream. Ask jurors what their personal goals were in high school, whether they achieved them, and why they did or did not. Ask jurors what their goals are for the next five years. Answers to these kinds of questions often reveal jurors who are disappointed with life, feel that their situation in life is caused by others, and view life as basically unfair.

Authoritarians are people who fit easily into large organizations and know their place in them. They usually can be identified through their work history. Many have military backgrounds or work in governmental agencies or large businesses. They are deferential to authority. Ask the jurors to name three people they admire and why. Answers to these questions will frequently reveal an admiration of authority figures such as presidents and military leaders.

Holdout jurors are more likely to move frequently between jobs and be self-employed. Asking these jurors to name three people they admire and why will frequently reveal an admiration of independent persons, such as artists, writers, and entertainment figures. Their leisure-time activities frequently feature individual pursuits rather than group activities.

3.9 Questioning Techniques

We now have seen that jury voir dire should be directed toward accomplishing several goals:

- Creating a comfortable environment for self-disclosure
- Identifying juror attitudes on matters important in the case
- Determining the strength of these attitudes
- Determining if jurors are persuaders, participants, or nonparticipants
- Determining if jurors are punitives, authoritarians, or holdouts

How do you ask questions that accomplish these goals?

1. Create a Comfortable Environment for Self-Disclosure

In the first minute or two, you should introduce yourself; create a casual, friendly atmosphere; and get the jurors talking. Many lawyers today go directly to the jurors' life experiences, particularly if the judge has limited the amount of time each side has for questioning.

Example:

The judge has introduced the parties and lawyers, read the witness lists, and mentioned the date and location of the collision on which the case is based. None of the jurors knows the parties, lawyers, or witnesses, and none of the jurors has heard about the collision. The judge then turns the questioning over to the lawyers. The questioning is in open court, and both group and individual questions are permitted.

JUDGE: Plaintiff's counsel, you may begin.
LAWYER: Thank you, your honor. [Stand up, leave counsel table, and stand a few feet in front of the jurors, unless local rules require that you stay at counsel table or a lectern.] Good morning, folks. How many of you have ever been involved in a collision involving two cars? [Several jurors raise their hands.] How many of you have ever been involved in a collision in which you or someone was hurt, hurt seriously enough to be taken to a hospital? [Two jurors raise their hands.] The first juror on the end, your name is Ruth Adams, right?
JUROR: That's right.
LAWYER: Ms. Adams, please tell us about that collision.
JUROR: I was driving to work and stopped for a red light. The driver behind me wasn't paying attention and plowed right into the rear of my car.
LAWYER: So it was the other driver's fault?
JUROR: It sure was. Wasn't any doubt about that.
LAWYER: What happened to you?

JUROR: The crash threw my head and body back, and I hurt my neck.
LAWYER: How badly?
JUROR: They took me to the emergency room, checked me out and x-rayed my neck, and kept me overnight. Nothing was broken, but all the muscles in my neck and back hurt like crazy.
LAWYER: How long did it take you to recover?
JUROR: Well, I missed a week of work, and it took about a month before all the pain went away.
LAWYER: How were you compensated for your expenses, lost income, and the pain?
JUROR: The insurance took care of all that. I assume the other man's insurance paid, but it was all handled by my insurance company.
LAWYER: How has that experience affected you?
JUROR: I guess it's made me a more careful driver. It certainly makes me appreciate good health more.
LAWYER: Thank you, Ms. Adams. The other juror who raised his hand, that was Mr. Baker?

And so on. However, some lawyers prefer to ask easy background questions as a way to get jurors talking about themselves. This is a common approach, particularly if the judge has not imposed time limitations on the voir dire.

Example:

LAWYER: Ms. Andrews, good morning. How long have you lived here?
JUROR: Five years.
LAWYER: What brought you to our town?
JUROR: I lived all my life in Nevada and went to college there. I got married after college, and my husband's job transferred him here.
LAWYER: What kind of work do you do?
JUROR: I work for a real estate firm. I do the accounting and some administrative work.
LAWYER: And your husband?
JUROR: He's an accountant for one of the big accounting firms.
LAWYER: Let me guess—you met your husband in college?
JUROR: Right. We were both accounting majors, but he was a year ahead of me.
LAWYER: Tell us about your family.
JUROR: Right now it's just me, my husband, and our two-year-old.

And so on. Getting jurors talking immediately, using group and individual questions, is important. Being friendly, showing interest in the jurors' lives, asking easy introductory questions, and asking logical follow-up questions all help create a positive atmosphere in which jurors are not afraid to speak up and talk openly about themselves.

2. Identify Juror Attitudes on Matters Important in the Case

The next objective is to identify juror attitudes important to the case. This requires two steps. First, look at the parties, claims, defenses, and facts to determine what the important issues and disputes in the case will be from the jurors' point of view. Second, identify the kinds of questions that are likely to elicit disclosure of the jurors' backgrounds, interests, and life experiences that will reveal the jurors' attitudes on those important issues and disputes.

Keep in mind the hierarchy of background information, the third being the most important:

1. Socioeconomic history
   - family
   - residence
   - education
   - job
2. Personal interests
   - hobbies
   - organizations active in
   - newspaper, magazine, and book reading interests
   - television viewing, radio listening, and internet searching
   - other information sources
   - bumper stickers and decals
3. Life experiences
   - personal, family, and close friends' experiences similar to event on which case is based

General socioeconomic history has little predictive value in most cases. (However, jurors who have achieved satisfaction in life, often by reaching a comfortable socioeconomic level, usually believe in personal accountability and responsibility, an attitude that is important in both criminal and personal injury cases.) Personal interests, especially personal experiences similar to the case being tried, are usually much stronger indicators of relevant juror attitudes. This does not mean that you should never ask jurors about their history, because doing so can get them talking and you can sometimes learn a great deal from it, and expressing interest in the jurors and their lives is always important. Rather, it means that when you are looking for background information that suggests juror attitudes on key issues, it is much more useful to focus on personal interests and, most importantly, life experiences.

Example:

This is an automobile collision case. The plaintiff's lawyer will want to know if any jurors have attitudes generally adverse to plaintiffs and the tort compensation system. The plaintiff's lawyer will also want to find out if any jurors have been on the defense side of a similar lawsuit and therefore might look skeptically at plaintiffs and the tort system.

LAWYER: How many of you have ever had a lawsuit brought against you? [Several jurors raise their hands.] Mr. Smith, tell us about that lawsuit.
JUROR: I own a small business, a hardware store, and we've been sued a few times.
LAWYER: What kind of suits?
JUROR: I've been sued twice over deliveries of goods that were defective so we didn't pay for them. We've been sued once for a slip-and-fall incident.
LAWYER: The lawsuits with the suppliers—how did they end up?

JUROR: They settled pretty quickly once it became clear to them that they didn't deliver the kind of quality merchandise we had ordered.

LAWYER: The slip-and-fall—how did that end up?

JUROR: In that case a customer, an elderly lady, claimed she slipped on the floor in one of the aisles. No one else saw it, and there was nothing obviously defective about the floor. But we settled it after the lawsuit was filed.

LAWYER: Were you satisfied with how that case ended up?

JUROR: Not really. We never thought there was a valid basis for the claim, but our insurance company said it would be cheaper to settle for a few thousand than go to trial over it.

LAWYER: How do these lawsuits make you feel about lawsuits in general?

JUROR: Well, I now understand how easy it is to bring a lawsuit, even if you don't have a valid basis for it.

LAWYER: Thank you, Mr. Smith.

Example:

This is a murder case and the defense is insanity. The prosecutor will want to know if any of the jurors, or their immediate families or close friends, have ever had any involvement with psychiatry and whether any of the jurors has any education or employment in the mental health field. This would indicate that they might be more receptive to the defense's psychiatric evidence.

LAWYER: Did any of you study psychology, sociology, or similar fields in college? [Two jurors raise their hands.] Mr. Adams, what did you study?

JUROR: I was a sociology major in college.

LAWYER: Did you ever take courses in psychology?

JUROR: Nothing beyond Psych 101.

LAWYER: Ms. Williams, how about you? You also raised your hand.

JUROR: Yes, I was a psychology major at the university.

LAWYER: Did you ever study psychology after your undergraduate years?

JUROR: No.

LAWYER: What part of psychology were you interested in?

JUROR: Child development.

LAWYER: What attracted you to that area?

JUROR: I just find it fascinating how the brain develops from infancy through the first few years. The changes, the growth in mental abilities, are so fast and remarkable.

LAWYER: Thank you, Ms. Williams. Have any of you ever worked in the mental health field? [One juror raises her hand.] It's Ms. Henderson, right?

JUROR: That's right.

LAWYER: Ms. Henderson can you tell us about that experience?

JUROR: Sure. I worked for the Department of Mental Health for a year after college. I helped test children and adults who had various levels of intellectual impairment to determine what kind of training program would be best for them.

LAWYER: Did you find that work rewarding?

JUROR: Rewarding and tiring. It's very satisfying to see someone with limitations learn to be self-sufficient and able to go about daily life with minimal help.

LAWYER: Did you ever deal with children or adults who had behavioral problems?

JUROR: No, that was another department.

These kinds of questions, pleasant and nonjudgmental, elicit the kind of information that helps determine if jurors have receptive or resistant attitudes to your side of the key issues in the case.

If the court will allow it, ask questions to test the jurors' reactions to the key concepts and themes you plan to use during the trial. For example, in a personal injury case, you might ask: "Have any of you ever seen a driver who just couldn't wait to make a left-hand turn?" In a criminal case, you might ask: "Have any of you ever been frozen by fear?" Some judges bar such questions on the ground that they are designed more to convey concepts than to elicit information. Other judges permit such ways, and they can be good ways to determine if jurors will be receptive to—or at least open-minded about—your themes.

3. Learn the Strength of Juror Attitudes

Merely learning the likely juror attitudes about key issues in the case is not enough. You also need to determine the strength with which the jurors hold those beliefs. This is where the "what-why-how" questions become important. The what questions get the facts; the why questions get the explanations; and the how questions get the feelings.

Example:

This is a personal injury case in which the plaintiff's negligence claim is based on the defendant's drinking. The defense is that although the defendant had been drinking socially at a business reception, his drinking did not impair his driving. The defense lawyer will want to learn the jurors' attitudes about alcohol and how strongly they hold those attitudes.

LAWYER: How many of you sometimes drink alcohol at social gatherings or business functions? [A number of jurors raise their hands.] Are there any of you who never drink alcohol at any time? [Two jurors raise their hands.] Ms. Iverson, you raised your hand. Could you share with us why you never drink alcohol?

JUROR: Sure. I don't approve of it, so I don't do it.

LAWYER: Why don't you approve of it?

JUROR: I've seen too many lives ruined by alcohol.

LAWYER: Does that include anyone in your immediate family or close friends?

JUROR: Yes, my father was an alcoholic.

LAWYER: How did that make you feel?

JUROR: I alternated between feeling sorry for him and hating him. Our entire family suffered because of his drinking while I was growing up.

Here, simple, gentle, follow-up questions developed not just the juror's attitudes toward alcohol, but also the level of her feelings and the reasons for them.

This also is a good way to test the jurors' reactions to your themes (which some judges permit) and gauge the strength of juror attitudes.

Example:

> This is a civil fraud case. The plaintiff corporation claims that when it bought a subsidiary of the defendant corporation, the defendant misrepresented the financial condition of the subsidiary by submitting false financial statements. One of plaintiff's themes is that defendant "cooked the books."
>
> **LAWYER (plaintiff):** Mr. Gilbert, do you own stock?
> **JUROR:** Well, I guess I do through my company's retirement plan.
> **LAWYER:** Who decides what stocks are in your plan?
> **JUROR:** The managers of the plan do that.
> **LAWYER:** Do the managers rely on financial statements to decide what stocks to buy for the plan?
> **JUROR:** I suppose so.
> **LAWYER:** What does the term "cook the books" mean to you?
> **JUROR:** It means the financial records have been altered.
> **LAWYER:** By accident, or on purpose?
> **JUROR:** On purpose.
> **LAWYER:** Is this a common problem today?
> **JUROR:** You certainly hear enough about it.
> **LAWYER:** Why do some companies cook their books?
> **JUROR:** To look better than they really are.
> **LAWYER:** How do you feel about that?
> **JUROR:** It's dishonest. The people that do it should go to jail.

There is a cardinal rule you must always obey when delving into juror backgrounds and experiences: *do not embarrass a juror.* Jurors will let you know if you are getting into sensitive or private territory, either by telling you directly or by their inflection and body language. When jurors hesitate to answer, look to the judge before answering, refuse to make eye contact, or turn sideways and cross their arms, these are usually defensive and negative reactions to your questions. When that happens, don't pry, because that juror, and all the other jurors watching, will immediately resent you. If the information is important, ask the judge if the juror can be questioned at the bench on the sensitive matter so that the other jurors cannot overhear the conversation.

Example:

> This is a criminal case in which the defendant is charged with sexual assault. The defense will want to know if any of the jurors has been a victim of a serious crime.
>
> **LAWYER:** Have any of you or your immediate family ever been the victim of a crime? [Several hands go up.] How many of them were burglaries of a home or business? [Two hands go up.] How many of them were break-ins or thefts of cars? [Two hands go up.] Anyone else been a victim of a crime not involving burglaries or cars? [One hand goes up.] Mr. Avery, could you tell us what happened?
> **JUROR:** Well, it involved my sister.
> **LAWYER:** What happened?
> **JUROR:** It's rather personal.

LAWYER: Your honor, could Mr. Avery discuss this with us at the bench?

JUDGE: Very well. Mr. Avery, please come up to the bench. [Juror and law-yers walk to the judge's bench and speak in lowered voices.]

LAWYER: Mr. Avery, now that we're up here, can you tell us what hap-pened to your sister?

JUROR: My sister was sexually assaulted in her dorm room when she was a student. There were never criminal charges brought, but the guy was expelled from the university. She's wanted to keep that private, since she still lives here.

LAWYER: Of course, Mr. Avery. We understand. Thank you for sharing this with us.

JUDGE: Mr. Avery, do you think that what happened to your sister might affect how you view this case, since it also involves a sexual assault charge?

JUROR: I don't think so. This case depends on its own evidence.

JUDGE: Very well. Let's have everyone return to their seats.

4. Learn if Jurors Are Persuaders, Participants, or Nonparticipants

Identifying the persuaders in the jury pool is particularly important, because they tend to dominate the discussions and have a disproportionate influence over the other jurors. Persuaders are talkative, willing to speak in front of strangers, and freely express their thoughts and opinions. Ask group questions to see who volunteers to speak. Find out who has supervisory experience over others.

Example:

LAWYER (plaintiff): How many of you think there are problems with our trial system, the system that allows persons to file lawsuits and have their cases heard before a jury? [A few jurors raise their hands.] Ms. Johnson, you raised your hand. What are the problems?

JUROR: I think it's too easy to file lawsuits.

LAWYER: Why do you feel that way?

JUROR: My company is constantly being sued, and most of the lawsuits are complete nonsense.

LAWYER: What company do you work for?

JUROR: I work for Robinson's, the department store chain.

LAWYER: What's your job with Robinson's?

JUROR: I'm in the accounting department.

LAWYER: Specifically, what do you do?

JUROR: I'm in charge of the receivables section. We make sure that all income is accounted for and that people and businesses who owe us money actually pay us.

LAWYER: How many people work for you in your section?

JUROR: It varies. Right now I've got 18 employees.

LAWYER: Thank you. Mr. Williams, you also raised your hand. Do you feel there are problems with our trial system?

JUROR: Yes.

LAWYER: In what way?

JUROR: It's so slow and expensive. It seems to take forever to get a case to trial, and it seems you have to be rich before you can afford a lawyer to take a case in the first place.

LAWYER: Any personal experience that got you to that view?

JUROR: I was in the rental real estate business for a while, and we were constantly filing lawsuits against persons and businesses who had breached their agreements, usually by failing to pay the rent. There was always a question of whether it made sense to file a lawsuit or whether it was cheaper just to take the loss.

LAWYER: Who had to make those decisions?

JUROR: I did.

5. Learn if Jurors Are Punitive, Authoritarian, or Holdouts

Finally, you might need to identify if any jurors are punitives, authoritarians, or holdouts, because these are important characteristics in certain kinds of cases.

Punitive jurors are dangerous in civil cases to defendants who are corporations, governmental entities, or wealthy individuals. Punitive jurors have a need to strike out against a system that they see as fundamentally unfair, especially to the "little guy," and they do it by returning large damages awards against such target defendants. Punitive jurors are often at the bottom of the socioeconomic scale; they are are frequently loners who feel alienated from the mainstream. Sometimes they have had traumatic experiences in their personal or work lives.

Example:

> This is a lawsuit against a large automobile dealer. The plaintiff claims that the dealer fraudulently sold him a used car knowing that it had been involved in a major collision and had not been properly repaired, but nevertheless represented that the car was in perfect condition. The plaintiff is seeking both compensatory and punitive damages. The defendant's lawyer will want to know if any jurors will be receptive to returning a large damages award against the dealership.

LAWYER (defendant): Mr. Belkin, when you were in high school, what did you want to be?

JUROR: A pilot.

LAWYER: Did you become a pilot?

JUROR: No.

LAWYER: Did you change your plans?

JUROR: No. You've got to have money to get the training. I wasn't born rich, so it never happened.

LAWYER: What kind of work are you doing now?

JUROR: This and that. I've been a waiter and done maintenance and yard work.

LAWYER: Where do you see yourself in five years?

JUROR: Probably about where I am now.

Authoritarians are dangerous to defendants in criminal cases. They are deferential to the government and authority figures and believe that "rules are rules" and are there to be followed. Authoritarians frequently have military and law enforcement experience or are career government and corporate employees.

Example:

This is an armed robbery prosecution. The defense is mistaken identification.

LAWYER (defendant): Mr. Mason, what did you do after high school?
JUROR: I enlisted in the Army.
LAWYER: How did you like your Army years?
JUROR: They were good. The Army made me grow up and become responsible.
LAWYER: What was the best thing about the Army?
JUROR: Well, it trained me in electronics. But I guess the best thing is that in the Army you learn what the rules are and what you're supposed to do, and if you do that everything will work out.
LAWYER: What did you do after the Army?
JUROR: I left after my three years were up, but I'm still in the Reserves. I went to work for Raytheon, the military supplier.
LAWYER: And you've been there ever since?
JUROR: Right. It'll be 15 years next month.
LAWYER: Mr. Mason, if you were to pick one person, other than your parents, whom you admire, who would that be?
JUROR: I guess I'd pick General Eisenhower.
LAWYER: Why Eisenhower?
JUROR: He put everything together to make the invasion of Normandy during World War II possible. That wasn't easy. And he was a pretty good president.

Holdouts are dangerous to prosecutors in criminal cases, because the prosecution in almost every jurisdiction needs a unanimous verdict to win. They are dangerous to plaintiffs in civil cases in jurisdictions that require unanimous verdicts. Holdouts are the underdogs, free spirits, and nonconformists. They often have individual, rather than group, interests and admire independent persons.

Example:

This is a burglary case. The defendant was arrested one day later with goods taken from the scene of the burglary, but claimed he'd obtained the goods from someone else without knowing they were stolen.

LAWYER (prosecutor): Ms. Adams, what kind of work do you do?
JUROR: I'm a freelance photographer.
LAWYER: What do you like best about that work?
JUROR: The independence. I can set my own hours, take the jobs I like, and I don't have to answer to anyone except myself. Being your own boss is the best. You may not earn the big bucks, but you get to control your own life.
LAWYER: Ms. Adams, I've asked this of other jurors, so I'll ask you as well: If you had to pick one person, other than your parents, whom you admire, whom would you pick?
JUROR: I'd probably pick a painter like Picasso.
LAWYER: Why?
JUROR: Because he decided what he wanted to do with his life and how to live it. No one dictated to him, no one told him what to do.

Identifying any punitive, authoritarian, and holdout jurors in the jury pool is the last step in evaluating the potential jurors. You have now focused on four key juror attributes:

- Juror attitudes
- Strength of juror attitudes
- Persuaders, participants, and nonparticipants
- Punitives, authoritarians, and holdouts

You are now ready to use your limited number of peremptory challenges to deselect those jurors who are persuaders holding strong attitudes unfavorable to your side, and any other jurors who are particularly dangerous to your side.

3.10 Exercising Cause and Peremptory Challenges

For an overview of the jury selection process, please watch Video B.1., "Mauet on Jury Selection."

During the jury selection process, you will need to make cause challenges and exercise your allocated peremptory challenges (sometimes called *strikes*). How you do this depends largely on the method by which jurors are questioned and the practice of the trial judge. Section 3.2 discussed the law governing challenges; this section discusses when and how to make cause and peremptory challenges.

1. Challenges for Cause

Challenges for cause can be made either in the presence of the jury or out of the jury's hearing, depending on local practice.

a. Strike System

Under the strike system, used in federal courts and some states, the judge and lawyers usually question all the jurors before any challenges for cause are made. After all the jurors have been questioned, the judge usually calls the lawyers to the bench or calls a short recess. The judge then asks if either side challenges any juror for cause.

The usual reason for a challenge is that the juror already has a fixed opinion of how the case should be decided or has a close relationship to a party, and cannot be fair and impartial. After both lawyers have argued the point, the judge rules. For example, if the juror is a close friend of a party, or works for one of the parties, most judges will excuse that juror for cause. If any juror is struck for cause, the judge and lawyers simply draw a line through that juror on the jury list.

Example:

JUDGE: Counsel, please approach. [Lawyers come to the bench.] Any challenges for cause?

LAWYER: Just one for the plaintiff, your honor. Mr. Mendez is a registered nurse who used to work at Mercy Hospital, the defendant in this case. He said he knows the doctors and nurses who are on the witness list, and said that knowing those witnesses would probably influence his judging the case. We ask that he be excused for cause.

JUDGE: Defense, any objection?

LAWYER: No, your honor.

JUDGE: Very well. Mr. Mendez will be excused for cause.

If there is some personal or health reason why a juror cannot serve on the case, or when service would be a hardship, the judge may excuse the juror on the spot and send the juror back to the jury assembly room. For example, if a juror has surgery scheduled, a wedding date set, or a nonrefundable vacation planned, the juror will usually be excused. Although this is not technically a challenge for cause, its effect is the same: The juror is excused from sitting on this case, and will probably be called for jury duty at a later time.

b. Panel System

Under the panel system, used in many states, the jurors in the jury box are questioned, and then the lawyers exercise their challenges. Dismissing a juror for cause can be a sensitive moment, so many judges direct the lawyers to come to the bench after one or more jurors in the jury box have been questioned. The judge then asks if either side challenges a juror for cause, hears the basis for the challenge and any opposing argument, and rules. After the bench conference, the judge excuses any juror who has been successfully challenged and directs the juror to return to the jury assembly room. Under this method, the jurors watching do not know which party challenged the juror.

In some courts, challenges are made in open court in front of the jurors. After the judge asks if there are any challenges, most lawyers say something like: "Your honor, we ask that Ms. Johnson be excused for cause from serving on this particular case." If the reason is obvious, the judge may rule immediately. If the judge wants to hear arguments, she may direct the lawyers to come to the bench. If the judge wants to hear arguments in open court, diplomacy is obviously called for.

Example:

JUDGE: Counsel, any challenges?

LAWYER: Yes, your honor, we ask that Ms. Williams be excused for cause.

JUDGE: What's your basis?

LAWYER: Ms. Williams has worked as a manager for a drug company for many years. The defendant in this case is a drug company, and the defense witnesses are primarily from the company. Ms. Williams candidly told us that she believes people who work for drug companies are highly qualified and credible people. It seems clear that Ms. Williams will find those witnesses from the defense automatically credible, and that's unfortunately not consistent with judging witness credibility at arm's length. Therefore, we ask that Ms. Williams be excused from sitting on this case, and that she be sent back to the jury assembly room so she can serve on a case not involving a drug company.

If the judge grants the challenge, the juror is excused. If the judge denies the challenge, the juror remains in the jury pool. If that occurs, because the jurors know which party made the challenge for cause, that party usually will have to use one of its peremptory challenges to remove the hostile juror.

The situation in which disputes most commonly arise over challenges for cause is when a juror clearly shows a tendency to favor one side, and the question is whether that juror has a sufficiently fixed opinion about how the case should be decided that he should be dismissed for cause.

Example:

This is an armed robbery case. The prosecution claims that the defendant gave a voluntary statement following his arrest in which he admitted committing the robbery. The defense claims that the statement was a result of police threats and trickery. The credibility of police officer testimony is, therefore, an important issue in the case.

LAWYER (defense): Mr. Jackson, do you have any family, close relatives, or friends who work in law enforcement?

JUROR: Yes.

LAWYER: Tell us about them.

JUROR: My brother-in-law is a police officer in the city, and my next-door neighbor is a deputy sheriff.

LAWYER: Do you see them often?

JUROR: I see my brother-in-law maybe once a week, the neighbor once or twice a month.

LAWYER: Do you consider your brother-in-law and neighbor good police officers?

JUROR: Sure.

LAWYER: Honest?

JUROR: Sure.

LAWYER: Mr. Jackson, in this case we're going to be hearing from several police officers. Would you tend to give the testimony of police officers more weight because they are police officers?

JUROR: Well, the police officers I know are pretty straight people.

LAWYER: I guess my question is, would you give the testimony of police officers you don't personally know more weight than the testimony of other persons?

JUROR: I might, depending on the situation.

LAWYER: What kind of situation would that depend on?

JUROR: Well, like I said, the police officers I know are pretty straight, and I'd believe what they say, but if a police officer testified in a way that didn't make sense, I guess I'd have to think twice about him.

LAWYER: Your honor, may we come to the bench for a moment?

JUDGE: Yes. [Lawyers come to the bench.]

LAWYER: Your honor, in light of Mr. Jackson's responses, we ask that he be excused for cause. He's clearly indicated that he will generally give police officer testimony greater weight than other witnesses. Given the credibility issues in this case, Mr. Jackson can't be fair and impartial.

JUDGE: Any response from the state?

LAWYER (prosecutor): Your honor, Mr. Jackson did not say he could not be fair and impartial or that he has a fixed opinion of how this trial should come out. That's not enough for a challenge for cause.

JUDGE: The motion is denied at this time. If further questioning of Mr. Jackson changes things, you may renew your motion.

Most judges are reluctant to grant requests to dismiss a juror for cause unless it is clear that the juror cannot be fair and impartial. In fact, some judges (and opposing counsel, when they question the juror) try to "save" questionable jurors from being challenged for cause by asking the juror a rehabilitating question, such as: "Your relationship with other police officers, that wouldn't keep you from being fair and impartial in deciding this case, would it?"

In the preceding example, in which the judge denied the request, the lawyer probably should use one of her peremptory challenges to eliminate this clearly unfavorable juror.

2. Peremptory Challenges

How peremptory challenges are exercised is also controlled by the trial judge, and is largely based on whether the judge uses the strike or panel system to question the prospective jurors. As discussed in Section 3.2, each side has a limited number of challenges that can be exercised for almost any reason. Whatever the number, each side needs to use its available challenges to remove those persuaders who appear to have beliefs and attitudes unfavorable to that side, especially persuasive, punitive, authoritarian, and holdout jurors holding unfavorable attitudes. Jury selection, then, is the process of using your available challenges to deselect the most unfavorable jurors.

a. Strike System

Under the strike system, which is used in most federal and some state courts, each party receives a list of all the prospective jurors in the jury pool. After all the jurors have been questioned and the judge has ruled on any cause challenges, each side exercises its available peremptory challenges (strikes) by drawing a line through the name of each juror challenged and placing the lawyer's initials by the line.

In some courts, each side exercises its challenges on its own list. With this method, duplicate challenges between plaintiff and defendant are possible. In other courts, plaintiff and defendant work off one list, alternating challenges until each side has used its available challenges. With this method, duplicate challenges are impossible, as each side can see who the other side has already challenged. The judge or court clerk then calls the appropriate number of jurors, starting from the top of the list, who have not been challenged by either side, so that the proper number of jurors (and any alternates) are seated and sworn to try the case. Any jurors not called are then dismissed and sent back to the jury assembly room.

In recent years, the strike system has become the standard system in federal courts, and more states are adopting it. There are clear advantages to this system: It allows the lawyers to learn about the entire jury pool before they exercise their peremptory challenges, and it avoids much of the gamesmanship of the panel system.

b. Panel System

Some version of the panel system is still used in some states. In the panel system, the required number of jurors (or the required number of jurors plus alternates and peremptory challenges) is called to fill the jury box, and only those jurors are initially questioned. The lawyers then make any peremptory challenges they wish to make, either at a bench conference or in open court. The challenged jurors are then excused, and, if necessary, new jurors sitting in the spectators' seats are called to replace the excused jurors. Those new jurors are then questioned, and the process is repeated until the jury box is filled with the required number of jurors not challenged by either side. Any alternate jurors are selected the same way.

When peremptory challenges are made in front of the jurors, tact is obviously called for. After the judge asks if there are any peremptory challenges, most lawyers say something like: "Your honor, we thank but excuse Ms. Johnson." The judge then excuses the juror and directs the juror to return to the jury assembly room.

The panel system allows more gamesmanship than the strike system. For example, a lawyer may decide not to use a peremptory challenge against a juror, thinking that the other side will use a challenge against the same juror. Some jurisdictions allow the lawyer to reinvade the jury, or back-strike, meaning that the lawyer can use a peremptory challenge against a juror whom the lawyer initially accepted. Where this is allowed, the gamesmanship involved in deciding whether and when to challenge a juror also increases.

There is a cardinal rule in using peremptory challenges under the panel system: Do not run out of challenges! In the panel system, lawyers are constantly checking how many challenges they have left, how many the other side has left, and what the rest of the jury pool (not yet examined) looks like. Cases are legion in which a lawyer used her last challenge to excuse an unfavorable juror, only to see that juror replaced with an even more unfavorable juror. Save one of your peremptory challenges for just such a disaster. However, this rule has one important exception. Case law in most jurisdictions generally holds that a party may not raise, on appeal, error based on the trial court's denial of cause challenges or overruling your *Batson* objections unless that party has used all its available peremptory challenges.

As noted earlier, the lawyers' right to use their available peremptory challenges for almost any reason has one important limitation: *Batson.* Under the *Batson* line of Supreme Court cases, lawyers in civil and criminal cases may not challenge jurors solely because of their race or gender. When a peremptory challenge is objected to on *Batson* grounds, the judge must determine if there is a prima facie showing of a violation; if so, whether there is a race- or gender-neutral explanation for the challenge; and, if there is, whether the explanation is pretextual. Some lower federal courts and state courts have extended the *Batson* analysis to ethnicity, national origin, and other characteristics. Most *Batson* issues arise in criminal cases.

Example:

This is a sexual assault case. The defendant is charged with sexually assaulting another college student. The defendant claims he met the victim at a party and that the sex was consensual. The case is being tried in state court, which uses the strike system, and the prosecution and defense are alternating strikes from one jury list. The jurors are not in the courtroom. The prosecution strikes three male jurors with its first three strikes. When the prosecution uses its fourth strike against another male juror, the following happens:

LAWYER (defense): Your honor, I object to the prosecution using a peremptory strike against Mr. Williams on *Batson* grounds. They've already struck three men, and it looks like they intend to use all their strikes to eliminate any men from the jury. Striking a juror because of gender violates *Batson*.

JUDGE: Prosecution, what's your response?

LAWYER (prosecution): Your honor, the juror we just struck, Mr. Williams, grew up in the same neighborhood as the defendant. In addition, he stated during questioning that he believed that date rape was not a serious problem on college campuses and that people were making a big deal of it. That's the reason we struck him, not because Mr. Williams is a male.

JUDGE: Defense, what's your response to the state's explanation?

LAWYER (defense): That explanation is pretextual, your honor. They've used their first three strikes to get rid of the first three men on the jury list. Their conduct shows what they're up to: They're trying to get an all-woman jury. That violates *Batson*.

JUDGE: The motion is denied at this time, and the strike against Mr. Williams will be allowed. However, you may renew your *Batson* motion should the prosecution continue to use its peremptory strikes without a credible gender-neutral reason for doing so.

Batson objections are difficult to win. In most situations, such as the one in the example, the judge will overrule the objection but pay closer attention to the issue as the parties continue to use their peremptory challenges.

3.11 Example of Voir Dire

Example:

This is a products liability claim brought by Helen Smith, who used the prescription weight loss drug "Wate-Off" sold by the defendant, Global Pharmaceutical. Following prolonged use of Wate-Off, Ms. Smith contracted liver cancer, for which she is undergoing treatment. Plaintiff claims that defendant put the drug on the market without adequate long-term testing, that prolonged use of the drug significantly increases the chance of liver cancer, and that consumers were not warned of this fact. Defendant claims that it did all testing required by government agencies and that the drug received FDA approval before being put on the market.

The case is being tried in federal court. The judge does the preliminary voir dire, then turns questioning over to the lawyers with time limitations. The strike system is being used, and plaintiff and defendant alternate their strikes using one list. The jury panel has just been brought into the courtroom and is sitting in the spectator section. No written jury questionnaire has been used.

Introduction. The judge's first step is to introduce the case, the parties, and the claims. Most judges also introduce the court personnel and what they do during the trial.

JUDGE: Good morning. I'm Sandy Jones, and I'll be your judge for this trial. Our case is called *Helen Smith versus Global Pharmaceutical*. Ms.

Smith claims that she took Global's prescription drug called Wate-Off, a weight reduction medication, and that later she contracted liver cancer as a result of taking the drug. Ms. Smith claims that Global did not adequately test the drug before putting it on the market and that if Global had adequately tested it, Global would have known that Wate-Off increases the risk of getting liver cancer.

Global denies the plaintiff's claims. Global claims that Wate-Off is a safe drug, and claims that it did all testing required by government agencies and received FDA—that's the federal Food and Drug Administration—approval before putting Wate-Off on the market.

Jurors sworn in to answer questions.

Before we go any further, we need to swear you in as jurors to answer questions. Please stand. [Jurors stand.] Our court clerk, Ms. Adams, will administer the oath. [Clerk administers oath.] Please sit down. [Jurors sit.]

Judge questioning. If jurors raise their hands, the judge will ask follow-up questions to learn the extent of the jurors' knowledge and if that knowledge would prevent the jurors from fairly trying the case.

Have any of you heard anything about this lawsuit? If so, raise your hand. Do any of you know the plaintiff, Helen Smith? How about the defendant, Global Pharmaceutical? The lawyers in this case are Pat Fields, who represents the plaintiff, and Chris Jones, who represents the defendant. Do any of you know the lawyers? Have any of you or your family used the prescription drug Wate-Off? Have any of you heard or read anything about Wate-Off? Is there anything about this lawsuit that would prevent any of you from listening to the evidence with an open mind and being fair and impartial to both sides?

I'm going to read a list of the names of witnesses who may testify in this case. If any of you know any of these witnesses, raise your hand.

Most judges will ask the jurors if they have had previous jury service, what kind of cases they served on, and whether that experience would influence them in this case.

Have any of you previously served as jurors in any court? If so, raise your hand.

Standard juror background topics include: name, residence, marital status, spouse and children, education, job history, reading, television, and radio habits, hobbies, and personal interests. Some judges may include military service, family or friends in law enforcement, bumper stickers and decals, and other personal information.

The next step is to learn a bit about each of you. What we're going to do is ask questions about each of your backgrounds—your name, where you live, your family, education, job, and hobbies and other personal interests. To make things easy, we're going to use the checklist on the poster board that's been set up so all of you can see it. Does anyone have any trouble reading the checklist? I'm going to ask each of you to stand up, introduce yourself, and use the checklist to go over your backgrounds.

The first juror in the first row, let's start with you. Please stand, introduce yourself, and use the checklist to talk a little about your background and history.

JUROR: I'm John Zamora. I've lived here all my life and live in Pine Hills. I'm married and have two children. My wife is a homemaker right now, and the children—that's Mark, who's eight, and Sarah, who's five—are in elementary school. I graduated from high school and went into the Army for three years. I'm a jet mechanic working for Southwest Airlines at the airport. As far as reading, TV, and radio are concerned, I read the morning paper, get *Sports Illustrated*, watch mostly sports events and movies on TV, and listen to popular music on the radio driving to and from work. I like to work on cars, go camping with the family, and hunting during the season. That's about it.

JUDGE: Thank you, Mr. Zamora. Let's hear from our next juror.

[Each juror then stands up and states his or her background, using the poster board as a checklist, with the judge asking follow-up questions as necessary.]

This background questioning may take 30 to 60 minutes, depending on the number of jurors in the pool. When the lawyers do the questioning, time limitations of 30 to 60 minutes per side are common.

JUDGE: The lawyers now have the opportunity to talk with you, within the time limitations I've previously set. The plaintiff's lawyer will go first, followed by the defendant's lawyer. Counsel, please proceed.

Plaintiff questioning.

LAWYER (plaintiff): Thank you, your honor. Good morning, folks. I'm Pat Fields, and I'm here for Helen Smith, who has brought this lawsuit against Global Pharmaceutical.

Plaintiffs usually want to identify jurors who believe there is a "litigation explosion" of frivolous lawsuits.

LAWYER: How many of you think that there are too many lawsuits being brought in the courts? [Several jurors raise their hands.] Of those who just raised their hands, how many of you think that many of those lawsuits have no merit and are brought just to try to get money from someone else? [Two jurors raise their hands.] Ms. Chen, you raised your hand. How do you feel about that?

Notice the how and why questions; they get more information than the what questions.

JUROR: I think that many people today file lawsuits without any basis for them.

LAWYER: Why do you think that?

JUROR: The papers and TV are always full of stories about people who bring lawsuits and collect money without really having proved that somebody else is responsible for what happened.

LAWYER: Mr. Woods, you also raised your hand. How do you feel about this?

JUROR: I used to work for an insurance company, and we constantly saw lawsuits that were a joke. Too many people seem to think that you can get money simply by bringing a lawsuit against another party, even if what happened is your own fault. That's a real problem today.

LAWYER: How did you figure out which lawsuits were a joke and which ones had merit?

JUROR: We had to investigate everyone to find that out.

LAWYER: You had to look at the evidence?

JUROR: I guess you could put it that way.

Supervisory experience at work is a strong indicator that a juror is likely to be a persuader during jury deliberations.

LAWYER: How many of you have work that requires you to supervise the work of other employees? [A few hands go up.] Mr. Lynch, tell us about your work.

JUROR: I run the credit department of a local department store. I supervise about 20 employees.

LAWYER: How do you supervise them?

JUROR: Most of our employees do credit checks as part of the credit card application process, and some deal with delinquent accounts—slow pays, we call them. My job is to make sure they follow the required procedures, and I may handle problem situations from time to time.

LAWYER: Ms. Sherman, how about you?

JUROR: Yes, I'm a unit director in the city building department. My unit reviews building applications, and we have about 10 employees.

LAWYER: Describe what your supervisory job involves.

JUROR: I basically review the work of my employees, make sure that they don't miss anything important, and answer questions and solve problems when they pop up.

In this case, you will want to ask jurors about their attitudes about drugs.

LAWYER: How many of you regularly take drugs of any kind, either prescription or over-the-counter? [Almost all hands go up.] How many of you expect those drugs to be safe? [All hands go up.] Ms. Robertson, whose responsibility is it to make sure that the drugs are safe?

JUROR: That should be the responsibility of the company that sells it.

Here the lawyer is testing plaintiff's themes: safety, responsibility, and drug testing.

LAWYER: Why is that?

JUROR: The company that makes it should know what the drug does. They should test it to make sure it's safe.

LAWYER: Do any of you feel that the person using the drug should take the risk that the drug might actually hurt him? [One juror raises his hand.] Mr. Weiss?

JUROR: I don't know about taking the risk, but the person using the drug has the responsibility to read the warnings and use the drug correctly. He shouldn't be allowed to misuse or overuse the drug and then blame the maker if something bad happens to him.

LAWYER: What if he takes the drug the right way and it still hurts him?

JUROR: I guess it would still depend on the warnings. All drugs can have side effects, and you take drugs hoping they will do more good than bad. If the person taking the drugs was warned about possible side effects, then he shouldn't be able to blame the maker if he gets those side effects later on.

LAWYER: What if the person is never warned about a side effect?

JUROR: That's a different story. The maker ought to know what the side effects of a drug are and warn people about them.

The plaintiff will also want to explore attitudes about FDA regulation of the drug industry and its approval of a drug for sale to the public.

LAWYER: Let's talk a little about government regulation. The federal government, through the Food and Drug Administration, regulates the drug industry. How many of you have heard of the FDA? [Several hands go up.] Ms. Anderson, let me ask you: Is making sure drugs are safe the job of the maker, or the FDA?

JUROR: I don't know, but I would guess both.

LAWYER: Do you think a drug maker should be able to avoid responsibility for the harm its drug causes because the FDA has approved the drug for sale to the public?

JUROR: No, I think the manufacturer should still be responsible. They're supposed to test it, aren't they?

LAWYER: Let me ask all of you: Do any of you believe that a drug manufacturer should be able to avoid responsibility for harm caused by a drug it sells to the public because the FDA approved it for sale to the public? [One juror raises her hand.] Ms. Baird?

JUROR: It seems to me the question is who does the testing? If the FDA tested the drug and failed to discover that the drug could be dangerous, it seems that should be the responsibility of the FDA. But if the drug company was responsible for the testing, and failed to discover that the drug could be dangerous, then that should not be the responsibility of the FDA.

LAWYER: It all depends on who's responsible for the testing?

JUROR: That's right.

Work history in industries related to the defendant should always be explored.

LAWYER: Have any of you ever worked for an insurance company, other than Mr. Woods? Have any of you ever worked for a drug or pharmaceutical company? Have any of you ever worked in a hospital or doctor's office? How about working for a chemical company? [One juror raises his hand.] Mr. Cruz?

JUROR: I used to work for a paint company, if that counts.

LAWYER: Sure. Tell us about your work at the paint company.

JUROR: I worked on the finishing line, where the paint was taken from the tanks and put into the paint cans and sealed.

LAWYER: Was that dangerous work?

JUROR: Not unless there was a spill. The main concern was that the ventilation system worked right, so we didn't breathe the paint fumes.

LAWYER: Could that be dangerous to your health?

JUROR: Sure.

LAWYER: Whose job was it to make sure that the workplace was safe?

JUROR: That's the company's job. Our job was to tell the bosses immediately if anything was not working properly.

LAWYER: Thanks very much, folks. Your honor, I have no further questions.

Defense questioning. The defense will want to explore attitudes about lawsuits, burdens of proof, and corporations.

JUDGE: Defense?

LAWYER: Thank you, your honor. I'm Chris Jones, and I represent Global Pharmaceutical. How many of you think that because we were sued, there must be something to it? [Two hands go up.] Mr. Pollock?

JUROR: Well, something must have happened, otherwise nobody would have sued.

LAWYER: Of course. I guess my question is, because we were sued, does that mean we must be responsible?

JUROR: No.

LAWYER: Ms. Franklin, you raised your hand. How do you feel about this?

JUROR: The fact that you were sued means, I guess, that the plaintiff thinks your side did something wrong.

LAWYER: So who should be required to prove it?

JUROR: The plaintiff should have to do that.

The defense might as well discuss this now, in front of all the jurors, because they will certainly discuss this during their deliberations.

LAWYER: Let me ask all of you that: The law says that the plaintiff, who brought this lawsuit, must prove her claims by the greater weight of the evidence. Do any of you have any problems with that law? Do any of you think that it should be our—Global's—job to disprove her claims? [One juror raises her hand.] Ms. Abraham?

JUROR: Well, if the question here is whether that drug was safe, it seems to me that the company should have to show that it was safe. After all, they made it and sold it.

This may not be enough to get the juror struck for cause, but the defense will probably need to strike her.

LAWYER: Thank you, Ms. Abraham. Do any others of you feel that once the plaintiff brings a lawsuit, it should be the defendant's job to disprove the claims?

The defense needs to explore the "David vs. Goliath" issue and attitudes.

LAWYER: Then let's turn to another subject. My company, Global Pharmaceutical, is a large company. How many of you feel that the fact that Global is big is an important fact in this case? [One juror raises his hand.] Mr. Woods?

JUROR: I'm thinking that if the question here is whether that drug was properly tested, the size of the company might have something to do with that.

LAWYER: Why is that important?

JUROR: A big company probably has a bigger and better lab to do that testing.

LAWYER: Do any others of you have feelings about the size of a company in a lawsuit?

The defense will also want to learn about any juror involvement in lawsuits, prior jury and grand jury experience, and attitudes formed from those experiences.

LAWYER: How many of you have ever been a party to a lawsuit? [A few jurors raise their hands.] Ms. Winston?

JUROR: I was the plaintiff in a divorce.

LAWYER: Other than a divorce or custody case, any others? [Two jurors raise their hands.] Mr. Johnson?

JUROR: I was charged in juvenile court when I was 15.

Always suggest discussing a sensitive matter out of the presence of the other jurors, to avoid embarrassing any juror.

LAWYER: Mr. Johnson, would you feel more comfortable talking about that in private?

JUROR: No, it was a good thing that happened to me. I was caught smoking marijuana, and I was put on probation for a year. That pretty much straightened me out.

LAWYER: Our other juror who had her hand up?

JUROR: Yes, I'm Shirley Martin. I was involved in a car crash and hired a lawyer to sue the other driver. They settled before trial.

LAWYER: Were you satisfied with how that case was handled and how you were treated?

JUROR: Definitely, although it took over a year to get the case settled.

The defense usually wants to tackle the sympathy factor candidly.

LAWYER: It's natural to feel sympathy for anyone who suffers from liver cancer. How many of you feel sympathy for Ms. Smith? [Several hands go up.]

LAWYER: Ms. Pollock, you raised your hand. How do you feel?

JUROR: I feel terrible for her. No one wants to get cancer.

LAWYER: The others who raised their hands, you feel pretty much the same? [Jurors nod their heads.] That's only natural. My concern is that your natural sympathy will start you off feeling that the plaintiff starts with an advantage. Who thinks he or she might have any problem following the law that says that the plaintiff has to prove her case by the greater weight of the evidence? [One hand goes up.] Ms. Pollock?

This may not be enough to get the juror struck for cause, but the defense will obviously need to consider striking her.

JUROR: I'd certainly be concerned that Ms. Smith might not be able to get proper medical care unless she recovered something here.

LAWYER: You think that Ms. Smith should get something, given her situation?

JUROR: I'm not sure, but I have to be honest. It's on my mind.

LAWYER: Thank you for your candor, Ms. Pollock. Anyone else feel like Ms. Pollock?

Drug history, particularly with weight loss drugs, must be explored.

LAWYER: Let me ask another question of all of you: How many of you take a prescription drug now? [Several hands go up.] Have any of you had problems in taking your medication? [One hand goes up.] Ms. Kavanagh, could you share with us what happened?

JUROR: Sure. I was taking a drug for high blood pressure. It made me very nervous, so my doctor switched me to another prescription. That drug worked much better.

LAWYER: Did you blame the first drug for making you nervous?

JUROR: Yes, but that was one of the possible side effects my doctor warned me about.

LAWYER: Have any of you ever taken a prescription drug for weight loss? Have any of you ever taken an over-the-counter drug for weight loss? [Two jurors raise their hands.] Mr. Adams?

JUROR: I took diet pills back in college when I was trying to lose weight. It worked, but then people told me that it was dangerous because it contained speed, so I stopped taking it.

LAWYER: Who told you?

JUROR: Other college students.

LAWYER: Didn't the package tell you what was in the medication?

JUROR: I suppose so, but no one really reads all that stuff.

LAWYER: Ms. Helm, you also had your hand up.

JUROR: Yes, I've done the same thing, taken over-the-counter weight loss drugs.

LAWYER: Do you remember which one?

JUROR: It was Dexatrim.

LAWYER: How often have you used it?

JUROR: Three or four times during the past several years.

LAWYER: Did you have any problems in using it?

JUROR: No.

This final question can sometimes get revealing responses.

LAWYER: I've just about used up my time, so let me end by asking one final question. Is there anything you feel we should know about you, that we don't already know, that you would want us to know if you were in our position, the parties and lawyers? [One hand goes up.] Yes, Mr. Wills?

JUROR: I don't know if this is what you want, but I had a nephew who died of a drug overdose a few years ago.

LAWYER: Was that from a prescription drug?

JUROR: No, it was some illegal drug. He'd had drug problems since his teenage years, and it caught up to him.

LAWYER: Thank you for sharing that, Mr. Wills. Your honor, we have no further questions of the panel.

Judge.

JUDGE: Members of the jury, we're going to take a recess at this time. It shouldn't be more than about 15 minutes. Please wait outside and be ready to come back into the courtroom at 11:30, and please don't discuss this case among yourselves or others. [Jurors leave the courtroom.] Counsel, does either side have any challenges for cause you wish to make?

Cause challenges are made.

LAWYER (plaintiff): No, your honor.

LAWYER (defendant): Yes, your honor. We ask that Ms. Pollock be struck for cause. She was the juror who said that she was influenced by sympathy for the plaintiff and that it would be on her mind. That's not being fair and impartial.

JUDGE: Plaintiff, any argument?

LAWYER (plaintiff): Yes. Ms. Pollock said she felt sympathetic, but she never said she could not be fair and impartial. That's not enough to strike her for cause.

Peremptory challenges are made.

JUDGE: The motion is denied. Counsel, make your allotted strikes on the one jury list, alternating strikes, beginning with plaintiff, and initial your strikes. When you're done, let me know. I'll be in my chambers. [Judge leaves courtroom. The lawyers exercise their strikes on the jury list. When done, they notify the judge, who comes back to the courtroom and checks the list. The bailiff then brings the jurors back into the courtroom and again has them sit in the spectator section.]

Trial jurors are announced. If alternate jurors are needed, the judge will have the clerk call the appropriate number of additional jurors from the list.

JUDGE: Members of the jury, we are now going to call out the names of those jurors who will hear the evidence and decide the case. The clerk will call the first 12 names from the list. When your name is called, please take any seat in the jury box. [Clerk calls the names of the jurors, who fill the jury box.] Those jurors who did not get to sit on this case, the bailiff will now take you back to the jury assembly room, and hopefully we can find another case in which you will be able to serve as jurors. [Bailiff escorts the remaining jurors out of the courtroom.]

Jurors sworn to try case.

Those jurors in the jury box, please stand and the clerk will swear you in as trial jurors. [Jurors stand, and the clerk administers the oath for jurors.] Please be seated. [Jurors sit.]

Preliminary instructions of law.

Members of the jury, I am now going to give you some preliminary instructions about your duties as jurors, how the trial will proceed, a few things you need to do and cannot do during the trial, and the law that applies to the claims and defenses in this case. When we are done with that, the lawyers will give their opening statements. [Judge then reads the preliminary instructions to the jury.]

Notice what the lawyers did not do: spend time on general juror backgrounds, and ask useless questions such as whether jurors can be fair and impartial. Instead, they went directly to the jurors' significant experiences in life and asked questions designed to learn the jurors' attitudes, and the strength of those attitudes, about key concepts and issues important to the case. When each side is limited to perhaps 30 to 60 minutes, time is precious, and you need to focus immediately on the high-yield questions.

3.12 Trial Notebook

The jury selection section of your trial notebook should have everything you need to pick a jury in a particular case. First, put a copy of the applicable federal or state rules and statutes in this section. Disputes over the number of peremptory challenges, discretionary additional challenges, the number of alternates, and whether multiple plaintiffs and defendants get additional challenges or can pool their challenges, are surprisingly common.

Second, develop a good-versus-bad juror profile. This should identify the background characteristics and experiences of the jurors you want (those who will be receptive to your themes, theory of the case, party, witnesses, and evidence) and, more importantly, of the bad jurors you need to strike. In civil cases, you might also refine the good-bad dichotomy for the issues of liability and damages, because jurors who may be good on liability may not always be good on damages. Many lawyers prepare a simple diagram like the following:

Example:

JUROR PROFILE—PLAINTIFF

Bad jurors	Good jurors
▨ Nondrivers or occasional drivers	▨ Commuters and city drivers
▨ Young	▨ Senior citizens
▨ Non-drug takers	▨ Prescription drug users
▨ Business management or ownership	▨ Medicare/Medicaid enrollees
▨ Insurance, drug, health industry experience	▨ Employees/lower incomes

The defendant's juror profile should resemble the opposite of the plaintiff's. Developing a profile of good and bad jurors will get you focused on asking the kinds of questions needed to elicit the information that will enable you to categorize the jurors appropriately.

How do you develop the juror profile? This is where experience comes in, because trial lawyers learn through experience what kinds of people are "good" and "bad" jurors in particular kinds of civil and criminal cases. Jury consultants frequently research community attitudes and help the trial lawyers ask the right questions to identify jurors who hold attitudes strongly unfavorable to their side. What do you do if you don't have experience, and you don't have a litigation budget that permits hiring a jury consultant? Ask experienced lawyers. Tell them what your case is about legally and factually; what your party, the other party, and the key witnesses are like; and what the issues on liability and damages are, so they can help you identify the kinds of jurors likely to be unfavorable to your side.

Third, develop a list of specific questions you want to ask, or, if the judge will do all the questioning, specific questions you will request the judge to ask in a written motion. Be prepared to ask appropriate follow-up questions.

Example:

SPECIFIC QUESTIONS

Q: Do any of you presently take prescription drugs?
Q: Have any of you ever taken prescription diet drugs?
Q: Have any of you ever taken over-the-counter diet drugs?
Q: Have any of you ever worked for an insurance company, hospital, doctor, or drug company?
Q: Have any of you ever had a reaction from taking a prescription drug?
Q: Name one person, other than a parent, whom you admire greatly.

Fourth, develop a note-taking method to efficiently and accurately collect information about the jurors as they are questioned. Note-taking should be done by someone else (another lawyer, paralegal, or assistant), because taking notes while talking with jurors strongly interferes with creating an environment that promotes juror self-disclosure. You need to watch and listen during the voir dire, not take notes, because what jurors say as they answer is important, but *how* they say it and how they act as they say it are even more important.

How your assistant takes notes will depend largely on whether the strike or panel system is used to question the jurors. Under the strike system, the jurors usually sit in the spectator rows of the courtroom and all the jurors are questioned in succession. Taking notes is simply a matter of jotting down the key information about each juror on a notepad or form. Many lawyers create a customized juror form to record juror information pertinent to civil or criminal cases.

Example:

JUROR FORM

Name:
Address:
Family:
Education:
Job:
Military:
Reading, TV, radio:
Computer use:
Hobbies and interests:
Knows parties/witnesses/lawyers:
Prior jury service:
Friends in law enforcement:
Victim of crime:
Involved in similar accident:
Similar physical injuries/conditions:
Experiences similar to present case:

Under the panel system, many lawyers simply draw a representation of the jury box, usually 12 boxes in 2 rows (and perhaps 2 extra boxes for alternate seats) reflecting the physical arrangement of the jury box. As jurors are questioned, the information about each juror is summarized in the appropriate box. The difficulty with this system is that jurors get replaced, and jurors may sometimes be moved over as jurors are excused. This makes keeping the correct position for each juror over time an important matter.

Some lawyers use self-stick notes or three-inch by five-inch file cards for each juror and put them in the correct location. If a juror is excused, that sticky note or file card is taken away and replaced with a new note or card for the new juror. Other lawyers use a juror form and replace or move the forms around to match where the jurors are sitting. Still other lawyers use a laptop computer to create fields on which juror location and information can be recorded. A spreadsheet works well for this purpose.

The important thing is to have a system that not only records information about each juror, but also shows where that juror is sitting. Under the panel system, it is easy for lawyers to strike the wrong juror, because the juror they thought they were striking has moved from his original seat in the jury box.

Finally, you need some sort of rating system to evaluate the jurors and make intelligent decisions on the worst jurors to deselect by striking them with your available peremptory challenges. The system has to be simple and efficient, because the judge will not give you much time during the jury selection process to decide whether to accept or strike a juror.

Many lawyers use a simple checklist and rating system. First, are the juror's attitudes on the important liability and damages issues good or bad for my side? Second, is the juror a persuader, participant, or nonparticipant? Third, is the juror a punitive, authoritarian, or holdout? Finally, does the juror like or dislike my client, key witnesses, and me? Some lawyers use a simple yes or no on these questions; others use a sliding scale to rate how favorable or unfavorable the juror is on these questions. The point is that you need a simple system to evaluate and rate each juror quickly so that you can use your limited peremptory challenges on those jurors who are persuaders and are most likely to strongly favor the other side. The rating system should be summarized on your juror form.

> An example of a trial notebook, with shell forms and completed forms, is on the website that accompanies this book.

Example:

Juror rating:

- good/bad: background & attitudes
- persuader/participant/nonparticipant
- punitive/authoritarian/holdout
- like/dislike: client, witnesses & me

Overall rating: 1 2 3 4 5

3.13 Common Problems

Lawyers commonly encounter several recurring problems during jury selection.

1. Interrogation Environment

An interrogation environment destroys the atmosphere necessary for candid juror self-disclosure. Put away the notepad, get away from counsel table, stand in front of the jurors whenever possible, and talk to them as you would at a social gathering. Act how you naturally act and interact when you meet a new person. Take someone, preferably a non-lawyer, with you to take notes, observe the jurors, listen to their responses, and give you feedback before you use your strikes.

> For a discussion of varied approaches to jury selection and common problems practicing attorneys experience during jury selection, please watch Video B.3, "Wyo STI: Voir Dire and Jury Selection Panel."

2. Too Much Lawyer Talking

Effective jury selection requires that the jurors talk, not the lawyers. Try to do 10 percent of the talking, and let the jurors do 90 percent, much like a good direct examination. Use short, nonleading questions that invite the jurors to talk and reward those jurors who talk with positive verbal and nonverbal feedback.

3. Useless and Intrusive Questions

Some frequently asked questions produce almost no yield. Asking: "Can you be fair and impartial?" or "Can you wait until you've heard all the evidence before deciding the case?" rarely gets anything other than the obvious answer. Even worse, many jurors are offended by the lawyer even thinking it is necessary to ask such questions. Intrusive questions have the same result. You need the jurors' permission to pry into their lives. If jurors are hesitant to discuss something in the courtroom, don't press and embarrass them. Either seek the judge's help so you can discuss the matter in private, or move on to something else.

4. Too Much General Background, Too Little Life Experiences

Many lawyers spend most of their time obtaining general socioeconomic information from the jurors. Such information, however, has little predictive value in most cases. Focus your time and questions on getting the information that matters: the jurors' reading, TV, radio, and computer habits; their hobbies and personal activities; and—by far the most important—their experiences in life that are similar to the event on which the trial is based.

5. Too Much "What," Too Little "Why" and "How"

The what questions get the facts, and that's a good start. But it's the why and how questions that get the explanations and feelings and generate much more revealing information about juror attitudes and the depth of those attitudes.

6. Not Using All Peremptory Challenges to Preserve Error

Case law generally holds that a party may not raise on appeal error based on the court's denial of cause challenge requests or *Batson* objections unless all available peremptory challenges have been used. The usual advice—never run out of peremptory challenges—has one important exception: If you want to raise these errors on appeal, you must exhaust your peremptory challenges.

CHAPTER 4

OPENING STATEMENTS

4.1 Introduction

First impressions are lasting impressions. That's true in life, and it's true in trials. The opening statement is each side's first opportunity to tell the jury its themes, what the case is all about from its point of view, and why the jurors should return a favorable verdict. It forms the framework from which the jurors will evaluate the evidence, the parties, and the lawyers for the rest of the trial. Because of this, opening statements have a powerful influence on the eventual verdict.

To make effective opening statements, trial lawyers must know the applicable law; the jury's perspective; how to choose and use themes and labels that send compelling emotional messages; and storytelling techniques that engage the jurors' hearts and minds, communicate "what really happened" from their point of view, and show why their party is the good side that deserves the jury's support. Done well, an effective opening statement is a preview of reality that creates a preference in the jurors' minds—a preference that will influence how the jurors will view the evidence that is presented later. Done poorly, the opening statement only confuses, bores, or alienates the jurors.

4.2 The Law

There are no federal rules or statutes governing opening statements. The states are largely silent as well, either having no rules or having only general rules permitting an opening statement. The real rules that govern opening statements are found in federal and state case law.

1. Procedure

There is no inherent right to make an opening statement in federal court, as no federal rule or statute expressly confers such a right. When state rules exist, they usually simply permit the parties to make a "brief statement" of their anticipated evidence. Nonetheless, trial judges invariably allow opening statements in jury trials, recognizing that opening statements give the jury an overview of the anticipated evidence and each party's positions on the disputed issues.

The standard procedure is that the plaintiff, having the burden of proof, presents its opening statement first, followed by the defendant. However, if the plaintiff's case has already been proven or admitted, so that the only trial issues involve the defendant's counterclaims or defenses on which the defense has the burden of proof, judges usually permit the defendant to go first, followed by the plaintiff.

Can a defendant reserve its opening statement to the beginning of the defense case-in-chief? Again, this is discretionary with the judge, but judges frequently grant a defense request to reserve its opening statement. Defendants, particularly in criminal cases, may not want to alert the prosecution to the details of its defense, and reserving the opening statements may accomplish that. However, some judges require opening statements to be made at the beginning of the trial, or else they are waived.

Some judges routinely impose time limitations on opening statements, whereas others impose limitations only in complicated cases when they think limitations are needed. When judges impose time limitations, they frequently limit each side to between 10 and 30 minutes.

2. Content

The traditional view of opening statements was that they were restricted to what the parties expected to prove during the trial through witnesses and exhibits. The modern view is broader and permits themes and the parties' positions on disputed facts and issues. The modern view recognizes the significance of opening statements in informing and orienting the jury to the facts of the case and the disputed issues.

An opening statement can only refer to the anticipated evidence. That evidence must be properly admissible, and the parties must actually be able to get the evidence admitted during the trial. This is an ethical requirement under Model Rules 3.3 and 3.4. When in doubt about the admissibility of witness testimony or exhibits, raise the issue before trial and get a ruling whenever possible. This is particularly important with exhibits you intend to use during your opening statement. If you get your exhibits admitted before or at the beginning of the trial, your opponent cannot object to them during your opening statement.

Some jurisdictions require the opening statement to establish a prima facie case as to the claims and defenses on which that party has the burden of proof. When this requirement exists, make sure your opening statement clearly and explicitly states each element of each claim and defense, and shows how you will prove each element.

3. Improper Opening Statements

What is improper in opening statements? Case law focuses on several areas:

- Mentioning inadmissible evidence
- Mentioning unproveable evidence
- Arguing
- Stating personal opinions
- Discussing the law
- Mentioning the opponent's case
- Appealing to sympathy or prejudice

a. Mentioning Inadmissible Evidence

Opening statements may not mention inadmissible evidence. The standard is one of good faith: Do you have a reasonable, good-faith belief that the evidence you are mentioning now will be admissible later? If so, you may mention it in the opening statements.

This means that the evidence mentioned in the opening statements must be relevant (to the claims and defenses being tried), reliable (meet the hearsay rule requirements), and right (meet the witness examination and exhibits foundation requirements).

Keep in mind that relevance is controlled by the pleadings. In civil cases, both liability and damages are usually in issue. In criminal cases, however, the lawyers may not discuss the sentencing consequences of a verdict, because any sentence following a guilty verdict is usually the function of the judge, not the jury. ✱

b. Mentioning Unprovable Evidence

Opening statements may not mention unprovable evidence. A lawyer who mentions a fact in the opening statement is then obligated to present evidence of that fact during the trial. If you can't prove it, you can't mention it. For example, if you know that a fact is unprovable because a necessary witness is unavailable or a necessary exhibit has not been located or cannot be qualified for admission in evidence, you cannot mention that fact in your opening statement.

What happens if your opponent (or, for that matter, you) mentions unprovable or unproven evidence in the opening statement? This will usually become apparent only after your opponent has presented his evidence in his case-in-chief and rested. If the failure is important, you must then make an objection, ask for a sidebar, and tell the judge that the other side failed to prove something important that he mentioned in his opening statement. Move to strike the unproven matter and ask that the jury be instructed to disregard it. In egregious cases, ask for a mistrial. The other option is not to object, but use the other side's failure to prove what it said it would prove in closing arguments. This is discussed in Section 9.5.

c. Arguing

It is settled law that opening statements should not contain "argument." Less clear, however, is what constitutes impermissible argument. Some judges limit opening statements to what witnesses will say or exhibits will show and

For a discussion of both opening statements and closing arguments, please watch Video C.1, "Mauet on Opening Statements and Closing Arguments."

bar attempts to characterize the credibility of those witnesses and exhibits; other judges take a broader view. The line between what is proper and improper is blurry and is often drawn by the custom in a particular jurisdiction and the attitude of a particular judge.

d. Stating Personal Opinions

A lawyer may not state personal opinions at any time, such as vouching for the credibility or lack of credibility of any witness, or stating personal knowledge of facts. "I believe," "I know," and "I think" are phrases best deleted from a trial lawyer's vocabulary. However, many courts treat such statements as harmless if the principal point being made is the expected evidence, not the lawyer's opinion of the evidence.

e. Discussing the Law

Case law frequently holds that an opening statement should not discuss or quote the law. However, because an opening statement's purpose is to help the jury understand the evidence, it is usually helpful to tell the jury what the applicable law is, because the jury must later relate the evidence to the law to decide the case.

Most judges recognize this and permit general references to what a party is legally required to prove. This includes references to the pleadings and summaries of the legal elements of claims and defenses. However, detailed or lengthy quotations from statutes or elements instructions are not permitted. This should not be an issue in jurisdictions where the practice is for the judge to instruct the jury on the claims, defenses, and applicable law immediately before the opening statements.

Can the lawyers talk about the applicable burden of proof? Some judges permit it, whereas others feel that this is judicial turf and bar it. In contrast, it is common practice in criminal cases for the defense to mention the prosecution's burden of proof beyond a reasonable doubt. This issue should be raised before trial to determine what references to the law the judge will permit.

f. Mentioning the Opponent's Case

A lawyer during opening statements can mention only the facts that she in good faith expects to prove with admissible evidence. It follows, then, that a lawyer cannot anticipate and comment on the opponent's case, as she has no control over what the opponent will do in his case.

This prohibition is particularly important in criminal cases. Because the defendant has a constitutional right not to present evidence, it is always improper for the prosecutor to mention the anticipated defense evidence. In civil cases, however, if the opposing party has committed itself, through pleadings, discovery, pretrial statement, or stipulations, to presenting certain evidence at trial, many judges permit lawyers to refer to that expected evidence.

g. Appealing to Sympathy or Prejudice

Direct appeals to sympathy, prejudice, or other emotions of the jury are improper at any time. Direct attacks on the character of the parties and witnesses are improper in opening statements.

For a detailed discussion of the law on opening statements, *see* Mauet & Wolfson, *Trial Evidence* (7th ed., 2020). Take a look at that sec.

4.3 The Jury's Perspective

What are the jurors feeling and thinking as the lawyers give their opening statements? First, the jurors in the jury box have just survived the jury selection process, and most feel good about being selected. Second, they are mentally fresh and open to receiving new information. Third, they are still mostly ignorant about the parties, the facts of the case, what really happened and why it happened, and what the parties are disputing. Fourth, they have not yet decided which side should win, and they want to reach the "right" verdict. This creates uncertainty and anxiety, which is stressful.

the jury is the 'cinnastic'/ 'this trial' voice

This means that the jurors are now highly interested in finding out what the case is all about. It also means that jurors subconsciously look for ways to reduce the stress they are experiencing. They do this by rapidly creating "stories" in their minds to make sense of the information they get from the opening statements and by quickly developing first impressions about the parties and what really happened. These first impressions usually become conscious or subconscious preferences for one side's point of view, and these preferences influence whether jurors accept, distort, or reject the evidence they hear and see from the witnesses and exhibits. In short, the jurors' first impressions, developed during the opening statements, usually become lasting impressions, and those impressions have a powerful influence on the eventual verdict.

Is it more like theater/ why

Effective trial lawyers recognize the jury's needs, interests, and expectations at this stage of the trial. They respond to them by preparing and delivering opening statements that capture and hold the jury's interest, tell an engaging people story, create a story of what really happened from their point of view, and show why their side wears the white hat and deserves the jury's verdict. An effective opening statement doesn't try to force a conclusion; it shows the jurors the facts that make them want you to win, because that will right a wrong. Opening statements, in short, are a competition to see which side can better draw the jurors emotionally into its version of what really happened, so that the jurors will develop a preference for that side and accept the evidence supporting that side's point of view during the trial.

4.4 Content of Effective Opening Statements

An effective opening statement must accomplish several goals. It must grab the jurors' attention; show them what the case is about from your point of view; anchor the facts and issues of the case to memorable themes and labels; tell an engaging people story that captures and maintains juror interest; and create a preference in the jurors' minds for you, your client, your story, and your themes. Furthermore, it must do all these things quickly and efficiently.

An effective opening statement must dramatize, humanize, and organize. It is not a recitation of anticipated witness testimony, and it should never be a repetition of "The evidence will show" statements. It must draw the jurors into the story, engaging their hearts and minds, so that they "see" what happened from your point of view and develop a preference for your side.

Remember the principles of persuasion discussed in Chapter 2. They apply to opening statements as much as the other stages of a trial.

- Think like a juror
- Select a theory of the case
- Select your themes and labels
- Focus on the people, not the problem
- Use storytelling techniques
- Focus on the key issues

Remember that you, an advocate, are like the director of a play. Though limited to the admissible evidence (the testimony and exhibits) and restricted by the applicable law, you have great flexibility in how you portray and present your case. Effective advocates see opening statements as a creative process. What themes will effectively summarize my case? What is the most persuasive way to present my theory of the case—what really happened from my point of view—to the jurors? How can I best portray my party? What kind of storytelling will engage them? What are the critical issues I need to focus on? Like all good stories, opening statements have a beginning, middle, and end.

1. Impact Beginning

You have one or two minutes—that's all—to capture the jury's interest. That's the reality of jurors whose expectations come from watching television and movies and reading popular magazines. Opening statements today have to grab the jurors' attention immediately, state the themes, and give a brief overview of the case.

This means that the traditional way of starting an opening statement—thanking the jurors for being there, introducing the parties, analogizing the opening statement to an "overview," comparing the evidence to "pieces of a jigsaw puzzle," and eventually getting to "what we expect to prove"—does not work today. Jurors will quit listening before you ever get to anything important.

How do you make an immediate impact? You must decide how best, and in what order, to do three things in the first minute: grab attention, state your themes, and give a short overview of the case that draws the jurors into the story. However you start, what you say must convey one clear message: I'm going to be worth listening to. This message must be sent by both plaintiffs and defendants in every kind of case.

Where do the good impact beginnings come from? They come from your own creativity, but you can get guidance from the professionals. Watch television news and advertisements. Read the first few paragraphs of a newspaper story or the back covers of paperback novels. Notice the first two or three sentences. All of them are designed and delivered to accomplish one thing: grab your attention and hold your interest.

a. Present a Short Re-creation of the Case

One way to grab attention is to immediately re-create the central event. This is effective if the central event in the trial is traumatic, as is often true in criminal and personal injury cases. Make the re-creation visual and visceral, from your side's point of view.

Example (Prosecution in Armed Robbery Case):

Members of the jury, let's go back to June 1, 2020, at 9:00 p.m. We're at the Chicken Shack, a take-out shop at Main and Broadway. Inside are two employees and one customer. Suddenly, the front door swings open. A man, carrying a shotgun and wearing a mask, bursts in and yells, "Don't anybody move. It's a stickup." That man, the man who held the gun, the man who spoke those words is the defendant, the man sitting right there [pointing].

Example (Defense in Murder Case):

Bobby Jackson is lucky—lucky to be alive. He's alive only because he defended himself when that other man, without warning, without reason, and without provocation, attacked him with a pool cue. Bobby did the only thing he could do to save his life: He used his gun to shoot the man who was trying to kill him. That's self-defense. That's why Bobby's alive today, instead of the other way around. That's why Bobby's not guilty—not guilty of murder, and not guilty of any other crime.

Example (Plaintiff in Automobile Collision):

On June 1, 2020, at about 9:00 p.m., that defendant [pointing] finished his sixth martini at the Lucky Lounge. He staggered out the door, fumbled for his car keys, and crawled behind the wheel of his Cadillac. He pulled onto Elm Street and drove westbound. He had only gone two blocks when the light at Maple turned red. That defendant was too drunk to notice the light, too drunk to slow down, and too drunk to see the station wagon going down Maple with the entire Smith family. Within one minute of leaving the Lucky Lounge, that defendant drove his Cadillac through a red light and smashed broadside into the Smith's station wagon. That defendant fatally crushed Mrs. Smith and one of her children and destroyed the lives of her other children.

b. Present Your Themes

Another way, perhaps the most common way, is to start with the themes that you have carefully selected and refined well before trial. Most cases have two to four themes: one for liability, one for damages (in civil cases), and one or two more for key issues such as credibility and motive. Themes tell the jurors what the case is all about, identify the issues from your point of view, and show why your side deserves to win. Themes turn complex facts into simple universal concepts.

Where do the good themes come from? Good themes are simple, universal, and timeless. They are about people, their motives, and how life actually works. Good themes are found in many places. Traditional sources are the Bible, Aesop's Fables, Americana sayings, and quotes from Shakespeare and other notable authors. They can be found in current events, even popular sayings and advertisements. Good themes catch the ear, make a vivid and visceral connection, and send a clear message. They complete the sentences: "This is a case about _____";

"This happened because _____"; "Plaintiff/defendant is a _____"; "We win because _____ ."

Themes can be simple but powerful words: love, hate, revenge, fear, cheating, greed, power. They can be short phrases: taking responsibility; playing by the rules; changing the rules after the game starts; stacking the deck; profit over safety; haste makes waste; David versus Goliath; taking advantage of the little guy; cutting corners; and so on. They can be rhetorical questions: Why didn't that man wait? Why did he take matters into his own hands? Does a handshake still mean something in America? Good themes are limited only by your imagination.

A good theme is memorable, and when you find the right themes for your case you will want to repeat them periodically, perhaps three to five times, during your opening statement. Inexperienced lawyers often state their themes in the beginning of the opening statement and never use them again. This is a good sign that you have not yet found your best themes. Compelling themes beg to be repeated.

Example (Prosecution in Criminal Case):

This is a case about revenge. You see, ever since Frank North beat the defendant in a fight three weeks before, the defendant had been planning his revenge. And on June 1, at 2:00 a.m., in a dark alley, that defendant took revenge.

Example (Defense in Criminal Case):

Once again, it's happened. An innocent man stands accused of a serious crime because of a mistaken identification and shoddy police work. And only you can prevent an injustice from happening.

Example (Plaintiff in Personal Injury Case):

Members of the jury, this case is about two things: failure to yield the right of way and a shattered future. On June 1, 2020, that defendant failed to yield the right of way to Ms. Anderson's car, made an illegal left-hand turn, and caused the crash. That crash broke her back, destroyed her health, and shattered her future.

Example (Defendant in Personal Injury Case):

This is a case about a man who couldn't wait, couldn't wait two seconds before making a turn. Couldn't wait two seconds until that traffic light changed from yellow to red. Couldn't wait two seconds to make sure oncoming traffic had stopped. Because that plaintiff couldn't wait, he made a left turn right in front of Mr. Balboa's oncoming car, causing the crash. And now he's trying to blame Mr. Balboa for his own negligence.

Example (Plaintiff in Contract Case):

Folks, this case is about broken promises. You see, Mr. Adams made a contract with that defendant. He paid the defendant in full. Mr. Adams lived up to his promise. But what did that defendant do? Instead of living up to his end of the deal, he broke his promise. He refused to do what he had promised to do.

Example (Defendant in Contract Case):

> This case is about a low-ball bid. The plaintiff won the contract by low-balling his bid, making an artificially low bid to beat the other people competing for the contract. The plaintiff figured that once he got the bid, he could threaten to walk off the job and get us to pay more money to do what he was already obligated to do. But the plaintiff figured wrong. We refused to pay more than what the contract called for and we insisted that plaintiff do what he agreed to do at the agreed price. Not a penny more.

Example (Plaintiff in Products Liability Case):

> This is a case about a cat. No, it's not the cat that's a house pet. This case is about *C* [writes C on poster board]: a conspiracy; *A* [on board]: to addict; and *T* [on board]: teenagers. Those corporations masterminded a conspiracy to addict teenagers to cigarette smoking. And they started it a long time ago.

c. Present Building Tension

Yet another way to grab attention is through strong, detailed imagery and building tension. Human conflict, the essence of a good story, always triggers interest and gut reactions. Where do the good images come from? Again, look at popular magazines and novels. Watch television news programs. People love to become emotionally involved in the life of another human being. Notice how each article and story begins. There's always an immediate hook, something that catches your attention and holds your interest.

Example (Plaintiff in Personal Injury Case):

> The morning of June 1, 2020, started as a beautiful day. The grass was still wet from a morning shower. The sun was beginning to shine. The birds were chirping. The day started that way for Shirley Johnson as well. She had just moved to the city and started a new job. She was full of life, full of dreams, planning an exciting future. She didn't know that, at the same time, a man—that defendant—was having his fourth martini at a neighborhood bar.

Example (Plaintiff in Medical Malpractice Case):

> Every morning a little elderly man gets up, gets dressed, and goes down to the kitchen for a bowl of corn flakes. At 7:30 he walks to the corner, catches the bus downtown, and gets off at the University Hospital. He walks into the hospital, rides the elevator to the fourth floor, and walks to room 412. He pauses for a moment and listens, but there's no sound from the room. He knocks, but there's no response. He then pushes open the door, and sees a little elderly woman lying motionless under a white sheet. He says "Good morning, Mary," but there's no answer. He then walks to the foot of the bed, places his hand gently on her foot, squeezes it softly, and says "I'm here, it's me." Members of the jury, Mary didn't see him. Mary didn't hear him. And Mary couldn't even feel her own husband's touch. The reason we are here today is to answer one question: What did those doctors do to Mary Smith?

Example (Plaintiff in Contract Case):

> Frank Martin thought he was living his dream. He had just signed the contract that would put his small company into the big leagues. As he blew on the signatures on the contract to make sure the ink was dry, he began dreaming of the future. Members of the jury, Frank Martin didn't know that his dream was about to turn into his worst nightmare.

Grabbing attention is particularly important for the defendant, whose opening statement follows the plaintiff's. The defense needs to jar the jurors away from the impressions, atmosphere, and focus created by the plaintiff's opening statement. It needs to contest the plaintiff's account and let the jurors immediately know what really happened from the defense point of view. A common approach is to take issue with the plaintiff's statement of the issues and redirect the jurors' attention to what the "real issues" are.

Some jurisdictions allow the defense to reserve its opening statement until the beginning of the defense case. In rare cases this is done—almost always in criminal cases in which the defense has an undiscovered affirmative defense and wants to preserve the element of surprise. However, in almost all cases the defense will want to give its opening statement immediately after the plaintiff's; otherwise, the plaintiff's account goes unchallenged in the jurors' minds.

Example (Defendant in Criminal Case):

> The prosecution wants you to believe that this case is about eyewitness identifications. But it's not. This case is all about police practices—shoddy, misleading, and improper police practices that caused an innocent person to get arrested for a crime he didn't do. And only you can make it right.

Example (Defendant in Construction Case):

> Plaintiff wants you to think that this is a simple contract case in which we didn't do what we agreed to do. But that's not it at all. What this case is really about is reasonable access. It's about a general contractor—that plaintiff—who refused to give us reasonable access to the job site so we could do the job we were hired to do. And the reason the plaintiff didn't give us reasonable access to the job site is simple: He was cutting corners and saving money. And now he wants to hide the fact that he botched his job as general contractor by blaming us for the scheduling problems he created. That's not right, and we won't stand for it.

Grabbing attention is obviously essential for any opening statement. Regardless of how you start—by stating your themes, giving a summary of the facts from your point of view, or building tension—and regardless of whether you are plaintiff or defendant, it is effective only if you draw the jurors into the story and make them want to hear more.

2. Storytelling

An attention-grabbing beginning tells the jury that you and your side are worth listening to. The next step is also crucial: Tell the story of your case—what really happened from your point of view—through people stories. Regardless of whether the case is criminal, personal injury, or commercial, you need to create a people story that the jurors can understand, identify with, and ultimately prefer. Good people stories dramatize, humanize, and organize, and they pull the jurors into the story.

Putting your case in the form of a story is the key concept. Jurors instinctively think in stories. It's almost as if storytelling is hard-wired into our brains. If you don't create a compelling story that appeals to the jurors, the jurors will create their own stories. Your story must account for the important facts that will come out during the trial, and that story must be acceptable to the jurors. So how do you create effective stories?

First, understand that jurors want to learn about the facts through storytelling. Telling the jury a series of facts or listing your witnesses and reciting the facts each will testify about is not effective. Focus on creating a dramatic story about what happened between your party and the other party, not on reciting the facts.

When telling the story, use appropriate labels for the parties and other important people and things, and use them consistently. *Labels* are the tags we put on people, events, and things. Select labels for your party, the other parties, and the key witnesses, and use them consistently. Labels send messages. Personalize your characters and depersonalize the other side's. For example, prosecutors commonly refer to the "victim" (if allowed) and "defendant." In civil cases, plaintiffs commonly refer to "Mary Jones" and "that corporation." Inexperienced lawyers frequently mix their labels for the same person (e.g., using "plaintiff," "Ms. Jones," "Mary," and "my client" interchangeably), thereby confusing everyone.

> For a discussion of storytelling and other aspects of opening statements, please watch Video C.2, "Wyo STI: Opening Statements."

Pick labels for the events and things central to the trial. For example, plaintiffs usually call it a "crash" or "collision," whereas defendants call it an "accident" or "incident." For plaintiffs, the truck involved in the collision is a "40,000 pound semi" or "fully loaded 18-wheeler," but for defendants it's a "truck" or "vehicle." For plaintiffs, it's a "time bomb waiting to explode"; for defendants, it's a "gas storage tank." Decide on the best labels before trial, and stick with them throughout the trial. Although you should stick with the same labels and use them throughout the trial, do not overuse them. Consider variations that convey the same meaning or image. For example, "the big black Jaguar sports car" can also be "the big Jaguar" or "that Jag."

Second, understand that jurors want information about the people involved in the story. Telling the jurors about the various legal claims and theories of recovery is not effective. It's the human element that captures interest. Jurors want to become emotionally involved in the lives of other people. That's what pulls them in and keeps them engaged. In the news business, there's an adage: "It's not a story about a fire, it's about the people caught in the fire." The same is true for trials. Focus on the people, not the problem.

Third, understand that jurors see trials in moral terms. Which side is the good guy, which side is the bad guy? Who's wearing the white hat? Effective opening statements focus on the other side's misconduct and at the same time show that your side was wronged. Jurors need to make a decision that is legally correct, but their primary emotional need is to reach a decision that they feel is fair and just.

Finally, jurors need to feel that their decision is consistent with universal truths. Themes tie the story of your case to those universal truths and have high persuasive impact. It's not a breach of contract case; it's a case about keeping your word. It's not a case about an assault; it's a case about revenge. It's not a case about a vehicle collision; it's a case about taking responsibility. Themes make the connection between the events of the case and those universal truths and provide the moral basis to motivate the jurors to return a favorable verdict.

If engaging people stories are the key to effective opening statements, how do we create such stories? Good stories dramatize, humanize, and organize. They have characters, plot, conflict, crisis, and resolution. They portray the central characters as real people. They make the events vivid and visceral by using sensory language and providing lasting images. They tell the story in real time, using the present tense. They organize the story in chronological or other sensible order, always moving the story forward. They start and end the story on strong points. They provide enough important facts to follow the story without bogging down in unnecessary detail. They answer the questions: what happened, who did it, why did she do it, what will make it right? They create memories, reaching both the jurors' hearts and minds. And they show that a happy ending—a favorable verdict—will be consistent with the themes and give the jurors an opportunity to see that justice is done and fairness wins the day.

Doing this effectively means you need to have the proper mindset. Step back from all the details and take an arm's length view of the evidence. Creating an engaging opening statement requires understanding that the jurors know nothing about the case and need to see the big picture. Start at the very beginning. Identify the key central facts that you will prove through witness testimony and exhibits, determine which of those facts the other side will dispute, and put your version of the key facts into an engaging people story that the jurors can immediately understand. It's your theory of the case, translated into a people story, containing the key facts that you need to prove or disprove. Jurors must understand that your party is the good guy who was wronged, so the jurors will prefer your side and be motivated to right the wrong through their verdict. If you have already prepared an outline of your closing argument first, you can draft a story in your opening statement that will parallel your closing argument.

The following examples illustrate effective storytelling from the plaintiff's and defendant's points of view.

Example (Plaintiff in Wrongful Death Case):

During the summer, 4:00 p.m. is a happy time for the children on the 800 block of Maple Street. That's the block where the school playground is. It's a busy place whenever the weather is good. And 4:00 is the best time of all, because that's when the Good Humor ice cream truck comes down the street, music playing, bells jingling. The minute the kids hear those sounds, they dig in their pockets or run to their parents for money to get a popsicle, chocolate bar, or ice cream cone. If you're quick, you get to be first in line when the truck stops.

June 1, 2020, was a happy time for little Jenny Smith. Six years old, she was the apple of her parents' eyes, a lively, cheerful kid, full of life. She was there at the playground, playing with her friends, while her mother sat on a bench near the swings, chatting with friends.

It was just after 4:00 when they first heard the familiar sound, the bells jangling. Jenny, like several of the other kids, ran to her mother and said: "Mommy, can I get an ice cream?" Jenny's mom reached into her purse, took out a dollar bill, gave it to her, and said: "Be careful." Jenny grabbed the dollar and ran toward the opening in the chain-link fence.

By this time, the Good Humor truck had stopped on the far side of Maple, across the street from the playground. Jenny ran to the opening in the fence and started across the crosswalk to get to the truck.

At that moment, that defendant, driving a big, new Cadillac, was zooming down Maple, going at least 25 miles per hour, at least 10 miles per hour over the posted speed. He drove right past the sign that said: "School Zone—15 m.p.h." He drove right past the sign that said: "Look Out for Children." He drove right past the sign that said: "School Crosswalk Ahead." Instead, he was busy talking on his cell phone. Too busy to go 15 miles per hour. Too busy to look out for children. Too busy to even see little Jenny crossing in the crosswalk.

The impact of the Cadillac against Jenny's little body was horrible. It crashed into her ribs, crushing her chest, lungs, and other organs, threw her up in the air, to the curb, where she landed with a thud. Jenny didn't even have time to scream.

But others did. The other children reaching the crosswalk screamed. Their screams alerted the parents, who ran over to the crosswalk. Jenny's mom also ran over, and when she saw it was Jennifer lying crushed and motionless in the street, she started to scream too.

There was little they could do. The damage had been done. The police came, the ambulance came, but all they could do was take Jenny to the hospital. Even that was too late. Before they got her to the hospital, little Jenny Smith was dead.

Example (Defendant in Same Case):

Ed Johnson lives in the neighborhood. His children, before they grew up, used to play in that same playground, and Mr. Johnson would sit in the playground watching them. He still lives on Maple, a few blocks up the street.

Whenever Mr. Johnson's business takes him downtown, he goes down Maple. Partly it's the convenience, since Maple goes directly from his house to downtown. Partly it's the memories, because when he goes down Maple, he sees where his own children grew up, the school they went to, the playground where they played.

That afternoon, Mr. Johnson had to go downtown for a 4:30 meeting. Just before 4:00 he left his house, got in his car, and began driving. He gave himself plenty of time to get there in case traffic was heavy. The speed limit on Maple is 25 miles per hour. He put his headlights on even though it was daytime. When he got to the 800 block of Maple, where the school playground is, he slowed down to 15, just like he always does, ever since his own children went there. He had received a call on his cell phone a minute or two before. It was his wife, calling to make sure everything was all right. Just a routine call.

At the playground, there's parking on both sides of the street, and the parking spots are usually full. That's the way it was that afternoon. As he travels down Maple, at 15 miles per hour, he sees the Good Humor truck, looks around for children. There are children in the playground, but none on the sidewalk, in the crosswalk, or by the truck. So Mr. Johnson keeps going.

It was right at the crosswalk when it happened. Suddenly, without warning, when he was just a few feet away, a little girl ran out between two vehicles, one an SUV. Mr. Johnson couldn't possibly see her, because she was short, shorter than the SUV she'd been behind. She didn't stop, she didn't look. She just ran right across the street directly in front of Mr. Johnson's car. Before he could even react, before he could even slam on his brakes, it happened. It happened that fast. And there's nothing Mr. Johnson, or anyone else, could have done to prevent it from happening.

Example (Prosecution in Armed Bank Robbery Case):

The Second Federal Savings Bank has a small branch office at the corner of Central and State. It looks like a typical bank building: one-story brick, glass picture windows on the side facing Central, two drive-up bays, and parking on all sides.

June 1, 2020, started like a typical day for Sarah Hughes, the manager, and three tellers and receptionist. They had all gone into the bank around 8:30 through the employee entrance on the side and were setting up for the 9:00 a.m. opening.

At 9:00 a.m., Ms. Hughes unlocked the front door and returned to her office next to the teller's counter. A few minutes passed. She was doing paperwork when she heard something that no bank manager ever wants to hear. She heard a man's voice yell: "Everybody down on the floor." Ms. Hughes immediately tripped the silent alarm, then left her office and entered the lobby.

She saw a man pointing a shotgun at her tellers. The tellers were already getting down on the floor. The man looked right at Ms. Hughes, not more than ten feet away. The man was a slender white male, about five feet ten inches tall, weighing perhaps 150 pounds. The man was dressed in blue jeans, a white tee shirt, and sneakers. He did not wear a mask. His face was not disguised in any way. He had no beard or mustache, and wore short brown hair, almost a crew cut. He had no visible scars or tattoos. That man, members of the jury, was the defendant, the man sitting right there [pointing] at the table. The defendant then pointed the shotgun at Ms. Hughes and said "You too. On the floor." Ms. Hughes got on the floor.

The defendant then climbed over the teller's counter, removed the cash from each of the teller's drawers, then jumped back over the counter. From where she was on the lobby floor, Ms. Hughes could see the defendant moving from station to station, scooping out the money, stuffing it into his bag. One of the tellers, Jane Smith, was on the floor behind the counter, and she could see everything the defendant did as well.

The defendant then said: "Stay on the floor," and ran out the front door to a car and took off. The car looked old, a blue four-door sedan.

Within two or three minutes, the police were there. Ms. Hughes and Jane Smith gave the police a description of the defendant and the getaway car, which was broadcast over the police radio.

Less than one hour later, a police officer, Officer Wilson, pulled over a speeding car a few miles away. It was a 2018 blue Ford sedan. Officer Wilson noticed the driver was acting nervous and that he was a slender white male, about five-ten tall, about 150 pounds, wearing blue jeans and a white tee shirt. He fit the description of the bank robber. Officer Wilson asked him, "Where were you at 9:00 a.m.?," and the defendant didn't answer. Officer Wilson, believing that this might be the bank robber, handcuffed him and took him to the police station. Another officer came to the scene, drove the defendant's car to the police station, and searched it. No shotgun or money was found in the car.

That afternoon the police conducted a lineup. In the lineup was the defendant and five other young white males. You'll see the photograph of the lineup. Each person was told to say the words "Everybody down on the floor" and to turn around once. Ms. Hughes and the three tellers were present. After the lineup, each was interviewed separately. Two tellers, because they could not see the robber as they were lying on the floor, were unable to make an identification. Both Ms. Hughes, the manager, and Ms. Smith, the third teller, could see everything as it happened, and both positively identified that defendant as the man who robbed them at gunpoint that morning.

Example (Defense in Same Case):

Members of the jury, Frank Johnson is the victim of a horrible mistake, a horrible mistake made by the police. June 1 was another work day for Frank. He got up around 8:30 that morning in his studio apartment. He got dressed, made a cup of coffee, ate a couple of doughnuts, and got ready for work.

Around 9:30 Frank left his apartment and drove his car, a 2018 blue Ford, to his job at the Landscape Center. The Landscape Center is about five miles from his apartment, but west of his apartment—the *opposite* direction of that bank.

You see, Frank works as a gardener, and has for the last three years, since he graduated from high school. He loves working with plants, and he loves working outdoors. He was dressed in yellow construction boots, blue jeans, and a white tee shirt, the same clothes he wears every day during the warm months. That day he punched in at work at 9:30, his normal starting time. So far it had been an entirely normal work day for Frank. The boss assigned Frank and another worker to a job, and both got into their cars to drive there.

It was around 10:00, on his way to the job site, that a squad car pulled up behind him, lights flashing. Frank pulled over, immediately wondering what the problem was, since he was driving within the speed limit. The police officer asked for his license and registration, and Frank gave it to him. Frank asked: "What's the problem, officer?" but the officer didn't reply. The officer talked on his radio for a moment, but Frank couldn't really hear. He hoped it wouldn't take long, so he could get to the job site and start working. The officer then told Frank: "Please step out of the car, walk to the trunk, and put your hands on the trunk." Frank kept asking: "What's going on?" but the officer refused to answer. Frank asked. "Officer, could you tell me what this is all about?" No answer. When

Frank went to the rear of the car, the officer suddenly snapped handcuffs on Frank, pushed him to the squad car, and told him to get in. Frank kept asking: "Why are you doing this?" The officer refused to answer.

On the way to the station the officer asked him where he was at 9:00 that morning, and Frank told him. Frank told him the truth: that he was getting ready to go to work and left the house shortly after 9:00. The officer asked him where he lived, and Frank told him. At the station Frank was handcuffed to a chair that was bolted to the floor. Other plain-clothes police grilled him some more, and Frank kept telling them the same thing. Still nobody told him what it was all about. Frank had no idea why this was happening, and every time he asked he was ignored.

Around 3:00 that afternoon—*five hours* after being arrested, and after being fingerprinted, photographed, and interrogated—the police told him he was going to be put in a lineup. Again Frank asked why, and again they refused to answer. The lineup was held in a room with a big mirror. The only other person in the room was a police officer. The officer told everyone to step forward, turn around, and say "Everybody get on the floor." Everyone did that, and then everybody was taken away—except for Frank. A few minutes later another police officer came in and said: "You've just been identified as the person who robbed the Second Federal Savings this morning." Needless to say, Frank was stunned.

Members of the jury, that's the first moment Frank even knew that the bank had been robbed that day. And it's the moment that Frank knew that a terrible mistake had been made. He was being accused of committing a crime he didn't commit.

Example (Plaintiff in Contract Case):

Andrews Properties is a small real estate company owned by Arthur Andrews, who is a self-employed real estate agent. Arthur inherited a vacant lot at Main and Broadway when his father died ten years ago. Some of you may know where the Johnson Shoe Store now is—that's the lot. He planned to develop the lot when his finances were stronger. As far as Arthur knew, that lot had always been vacant. As far as Arthur knew, that lot had never had anything built on it.

Three years ago, Arthur finally decided the time was right to build a small retail store on the lot. The area had become ripe for commercial development, and Arthur could now afford to spend money on its development. Arthur decided to act as his own general contractor. He got bids for all the work: the foundation excavation, the building construction, the electrical, plumbing, heating, and air conditioning, and so on. Arthur was ready to go. Like all construction, there was a timetable for the various jobs, and Arthur had even gotten a local hardware company to lease the store when it was completed. Arthur also had gotten a construction loan from his bank for $400,000.

The excavation contract went to the defendant, Asher Construction, the low bidder. Under the contract, Asher agreed to do the excavation work and have it completed by February 1, 2019. That was important, because other construction was already scheduled to begin on that date. Upon completion of the work, Asher would be paid $40,000.

On November 1, one day before they signed the contract, Mr. Andrews and Mr. Asher had an important conversation. They were talking on the telephone, and Asher said that he was going to submit a bid the next day. Asher asked if there was anything unusual about the lot, and Mr. Andrews said: "I don't know. It's always been a vacant lot as long as I've had it. But check it out if you have any concerns. You're the excavator."

Folks, Asher never did that. He never inspected the lot, never did any test drilling, and never checked any public records to see if there had ever been a building constructed there. He did nothing to check the ground conditions at the job site and simply assumed that the ground would present no problems. That was a mistake, because after he agreed to do the job, after he signed the contract, and after he began excavating the foundation, that's when Asher first found out that it was not a usual job.

You see, many years ago, there had been a gas station on that lot. The gas station had been leveled more than 20 years ago, leaving large gas tanks buried underground and large slabs of concrete below the surface. Mr. Andrews didn't know this, and there was no way to learn it simply by standing on the lot. Everything was below the surface. In January, when Asher encountered these problems, he simply walked off the job. When Mr. Andrews learned of this, he called Asher and insisted that he complete the job under the contract. All Asher ever said was "I'm an excavator, not a demolition man," and he refused to do the job he had agreed to do. Refused to complete the job he had promised to complete.

So Mr. Andrews was faced with a half-completed job, and it was getting close to February 1. Finally, he hired another company, one of the other original bidders, to complete the job, but had to pay twice as much to get it done—$80,000—and the work couldn't be completed until May. By this time all the other construction work was late and backed up, which also cost money. The bank financing was extended longer, and that cost money. The building was completed almost six months late, and by that time the hardware store that had planned to occupy the new store had found another location. It took Mr. Andrews another six months to find a new tenant. Because Asher walked off the job and refused to do what he had promised to do, Mr. Andrews almost went broke, almost lost everything.

Example (Defendant in Same Case):

Members of the jury, Mr. Asher agreed to do one thing, and one thing only: He agreed to use his bulldozer and backhoe, the only equipment he owns, to remove dirt from Andrews's vacant lot, remove the dirt down to a level of 10 feet below grade, in an area 60 by 80 feet, and then haul the dirt away, and do that by February 1. And he was prepared and willing to do that. That's what he does every day, and that's all he does.

What Mr. Asher was not prepared to do, what was impossible to do, and what he never agreed to do, is do what Andrews later discovered he needed: demolition work, removing the large gasoline tanks and huge concrete slabs that were discovered under the ground. Mr. Asher never agreed to do that, because he doesn't have the equipment or the expertise to do that kind of work. That requires cranes, industrial jack hammers and saws, perhaps even explosives.

In short, what we have here is a situation where two people both made a fundamental mistake about the nature of the work involved. When it turned out the work was impossible to do, because of that fundamental mistake, Mr. Asher was fully entitled to stop work. It's that simple.

But it gets worse. This is also a case of Andrews trying to take advantage of Mr. Asher, trying to park all his problems on Mr. Asher's doorstep. Instead of simply asking for $80,000, the cost of the contract with the demolition company that actually did the work, Andrews is trying to recover all his other cost overruns from Mr. Asher. Those cost overruns were Andrews's fault, because he had a work schedule that was unrealistic. The construction work the various other contractors had to do to finish the store couldn't possibly have been completed in the time scheduled. That means the store couldn't possibly have been completed when the hardware company was supposed to move in.

The fact of the matter is, if Andrews wanted Mr. Asher to be responsible for any of these cost overruns, they could have put that in their contract. But look at the contract they signed. Not one word about cost overruns. That's why Mr. Asher is not responsible for those cost overruns. That's why this is also a case of a man who is trying to get someone else to pay for his own mistakes.

3. Ending

[handwritten margin note: Think of some great climaxes & endings in the film.]

The ending, the last minute of the opening statement, must also accomplish several things quickly: Repeat the themes one last time; summarize the basis for liability or nonliability, or guilt or innocence, by tying the key facts to the key issues; tell the jurors what you want them to do through their verdict; and, finally, motivate the jurors to see that fairness is served and justice is done. There are several ways that this is commonly done.

Example (Prosecution in Criminal Case):

Members of the jury, because that defendant planned it in advance, and because he intentionally shot and killed Bobby Wilson with revenge on his mind, at the end of the case we will come back and ask you to do what this evidence compels and justice demands: Find that defendant guilty of premeditated murder.

Example (Defense in Criminal Case):

When you hear all the evidence—their evidence and, just as important, our evidence—you will see that this is a case about shoddy police work, a case about mistaken identification, and a case of a rush to judgment. The evidence will point to only one conclusion: Frank is not guilty of anything, and Frank is certainly not guilty of robbery.

Example (Plaintiff in Personal Injury Case):

What are we asking you to do? Tell that defendant: Two years of denial is enough. Two years of failing to take responsibility for what your negligence did to Karen Adams is enough. When this trial ends, we will ask you to sign the verdict form that reads: "We, the jury, find the defendant negligently caused the plaintiff's damages." We will ask you to fill in the next line: "We find plaintiff has proven damages in the amount of —." We will ask you to fill in the amount that will return to Karen what that defendant took away. In short, we will ask you to do what only you have the power to do: Make it right.

Example (Defendant in Personal Injury Case):

When you've heard all the evidence, you will know that this accident happened for one reason: that plaintiff was in a hurry, took a chance, made an illegal left-hand turn in front of Mr. Jackson's car, and caused this collision. Ever since that day, the plaintiff has tried to blame Mr. Jackson. That's not what the evidence will prove, and that's simply not right. That's why we will ask you to sign the verdict that says: "We find in favor of the defendant and against the plaintiff."

Example (Plaintiff in Product Liability Case):

Members of the jury, what all this evidence will prove is that the defendant manufactured a dangerous, defective lighter and put it in the marketplace. They sold a dangerous, defective lighter without adequate warnings that the lighter might flare up and burn and injure the user. And they did it because it was cheaper and more profitable to sell a dangerous lighter than a safe one. In short, we will prove that they put profits over safety. Through your verdict, they will be forced to do what they have refused to do: own up to what they did, and pay for what they did.

Example (Defense in Product Liability Case):

This trial, when it's over, will teach us one thing: You can't force people to be safe. If people ignore instructions, if they ignore product warnings, and if they ignore common sense, people can misuse almost anything, and they can certainly misuse a lighter. Once you make a safe product, tell people how to use it, and warn people how not to misuse it, then it's up to them. That's exactly what the evidence will show happened here: The plaintiff failed to read the instructions, failed to heed the warnings, misused the lighter, and is now trying to blame us for what he caused. Through your verdict, we will ask you to tell the plaintiff exactly that.

4. Additional Considerations

Impact beginnings, engaging storytelling, and crisp endings are the hallmarks of effective opening statements. In addition, keep in mind the following.

a. Focus on Liability, Not Damages

In civil cases, particularly personal injury cases, where both liability and damages are usually in dispute, plaintiffs usually focus on liability, describing the event and the personal consequences to the plaintiff, but do not detail the damages or talk about money. The conventional wisdom is that plaintiffs need to demonstrate the basis for liability first, and that talking about money damages will sound greedy and appear to be putting the cart before the horse. (In closing arguments, by contrast, plaintiffs usually spend substantial time detailing the damages and justifying the dollar amounts requested.)

Defendants usually discuss only the liability evidence during the opening statements. In closing arguments, defendants then can still choose either to deal with liability alone or address damages as well.

b. Deal Candidly with Weaknesses and Avoid Overstating the Evidence

Opening statements require candor about all the evidence, not just the evidence that helps your side. A common mistake inexperienced lawyers make is to ignore the important facts that hurt you. Every case that gets tried will have weaknesses. Dealing candidly with weaknesses minimizes their impact and maintains your credibility before the jury. Minimize the unfavorable evidence by disclosing it, even embracing it, and making it part of your story. The order in which you disclose it—*order effects*—is important. Putting the unfavorable evidence in the middle of the story, after creating an overall good impression, reduces its impact.

Dealing candidly with weaknesses is particularly important for the plaintiff, who goes first. If plaintiff avoids or glosses over unfavorable facts, the defendant will immediately point this out in the defense opening. Opening statements are not a good place to have your credibility and candor put in doubt.

Do not unintentionally create a weakness by overstating the evidence you have. Inexperienced lawyers sometimes tell a better story during the opening statements than the evidence will later support. Experienced lawyers take careful notes on their opponent's opening statement, and during closing arguments will point out where the opponent promised to present evidence but failed to deliver on that promise. Always make sure you can prove what you say in your opening statement you will prove.

Example (Plaintiff in Personal Injury Case):

What happened at the end of the work day? Mr. Johnson and the other workers at the plant punched out at 5:00 p.m., and they walked over to Gene's, a local tavern, as they usually do. They had a beer, watched the five o'clock news, waited for rush hour to slow down, and left about 30 minutes later to have dinner with their families. It was on the way home that the defendant ran the red light and crashed right into Mr. Johnson's car. Having a beer after work had nothing to do with this collision.

Example (Defendant in Criminal Case):

Life hasn't always been easy for Bobby. His father left when he was a young boy. His mother struggled to provide a home for Bobby and his two sisters. There was never enough money, even for the basics. But

Bobby stayed in school, worked hard, and got his high school diploma. It was in his final year that Bobby got in trouble with the law. He and some other classmates were caught with drugs at a party, and they were charged with possession of amphetamines. Bobby admitted it and was put on probation for three years. He successfully completed his probation. Since that time, Bobby has never been in any kind of trouble, he has held a steady job, and he recently got married. Bobby's learned from his mistake and become a solid member of our community.

c. Use Exhibits and Visual Aids

Always consider using exhibits and visual aids during the opening statement. You may use any exhibit you believe will be admissible during the trial and any visual aid that accurately reflects admissible evidence. However, to avoid objections that would interrupt your opening statement, it is usually a good idea to show any exhibits and visual aids you intend to use in your opening statement to the other side just before you give it, so that any objections can be raised and ruled on by the judge before you start.

Making information visual enhances its impact and retention, which is particularly important at the beginning of a trial. In multiple-party cases, it is helpful to the jurors to see a chart showing the parties, their positions in the lawsuit, and the names of the witnesses from the parties who will testify during the trial. In commercial cases, it is helpful to have the key provision of the contract enlarged on a poster board and a timeline showing when the various meetings and events occurred. In personal injury and criminal cases, it is helpful to see a diagram of the accident or crime scene. Such exhibits, charts, and diagrams help the jurors understand what the case is all about, help them understand your opening statement, and establish you as the source for helpful information. However, do not use too many exhibits and visual aids during opening statements. Remember that opening statements must accomplish two things: present your story, and establish you as a reliable source of information. Make sure any exhibits or visual aids further these objectives.

Keep in mind that once used in the opening statements, an exhibit or visual aid will no longer be new when it is used again during the trial. For that reason, many lawyers create visual aids that they will use only during the opening statements (just as they create visual aids solely for closing arguments) and save other exhibits for the case-in-chief. The visual aids must be clear, understandable, and look professionally made. Many lawyers today use PowerPoint or other presentation software to make visual aids for their opening statements (and closing arguments). As long as these visual aids can be smoothly coordinated into the overall presentation, jurors appreciate and respond favorably to them.

Example (Diagram of Parties and Witnesses in Business Tort Case):

Please take a look at this diagram, and things will become clear. My company, Acme Gift Center—here [pointing]—leased a store in the Landmark Shopping Center [pointing]. Acme had been there for almost five years. The store was successful. It was making money. Acme and the owners of Landmark were negotiating to renew the lease, which was up soon. That's when these three defendants [pointing] stepped into the picture, and intentionally and wrongfully interfered with Acme's negotiations with Landmark. Who are they, and what did they do? First, there's

College Fashions [pointing], which leased a store next to Acme. Second, there's Roger Johnson, a loan officer at First National Bank [pointing]. And finally, there's Helen Adams, a commercial real estate broker [pointing]. All three of these defendants got together and started giving false and harmful information about Acme to Landmark. They did it to keep Landmark from renewing Acme's lease, because College Fashions wanted to expand by getting Acme's store. Here's what these defendants did.

d. Establish a Prima Facie Case

Some jurisdictions require that the opening statement make out a prima facie case on each element of that party's claims or defenses. This is based on the concept that a lawyer is an agent of the party and can make admissions binding on the party. If the lawyer's opening statement fails to make out a prima facie case, the other side is entitled to a directed verdict. If this is so, tell the jurors expressly what the law requires you to prove, and show how you will prove each element.

Example (Plaintiff in Contract Case):

Members of the jury, we brought this lawsuit which charges that the defendant breached the contract with us. In a breach of contract case, we have to prove that there was a contract that we and the defendant signed; that we did everything we were required to do under the contract; that the defendant failed to do what he was required to do under the contract; and, finally, that we were damaged as a result of the defendant's failure. Here's what the evidence will be that proves each of these things.

e. Keep Opening Statement Short

How long should an effective opening statement take? If the judge sets time limits, that will provide the outside limit. Remember that the opening statements must accommodate the jurors' limited attention spans and limited capacities to absorb and make sense of the facts. Most opening statements, in routine trials that last 2 to 4 days, are in the 10- to 20-minute range. That is enough time to tell the jury what the case is about from your point of view, yet not so lengthy that jurors lose interest or become overwhelmed by details.

5. The Defense Opening

The defense has an obvious disadvantage: It goes second. The danger is that the jurors, having heard the plaintiff's opening statement first, will accept the plaintiff's version of what happened before the defense gets a chance to present its case. How do you deal with this reality?

One approach is to remind the jurors that they heard only the plaintiff's version, and that they need to hear the defendant's side before they will know the entire story. The defense may go second, but the second half is just as important.

Example:

Folks, you've all heard the expression: There's two sides to every story. And that's true. The plaintiff just told you one side, the side they want you to hear. But you need to hear both sides before you can know what really happened that evening. Here's what you'll find out, when we get our chance to present evidence.

Another way is to deny the plaintiff's allegations explicitly, then turn immediately to the defendant's version of what happened.

Example:

Plaintiff claims that this collision happened because Mr. Johnson was not paying attention. Well, that's not true, and it's not what the evidence will show. What really happened that night? We will prove to you that . . .

Example:

The prosecution wants you to believe that Bobby shot Frank Smith intentionally, with premeditation. That may sound good, but there's a problem: That's not how it happened. We will show you, when it's our turn to present evidence, that . . .

If the plaintiff omitted an important fact, point this out explicitly.

Example:

Today the plaintiff wants you to believe that the traffic light was green when the accident happened, and that the plaintiff saw it clearly. But the plaintiff in her opening statement didn't tell you something important: In the hospital emergency room, when Mr. Johnson was asked by the nurse how he got hurt, he said: "I don't know; it all happened so quickly." It's right there, on the emergency room report, and we'll show you that report when it's our turn to present evidence.

Example:

The prosecutor just told you what happened on June 1 at 2:00 in the afternoon. That's part of what happened, but that's only part of the story. What's critical is what happened between 10:00 and 2:00 that day. That's the part the prosecutor didn't tell you about, and it's the part you have to know to understand what was really going on that day.

If the plaintiff did not talk about the burden of proof, this is always fertile ground, especially in criminal cases having a high burden of proof.

Example:

Her honor will tell you, the party that does the suing has to do the proving. In a civil case, the plaintiff has to prove everything it is required to prove by what is called a preponderance of the evidence. The question you will ask throughout the trial is: Did they really prove what the law requires them to prove?

Example:

Members of the jury, the most important thing you need to remember in this case is the one thing the prosecutor didn't even mention in his opening statement. This is a criminal case. Under our Constitution, the prosecution has the burden of proof. They have to prove everything beyond a reasonable doubt.

Above all, remember that the defense opening statement cannot be defensive. Although the defense must deal with the fact that it goes second, and should take the plaintiff to task for omitting any important evidence, it cannot merely respond to what the plaintiff has said. The defense opening statement must tell a story that is assertive and positive, engages the jurors, and reminds them that your evidence, which they will hear only after the plaintiff has presented her case, is just as important and necessary for the jurors to fully understand what happened.

Perhaps the most difficult opening statement is the defense opening in criminal cases when the defense will not present evidence. In this situation, the defense often talks about the presumption of innocence, that the burden of proof in a criminal case is beyond a reasonable doubt, that the defense is not required to prove anything, and so on. Most judges permit this if it is part of a discussion of the evidence (or lack of evidence), although some feel that this amounts to discussing the law, or constitutes argument, and bar it. The defense also commonly talks about its theory of the case and its themes and points out that the defense "evidence" will come during cross-examination of the prosecution's witnesses. This is an effective approach, because it focuses the jurors' attention on issues that help the defense, does not involve any extensive discussion of legal concepts, and ties the legal concepts to the evidence. Drawing the jurors' attention to the prosecution's weaknesses, telling them what to look for as the witnesses testify and are cross-examined, and why those things are important, also sets up the discussion of the defense themes in closing argument.

Example (Defense in Criminal Case):

> The testimony from the prosecution's witnesses will raise many doubts that the right person was arrested. Listen when we cross-examine those witnesses. You will learn as much during our cross-examinations of those witnesses as you do from the direct examinations. Did they have a good opportunity to see the robber? How dark was it in that alley? How fast did it happen? What kind of descriptions did they provide? Listen when we cross-examine the police officers. Were any of the things taken in the robbery ever traced to Mr. Williams? Was there any physical evidence of any kind connecting Mr. Williams to the robbery? Was the lineup reliably conducted? Once you hear all the evidence, including our cross-examinations, if it convinces you of anything, it will convince you that the wrong person was charged and that a grave injustice has happened.

4.5 Delivery of Effective Opening Statements

The delivery of the opening statement is just as important as its content. A common mistake inexperienced lawyers make is spending too little time and effort on delivery. Remember that the jurors are acutely aware that you are being paid to be an advocate, and they are always asking: Are you just saying the words because you've been hired to say them, or do you really believe them? An effective delivery emphatically answers that question.

First, project a positive attitude. Jurors are sensitive to the courtroom atmosphere and quickly detect which lawyer appears glad to be here and which lawyer appears defensive; they draw conclusions from this as to who has the better case. When the judge says "Counsel, you may proceed with your opening statement," get up immediately, thank the judge, walk confidently and assertively to a spot a few feet away from the middle of the jury box (unless restricted to a podium), recite a quick "May it please the court," if local custom requires, pause, then start. From that moment until the jury has returned the verdict, always project a consistent and confident image: you are competent, sincere, and fair; you are committed to your cause; and you expect to win.

Second, avoid using a podium, unless required by the court. A podium is a physical barrier between you and the jurors. You won't use reinforcing body language, gestures, and eye contact if you are standing behind a podium, particularly if you are looking at notes. If you are required to use a podium, try to stand to one side, so the jurors can see all of you. If you like the security of a podium, practice without it so you can eventually give your opening statements without this prop.

Third, keep your vocabulary simple and your sentence structure clear. Get rid of the legalese! Effective opening statements use the language of oral storytelling: simple, clear language that is visual and visceral. A common mistake inexperienced lawyers make is to write out the planned opening statement, then practice delivering it. This rarely works, because written language is fundamentally different from spoken language. [Written language is more formal, uses a more sophisticated vocabulary, and uses more complex sentence structure.] Written language may read well, but it does not sound genuine. Instead, reverse the process. Practice giving the opening statement, using the words and phrases you naturally use when speaking with others, then outline it afterward.

Fourth, practice giving the opening statement without notes, or, at most, with a one-page outline in large print. Notes are a serious impediment to persuasive communication. Notes keep you from focusing on *how you deliver the* opening statement, prevent you from making eye contact with each of the jurors, and inhibit the natural body language that reinforces what you are saying. Notes remind the jury that what you are saying has all been planned and written out in advance, rather than coming from the heart. Speaking without notes conveys positive messages about you and your belief in the rightness of your cause. That's important, particularly in opening statements.

Finally, learn and practice all components of effective oral delivery. Effective advocates acquire effective communication skills. They learn to use memorable words and phrases because these have an impact. Verbal content—powerful, clear, simple speech, devoid of clutter and distractions—is the beginning. Effective advocates learn to use reinforcing paralinguistics, because how you say it is as important as what you say. [Nonverbal delivery—varying volume, pace, pitch, articulation, pronunciation, pauses, and silence—gives texture and depth to the verbal content.] Nonverbal delivery is the punctuation and emphasis for the content that captures and maintains interest. Effective advocates learn to use reinforcing kinesics. Body language—appropriate clothing and grooming, breath control, posture, position, facial expressions, eye contact with each juror, hand and upper body gestures, and controlled movement—provides additional emphasis and interest. Body language must reinforce the opening statement, not compete with it. When you talk, don't walk; when you walk, don't talk. When talking, face the jury and maintain eye contact with them, a few seconds with each juror, and use facial expressions, hand gestures, and upper body movement to punctuate what you say. All three components—verbal content, nonverbal delivery, and body language—must work together before an opening statement will be persuasive.

4.6 Examples of Opening Statements

Gable v. Cannon (personal injury)

This case involves a collision between two cars at the intersection of Main and Elm Streets. Gable was driving southbound. Cannon was stopped in the northbound lane at the intersection, then made a left-hand turn in front of Gable's car. The two cars collided, and Gable dislocated his right elbow. Each driver claims the other was negligent. Gable claims that the traffic light at the intersection was yellow at the time of the collision, and that he had the right of way. Cannon claims that when he made his left turn the light had already turned red, and that Gable ran the red light.

> For additional examples of opening statements (and closing arguments), see Video C.5, "Wyo STI: Demonstration of Problem 9.4."

PLAINTIFF'S OPENING STATEMENT

Introduction. This introduction immediately brings out the three themes, what happened, and the basis for liability.

May it please the court, counsel, members of the jury.

This case is about three things: success, failure to yield the right of way, and 15 percent. It's about success, because Jim Gable's life was a success story, until June 6, two years ago, when that defendant, Douglas Cannon, broke the rules of the road, violated the law, and made an illegal, dangerous, left-hand turn in front of Jim's oncoming car. That illegal, dangerous, negligent left-hand turn caused the crash with Jim's car, that crash ruined Jim's elbow, ruined his career as a diesel mechanic, and ruined his life.

Telling the jurors you need their help to see that justice is done is always a good message.

Folks, we're here for one reason: We need your help. We need your help to tell that defendant: Two years of denial is enough. Today is the day when—finally—you take responsibility for what you did to Jim, his career, and his family. Today is the day you own up to what you did, and you pay for what you did. Only you can make him do that.

The first theme—success—personalizes the plaintiff, and is important for the damages issue.

Personalizing your party is always important, because jurors must see him as a real human being they can relate to on a personal level.

I said Jim was a success story. Who is Jim Gable? He's one of us. He grew up here, went to school here. Jim will be the first one to tell you he wasn't a great student in high school. Some things were tough. But Jim's not a quitter. He never quits. He finished high school, and had to decide what to do with his life. Like a lot of guys his age, Jim liked cars, so he decided to become a mechanic. He went to vocational school and became a certified diesel mechanic. He then married his high school sweetheart, Karen, and they now have two children, Sandy and Kim, who are students at Ridge Middle School.

Jim then went to work at Rudy's, the diesel repair shop he's been working at since he got certified. For almost all of his adult life Jim has been doing the one thing he has been trained to do, the one thing he's good at, the one thing that's made his life what it is: working as a certified diesel mechanic. Until June 6, life was good, and Jim was a success.

The second theme—failure to yield—is the liability theme.

I said this was also a case of failure to yield the right of way. You see, every morning Jim drives up Main Street to Rudy's, where he works, and every afternoon around 5:00 or 5:30 he drives back down Main Street—southbound—on the way home to have dinner with his family. For Jim, that June 6 was like every other work day. Go to work in the morning, go home in the evening. The only thing different about that day, different from the thousands of other times Jim has gone home on Main Street, is that on that day, that defendant, Douglas Cannon, was also at the intersection of Main and Elm.

What Happened.   The event is acted out, using present tense, so the jurors are drawn into the story and see the collision from the plaintiff's point of view. Some lawyers would use a diagram here to help show what happened.

So what happened? You've all seen this happen any number of times, because all of you drive. Jim's on Main Street, driving his pride and joy, the Jaguar sedan that he bought for almost nothing after it was badly damaged and rebuilt on his own time. Jim's driving southbound [gesturing] on Main Street, his daily commuter route. It's rush-hour traffic, crawling along at 20 to 25 miles per hour. Jim's in a string of cars, cars in front of him, cars behind him, the way it always is. Jim can see the intersection with Elm Street, and he can see the traffic light there. The light is green, so Jim and the other cars just keep going. Jim sees that the northbound traffic on Main Street, the traffic coming toward him, has stopped, because there's a Chevy at the Elm Street intersection trying to make a left turn [gesturing], but it can't. That's the Chevy driven by that defendant.

This anticipates the expected defense position: Plaintiff could have, and should have, avoided the accident.

When Jim gets about 40 feet from the intersection, the light for Main Street turns yellow. It's too late to slam on his brakes, so Jim does what he's entitled to do, what he's done many times over the years: He rolls into the intersection on the yellow light, because he knows he can enter and go through the intersection on the yellow—safely and legally.

The focus now shifts to the defendant's misconduct.

> The only thing different about that day, folks, is that on that day, driving that Chevy, was a man who couldn't wait. You see, the defendant's wife was pregnant, she'd been having morning sickness, and it became severe enough that they'd made an appointment with their doctor and were on their way to the hospital to see him. That's what was on his mind at that intersection.

The description here is well-paced and visual.

> And then it happens. What Jim didn't expect, and shouldn't have expected, was that when Jim's car got just about to the crosswalk, that defendant—for whatever reason—suddenly turned left, directly in front of Jim's car—on the yellow light, when Jim has the right of way. Jim does the only thing he can: react as fast as possible, slam on the brakes, lay down some rubber, but there was nothing else he can do. Jim's car smashes into the side of the Cannon car, the impact throws him forward, and that's when Jim feels it, and hears it—his elbow snaps. And Jim sits there, dazed, not yet knowing that the life he had worked so hard to create was now over.

This can be an effective technique: asking rhetorical questions that will be difficult for the other side to answer.

> Folks, when you hear that evidence you are going to ask: Why didn't that defendant just wait? Why didn't he wait for just two more seconds? Why didn't he wait until the light not only turned to yellow but also changed to red, when it was safe and legal to complete his left-hand turn? And you are going to wonder: Where was that defendant looking? What was he thinking? Where was his mind at? Why didn't he wait until the oncoming traffic stopped before completing his left-hand turn? See if they ever answer those questions.

Aftermath.   This forewarns the jurors about a prior inconsistent statement.

> You know what happened afterwards. The police come, the ambulance comes. Jim is taken to the hospital. He's dazed, in shock, and people at the hospital are poking, prodding, questioning. Jim doesn't remember all that much about what happened in the hospital. But watch what they try to make of what nurse Reynolds jots down on one of the reports. Wait for it. And listen when Jim tells you about that.

The opening statement now shifts to medical treatment, therapy program, and damages.

> Jim finds out that the impact of the crash has torn his right elbow socket out of joint. He's taken up to surgery, knocked out with a general anesthetic, and wakes up in a cast. The next day, after his vital signs stabilize, his wife takes him home.
> For the next few weeks Jim is at home with his elbow raised to keep down the swelling. He can't do anything other than take the painkillers they gave him at the hospital. A few weeks later he goes to Dr. Klein—you'll hear from her as well. She cuts the cast off, and then Jim

discovers what the doctors had warned him about. When the cast came off they said: Jim, you're not going to be able to move your arm more than an inch or two either way. That's what happens when an elbow gets damaged, when those ligaments are torn and ruptured the way yours were, and your elbow's been in a cast that long. Jim, you're going to have to do therapy to try to get your arm back as far as it can get.

Showing plaintiff was motivated to do the therapy is important. Plaintiff raises another fact the defense will try to use.

And Jim did. You bet he did—he had to get back to work. Three times a day, for about 15 minutes, Jim would soak his elbow in hot water, as hot as he could stand, and then slowly stretch his elbow back and forth [demonstrating]. Was that painful? You bet. And you know what else? Jim did it without prescription pain medication, because he didn't like the stuff they gave him at the hospital, and he didn't need it to do the therapy. And you know what? The elbow got better. It got a lot better pretty quickly. Within a few weeks Jim could go from just an inch or two either way to bending his elbow all the way up pretty much like before [demonstrating], and he could straighten it out most of the way [demonstrating].

And then it stopped. Jim just hit a wall. No matter how much he did that therapy—and he did—it didn't get any better, and after a while he stopped. He told Dr. Klein about it, and Dr. Klein said: Jim, keep doing the therapy. Let's make sure. And Jim did the therapy some more, but it never got better. Jim could never straighten out his arm the way he used to, he never got that last 25 or so degrees [demonstrating]. That's the way his right arm is today, and how it'll be for the rest of Jim's life.

This is plaintiff's third theme—15 percent—which relates to damages, the issue plaintiff is most concerned about.

Folks, when you hear from Dr. Klein and she tells you how many people with that kind of damage to an elbow never regain full range of motion, never regain full strength, never regain full use; you are going to know why this is a case not just about success, not just about failure to yield, but it's also a case about 15 percent.

But it gets even worse. Does Jim go back to work? Of course. Jim is dying to get back to work. What happened when he got there? Ah, this is when it really became clear to Jim how bad it was. Jim would start working, and within a couple of hours his elbow would get tender, sore, start swelling, puff up, and Jim would have to stop. His boss, Rudy, was real good about it. Rudy said: Jim, take some time off. When you feel ready, come back and we'll try it again. You know what happened? Every time Jim tried to work, the same thing would happen. The arm would get sore, get tender, get stabbing pains, swell, and puff up.

Note the graphic language.

The fact of the matter, folks, is that there's been too much damage to the ligaments in Jim's elbow. Those ligaments are like nylon straps, and they hold the elbow joint together. When Jim's elbow joint was ripped apart, the ligaments that hold the joint together were stretched and torn. When they heal, they develop scars, and they're never as strong as before. Jim's elbow just isn't up to the heavy physical work being a diesel mechanic involves. That job requires 100 percent of both arms. Finally, Rudy, his boss and his friend, had to let him go, and Jim lost the only job he's ever had.

This is an important fact on the mitigation-of-damages issue.

Note that plaintiff does not mention dollar amounts. This is the common approach in personal injury cases.

Jim tried to find other work, but you know how that goes. Jim wasn't going to lie to people about his arm. With the world full of people who have 100 percent of both arms, how many repair shops will hire a mechanic with only one good arm? Jim found out the hard way. Since that June 6th, Jim can't work any longer as a diesel mechanic, and he hasn't been able to find other work either. That's the Jim Gable of today.

Conclusion.   This conclusion again emphasizes defendant's negligence and the impact the collision had on plaintiff's life.

So why are we here today? As I said in the beginning, we need your help. We need your help to tell that defendant: Two years is enough. Two years of denial is enough, two years of not taking responsibility for what your negligence did to Jim is enough. Today's the day when that defendant finally has to own up, and yes, pay up for what he did to Jim, Jim's career, Jim's family, and Jim's life. We're asking you, in short, to give Jim his life back. Thank you.

DEFENDANT'S OPENING STATEMENT

Introduction.   Defendant immediately shifts the perspective to the defendant's point of view.

May it please the court, counsel, ladies and gentlemen of our jury.

It's 5:30 p.m. on a beautiful June 6 day. In his Chevy is Douglas Cannon and his wife Marsha, pregnant with their first child. Doug sits in the Chevy, waiting at the corner of Main and Elm, looking at the light, foot on the brake, left turn blinker on, talking to Marsha. They were on the way to the doctor's office for a checkup. They were early for the appointment, no rush. It's been a good day so far.

Notice the label—*big black Jaguar sports car*—and the image it creates of the plaintiff. The label is used repeatedly.

The defense themes.

They didn't know that at that moment, coming down the street, is a big black Jaguar sports car driven by someone who will, in just seconds, refuse to give Doug and Marsha what they are both entitled to. They don't know that the driver of that big black Jaguar will refuse to give Doug and Marsha even one second of safety, one moment of caution, not even one foot of care. Because on that afternoon, the driver of the big black Jaguar dashes into the intersection, runs through the light that's turned from green to yellow to red, and slams into Doug Cannon's Chevy. Doug grabs Marsha, they hear the metal crumpling and the glass shattering, and they spin around.

Then it's quiet. Doug looks out and there he sees it: the big Jag slammed into his right rear quarter panel. Doug made sure Marsha was okay, picked up his phone, and called the police.

The defense themes again.

Members of the jury, this case is about the driver of the big black Jaguar sports car, who ran through a light that had turned from yellow to red, and refused to give Doug the one second it takes to take a foot off the gas and put it on the brake.

Personalizing your party is always a good tactic.

Before I tell you the evidence, I want you to meet Doug Cannon. Doug, stand up. [Stands up.] Now look at him. The other side wants you to say: Douglas Cannon, you're the kind of driver, with your wife in the car and your unborn child, who is stupid enough, negligent enough, reckless enough to make a left-hand turn in rush-hour traffic in front of a big black Jaguar sports car, when you are in no hurry to be anywhere. That is what they want you to say. Thank you, Doug. [Sits down.]

Here the defense emphasizes the eyewitnesses, because the defense has more of them.

You know, it wasn't all bad that day, because there were witnesses. Who will I bring to you? Well, there were a number of people there. First you'll hear from Doug, and you'll hear from Marsha. Marsha was in the passenger seat, and the traffic light was right in front of her, and she'll tell you how that light turned from green to yellow to red. There was a pedestrian standing on the southeast corner. His name is Bozza, John Bozza, and he saw it happen. As he stepped off the curb to cross Main Street, he looked up, and you'll hear him tell you what color the light was for Elm Street. And because Doug had a cell phone and called the police, a police officer came to the scene quickly. He got down on his hands and knees and looked for clues. When I ask Sergeant Tracy, how much rubber did the big black Jaguar lay down, where did the rubber start and where did the rubber end, you'll understand why Doug Cannon is completely innocent.

The defense is contesting liability, but is just as concerned with limiting damages.

Here the defense is "teasing" the jurors with upcoming evidence without actually disclosing it.

You heard that the driver of the Jaguar was injured. He was. We don't say he wasn't. Fortunately, there were no bones broken. He didn't hit his head. He had the seat belt on. What he got is called a dislocation, that's all. He went to University Hospital, and when he went into the emergency room, a nurse was on duty. You'll hear from nurse Reynolds. Nurse Reynolds is thorough. I'm going to put in your hands a business record of the hospital, the official record of the emergency room, because nurse Reynolds writes down everything. Nurse Reynolds put on here [holding up report] what really happened, and you'll hear from her.

Mr. Gable was treated and released the next morning. And he was told by the doctor in the emergency room to go to his own doctor for follow-up care and therapy. Do you have a good doctor? I do. Who is that doctor? Dr. Klein. Good. Dr. Klein will know what needs to be done and tell you what to do. And this, members of the jury, is what the doctor's order was: Mr. Gable, in order for you to get 100 percent well— not 10 percent or 20 percent, not 80 percent or 90 percent, but 100 percent—this is all you have to do, 3 times a day for 15 minutes [gesturing by bending the arm back and forth]. If you do that, you're going to be 100 percent.

This is the defense theme on damages: not following the doctor's orders. This is a reference to the defendant's medical expert.

Members of the jury, this case is about that one second of care that the driver of the big black Jaguar sports car wouldn't give. It's also about not following your doctor's orders. You may wonder why I walked up in front of you with a glass with nothing in it. This glass has meaning [holds up water glass]. It's a symbol of what that driver didn't do, refused to do, stopped doing, and it's also a symbol of a tale he told. He's going to tell you something today. He is going to tell you, I believe, that he stopped doing this [gesturing] because his arm stopped getting better. But he told somebody else, another doctor, Dr. Smith, that he stopped doing this [gesturing] because it hurt too much.

An important point for the defense is that the plaintiff never took prescription pain medication while doing the therapy.

The damages theme again.

You'll also hear, when Dr. Klein testifies, that Mr. Gable never asked her even for so much as an aspirin. Never asked her for any help dealing with the pain. And never told her that he stopped doing this [gesturing] because of pain. I promise you, members of the jury, if there's even one aspirin in this glass, a Tylenol, an Advil, anything in here at the end of this trial, I will stand up in front of you and I will tell you: Do what they want you to do. Because this case is also about Mr. Gable not following his own doctor's orders.

Conclusion. The *big black Jaguar sports car* label one last time.

For additional examples of opening statements in criminal (*State v. Rausch*) and commercial (*Thompson v. Thermorad Corp.*) cases, see Chapter 4 on the accompanying website.

Doug asks for one thing: Put the blame where it belongs. Tell the driver of that big black Jaguar sports car, that when you come to an intersection in rush-hour traffic, take your foot off the gas and slow down just for a second. That's all. That's all you've got to do.

Doug, Marsha, Mr. Bozza, nurse Reynolds, officer Tracy, and I look forward to giving you what you need to know so you can decide this case fairly. So you can look Doug in the eye when you come out of the jury room, and tell him that you have reached a fair verdict. Thank you.

4.7 Trial Notebook

The opening statements section of your trial notebook should have everything you need to give your opening statement and take notes on the other side's opening.

First, have a few blank sheets of paper in this section. Use them to take notes on your opponent's opening statement. Another common method is to have a yellow pad that is already three-hole punched, take notes on the pad, and then insert them in the section. These notes will be useful when you refine your closing argument, because experienced lawyers frequently refer to the other side's misrepresentations, overstatements, and unkept promises made during the opening statement.

Second, have the outline of your opening statement in this section. This should be a one- or two-page outline, that you can refer to if the need arises. It will contain your themes and labels, the visual aids and exhibits you plan to use, and bullet points of the key ideas in your opening statement. It should be in large print, so that you can glance at it quickly if you need to. However, keep the outline out of your line of sight as you give your opening statement. If it is too close to your line of sight, you will constantly look at it even if you don't need to and seriously detract from your delivery. The outline is there if you lose your train of thought and need to glance at it to get back on track.

Example (Plaintiff in Automobile Collision):

OPENING STATEMENT

Themes: 2 sec, failure to yield, 15%
Exhibits: intersection diagram

- Intro—This is a case about three things:
  For two years, Jim hasn't . . .
- Who is Jim Gable?
  Success: schooling, mechanic, family, job
- What happened on 6/6/2020?
  Jim is southbound on Main heading toward Elm . . .
- That defendant couldn't wait 2 sec
  Failed to yield right of way
  Why didn't he wait 2 sec? What thinking? Where looking?
- Hospital
  Therapy—followed Dr. Klein's orders
  No prescription pain killers—why
- Problems with arm
  Tried to return to work
  Lost job, can't find work
  Jim's state of mind & family
- Ending—Make it right. Give Jim his life back.

> An example of a trial notebook, with shell forms and completed forms, is on the website that accompanies this book.

4.8 Common Problems

What are the recurring problems that inexperienced lawyers encounter during opening statements?

1. Weak First Minute

The first minute should grab the jurors' attention, state your themes, and present a short synopsis of the case from your point of view. It should establish you as the lawyer the jurors want to hear as the case progresses. The slow, traditional start just doesn't work with today's jurors.

2. Weak Themes, Not Repeated Enough

A common mistake inexperienced lawyers make is to state their themes once and then never repeat them. The most important thing in opening statements is to have the jurors remember your themes, so repeat them three to five times. When lawyers don't do this, it usually means that their themes are weak. Strong themes beg to be repeated.

3. Weak Labels

Labels convey impressions: about the parties, event, and other things important in the case. Calling the plaintiff "my client" creates a different image than calling her "Helen Johnson." Calling the defendant "that corporation" is different from calling it "Mr. Smith's company." A "collision" conveys something different than an "accident." A "truck" is different from a "40,000-pound 18-wheeler." Like themes, labels must be carefully selected before trial to create strong images, and then be used consistently throughout the trial.

4. No People Stories

Jurors don't want bare, disjointed facts. They don't want to hear what each expected witness will say. Instead, jurors want interesting stories about people so they can make an emotional connection with the case. Inexperienced lawyers frequently present the jurors with a series of facts, but fail to put them together into a coherent, engaging story. It's the story that's important, not the facts that make up the story.

5. Weak Delivery

Delivery is just as important as content. Inexperienced lawyers usually spend too much time preparing the exact wording of their opening statement and too little time on practicing a forceful delivery. The result is an opening that reads well in transcript form but fails to impress the jurors in the courtroom. Don't worry so much about your exact words, and get away from your notes. Jurors will forgive and ignore stumbling over words or losing your train of thought, as long as what you say is from the heart.

6. Not Dealing with Weaknesses Candidly

It happens all the time: A plaintiff's opening statement sounds good, and then is followed by the defendant's opening that begins, "Members of the jury, what they just told you is only half the story. Here's the other half, the part they didn't want you to hear." If the jurors think that you are not being candid and up front about all the evidence, both good and bad, your credibility erodes. An effective opening statement embraces all the evidence. It weaves the bad evidence into the story to candidly disclose it, yet minimizes its impact, all the while maintaining a positive tone.

7. Forgetting That Jurors Know Nothing About the Case

Jurors know nothing about your case, so your opening statement must start at the very beginning. Inexperienced lawyers sometimes forget this, because they have been thinking about the case for months and talking to others who already know the case. Good opening statements involve good storytelling, and good storytelling always recognizes that the listener starts out as a blank slate.

8. Not Using Visual Aids

Visual learning always improves understanding and retention. That's true everywhere, including the courtroom, and it's particularly important during opening statements, when the jurors rapidly create first impressions of the case. Many lawyers are reluctant to use exhibits and visual aids during opening statements, believing that if they use them now, they will no longer be fresh and interesting if used again during the party's case-in-chief. Though this is a concern, it can be easily resolved by using some exhibits and visual aids during the opening statement and introducing others during the case-in-chief.

9. Evidentiary Violations

Finally, watch for common evidentiary violations during the opening statement. The more important ones include directly arguing witness credibility issues (which is proper only in closing arguments); misstating the applicable law on claims, defenses, or burdens of proof; and anticipating and referring to what the other party is expected to present during the trial (which the prosecutor in a criminal case can never do, because the defendant has a constitutional right not to testify or present any evidence).

Do not be afraid to make an objection during your opponent's opening statement. Some lawyers feel that this is ineffective or improper. However, if your opponent is making serious misstatements of the law or improperly shifting the burden of proof to your side, you must object forcefully and quickly.

CHAPTER 5

DIRECT EXAMINATIONS

5.1 Introduction

Direct examination is the riskiest part of a trial—i.e., the portion that most often goes wrong—because it relies upon another human being, the witness. It is where most of the evidence rules come into play; it requires training and practice with the witness so that the testimony is presented clearly, efficiently, and memorably; and it requires the lawyer to take a back seat, give up control, and let the witness be the star.

Effective direct examinations do not tell the jurors what happened. Rather, they recreate what happened through the witnesses' eyes so the jurors experience what the witnesses previously experienced. Persuasive examinations engage the jurors' hearts and minds, so they not only understand what happened, but also make an emotional connection with the witness and what the witness experienced.

To present effective direct examinations, trial lawyers must know the applicable law and the jury's perspective. They must understand the jurors' interests, needs, and limited attention spans. Jurors want to know what happened, how it happened, why it happened, and what effect it had on the witness. They want to "feel" what happened so they can make a visceral connection with the witness's experience. They want to "see" what happened, so they can form pictures in their minds as they hear the testimony. They want it fast, easy to understand, and visual. And they want witnesses who are knowledgeable, impartial, and dynamic.

> ▇◀ For an overview of direct examination of fact witnesses, please watch Video D.1, "Mauet on Direct Examination of Occurrence Witnesses."

Done well, the direct examination draws the jurors into the life of another human being, engages their hearts and minds, and allows them to re-experience an event previously experienced by the witness. Done poorly, the direct examination bores, confuses, or overloads the jurors with unnecessary details.

5.2 The Law

Direct examinations must comply with the applicable rules of evidence. The witness himself, the lawyer's questions, and the witness's answers all must survive evidentiary scrutiny. The following are the rules that most commonly come into play during direct examinations.

1. Witness Competency

Every witness must be competent to testify. Federal Rule of Evidence (FRE) 601 eliminates the traditional common law limitations on witness testimony. However, some states still retain some competency restrictions, such as barring testimony by young children, persons of unsound mind, and interested parties under dead man's acts. Those state competency rules apply not only to state court cases, but also to civil diversity jurisdiction cases in federal courts.

Every witness must take an oath to tell the truth. FRE 603 requires that every witness swear or affirm to tell the truth, but the oath need not be in the usual form if the witness has personal or religious reasons for refusing to take the usual oath. The important point is to have the witness declare that she will testify truthfully, which then subjects her to the penalties of perjury for testifying falsely.

Every witness (except experts) must have personal knowledge of the event or transaction about which the witness will testify. FRE 602 requires that a witness be shown to have personal knowledge before that witness can testify about the event or transaction.

The special rules governing expert witness testimony, FRE 702 to 706, are discussed in Chapter 8.

2. Lawyer's Questions

The lawyer's direct examination questions must meet certain evidentiary requirements. The lawyer's questions must elicit testimony that is relevant (FRE 401 to 415) and reliable (FRE 801 to 807), and there are rules that control the form and content of direct examination questions. That is, relevant and reliable testimony must be elicited in the right way.

It is commonly said that leading questions should not be used during the direct examination. Under FRE 611(c), however, leading questions may be asked "as necessary to develop the witness's testimony" and when a party calls a "hostile witness" or an "adverse party." In practice, the rule is even broader, and judges commonly permit leading questions that bring out witness backgrounds, preliminary and introductory matters, matters not in dispute, matters already proven, and foundations for exhibits. Judges recognize that leading questions on these kinds of matters are an efficient way to elicit this information. However, when testimony moves to central, disputed matters, lawyers must ask nonleading questions. In short, you may lead on background, preliminary, undisputed, and foundational matters, or if the witness is adverse, hostile, young, or forgetful. But you may not lead an ordinary witness when you get to the substance of the witness's testimony.

Direct examination questions cannot violate other "form" rules. Although there is no specific evidence rule, courts will not allow questions that are compound, confusing, or unintelligible; that ask the witness to guess or speculate; or that assume facts not in evidence.

Direct examination questions can properly elicit lay (nonexpert) witness opinion testimony. Under FRE 701, a lay witness can testify in the form of an opinion if the testimony is "rationally based on the witness's perception" and the opinion is "helpful" to the jury in understanding the testimony and resolving factual issues.

Direct examination questions can properly refresh a witness's recollection. Under FRE 612, if a witness fails to remember something while testifying, the witness can be asked if anything would refresh his memory and then be shown the document or exhibit that the witness says will jog his memory. Once the witness's memory has been refreshed, the witness then continues testifying without further assistance from the document or exhibit used to remind him. However, using a writing to refresh memory comes at a cost, because FRE 612 requires that "when a witness uses a writing to refresh memory," the adverse party "is entitled to have the writing produced at the hearing, to inspect it, to cross-examine the witness about it, and to introduce in evidence any portion that relates to the witness's testimony." Many courts hold that FRE 612 trumps claims of work product.

Finally, direct examination questions can impeach the witness. Under FRE 607, the credibility of any witness can be attacked by any party, including the party calling the witness. This means that the direct examination can anticipate impeachment and "draw the sting" by bringing out the impeachment during the direct examination.

3. Witness Testimony

Testimony must be relevant. This involves a two-step analysis. First, under FRE 401 to 402, the testimony must have "any tendency" to make a fact that is "of consequence" to the case "more or less probable." In other words, if the testimony proves or disproves something in issue in the case, it is relevant. Second, even if evidence meets this general relevance standard, other specialized relevancy rules may still exclude the testimony. These rules include FRE 403, which excludes relevant evidence if its "probative value is substantially outweighed by a danger of . . . unfair prejudice, confusing the issues, [or] misleading the jury," or by considerations of judicial economy. These rules also include the character trait rules (FRE 404 to 405), the other acts rule (FRE 404(b)), the habit rule (FRE 406), policy exclusions (FRE 407 to 411), the sexual assault rules (FRE 412 to 415), and the privileges rules (FRE 501 and 502).

The testimony also must be reliable. The reliability rules, FRE 801 to 807, govern the admissibility of hearsay. If a witness is asked to repeat in court a statement previously made out of court, the testimony must survive the scrutiny of the hearsay rules. The statement may be nonhearsay because the statement is not an assertion, because the statement is made by a party-opponent, or because the statement has probative value because it was made (its probative value does not depend on the truth of the statement). Common examples of nonhearsay include party-opponent statements (FRE 801(d)(2)); words of contract, defamation, and permission; and statements that reveal the listener's state of mind. Also, a statement may be hearsay (its probative value depends on the statement being true) but fall within a recognized hearsay exception. Common examples of hearsay exceptions include present sense impressions (FRE 803(1)), excited utterances (803(2)), and statements made for the purpose of medical diagnosis or treatment (803(4)).

Because most of the evidentiary rules come into play during direct examinations, you must prepare accordingly. Assume that every question you ask will be objected to, and be mentally ready to show why the question is proper. Assume that every answer the witness gives will be objected to, and be mentally ready to show why the answer is proper. If an objection to a question or answer is made and sustained, be prepared to overcome the objection so you can bring out all the important testimony from each witness.

For a detailed discussion of the law on direct examination, *see* Mauet & Wolfson, *Trial Evidence* (7th ed., 2020).

5.3 The Jury's Perspective

When a new witness is called to the stand, the jurors' interest heightens. They watch as the courtroom doors open, the witness walks through the spectator section to the front of the courtroom, is sworn in by the clerk or court reporter, and sits down in the witness chair. As they watch, the jurors want to know three things: Who is this person? Why is he here? Can I believe him? Jurors want answers to these questions quickly because they form impressions quickly—in the first minutes of any direct examination.

Most jurors want testimony presented as "people stories" that involve them emotionally and let them become involved in the life of another person. That's the kind of testimony most jurors connect with and remember. The best witnesses are those whose testimony is visceral and triggers emotional responses. Jurors want witnesses to tell their stories in real time, using sensory language, so they can "see" and "feel" what happened and connect emotionally with the witness and the event. This also means that lawyers should use exhibits and visual aids during witness testimony whenever possible, to highlight and make visual the information the jurors are hearing.

Finally, during direct examination jurors subconsciously test the witness's testimony against the stories they have created in their minds of what really happened. If the witness's testimony is consistent with the jurors' stories, they find the witness credible and accept the testimony. If the testimony is inconsistent, the testimony is either rejected or distorted. In this way, jurors subconsciously reconcile the testimony of witnesses with the stories the jurors have already created mentally.

Effective trial lawyers understand that direct examination involves much more than getting a witness to describe what she saw, heard, and did. Persuasive direct examinations meet the jurors' interests, expectations, and needs. They are efficient, organized, and easy to understand. They recreate what happened so that jurors can picture the events in their minds and relive the experience through the witness. They use sensory language, create vivid mind pictures that draw jurors into the story, and use exhibits and visual aids to make testimony visual. They tell a story that is consistent with the jurors' understanding of how real life works.

Planning and executing a direct examination that accomplishes all these goals is difficult, as difficult as any aspect of trial work. Nevertheless, direct examinations of well-prepared, persuasive witnesses who connect with the jurors often make the difference in the outcome of a trial.

5.4 Structure of Direct Examination

An effective direct examination is a *directed* examination. It must have a structure that is simple, clear, and logical. It should break up the examination into simple chapters that say: This is where we were, this is where we are, this is where we're going. It must be efficient, because juror attention begins to wane after about 20 minutes of listening to anything, including direct examinations, if not earlier. There are two basic ways to structure a direct examination: chronological and impact.

1. Chronological

Most storytelling is chronological. That's the way life works, and that's the way we're used to hearing stories told. Because most trials involve a sequence of events, it makes sense to tell the story in the order in which the events occurred. That's what jurors expect.

Direct examinations structured chronologically usually divide the examination into several digestible topics:

- Introduction
- Background
- Scene
- Action

■ Supporting exhibits
■ Aftermath
■ Ending

Inexperienced lawyers often have difficulty starting the direct examination and moving from topic to topic. This is where introductory and transition questions come in. They do what their names suggest: They introduce a new topic and move from one topic to another.

Examples:

> Q: Ms. Jones, let's begin by having you introduce yourself and telling us where you live.
> Q: Let's turn now to the next time you and the defendant had a meeting.

Introductory and transition questions orient the jurors by dividing the direct examination into easily followed parts, so the jurors always know that you have ended one topic and are now moving to a new topic.

a. Introduction

The first minute of any direct examination must make an impression. Whenever a witness walks into the courtroom, takes the oath, and sits in the witness chair, the jurors ask three questions: Who is she? Why is she here? Should I believe her? The first minute has to address these questions, because impressions about other people are formed quickly.

Remember that the first minute of any direct examination is largely nonverbal. The jurors watch as the courtroom doors open, a person walks in, comes to the front of the courtroom, is sworn in, goes to the witness stand, and sits down. All this happens before the witness answers the first question. How the witness appears, how he walks into the courtroom, how he acts when taking the oath, and how he sits on the witness stand are all important to the jurors in sizing up the witness, because impressions are made quickly. For the most part, those first impressions become the jurors' lasting impressions.

Once the nonverbal first minute is over, the actual direct examination begins. The traditional way of starting a direct examination does not address the jurors' needs. Asking: "State your name for the record," "Where do you reside?" and "By whom are you employed?" is stilted and awkward. Today, direct examinations by effective lawyers directly and immediately address the jurors' needs.

Example (Personal Injury Case):

> Q: Please introduce yourself to the members of our jury.
> A: I'm Helen Johnson. I'm a schoolteacher at Davis Elementary.
> Q: Why are you here?
> A: I saw the collision at Main and Elm on June 1, 2020, at around 3:00 in the afternoon.

A warning: Why questions require careful preparation with the witness.

Example (Commercial Case):

> Q: Please introduce yourself, tell us where you work, and what you do there.

A: I'm Robert Williams. I work at Higgins Electric as the vice president for sales.

Q: Were you present at the board meeting of Higgins Electric on June 1, 2020?

A: Yes.

Q: Do you remember who else was present and what was said at that meeting?

A: Sure.

Example (Criminal Case):

Q: Sir, please tell us who you are and where you live.

A: I'm Jack Anderson. I live at 234 Elm Street here in town.

Q: Is that near the Circle K store at Elm and Maple?

A: My house is only a block from the store.

Q: On June 1, 2020, around 9:00 in the evening, where were you?

A: I was walking from my house. I'd just gotten to the front of the Circle K store when the robbery happened.

Q: Did you see the actual robbery in the store?

A: Right though the plate-glass windows.

This kind of introduction lets the jurors know immediately what role the witness plays in the story of the trial. That's what they want to know *now*, not several minutes later.

Should this kind of introduction be used with every witness? Of course not. When calling the plaintiff or defendant, the jury already knows the role that person plays in the trial, so this introduction may be unnecessary. When calling a police officer in a civil or criminal case, the jury can usually guess why the officer is being called as a witness. For most lay witnesses, though, this kind of introduction works well.

b. Background

The third question jurors ask when a witness first takes the stand is: Can I believe him? The most credible witnesses are likeable, knowledgeable, and impartial. Credibility comes from a person's background, demeanor while testifying, and whether the testimony makes sense in light of the other evidence and the jurors' experiences in life.

Witnesses who lead responsible, stable lives; who are members of the community; who have resided in it for a substantial period; and who have served their community or country are more believable. Such witnesses meet the jurors' comfort level because they are "just like us." Common background information usually includes residence, family, education, job, and perhaps military and public service.

After the introduction, use a transition question to move to the witness's background. This tells the jurors that the previous topic is finished, and you're now going to move to the next topic.

Example (Witness in Personal Injury Case):

Q: Mrs. Atkins, let's turn now and learn a little about you and your life. Where do you live?

A: On Jenkins Road, just past the high school.
Q: How long have you been there?
A: Almost 20 years now.
Q: Tell us about your family.
A: My husband's name is Bob, and he's a teacher at the high school.
Q: What does he teach?
A: Algebra and physics.
Q: How about children?
A: We have two daughters. They're both adults now and out of the house. Sarah's a schoolteacher as well, Jenny's a legal secretary. But they're still both in town.
Q: Are you working outside the home at present?
A: I was also a teacher, but I retired last year.
Q: What did you teach?
A: English literature.
Q: Where did you go to school?
A: Right here. I went to Central High, and then to the university, where I majored in English. A few years later I got my masters in education.

Demeanor, of course, counts as well. We like people who are likeable, pleasant, courteous, and friendly, and who have a positive attitude about life. Likeability is a major component of credibility. How witnesses say it—their vocal inflection and body language—is at least as important as what they say, and that includes background information.

How long and detailed should the background be? That depends on the importance of the witness, the jurors' expectations, and the judge's attitude. With key witnesses, such as the plaintiff in a personal injury case, and the victim and defendant in a criminal case, judges usually permit more thorough background expositions, because jurors want to know more about the witnesses they will be judging. A key witness requires the development of a three-dimensional person the jurors can relate to, understand, and trust. Jurors want to know if the witness is a reliable member of the community or society and has attained notable goals, worked hard, and overcome adversity along the way. Those are the people we admire, and the ones we believe when they become witnesses during trials.

Example (Plaintiff in Personal Injury Case):

Q: Ms. Atkinson, let's start by learning a little about you, what you've done in your life, and what you hope to do. Where did you grow up?
A: Right here. I was born here, and we've never lived anywhere else.
Q: Tell us about your family.
A: There's my mom and dad, and I have a younger brother, Ken, who's 16.
Q: What do your parents do?
A: My dad's an administrator for Royal Life Insurance, and my mom's a substitute teacher in the public school system.
Q: You went to school here?
A: Yes, I went to University High and then the university.
Q: What kind of school is University High?
A: It's the honors high school for the city.
Q: What kind of student were you?
A: I graduated in the top 25 in my class, and I was a member of the National Honor Society.

Q: How about school activities?

A: I was on the cross-country team in the fall, and the soccer team in the spring.

Q: What made you decide to go to the university?

A: I was admitted early, and the in-state tuition was real attractive to my family, so I didn't really consider anywhere else.

Q: What did you study at the university?

A: Biological sciences.

Q: Why that particular field?

A: My dream was to be a researcher for a drug company. I always wanted to be involved in discovering new drugs. That's exciting.

Q: When you graduated, what did you do?

A: I looked for work with a drug company in their research division. I got a job in the lab of Johnson Pharmaceuticals, a small company that develops vaccines.

Q: How long have you been there?

A: Over three years now.

Q: Do you like your work?

A: I love it.

Q: What's the best part of your work?

A: It's exciting, and it's important. Developing new vaccines is the best work I can imagine being part of.

Example (Defendant in Criminal Case):

Q: Bobby, tell us about your family.

A: There's my mom, me, and my two sisters.

Q: Where do you live?

A: In the Keller Apartments. That's the public housing on Taylor Street.

Q: What does your mom do?

A: She works in housekeeping at one of the hotels by the airport.

Q: How long has she been working there?

A: Several years. Almost as long as I can remember.

Q: Tell us about your sisters.

A: There's Karen and Katherine. They're 16 and 12. Both go to public school. Karen gets really good grades.

Q: Bobby, how far did you get in school?

A: I finished high school last year. I got my diploma.

Q: How did you do in school?

A: Okay, I guess. I was an average student.

Q: How about sports and other school activities?

A: I love sports. I was on the basketball and track teams.

Q: What position did you play in basketball?

A: I was a guard. I started the last two years.

Q: How about track?

A: I ran the 200-meter dash and was on the relay team.

Q: Did you work during school?

A: Sure. We all worked. I was a bagger at the Grand Union, after school and on Saturdays.

Q: How about summers?

A: Same thing. I worked at the Grand Union every summer for three years.

> Q: Bobby, when you finished high school, what were your plans?
> A: I was planning to get into the Marine Corps.
> Q: What's happened to those plans?
> A: I got arrested, so everything is on hold until this is over.

Not all of this information, of course, has a direct bearing on the witness's credibility, but judges are usually lenient in admitting it (if it doesn't go on too long) because they understand that jurors want to know these things about the key persons in the trial.

c. Scene

In a chronological direct examination, a crisp introduction and appropriate witness background are usually followed by a description of the scene. The jurors cannot follow the action unless they have a clear picture of where the action took place. Like a play, the stage must be set before the action can begin.

Use transition questions when going from the witness's background to the scene. The jurors always want to know that you have finished one topic and are now moving on to the next one.

Examples:

> Q: Let me take you back in time to June 1, 2020, in the back room of the Four Aces Bar.
> Q: Let's return to the board room of Applied Chemicals, and go back to June 1, 2020.

These transition questions are effective because they invite the jurors to make the mental shift from the previous topic (the witness's background) to the next topic (the scene where the action happened). These questions are more effective than the traditional way (e.g., "Directing your attention to Main and Elm, do you know that intersection?" or "Are you familiar with the corner of Main and Elm?"). Although these traditional questions are proper and establish the witness's firsthand knowledge, they sound stilted and do not start the process of making mental pictures.

Make sure the witness demonstrates her firsthand knowledge of the scene at the relevant date and, if important, time. When in doubt, demonstrate that knowledge expressly.

Examples:

> Q: Were you in the board room of Applied Chemicals on June 1, 2020, when the board meeting took place?
> Q: Were you in the Four Aces Bar on June 1, 2020, at 11:00 in the evening?

Should you have the witness describe the scene, or should you use an exhibit such as a photograph or diagram to show the scene? There are pros and cons to either choice, so the important thing is to think about the benefits and liabilities of each approach. The biggest advantage of using an exhibit is that it quickly and clearly shows the scene to the jurors. In addition, some situations may be difficult for a witness to describe, and the jurors to understand, if the witness does so without using an exhibit.

However, there are important countervailing considerations. First, because exhibits attract attention, they take attention away from the witness, which is not a good thing with an important witness. Once an exhibit is introduced in the courtroom, jurors will concentrate on the exhibit, not the witness. When you have a key witness on the stand, keep the spotlight on the witness, not the exhibit. Second, the exhibit is often a distraction for the witness as well. Once the exhibit is on an easel, the witness has a tendency to look at and talk to the exhibit, rather than maintaining eye contact with the lawyer or jurors.

Third, many lawyers have witnesses testify in conjunction with the exhibit, often by having the witness stand by the exhibit as they testify. This usually detracts from the testimony. Most witnesses, certainly the inexperienced ones, feel and look awkward standing and talking by an exhibit, and much prefer to testify from the relative safety of the witness chair. Fourth, exhibits tend to detract from dramatic oral testimony. Jurors prefer to hear dramatic testimony from the witness, because they can relate better to what the witness experienced if they can concentrate on the witness and not be distracted by visuals. Finally, many lawyers use a scene description as an opportunity to settle the witness down and build up credibility before getting to the more difficult action part. After all, if the witness can clearly describe the scene where the action happened, it builds up the witness's credibility for the rest of her testimony.

For these reasons, most lawyers do not initially use exhibits when the witness is important and the testimony is dramatic. They do use exhibits *after* the witness has told the dramatic story, because exhibits then can be used to highlight, repeat, and visualize key parts of the story. For example, the plaintiff in a serious automobile collision case, or the victim in an aggravated assault case, can testify about the collision or assault without using exhibits. Once they tell a dramatic story, exhibits can be used to highlight and repeat the key points of the testimony.[1]

Later witnesses, whose principal function is to corroborate the earlier witness's story, can testify while using exhibits. For example, police officers in civil and criminal cases frequently testify while using diagrams. The jurors already know the story, the police officers are usually experienced and comfortable as witnesses, and they can testify while standing by a diagram or photograph without feeling and appearing awkward.

If you decide to have the witness tell a dramatic story without exhibits, the witness (if the first occurrence witness) must describe the scene where the action happened. The stage must be set before the action will make sense. How do you do this?

Think of scene description as the zoom lens of a camera: A zoom lens starts out at a wide-angle, showing the general area. It then moves in and focuses on the key details, making them large enough that the viewer can see them clearly. People make mental pictures the same way. They create a general picture first, then make specific images of the key things in the scene that are important. They visualize just enough to "see" where it all happened. Watch how movies and

---

1. Junior co-author Easton believes that, in this age when jurors are used to seeing pictures, it can sometimes be best to start with the exhibit. In Easton's view, that is often the best approach, because it gets the jurors oriented to the scene quickly—faster than an attempt to explain the scene with testimony. If you ask the witness to describe the scene and then introduce the picture later in the direct, some jurors might ask themselves why you did not simply use the picture in the first place, to speed things up.

television introduce scenes. They start out with an "establishing" shot, which lets the viewers know in general terms where the later action will be. They then zoom closer to the key places and objects that will be important to the story.

Experienced trial lawyers do the same thing when they have witnesses describe scenes orally. They go from wide-angle to narrow, from distance to closeup, focusing only on those things that are important—and they do it efficiently.

Example (Automobile Collision Case):

Q: What's the area around Broadway and Main like?

A: It's a commercial area. There are strip malls on all four corners, with food stores, hardware stores, fast food restaurants, things like that.

Q: Describe Broadway, the north-south street.

A: It's a big street. It has three lanes of traffic in each direction. There's a big median strip, and it has a left turn lane for both directions.

Q: How about Main Street, the east-west street?

A: It's not quite as big. It has two lanes of traffic for each direction, a median strip, and a left turn lane in each direction.

Q: What about road markings?

A: All the lanes are marked with white dotted lines. The left turn lanes are also marked, and have turn arrows painted on the lanes. There are also crosswalks across both streets.

Q: What about traffic signals?

A: There are lots of traffic lights. There are probably two or three lights in every direction. And the turn lanes have separate arrow lights. At this corner, the left turn arrows turn green after the main lights in that direction turn red.

Q: What's traffic like at 8:30 in the morning?

A: It's busy. Both Broadway and Main are commuter routes to downtown and the business parks out by the airport. The traffic is heavy, and around 8:30 it often backs up at that corner.

Q: How did Broadway and Main look on June 1, 2020, the morning of the collision?

A: Very busy. A lot of traffic backed up.

Q: What was the weather like?

A: It was a bright sunny morning.

Q: What were the road conditions like?

A: The roads were completely dry. It hadn't rained for days.

Example (Criminal Case):

Q: Mr. Williams, in what part of town is your tavern, the Lucky Strike?

A: It's on South State Street, near Porter Avenue.

Q: What kind of area is that?

A: It's an older neighborhood. Lots of small shops on the street, and lots of two- and three-story apartment buildings.

Q: If you're standing on State Street, across from the Lucky Strike, looking toward your tavern, what do you see?

A: My tavern is in a typical single-story brick building with a plate-glass front. There's a shoe repair store on the left, and a secondhand clothing store on the right. There are small stores on the entire block, and the tavern is about in the middle of the block.

Q: When you walk through the front door to the tavern, what do you see?

A: The door is in the middle of the front, so when you walk in there's the bar on the left wall, with about eight bar stools along the counter. On the right wall there are four tables, booths really.

Q: Is that the only room to the tavern?

A: No. If you walk between the bar area and the booths, there's an arched opening that leads to the back room. That has several more tables. Behind that there's a bathroom on the left, and a store room on the right.

Q: What's the lighting like in the front room of the tavern?

A: It's typical bar lighting. There are lights over each booth, lights over the bar counter, and lights on the bottles on the wall. There's a TV hanging from the ceiling against the wall at the front.

Q: Mr. Williams, if you're behind the counter in the front room, and one of your regulars walks in, can you recognize him when he walks in?

A: Sure. There's plenty of light. Enough to recognize people.

Q: Is that the way the lights were the night of the robbery?

A: Yes.

In two or three minutes, the witness can describe the scene, giving the jurors enough information so that they can form a mental picture of it and follow the action. If weather, lighting, or a particular thing is important to the story, describe it. However, keep it short. Do not cover every detail about the scene. Instead, give the jurors only those things that help them understand where the event happened so that they can visualize it.

Note also that describing the scene builds up the witness's credibility. If the witness can describe the scene clearly and remembers details, it stands to reason that the witness will also remember the details of what happened.

d. Action

The critical part of the direct examination is the action. Most lawyers have the witness tell the jurors what happened, but effective lawyers do more than that. Effective lawyers have the witness *show*, not tell, what happened. They have the witness recreate the event, so that the jurors can relive reality through that witness's eyes. They make the testimony visual and visceral, so that it has emotional impact and draws the jurors into the story. They make sure that the testimony supports their theory of the case, themes, and labels.

FRE 602 requires that the witness have firsthand knowledge of the event the witness is testifying about. If there is any question about this, establish it clearly.

Examples:

Q: Did you see the collision at the intersection of Main and Elm on June 1, 2020, around 3:00 in the afternoon?

Q: Where were you when the shooting happened in the front room of the Lucky Strike tavern?

Persuasive witnesses recreate an event in the courtroom. But how does that happen? There are several basic tools effective lawyers use:

- Witness's point of view
- Present tense
- Pace

- Sensory language
- Witness demonstration
- Selective repetition
- Challenging one's own witness

Witness's Point of View. First, the story can be told through the witness's eyes, much like a movie camera shows the perspective of the person shooting the film. A good way to do this is to set up the perspective clearly, so the jurors "see" what the witness saw. If the jurors see the action the way the witness did, the jurors are more likely to accept the witness's account.

Examples:

Q: Mr. Edgerton, please describe what you see through the windshield of your car as you're driving down Broadway that afternoon.

Q: Mrs. Henderson, when you're standing at your teller station, looking out into the lobby area of the bank, what do you see?

When jurors see the action through the witness's eyes, it becomes more vivid and has a stronger emotional impact.

Present Tense. Second, the story can be told in the present tense. Present tense makes the story come alive, and lets the jurors relive the event in real time. Present tense draws the jurors in and helps them make emotional connections with the event and the witness's experience.

Example (Personal Injury Case):

Q: When you hear the screech, what's the first thing you do?
A: I look around, trying to figure out where it's coming from.
Q: What do you see?
A: I see a large black car racing down Maple toward me.
Q: How fast?
A: It's got to be going 60 at least.
Q: What's the next thing the black car does?
A: It suddenly slams on its brakes.
Q: How do you know that?
A: I can see the tires smoking, and I can hear the tires screeching again.
Q: What does the black car do?
A: It starts skidding, then it starts to spin around and slide sideways into the intersection, coming right at me.

Example (Criminal Case):

Q: From where you're sitting at the bar, can you see everyone there?
A: Sure, if I turn sideways.
Q: What's the first unusual thing you hear?
A: I hear a loud voice yelling "Hey punk!"
Q: What do you do?
A: I turn around to see what's going on.
Q: What do you see?
A: There's two guys standing face to face a few feet from me.
Q: What are they doing?

> A: The taller guy is pushing the little guy in the chest, and he's yelling "You want to get into it?"
> Q: What's the smaller guy doing?
> A: He's backing up, he's got his hands up, and he says, "What's the problem?"

Using present tense, for both the lawyer's questions and the witness's answers, makes the action sound and feel as if it's happening right now. This is usually much more effective than the traditional approach, which asks questions in the past tense (e.g., "What did you see?" "What did you hear?"), and causes the witness to answer in the past tense (e.g., "I saw . . . " "I heard . . .). However, effective use of the present tense requires witness preparation, because most people are used to talking about a past event in the past tense.

Pace. Third, the direct examiner also can control the pace of the direct examination. Pace is an important aspect of recreating what happened. Sometimes you will want to show that something happened quickly. In that case, you will want your questions, and the witness's answers, to reflect that suddenness. Here you might bring out the event in one or two questions, showing how quickly and unexpectedly it happened. For example, in an intersection collision case the plaintiff usually wants to show that the event happened quickly, through no fault of the plaintiff, and that there was simply no time to avoid the collision.

Example:

> Q: As you approach the intersection, what's your speed?
> A: About 25 miles an hour.
> Q: What's the first thing you notice?
> A: The car coming toward me suddenly makes a left turn right in front of me.
> Q: Do you expect that?
> A: Absolutely not.
> Q: What do you do?
> A: I hit the brakes as fast and hard as possible.
> Q: What happens?
> A: My car lays down rubber and my brakes are squealing. Before I even realize it, my car crashes into the car that is turning right in front of me. Other than slamming on the brakes, I don't even have time to react before the cars crash.

Sometimes you want to portray the event more slowly. For example, in a robbery case, the prosecutor will want to show that the robbery took long enough for the victim to get a good look at the defendant.

Example:

> Q: When the man says "Give me your wallet," how far is he from you?
> A: No more than three or four feet away.
> Q: What do you notice about him?
> A: He's about my height and weight. He's white. He has short, straight, dark hair, either dark brown or black.
> Q: Any beard or mustache?
> A: No.

Q: Any earrings or jewelry?
A: Not on his face.
Q: Any tattoos?
A: I didn't see any on his face or neck.
Q: Please describe his clothing.
A: White tee shirt, nothing on the front, and dark pants.
Q: After the man says "Give me your wallet," what do you do?
A: I stare at him and say "What?"
Q: What does the man say or do next?
A: He says, "I said, give me your wallet," and he reaches into his pants pocket and pulls out a knife.
Q: Which pocket?
A: The right front pocket.
Q: What is his tone of voice like?
A: It sounds low, very deliberate.
Q: Anything unusual about his voice?
A: No, no accent or anything unusual.
Q: What's the next thing that happens?
A: I take my wallet out of my back pocket.
Q: What's the man doing during this time?
A: He's just standing in front of me, watching me, holding the knife in his hand.

Here the robbery is portrayed, step by step, to demonstrate that the victim had enough time to watch and make a series of mental impressions about the man who robbed him, lending credibility to his later identification of the defendant as the robber. (On cross-examination the defense will want to portray the robbery as having happened quickly, in poor light, creating the circumstances in which a mistaken identification occurred.)

In commercial cases, the action is frequently a key meeting in which an agreement was reached or a decision was made. Exactly what happened during that meeting is now in dispute, and plaintiff and defendant will present conflicting versions of the meeting. Jurors are more likely to accept the version of the witness who has a better recall of the event, describes details confidently, and has a particular reason to remember the meeting.

Example (Plaintiff in Contract Case):

Defendant is sued for breach of a loan agreement. Plaintiff claims that the bank's loan officer orally agreed to modify the agreement, which the bank now disputes.

Q: Mrs. Jacobson, let's turn now to the meeting you had with Mr. Brown, the loan officer at the bank. Do you remember that meeting?
A: I certainly do.
Q: How is it you remember the meeting so well?
A: This was the only time in my life I ever talked to a loan officer about borrowing money from a bank.
Q: When was your meeting?
A: On June 1, 2020.
Q: Where?

A: At the bank.

Q: What time?

A: It was scheduled for 2:00 p.m., but it didn't get started until 2:20.

Q: Why was that?

A: I was there before 2:00, but Mr. Brown said he was running late because he'd been with loan applicants all day.

Q: How did he appear to you?

A: Very busy, almost preoccupied.

Q: Where at the bank did you meet him?

A: We met at Mr. Brown's desk, but after saying hello, Mr. Brown took me to a small conference room down a short corridor.

Q: What did the conference room look like?

A: It was a small room, no windows, with an oval wooden table and four wooden chairs. The walls were white, with some framed prints on them. I'd call it a basic, functional room.

Q: What happened there?

A: It was just the two of us. We sat across from each other on the long sides of the table. We went over the loan agreement, and then he asked me if I had any questions.

Q: Did you have any?

A: Only one.

Q: What was that?

A: I told him since I'm self-employed, my income varies from month to month, and it comes at irregular times. I told him that I needed a longer grace period than the 15 days provided for in the contract before incurring late charges or being considered in default. I told him that was very important to me.

Q: What did he say?

A: He said, "Oh, that won't be a problem, because the bank never does anything unless a customer is over 30 days late."

Q: What did you say?

A: I said, "Are you sure?"

Q: How did he respond?

A: He said, "You don't have a thing to worry about. The computers in the loan department don't even flag your account until you're 30 days late on any payment."

Q: Mrs. Jacobson, are you sure that's what Mr. Brown told you during that meeting?

A: I'm positive. I would never have signed the loan agreement unless he had told me that.

Sensory Language. Fourth, the direct examiner can use, and teach the witness to use, common sensory language. Sensory questions compel sensory answers, once again making the testimony come alive, creating word pictures, and stimulating the jurors' emotional involvement.

Example (Civil Case):

Q: When your car smashes into the defendant's car, what do you hear?

A: I hear this loud crunching sound as the fenders crumple. I hear the headlight glass shatter, kind of a tinkling sound.

Q: What's the first thing you feel?

A: I'm thrown forward, my face crashes into the support column between the door and the windshield, I can feel my head being twisted, and I feel this stabbing, shooting pain in my forehead and going down my neck. And it keeps getting worse.

Example (Criminal Case):

Q: Mr. Wilson, when the defendant attacks you with the tire iron, describe how he does that.

A: He's holding the tire iron in his right hand, and he's got it over his head. He then swings it straight down toward me.

Q: What do you do?

A: I'm holding my arms out, trying to figure out where he's going to swing so I can block it.

Q: Do you?

A: Not really. The tire iron hits my left hand, and it bends the little finger back, and it snaps, like a stick. Before I can even react, the tire iron hits my head.

Q: What do you feel?

A: There's this instant flash of pain, a stabbing pain, kind of like getting jolted by electricity. I feel blood oozing down the side of my face. Then I just go limp, and fall down. That's the last thing I remember.

Sensory questions—those that ask the witness what she saw, heard, smelled, tasted, or felt—naturally trigger sensory responses. They are much more effective than the commonly asked unfocused questions (e.g., "What happened?" and "What happened after that?"), which usually get flat conclusory responses (e.g., "My car hit his" and "I got hurt").

Witness Demonstration. Another way to show, not tell, is to have the witness physically show or demonstrate something important. Plaintiffs in civil cases are sometimes asked to stand in front of the jurors to show scars or to demonstrate limited range of motion in joints. Victims in criminal cases are sometimes asked to demonstrate how a weapon was held against them during an assault or how they were made to lie on the floor during a robbery. These demonstrations have more impact than an oral description.

Example:

Q: Your honor, may Mr. Jackson step down and stand before the jury while I ask questions?

JUDGE: Certainly. [Witness stands in front of the jury box.]

Q: The facial scars you just testified about, could you point them out to the jury?

A: Sure. One scar runs from my left ear [pointing] down below my jaw to my neck [pointing]. The other scar is on the top of my head, from here to here [pointing]. It's hard to see because my hair has mostly grown back, except for where the scar is.

Q: On the second scar, you were starting at the top of your head and moving to just above your ear?

A: Yes.

Q: Thank you, Mr. Jackson. Please take your seat again. [Witness returns to the witness stand.]

If the witness uses imprecise expression like "from here to here," remember that the transcript will be unclear unless you define "here" and "here."

Example:

Q: Your honor, may Ms. Jefferson step down?

JUDGE: Yes.

Q: Ms. Jefferson, please come over to the jury box. [Witness stands in front of the jury box.] Please show the jury how far you can bend your back today.

A: I can bend over this far [demonstrating] so I can just about touch my knees with my fingers.

Q: What happens if you try to bend over further than that?

A: I get a horrible stabbing pain in the small of my back. I never do that because of the pain.

These demonstrations are effective because they show, not just tell, what happened, and leave a lasting impression with the jurors. Make sure you practice beforehand, so that the demonstration in fact shows what you want it to show. Make sure that the demonstration does not embarrass the witness or jurors and make a record of what the demonstration did.

Selective Repetition. Repetition is sometimes an effective tool, as long as it does not repeat exactly the same testimony, and it is not overused. For example, a series of related questions can drive home the point better than one summary question.

Example:

Q: When you first saw the defendant, how was he dressed?

A: He had on baggy black pants and a baggy Raiders shirt.

Q: When you first saw the defendant, what was he doing?

A: He was yelling at another guy.

Q: And when you first saw the defendant, what was he saying?

A: He said "I'm going to get you when this is over."

In this example, using three parallel questions puts emphasis on the fact that the witness saw the defendant.

Sometimes you can get the witness to repeat the same answer to a series of different, but related, questions.

Example:

Q: Officer, when you saw Mr. Adams at milepost 20, how was he driving?

A: He was going over 80 in a 55 mile per hour zone.

Q: At milepost 21, how was he driving?

A: He was still going over 80.

Q: When you pulled him over at milepost 22, how was he driving?

A: He was still going over 80.

Looping back is another repetition technique. When you get a great answer, use the answer to form part of your next question.

Example:

> Q: What did the man do next?
> A: He pulled out a handgun and stuck it in my face.
> Q: After he stuck the handgun in your face, what did he do?
> A: He said, "Give me your money."

Repetition and looping back are useful techniques, but use them sparingly to highlight key information. Used too often, these techniques quickly become tiring and even annoying. Jurors commonly complain about lawyers who engage in direct repetition, especially when they do it too often. Direct repetition conveys a horrible message to jurors—that you did not think they were paying attention to the original testimony.

Challenging One's Own Witness. Whenever a witness testifies to something that doesn't make sense, or seems improbable, the jurors will question it. Use the opportunity to enhance your credibility, as well as the witness's credibility. Challenge the witness's answer; ask the questions the jurors would ask if they could.

Example:

> Q: Ms. Williams, after the shot went off, what did you do?
> A: I just stood there.
> Q: Why didn't you run?
> A: I was just numb.
> Q: Didn't you call the police?
> A: No.
> Q: Why not?
> A: At the time I was just frozen.

Example:

> Q: Mr. Adams, when the car started to turn in front of you, why didn't you slam on your brakes?
> A: There wasn't time. By the time I could react, he had already crashed into my car.

e. Exhibits

Exhibits are another opportunity to make testimony visual, which helps jurors to understand, experience, and remember what happened. As discussed earlier, exhibits should be integrated into the direct examination so that they reinforce, rather than distract from, the oral testimony. With key witnesses, some lawyers bring out the testimony about the scene and action first, then introduce exhibits that repeat, highlight, and reinforce the testimony.

Exhibits have high psychological value. Some have high emotional value, such as photographs of accident and crime victims. Some have high informational value, such as diagrams and models of accident and crime scenes. Their value depends, in part, on how individual jurors react to different kinds of information.

Most jurors are right-brained (*affective* decision makers), and prefer to hear information, particularly dramatic testimony, directly from witnesses. For them, emotional exhibits have more impact than informational exhibits. A minority of jurors are left-brained (*cognitive* decision makers) and usually prefer to receive information through exhibits that they can analyze. For them, diagrams, models, and charts that organize and visualize information have higher impact.

Because juries usually will contain both right-brained and left-brained decision makers, effective direct examinations are planned to reach both kinds of jurors through their preferred channels. Oral testimony, particularly of dramatic or traumatic events, and graphic exhibits influence the right-brained jurors. Exhibits such as diagrams, models, maps, and flowcharts influence the left-brained jurors. Hence, having a witness describe what happened, and then highlighting the key parts of the testimony with photographs, diagrams, models, or charts, effectively reaches and influences both kinds of jurors.

Developing a visual strategy and deciding what exhibits and visual aids to use during the various stages of the trial is a key part of trial strategy. Deciding how to integrate exhibits into a direct examination is an important part of structuring the direct examination of any witness. Chapters 7 and 11 discuss these matters in detail.

f. Aftermath

After the action comes the aftermath. Some occurrence witnesses testify only to the action, because they were not involved in what happened after the event on which the trial is based. Key witnesses, such as the plaintiff and investigating police officer in a personal injury case, and the arresting police officer and the defendant in a criminal case, can also testify about what happened after the collision or arrest occurred. In civil cases, such testimony is frequently critical evidence on the issue of damages. In criminal cases, it frequently includes inculpatory statements and conduct by the defendant.

As always, use transition questions to let the jurors know you are moving to the next topic.

Examples:

    Q: Mr. Johnson, let's turn now to what happened right after the collision.
    Q: Officer O'Brien, let's go next to when you conducted the lineup.
    Q: Ms. Williams, we're going to focus now on the time between when you left the hospital and when you returned to work.

In personal injury cases, the plaintiff's (and plaintiff's family's) testimony about the plaintiff's life from the time of the injury to the present time must be developed persuasively. This testimony is important to several elements of damages, including pain and suffering, extent and permanence of injury, past and future medical expenses, and loss of income. The plaintiff needs to testify about some of these elements, but in a way that is positive and commands the jurors' respect. Nobody likes a whiner or complainer; everybody admires the person who deals as best he can with a bad situation. Jurors like to help those who have done as much as possible to help themselves, and that is particularly true of plaintiffs in personal injury cases.

Consequently, the direct examination must show what the plaintiff experienced on the road to recovery. It must show the permanent physical and mental effects, and how these changed her work and personal life. The direct examination should sound positive, even uplifting, while describing the plaintiff's experience. The key is to understand what most jurors feel about plaintiffs and other victims: If they did everything possible to recover as fully as possible (and mitigate their damages), the jurors will take care of the rest. Understatement, not exaggeration, is the effective way to portray the aftermath from the plaintiff's side.

What happened afterward also can be important from the defense side. For example, in personal injury cases the defense can show that the defendant driver remained at the scene, called the police and ambulance, tried to help the plaintiff driver, and cooperated with the police and medical personnel when they arrived. In a criminal case, the defense can show that the defendant did not try to flee the scene, remained there until the police arrived, cooperated with the police, and freely gave a statement about what happened.

g. Ending

Ending strong is just as important as starting strong. The reason is the principles of primacy and recency. We tend to remember better the things we hear first and last. Therefore, the last thing a witness says on direct examination should be important and linger in the courtroom, so that every juror will remember it.

What should the last question and answer be about? That depends on what is important. What is the most important point the witness can make during the direct examination, the one you want to be sure the jurors never forget? Once you have identified that, make it part of your last question. For example, if the principal concern is liability, ask a key liability question; if damages, ask a key damages question; if identification, end on that issue. After the witness answers, pause, let the answer sink in, then tell the judge that your direct examination has ended.

Example:

Q: Mr. Williamson, I have one last question. At the moment your car collided with that defendant's car, what color was the traffic light for Main Street?
A: It was green.
Q: [Pause] Your honor, we have no further questions for Mr. Williamson.

Example:

Q: Since the collision, have you ever been able to return to your job as a steelworker?
A: No.
Q: Have you been able to find other work?
A: No.
Q: Have you been able to support your family?
A: No.
Q: [Pause] Your honor, we pass the witness.

Example:

Q: Ms. Swain are you sure that the defendant, the man sitting over there, is the man who robbed you at gunpoint that day?
A: I'm positive. I'll never forget his face.

Q: [Pause] Thank you, Ms. Swain. Nothing further on direct.

Many direct examinations end simply because the lawyer has run out of questions. Effective lawyers identify the key facts and disputes and structure their examinations so that the last question always brings out a key fact important to a key issue. That's the last question and answer the jurors should remember. Try, also, to ask a final question that has little chance of drawing a sustained objection. You want to end on a high note, not the dud of an objection by your opponent that the judge upholds.

h. Incorporating Weaknesses and Anticipating Cross-Examination

People have a natural tendency to emphasize the positive and ignore the negative. Lawyers are no exception. However, the opposing side has the opportunity to bring out all negative information, both during cross-examination and during the opposing side's case-in-chief or rebuttal case. Thus, the better approach is to anticipate the negative information and incorporate it into the direct examination story. Trial lawyers call this "drawing the sting" or "fronting the problems." Because FRE 607 permits any party to impeach any witness, there is no evidentiary barrier to bringing out bad facts or impeaching your own witness. When and how you do this, however, makes a big difference.

The order in which you present information—*order effects*—has a great deal to do with impression formation. People tend to make impressions quickly, based on little information. Once made, people resist changing their impressions, even in the face of substantial contrary information. In addition, jurors expect and value candor from the lawyers. Once they believe that a lawyer is telling them only half the story—the favorable half—that lawyer won't be trusted and quickly loses any capacity to influence the jury.

The conclusion is clear. Lawyers need to disclose weaknesses candidly, and they need to do it in a way that minimizes the impact of the bad facts. The best approach is to bring out the bad facts and make them part of a story, but only after the jurors have formed an initial good impression of the witness.

Sometimes the weakness involves the witness's background. Most commonly this is a criminal conviction that, under FRE 609, can be used to impeach the witness's credibility. In this situation, lawyers usually bring out the prior conviction during the direct examination, after first bringing out facts that create a good impression. Most courts permit bringing out the date, location, and crime of which the person was convicted; many bar bringing out the facts underlying the conviction.

Example:

In this case, an important eyewitness for the plaintiff has been convicted of a felony theft. The direct examiner has spent time developing the witness's positive background. The following then happens.

Q: Mr. Johnson, before we go any further into your family and work, let's talk about the time you got in trouble with the law. When was that?
A: It was eight years ago, when I was a senior in high school.
Q: What were you charged with?
A: Theft. I stole a computer from an electronics store.
Q: What happened to that charge?

A: I pleaded guilty and was put on probation for three years.

Q: Did you finish that successfully?

A: Yes. In fact, my probation ended early.

Q: Since that time, what have you done with your life?

A: I haven't done anything stupid like that again, that's for sure. I got married, and we started a family, like I've just told you. I went to vocational school, got certified as an automotive mechanic, and I've worked for the GM auto dealership here for the past seven years.

Q: You like your job?

A: You bet. It's good work, and they're good people to work for.

Sometimes the weakness involves the witness's story. Frequently this involves the witness's drinking before being involved in a collision. In this situation, lawyers usually bring out the fact of drinking during the direct examination, making it part of the story and showing that the drinking had nothing to do with the collision.

Example:

In this case, the plaintiff had some champagne before driving her car and being involved in a collision. The direct examiner will spend time showing what the witness did during the day of the collision and weave the fact of drinking into that story.

Q: Ms. Griggs, when did you go to work that day?

A: The usual time. Around 9:00.

Q: Anything unusual about that day?

A: No, not at work.

Q: How about after work?

A: We planned a surprise shower for one of my co-workers. She was getting married in a couple of weeks.

Q: Where was the shower?

A: At Jason's, a restaurant about a block from work.

Q: You went to the shower?

A: Sure. Barbara's a good friend of mine.

Q: When did you get to the shower?

A: Probably around 5:15.

Q: And how long did you stay?

A: About 45 minutes.

Q: While you were there, did you have anything to eat or drink?

A: Both. They had finger sandwiches, and I ate three of them. I also had a glass of champagne—actually it was one of those plastic glasses—and had part of a second glass, then I had to leave.

Q: What did you do after you left?

A: I walked back to my building, picked up some things from my office, and got my car from the garage.

Q: Where were you going?

A: Home. I was going to meet my husband, and we were planning to have dinner out. It was on the way home when all this happened.

In short, bring out the bad facts, make them part of the story, and don't sound defensive about them in the process. If the jurors already have a good impression of the witness, they will minimize the significance of the bad facts and will appreciate the witness's candor. Of course, you can't make bad facts disappear. But volunteering them on direct, in a candid way, will lessen their impact over the effect they would have if first brought out during cross-examination.

2. Impact

Chronological direct examinations are the most common way to structure direct examinations. There is another way, though: the impact direct examination. The impact direct examination puts the dramatic testimony at the very beginning of the examination, where it will grab and hold the jurors' attention. After the dramatic testimony is revealed, the direct examination then loops back to the other elements of the chronological approach.

The impact approach is frequently used with key witnesses to a traumatic event, and with defendants in criminal cases. For plaintiffs, the idea is to jolt the jury and make a lasting impression. For defendants, the idea is to jolt the jurors away from the plaintiff's version and see it from the defense point of view. Obviously, the witness must be prepared carefully so that the drama unfolds as you intend it to unfold.

Example:

The witness is the plaintiff in a wrongful death case. The direct examination begins with the telephone call informing him that his wife has been seriously injured in an accident.

Q: Mr. James, where were you on June 1, 2020, when you received the call?
A: I was in my office.
Q: When the telephone rang, what happened?
A: I picked it up, said hello, and a voice said "Mr. James, your wife has been in an accident, she's been seriously hurt, and they've taken her to St. Mary's Hospital."
Q: What did you do?
A: I ran from my office, got in my car, and drove as fast as I could to the hospital.
Q: What did you see?
A: When I got to the emergency room, I couldn't recognize her. There were bandages, tubes, and wires all over, and nurses and doctors everywhere. I couldn't believe that I was seeing Judy.
Q: What did you do?
A: I started praying.

Example:

The witness is the defendant who is charged with armed robbery of a liquor store. The defense is misidentification.

Q: Bobby, the prosecution charges that you used a .38 caliber gun and robbed Cut Rate Liquors on June 1, 2020, at 11:00 in the evening. Did you do that?
A: No sir, I did not.

Q: Were you anywhere near the store at that time?
A: No sir.
Q: Do you know who robbed the store?
A: No, but I know it wasn't me.
Q: Tell the members of the jury where you were at 11:00 p.m. on June 1, 2020.
A: I was at home.

After the impact beginning, the direct examination can then loop back, develop the witness's background, and follow the chronological approach throughout the rest of the examination. Consider an impact beginning whenever you have dramatic testimony that will grab the jurors' attention. From the defense side, consider an impact beginning when you want to jolt the jurors away from the impressions they have developed from hearing the plaintiff's case-in-chief.

5.5 Language of Direct Examination

Direct examination is an interplay between lawyer and witness that is designed to influence the jurors. It is a three-way conversation, with jurors being the silent participants. Both the lawyer's questions and the witness's answers have to use the language of effective direct examinations. This involves both form and content.

1. Lawyer's Questions

First, the lawyer's questions must be in the proper form. The general rule is that the lawyer's questions should be nonleading, but that rule has a number of exceptions. Leading questions usually are permitted on witness backgrounds, preliminary and introductory matters, matters not in dispute, matters already proven, and foundations for exhibits. Leading questions may be used if the witness is an adverse party, hostile, young, or forgetful. In practice, the nonleading rule is a rule of preference: With most witnesses, the direct examiner may use leading questions on preliminary matters not in dispute, but must use nonleading questions when the testimony turns to important and disputed facts.

A *leading question* is one that suggests the desired answer. Questions can be leading because of content, but they can also be leading because of tone. Just because a question has detailed content does not necessarily make it leading. For example, some believe asking "Were you in Las Vegas in 2020?" is not a leading question, because it does not suggest the desired answer. By contrast, asking "You were in Las Vegas in 2020, right?" clearly suggests the desired answer and is improperly leading. Tone can also make a question leading. For example, asking "You're 38 years old?" with a rising intonation and an accompanying head nod suggests the desired answer and is improperly leading. Judges vary widely in their definition—and tolerance—of leading questions.

Effective lawyers rarely object to each other's direct examinations on leading grounds, because effective lawyers rarely ask improperly leading questions. They know that asking leading questions during direct examination is not an effective technique, because leading questions detract from the credibility of both witness and lawyer. Jurors will always think: "That lawyer doesn't trust his own witness, otherwise he wouldn't spoon feed her the right answers." And jurors will always ask, "Would the witness ever have said all the things she said if that lawyer hadn't put those words in her mouth?" Leading questions prevent the witness from doing the most important thing during direct examination: telling the story in the witness's own way, in the witness's own words, with minimal control from the lawyers.

Second, effective lawyer's questions are short, particularly when the testimony gets to core, disputed matters. Think of direct examination as a 10–90 percent rule. The lawyer should be questioning 10 percent of the time, and the witness should be answering 90 percent of the time. A good test of how well the direct examination is going is to ask: How much is the lawyer talking? When the lawyer asks only simple, clear questions and merely directs the witness from one topic to another, the jurors' focus stays on the witness, where it should be. Simple questions are the who, what, where, when, how, and why questions we all use in our daily lives. These are nonleading and get the witness talking, which is essential to an effective direct examination.

Effective questions also use simple words. This means that trial lawyers need to use common language, not lawyer talk. When lawyers use lawyer language, two things happen: The jurors don't understand the question, and the jurors think that the lawyer is being condescending. Just as bad, the witnesses may think that lawyer talk is the way they should answer the questions. Think of how you used to talk before you went to law school and translate the lawyer talk back into the language of normal people. Common examples:

Lawyer talk	*Normal talk*
Prior to	Before
Subsequent to	After
With respect to	(omit the phrase)
Did you have an occasion to	Did you
Exit your vehicle	Get out of your car
By whom are you employed	Where do you work
State your full name	What's your name

Always ask yourself: How would I have asked that question when I was "normal," before I learned my new lawyer vocabulary? Then ask the question that way. Jurors prefer plain English from everyone, including lawyers.

Third, lawyers should ask questions that ask for sound bites. Lawyers cannot ask questions that ask the witness to give long narratives, because such answers do not give the other side a reasonable chance to object to improper testimony. For example, asking "Tell us what you saw, heard, and did that morning" is improper, because the witness may give a long, rambling answer. More importantly, these questions are usually ineffective, because they ask for too much information, too fast.

The solution is to ask questions that elicit sound bites. These are the 10- to 15-second answers that present the testimony in digestible bites. This means that the questions, instead of asking for long narratives, are more focused. For example, instead of asking: "What did you see at the time of the crash?," ask: "What's the first thing that drew your attention?," "What did you notice about the green car?," and "What did the driver of the red car do next?"

Fourth, lawyers need to ask vivid questions, because these questions bring out the visceral and visual answers. Remember that witness testimony should create word pictures. As the witness testifies, the jurors are making mental pictures of the testimony and organizing those pictures into a story. Sensory questions are exactly that; they use the five senses. Instead of asking "What happened next?," ask "What do you see next?" and "What's the next thing you hear?" Instead of asking "What happened to you?," ask "What do you notice about yourself?" and "What's the first thing you feel?"

Finally, show interest in the witness and the witness's testimony. Everyone in the courtroom, including the jurors, knows that the direct examination has been planned and, at least with parties, practiced beforehand. However, this doesn't mean the direct examination should feel and sound scripted. Energy, enthusiasm, and dynamism make a difference. Effective trial lawyers understand that jurors naturally adopt the attitude of the active participants in a conversation. If you, the direct examiner, sound genuinely interested in the witness, so will the jurors. If you sound genuinely surprised by some of the testimony, so will the jurors. If you maintain eye contact with the witness and use reinforcing gestures and body language, this will influence the jurors. At the same time, you also influence the witness, who will subconsciously adopt your attitude and demeanor. Even though you have practiced the direct examination many times, in the courtroom (like on a stage) it must look, sound, and feel fresh.

2. Witness's Answers

The witness's answers also have to use the language of effective direct examinations. This means several things. First, witnesses need to testify using their own natural vocabulary and expressions, because only those will sound natural in the courtroom. The witness's own vocabulary, however, should avoid slang, stilted language, and offensive terms. Research shows that jurors prefer plain English — simple vocabulary, proper grammar, short sentences. Slang (e.g., "He done good"), police talk (e.g., "I exited my vehicle and approached the subject"), and lawyer talk (e.g., "Subsequent to that conversation, I contacted him again") all detract from the witness's credibility.

Second, make sure that the key words and descriptions come first from the witness, not the lawyer. Testimony has impact when it comes from the witness, not the lawyer's suggestion. For example, asking a witness: "Was the car going fast?" is not as effective as asking: "What was the speed of the car?" and the witness answers: "Fast." Make sure the key word — "fast" — comes first from the witness. Once the witness has used a key word or description, then you can use it in follow-up questions. For example, you ask a witness, "What did the knife look like?" and the witness answers, "It looked like a six-inch-long hunting knife." You can then ask, "What did the defendant do with that hunting knife?"

Third, try to have the witness answer in sound bites, those 10- to 15-second answers that give the jurors a digestible amount of information. You get sound-bite answers by asking sound-bite questions.

Fourth, try to have the witness's answers create word pictures by using sensory words rather than conclusory words. In large part, this is controlled by the questions. Asking a witness: "What happened?" will usually get a bland, conclusory answer. Asking a witness: "What did you see?," "What did you hear?," "What did you feel?," and "What's the first thing you noticed about yourself?" will usually get visceral and vivid answers.

Finally, the witness's answers should be given in a clear, positive, confident manner. How witnesses say it is as important as what they say, and this takes practice.

5.6 Preparing the Witness and Yourself

Direct examination is the most difficult part of a trial to do well. In part, this is because direct examination is the only part of the trial in which the lawyer must give up center stage to let someone else—the witness—be the center of attention. In part, it is because doing a direct examination well requires substantial preparation time from both lawyer and witness. Compelling direct examinations don't happen simply because you have good witnesses; they happen because of planning and preparation.

1. Prepare Yourself

First, your organization of what the witness will say must serve your theory of the case, themes, and labels. Inexperienced lawyers frequently have witnesses tell everything they know about the case during the direct examination; effective direct examinations are much more focused. They have the witness testify only to those facts that persuade the jurors to accept your theory of the case, that support your themes, and that validate your labels. In short, you need to review what the witness *can* say, based on what you know from your formal and informal pretrial discovery, and then decide what the witness *will* say. This involves reducing the 100 percent of what the witness knows down to the perhaps 20 percent that is important enough to bring out during the direct examination. Only then can you move to the next step: deciding how to organize that testimony into a cohesive and compelling story. This must all be done before you meet with the witness to prepare for the trial.

> 🎥 For a discussion of drafting of direct (and cross) outlines, please watch Video D.2, "Wyo STI: Direct & Cross-Examination Outlines."

For example, consider an important eyewitness whose deposition took three hours. You need to review that deposition and any other sources of information, determine the facts about which the witness can testify, and then decide which of those facts are sufficiently important to bring out during the witness's direct examination. Those three hours have to be organized and condensed into a twenty-minute story. Jurors have a limited attention span and a limited ability to absorb information. Effective direct examinations recognize these realities by structuring the examination to focus on the key information that will make a difference to the jurors.

Second, the lawyer must have the right mindset. Direct examination requires that you take a back seat and let the witness be the center of attention. Think of yourself as a director whose job is to make sure the witness efficiently moves from one topic to another and testifies persuasively, so that jurors create mind pictures as they hear the testimony. This requires that you show genuine interest in the witness, actively listen and ask appropriate follow-up questions, maintain eye contact, and use reinforcing gestures and body language so that the witness becomes a more confident, dynamic witness.

Direct examination is a three-way conversation that includes the jurors, although they are passive participants. Think of the body language you use when you talk with another person and a third person joins in. You reposition yourself appropriately. You use gestures and body language to show interest in the third person, making sure he is listening and feels involved, even though he is not actively participating in the conversation. Effective direct examinations always include the jurors by making them part of the conversation between you and your witness. If allowed, conduct direct examination near the corner of the jury box furthest from the witness stand. When looking at you, the witness will have incidental eye contact with the jurors.

2. Prepare the Witness

Next, you as the lawyer must prepare the witness. How this should be done depends, in part, on who the witness is and what you will be using to prepare. Your confidential conversations with your client are privileged and protected from disclosure, so you can freely discuss anything with the client. In contrast, your conversations with other witnesses are not privileged. Talk to nonclient witnesses as though the jurors were present and listening, because your conversations with these witnesses may be brought out during cross-examination. In addition, no witness is obligated to work with you before trial to prepare for testifying at trial. Although cooperative witnesses will want your help, neutral and hostile witnesses can and often do refuse. With such witnesses, your only right, except for the opposing counsel's client (Model Rule 4.2), is to request to speak with them. But they are free to refuse. (You can bring out a witness's refusal to talk to you during direct or cross-examination, since this suggests bias.)

Witness preparation also involves having the witness review documents, records, and other written matter. Be careful about what you show witnesses—your client as well as any other witness. Under FRE 612, if a witness before trial uses any writing to refresh memory for the purpose of testifying, the court has discretion to require that it be turned over to the other side, which can then use it to cross-examine the witness and introduce relevant portions in evidence. The disclosure requirement of the rule usually trumps claims of work product and may even trump claims of privilege. If you show it to any witness to prepare for testifying at trial, it may end up in the other side's hands. Therefore, show witnesses only those documents, records, deposition transcripts, exhibits, and visual aids the other side has already obtained during discovery and pretrial disclosures, or that you don't mind the other side getting.

Explain to the witness what your purpose is during a preparation session. Many witnesses don't understand that it is perfectly proper for a lawyer to talk with a witness for the purpose of preparing to testify at trial. In fact, jurors are sometimes given a jury instruction to that effect. Explain to the witness that you need to learn what the witness can say at trial; show how her testimony is an important part of your proof; and help the witness be a knowledgeable, impartial, and dynamic witness. Only the witness knows what facts she can testify about. Only you know what parts of the witness's personal knowledge are important to the presentation of your case. Your job on direct examination is to bring out the important facts so they are clearly and credibly presented to the jurors.

Find out the witness's goals and concerns. For example, an employee for a corporation may be concerned about how her testimony will be assessed by her supervisors. Some witnesses may be concerned about a particular part of their testimony. Direct examinations will be more successful if you keep in mind that witnesses also have needs that should be addressed.

Witnesses are persuasive because of *what* they say (content) and *how* they say it (delivery). The key to effective testimony is to make sure the content comes from the witness, not the lawyer. Develop the testimony through the witness's own natural vocabulary and plain English. Ask sensory (e.g., "What did you see, hear, smell, taste, and feel?"), not conclusory, (e.g., "What happened?") questions. Above all, don't suggest words that the witness might use, unless you need to advise a witness to not use a derogatory term. Outside of this limited exception, when you suggest the words, they will be your words, not those of the witness, and they won't sound genuine in the courtroom. Instead, prod the witness's natural sensory language out of him. A witness should sound and look prepared, not rehearsed.

Most importantly, always advise every witness that he will testify under oath and that his primary obligation as a witness is to tell the truth. Repeat this message often in your preparation sessions with witnesses.

Example (Lawyer Preparing Client):

LAWYER: John, describe in your own words how the crash happened.

CLIENT: His car ran the red light, hit my car, and I got hurt.

LAWYER: John, that's a start, but we need to show the jury what happened, so that they can see what you saw, hear what you heard, and feel what you felt. Let's talk about his car hitting yours. Did you hear anything?

CLIENT: Sure. There was a huge crash.

LAWYER: What did it sound like?

CLIENT: A loud crunching sound, from all the metal crunching.

LAWYER: What metal?

CLIENT: The fenders, bumper, and grill all got smashed in, and the radiator was crushed.

LAWYER: Could you actually see it happen?

CLIENT: Sure. It was right in front of me.

LAWYER: What did you see?

CLIENT: The front of his car hit the left front of my car right about at my left headlight.

LAWYER: What did you see happen to the two cars?

CLIENT: The left front of my car got smashed in, my left fender got peeled back, the headlights broke, you could hear the tinkling, the grill, bumper, everything was smashed in. The same thing happened to the other guy's car, and his hood popped up. Oh yeah, his horn started going and wouldn't stop.

LAWYER: John, that's good. The jury can get a much better idea of what happened when we talk about what you actually saw, heard, and felt. Let's go over that again, and this time let's go over it as though it's actually happening again, in real time.

Making testimony come alive takes time. It requires repeatedly going over all parts of the testimony and drawing out the witness's natural language so the jurors can see, hear, and feel what happened.

Once you develop the content of the testimony, work on the delivery. How witnesses say it and how they look as they're saying it are as important as the content. Nonverbal communication begins when the witness first walks into the courtroom and ends only when the witness leaves.

Decide what the witness should wear. Don't tell the witness to "wear appropriate clothing for court," because the witness may not know what that means. Suggest a suit or slacks and jacket for men and business attire for women. If the witness is in the police or military, suggest the regular uniform. If the witness is in another line of work relevant to the trial that features uniforms, like mechanical repair, it might be appropriate to testify in the uniform, as long as it is clean. If the witness is a child or adolescent, suggest plain trousers and shirt, or similar clothing. Avoid jewelry other than watch, wedding ring, and other basics. Avoid excessive makeup or extreme hairstyles. Find out exactly what the witness will look like in court; don't guess. Witnesses need to feel comfortable, but they also need to show, through their attire and grooming, that they take the courtroom and their role as witness seriously.

Practice the first minute of the witness's appearance in the courtroom, which is mostly nonverbal. How the witness enters the courtroom, how he walks to the witness stand, how he takes the oath to tell the truth, how he makes eye contact with others, and how he sits in the witness chair all send strong signals at a time when the jurors are sensitive to such signals. Witnesses who appear confident, knowledgeable, and dynamic are more credible. Let the witness know that this first minute is important.

Practice the nonverbal aspects of testifying. How words are spoken is as important as the words themselves. Appropriate volume, speech rate, articulation, and pauses make the witness appear more confident and powerful. Work on identifying weak speech patterns, such as using hollow intensifiers ("very," "really," "clearly," "obviously," "you know"), hedges ("I think," "well, ah"), and uncertainty ("it seemed like," "sort of"). Finally, practice the body language. The witness's posture, eye contact, facial expressions, gestures, and body movement should reinforce, not detract from, the testimony.

Practice where the witness should look. Most witnesses look best when they look at the direct examiner as the questions are asked and when the witness answers them. However, when you have a particularly important question, have the witness turn and look at the jurors when answering. For example, when asking the defendant in a robbery whether he robbed the victim, have the defendant face the jurors as he emphatically denies the charge. ("Bobby, tell the members of the jury, did you rob Helen Smith on June 1, 2020?") When asking an expert to explain something, again ask the expert to talk directly to the jurors. ("Dr. Adams, explain to our jurors why Mr. Johnson will never be able to work as a carpenter again.") In this way, looking at the jurors seems natural, and the witness makes eye contact with the jurors on key questions.

Inexperienced lawyers usually spend too much time on the verbal content of the witness's testimony and too little time on the delivery. For jurors, how the witness sounds and looks when he testifies is at least as important as what the witness actually says. A word of caution, however. Some witnesses will sound and look great; others will not. With the latter, you can only change so much. Identify one or two mannerisms that stand out and work on improving them. For instance, many witnesses use too little volume and let their voice drop off at the end of sentences. Many witnesses slouch and hide their hands while testifying.

These problems can usually be improved. However, trying to fix too many things often results in the witness becoming confused and distracted.

> For a discussion of witness preparation and other aspects of direct examination, please watch Video D.3, "Wyo STI: Direct Examination, Including Witness Preparation."

Finally, practice with the witness. Really practice! Practice means practicing the direct examination in a courtroom setting. If the witness is important, take the witness to the courtroom where the trial will be held and practice entering the courtroom and testifying from the witness chair. (If necessary, get the judge's or clerk's permission to use the courtroom.) If a courtroom is not available, practice in a room that has been set up to replicate the courtroom. If the courtroom is in use, take the witness inside it so the witness can see the courtroom layout, the judge, court reporter, clerk, bailiff, and other people.

Practice means practicing the direct examination with the lawyer who will be conducting the examination during the trial. If someone other than the trial lawyer does the practice sessions, neither the witness nor the trial lawyer gets a feel for the other, and that's important. Practice means asking the questions the lawyer will ask and hearing the actual answers the witness will give. It means practicing enough so that the witness understands how to testify, understands what you will bring out during the direct examination and why you are doing it, and understands how to answer questions confidently and clearly, until the witness becomes comfortable in that role. However, practice should not go on so long that the witness's testimony sounds rehearsed or memorized. In most cases, though, the enemy of effective direct examinations is underpreparation, not overpreparation.

5.7 Occurrence Witnesses

Occurrence witnesses are the most common witnesses in civil and criminal trials. The key concept with occurrence witnesses is to recreate the action so that the jury becomes involved in the story and relates to what happened from the witness's point of view. This means that the testimony must capture the jurors' attention quickly, set the scene efficiently, and use the tools of re-creation—point of view, present tense, pace, and sensory language—so that the jurors understand what happened and get a feel for what the witness experienced. The following examples illustrate effective direct explanations of commonly encountered occurrence witnesses.

1. Example (Plaintiff in Personal Injury Case)

Introduction. This introduction immediately brings out what happened and the devastating impact on the plaintiff.

Q: Mr. Smith, please introduce yourself to the members of our jury.
A: I'm Robert Smith. I live here in town. I'm a diesel mechanic.
Q: Mr. Smith, were you injured during the collision on June 1, 2020, at the corner of Main and Elm?
A: Yes, I broke my arm at the elbow.

Q: How has this affected your life?
A: I can't work as a mechanic, and I haven't been able to find other work even though I've tried.
Q: Have you been able to support your family?
A: No.

Background. This background shows how "normal" the plaintiff is, and why jurors should relate to him as a person.

Q: Let's begin by learning a bit about yourself. Where did you grow up?
A: Right here. I've lived here all my life.
Q: What kind of a student were you in high school?
A: Average. Some courses were tough, but I stuck with it and graduated.
Q: When you graduated, what did you decide to do?
A: I thought about going in the military, but then decided to go to vocational school to be a mechanic. I've always been interested in cars, things like that.
Q: Which vocational school did you go to?
A: ABC Technical, right here. It took two years, but I got my certificate in diesel mechanics.
Q: What did you do after graduation?
A: I went to work at the GM dealership. They have a large service department, and they have a lot of diesel trucks that come in. I was there for over five years.
Q: Let's go back to your time there. Did you like working at the GM dealership?
A: Sure did. The work was good, the pay was good, the benefits were great, and the guys working there are good guys.
Q: What kind of work did you do?
A: A little of everything. Tune-ups, repair and maintenance, all the way up to complete engine rebuilds.

Because this is the plaintiff, jurors will want to know something about the plaintiff's family, and judges usually allow this even though it has little to do with witness credibility.

Q: Let's talk a bit about your family: You're married?
A: That's right.
Q: Tell us about your wife.
A: Her name's Vicky—Victoria, actually, but everyone calls her Vicky. We met in high school, went steady my senior year, and got married two years later right after I got my certificate at ABC Technical.
Q: Your children?
A: We've got two, a boy and girl. Bobby is four, Shirley is three.
Q: Does Vicky work outside the home right now?
A: Yes. She was home taking care of the kids, but after I couldn't work, she got a job at Wal-Mart as a sales clerk. It's not full time, but it sure helps. I look after the kids now.
Q: Bob, how was life for you and the family before June 1, 2020?
A: Pretty good. I had a good job and took care of everything we needed. Life was good.

Scene. Notice that the scene description is done orally, rather than by using a diagram or photograph as an exhibit. This keeps the spotlight on the plaintiff. Notice also how the scene description goes from general to specific, much like a zoom lens.

> Q: Let's turn now to the intersection where the collision happened, Main and Elm. Do you know that intersection?
>
> A: Sure. That's the way I went to and from work every day for the last five years.
>
> Q: What kind of area is that intersection in?
>
> A: It's mainly residential, single family houses. Right on the corner there's a gas station and a convenience store on opposite sides of the intersection.
>
> Q: Main Street, the north-south street, what's that like?
>
> A: Main's a two-lane street, one lane of traffic in each direction.
>
> Q: Any parking lanes?
>
> A: No.
>
> Q: Show us what Elm Street's like.
>
> A: Pretty much the same. One lane of traffic in each direction, no parking lanes.
>
> Q: Any turn lanes on Main or Elm?
>
> A: No.
>
> Q: Are there any traffic controls?
>
> A: Yes, there's a traffic light.
>
> Q: Describe the traffic light.
>
> A: It's one of the old-fashioned ones, the kind that hangs right over the middle of the intersection.
>
> Q: Does that traffic light have any turn arrows?
>
> A: No. It's just a simple green-yellow-red light.
>
> Q: The day of the collision, June 1, 2020, what was the weather like around 5:00 in the afternoon?
>
> A: It was sunny and dry, and had been the whole day.

Action.

> Q: Let's turn now to what happened on June 1. Where are you about 5:00 in the afternoon that day?

The action is portrayed from the plaintiff's point of view. This gets the jurors to see what happened through the plaintiff's eyes.

Note the use of present tense, which is possible only if practiced in advance. The present tense makes the testimony more "alive."

> A: I'm in my car, a Toyota Corolla, going south on Main Street.
>
> Q: Where are you going?
>
> A: I'm on my way home from work, to have dinner with the family.
>
> Q: Anyone else in the car with you?
>
> A: No, just me.
>
> Q: Mr. Smith, let's see what you see as you're going south on Main Street. What do you see in your lane of traffic?
>
> A: There's a string of cars in front of me.

Q: When you look in your rear-view mirror, what do you see?
A: There's a string of cars behind me.
Q: What's your speed and the speed of the other cars?
A: We're going maybe 25 miles an hour. That's the way it usually is during rush hour.
Q: What's the speed limit there?
A: 35 miles an hour.
Q: When you first see the Elm Street intersection, what's the color of the light?
A: It's green for me, for Main Street.
Q: What do you do?
A: I keep going south at 25 miles an hour.
Q: Do you notice anything about the northbound traffic, the traffic facing you?
A: Not at first. But as I get closer to the Elm Street light, I see that the traffic on Main going toward me has stopped.
Q: Why?
A: There's a car in the intersection, a Chevy sedan, trying to make a left-hand turn onto Elm.
Q: How do you know that?
A: He has his left turn signal on.
Q: Can he make the left turn?
A: No, my traffic going south on Main Street is keeping him from making the turn.

Now the pace quickens.

Q: As you get closer to Elm Street, what happens?
A: My light goes from green to yellow.
Q: Mr. Smith, how far from the intersection are you when the light turns yellow?
A: About 30 feet, certainly not more than 40. About two car lengths.
Q: When the light first turns yellow, what do you do?
A: I keep on going.
Q: Why?
A: I'm too close to the intersection to slam on my brakes suddenly. I don't want to get rear-ended. And I know I can go through the intersection on the yellow.
Q: What happens as you get to the intersection?
A: Suddenly that Chevy, the one facing me in the intersection, makes a left turn right in front of me.
Q: Do you expect that?
A: No. I've got the right of way.
Q: What do you do?
A: I slam on my brakes as fast and as hard as I can.
Q: And then what happens?
A: I'm laying down rubber, the Chevy goes right in front of me, and before I even realize it, my car crashes into him.

Note the sensory language.

Q: What do you hear?

A: There's my brakes screeching, there's a huge "whump" as the cars crash, and I can hear the lights breaking, a tinkling sound.

Q: What do you feel?

A: I'm thrown forward, I can remember trying to brace myself, and then I hear it and feel it: My right arm breaks, kind of a snapping sound.

Q: What do you do?

A: Everything comes to a stop, then everything's silent, and I'm sitting in the car, dazed. I can feel these sharp shooting pains, a burning sensation, shooting up and down my arm.

Q: And then what do you see?

A: I'm just sitting in the car, holding my arm. I can see people outside my car. After a while the police arrive, and they tell me to stay in the car until the ambulance comes. After a while, the ambulance arrives, they put me on a stretcher and take me to University Hospital.

Exhibits. Once the witness has shown what happened, exhibits are then introduced to highlight and emphasize the key facts.

Q: Mr. Smith, I'm going to show you a diagram of the intersection of Main and Elm, Plaintiff's Exhibit No. 1, already in evidence. Does that diagram look accurate to you?

A: Yes.

Q: Your honor, may Mr. Smith step down and continue his testimony by the diagram? [Lawyer puts diagram on easel in front of jury.]

JUDGE: Certainly. [Plaintiff walks to diagram, stands to one side, facing the jurors.]

Notice how the lawyer expressly tells the witness what to do and how to do it. This helps the witness, and it makes a clear appellate record at the same time. This must be practiced so the plaintiff can do it smoothly and confidently.

Q: Mr. Smith, I'm going to ask you to mark the diagram, using these sticky car figures and felt-tip markers. First, using the green car figure with the number one on it, please place the car where your car was when the Main Street light first turned yellow.

A: Sure. I was right here. [Places car figure on diagram.]

Q: Using the red car figure with the number one on it, please place the car where the defendant's car was when the Main Street light first turned yellow.

A: Sure. He was right here under the light. [Places car figure on diagram.]

Plaintiff is now using exhibits to highlight and repeat key liability facts.

Q: Now, using the green car figure with the number two on it, please place the car where your car was when it collided with the defendant's car.

A: I was right here. [Places car figure on diagram.]

Q: Finally, using the red car figure with the number two on it, please place the car where the defendant's car was when it collided with your car.

A: His car was right here, right in front of my car. [Places car figure on diagram.]

The dotted lines and arrows show the direction of the cars.

Q: Using the green and red felt-tip markers, please draw dotted lines with arrows, showing the direction of your car and the defendant's car during this time.

A: Sure. [Places dotted green and red lines on diagram.]

Because car speed and distance are important to plaintiff's liability case, these are also put on the diagram.

Q: Two more things, Mr. Smith. What was the speed of your car when the light first turned yellow?

A: About 25.

Q: Using the blue felt-tip marker, please label your car "25 mph."

A: Sure. [Puts "25 mph" by green car.]

Q: How far was your car from the crosswalk at Elm Street when the light first turned yellow?

A: 30, tops 40, feet.

Note that the diagram is now a visual summary of plaintiff's liability case.

Q: Using the blue felt-up marker, please draw a line between the front of your car #1 and the crosswalk, and label it "30–40 ft."

A: Sure. [Puts "30–40 ft." by green car.]

Q: The things you just marked on the diagram, do they accurately show what happened on June 1, 2020, at the time of the collision?

A: That's the way it happened.

Medical Treatment and Rehabilitation.

Q: Please return to the witness stand. [Returns to chair.] Let's finally turn to the therapy and rehabilitation period after the collision, and your life since the collision. What happened at the University Hospital?

A: They took me to the emergency room, various people examined me, I remember they took x-rays, and after a while they took me to an operating room, put me under, and that's the last thing I remember.

Q: When you woke up, where were you?

Again, sensory language.

A: In a recovery room. My arm was in a cast from my armpit to my wrist, it hurt, a steady aching pain, as if my heart was right in my arm.

Q: How long were you there?

A: It seemed like two or three hours, they said it was to make sure the anesthesia wore off right. Later that night my wife drove me home.

Q: The next few weeks, what were you able to do?

A: Not much. Most of the time I was sitting on the couch. I kept the elbow as high as possible, that helped keep the swelling down. That was about it.

Therapy and Rehabilitation.

Q: Let's talk about the time your doctor, Dr. Klein, removed the cast and you started the therapy. Do you remember that?
A: I sure do. Will never forget it.
Q: What did your arm look and feel like when she cut the cast off?

Note again the visual language.

A: It had shrunk. It looked as if it was half the size of my other arm. All the callouses on my hand peeled off. And I could only move the arm back and forth a couple of inches in either direction, like this [indicating]. The elbow felt frozen.
Q: What did Dr. Klein tell you to do to get your arm back to the way it was before?
A: She said soak the elbow in hot water, as hot as you can stand. After soaking it for a while, move the arm back and forth to stretch the elbow as far as it would go in both directions. She said to do that 3 times a day, for maybe 15 minutes each time.
Q: Did you do it?
A: Of course.
Q: Why?

Plaintiff's motivation is an important point.

A: I had to get back to work. I've got a family to support.
Q: Was the therapy painful?
A: Sure, but doing therapy is always painful. You just deal with it.
Q: Did the therapy work?
A: It worked great, for a while.
Q: What do you mean?
A: The first few weeks it worked great. It got where I could move my arm up all the way [indicating], and I could straighten it out most of the way [indicating]. But then it stopped getting better.
Q: What do you mean?

Much of plaintiff's damages case is based on plaintiff's incomplete recovery, and the effect it had on his job and career. This must be spelled out clearly.

A: No matter how much I did the therapy, the arm never got straighter than this [indicating]. Before I got hurt, I could straighten it out all the way, like I can with my left arm [indicating].
Q: Did you tell that to Dr. Klein?
A: Sure. She said that some people never recover fully, even though they do the therapy.
Q: Is that the way your right arm is today?
A: Yes. It's never gotten better than that.

Attempting to return to work is important.

Q: Let's talk about going back to work at the GM dealership. How did that work out?

This establishes that the limitations are permanent.

A: Not well. I'd go back, start working, and after two or three hours, my arm would swell up, get stiff, and start throbbing, and I'd have to stop. That happened every time I tried to do my job.

Q: Do you have your job today?

A: No. Karl—that's my boss—was pretty good about it, but it was obvious I couldn't do the work anymore. One day Karl said he had to let me go, and I lost my job.

Q: Have you been able to find other work?

A: No. I've looked, but I'm not going to lie to people. I told them about my arm, and that I was looking for light work, desk work, something like that. But nobody wants to hire me with my arm the way it is.

Ending. The focus ends on the plaintiff and the impact of this collision and injury on plaintiff's life.

Q: Mr. Smith, one last question. How do all these changes in your life since the collision make you feel about things?

A: Not good. I'm supposed to be taking care of my family, and instead they're taking care of me. I guess I'm a little down right now.

2. Example (Defendant in Personal Injury Case)

Introduction and Background.

Q: Ms. Jones, please introduce yourself.

A: I'm Helen Jones. I'm a schoolteacher at Washington Elementary. I've lived here for the past ten years.

This introductory question is becoming common.

Q: How long have you been teaching at the school?

A: Ten years. I moved here to take the job.

The usual background includes family, residence, and job.

Q: Tell us about your family.

A: My husband's Mike, and he's also a teacher, at Central High. He teaches algebra and physics and coaches the tennis team. We have a daughter, Shannon, she goes to Washington Elementary. That's very convenient, since I take her to and from school every day.

Q: Where do you live?

A: We have a house in the University Heights neighborhood. We've been there ever since we came here.

Scene. Because the jurors have already heard and seen the intersection in the plaintiff's case, it need not be described again.

Q: Where is your house in relation to your school?

A: My house is north of the school, about three miles away. But it's a convenient commute, since I can take Main Street almost the entire way.

Q: How often do you go through the Main and Elm intersection?

A: Twice a day on school days. On the way home, that's where I take a left turn on Elm to get to my house. It's only about three blocks from that corner.

Action. Notice that defendant is also using the present tense, and describing the action through the defendant's eyes.

Q: Let's turn back in time to June, 1, 2020, at about 5:00 pm. Where are you at that time?

A: I'm driving home from school.

Q: What car are you driving?

A: My 2015 Chevy sedan.

Q: Anyone with you in the car?

A: Yes, Shannon, my daughter, is in the front seat with me.

Q: Are you wearing seat belts?

A: Of course. We always wear them.

Notice that the pace here is deliberate.

Q: Let's talk about the time you reach the intersection of Main and Elm. What's traffic like at that time?

A: It's busy. It's rush hour, and Main is a busy commuter route.

Q: How fast is the traffic moving?

A: That depends. Sometimes it goes the speed limit, sometimes it's stop-and-go, but most of the time it's moving, but under the speed limit.

Q: When you get to the Elm Street intersection, what do you do?

A: The light's green for Main Street. I put on my left turn signal and slow down, then come to a stop in the intersection.

The pace of the testimony is still deliberate.

Q: Why do you stop?

A: There's a steady stream of traffic coming toward me on Main, so I can't make the turn.

Q: What's happening to the traffic behind you?

A: It's backing up, because there's no left turn lane, and my car is keeping the traffic from moving. That's the way it is every day at that corner.

Q: When does the light change?

A: I was there in the intersection for perhaps 10 to 15 seconds, then the light turns yellow.

Q: You can see the light?

A: Sure. I'm partly in the intersection, but I can still see the traffic light in front of me.

Q: When the light turns yellow, what do you do?

A: Nothing. I still can't make the left turn, so I just wait.

Q: Wait for what?

A: For the light to turn red. That's when I usually complete the turn. That's just the way it is during rush hour at that corner.

Now the pace picks up, because things are now happening quickly.

Q: When the light finally turns red, what do you do?
A: I'm watching the light, it turns red, there's no one else in the intersection, and I start to make the left turn.

Notice the sensory questions and answers. The defense needs to show that the accident was just as traumatic for the defendant and her daughter as it was for the plaintiff.

Q: What do you see next?
A: I've started the turn, my car is about halfway through the turn, and I realize that a car, coming down Main toward the corner, is not slowing down at all, and is going into the intersection right toward me.
Q: What's the first thing you do?
A: I remember screaming, because the car is coming right at us. I remember reaching for Shannon, trying to protect her, but it all happens so fast.
Q: And then what happens?
A: That car crashes right into the side of my car. Thank God it didn't hit the front door where Shannon was sitting. It crashes into the rear of my car, right about at the right rear wheel.
Q: What do you hear?
A: There's this huge crash, a big thumping sound, I hear myself screaming.
Q: And what do you feel?
A: The crash spins my car around, so now it's facing north again. The impact throws me toward Shannon, and it throws her against the passenger side door.
Q: And then?
A: Finally, everything stops, and it gets quiet.
Q: What do you do?
A: Shannon's crying, and I'm trying to comfort her, see if she's all right. I'm hugging her, then looking at her, then hugging her again.
Q: Was she all right?
A: I can't see anything wrong, but I don't know for sure.
Q: What about yourself?
A: Other than being scared to death, I'm all right.
Q: What do you do then?
A: For a minute or two, we just sit in the car, trying to calm down. I get my cell phone from my purse and call 911. The police arrived pretty quick, so maybe others called as well.
Q: When the police arrived, did you talk to them?
A: Yes. They wanted to know if we were all right, and they asked me what happened, so I told them.
Q: What happened to your car?
A: The right rear side from the rear door to the rear bumper was all smashed in. The front of the other car looked as if it was stuck in the right rear of my car. It looked awful.
Q: Could you drive your car?
A: No, it was way too damaged for that. The police called a tow truck, and they towed it away.

Q: What happened to the other driver?

A: I'm not sure. He was just sitting in his car. When the ambulance arrived, I could see the attendants talking to him, then he got out of his car, holding his arm, and he walked over to where they had a stretcher. He sat on the stretcher, they put a seat belt around his waist, and put the stretcher in the back of the ambulance and drove off.

Q: How did you get home?

A: After the tow truck hauled our car away, Shannon and I walked home, since it was just three blocks away.

Exhibit and Ending.

Q: Ms. Jones, I'm showing you Defendant's Exhibit No. 1, a diagram of the intersection. It's already in evidence. Does that diagram accurately show where your car was when you first started to make your left turn?

A: Yes.

This is the crux of the defendant's liability case, so the defense wants to end on the most important facts from the defense perspective.

Q: Does it accurately show where the plaintiff's car was when you first started to make your turn?

A: Yes.

Q: Ms. Jones, when the cars were in those locations, and you started to make your left turn, what color was the light for Main Street?

A: It already turned red.

Q: Are you sure?

A: I'm positive.

Q: What color was the light when the plaintiff's car entered the intersection?

A: It was red.

Q: Are you sure?

A: I'm positive.

Q: And what color was the light when the plaintiff's car ran into your car?

A: It was red.

3. Example (Eyewitness in Personal Injury Case)

Introduction. This introductory question is becoming a more common beginning for occurrence witness.

Q: (by plaintiff's lawyer): Mr. Ginsberg, why are you here today?

A: I was a witness to the collision at the corner of Main and Elm on June 1.

Q: Did you see the actual crash?

A: Yes. It happened right in front of me.

Q: Are you prepared today to tell us what you saw, heard, and did at that time?

A: Yes.

Background.

Q: Mr. Ginsberg, where do you live?

A: I live about two blocks from the corner of Main and Elm.

Q: For how long?

A: Almost 30 years.

Q: What kind of work do you do?

A: I'm retired now, but I used to be a reservations agent for American Airlines.

Q: Tell us about your family.

A: My wife is also retired. She was a flight attendant for American for many years. We have three children, and they're all grown up and on their own.

Because the scene has already been described by other witness and exhibits, it need not be described again.

Q: Let's turn now to what you saw that afternoon. What were you doing when the crash happened?

A: I had walked to the convenience store to get some milk. I was on my way home when it happened.

Q: Where's the convenience store at the corner?

A: It's on the southeast corner.

Q: To get from the convenience store to your house, how do you go?

A: The store's on the southeast corner, and my house is about two blocks west just off Elm, so I just walk straight west, on the south side of Elm.

Q: Is that the way you went on June 1?

A: Yes.

Q: How far had you gotten when the crash happened?

A: I had just left the convenience store, and I was standing on the southeast corner of the intersection, waiting for the light to change so I could walk across Main.

Action. Notice the present tense in both the question and answers.

Q: Mr. Ginsberg, as you're standing on the corner, waiting for the light to change, what do you see in the intersection?

A: Well, it's rush hour. There are cars going up and down Main Street. The traffic going south is moving, but the traffic going north has stopped.

Q: Why?

A: There's a Chevy that's trying to make a left-hand turn, but can't.

Q: How do you know the Chevy's trying to turn left?

A: She's stopped, standing right over my crosswalk, part way into the intersection.

Q: Why can't she complete the left turn?

A: Because there's a solid line of cars going south on Main.

Q: What's the traffic doing behind the Chevy?

A: It's backed up, since there's only one lane of traffic and no turn lane.

Q: You can see all this?

A: Sure. The Chevy is only maybe ten or fifteen feet from me, directly in front of me.

The pace now picks up.

Q: When the light changes for Main, what happens?

A: The light changes from green to yellow. I'm still standing on the corner. Then the Chevy turns left, pretty fast, and I hear a screech of brakes. I see a car in the southbound lane of traffic—a Toyota—skidding across the crosswalk, just as the Chevy is cutting in front of him. And then the Toyota crashes into the side of the Chevy, and there's this loud crashing sound. And then everything is still.

Q: Mr. Ginsberg, when the Chevy makes the left turn, what color is the Main Street light?

A: It had just turned yellow.

Q: When the two cars collide, what color is that light?

A: Still yellow.

Q: Are you sure?

A: Sure. I was still on the corner, waiting for it to turn red so I could cross Main, and it hadn't turned red yet.

Ending.

Q: After the two cars crash, what do you do?

A: I stand there on the corner, just watching. There's people standing by the cars, talking to the people inside. Someone starts to direct traffic around the cars, and after a few minutes the police come, and there's an ambulance a little after that.

Q: Did you talk to the police?

A: Sure. I told them I saw the whole thing.

4. Example (Victim in Criminal Case)

Introduction and Background.

Q: Mr. Appleton, introduce yourself to our jury.

A: My name is Mark Appleton.

Q: Where do you live?

A: Here in the city.

Q: For how long?

A: All my life. I still live at home with my parents.

Q: You went to school here?

A: Central High School.

Q: After high school, what did you do?

A: I apprenticed to be a bricklayer with a masonry company, and that's what I've been doing for the past five years.

Scene.

Q: Let's turn to the place where everything happened, the Country Tavern. First, where is it?

A: It's on Broadway, near Park.

Here the prosecutor decides to have the witness describe the scene, rather than use exhibits.

Q: What kind of place is that?

A: It's a neighborhood tavern with a bar room, a game room, and on weekends they have live country music.

Q: Do you go there often?

A: I wouldn't say I'm a regular, but I probably go there maybe twice a month, usually when they have live music.
Q: The game room, what's that like?
A: That's behind the bar room. It's got two pool tables, and a bunch of video game machines against the walls.

Lighting is often important.

Q: What's the lighting like in the game room?
A: Pretty good. The pool tables have lights directly over them, and the video games all are pretty bright. You can see what's going on there without any problem.

Action.

Q: Let's turn now to June 1, 2020, around 10:00 that night. Where were you at that time?
A: I was shooting pool in the game room.
Q: How long had you been there?
A: Probably an hour.

Drinking is brought out now, before the cross-examiner can go into it.

Q: Were you drinking anything?
A: Sure, beer.
Q: How many beers had you had that night?
A: Two. I had pretty much finished the second when this happened.
Q: What kind of beer?
A: Bud Light, from the bottle.

The prosecutor will need to have the witness identify the defendant in court at some point.

Q: When was the first time you noticed the defendant?
A: He was standing by the tables, waiting to play.
Q: How did you know that?
A: He said he wanted to play the winner.
Q: Had you ever seen him before?
A: I don't think so.
Q: Let's go back to the game room on that night. Are other people in the game room?

Notice the details the witness provides during his testimony. This shows the witness remembers the event well. Also, notice the present tense.

A: Yeah, probably six or seven. I know the other pool table is being used, and there are two or three other people playing video games on the machines.
Q: What do you tell the defendant?
A: I tell him he could play the winner, when we had a winner.
Q: What does he say?
A: Nothing. He just stands by the wall watching the game.
Q: Do you notice anything unusual about the defendant?
A: No. He looks and acts like you'd expect.

Q: When's the next time you speak with him?

A: When our first game is over. I'm racking up the balls for the second game and taking a swig from my beer.

Q: Who says what?

A: He comes over to the end of the table where I was and says, "I've got the winner." I say, "This is best out of three. That was the first game." He says, "That's not the way it goes."

Q: What happens next?

A: I bend over, get the balls from under the table and put them in the rack on the table. When I stand up, the defendant kind of pushes me sideways with his forearm, away from the table, like this [showing].

Q: What do you do?

A: I say, "Look pal, we're playing best out of three," and push him back with my right hand, like this [showing].

Q: What do you do with your beer?

A: Nothing. I'm just holding it in my left hand.

Q: And then what happens?

Notice the pacing as the witness emphasizes the key moments.

A: Suddenly he swings at me. I think he's trying to punch me, but then I have an instant stinging feeling across my stomach, and I realize I've just been cut.

Q: What do you do?

A: I yell, "He's got a knife," and back away. I look down at my shirt and I can see blood from where he's cut me.

Q: What's the defendant doing?

A: He's just standing there, sort of grinning at me, and some of the guys jump him and wrestle him down on the floor. One of the guys takes the knife from him.

Q: What are you doing?

A: I'm just standing there. Once he's down on the ground. I open up my shirt, and I see that he's cut me across my stomach, and it's bleeding. Then I take my shirt off and hold it against my stomach to help stop the bleeding.

Q: What happened after that?

Notice the shift to past tense, which is more natural for the witness, now that we are past the key moments.

A: The police came, and then an ambulance took me to the hospital.

Q: What happened there?

A: The doctors and nurses checked me out. They cleaned the cut and said they'd have to stitch me up.

Q: How did they do that?

A: They put some stuff on the cut and then put the stitches in.

Q: Did you see them do it?

A: No. I was lying flat on my back, but I could sure feel it.

Q: How many stitches did you get?

A: Eighteen. The cut was about half a foot long.

Q: Mr. Appleton, did you miss work because of this?

A: Yes, I stayed out a week waiting for it to heal. The next week I went back to work, but the stitches weren't removed for another week after that.
Q: How did the cut heal?
A: It healed just fine, but I've still got the scar.

Exhibits and Demonstration.

Q: Your honor, may Mr. Appleton step down and show the jurors the scar on his stomach?
JUDGE: He may. [Witness leaves stand and walks to jury box with lawyer.]

Here the prosecutor decides to have the victim display his wound.

Q: Mr. Appleton, please open up your shirt and show the members of the jury the scar.
A: Sure. It's right here [pointing], and runs from my left side to my right side [pointing].
Q: You were first pointing to a spot near where your left elbow meets your chest when it is against the chest, then to a spot about an inch to the right of the midline of your chest?
A: That seems about right.
Q: Thank you. Please return to the stand. [Witness returns.] I'm now showing you State's Exhibit No. 7. [Lawyer hands exhibit to witness.] Please take a look at it. Do you recognize Exhibit No. 7?

This testimony may not be enough to have the knife admitted in evidence.

A: Well, it looks just like the knife the defendant cut me with, but I can't say for sure that's the same knife.

Ending.

Q: Two final questions. That evening, in the Country Tavern, did you do anything to cause that defendant to cut you?
A: No.
Q: Did you attack him with anything before he cut you?
A: No.

This anticipates the defense claim of self-defense.

Now the prosecutor decides to end with the in-court identification of the defendant. (Some prosecutors would do it early in the testimony.)

Q: Mr. Appleton, please look around the courtroom. If you see the man who cut you in the courtroom, please point him out and describe what he's wearing today.
A: He's right over there sitting at the table [pointing to the defendant] next to the lawyer in the dark suit. He's wearing the gray pants and the blue shirt.

5. Example (Defendant in Criminal Case)

Introduction. This dramatic introduction is designed to jar the jury away from the prosecution's picture of what happened. It is an example of the impact direct examination structure.

Q: Mr. Jackson, let's get right to the point. Did you cut Mark Appleton with a knife?

A: Yes, I did.

Q: Why?

A: Because he was coming at me with a beer bottle. I thought he was going to hit me over the head with it.

Q: Why did you think that?

A: Because he had the bottle by the neck, he shoved me back, and he raised the bottle in his hand. It looked like he was trying to hit me. I only cut him to defend myself.

Background. The defense in criminal cases often spends time bringing out the defendant's background, so jurors can relate to him as a human being.

Q: Let's turn the clock back and first learn a bit about you. Where do you live?

A: Here in the city.

Q: For how long?

A: Five years.

Q: Where are you from originally?

A: I grew up in Nevada, in Reno.

Q: You went to school there?

A: Yes. At Reno High School. I graduated in 2015.

Q: What did you do after that?

A: My parents moved here right after I graduated, so I came with them and started looking for work.

Q: What work did you find?

A: I got a job at Barnes and Noble. That's the big chain bookstore. I started as a sales clerk, and then became the manager of the fiction department.

Q: When was that?

A: About two years ago.

Q: What's involved in being the manager of the fiction department?

A: You decide how the books will be displayed, keep track of inventory, assign hours for your sales clerks, and solve any problems that come up. Basically, my job is to make sure the department runs smoothly and profitably.

Q: Do you still live with your parents?

A: No, I finally got my own place when I got promoted to manager of the fiction department.

Scene. This testimony shows the defendant is a normal guy doing normal things.

Q: What had you been doing earlier in the day on June 1, 2020?

A: I was working at Barnes and Noble from noon to 9:00 in the evening.

Q: What clothes were you wearing?

A: My usual work clothes. Khaki pants, plain white shirt. I wear my employee identification tag on a key chain I wear around my neck.

Q: After 9:00 that evening, what did you do?

A: I made sure that my department was properly closed up, the registers were off, and I left around 9:20.

Q: Where did you go?
A: I went through the drive-thru at McDonald's, got a Quarter-Pounder and a Coke, and ate in my car.
Q: And after that?
A: I stopped at the Country Tavern. It's near my apartment.
Q: What did you do when you arrived there?
A: I walked in and went through the bar area to the pool room. I wanted to shoot some pool.
Q: Did you?
A: Not right away. Both tables were being used.
Q: So what did you do?
A: I told the guys at the tables that I had winners.

The "standard rules" are important to the defense.

Q: What's that mean?
A: That's standard pool table rules. If people are waiting to play, when a game is over, the winner stays, the loser gets replaced by the next person waiting.
Q: Who makes those rules?
A: I don't know. Those are just the rules everywhere. That way people can't hog a table when others are waiting.

Exhibits.

Q: Mr. Jackson, let me show you State's Exhibit No. 7. Is that your knife?
A: Yes, it is.
Q: Why were you carrying this knife on you on June 1?
A: That's the knife I always have when I'm working.

An innocent explanation for carrying a knife is also important to the defense.

Q: You use a knife at the bookstore?
A: You bet. We're constantly cutting open boxes with books and putting them on the shelves or on special displays. That's why I have that knife.
Q: Why this kind of knife?
A: Because it's small, and fits easily in my pocket. It has a blade only two inches long, but that's enough. There's a small knob on the blade, so you can swing the blade out with your thumb. That's real useful if you're holding a box in one hand and cutting it open with the other hand. It's not much good for anything else, but it's a perfect utility knife at the store. I've had it all the time I've been working there.

Action. Note the transition question and the transition to present tense.

Q: Let's turn now to what actually happens in the pool room around 10:00. What are you doing?
A: Just standing, watching the games, waiting for either table to finish a game.

The drinking testimony favors the defendant.

Q: Are you drinking anything?
A: No.
Q: Is Mr. Appleton drinking anything?

A: He keeps chugging from a bottle of beer.

Q: So what's the first thing that happens?

A: He finishes the game on his table. He then puts money in the slots, the balls drop into a bin under the table, and he starts to put the balls into the rack on the table.

Q: When you see this, what do you do?

A: I walk over to him and say, "I've got the winner."

Q: What's he say?

A: He says, "We're playing two out of three."

Q: What do you say?

A: I say, "That's not the rules" or something like that.

Q: Where are you standing when this is going on?

A: I'm standing right next to him at the end of the table.

Now the pace picks up.

Q: Then what happens?

A: He takes his hand—his right hand—and he's grabbing at my chest. He's got the beer bottle in his other hand, holding it in his other hand by the neck, and he's starting to raise it up.

The defendant's state of mind is important in a self-defense case and should be brought out explicitly.

Q: What are you thinking as you see this?

A: I know he's not getting ready to take a hit from the beer bottle, cause he's holding the neck the wrong way. I suddenly realize that he's going to hit me with it.

Q: What do you do?

A: I'm standing there with my hand in my pocket, and I grab my pocket knife, flick it open, and swing it at him before he can hit me with the bottle.

Q: What's he do?

A: He never hits me with the bottle. He drops the bottle and starts yelling. I just stand there looking at him.

Q: What happens after that?

A: A couple of guys jump me from behind and throw me on the floor. Somebody takes the knife from my hand.

Q: What are you doing?

A: Nothing. I'm just watching that guy to make sure he doesn't try to attack me again.

Aftermath.

Q: Let's turn to when the police come. What did they do when they arrived?

A: They talked to the other guy and me.

Q: Did you talk to them?

A: Sure. They wanted to know what happened and I told them.

Ending. The direct examination ends on a key point: the defendant's state of mind.

Q: Mr. Jackson, why did you swing your knife at Mr. Appleton on June 1, 2020?

Q: I was just defending myself. He was about to attack me with the beer bottle.
Q: Any other reason?
A: No.

6. Example (Police Officer in Criminal Case)

Background.

Q: (by plaintiff's lawyer): Sergeant Kane, tell us your name, how long you've been a police officer, and where you're assigned.

This is enough background for the police officer under these circumstances.

A: My name's Michael Kane. I've been a police officer with the city for 12 years, and right now I'm a supervising sergeant in the patrol division of the central district.

Action.

Q: Were you on duty on June 1, 2020?
A: Yes.
Q: Which shift?
A: The afternoon shift, 3:00 to 11:00.
Q: What was your assignment that day?
A: I was on routine patrol in my sector.
Q: What area is that?
A: I'm responsible for several patrol officers in the northern sector of the central district.
Q: Does that cover the area around Broadway and Park?
A: Yes.

Notice how efficiently this examination gets to the important testimony. The police officer here corroborates a few things, and that can be done quickly.

Q: Around 10:00 that evening, did you receive a call?
A: Yes, the radio dispatcher put out a call to respond to the Country Tavern.
Q: What did you do when you heard the call?
A: Another unit responded, but I called in that I was also responding, since there was a possibility someone was injured.
Q: How long did it take you to get there?
A: About three minutes.
Q: When you got there, what did you see?
A: The other patrol unit was already there. I went inside and was directed to the back room. There I saw my two uniformed officers. One officer was kneeling by a person who was sitting on the ground and bleeding through his shirt. The other officer was standing over another man who was being held by some of the patrons of the bar.
Q: What did you do?
A: I talked to my officers to find out what they knew. I talked to a couple of the patrons to find out what had happened. I also called for an ambulance to take the injured man to a hospital.

Q: What happened after that?
A: The emergency medical technicians came, checked the man—a Mark Appleton—bandaged him, and walked him outside to the ambulance.

This is the key part of the police officer's testimony that corroborates the victim's testimony.

Q: What did you do with Mr. Jackson?
A: I told him that he was under arrest for assault, and I directed one of the patrolmen to handcuff him.
Q: Did you talk with Mr. Jackson?
A: Yes. I first gave him the Miranda warnings, and asked him if he was willing to give up those rights and tell me what happened. He said he was willing.
Q: What did Mr. Jackson say?

The defendant's statement does not demonstrate justifiable self-defense.

A: Basically, he said that they had an argument over who was going to play the next game of pool, and that after Mr. Appleton grabbed and shoved him, he cut Mr. Appleton with his knife.

Exhibits.

Q: I'm showing you State's Exhibit No. 7. Do you recognize it?
A: Yes, that's the knife I obtained from one of the patrons of the bar who was standing behind Mr. Jackson when I first walked into the back room. That's my inventory tag on it.

Ending. The direct examination ends on a key point.

Q: Sergeant Kane, did Mr. Jackson ever tell you that he cut Mr. Appleton because Mr. Appleton was going to hit his head with a beer bottle?
A: No. He never mentioned to me that Mr. Appleton even had a beer bottle.

5.8 Transaction Witnesses

The key concept with transaction witnesses is to recreate the events that are at the core of most commercial cases. These cases usually involve disputed versions of meetings, telephone calls, and conversations, usually between officers and employees of the opposing parties in the lawsuit. For example, plaintiff's and defendant's chief executive officers may have different versions of the key meeting in which they entered into an oral contract or contract modification. They may have different versions of a telephone conversation during which certain representations were made that are the basis of a fraudulent misrepresentation case. Plaintiff and defendant's employees may have different recollections of a meeting during which decisions were made on how to proceed during the construction of a commercial building. In all these cases, jurors have to decide a key issue: Which version of the disputed meeting, telephone call, or conversation is more credible, the plaintiff's or the defendant's?

What makes one witness more credible than the other in these situations? In addition to the usual witness credibility factors, consider the following: Who remembers details of the meetings—not just the key conversations, but the surrounding facts? Was this meeting or conversation an important, unusual event that the person is likely to remember, or does the person hold meetings and conversations like this on a regular basis? Who made a memo or record of the meeting or conversation, or sent a confirming letter? Whose subsequent conduct is consistent with the meeting or conversation? Whose conduct followed standard procedure?

Your witnesses must present your version of those disputed meetings, telephone calls, and conversations more vividly than the other side's witnesses. Have your witness draw a picture of the event with all the surrounding details, not just the key conversation or words, to demonstrate that the witness has an excellent memory of the event, so that her version of the actual meeting and conversations will be accepted over the other side's version. Have your witness show that her conduct followed standard procedure and that her actions following the meeting and conversation were consistent with the meeting and conversation.

1. Example (Plaintiff in Contract Case)

Introduction. This introduction gives the jury an overview of what the witness will be talking about.

> Q: Ms. Jacobson, what role did you play in the contract between your company, Ace Hardware, and the defendant, Acme Supplies?
> A: I did all the negotiating for Ace.
> Q: Do you remember the meeting in which the negotiation was conducted?
> A: I certainly do.

Background.

> Q: Let's begin with your professional background and history with Ace Hardware. You're an accountant by training?

Notice that the background is entirely professional. This is appropriate, because the witness is testifying as a corporate officer.

> A: Yes. I majored in accounting in college, and then became a certified public accountant.
> Q: When was that?
> A: Fifteen years ago.
> Q: When did you join Ace Hardware?
> A: I've been with Ace for over 12 years now.
> Q: What kind of company is Ace Hardware?
> A: Our company owns about 15 stores in the city and suburbs, and all of the stores are full-service hardware stores. We sell tools, paint, building supplies, appliances, lights, almost everything for the home.
> Q: What did you start out as when you started at Ace?
> A: I started out in the accounting division in the headquarters office, and then moved to the administrative side about two years later.
> Q: What's your position with Ace now?
> A: I'm a vice president in charge of purchasing.
> Q: Was that your position in 2020?
> A: Yes, I'd been promoted to vice president just before the negotiation with Acme.

Scene.

Q: Ms. Jacobson, when did the negotiation with Acme take place?
A: On June 1, 2020, shortly after 1:00 p.m.
Q: Where did it take place?
A: In our conference room, at Ace headquarters.

The witness paints a picture of the conference room, who was present, and other details. This shows that the witness has a good memory for details, building up her credibility.

Q: Describe the conference room.
A: It's off an internal corridor, so the room has no outside windows. It's a wood-paneled room, light wood, with a matching wood conference table and chairs. The table is large enough for ten persons, four on each side, one on each end.
Q: Who was in the conference room during the negotiations?
A: I was there and my administrative assistant, Herb McGuire, was there. We were sitting in the chairs on one side of the conference table. The president of Acme, Kenneth Doyle, and one of his officers, Roberta Johnson, arrived and sat on the other side of the conference table.
Q: It was just the four of you?
A: Yes, except one of my assistants came in once or twice to see if anyone needed anything.
Q: How long did the meeting take?
A: It was quite short, less than 30 minutes. Things moved quickly.
Q: Do you remember who said what during the meeting?
A: Yes, I do.

An important question and answer, because this witness's testimony will conflict with that of the other side's witnesses.

Q: How is it that you remember the meeting so well?
A: This was the first negotiation I did after I was promoted to vice president at Ace, and it's still clear in my mind.
Q: How did the meeting start?
A: When Mr. Doyle arrived, I introduced myself and Herb, and he introduced us to Ms. Johnson. We did small talk for a few minutes, then got down to business.
Q: When it got down to business, who did the talking?
A: It was mainly between me and Mr. Doyle. Every now and then Herb or Ms. Johnson would add something.
Q: Tell us what you said and he said during the negotiation.

Again, the witness testifies to the details of the conversation.

A: Sure. I started by telling Mr. Doyle that we were very interested in his earlier proposal which he had submitted to us by letter, and that I hoped to finalize a deal today. He said that was great, that he was hoping for the same thing.
Q: What was his earlier proposal?
A: He offered to sell us 1,000 toolbox kits at $100 per box.
Q: What was said next?

A: I told him that we had two concerns. First, we needed to make sure that he could deliver the 1,000 units to us before the last day of August, because we were going to promote the toolboxes as part of a big Labor Day ad campaign for home improvement projects. Second, I told him that because we were buying a large quantity we would insist on some bulk discount.

Notice how many of the answers are in 10- to 15-second sound bites.

Q: How did Mr. Doyle respond to that?
A: He talked to Ms. Johnson privately for a few moments, then he said that he could offer the toolbox kits at $94 each, but not unless we agreed to buy at least 1,000 boxes.
Q: How did you respond?
A: I told him that the price was acceptable, but we still needed a guarantee that we would have all 1,000 by the end of August. I told him that if he couldn't guarantee that, it would be a deal buster. I told him that because of our planned ad campaign for Labor Day, time was of the essence.
Q: How did he respond?
A: He again talked to Ms. Johnson privately, then he asked if they could deliver the boxes between now and the end of August, rather than all at one time. I told him yes, because storage at our stores was not a problem, but he still had to get the 1,000 boxes to us by the end of August or there would be no deal. I told him that to guarantee we received all 1,000 boxes on time, we would only pay him what was due—$94,000—within 30 days of the delivery of the last of the 1,000 boxes. And I told him that if the boxes were not delivered on time, we would have to return them at his cost.
Q: How did he respond?
A: He thought about it for a while, then said that we have a deal.
Q: Those were his exact words?
A: Yes, he said: "We have a deal."
Q: What happened after that?
A: I said good, place the order, and he reached across the table, extended his arm, and we shook hands. We then chatted for a couple of minutes, and they left.
Q: What did you do after the meeting?

It's always a good idea to show that a confirming memo and letter were written and sent.

A: I dictated a memo to the file about the meeting, and sent a confirming letter to Mr. Doyle setting out the terms of our agreement.

Aftermath.

Q: Ms. Jacobson, did you get the 1,000 toolboxes from Acme Supplies by the end of August?
A: No, we did not.
Q: What happened?
A: We got small deliveries in June and July, but nothing close to the 1,000. In early August, I talked to Mr. Doyle about it.

Q: When was that?
A: Around August fifth, or within one or two days of that.
Q: Who called whom?

The telephonic conversation is treated the same way: details are brought out.

A: I called him from my office, in the afternoon.
Q: Was anyone else on the line with you?
A: Not as far as I know, just the two of us.
Q: Tell the members of the jury what you said and he said during the call.
A: I told him that we had received only about 300 toolboxes to date, with the deadline for delivery only three weeks away. He said he was very aware of that, and that he'd been having problems with some of his suppliers. I told him that I understood his problems, but our agreement called for delivery of all 1,000 boxes by the end of August. He said he was very aware of that, and would do everything he could to make the delivery on time. I told him that if he could not guarantee delivery on time, we would drop our ad campaign for Labor Day, return the 300 boxes he had delivered, and bill him for the costs we had incurred. He said that wouldn't be necessary, he'd make sure we got the rest of the boxes on time. And that was the extent of it.
Q: What did you do after the phone call?

Again, a confirming memo.

A: I made a note of the conversation and put it in my file.
Q: Did you talk to Mr. Doyle again?
A: I tried again, the last week of August, but their receptionist said he was out of the office. I left a message that I called, but he never called back. I tried again on August 31, but the same thing happened. He never called back.
Q: What did you do?

This testimony is relevant to damages.

A: By that time our ad campaign—newspaper ads and some TV spots—had already begun to run. Of course, we ran out of the toolboxes, since we only had 300 to spread around 15 stores, which amounted to 20 per store. Lots of customers were unhappy, but we honored our standard commitment to customers: If we run out of an advertised special, we will give customers a voucher for the item at the advertised price and notify them when we have it in stock. Of course, we didn't get the 700 toolboxes from Acme Supplies, we had to get them from another supplier at a higher price.
Q: What did you do after that?
A: I sent a letter to Mr. Doyle about what had happened.
Q: Did he ever reply to your letter?
A: No.

Ending.

Q: Ms. Jacobson, I have one last question. After Mr. Doyle didn't return your calls or reply to your letter, what did you do?
A: That's when I decided to call you.

Many commercial cases involve transactions that are largely recorded in documents and business records. Your witnesses must walk the jurors through the paperwork so that a vivid story of the transaction unfolds. When necessary, the witness must explain or interpret any important terms and symbols on the records that may not be obvious to the jurors.

2. Example (Records Witness in Contract Case)

Introduction and background. The witness's professional background is brought out.

> Q: Mr. Jones, please introduce yourself.
> A: I'm Bart Jones, and I'm the head of the billing department at my company, the ABC Trucking Company.
> Q: What's the business of ABC Trucking Company?
> A: We're what's known as a long-haul mover. We move both home and business contents in the lower 48 states. We can pick up almost anything and deliver it almost anywhere.
> Q: How long have you been with ABC?
> A: Six years.
> Q: What kind of jobs have you had with the company?
> A: I started out in the sales department, where I booked and priced moving orders. About two years ago I went to the billing department.
> Q: What does the billing department do?
> A: We're in charge of all the paperwork and seeing to it that we get paid for our work.
> Q: During your years at ABC Trucking, have you become familiar with the documents your company creates when it gets a move order?
> A: Sure. I handle those documents every day.

Exhibits. Here the business records are the evidence, so they are put on easels and the witness takes the jurors through the transaction, explaining things on the records along the way.

> Q: I'm now showing you three exhibits—Plaintiff's Exhibits Nos. 1, 2, and 3—already admitted in evidence. Take a look at them for a moment. Are you familiar with these three types of records?
> A: Sure. These are our order, shipping notice, and invoice forms. They get filled out for each move we do.
> Q: Your honor, may we put these three exhibits on the easels in front of the jury and have Mr. Jones step down and continue his testimony before the jury?
> JUDGE: Of course. [Witness stands to side of first exhibit.]
> Q: Mr. Jones, can you walk us through these exhibits and show us what happened, starting with the first exhibit?

(1) The order form

Who makes the record, and how, are important to show that the record is reliable.

> A: Sure. This first exhibit is an order form. It's prepared by our estimator who goes out to the home to book a move. He fills out the order

form. It records who ordered the move, the location, what's to be moved, where it's going, target dates for the pickup and delivery, and estimated cost.

Q: Why estimated cost?

A: Cost of the move is based both on total weight of the goods, and the exact mileage. We won't know the exact figure until the move is made.

Q: Does this first exhibit show who ordered the move?

Important entries on the record are pointed out. The witness could also be asked to highlight those entries using a yellow or red highlighter.

A: Yes, that's right here [pointing]. Mr. Ralph Madison, and his signature. We always have the customer sign the order form.

Q: What's to be moved?

A: That's here [pointing]. Entire contents of one-story home.

Q: From where to where?

A: That's also here [pointing]. From Mr. Madison's home in town to an address in Elko, Nevada.

Q: When?

A: Target pickup date is June 1, 2020, and target delivery date is June 5, 2020. That's right here [pointing].

Q: And estimated cost?

A: It was estimated at $3,450.

(2) Shipping notice

Q: Let's turn to the second exhibit, the shipping notice. What's that show?

A: It shows that the contents of Mr. Madison's house were picked up on June 2, 2020, and were delivered to the address in Elko, Nevada, on June 7, 2020. That's prepared by the driver.

(3) Invoice

Q: Finally, let's turn to the third exhibit, the invoice. What's that show?

A: It shows that an invoice—a bill—for $3,644 was mailed to Mr. Madison on June 15, 2020, at his new address in Elko, Nevada.

Aftermath.

Q: Mr. Jones, was your company, the ABC Trucking Company, paid for this move?

A: No, we were not.

Q: How do you know that?

Here the absence of a record is used to show the absence of an event— payment of the invoice.

A: Because the file on this move has no indication of payment. When we get a payment, we make a photocopy of it and put it in the file before we deposit the check into our bank account. This file has no copy of any payment check.

Q: Did you do anything else to determine if the invoice was ever paid?

A: Yes, I double-checked the file to see if the invoice had been returned undelivered. Our office practice is that if any mail is returned undelivered we put it into the file. Here there was no returned mail. In addition, I checked our bank deposits since June 15, 2020, to see if we deposited any check in the amount of $3,644, which was the amount of the invoice. We didn't.

Ending.

Q: Mr. Jones, my last question is: These three exhibits—the order, shipping notice, and invoice—and your search of the file and bank records, what do they tell us?

A: They show that we did the moving job we were asked to do, and we never got paid.

5.9 Character Trait Witnesses

The rules of evidence heavily regulate and limit the circumstances under and methods by which character evidence can be presented during trials. Substantial differences may exist between the Federal Rules of Evidence and the rules in states that have not adopted the federal rules. In addition, character witnesses must be well-qualified and able to testify forcefully before this kind of evidence will have any effect on the jurors.

FRE 404, 405, and 608 regulate the admissibility of character evidence. Under the rules, there are two different uses the parties can make of character evidence. First, character evidence can be used under FRE 404(a) and 405 in some instances, because someone's character is relevant to the claims, charges, or defenses raised in the pleadings. Second, character evidence may be used under FRE 608(a) to attack the credibility of any testifying witness.

1. Character Traits Relevant to Claims, Charges, and Defenses

There are two distinct ways that character trait evidence can be used that are relevant to the claims, charges, or defenses: the essential element rule and the circumstantial evidence rule. Each has several technical requirements that must be followed closely.

a. Character Trait as an Essential Element

Character or a trait of character is sometimes, although infrequently, an "essential element" of a claim, charge, or defense. In these circumstances, when character itself is at the heart of a claim, charge, or defense, such character evidence is admissible in both civil and criminal cases if offered by a proper party at a proper time. Look to the definition of the claim, charge, or defense and see if it *requires* proof of someone's character trait. A good place to start is with the statutory or case law definition of the claim, charge, or defense and the jurisdiction's pattern jury instructions.

A character trait is sometimes an essential element of a claim or charge. For example, if the plaintiff claims that the defendant trucking company hired a driver it knew to be incompetent or reckless, the plaintiff, in its case-in-chief, must prove that the truck driver has the character of being incompetent or reckless. If the plaintiff claims that a nursing home hired a nurse it knew to be violent, the plaintiff, in its case-in-chief, must prove that the nurse has a violent character.

A character trait is sometimes an essential element of a defense. For example, if the plaintiff brings a defamation claim alleging that the defendant falsely said that the plaintiff is a drug addict, and the defendant raises truth as an affirmative defense, the defendant, in his case-in-chief, must prove that the plaintiff is a drug addict. If the plaintiff brings a wrongful termination case alleging that the defendant improperly fired her because of her race or gender, and the defense is that the plaintiff was properly fired for being dishonest or incompetent, the defendant, in its case-in-chief, must prove that the plaintiff is dishonest or incompetent.

A character trait can also be an element of a rebuttal case. For example, if the defendant is charged with the sale of drugs, and the defense is entrapment, in some jurisdictions this raises the defendant's predisposition to commit illegal drug sales, and the prosecution may rebut the defense by offering evidence of the defendant's preexisting illegal drug sales.

When a character trait is an essential element of a claim, charge, or defense, the trait can be proven in three ways: (1) general reputation, (2) personal opinion, and (3) specific instances of conduct. *Reputation* is the community's collective belief about the kind of person someone else is. *Opinion* is an individual's personal belief about the kind of person someone else is. *A specific instance of conduct* is evidence of conduct at a particular time that shows someone's character.

The plaintiff presents character evidence during the plaintiff's case-in-chief if character is an essential element of the plaintiff's claim or charge. The defendant presents such character evidence during the defendant's case-in-chief if character is an essential element of the defendant's defense. The other side, of course, can then present rebutting character evidence.

Example (Character Witness in Civil Case in Which Plaintiff Claims That Defendant Nursing Home Hired an Orderly It Knew Was Violent):

[REPUTATION]

Q: (by plaintiff's lawyer): Mr. Dickens, have you heard of Mark Johnson's reputation in this community for violence as of June 1, 2020?

A: Yes, I have.

Q: How have you come to know his reputation?

A: I've heard dozens of people talk about him over the past ten years.

Q: What's his reputation in the community for violence?

A: He's known as an aggressive, violent person.

[PERSONAL OPINION]

Q: Do you have a personal opinion as to whether Mark Johnson is a violent person?

A: Yes, I do.

Q: How have you formed your personal opinion?

A: I've known him for ten years. He lives across the street from me.

Q: What's your personal opinion as to whether Mark Johnson is a violent person?

A: I think he's extremely aggressive and violent.

[SPECIFIC INSTANCE OF CONDUCT]

Q: Mr. Dickens, were you in the Tap Root Pub on June 1, 2020, during the early evening?

A: Yes.

Q: What's the Tap Root Pub?

A: It's a popular neighborhood restaurant and bar.

Q: Was Mark Johnson there?

A: Yes.

Q: Tell us what Mark Johnson did at that time.

A: He was standing at the bar, having a drink, and he suddenly pushed another man off a bar stool, started yelling at him, and started punching and kicking him.

Q: What had the other man been doing?

A: Nothing. He was just sitting there having a beer and watching the television.

b. Character Trait as Circumstantial Evidence

Character trait evidence also is admissible, in limited circumstances, as circumstantial proof that a person acted consistently with his character at a particular time. For example, if the defendant in a criminal case is charged with assault, evidence that the defendant is a peaceful kind of person makes it less likely that he would have assaulted the victim.

This use of character trait evidence is severely limited by the evidence rules, which are based on policy and efficiency considerations. First, such evidence is admissible only in criminal cases. Second, it is the defendant's choice whether to introduce character evidence in the trial. If the defendant does, he is said to "put his character in issue," and the prosecution may rebut with contrary character evidence. If the defendant chooses not to go into character evidence, the prosecution may not do so. (The only exception is FRE 404(a)(2)(C), which provides that when the defendant in a homicide/self-defense case presents evidence that the victim was the first aggressor, the prosecution may rebut with evidence of the victim's good character for peacefulness.) Third, the circumstantial evidence rules allow proof of character in only two ways: general reputation and personal opinion (not specific instances of conduct).

Fourth, the character must be a pertinent character of the defendant or, if relevant, the victim. The common character traits are peacefulness or violence in crimes involving violence (murder, assault, etc.), honesty or dishonesty in crimes involving theft or fraud (burglary, theft by deception, etc.), and truthfulness or untruthfulness in crimes involving truth-telling (perjury, false statement, etc.). For example, if the defendant is charged with assault, the defendant may introduce evidence of his own peaceful character. If the defense is self-defense, the defendant may also introduce evidence of the victim's violent character.

Fifth, the prosecution may rebut to the extent that the defense has opened the door by presenting character trait evidence of the defendant or victim. (The only exception is FRE 404(a)(2)(B)(ii), which provides that if the defense attacks the *victim's* character for a pertinent trait, the prosecution may rebut with evidence of the *defendant's* character for the same trait.)

You should not present character trait evidence in criminal cases unless you understand the technical rules governing the admissibility of such testimony.

You must also understand that calling such witnesses opens the door on cross-examination to specific instances of conduct inconsistent with the claimed character, which can have an extraordinary impact on the jurors.

Example (Character Witness in a Criminal Assault Case in Which the Defense Is Self-Defense):

[DEFENDANT'S GOOD CHARACTER FOR PEACEFULNESS— GENERAL REPUTATION AND PERSONAL OPINION]

Q: (by defense lawyer): Mr. Cohen, do you know [defendant] Bob Johnson's reputation in the community for peacefulness as of June 1, 2020?

A: Yes.

Q: Have you heard others talk about the kind of person he is?

A: Yes.

Q: How many, and over what period of time?

A: I've probably heard a couple dozen neighbors discuss him over the past several years.

Q: What is Mr. Johnson's reputation for peacefulness?

A: It's excellent. He's known as a quiet, peaceful guy.

Q: Do you also have a personal opinion about his character for peacefulness?

A: Yes.

Q: What is that based on?

A: He's been a neighbor and a friend for many years.

Q: What is your personal opinion about Mr. Johnson's character for peacefulness?

A: The same. I believe him to be a very peaceful, calm kind of person.

[VICTIM'S BAD CHARACTER FOR PEACEFULNESS— GENERAL REPUTATION AND PERSONAL OPINION]

Q: Let's turn to [alleged victim] Tom Dorr for a minute. Do you know the reputation of Mr. Dorr in this community for peacefulness as of June 1, 2020?

A: Yes.

Q: How have you come to know his reputation?

A: By hearing a number of neighbors talking about him over the past five years.

Q: What is Mr. Door's reputation for peacefulness?

A: Not good. In fact, it's bad. His reputation is that he's a violent, aggressive man.

Q: Do you have a personal opinion of Mr. Door's character for peacefulness as well?

A: Yes.

Q: And what is that based on?

A: I've known him through living in the same neighborhood for several years, and having had many personal contacts with him over those years.

Q: What's your personal opinion of Mr. Door's character for peacefulness?

A: It's bad, I'm sorry to say. I think he's quite violent.

Note that the witness was *not* asked about the basis for his opinions, which would be asking for specific instances of conduct. This conduct would be improper on direct examination. Raising specific instances of conduct is proper only during cross-examination of such a witness.

2. Character for Truthfulness to Impeach Credibility of Testifying Witnesses

Character trait evidence can also be used in another way. Whenever any witness—plaintiff or defendant, party or nonparty—testifies in any civil or criminal trial, the jurors must assess the credibility of that witness. Under FRE 608(a), the credibility of a testifying witness can be attacked by calling a character witness to testify to the testifying witness's bad character for truthfulness. Only then can the other party (the one that called the testifying witness) call a character witness to testify to the testifying witness's good character for truthfulness. In other words, a testifying witness must first have her credibility attacked before she can have her credibility accredited. Although the attack usually comes in the form of testimony as to bad character for truthfulness, a witness can also have her credibility attacked through a cross-examination that suggests the witness is not a truthful person. Such a cross-examination usually raises the witness's prior conviction, or prior inconsistent statements, that suggest the witness is not being truthful.

For this use of character trait evidence, two forms of testimony are allowed: general reputation and personal opinion (not specific instances of conduct). However, on cross-examination the reputation witness can be asked about specific instances of conduct that are inconsistent with the claimed reputation or opinion.

When calling a character trait witness on the issue of truthfulness, the proper foundation for both general reputation and personal opinion can be quickly established. In practice, such witnesses frequently testify about both general reputation and personal opinion.

Example:

> Q: (by defense lawyer): Ms. Sullivan, during the plaintiff's case-in-chief, plaintiff called Matthew Wilson to be a witness. Do you know Mr. Wilson?
>
> A: Yes, I do.
>
> Q: How have you come to know Mr. Wilson?
>
> A: He worked for several years at my company. He left the company recently.

> *[GENERAL REPUTATION]*

> Q: Do you know the reputation of Mr. Wilson in the community for truthfulness?
>
> A: Yes.
>
> Q: How have you come to know it?
>
> A: From a number of employees talking about him over those years. You know, office talk.
>
> Q: What is the reputation of Mr. Wilson in the community for truthfulness?
>
> A: Unfortunately, it's not very good. He's not known to be very truthful.

[PERSONAL OPINION]

Q: Do you have a personal opinion as to whether Mr. Wilson is a truthful person?

A: Yes, I do.

Q: What is your personal opinion based on?

A: As I said, Mark Wilson worked for my company for a few years, and I had business dealings with him on a regular basis.

Q: What is your personal opinion as to whether Mr. Wilson is a truthful person?

A: It's the same as his reputation. I don't think Mr. Wilson is very truthful.

Jurors are naturally suspicious of character witnesses, particularly if they are prominent members of the community but have little solid basis for their reputation or opinion testimony. Hence, it is usually better to find witnesses who are "regular people"—the next-door neighbor or a co-worker—with whom jurors can identify, and who have a solid knowledge of the person whose character they are testifying about.

5.10 Adverse Parties, Hostile Witnesses, and Problem Witnesses

1. Adverse Parties

Each party may call the opposing party as an adverse witness. FRE 611(c)(2) specifically provides that when a party calls an "adverse party, or a witness identified with an adverse party," ordinarily "the court should allow leading questions." This rule recognizes that examination of an adverse party is essentially like a cross-examination and that leading questions are necessary to elicit meaningful testimony. A "witness identified with" an adverse party includes directors, officers, and managerial employees of an adverse party (whose statements would be admissions imputed to the party), other employees, other persons having a special relationship to the party (such as spouse and family members), and anyone else with a relationship close enough to support a reasonable inference of bias.

There are three reasons why you might wish to call an adverse party as a witness at trial. First, the adverse party may be surprised and be unprepared to testify. Second, the adverse party may be arrogant and argumentative, and will make a bad impression on the jury. In these situations, the adverse party may already have made inconsistent statements in depositions, memoranda, and reports, which you can use effectively. When these are the reasons, the adverse party is often called as the first witness. For example, in medical malpractice and wrongful termination cases, plaintiffs sometimes call the defendant doctor or employer as the first witness in the plaintiff's case-in-chief.

Third, the adverse party must be called as a witness to establish a necessary item of proof. When this is the reason, always see if there is another way to establish that proof, such as through requests to admit facts, interrogatory answers, deposition transcripts, exhibits, or other witnesses. If none of these exists, and you are faced with the prospect of failing to establish something critical (usually something that will mean a failure to establish a prima facie case), you must call the adverse party. When this is the reason, it is usually safer to call the adverse witness in the middle of your case-in-chief.

Either party can call an adverse party, but it is much more common for plaintiffs to call defendants as adverse witnesses in the plaintiff's case-in-chief. (Of course, a prosecutor could never call the defendant to the stand in a criminal trial, because this would violate the Fifth Amendment.) When calling the adverse party, the safer practice is to make it short—establish what you need to establish through simple, leading questions, then stop. Do not give the witness opportunities to say things that will hurt you.

Example (Defendant Called as an Adverse Witness):

LAWYER (plaintiff): Your honor, we call Mr. Phillip Johnson as an adverse witness. [Witness is sworn in and takes the stand.]

Q: Mr. Johnson, you're the vice president of the Acme Manufacturing Company, right?

A: Yes.

Q: Your job includes negotiating contracts for Acme?

A: That's one of my duties.

Q: You have authority from your company to negotiate contracts on behalf of the company, right?

A: Yes.

Q: Mr. Johnson, I'm showing you what has previously been marked as Plaintiff's Exhibit No. 1. You've seen that document before, right?

A: Yes.

Q: That's a contract you negotiated for your company?

A: Yes.

Q: In fact, on page five of the contract, that's your signature at the bottom of the page?

A: Yes.

LAWYER: Nothing further from this witness at this time, your honor.

What does the adverse party do after the adverse examination? It has two choices. It can examine its own party now, or it can recall the party as a witness in its own case-in-chief. If it examines its own party now, many judges believe nonleading questions should be used, and the examination must be within the scope of the first examination. If the first examination had a narrow scope, it will significantly limit what can be brought out now (unless the judge permits examination into additional matters). If scope is not a problem, some lawyers do a full examination at this point, because it gives the adverse party the opportunity to tell its story in the middle of the other side's case-in-chief. The other option is to ask no questions now, but let the court and jury know that the party will be called again in your case-in-chief.

Example:

JUDGE: Counsel, any examination?

LAWYER (defendant): Not at this time, your honor. We'll call Mr. Johnson later when Acme presents its case.

JUDGE: Very well. Mr. Johnson, you're excused for now.

2. Hostile Witnesses

FRE 611(c)(2) also provides that when a party calls a "hostile witness," the examination may be by leading questions. There are usually two reasons why a witness is hostile. First, the witness is extremely biased in favor of the other side. Second, the witness is unhappy about being involved and is reluctant to testify. Leading questions of such witnesses are practically necessary to develop their testimony.

Some new trial lawyers mistakenly believe that the mere fact that the witness will present testimony harmful to their case is enough to make the witness hostile. Knowledgeable judges reject this notion.

The rule does not define hostility, but case law generally requires a demonstration of hostility on the stand. The usual procedure is to start the examination with nonleading questions and, when the futility of that approach becomes apparent, ask the judge to permit examining the witness as if on cross.

Example:

Q: (by plaintiff): Mr. Atkins, did you see the crash?
A: I may have.
Q: Did you see the two cars that were involved in the crash?
A: It's possible.
Q: How fast was the plaintiff's Chevy going?
A: I'm not sure.
Q: How fast was the defendant's Ford going?
A: I'm not sure.
LAWYER (plaintiff): Your honor, may I approach?
JUDGE: Please. [Lawyers come to the bench.]
LAWYER (plaintiff): Your honor, may I have permission to lead? Mr. Atkins is the defendant's next-door neighbor, and he had no trouble recounting what happened when he was interviewed by the police about the accident the day after it happened.
JUDGE: Very well. Permission granted.
Q: Mr. Atkins, the defendant in this case is your next-door neighbor, right?
A: Yes.
Q: You told the police how this accident happened?
A: Yes.
Q: In fact, you gave a written statement to the police the day after the accident, isn't that right?
A: Yes.
Q: Mr. Atkins, isn't it true that the plaintiff's Chevy was going 20 miles per hour?
A: Yes.
Q: And your neighbor's Ford was going over 50 miles per hour, isn't that true?
A: Yes.

In some jurisdictions that do not follow the federal rules, having a witness declared hostile also requires demonstrating that you are surprised at trial by the witness's hostility. These jurisdictions take the view that, if you know that the witness is going to be hostile before trial, you may not examine the witness at trial

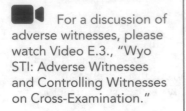
For a discussion of adverse witnesses, please watch Video E.3., "Wyo STI: Adverse Witnesses and Controlling Witnesses on Cross-Examination."

with leading questions, because you had the option not to call the witness at all.

3. Problem Witnesses

In addition to adverse and hostile witnesses, certain persons may create additional problems during direct examinations. These include children, the elderly, persons with mental disabilities, persons with language difficulties, and other witnesses who are forgetful, frightened, or angry. What should the direct examiner's approach be with such witnesses?

First, use leading questions if necessary. FRE 611(c) provides that leading questions may be used during direct examination if "necessary to develop the witness's testimony." The request can be made before the witness begins testifying, if the need is obvious, or during the direct examination, when the need becomes apparent. Leading questions, of course, give you more control, but use the right sparingly. Remember that if you spoon-feed the desired answers through leading questions, the witness's credibility (and yours) will suffer. Lead selectively, when it becomes necessary, rather than just because the judge permits it.

Second, make your questions simple by using basic vocabulary and sentence structure. Short, simple questions that call for short answers—one or two words or, at most, a sentence—improve your control.

Third, use exhibits and visual aids. For example, child victims in criminal cases sometimes are given dolls to help demonstrate what happened to them. Other witnesses can use photographs or models of a scene to help them present and explain their testimony. Still other witnesses can be shown their prior statements to help them remember the facts.

Finally, make it short, then stop. Stick to the basics and don't try to get more information or details from the witness than you can easily obtain.

5.11 Lay Witness Opinions

Lay witnesses are frequently asked to give opinions during trials. FRE 701 provides that a lay witness may testify in the form of opinions or inferences if those opinions are "(a) rationally based on the witness's perception; (b) helpful to clearly understanding the witness's testimony or to determining a fact in issue; and (c) not based on scientific, technical, or other specialized knowledge within the scope of Rule 702." This rule should be read with FRE 602, which requires that a witness have "personal knowledge" of the matter about which the witness is testifying. In trial lawyers' language, lay witness opinions are proper if the witness has firsthand knowledge based on the witness's perceptions and the opinions are "helpful" to the jury. The federal rules recognize that a rigid line between "facts" and "opinions" is not a useful distinction in the courtroom. What matters is testimony that is based on reliable observation and perception.

A proper foundation must be established before lay witness opinions are admissible. The witness must demonstrate his firsthand observations and perceptions before he can give his opinions. This is usually done by having the witness testify that he saw and heard the matter on which he has an opinion. For example, before a witness can give an opinion about a car's speed, the witness must testify that he actually saw the car.

Lay witnesses are commonly permitted to give opinions that someone looked angry, irritated, in pain, rushed, happy, delirious, disoriented, nervous, frightened, or intoxicated. They can give opinions on degrees of lightness or darkness, size, weight, distance, and speed. They can give opinions on handwriting and identity. The only necessary predicate is that the witness have sufficient observations and, if logically necessary, experience to make the opinion helpful to the jurors. This can be easily established.

Example:

Q: Ms. Evert, did you see the driver of the Chevy after the two cars collided?

A: Yes, I did.

Q: What did the driver do?

A: I saw him get out of his car, stagger around, and mumble to himself. He kept walking in circles.

Q: Before the day of the collision, have you seen people who appear to be intoxicated?

A: Of course. Many times.

Q: How did the driver of the Chevy appear to you?

A: He looked intoxicated—quite intoxicated, in fact.

Always consider doing more than the minimum necessary to admit the opinion testimony. Remember that you must satisfy the judge (who rules on admissibility) and convince the jurors (who decide weight). The jury's job is to assess the credibility of the witness and the weight of her testimony, so make sure that you provide a solid foundation for the opinion—more than the minimum the judge will require for admissibility, particularly if the testimony will be disputed.

Example:

Q: Mr. Wilson, do you know the defendant, Arthur Jackson?

A: Yes.

Q: Have you ever seen Mr. Jackson sign his name?

A: Yes, several times.

Q: Under what circumstances?

A: I've had business dealings with Mr. Jackson, probably seven or eight over the past year or so, and Mr. Jackson has signed business checks in my presence and then given the checks to me during each deal.

Q: Can you recognize his signature when you see it?

A: Yes. His signature is quite distinctive.

Q: How so?

A: Well, it's a large, bold signature, written with a flourish, and the first letters of his first and last name are much larger than the rest of the signature.

Q: I'm showing you what has been marked as State's Exhibit No. 1. Do you recognize the signature at the bottom of that check?

A: I certainly do.
Q: Whose signature is it?
A: That's Arthur Jackson's signature.
Q: Are you sure?
A: I'm positive.

5.12 Conversations, Telephone Calls, and Other Communications

Conversations, telephone calls, and other communications are frequently introduced during direct examinations, but they must be properly admissible in evidence. They must be relevant, reliable, and authenticated. Although relevance is usually obvious, conversations, telephone calls, and similar communications frequently raise hearsay and authentication issues. Satisfy the judge (who rules on admissibility), but also convince the jurors (who decide weight).

Keep in mind the threshold standard for admissibility for conversations and other communications. Under FRE 901(a), the authentication requirement is satisfied if the proponent presents "evidence sufficient to support a finding that the item is what the proponent claims it is." This is sometimes called the *prima facie standard*. The admissibility standard under FRE 901(a) is identical for civil and criminal cases.

1. Conversations

When a witness testifies to a conversation he had with another person, whether in person, over the telephone, or through electronic means, hearsay issues often arise. After all, the witness is usually asked to repeat both his own and the declarant's out-of-court statements. Therefore, both the witness's and the declarant's statements must be shown to be either nonhearsay or subject to a hearsay exception.

For example, consider the common situation in which a plaintiff's witness is being asked to recount a conversation he had with the defendant. The witness will testify, if permitted, that he said: "Did you reach an agreement with Smith [the plaintiff]?" and the defendant replied: "Yes, I did." The witness's part of the conversation is nonhearsay (it is not an assertion, and it is not being offered for its truth); the defendant's part of the conversation is also nonhearsay (it is a party admission). Hence, both sides of the conversation should be admissible over a hearsay objection.

You must always be ready to respond to hearsay objections to each participant's part of any conversation you intend to introduce in evidence. Common nonhearsay reasons (under FRE 801) for admission include party admissions, words having independent legal significance (words of contract, defamation, permission, etc.), and words indicating or affecting the listener's state of mind (notice, knowledge, fear). Common hearsay exceptions (under FRE 803 and 804) include present sense impressions, excited utterances, and statements made for diagnosis and treatment.

Whenever a witness testifies to a conversation she had with another person, authentication issues also arise. Conversations must be authenticated. Case law discusses the following foundational elements:

1. When the conversation was held
2. Where it was held
3. Who was present
4. What was said by each participant

The identity of each person participating in the conversations is necessary to establish relevance and resolve hearsay issues. The surrounding details—when and where the conversation took place—are necessary to avoid confusion and give other parties an opportunity to verify or contradict this witness's version of the conversation. Most courts also require that the witness testify to the actual words of the conversation, rather than a summary, whenever this is possible. Of course, most witnesses cannot recount a conversation word for word and testify instead to their best recollection of the conversation. Courts usually permit this, as the degree of the witness's memory goes to weight, not admissibility.

The when, where, who, and what requirements can easily be established in most cases.

Example:

Q: (by plaintiff's lawyer): Ms. Drake, did you have a conversation with the defendant, William Patterson, on June 1, 2020?
A: Yes, I did.
Q: Where did you talk with the defendant?
A: Outside the office building where we both work.
Q: Where is that?
A: The First National Bank Building, at State and Main.
Q: When?
A: We talked on June 1, right after lunch.
Q: Was anyone else present when you and the defendant talked?
A: No, it was just the two of us.
Q: Ms. Drake, tell us what you said and the defendant said at that time.
Q: We had been talking about the economy in general. Then he said: "If the economy doesn't turn around soon, we're in trouble." I said: "What does that mean for the company?" And he said: "We'll probably have to declare bankruptcy in the next six months."

Remember that you need to satisfy the judge (who rules on admissibility) and convince the jury (which determines weight). If the conversation is particularly important, have the witness provide details that show she has a good recall of the conversation itself.

2. Telephone Calls

Telephone calls present the identical hearsay issues as conversations. However, telephone calls present an additional authentication issue: identification of the other person or persons participating in the telephonic conversation. FRE 901(b) refers to two common ways in which the identity of the other person can be established: voice identification and calling a telephone directory number.

Telephone calls, then, require the following foundation:

1. When the conversation was held
2. Where it was held (location of witness and, if known, other person)

3. Who was present (who else participated in the conversation or was on the line listening)
4. What was said by each participant

a. Call Made to or from a Known Person

When a telephone call is made to, or received from, a known person, no problems arise. Voice recognition is the common way the identity of the other person on the line is established. The usual witness is one of the participants in the conversation, although it could be any person who listened in on the conversation.

Example:

Q: Mr. Quigley, do you know the plaintiff, Jack Sarnoff?
A: Yes, I do.
Q: How have you come to know him?
A: We've had a number of business dealings, and we've talked at length, both in person and on the telephone, over the past two years.
Q: When you hear his voice, can you recognize it?
A: Oh yes, he has a distinctive voice.
Q: Let's turn to June 1, 2020, at around 2:00 in the afternoon. Where were you at that time?
A: In my office.
Q: What happened at that time?
A: The telephone rang, and I picked it up.
Q: Did you recognize the voice on the other end?
A: Yes.
Q: Whose voice was it?
A: It was Jack Sarnoff.
Q: Did anyone else participate in the conversation?
A: Only the two of us talked, and no one else was listening in on my end.
Q: Tell us what you said and Jack Sarnoff said at that time.
A: I said: "Hello" and he said: "Tom, it's Jack Sarnoff." I asked: "What's up?" and he said: "We're having problems with the shipment date." I said: "What's the problem?" and he said: "We're having manufacturing problems, and that will push back the delivery date by several weeks." I said: "You know, that's going to trigger the penalty provisions of our contract," and he said: "I know, but it can't be helped." I told him: "Thanks for letting me know," and that was the end of our conversation that day.

b. Call Made to an Unknown Person

When a telephone call is made *to* an unknown person, FRE 901(b)(6) permits identification of the other person on the call through proof of the number called. This is done by showing that "a call was made to the number assigned at the time to: (A) a particular person, if circumstances, including self-identification, show that the person answering was the one called; or (B) a particular business, if the call was made to a business and the call related to business reasonably transacted over the telephone."

The business telephone number foundation is frequently used and can easily be established.

Example (Business Telephone Number):

Q: Ms. Marlowe, on June 1, 2020, about 2:00 in the afternoon, where were you?

A: I was at home.

Q: What did you do at that time?

A: I made a telephone call.

Q: What number did you call?

A: I called 888-1234, a local number.

Q: How did you get that number?

A: I googled Acme Plumbing and got its telephone number.

Q: What did you do then?

A: I called the number, and someone answered the phone and said: "Acme Plumbing."

Q: Who answered?

A: I don't know the person, but it was a woman's voice.

Q: What happened after that?

A: I had a conversation with the woman on the other end.

Q: Did anyone else participate in the conversation?

A: No, not that I was aware of.

Q: What did you and the other person say at that time?

A: I said: "I have an emergency. I've got a leak in a pipe, and there's water coming through the plasterboard in my laundry room." She asked me for my address and telephone number, and I gave it to her. I then asked: "When can you get here?" and she said: "We can get a truck out there within an hour." I said: "Great, I'll be waiting," and hung up.

c. Call Made by an Unknown Person

Finally, when a telephone call is received from an unknown person, the identity of the caller can sometimes be established circumstantially. (Note that self-identification under FRE 901(b)(6) only applies to calls made *to* a number.) That is, there may be circumstances, either before or after the call, that identify the caller. For example, you go to a store, talk to the manager and place an order for a specific item, and the manager says she will call you when the item is available for pickup. When a "person" later calls you and tells you that your item has arrived and may be picked up, you have identified the manager of the store as the person who called you, even if you cannot recognize the voice as being of the manager. In such a case, the basis for the later voice identification is the content of the earlier conversation with the manager.

Telephone callers can also be identified on the basis of subsequent conduct. The logic is the same.

Example:

Q: Ms. Adams, on June 1, 2020, around 2:00 in the afternoon, did you receive a telephone call?

A: Yes.

Q: Where were you?

A: In the kitchen of my home.

Q: Anyone else with you?

A: No.

Q: When the phone rang, what did you do?

A: I picked it up, said hello, and listened to the other person.

Q: At that time, did you recognize the other person's voice?

A: Not at that time, no.

Q: Let's turn to the next day, June 2. Were you at home on that day?

A: Yes.

Q: Around 2:00 in the afternoon, what happened?

A: The doorbell rang, and I went to the front door to see who it was.

Q: Who was it?

A: The defendant, Mr. Bryant.

Q: Did Mr. Bryant say anything?

A: Yes, he said he was ready to start trimming the palm trees around my property.

Q: Let's turn back to the telephone call the previous day. Do you now know who was on the telephone during that call?

A: Sure. It was Mr. Bryant.

Q: Tell us the conversation you had with Mr. Bryant during the telephone call.

A: He said: "My name is George Bryant, and I'm doing tree trimming in your neighborhood. Your palm trees look as if they need trimming, and I'm willing to do them for $50 per tree." I said: "When can you do it?" and he said: "I can start tomorrow afternoon, and it will probably take me that day and the next day to complete the job." I said: "That sounds good, you've got a deal." That was the extent of our conversation.

Another common situation in which a telephone caller is identified through subsequent conduct is when the caller sends a follow-up or confirming letter. If the signature on the letter is identified as the caller's signature, and the letter refers to the previous telephone conversation, the person who signed the letter has been shown to be the previous caller.

Caller identification is a built-in function of cell phones and smart phones. Identifying an unknown caller through a caller identification unit may involve three steps. First, the person called must remember the telephone number displayed on the unit (or rely on the call history that stores this information) and testify to that number. A representative of the telephone company may need to testify that the caller identification unit is a reliable or generally accepted system for displaying the number from which a call originates (although some judges may take judicial notice of this fact). Finally, a commercial telephone directory (self-authenticating under FRE 902) or telephone company records (business records under FRE 803(6)) may have to be introduced to prove that the displayed telephone number belongs to a particular business or home. This foundation should be adequate if the call is made from a business telephone (as proof that someone from the business called), but may not be adequate if the call is made from a residence telephone, because many people, in addition to the person to whom the number is assigned, may have access to a residence telephone.

Voice messaging, increasingly common, involves the same foundation as live telephone calls. When persons leave messages and reply to messages for each other, instead of talking to each other directly, the same kind of voice recognition or voice identification foundation is required.

3. Computer-Based Conversations

The electronic age has created additional ways in which people can have "conversations," and these new ways have raised new authentication issues. In particular, instant messaging (IM) has become a popular way for people to communicate, and the question of what foundation is needed to admit such messages in evidence arises frequently.

IM requires that a person have a "screen name" through an Internet service provider (in practice, the screen name used may not be the person's real name). Messages are sent to the screen name address, and if that person is on-line, the person can send a return message. The messages are normally sent and received within seconds, so that two persons can have a conversation that is close to being in real time.

IM can be in text, voice, or video form. If in voice or video form, the other person usually can be identified through voice or visual recognition. When the IM message is in text form, however, authentication issue arises. How does the person on one end of the conversation know that the person on the other end is actually the person he purports to be? In some situations, prior or subsequent conduct will identify the person in the same way that prior or subsequent conduct can identify the other person on the telephone. If this situation does not exist, can IM messages be adequately authenticated?

A foundation for text IM would necessarily include the testimony of a witness that she sent an IM to a particular screen name address, and that she received an IM back from that address. The foundation might also include evidence from the provider that the particular screen name is registered to a particular person. That foundation should be enough to admit the content of the conversation over foundation objections. After that, the issue of weight is for the jury.

Technology will undoubtedly create different vehicles for communication in the future. Regardless of the vehicle, the evidentiary issues that arise will remain the same: Is the communication relevant? Is it reliable? Has the communication been adequately authenticated?

5.13 Refreshing Memory

It's an everyday trial event: During the direct examination, a witness simply forgets something important. Whatever the cause, the problem has to be fixed *now*, and one vehicle for fixing it is FRE 612, the refreshing memory rule (also called the *refreshing recollection rule*). Whenever a witness forgets something, you can refresh — "jog" — the witness's memory. FRE 612 controls when you can do it, how you do it, and the consequences of doing it.

First, FRE 612 controls refreshing memory "while testifying." If a witness uses a "writing" to refresh memory, an adverse party is entitled to see the writing, use it during cross-examination, and introduce in evidence relevant portions of the writing.

Before refreshing memory, you must demonstrate that the witness in fact needs his memory refreshed. The key is to have the witness say "I don't remember" or "I don't recall" (not "I don't know") in response to one of your questions, or to ask the witness "Do you recall anything else?" and have the witness answer

"No." Once that is established, the writing used to refresh memory is marked as an exhibit, shown to opposing counsel, and then shown to the witness. The witness looks at the writing and, after it jogs his memory, returns it to the lawyer. The witness then testifies about the matter on which his memory has just been jogged. Although FRE 612 controls refreshing memory with a "writing," case law makes it clear that anything can be used to refresh memory. It need not be a writing, and it need not have been made by the witness. As a practical matter, the most common things used to refresh memory are the witness's deposition transcript, the witness's own report, someone else's report, business records, and trial exhibits.

Example (Direct Examination):

> Q: Officer Tracy, when you searched the defendant's bedroom, what did you find?
>
> A: I found a Smith and Wesson revolver, a .38 caliber.
>
> Q: Did you find anything else?
>
> A: Well, not that I can remember right now.
>
> Q: Would anything jog your memory?
>
> A: I'm sure my report would.
>
> Q: [Have the report marked, show it to opposing counsel, and hand it to the witness.] I'm showing you what has been marked Government Exhibit No. 8. Do you recognize it?
>
> A: Yes, that's the report I wrote about this case.
>
> Q: Officer Tracy, please read it to yourself. [Witness reads the report.] Does that help jog your memory?
>
> A: It sure does.
>
> Q: May I have the report back, please? [Witness returns report.] What else did you find in the defendant's bedroom?
>
> A: In addition to the revolver, I found a box of .38 caliber shells in the top dresser drawer.

Prepare your witness for the memory-refreshing routine. Asking the witness "do you remember" or "do you recall" tells the witness that she has forgotten something important and should be prepared to say that her deposition, report, other records and writings, or other exhibits would help jog her memory.

Because the exhibit was used to refresh memory, the opposing party is entitled to use the report or file during cross-examination and to introduce relevant portions of the report or file in evidence. For the direct examiner, this means that you should never use anything to refresh recollection that will give the opposing side additional ammunition for cross-examination.

Second, FRE 612 also governs refreshing memory "before testifying." Although the opposing party's right to see the writing used to refresh memory is discretionary ("if the court decides that justice requires the party to have those options"), if the item was used before testifying, the court may order its production. In practice, if the court thinks that a witness has used something to prepare for testifying, and is trying to keep it confidential or secret, the court may well order production if requested.

Example (Cross-Examination):

> Q: Mr. Quigley, before coming to court to testify today, did you look at any records, documents, or other things to prepare for testifying?

A: Well, I looked at my private diary.

Q: Did that private diary help you remember the exact dates on which you had the conversations you have been testifying about?

A: Well, not all of them, but some.

LAWYER: Your honor, may I approach?

JUDGE: Yes. [Counsel approach.]

LAWYER: Your honor, at this time we ask for production of the witness's private diary.

JUDGE: Plaintiff, any response?

LAWYER (plaintiff): Yes, your honor, the witness didn't use the diary today in court.

JUDGE: Under Rule 612, I have discretion in this matter, and I'm going to order that the diary be produced. Mr. Quigley, do you have the diary with you?

WITNESS: No, I don't.

JUDGE: We'll suspend the cross-examination at this time. Mr. Quigley, you're ordered to produce the diary. How quickly can you get it?

WITNESS: It's in my office. I can probably get it and come back in about one hour.

JUDGE: Very well. We'll take our lunch break now and resume with Mr. Quigley's cross-examination at 1:00.

Finally, make sure you understand the relationship between FRE 612, the refreshing memory rule, and FRE 803(5), the recorded recollection rule. If a witness, after being shown a writing, says it refreshes memory, FRE 612 controls. However, if a witness, after being shown a writing, says it does *not* jog the witness's memory, you should be able to qualify the writing under FRE 803(5) as recorded recollection if the witness made or adopted the writing. If it qualifies, the contents of the writing may be read to the jury to substitute for the witness's forgotten memory.

What are the common mistakes lawyers make when refreshing recollection? First, they forget to have the document used to refresh recollection marked as an exhibit and to show it to opposing counsel. Second, they try to show the document to the witness before they establish that the witness's memory needs to be refreshed. Third, they leave the document with the witness, which usually causes the witness to read from the document (which has not been admitted as an exhibit) rather than testify from memory. Finally, they fail to realize that the consequences of refreshing a witness's memory with a document gives the other side an opportunity to see the document, use it during the cross-examination, and introduce pertinent portions in evidence. FRE 612 is an important rule and it must be understood thoroughly.

5.14 Anticipating Cross-Examination and Judge's and Jurors' Questions

This chapter has discussed how effective direct examinations must be organized from the jurors' point of view and emphasized that the examinations must comply with the technical rules governing witness testimony. There is another consideration that should never be overlooked: What is the opposing lawyer likely to do during cross-examination, and how can you defuse it?

Your witness certainly has been thinking about cross-examination and will have concerns. Your witness wants to know what the other lawyer is like, and what to expect on cross. Witnesses have seen enough courtroom dramas on television and in the movies to believe that witnesses are routinely "destroyed" during cross, and they worry that it will happen to them. Witnesses need to know what they can realistically expect during cross-examination, and you need to show them that you have planned for and anticipated these occurrences. You must prepare each witness you call for what to expect on cross-examination.

There are three reasons you should always anticipate the cross-examination. First, anticipating the cross-examination—in trial lawyers' language, *drawing the sting*—will lessen its impact. Psychological research on order effects, fore-warning, inoculation, and counterargumentation shows that you can substantially lessen the impact of points made on cross-examination by anticipating and addressing them during the direct. Second, anticipating the cross-examination will preserve your credibility with the jurors. If jurors believe that you are telling them only half the truth, (the half that helps you) and are avoiding the other half (the half that hurts you), your credibility will plummet. Third, anticipating the cross-examination, both the content and the cross-examiner's style, will help your witness to anticipate the questions and atmosphere and to answer the questions truthfully and calmly. You may want to prepare cross-examination questions and have another lawyer conduct a mock cross-examination of your witness.

What should you anticipate? Always think: If you were doing the cross-examination of this witness, what things would you go into? If so, can you raise these matters during the direct examination and defuse them? Two common areas are impeachment and facts that limit the witness's testimony.

If you have done your homework on the witness, you will know if any impeachment is possible. For example, the witness may have a prior conviction; a bias, interest, or motive to testify a certain way; or have made prior inconsistent statements. These are obvious things the cross-examiner will explore and things you can and should defuse on direct. Under FRE 607, you can impeach your own witness during the direct examination, and drawing the sting involves doing just that: impeaching your own witness, but gently and with an understanding tone, and teasing out explanations when appropriate.

Example (Prior Conviction):

Q: Mr. Smith, before we go any further, let's talk about what happened to you five years ago. You got in trouble?

A: Yes, I did, I'm sorry to say.

Q: What happened?

A: Some friends and I took some beer from a convenience food store. We were caught and charged with theft.

Q: What happened in court?

A: I pleaded guilty and received a suspended sentence, probation for one year.

Q: Did you complete the probation?

A: Yes.

Q: How old were you when this happened?
A: I was 18.
Q: Since that time, have you ever gotten in trouble again?
A: No, sir. I learned from that experience.

Example (Prior Inconsistent Statement):

Q: Ms. Adams, at the time of the crash, how far were you from the place where the two cars crashed?
A: I was 50 feet away.
Q: Are you sure?
A: Oh yes.
Q: Ms. Adams, didn't you talk to a police officer right after the crash?
A: Yes, that's true.
Q: And didn't you tell that officer that you were about 25 feet away when the crash happened?
A: Yes.
Q: Then why are you telling us today that you were 50 feet away?
A: A few days later, I went back to that corner. I walked off the distance from where I was standing to where the two cars collided. It was 25 steps, and I take about 2-foot steps.

If you have done your homework, you should also know the ways in which the cross-examiner will try to limit the witness's testimony. For example, cross-examinations of eyewitnesses to accidents and crimes often point out that the event happened quickly, that it was unexpected, that it occurred at night and in poor lighting conditions, and that the witness made no report or written memorandum of what happened. Once again, decide if you want to "front" these limiting facts during the direct examination. If you do, bring out the facts gently and then return to your strong points.

Example:

Q: Mr. Giambi, when you saw the accident, what time was it?
A: Almost 9:00 in the evening.
Q: Was it dark?
A: Yes.
Q: Did you expect to see a collision between two cars that evening?
A: Not at all.
Q: Were you surprised when it happened?
A: Definitely.
Q: And Mr. Giambi, you were walking from the restaurant where you just had dinner?
A: That's right. I was walking to where my car was parked.
Q: Dinner included wine?
A: Yes.
Q: How much wine did you have?
A: I shared a bottle of wine with my boss.
Q: Mr. Giambi, did you have any difficulty seeing the collision when it happened?

Q: No. It happened no more than 50 feet from where I was walking, right in front of me, and there were plenty of streetlights and other lights to see what happened.

Example:

Q: This meeting, Ms. Boxer, how long did it take?
A: About one hour.
Q: How many persons were present?
A: Four.
Q: All of them talked?
A: Yes.
Q: This meeting took place how long ago?
A: It's been just over two years now.
Q: Did you take any notes during the meeting?
A: No.
Q: Did you make any notes after the meeting?
A: No.
Q: You're testifying today about the meeting based on your memory?
A: That's right.
Q: How is it, Ms. Boxer, that you remember this meeting so well?
A: This was the most important meeting that year. This contract could make or break us, and the negotiations were critical. I remember that meeting as if it were yesterday.

Where in the direct examination should you defuse the anticipated cross-examination? Here, *order effects*—the order in which information is disclosed—are important. Most people form impressions quickly and then become resistant to changing them, even when confronted with reasons to change. This means that you should always make an initial good impression about the witness and the testimony before drawing the sting by "volunteering" the weaknesses. Don't wait until the very end of the direct examination, though, because jurors will notice it more when it comes late. Instead, bring out the weakness in the middle of the witness's testimony, and make it part of the story, without emphasizing, apologizing for, or hiding it. Jurors will make less of the bad fact if they already have an initial good impression of the witness and the testimony, and they will appreciate your candor in telling them the entire truth, rather than just those parts that help you.

Example:

Q: The color of the light when your car and the defendant's car collided, what was it?
A: The light was yellow for my street, Main Street.
Q: Are you sure?
A: I'm positive.
Q: Mr. Gable, let's turn next to what happened when the ambulance took you to the emergency room at Mercy Hospital. Do you remember being in the emergency room?
A: Yes.
Q: Do you remember what happened when you were there?

A: Some, sure. I remember there were a bunch of nurses and doctors checking me out, asking me questions, taking blood, taking x-rays, things like that. But I was in a lot of pain, and a little stunned by what had happened, so I'm not sure about everything that was going on.

Q: Do you remember talking to a nurse by the name of Smith?

A: No.

Q: Do you remember her asking you what happened?

A: No.

Q: Mr. Gable, the reason I'm asking you about nurse Smith, in the emergency room record she wrote down that you said: "When the cars collided, I had the green light." Do you remember saying that to her?

A: No, I don't. If I did, it was a mistake, because that's not the way it happened.

Q: What color was the light when your car and the defendant's car actually collided?

A: My light, for Main Street, had just turned yellow.

There is a final area you need to think about: questions from the judge and jurors. Some judges, particularly federal judges, may ask questions during or at the end of the direct or cross-examinations. These are most commonly clarifying questions or questions that fill in missing information.

In some jurisdictions today the jurors are permitted to ask witnesses questions. Practices vary widely. Some trial judges like juror questioning; others dislike it. Some allow juror questioning only in civil cases, while others permit it in both civil and criminal cases. In state courts, the trend is toward permitting juror questioning in civil and, less frequently, criminal cases.

If the trial judge will permit juror questioning, make sure you know the procedure the judge will follow. A common procedure is for the judge to tell the jurors at the beginning of the trial that they may submit questions in writing, and that the judge will decide if the questions are proper and can be asked. After a witness has testified, the jurors return to the jury room, where they can write down any questions they may want asked. The jurors send the questions to the judge, who confers with the lawyers to discuss whether the questions are appropriate. The lawyers can object and suggest other ways of asking the questions. The jurors are then brought back into the courtroom and the judge asks the approved questions of the witness. The lawyers may then ask follow-up questions.

Regardless of the procedure, make sure that your witness is prepared for such questioning, and make sure that your witness answers the queries accurately, candidly, and truthfully.

5.15 Stipulations

A stipulation is an agreement between the parties that certain facts are not in dispute, or that a witness would testify to certain facts if called as a trial witness. For example, prosecutors and defense lawyers in criminal cases frequently stipulate that all the events testified to during the trial occurred in a certain county and state (this proves proper venue). Plaintiffs and defendants in personal injury cases frequently stipulate that the plaintiff has a life expectancy of a certain number of years (this is necessary to determine future damages). The advantage of stipulations is that they eliminate the need to formally prove a necessary fact and streamline the trial.

Either side can ask the other to stipulate. Stipulations can be made orally or in writing (the better practice). If a matter is stipulated, the fact of the stipulation is brought to the attention of the judge, the stipulation is read or shown to the jury, and the judge instructs the jury on the effect of the stipulation.

Example (oral):

PROSECUTOR: Your honor, we have a stipulation we would like to present to the jury at this time.

JUDGE: Very well. Proceed.

PROSECUTOR: The prosecution and defense have stipulated that all the events testified about during the prosecution's case-in-chief occurred in Cook County, Illinois.

JUDGE: Defense, have you agreed with this stipulation?

DEFENSE LAWYER: We have, your honor.

JUDGE: Members of the jury, a stipulation is an agreement between the prosecution and defense that certain facts are true and are not in dispute in this trial.

The better practice is to put the stipulation in writing, put the court caption and heading on the document, and have it signed by the plaintiff's and defendant's lawyers. In some jurisdictions the practice is to mark the written stipulation as a trial exhibit. This is a good practice if you want the written stipulation to be included with the other admitted exhibits that go to the jury room during deliberations. The stipulation is then submitted to the judge and presented to the jury.

Example (written):

PLAINTIFF: Your honor, we have entered into a written stipulation with the defense and would like to read it to the jury at this time. I have marked the stipulation Plaintiff's Exhibit No. 9. Defense counsel and I have signed the stipulation.

JUDGE: Defense, is that correct?

DEFENSE LAWYER: It is, your honor.

JUDGE: Plaintiff, please read the written stipulation.

PLAINTIFF: The stipulation reads as follows: "Plaintiff and defendant hereby agree that a white male, presently 45 years of age, has a life expectancy of 35.6 years."

JUDGE: [Advises jury of the effect of a stipulation.]

Stipulations are more commonly made to facts, but they can also be made to witness testimony.

Example:

DEFENSE LAWYER: Your honor, may we present a stipulation to the jury at this time? It's in writing, signed by the lawyers, and has been marked Defendant's Exhibit No. 3.

JUDGE: Yes. Proceed.

DEFENSE LAWYER: This stipulation, Defendant's Exhibit No. 3, reads as follows: Plaintiff and defendant agree that if William Smith were called as a witness in this trial, he would testify under oath that he attended the board meeting on June 1, 2020, and abstained from voting on whether to approve the purchase of the Johnson Building.

Stipulations are entered into when both sides benefit. The proponent benefits by eliminating the need and expense of formally proving necessary facts; the other side benefits by not appearing to be an obstructionist on matters that are not seriously in dispute. In civil cases, if the other side will not agree to stipulate to something you want, send the other side a Rule 36 Request for Admission (if discovery has not yet been closed). This frequently has the effect of making the other side more reasonable. If the other side will not agree to stipulate to facts that are easy to verify from a reliable source (such as life expectancy from Department of Labor statistics), ask the trial judge to judicially notice that fact under FRE 201.

> For a discussion of stipulations, please watch the latter half of Video H.3, "Wyo STI: Profs. Easton and Younger on Judicial Notice and Stipulations."

5.16 Redirect Examination

If you have accurately anticipated the cross-examination, there should be little reason to conduct a redirect examination. Confidently standing up and saying: "No redirect, your honor" signals to the jurors that the cross-examination didn't hurt you and there is no reason to redirect. Conversely, conducting a redirect always implies that there is a problem that needs fixing. Too many inexperienced lawyers think that they should redirect just to repeat key parts of the direct and get in the last word. This is improper and does not accomplish anything positive in the jurors' eyes. In short, don't do redirect unless there is something important you need to address, and you can address it effectively.

What's important, and how can you address it? Redirect examination can do three things. First, it can explain new matters raised for the first time on cross. Second, it can correct mistakes and clarify faulty impressions created by the cross. Finally, it can explain the reason for prior inconsistent statements and rebut implications of recent fabrications or improper influence.

> For a demonstration of redirect examination after the cross-examination of an expert, please watch the last portion of Video F.2, "Wyo STI: Demonstration of Problem 5.10."

Remember that the rules governing direct examination apply to redirect as well. Questions should be nonleading, although judges customarily permit leading questions on preliminary and introductory matters. The redirect examination also must be "within the scope" of the matters gone into during the cross-examination. Most judges rule that the lawyer who conducted the direct examination must also conduct the redirect examination.

Cross-examination frequently raises new matters not mentioned during the direct examination. The redirect examination can then explain whatever has to be explained.

Example:

The cross-examination has pointed out that a victim of a sexual assault did not call the police for several hours after the attack. On redirect examination, the following happens.

Q: Ms. Smith, the other lawyer brought out that you called the police several hours after the defendant attacked you. Is that true?

A: Yes.

Q: Is there a reason you waited that long before calling them?

A: Yes.

Q: What's the reason?

A: He said he'd kill me if I called the police. He said he'd know if I called them. I just curled up in a fetal position trying to block it all out. It wasn't until it got light outside that I finally got the courage to make the call.

Cross-examination can also create faulty and misleading impressions. Redirect examination can correct them.

Example:

The cross-examiner has brought out that the witness told the police she was "half a block away" at the time of the crash, but she said she was "25 feet away" on direct.

Q: Ms. Jones, how far from the defendant were you when you heard him say: "I'm sorry, my mistake"?

A: About 25 feet away.

Q: Why did you tell the police you were half a block away?

A: I told them I was half a block away when the crash happened. I then walked over to the crash and was standing about 25 feet away watching what was happening. That's where I was when I heard the defendant say "I'm sorry, my mistake."

Cross-examination will frequently bring up prior inconsistent statements. Redirect examination can properly elicit the reason for the inconsistency. "Why" questions are proper here, because FRE 613(b) provides that a witness must be "given an opportunity to explain or deny" the prior inconsistent statement.

Example:

Q: Mr. Jackson, on cross-examination the other lawyer pointed out that in your deposition you stated that "there were three people in the room during the meeting." On direct examination you stated that there were six people in the room. Can you explain why you said six people today but said three people in your deposition?

A: Yes. There were a total of six people in the room. However, only three of them were doing any talking, and that's what I was asked about during the deposition.

Prior consistent statements are properly admissible under FRE 801(d)(1)(B)(i) if they rebut the implication of recent fabrication, improper influence, or motive. However, the prior consistent statement must have been made *before* the event giving rise to the implication of recent fabrication, improper influence, or motive arose.

Example:

Q: Ms. Anderson, what color was the light when the defendant's truck went into the intersection?

A: It was green for the truck.

Q: Remember when on cross-examination you were asked about being hired by the defendant company three months ago?

A: I sure do.

Q: Ms. Anderson, are you testifying today that the light for the truck was green because you were recently hired by the defendant company?

A: No.

Q: Tell the members of the jury what you told the police officer right after the crash.

A: I told the police officer that the truck had the green light.

Q: The same thing you're saying today?

A: The same thing.

FRE 801(d)(1)(B) was amended in 2014 by adding subsection (ii), which provides that a prior consistent statement is also admissible if offered "to rehabilitate the declarant's credibility as a witness when attacked on another ground." The scope of subsection (ii) is presently unclear, as there is little case law. For example, if a witness is impeached with a prior felony conviction under FRE 609, does subsection (ii) then permit bringing out any of the witness's prior consistent statements? Although the language of subsection (ii) suggests this is the case, many believe this wide scope was not intended.

5.17 Trial Notebook

The direct examination section of your trial notebook should contain the outlines of the planned direct examinations of each witness in your case-in-chief and, if necessary, rebuttal case. The outlines, of course, should be prepared before preparing the witnesses, then revised as developments warrant.

First, put the direct examination outlines in the order in which you intend to call the witnesses in your case. This makes it easy to find the outlines when you need them.

Second, create a witness folder for each witness. The folder will contain a copy of the direct examination outline, a copy of each exhibit the witness will qualify or use, and a copy of each statement the witness has made, whether deposition transcripts, written statements, or reports. The witness folder will then contain everything you need to prepare the witness for testifying. Put the witness folders in the order in which you intend to call the witnesses in your case.

Third, prepare the direct examination outlines for each witness. Two approaches are common, the Q&A method and the checklist method. With the Q&A method, each question you intend to ask and every answer you expect the witness to give is written down. The outline will look much like a trial transcript. During the direct examination, you simply follow the outline, asking the questions you have written down. The Q&A method is often used by inexperienced trial lawyers who like the comfort level provided by having the questions written out in advance. However, the Q&A method has serious weaknesses. It usually causes the direct examination to look and sound scripted and rehearsed, because that's what it is. It also causes inflexibility, because the script does not allow for variations and modifications during the examination. For those reasons, most trial lawyers give up the Q&A method as they become confident of their examination skills. If you are a newcomer to direct examination, it is far better to never use a Q&A direct examination outline in the first place, so you never become dependent on this type of outline.

The more common, and far better, method is the checklist method. With the checklist method, you organize the direct examination by putting down the key facts, dates, and events that will trigger the questions you will ask to bring out the testimony. The checklist method has advantages. It forces you to ask questions spontaneously, which helps make the direct examination look and sound like a fresh, dynamic exchange between you and the witness. It permits flexibility, because you can ask follow-up questions as necessary and not remain wedded to a script. It allows you to put the outline on one or two pages. For these reasons, the checklist method is used by most experienced trial lawyers.

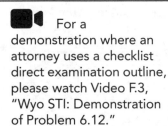

For a discussion of drafting of direct (and cross) outlines, please watch Video D.2, "Wyo STI: Direct & Cross-Examination Outlines."

For a demonstration where an attorney uses a checklist direct examination outline, please watch Video F.3, "Wyo STI: Demonstration of Problem 6.12."

How do you organize the direct examination using the checklist method? There's no one way. However, make sure the outline contains what you need to conduct the direct examination and that it has a visually clear sequence of the key facts the witness will testify about. Organize your bullet points under headings, with three to six (or maybe eight) bullet points per heading.

Many lawyers put at the top of the outline a short statement of the purpose for calling the witness; each exhibit the witness will use, in the order in which they will be used; and each prior statement the witness made (that may be needed to refresh memory during the direct, and which the opposing side may use during cross). Before you start the examination, make sure you have all the exhibits at hand, in the order in which you plan to use them, and the witness's statements, in case you need to use them. This shows the jurors that you are organized, prepared, and know what you're doing.

To complete your outline, try to identify your opponent's possible objections to your questioning. Add those objections, and your responses, to your outline.

Example:

SANDY JOHNSON—DIRECT EXAMINATION

Purpose: Johnson was standing on corner, saw collision, says plaintiff had yellow light.

<u>Exhibits:</u>

1. Intersection diagram (Ex. #7)
2. Intersection photos (Ex. #4, 5, 6)
3. Photos of Pl. and Def. cars (Ex. #14, 15)

<u>Statements:</u>

1. Written statement to police
2. Written statement to ins. investigator
3. Deposition transcript

Next, outline the content of the planned direct examination. Make the parts and sequence clear. Put on the checklist the key events and facts you want the witness to testify about. Note when you will use the exhibits and what you want the witness to do with them. Use bold print, capital letters, colored highlighting, and anything else that makes your outline visually clear and easy to use. If you need to use lengthy documents or transcripts during the direct examination, put page numbers for them on your outline. This should eliminate fumbling around trying to find the pertinent page.

Example:

Introduction
Kelly Johnson
1468 Park Street
Happyville, MD
Electrician with Crab State Electric
Witnessed the collision
Prepared to tell jury what saw

Background
Born here, Central High; BA, State University
Married, 2 children
Schoolteacher at Hughes Elementary, 6 yrs.

Scene
Knows Main & Elm, walks to work
Average neighborhood, busy streets, crosswalks, traffic light
6/1/20 at 5:30 pm
Weather clear and dry
Traffic heavy on Main—rush hour
On SW corner, waiting for light to change, to cross Main

What witness saw before crash
Traffic in NB lane stopped
Chevy (def.) trying to make left turn
Possible Objection: Speculation
Response: Valid lay witness opinion under Rule 701
Traffic in SB lane moving 20–25 mph
Light turns yellow
SB Ford (pl.) enters intersection on yellow
Chevy turns left, right in front of Ford

What witness saw during crash
Brakes screech, huge crash, Ford crashes into side of Chevy
Light yellow

What happened after crash
Everything quiet
Police come, ambulance comes, Ford driver carried off
Talked to police

Exhibits
Intersection photos (#4, 5, 6) show intersection from NB lane, SB lane, and SW corner witness standing on
Car photos (#14, 15) show Ford and Chevy and damage
Intersection diagram (#7)—mark position of witness, cars at point of impact, and color of traffic light at time

Ending
Positive light for Main yellow when Ford entered intersection
Positive light for Main yellow when two cars collided

There is no magic or perfect outline, because lawyers are different. However, the outline should be a checklist for the key facts the witness will testify about and the key things the witness will do. Make whatever notations will be effective reminders. If the witness needs to identify a defendant in court, put "ID DEF" on the outline. If the witness will demonstrate the range of motion in his elbow joint, put "Demo: range of motion" on the outline, and highlight them with colored markers.

An example of a trial notebook, with shell forms and completed forms, is on the website that accompanies this book.

Finally, don't be afraid to hold the outline while you conduct the direct examination. Jurors don't expect the lawyers to remember everything and will expect you to use some sort of checklist. Use the outline as though it's the most natural thing to do.

5.18 Common Problems

What are the recurring problems that inexperienced lawyers encounter during direct examinations?

1. Weak Introduction

The first minute should answer three questions: Who is he? Why is he here? Should I believe him? Answer these questions, grab the jurors' attention, present a likeable witness, and the jurors will stay with you. The slow, traditional beginning just doesn't work with today's jurors.

2. Too Long, Too Detailed

The attention span of today's juror is limited. Most people cannot maintain a high level of attention for more than 15 or 20 minutes. After that, sensory overload happens quickly. This means you need to get to the key facts quickly, while the jurors are still listening.

Watch the jurors. Are they listening and watching? Do they appear interested? Are they watching the witness, or looking elsewhere? When the witness is answering a question, look at the jurors and take in their body language. Jurors will let you know how the direct examination is progressing.

3. No Word Pictures

Direct examination testimony has to be visual, visceral, and focused on the people involved. Direct examination should not merely be a recitation of facts. Jurors want mind pictures to draw them into a story that involves human beings, so they can see the occurrence and experience it from the witness's point of view.

4. Not Enough Exhibits and Visual Aids

Visual learning improves interest, understanding, and attention. Think how you can use exhibits and visual aids to repeat and highlight the key testimony from the witness.

5. Not Enough Focus on Key Disputed Facts

Inexperienced lawyers frequently spend too much time developing undisputed or peripheral details and too little time developing the key disputed facts. Always ask: What's the key dispute, and how can this witness prove my side of that dispute?

6. Weak Ending

Direct examinations frequently end when the witness has finished telling the story. This is a mistake, because jurors remember best what they hear first and last. Always ask: What is the most important thing the witness said during the examination? How can I end the direct examination so that the witness makes an important point? Direct examinations should end on a high note.

7. Not Anticipating Cross-Examination

Cross-examination should never be a surprise. It can be anticipated, and it should be defused during the direct examination whenever possible. Anticipating the cross-examination reduces the impact of the cross-examination.

8. Inadequate Witness Preparation

Effective direct examinations require preparation—and there are no short-cuts. Many inexperienced trial lawyers do not spend enough time with witnesses preparing them for the direct examination. They do not spend enough time doing actual questions and answers in a courtroom or a courtroom atmosphere. As a result, the witness's testimony at trial does not come off as well as anticipated. The witness needs to be prepared and confident, but not so prepared that he appears rehearsed.

CHAPTER 6

CROSS-EXAMINATIONS

6.1 Introduction

Cross-examination is the opportunity to elicit favorable information and expose weaknesses in a witness's testimony. It can expose a witness's opportunity to observe, capacity to remember, and ability to recount. It can bring out mistakes, limitations, and omissions in the testimony. It can provide support for your positions and bolster the credibility of your witnesses. It can impeach by demonstrating the witness's bias, interest, or motive; revealing background details that attack the witness's truthfulness; and raising prior inconsistent statements.

Trial lawyers must know the law governing cross-examinations and understand the jury's perspective.

> ▶️ For an introduction to cross-examination, please watch Video E.1, "Mauet on Cross-Examination of Occurrence Witnesses."

They must understand the juror's attitudes and expectations about cross-examination and impeachment. They must be realistic about what cross-examination can accomplish and know the techniques that are necessary to achieve what they set out to accomplish. Done well, cross-examination can significantly erode or limit the testimony of many witnesses. Done poorly, it succeeds only in reinforcing the direct examination or, even worse, damaging your credibility and image.

6.2 The Law

Cross-examinations must comply with the applicable rules of evidence, which can be divided into two areas: cross-examination generally, and impeachment.

1. Cross-Examination

The information being brought out on cross-examination must be relevant, and determining relevance involves a two-step analysis. First, the information must be generally relevant under Federal Rules of Evidence (FRE) 401 and 402. Second, if relevant, the information must not be substantially outweighed by the FRE 403 concerns, and the information must not be excluded by the other relevancy rules in FRE 404 to 415 or the privilege rule in FRE 501. Because cross-examination is limited to the "subject matter" of the direct, which itself must meet the relevance requirements, general relevance is usually not an issue during cross-examination.

The information being brought out must also be reliable under FRE 801 to 807. This means that whenever the witness is asked to repeat in court a statement previously made out of court, the testimony must survive the scrutiny of the hearsay rules. The statement must either be nonhearsay or hearsay that falls within a recognized hearsay exception.

Cross-examination may use leading questions. FRE 611(c) provides that "[o]rdinarily, the court should allow leading questions" on cross-examination. This means that you can ask questions that suggest the desired answer to the witness.

Although the cross-examiner may use leading questions, this does not mean that anything goes. Under the ethics rules (Model Rule 3.4(e)), a lawyer may not "allude to any matter . . . that will not be supported by admissible evidence." This means that the cross-examiner cannot invent damaging facts and ask the witness to admit them. For example, you cannot ask a witness: "You had three double martinis just before witnessing the crash, right?" unless you have a good-faith basis to believe that this fact is true.

You cannot intimidate a witness by shouting, gesturing, or using other means to unfairly badger a witness. For example, you cannot simply walk up to the witness and yell your questions in his face. You cannot mischaracterize evidence or the witness's previous answers. For example, if the witness said that she pushed another person, you cannot then say: "After attacking the person, . . ." because this mischaracterizes what the witness said. You cannot assume facts not in evidence. For example, you cannot ask: "The skid marks were over ten feet long, right?" if there is no evidence that there were any skid marks. You cannot ask questions that are misleading, vague, compound, or simply unfair to expect a witness to answer.

How does the leading questions rule apply when the witness being examined is called as an adverse party or a witness identified with an adverse party? The lawyer calling the adverse party is permitted to use leading questions during the questioning. Thereafter, if the lawyer for the adverse party wishes to examine the party, many judges rule that she cannot use leading questions. Judges generally recognize that in this situation, the examination by the party's own lawyer is like a redirect examination, and leading questions are usually not allowed.

Cross-examination must be "within the scope" of the direct examination. FRE 611(b) provides, "Cross-examination should not go beyond the subject matter of the direct examination and matters affecting the witness's credibility." The federal rule, also called the *American* or *restricted scope of cross* rule, is followed in almost all states. (A few states follow the English rule, which allows cross-examination on any relevant matter.) If the cross-examiner wishes to go into "additional matters," this is discretionary with the judge, but if permitted must be conducted as if on direct examination (i.e., with nonleading questions). In trial lawyer's language, the cross-examiner "makes the witness his own."

2. Impeachment

Evidence law in the impeachment area focuses on two topics: impeachment procedures and impeachment methods.

a. Impeachment Procedures

Impeachment, which is bringing out matters that attack the witness's credibility, is always proper under FRE 611(b); this rule allows cross-examination on "matters affecting the witness's credibility." Otherwise proper impeachment is never objectionable as being beyond the scope of the direct. Under FRE 607, any party can impeach any witness, even the party that called the witness.

The rules are largely silent on the procedural requirements for impeachment, but most judges generally follow the established common law requirements. First, the cross-examiner must have a good-faith basis for raising any impeaching matter. That is, the cross-examiner must have a reasonable factual basis to believe the impeaching matter exists. It is unethical for the cross-examiner to suggest something to be true when there is no factual basis for the suggestion.

Second, impeaching matters generally should be raised during the cross-examination of that witness. This is sometimes called the confrontation or warning question requirement, and it makes impeachment fair and efficient. It gives the witness an opportunity to admit, deny, or explain the impeaching matter, which is fair to the witness. If the witness admits the impeaching matter, that ends the issue, which makes for efficient courtroom procedure.

Third, how significant must the impeachment be? Some judges in practice impose a materiality requirement. If the impeachment is marginal, some judges will sustain objections under a FRE 403 analysis.

Fourth, can impeachment be on "collateral" matters? The short answer is yes, because the collateral/noncollateral distinction has nothing to do with cross-examination. It deals solely with the question of whether, when a witness does not admit an impeaching matter, the cross-examiner is then permitted to prove up the impeaching matter with extrinsic evidence. Noncollateral impeachment is "important" impeachment under FRE 403 analysis and *may* or, in the view of some judges, *must* be proved up with extrinsic evidence; collateral impeachment is unimportant and *cannot* be proved up. When judges sustain objections to collateral impeachment, they are probably implicitly ruling that the matter is not materially impeaching under a FRE 403 analysis.

b. Impeachment Methods

The FRE and case law recognize seven categories of impeachment. The first five can be raised during cross-examination of lay witnesses.

- Bias, interest, and motive (no rule; case law)
- Prior inconsistent statements (FRE 613)
- Contradictory facts (no rule; case law)
- Prior convictions (FRE 609)
- Prior dishonest acts (FRE 608(b))
- Bad character for truthfulness (FRE 608(a))
- Treatises (FRE 803(18))

Bad character for truthfulness is not a cross-examination technique, and treatises can be used only during the cross-examination of experts. These techniques are discussed later.

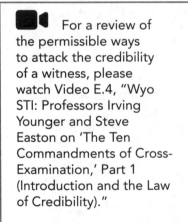 For a review of the permissible ways to attack the credibility of a witness, please watch Video E.4, "Wyo STI: Professors Irving Younger and Steve Easton on 'The Ten Commandments of Cross-Examination,' Part 1 (Introduction and the Law of Credibility)."

Bias, Interest, and Motive. The category of bias, interest, and motive, though not mentioned specifically by the FRE, is well recognized and may always be raised on cross-examination. Bias exists when a witness, through some relationship to the parties or attitude about the matter in dispute, has a frame of mind that might color her testimony. Interest exists when a witness's relationship to a party or the lawsuit is such that he stands to gain or lose, usually financially, from a particular outcome to the case, which may color his testimony. Motive exists when a witness has a particular reason, usually because of a history with one of the parties, to color her testimony a particular way. This category of impeachment also covers circumstances where a benefit of some kind, be it illegal like a bribe or legal like expert witness fees, has gone or will go from a party (or attorney) to a witness. Bias, interest, and motive are always considered noncollateral (important); if the witness does not admit them, the cross-examiner may prove them up later with extrinsic evidence.

Prior Inconsistent Statements. Prior inconsistent statements are the most commonly used impeachment method. Prior inconsistent statements can be by commission or omission. When a witness says one thing on the witness stand, but has said or written something different at an earlier time, this adversely affects the witness's credibility. When a witness says one thing on the stand, and has failed to say or write the same thing at an earlier time when the witness had such an opportunity, the witness's silence or omission adversely affects his credibility. Under FRE 613(a), the witness need not be shown his written statement before he can be cross-examined with it, but the opposing lawyer must still be shown the statement. Prior inconsistent statements are, as far as the collateral/noncollateral distinction is involved, taken on a case-by-case basis. If the witness does not admit it, the cross-examiner may prove up only the noncollateral (important) statements with extrinsic evidence.

The evidentiary status of prior inconsistent statements used to impeach is governed by FRE 801(d)(1). Prior inconsistent statements that were made under oath at a trial, hearing, or other proceeding are also admissible not just to impeach but also for their truth (as substantive evidence). Prior inconsistent statements that were not made under oath at a trial, hearing, or other proceeding are admitted only for the limited purpose of impeachment, but are not admissible for their truth. This means that whenever a witness is impeached with a prior inconsistent statement not made under oath, the jury must, on request of a party, be given an FRE 105 limiting instruction telling the jury that it may consider the statement only for the limited purpose of assessing the witness's credibility and for no other purpose.

Contradictory Facts. Contradictory facts, though not mentioned specifically by the FRE, constitute another firmly established impeachment method. Impeachment by contradiction occurs when a witness is asked to admit a fact that is inconsistent with what the witness has just testified about. Ethics rules are particularly important here. The cross-examiner cannot suggest a contradictory fact unless he has a good-faith basis for doing so and can prove the fact when required to do so.

Prior Convictions. Prior convictions are the basis of an important impeachment rule. Whenever a witness testifies, the witness's credibility can be attacked by showing that he has previously been convicted of certain crimes. The governing rule, FRE 609, has four core mandates. First, any witness can be impeached with any prior conviction (felony or misdemeanor) if a dishonest act or statement was an element of the crime. Second, a witness can be impeached with any prior conviction that is a felony in the jurisdiction where the conviction was entered, though there is a special balancing of probative value against prejudicial effect if the witness is a defendant in a criminal case. Third, evidence of any conviction is presumptively inadmissible if the conviction is more than ten years old (determined as of the date of conviction or the date of release from confinement, whichever is later), unless the judge determines that the probative effect of the prior conviction "substantially outweighs" its prejudicial effect. Prior convictions are always considered noncollateral (important). If the witness does not admit a prior conviction, the cross-examiner may prove it with extrinsic evidence.

Prior Dishonest Acts. Impeachment by prior dishonest acts is a permissible method recognized in most, but not all, jurisdictions. FRE 608(b) allows use of prior acts "in order to attack . . . the witness's character for truthfulness." However, if the witness does not admit the prior bad act, the rule expressly states that prior bad acts evidence may *not* be proved with extrinsic evidence. Although this is commonly referred to a "prior bad act" impeachment, only prior acts involving dishonesty, not other immorality, can be explored, so "prior dishonest act" impeachment is a better name.

Evidentiary objections during cross-examination are most common when the cross-examination delves into impeachment. Prepare accordingly. Assume that every question you ask will be objected to, and be prepared to show why the question and the information it seeks are proper.

c. Proving Up Unadmitted Important Impeachment

What happens if a witness is asked about an impeaching matter but does not admit it? The traditional analysis was based on the collateral/noncollateral distinction. If the impeaching matter is noncollateral and the witness denies it or equivocates, the cross-examiner is allowed to "prove up" the unadmitted impeachment with "extrinsic evidence" when the cross-examiner next has an opportunity to present evidence. Indeed, some believe the cross-examiner is required to do so, though this is rarely an issue because the cross-examiner is usually all too eager to do so if allowed. However, if the unadmitted impeaching matter is collateral, it cannot be proved up with extrinsic evidence.

Today, judges focus less on the technical collateral/noncollateral distinction and more on the importance of the unadmitted impeachment in determining whether it can or must be proven up. The real issue is judicial efficiency: In this case, given these issues and the significance of this witness, is the unadmitted impeaching matter important enough that it makes sense to use court time and require calling another witness or introducing another exhibit to prove up the impeaching matter? If the answer is yes, then the unadmitted impeaching matter may be proved through the later witness or exhibit. This importance analysis is actually an FRE 403 "wasting time" analysis.

Evidence law recognizes that some categories of impeachment are always important (noncollateral); others always unimportant (collateral); and others as being either, depending on case-specific circumstances. Bias, interest, and motive and prior convictions are always considered important. Prior dishonest acts are expressly classified as unimportant under FRE 608(b). Prior inconsistent statements and contradictory facts are taken on a case-by-case basis and are either important or unimportant, depending on the case-specific situation.

For a detailed discussion of the law on cross-examination and impeachment, *see* Mauet & Wolfson, *Trial Evidence* (7th ed., 2020).

6.3 The Jury's Perspective

Whenever a judge says: "Counsel, you may cross-examine," the jurors' interest heightens. From their perspective, cross-examinations should be chock full of moments of high drama. Jurors expect a mental duel—a fast-paced, exciting matching of wits where lawyers score points and witnesses break down quickly. After all, that's the way cross-examination is portrayed in movies and on television. That expectation, however, must be tempered by two other considerations. First, jurors do not like unwarranted aggression in the courtroom. Lawyers cannot be tough on witnesses without showing that their toughness is justified by the witness's testimony or conduct. Second, in cross-examination, ties go to the witness. After all, lawyers are supposed to be the courtroom experts, so any witness who holds her own during cross-examination will have won the contest in the jury's eyes.

Jurors, like all persons, soon forget most of the details of any cross-examination, the actual words of specific questions and answers. They do, however, remember the tone of the cross-examination and retain an overall impression of the examination and the witness. How you ask questions, your tone of voice, and your body language all convey the impressions about the witness that you want the jurors to adopt. The impressions, of course, are also driven by the content of the cross-examination, but cross-examination is about creating lasting impressions, not eliciting factual details.

Finally, jurors form impressions quickly, about both the witness and the cross-examiner. This means that the first few minutes of any cross-examination must capture the jurors' interest, show that the cross-examination is bringing out important new information, and create an appropriate atmosphere and tone for the rest of the examination. If you do not do this speedily, jurors will quickly conclude that you have nothing to add to what they already know from the witness, and they will tune out.

Effective trial lawyers understand that what they do during cross-examination, and how they do it, is largely driven by the jurors' expectations and interests. Good cross-examinations create impressions and convey emotions. They grab the jurors' attention, make the first point quickly, raise only meaningful matters, and demonstrate that this cross-examination adds something important to what they already know. They are efficient and make their points before jurors lose interest. They are realistic, and only attempt to do what is attainable and acceptable to the jurors.

Before cross-examining a witness, always ask three questions: Did the witness hurt you? Can the witness help you? Can you hurt the witness?

6.4 Purpose, Order, and Structure of Cross-Examination

Should you cross-examine a particular witness? Always ask: Can the witness help you? If the witness hurt you, can you hurt the witness? Unless you can answer yes to one of these questions, there's little point in cross-examining. An ineffective cross-examination—ineffective because it has no clear purpose—merely reinforces the direct, enhances the witness's credibility, and annoys the jurors when they realize you have nothing useful to add and are wasting their time.

> ▶ For an overview of cross-examination, please watch Video E.2., "Wyo STI: Brief Introduction to Cross-Examination."

Cross-examination can accomplish three things: (1) bring out facts helpful to your side, (2) attack or limit parts of the witness's testimony, and (3) attack the witness himself. If you are going to do all three things, you should usually proceed in that order. Start by bringing out helpful information, either by emphasizing facts the witness has already testified about on direct, or by bringing out new facts the witness knows but did not disclose on direct. Because bringing out helpful information is not an attack on the witness, this can usually be done in a neutral, nonconfrontational way. The witness will be more willing to testify to the new information if your attitude is pleasant.

After that, consider attacking specific parts of the witness's testimony. This includes exposing weaknesses in the witness's perception, memory, and ability to recount the events. It involves bringing out important prior inconsistent statements that contradict what the witness said on direct and showing that the witness's testimony is at odds with other evidence. Is the witness confused, mistaken, or forgetful? Or is the witness intentionally changing or fabricating her testimony? Your attitude should reflect the reasons for the changed testimony.

Finally, consider attacking the witness himself. Does the witness have a bias, interest, or motive to testify a certain way? Does the witness have an admissible prior conviction? Has the witness committed a prior bad act probative of truthfulness? Because these matters attack the witness's credibility, your attitude should reflect the attitude you want the jurors to adopt about the witness.

Next, keep your cross-examination structure simple and realistic. Cross-examination is largely the art of hitting singles and doubles; attempting to hit home runs usually leads to strikeouts. Pick the two or three best important points you can safely raise during the cross-examination. Too many points overload the jurors with information and dilute the impact of your best points. A good test is: Will I be talking about this point during my closing argument? If not, it usually means that it is not important enough to develop during cross-examination.

After that, arrange your points for maximum impact. The two best points should be at the beginning and the end of the cross-examination. This reflects the principles of primacy and recency. People remember best what they hear first and last.

Start big. Jurors will only give you one or two minutes to establish something important before they conclude that nothing significant will come out of the cross-examination and stop paying attention. Jurors are always asking: Why should I listen? Why should I make the effort? Cross-examination has to give jurors something good quickly to demonstrate that cross-examination will be worth it. Too many lawyers start weak. For example, saying: "I just have a few questions to ask on cross-examination," or "There are some things you said on direct that I didn't understand," merely tells the jurors not to expect much, or suggests that cross will simply be a rehash of the direct. Instead, start with something that grabs attention and tells the jurors that cross-examination will be interesting, informative, even exciting. For example, asking: "You didn't see the crash until *after* it happened, did you?" establishes something important immediately. Asking: "You're a convicted felon, right?" grabs attention immediately.

Your cross-examination must also end big. The last thing you bring out during cross-examination will have staying power, so it must be something important. Let the jurors know that you are ending, and let your tone of voice and attitude signal that this is your last important point. For example, questions such as: "You never saw a gun, knife, or weapon of any kind in Mr. Johnson's hands that evening, did you?," "All of this happened in *one or two seconds*, right?," "And you were *over 200 feet away* when it happened, isn't that right?," establish important points.

Cross-examination is about creating impressions and conveying emotions. Jurors may forget the details of the cross-examination, but they will remember the impressions formed during the cross about the testimony, the witness, and the lawyer.

6.5 Language of Cross-Examination

Cross-examination is also about control, and to control the witness's answers you need to control your questions. A good test is the 90 percent rule: During cross-examination you should be doing almost all of the talking (90 percent). Each time the witness gives a long answer, you have given up control. So, how do you control witnesses, most of whom don't want to be controlled?

1. Lead

First, ask leading questions. A leading question is one that suggests the desired answer. A question can be leading by form or by tone. For example, asking: "You signed the contract, right?" is obviously leading. It suggests that the desired answer is "yes." Making a declarative statement and adding "right?," "correct?," "true?," or similar language makes the question leading. A question can also be leading through inflection and gestures. For example, asking: "You signed the contract?" and using rising intonation and nodding your head also suggests that the desired answer is "yes."

> ◼◀ For an in-depth discussion of how to conduct cross-examination, please see Video E.5, "Wyo STI: Professors Irving Younger and Steve Easton on `The Ten Commandments of Cross-Examination,' Part 2 (How to Conduct Cross-Examination)."

You are not required to end all of your questions, which should actually be statements of fact, with "correct?" or "right?" Indeed, doing so quickly becomes monotonous, even annoying. With experience, you can even sprinkle in a few nonleading questions when it is safe to have the witness talk more freely (for example, when you are bringing out favorable facts). However, when you are asking questions about important matters, you should always control the exchange, and control begins with leading questions.

Example:

Q: The light was red when the two cars collided, right?
A: Yes.
Q: It was dark at the time?
A: Yes.
Q: Raining?
A: Yes.
Q: No street lights on that corner?
A: Right.
Q: And you were over 100 feet from the corner when the two cars collided?
A: Yes.

Avoid confusing negatives. For example, if you ask: "You never did enter the store, did you not?," neither a yes or no answer is clear. Instead, make an affirmative statement of fact and ask the witness to agree with it. This conditions the witness, and the jurors, to expect "yes" answers to your questions. It also conditions the jurors to look to *you* for all the facts, rather than the witness. In essence, you testify, while the witness merely ratifies.

Cross-examination requires active listening. Listen to the witness's answer carefully, then ask the next question. Too many cross-examiners are too busy thinking about their next question to listen carefully to the witness's answer. Focus on the answer you actually get, not the answer you expected or hoped to get. That answer will determine what your next question should be.

2. Factual

Second, make it factual. Use simple nouns and verbs. Avoid adverbs and adjectives, the characterizations that witnesses always quibble with. Characterizations are for you to make during closing arguments.

Example:

> Q: You saw the cars before the crash, right?
> A: Yes.
> Q: The Ford was going south on Main?
> A: Yes.
> Q: And the Chevy was going north on Main?
> A: Yes.
> Q: The Chevy stopped in the intersection?
> A: Yes.
> Q: The Chevy's left turn signal was blinking?
> A: Yes.
> Q: It then made a left turn?
> A: Yes.
> Q: The Chevy then collided with the Ford in the intersection, right?
> A: Yes.
> Q: At the time of the collision, the light for Main was yellow, right?
> A: Yes.

These are all factual questions. They don't ask the witness to agree that the Chevy was going "too fast," made an "illegal turn," "failed to yield" the right of way, or turned "quickly," all characterizations and conclusions that usually should be kept out of cross-examinations. These are the "quibble words" that witnesses rarely agree with. Those conclusions are what you will argue during closing argument, based on the facts you developed during the cross-examination.

3. Simple

Third, make it simple. Cross-examination is most effective if the questions are short, using basic nouns and verbs and avoiding complex vocabulary or structure.

Example:

> Q: Mr. Hanson, you attended the board meeting on June 1, 2020?
> A: Yes, I did.
> Q: That meeting started at 10:00 in the morning?
> A: Yes.
> Q: In addition to you, Mr. Baldwin was also there, right?
> A: Yes.
> Q: And Ms. Williams?
> A: Yes.
> Q: And Mr. Jackson?
> A: Yes.
> Q: The meeting lasted until noon?
> A: About then.
> Q: All four of you signed the contract, marked Plaintiff's Exhibit No. 2, that you have in front of you, right?
> A: Yes.
> Q: In fact, you saw Mr. Baldwin, Ms. Williams, and Mr. Jackson sign their names on the contract, right?
> A: Yes.

This simple language is better than using lawyer words such as "executing" or "ratifying" the contract.

4. Bit by Bit

Fourth, make your points bit by bit. Cross-examination is in part the art of establishing a point through several sequential questions, rather than jumping to the end right away. Asking questions that bring out information little by little makes it harder for the witness to deny or resist any of the questions that lead to the conclusion you want to reach.

Example:

Q: Ms. Adams, you've driven on Main Street many times?
A: Yes, that's the way I drive to and from work.
Q: You've been driving that route for several years?
A: Yes.
Q: You never saw a car crash at Main and Elm before, did you?
A: No.
Q: And you weren't expecting to see one there on June 1, were you?
A: No.
Q: This crash was a surprise to you, wasn't it?
A: It certainly was.
Q: It happened suddenly?
A: Yes.
Q: And it happened quickly?
A: Yes.

Avoid "why" questions. Why questions merely ask witnesses to give lengthy explanations, something that almost never works during cross-examination. Why questions give up control, and control is the hallmark of a good cross-examination.

Avoid asking what the witness "testified on direct examination." This invites the witness to disagree with your understanding of what the witness previously said.

Example:

Q: You testified on direct examination that the car was "approximately 40 feet from the intersection when the light turned yellow," right?
A: That's not exactly what I said.

The cross-examiner then loses control as she debates with the witness over what the witness said. Instead, avoid the "testified" question and rephrase it. Asking: "You say the car was about 40 feet from the intersection when the light turned yellow, right?" makes the same point without giving the witness an opportunity to quibble or nit-pick with you.

Avoid responding to witnesses who answer your question with a question. Witnesses who do this are usually trying to figure out where your questions are going and are trying to anticipate you.

Example:

Q: The Chevy entered the intersection before the Ford, right?
A: Are you asking me if the Chevy had the right of way?

When this happens, let the witness know you are not going to play this game. The best approach is simply to repeat your question (e.g., "My question is: The Chevy entered the intersection before the Ford, right?"). This lets the witness know that he cannot avoid answering a question you want answered.

Repetition can be an important part of cross-examination, but use it selectively. An effective way to use repetition is to use parallel phrasing in your questions to repeat and highlight an important point.

Example:

> Q: Mr. Jackson, you were carrying a gun that night, right?
> A: Yes.
> Q: The gun was a .38 caliber revolver?
> A: Yes.
> Q: You had that .38 in your pants pocket?
> A: Yes.
> Q: Where no one could see it?
> A: Yes.
> Q: It was concealed?
> A: I guess so.
> Q: You had that concealed .38 when you drove up to the store?
> A: Yes.
> Q: You had that concealed .38 when you went into the store?
> A: Yes.
> Q: And you had that concealed .38 when you walked up to the counter, right?
> A: Yes.

Another way to use repetition is to loop back when the witness gives a good answer and incorporate the good answer into your next question.

Example:

> Q: You said, "Give me the money," right?
> A: Right.
> Q: When you said "Give me the money," you intended to scare him, right?
> A: I guess so.
> Q: When you said "Give me the money," you intended to get the money from him?
> A: Yes.
> Q: And when you said "Give me the money," you intended to do whatever it took to get the money from him, right?
> A: I don't know.

Repetition is effective when it reinforces an important point or highlights a memorable phrase while also adding new information, but use it selectively. Constantly repeating points will draw objections ("asked and answered" or "repetitive"), and quickly bores and annoys jurors.

5. Stop

Finally, stop. Stop before you go too far. When you have established the facts that support your point, the temptation is to continue and try to force the witness to admit your conclusion. This almost never works. Save the conclusion for closing arguments, when the witness is gone. This division of labor usually works well and is safe. Cross-examination brings out the facts, closing argument brings out the conclusions.

How can you tell when you have gone too far? It's obvious when the witness gives you a bad answer that undoes the good work you just did. For example, if the cross-examination has shown that the crash happened quickly and unexpectedly and the witness was 100 feet away when it happened, you will be tempted to ask a conclusion question like: "So, you never got a good look at the actual crash, did you?" And the witness's likely response would be a bad answer: "No, I got a good look at it." Further questions then usually degenerate into argument between the lawyer and the witness, with the jurors usually siding with the witness. Save this conclusion for closing arguments, when you discuss the witness's testimony and summarize it by saying "he never got a good look at the actual crash." The conclusory statement that will cause trouble during cross-examination will help you in closing.

Questions that ask a witness to agree with a conclusion often start with "so," "therefore," "in other words," or "you would agree with me that." That's the signal that you are about to ask the witness to agree with a conclusion. Instead, just stop. Don't ask that one question too many; move on to something else. Later, during closing arguments, ask that question as a rhetorical question and answer it yourself, the way you want it answered.

6.6 Cross-Examination Topics

There are several topics you should consider when you plan cross-examination. There should be a checklist for every witness. (The topic of impeachment is discussed in the next section.)

- Favorable facts from direct
- Favorable facts not yet mentioned
- What witness must admit
- What witness should admit
- Attacks on the witness's perception
- Attacks on the witness's memory
- Attacks on the witness's ability to communicate
- Attacks on the witness's conduct
- The "no ammunition" cross

1. Favorable Facts from Direct

First, consider repeating favorable facts from the direct examination. It's a rare direct examination that does not bring out some facts that help the cross-examiner. Having the witness repeat those favorable facts highlights them for the jurors, who will remember the facts better because you repeated them. This does *not* mean you should repeat the entire direct examination; that is a common and serious mistake. Instead, note specific *facts* that the witness stated during the direct examination that help you, then have the witness admit those facts again during cross-examination.

Example:

> A witness has testified that she witnessed a vehicle collision during a rainstorm in the evening from a distance of about 100 feet. The cross-examination can repeat those specific facts, which cast doubt on her ability to see the details of how the collision actually happened.
>
> Q: Ms. Davis, this accident happened about 9:00 p.m.?
> A: Yes.
> Q: It was dark outside?
> A: Well, the sun was down.
> Q: It was nighttime?
> A: Yes.
> Q: Cars had their lights on?
> A: Yes.
> Q: And it was also raining?
> A: Yes.
> Q: Raining hard, right?
> A: It was coming down pretty fast, yes.
> Q: And you were about 100 feet away when it happened, right?
> A: That's right.

At this point, stop. Don't try to get the witness to admit that she was too far away to see clearly exactly what happened. The witness has just admitted specific facts that lead to this conclusion. Save that conclusion for closing arguments.

2. Favorable Facts Not Yet Mentioned

Second, consider what favorable facts the witness can provide that the witness knows but did not testify about on direct examination. Frequently the direct examiner does not go into details that the witness can testify about, usually because those details don't help. This is often a cue to the cross-examiner to get into those details.

Example:

> A witness has testified that he attended a meeting of several employees at his company. On direct, the witness testified about the fact of the meeting, but did not go into the actual conversations or qualify any of the business records made about the meeting. The cross-examiner can bring out the actual conversations of the employees in the meeting and can use the witness to qualify any business records created about that meeting.
>
> Q: Ms. Wilkins, the minutes of that board meeting were recorded, right?
> A: Yes.
> Q: That means that your company created a record of who attended the meeting, who spoke, and who said what?
> A: Yes.
> Q: One of the people at the meeting was Charles Crowe?
> A: Yes.
> Q: Mr. Crowe spoke during that meeting?

A: Yes.

Q: And during that meeting, Mr. Crowe said: "We might get in trouble with the regulators if we try to do this," right?

A: He said something like that.

Frequently you can limit the witness's testimony by showing that the witness was not present at an important event and has no firsthand knowledge of the event.

Example:

Q: Mr. Smith, you were not present at the board meeting held on June 1, 2020, right?

A: That's right.

Q: In fact, you were out of town that day?

A: Yes.

Q: You didn't return to your office until three days after the board meeting?

A: Yes.

3. What Witness Must Admit

Third, consider what the witness must admit. When witnesses have been interviewed or deposed, there is usually a paper record—a report, written statement, or question and answer transcript—containing their prior statements. Asking them to admit in court facts that they have already stated in their prior statements is a fertile source of additional favorable facts. If the witness does not admit the facts, you can always use the prior statements to impeach the witness.

Example:

A witness gave a statement to an investigator that he was "not sure" he could identify the person who robbed him because it "happened very quickly" and it was "pretty dark." The witness's statement is recorded in the investigator's report. On cross-examination you can simply ask the witness to admit those facts, knowing that you can impeach the witness with his prior statement if he now testifies differently. You can also remind the witness that you have the investigator's statement and are aware of it before you cross-examine on those facts. That makes it more likely the witness will not fight you over these facts.

Q: Mr. Lopez, two days after the robbery, you talked to an investigator about the robbery?

A: Yes.

Q: That was Mr. Taylor?

A: I think so.

Q: And he was taking notes on what you were saying?

A: It looked like he was.

Q: Mr. Lopez, the robbery happened quickly, right?

A: Yes.

Q: It was dark when it happened, right?

A: Yes.

Q: And you told Mr. Taylor you weren't sure you would be able to identify the person who robbed you, right?
A: Yes.

4. What Witness Should Admit

Fourth, consider what the witness should admit. Remember that jurors have
attitudes about how common events usually happen and will assume that the
event on which the trial is based happened the same way. In short, the way things
usually happen is the way this event probably happened. You can use this to your
advantage during cross-examination. Ask the witness to agree that something happened the way it usually happens; if the witness disagrees, the jurors will doubt the
witness. A common situation in which this technique is useful is when a witness to
an event wasn't expecting the event, and wasn't paying particular attention to it.

Example:

Q: The block where the collision happened, you walk on that block to
and from work every day, right?
A: Yes.
Q: Almost every day nothing unusual happens while you walk to and
from work?
A: That's right.
Q: You don't expect anything unusual to happen, do you?
A: No, I don't.
Q: And you didn't expect a collision between the two cars to happen
that day, did you?
A: No.

At this point, stop. You've established that the witness wasn't paying any particular attention to his surroundings. Don't ask the next question: "So, you
weren't paying attention, were you?" That's the point you want to save for closing arguments.

After obtaining favorable facts, consider how you can attack the witness's testimony. With eyewitnesses, cross-examination can frequently expose flaws in the witness's perception, memory, and communication. This cross-examination, the most
common kind with eyewitnesses, questions or attacks the reliability of the witness's
observations. As always, your attitude is an important part of the cross-examination.
It shows the jurors how you feel about the witness's testimony and how jurors
should feel about it.

5. Attacks on the Witness's Perception

When you can make an important point by doing so, attack the witness's perception. Cross-examination can expose weaknesses and flaws in the witness's ability to
perceive an event accurately. For example, if the witness was not wearing her prescription glasses, or has a condition that affects her vision, this should be brought out.

Example:

Q: Ms. Abraham, you wear glasses, correct?
A: Some of the time.

Q: But you didn't have them on at the time you saw the crash, did you?
A: No, I was just walking to my car.
Q: Your glasses correct for nearsightedness?
A: That's right.
Q: That means you can't see things well that are some distance away?
A: I can see them, I just see them better with my glasses.
Q: Your driver's license requires you to drive with prescription glasses, correct?
A: Yes.
Q: You wear your glasses when watching movies?
A: Yes.
Q: You wear your glasses when watching TV?
A: Yes.

If the witness was a substantial distance from the event, this should be brought out.

Example:

Q: The man you saw was about half a block away?
A: About that.
Q: And from that distance you think he was holding a knife in his hand?
A: That's what it looked like.
Q: Mr. Thompson, there are eight blocks to a mile in this city, isn't that so?
A: That sounds about right.
Q: Each block is one-eighth of a mile?
A: Right.
Q: That makes each block 220 yards long?
A: That sounds right.
Q: That makes half a block 110 yards?
A: Yes.
Q: This man you saw was 110 yards away?
A: Yes.
Q: That's further than the length of a football field, isn't it?
A: Yes.

If the event happened quickly, this is important to bring out.

Example:

The witness has testified that he estimated the speed of a car at 50 to 60 miles per hour. The cross-examination will show that the witness had very little time to see the car, and too little time to accurately estimate its speed.

Q: The car you saw going through the intersection, it was going from east to west?
A: Yes.
Q: You were looking north at the time?
A: Yes.
Q: You were about 100 feet from the intersection?
A: About that.
Q: Mr. Bryson, there are office buildings on each corner of that intersection, right?

A: Yes.

Q: The only time you saw that car was after it passed one office building and before it reached the next office building on the other side of the intersection, right?

A: That's right.

Q: You saw that car one or two seconds, isn't that right?

A: I'm not sure, but maybe.

If the case involves identification, showing that the witness had only a brief opportunity to see the person's face is often critical. This is a common cross-examination topic in criminal cases in which the central issue is identification.

Example:

Q: Mr. Ginsberg, you were sitting at the bus stop at the southeast corner of Main and Division, waiting for the Main Street bus, when the shooting happened?

A: That's right.

Q: Before you heard the shots, what were you doing?

A: I was looking at the advertisements on the sides of the bus stop shelter.

Q: When you heard the shots, you then looked around?

A: Yes.

Q: It was then that you saw two boys run right past you on Main?

A: Yes.

Q: They then ran west on Division Street, right?

A: That's right.

Q: You watched them run across Main?

A: Yes.

Q: And west on Division?

A: Yes.

Q: When the boys ran across Main and west on Division, they were running away from you, right?

A: That's right.

Q: And during this time you saw the two boys from their back sides, right?

A: That's right.

If the lighting conditions were poor, bring out this fact.

Example:

The victim has identified the defendant as the person who robbed him in an alley.

Q: Mr. Anderson, you say there was light in the alley where you were robbed, is that right?

A: Yes.

Q: The light came from street lights, right?

A: Yes.

Q: Those street lights were along Maple Street?

A: Yes.

Q: There weren't any street lights in the alley itself, were there?

A: Not in the alley.
Q: During the robbery in that alley, you were facing Maple Street?
A: Yes.
Q: Toward the lights?
A: Yes.
Q: The robber was facing you?
A: Yes.
Q: He was facing away from the street lights?
A: Yes.

At this point, stop. You've established that the light was not shining on the robber's face. Don't ask that one question too many: "So, you couldn't really see the robber's face, could you?" because the witness will give a bad answer. Instead, draw that conclusion during closing arguments.

If the witness's view of the event was obstructed, or there were other distractions, this is important.

Example:

A police officer has testified that he saw a minor buy a bottle of liquor at a liquor store.

Q: Officer Jones, you were watching what was going on inside the liquor store from outside the store, right?
A: Right.
Q: In fact, you were watching the liquor store from across the street?
A: Right.
Q: That street, Main Street, is a busy street?
A: It can be.
Q: You were watching the liquor store around 5:30 in the afternoon, right?
A: Yes.
Q: That's during the afternoon rush hour, isn't it?
A: Sure.
Q: Whenever a car or truck went by, it would block your view of the liquor store, right?
A: Well, maybe for a second or two.
Q: Let's talk about the store itself. There are plate-glass windows on the street side of the liquor store, right?
A: That's right.
Q: Those were the plate-glass windows you were looking through?
A: That's right.
Q: There were posters in the windows?
A: Some.
Q: There were decals in the windows?
A: Some.
Q: And there were flashing neon beer signs in the windows, isn't that right?
A: Yes.

If the witness was focusing on other things, this is frequently important.

Example:

> Q: The man who walked into the store immediately said: "It's a robbery, give me the money," right?
> A: That's right.
> Q: You then looked up, and he was right across the counter from you?
> A: Yes.
> Q: And you saw he had a handgun?
> A: He certainly did.
> Q: You were naturally worried about the gun?
> A: Of course.
> Q: He told you to get the money, right?
> A: Yes.
> Q: And you did get the money?
> A: Yes. That's how we've been trained.
> Q: While you're getting the money, you're looking at the drawer in the cash register?
> A: Yes.
> Q: But you're still worried about the gun, aren't you?
> A: Yes.
> Q: You keep looking to see what the gun is doing?
> A: Yes.
> Q: That gun is pointing at you, just above the counter, right?
> A: Yes.
> Q: Describe the gun.
> A: It looked big, it was a revolver, it was made out of dark metal.
> Q: How about the handle?
> A: It was made out of wood, a brown wood.
> Q: And whenever you moved, the gun would follow you?
> A: Yes.
> Q: And then the man grabbed the money from you, turned, and ran out the door, right?
> A: Yes.

In all these examples, the cross-examination has called into question the witness's ability to observe the event by demonstrating a limited opportunity to observe. This kind of cross-examination might be the most common during trials.

6. Attacks on the Witness's Memory

Consider attacking the witness's memory, but be careful in doing so because witnesses often claim a strong memory. If there are reasons why the witness's memory is questionable, this should be brought out. A common approach is to demonstrate that the event is a common event that should not particularly stand out in the witness's mind.

Example:

> Q: Officer Wilson, as part of the drug unit, you make arrests frequently, don't you?
> A: Unfortunately, that's true.

Q: This case involves marijuana?
A: That's right.
Q: You made the arrest in a public park?
A: Yes.
Q: That arrest happened almost a year ago?
A: Yes.
Q: You've arrested other persons during the past year?
A: Of course.
Q: How many?
A: Probably about three a week.
Q: Over the past year that adds up to around 150 arrests?
A: Yes.
Q: Some involved arrests in public parks?
A: Yes.
Q: Some involved marijuana?
A: Yes.

Example:

Plaintiff has sued a real estate brokerage, claiming that he asked the real estate agent to have the residence he bought inspected for termites. The agent has testified that this conversation never occurred.

Q: You claim Mr. Ellison never talked to you about inspecting for termites in the building?
A: That's right.
Q: Ms. Johnson, how many real estate clients do you have right now?
A: Oh, it depends, but I'd estimate around 100.
Q: How many did you have in June 2020?
A: About the same.
Q: You talk to all of those clients?
A: Of course.
Q: And you talk to each of those clients many times?
A: Not all of them, but most of them.
Q: Those conversations cover several common topics, right?
A: That's true.
Q: Such as financing and appraisals?
A: Yes.
Q: The conversations often deal with home inspections, right?
A: Yes.
Q: And one of the things that is frequently done in homes is a termite inspection, right?
A: That's often done, yes.
Q: You've talked to buyers about termite inspections dozens of times during the past year, haven't you?
A: I suppose so.

Again, this is the safe place to stop. Asking the next question: "You can't possibly remember all the buyers you've talked to about termite inspections, can you?" will get a bad answer or a plausible explanation, neither of which helps you.

If the witness is relying entirely on memory, bring out the fact that the witness made no record of the event and gave no statements near the time of the event.

Example:

> The witness is the manager of an apartment complex and handles all the leases. She has testified that she never orally agreed to make repairs to an apartment, as the plaintiff claims.

> Q: How many apartments are in your complex?
> A: About 150.
> Q: You're in charge of leasing all of them?
> A: That's right.
> Q: You do all the negotiations with all the tenants?
> A: That's right.
> Q: Over the past 18 months, how many times have you negotiated with tenants?
> A: Probably around 200.
> Q: This conversation with Ms. Rosenberg, you had it the same day she signed the standard lease agreement?
> A: I believe so.
> Q: You didn't make a memorandum of what the two of you said, did you?
> A: No.
> Q: You made no recording of that conversation, did you?
> A: No.
> Q: And you put nothing in your files about that conversation, did you?
> A: No.

If the witness has been interviewed by investigators or lawyers or has met and discussed the event with other witnesses, you can sometimes demonstrate that the witness's memory and recall have been influenced by these outside sources.

Example:

> Q: Mrs. Higgins, the collision on June 1, 2020, happened while you were outside waiting at the bus stop for the school bus to drop off your children, right?
> A: Yes.
> Q: There were several other parents waiting with you?
> A: Yes, it's the same group every school day.
> Q: The other parents that were there, they saw the collision too, didn't they?
> A: Yes.
> Q: Since that time, you've talked to the other parents about what happened that afternoon, right?
> A: Well, we sometimes talk about it.
> Q: About what happened, right?
> A: Yes.
> Q: How many times have you talked with the other parents since you knew you would be called to be witnesses during the trial?
> A: Maybe two or three times.

7. Attacks on the Witness's Ability to Communicate

Third, expose weaknesses and inconsistencies in the witness's communication abilities. Some witnesses have trouble communicating what they experienced and describing it accurately. If so, cross-examination can reveal these flaws.

Example:

> Q: Mr. Massaro, you say the car was going about 30 miles per hour, is that right?
> A: Yes.
> Q: And you watched it go from Washington to Jefferson Street, right?
> A: Yes.
> Q: A distance of one block?
> A: Yes.
> Q: Here in Chicago there are eight blocks per mile?
> A: That's right.
> Q: How long did it take that car to go the one block from Washington to Jefferson Street?
> A: I'd say ten seconds.

At this point, stop. You have established an important inconsistency which you can explain and use advantageously during closing arguments. (If the car was going 30 m.p.h., it would have traveled the one block—one-eighth of a mile—in about 14 seconds. The witness's 10 seconds means that the car was going about 45 m.p.h.) Witnesses frequently are "sure" of what they saw, but the details they also are "sure" of are inconsistent.

8. Attacks on the Witness's Conduct

Attacking the witness's conduct is another option. Sometimes witnesses say one thing, but act inconsistently. If so, cross-examination can effectively highlight the inconsistent conduct.

Example:

> Q: Mr. Byrd, you claim the sex with Ms. Williams was with her consent, right?
> A: It was.
> Q: But you heard the next day the police were looking for you, isn't that true?
> A: Well, I heard they wanted to talk to me.
> Q: The police came by your house and talked to your mother, didn't they?
> A: I wasn't there.
> Q: You heard about it from your mother?
> A: Right.
> Q: But you didn't call the police, did you?
> A: No.
> Q: And you didn't go home for three days, did you?
> A: No.
> Q: And you didn't go to work for three days, did you?
> A: No.
> Q: Instead, you stayed at a friend's house, isn't that right?
> A: Yes.

Q: And you didn't tell your mother where you were, did you?
A: No.

9. The "No Ammunition" Cross

Finally, what do you do if you have no effective ammunition with which to cross-examine the witness? The safe course is simply to stand up and say: "No cross-examination, your honor." That's the safe course, the one you should usually take. However, lawyers sometimes conduct a short "no ammunition" or "apparent" cross-examination. While this is usually a mistake, there are sometimes small points to be made.

Example:

A character witness has just testified that in her personal opinion the defendant is a peaceful person.

Q: Mrs. Johnson, you're a neighbor of the defendant?
A: Yes, we live on the same block.
Q: You're a friend of the defendant as well?
A: Not close friends, but we're friendly.
Q: You didn't receive a subpoena to come to court today, did you?
A: No.
Q: The defendant asked you to come?
A: Actually it was his lawyer.
Q: And you agreed?
A: Sure.
Q: You wanted to help?
A: Sure.
Q: Mrs. Johnson, did you talk to the police about what you're saying today?
A: No.
Q: But a police investigator came to your house a few days ago, right?
A: Yes.
Q: He asked you if you were willing to tell him what you knew about this case and about the defendant, right?
A: He said he'd like to know what I was going to testify about.
Q: But you didn't tell him, did you?
A: No.
Q: Or any other police officer, did you?
A: No.
Q: You didn't tell me, did you?
A: No.
Q: You didn't tell anyone in my office, the county attorney's office, did you?
A: No.
Q: But you told the defense lawyer, didn't you?
A: Yes.

6.7 Impeachment

Impeachment discredits the witness. It is a direct attack on a witness's testimony or the witness himself. The FRE and case law generally recognize seven impeachment categories:

- Bias, interest, and motive (no rule; case law)
- Prior inconsistent statements (FRE 613)
- Contradictory facts (no rule; case law)
- Prior convictions (FRE 609)
- Prior dishonest acts (FRE 608(b))
- Character for untruthfulness (FRE 608(a))
- Treatises (FRE 803(18))

In addition, FRE 806 governs impeaching out-of-court declarants.

The evidence rules and case law governing impeachment are discussed in Section 6.2. This section discusses the techniques lawyers should use to make impeachment effective.

Impeachment attacks the witness's testimony or the witness directly, but it is effective only if the jurors attach significance to it when it happens and remember it when they deliberate. For impeachment to be effective, lawyers must employ proper techniques and display appropriate attitudes. In addition, the impeachment must also be significant. Minor facts or inconsistencies have no impact or, worse, suggest that you have nothing significant to expose during your cross-examination. Impeach only if the jurors will perceive the impeachment as important.

> ▶ For a review of impeachment, please watch Video E.7, "Mauet on Impeachment."

1. Bias, Interest, and Motive

Bias, interest, and motive refer to relationships to the parties or the issues in the lawsuit that cause the witness, consciously or subconsciously, to slant her testimony toward one side.

Bias is a predisposition causing a witness to have a preference for one of the parties in the case. For example, a police officer testifying in a criminal case may have a bias toward the prosecution; a doctor testifying in a medical malpractice case may have a bias in favor of the defendant hospital. A witness may be related to, work for, or be a personal friend of the plaintiff or defendant. In these situations, the bias colors the witness's testimony.

Interest is a stake, usually but not always financial, in the outcome of the trial that causes a witness to prefer one side over the other. For example, the witness may be a business partner of the plaintiff, or the plaintiff may owe the witness substantial money. A witness may be an employee of a corporate party. A witness may work for an insurance company that insures the defendant. In these situations, the witness's interest in the parties or outcome of the case influences the witness's testimony.

Motive is a person's predisposition to testify a certain way because of personal reasons, such as love, hatred, or revenge. For example, if a witness was fired from his job, he has a motive to testify adversely to his former employer. If a witness is a jilted lover, he has a reason to testify adversely to the ex-paramour. In these situations, the witness's motive is a powerful influence causing his testimony to be slanted or even falsified.

Corruption is also within the general bias category. It is sometimes considered a subset of motive. It exists when a party or attorney has provided some sort of benefit to the witness. One possibility is an illegal benefit, like a bribe. More often, the benefit will be legal, such as the fees paid to a retained expert witness. You can explore both illegal and legal benefits on cross-examination, as long as you have a good faith basis for believing the opposing party or attorney provided (or will provide) a benefit to the witness.

Bringing out bias, interest, and motive can be easily done. Simply ask the witness, using leading questions, to admit the pertinent facts, accompanied with the appropriate attitude in your tone of voice and demeanor.

Example (Bias):

> Q: Mr. Asher, you work at Johnson Mills?
> A: Yes.
> Q: That's the defendant in this case?
> A: Yes.
> Q: The defense called you as a witness?
> A: That's right.
> Q: You weren't subpoenaed to come to court today?
> A: No.
> Q: You came because the defense asked you to come?
> A: Yes.
> Q: You've been working for Johnson Mills for over ten years, right?
> A: That's right.
> Q: And you plan to keep working for them, right?
> A: Yes.

At this point, stop. You've made the point that the witness is a captive who will say what the defense wants him to say. Don't ask the one question too many: "So, you're just trying to help your company, right?" Save that point for closing argument.

Example (Interest):

> Q: Ms. Adams, you're a business partner with the plaintiff?
> A: We have mutual interests, yes.
> Q: In fact, you started a small business together?
> A: Yes.
> Q: That business is called Investment Consulting?
> A: Yes.
> Q: In fact, you loaned $100,000 to the plaintiff to start that business, right?

A: Yes.

Q: You expect to get paid back?

A: Of course.

Q: Your getting paid back depends on the plaintiff being able to pay you that $100,000, right?

A: Yes.

Example (Motive):

Q: Mr. Smith, you were once a business partner of the defendant, John Adams, right?

A: Yes.

Q: And then you had a falling out?

A: You could call it that.

Q: In fact, you ended up suing each other?

A: That's right.

Q: There's no love lost between the two of you, is there?

A: No.

Example (Motive):

Q: Mr. Brown, you claim you saw the police beat up the plaintiff, is that right?

A: That's right.

Q: You don't like the police, do you?

A: I don't like some of them.

Q: In fact, you were arrested by the police two years ago, right?

A: That's right.

Q: At that time, you also claimed that you were being hassled by the police, right?

A: Right.

Q: And your two brothers have been arrested by the police in the past?

A: That's right.

Q: And some of your friends have been arrested as well, right?

A: That's right.

In practice, the direct examiner frequently brings out the facts showing bias, interest, or motive, knowing that the cross-examiner will otherwise do so, thereby drawing the sting.

Example (Direct Examination):

Q: Ms. Williams, who do you work for?

A: Sony Computers.

Q: That's the defendant in this case?

A: Yes.

Q: How long have you worked for Sony?

A: Ten years.

Q: Why are you here today?

A: I attended the board meeting on June 1, 2020.

Q: Did anyone at Sony tell you what to say today?

A: Absolutely not.

Q: Are you here trying to help Sony?
A: I'm here to testify about what was said during that meeting, and that's all.

A common source of impeachment by a showing of corruption happens when a settling party becomes a witness during the trial involving the remaining parties. Most frequently, this happens when a co-defendant in a civil or criminal case settles with the plaintiff and is later called as a witness by the plaintiff. In this situation, the remaining co-defendants will want to bring out the settlement or plea agreement the settling co-defendant entered into with the plaintiff. This is perfectly proper under FRE 408 and 410.

Example (Plea Agreement as Corruption):

Q: Mr. Jackson, you were once a co-defendant in this case, right?
A: Yes.
Q: Charged with armed robbery?
A: That's right.
Q: In fact, right after you were arrested, you told the police that you had nothing to do with any armed robbery, didn't you?
A: Yes.
Q: But then you cut a deal with the prosecutor, isn't that right?
A: We entered into a plea agreement.
Q: Part of the deal was that you would testify if called as a witness by the prosecutor, right?
A: That was part of it.
Q: And in return for your testifying, the prosecutor will drop the armed robbery charge, right?
A: Yeah, but I'm still looking at robbery.
Q: Before you were looking at serving at least ten years if you were convicted of armed robbery, right?
A: Something like that.
Q: Now that the armed robbery charge has been dropped down to simple robbery, you're looking at serving as little as one year, isn't that right?
A: Yes.
Q: In fact, you haven't been sentenced yet, have you?
A: No.
Q: That won't happen until this trial is over?
A: That's right.
Q: And at your sentencing, the prosecutor will tell the court about your cooperation, isn't that part of the deal?
A: That's right.

In practice, prosecutors usually bring out the details of a plea agreement on direct when they call a former co-defendant who has entered into a plea agreement as a witness at trial, to draw the sting and present the terms of the plea agreement in a softer way.

In civil cases, courts allow the fact of the settlement to be brought out, but sometimes exclude the dollar amount of the settlement, fearing that the jurors may misuse the dollar amount for an improper purpose (such as using it to figure what damages should be, rather than just using it to assess the witness's credibility).

Example (Settlement as Corruption):

> Q: Ms. Amos, you were once a defendant in this lawsuit?
> A: Yes.
> Q: Before trial, you and the plaintiff entered into a settlement?
> A: That's right.
> Q: In return for you paying him a sum of money, the plaintiff dismissed his lawsuit against you?
> A: That's right.
> Q: This means that regardless of what this jury decides, you'll never have to pay any more money in this case?
> A: Yes.
> Q: And whatever you say today, that will have no effect on you, will it?
> A: Not financially, no.

These kinds of cross-examinations develop the facts that will now support your closing argument: The only reason the witnesses are saying what they are saying is because they have cut a deal with the plaintiff, and under these circumstances the jurors should not believe them.

Finally, remember that bias, interest, and motive as an impeachment category is always considered important (noncollateral). This means that if the witness does not admit the impeaching fact, you may later prove it up with extrinsic evidence. Proving up is discussed in Section 6.12.

2. Prior Inconsistent Statements

Use of prior inconsistent statements is the most common impeachment method. Whenever a witness testifies about something during the trial, and the witness said something different (or failed to say anything) at an earlier time, the inconsistency detracts from the witness's credibility. Witnesses frequently make oral statements to police or other investigators. They make written and signed statements. They prepare reports and forms. They testify at depositions, hearings, and other proceedings. They fail to say something under circumstances in which they would be expected to say something. These are all potential areas for impeachment at trial. If the inconsistency is significant, bring it out.

> ◼◀ For a guide to the proper use of prior statements on cross-examination, please watch Video E.6, "Wyo STI: Proper Impeachment with Prior Inconsistent Statement."

Effective impeachment with a prior inconsistent statement requires two things: an effective technique and an appropriate attitude. Effective technique is necessary because impeachment must be simple and clear. It must create an impact *now*. The enemy of effective impeachment is complexity and confusion.

Think of impeachment with a prior inconsistent statement as holding up before the jurors two flash cards, one white, the other black. The white card contains what the witness said today; the black card contains what the witness said at an earlier time. If the flash cards are simple, the contrast is stark and clear. If the flash cards are complicated and muddled, they turn grey, and the contrast disappears. Effective technique is based on the 3 Cs, accompanied with an appropriate attitude. The 3 Cs are:

- Commit
- Credit
- Confront

First, *commit*. Commit the witness to the fact she said during the direct examination that you now want to impeach. Make it as specific, focused, and short as possible. Use the witness's actual words. Committing the witness is important because it reminds the jurors what the witness said on direct, and lets the jurors know that something important and interesting is about to happen.[1]

Examples:

Q: Mr. Jones, you say that the defendant's Chevy was going 30 miles per hour, is that right?

Q: Mr. Jones, you just said on direct that the defendant's Chevy was going 30 miles per hour, right?

Committing the witness must also communicate an appropriate attitude. In the preceding examples, the "you say" and "you just said on direct" questions are neutral. In most cases, however, you want to convey an attitude that signals to the jurors why the prior inconsistency happened. Is your position that the witness is confused, mistaken, or doesn't remember? If so, your questions, tone of voice, and body language must project that attitude.

Examples:

Q: Mr. Jones, as you remember it, the Chevy was going 30 miles per hour?

Q: Mr. Jones, you think the Chevy was going 30 miles per hour?

Is your position that the witness is intentionally changing his testimony, or even lying? If so, your questions, tone of voice, and body language must project that harder attitude.

Examples:

Q: Mr. Jones, are you claiming today that the Chevy was going 30 miles per hour?

Q: Did I hear you right? You want us to believe that the Chevy was going 30 miles per hour?

---

1. Junior co-author Easton avoids the commitment step. He believes time should not be used during cross to repeat the story told in direct examination, because the cross-examiner does not believe the story told on direct examination is correct. Instead, he almost always starts by asking the witness to admit the fact stated in the prior statement. For example, if the witness said the car "was going 50 m.p.h." in a prior statement and it is our position that the car was indeed going 50 m.p.h., co-author Easton's first question would be, "The car was going 50 m.p.h., right?" If the witness denies this or quibbles, the next step is to credit the prior statement by explaining the circumstances of the prior statement and the importance of telling the truth in that context.

These different forms—"as you remember it," "you think," or "are you claiming today," and "you want us to believe"—send clear messages about why the inconsistency happened, and must be accompanied with appropriate body language and tone of voice: soft and understanding, or doubting and accusatory. They tell the jury: Stay tuned, things are going to get interesting. Word choices, tone, and body language are all important here.

Second, *credit*. Build up the source of the impeaching statement. Jurors need to know where, when, and how the prior inconsistent statement was made. They need to know that the prior inconsistent statement was made in a serious environment, when the facts were fresh (or at least fresher) in the witness's mind. Create a picture of the place where the impeaching statement was made.

Example:

Q: Mr. Winston, you talked to a police officer after the crash?
A: Yes.
Q: That was Officer Smith, the uniformed police officer?
A: Yes.
Q: That was about 30 minutes after the crash?
A: About that.
Q: You talked to Officer Smith while sitting in her squad car?
A: Yes.
Q: You knew she was investigating the crash?
A: Sure.
Q: You told her that you were a witness?
A: Yes.
Q: You knew that it was important to tell Officer Smith what you saw?
A: Yes.
Q: As accurately as possible?
A: Yes.
Q: And as completely as possible?
A: Yes.
Q: As you were talking, Officer Smith was taking notes?
A: Well, she was writing things down, but I couldn't read it.

Example:

Q: Ms. Joseph, you had your deposition taken in this case?
A: Yes.
Q: A deposition is when you are asked questions under oath?
A: Yes.
Q: That's the day you came to my office?
A: That's right.
Q: We sat in a small conference room?
A: Yes.
Q: In the conference room were you, me, the other lawyer, Mr. Phelps, and a court reporter?
A: Yes.
Q: I asked you questions, and the lawyer for the other side asked you questions?
A: That's right.

Q: Before we started, a court reporter swore you in to tell the truth, right?
A: Yes.
Q: The same oath you took today in this courtroom?
A: Yes.
Q: And you knew it was important to tell the truth about what you saw, heard, and did when the crash happened, right?
A: Of course.
Q: You knew that the court reporter would write down everything that was said, word for word?
A: Yes.
Q: After the deposition was over, you had a chance to look at all the questions you were asked and the answers you gave?
A: Yes.
Q: Those questions and answers were in a booklet, what's called a deposition transcript?
A: Yes.
Q: You were given a chance to look over those questions and answers to make sure they were accurate, right?
A: Yes.
Q: And make any corrections if that was needed?
A: Yes.

Do you need to do this second C—credit—every time you impeach a witness with a prior inconsistent statement? No. Do it once, so that the jurors understand how a statement is made to a police officer or how a deposition transcript is created. After that, jurors will know why a statement to a police officer or a deposition question and answer is reliable. You can then abbreviate or even drop the "credit" step, and go immediately from committing the witness to what he said during direct examination and bring out the prior inconsistent statement. This makes the contrast cleaner and more immediate.

Third, *confront*. Bring out the prior inconsistent statement and ask the witness to admit making it.

Examples:

Q: Mr. Winston, didn't you tell that police officer that "the defendant's car was going at least 50 miles per hour"?
Q: Page 33, line 10, counsel. Mr. Adams, please read along silently with me as I read the question and your sworn answer aloud. "Question: How fast was the defendant's car going? Answer: At least 50 miles per hour." Did I read that correctly?

After you have finished with the 3 Cs—commit, credit, and confront—stop. Let the impeachment linger in the air for a few seconds to give the jurors a chance to absorb its importance. Don't ask follow-up questions that give the witness an opportunity to explain or start an argument. Let the redirect examiner bring out any explanation for the inconsistency.

When there is more than one inconsistency between what the witness says today and what the witness said in an earlier statement, bring out and contrast those inconsistencies one at a time, to keep things simple and clear.

Example:

> Q: You say today that the Chevy was going 30 miles per hour?
> A: Yes.
> [Build up the impeaching statement, then:]
> Q: You told Officer Jackson that the Chevy was going at least 50, isn't that right?
> A: Yes.
> Q: Today you say that the Chevy had the yellow light at the time the two cars crashed?
> A: That's right.
> Q: Back then you told Officer Jackson that you weren't sure what color the lights were at the time the two cars crashed, right?
> A: That's what I said then.
> Q: Today you say that the rain had stopped at the time of the crash?
> A: Yes.
> Q: Back then you told Officer Jackson that it was still raining at the time the two cars crashed, right?
> A: Yes.

In this example, the witness has been impeached with three separate inconsistencies. When you expose them one inconsistency at a time, the jurors will recognize them and understand their significance.

In many jurisdictions, judges permit lawyers to create a visual aid to make the contrast clear between what the witness says today and what the witness said earlier. As you start the impeachment, have a foam-core poster board or butcher paper set up on an easel. As you commit the witness to what he said on direct, and confront him with his earlier statement, write the key words on the board. Make sure that what you write is accurate and fair. Using a visual aid makes the inconsistency easy to see and understand.

Example:

> Q: Mr. Earl, you say today that the defendant's car was going 30 miles per hour?
> A: That's right. [Put a heading labeled "Today" on the right side of the board, then write "Def. going 30 mph" under it.]
> Q: You talked to a police officer right after the crash?
> A: Yes.
> Q: You told the police officer that day what you had just seen, right?
> A: Yes.
> Q: Didn't you tell the police officer that "the defendant's car was going at least 50"?
> A: I guess so. [Put a heading labeled "Day of crash" on the left side of the board, then write "Def. going at least 50" under it.]

Such a visual aid makes the impeachment obvious to everyone and keeps it before the jurors much longer. If there are additional prior inconsistent statements, they can be added to the board as you bring them out.

Sometimes it can be effective to vary the commit-credit-confront order. For example, you can begin with crediting the prior inconsistent statement, then committing the witness to the fact you want to impeach, and then confronting the witness with the inconsistent statement. This order—credit-commit-confront—puts the two statements immediately side-by-side for contrast. This order can be effective with lay witnesses who have little courtroom experience. It does not work as well for experienced witnesses like police officers and experts, who immediately recognize that you are setting them up for impeachment.

Example:

> Q: Ms. Jamison, you talked to a police officer after witnessing the crash?
> A: Yes.
> Q: You knew it was important to the officer investigating the crash to learn what the eyewitnesses saw?
> A: Sure.
> Q: And you told the officer what you had just seen as accurately as you could?
> A: Yes.
> Q: Ms. Jamison, today you tell us that the Chevy had the green light?
> A: That's right.
> Q: But you told the police officer right after the crash that you weren't sure what color the light was, right?
> A: I don't remember.

What happens if the witness does not admit making the prior inconsistent statement? Such statements are taken on a case-by-case basis: some are important (noncollateral), others are unimportant (collateral). This means that if the witness denies or equivocates about making an important prior inconsistent statement, you should later prove up the statement with extrinsic evidence.

Remember that effective impeachment with a prior inconsistent statement requires a clear technique (the 3 Cs) and an appropriate attitude. If you don't act as if the impeachment is important, neither will the jurors. There are four principal sources of prior inconsistent statements: oral statements; written or signed statements; sworn testimony in depositions, hearings, and other proceedings; and impeachment by omission.

a. Oral Statements

Impeachment with a prior oral statement is common. Witnesses frequently talk to police officers, investigators, family, friends, and co-workers about things they have witnessed. All those statements become potential impeachment material if the witness says something different when testifying.

Use the 3 Cs—commit, credit, and confront—when impeaching with an oral statement. Make sure you build up the circumstances under which the statement was made. Be specific. Let the jurors know that the statement was important and seriously made.

Example:

> Q: You say today that the Chevy involved in the accident had the yellow light?
> A: Yes.
> Q: Two days after the collision, on June 3, an investigator came to your house and asked to talk with you, right?

A: Yes.

Q: The two of you sat at your kitchen table?

A: Yes.

Q: He told you he had been assigned to investigate the collision and wanted to talk to the eyewitnesses?

A: Something like that.

Q: And you told him what you saw and heard that day?

A: Yes.

Q: You knew that what you told the investigator was important, right?

A: Sure.

Q: You told him what you saw and heard that day as accurately as possible, didn't you?

A: I tried to, yes.

Q: And the investigator was taking notes as you talked?

A: It looked like it.

Q: Mr. Rosen, didn't you tell the investigator that the Chevy involved in the collision ran the red light?

A: Yes.

Witnesses are more likely to deny or equivocate about making a prior oral statement, sometimes reasoning that it's their word against another person's. For that reason, it is important to bring out the details surrounding the oral statement. This shows the witness and the jurors that you know all about the prior statement, and the witness is more likely to admit making it.

> For a demonstration of a cross-examination based upon oral statements of a witness, please watch Video E.8, "Wyo STI: Demonstration of Problem 5.4."

Example:

Q: Ms. Quigley, your testimony is that the Chevy had the yellow light at the time the two cars collided, is that right?

A: That's right.

Q: Let's turn for a moment to where you work. You work at Webster Electronics?

A: That's right.

Q: At lunchtime most of you eat in the company's lunchroom?

A: Most of the time.

Q: The day after the collision, you ate in the company's lunchroom, didn't you?

A: I'm not sure, but probably.

Q: In the lunchroom that day were the usual co-workers?

A: Probably.

Q: And you were sitting with your usual friends at the large round table?

A: Probably.

Q: That day, the day after the collision, you talked to your friends about the collision, didn't you?

A: I'm not sure, but I may have.

Q: Ms. Quigley, didn't you tell your friends, at the round table in the lunchroom, the day after the collision, that the Chevy went right through the red light?

A: I may have.

A common impeachment mistake happens when lawyers try to impeach a witness with someone else's written report containing the witness's oral statement. For example, a police report contains a notation that "eyewitness said Chevy going 50 mph." The *report* cannot be used to impeach the witness, because the report is the police officer's statement, not the witness's. It is improper to ask the witness: "Didn't you say in the police report that the Chevy was going 50 miles per hour?" However, the witness can be impeached with her oral statement to the police officer. It is proper to ask: "Didn't you tell the police officer that the Chevy was going 50 miles per hour?" This is probably the most recurring mistake involving impeachment with an oral statement.

b. Written Statements

Impeachment with a prior written statement is also common. These can include statements that the witness herself writes or signs, as well as statements that are written or typed by someone else that the witness signs.

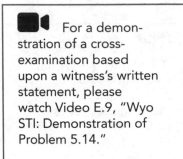
For a demonstration of a cross-examination based upon a witness's written statement, please watch Video E.9, "Wyo STI: Demonstration of Problem 5.14."

Use the 3 Cs—commit, credit, and confront—when impeaching with a written statement. Make sure you build up the circumstances under which the statement was made. Be specific. Let the jurors know that the statement was important and seriously made. With written statements, however, you also must have the statement marked as an exhibit, show it to opposing counsel, and show it to the witness, before using it to impeach. Although this procedure is only partially required by FRE 613, most judges require it, and it is the more effective impeachment technique.

Example (Written Statement):

Q: You say today that the Chevy was going 30 miles per hour?
A: Yes.
Q: Ms. Blumenthal, you made a written statement about the car crash you witnessed, right?
A: Yes.
Q: You did that two days after the crash?
A: I'm not sure of the exact date, but that sounds about right.
Q: You did that because an accident investigator came to your house and asked you to make a written statement about what you saw, right?
A: Yes.
Q: Please mark this document "Plaintiff's Exhibit No. 20." [Hands exhibit to court clerk, who marks it as an exhibit.] I'm now showing it to opposing counsel. [Hands exhibit to lawyer, who examines it and hands it back.] May I approach the witness? I'm now showing Plaintiff's Exhibit No. 20 to the witness. [Hands exhibit to witness.] That's the statement you made on June 3, 2020?
A: Yes, it is.
Q: It's in your handwriting?
Q: Ms. Blumenthal, follow along while I read from your statement, beginning here [pointing]. Make sure I read it right. Your statement says,

"I saw the two cars crash. The Chevy was going at least 50 miles per hour." Did I read it right, word for word?

A: Yes.

Note that the *lawyer* read the impeaching part of the written statement, not the witness. You always want to keep control over the impeachment, like everything else during cross-examination. When *you* read the impeaching part, you can read it with the volume, inflection, and body language that highlight the impeachment. This will not happen if the witness reads it. Note also where you should stand when impeaching. If permitted to position yourself anywhere in the courtroom, the best place is to stand next to the witness, where you will not block the jurors' view of the witness. You will then be next to the witness, facing the jury, and will be able to read the impeaching part, and still have the witness follow along.

The statement, because it is something used during the trial, is kept by the court clerk and becomes part of the trial record. The statement, however, has not been admitted as an exhibit and does not go to the jury when it deliberates (unless the statement has received a foundation that permits it to be formally admitted in evidence).

When impeaching from a writing, keep in mind the requirements of FRE 106, the so-called *rule of completeness*. It provides that when a writing or recorded statement is introduced, an adverse party "may require the introduction, at that time, of any other part—or any other writing or recorded statement—that in fairness ought to be considered at the same time." This rule prevents, among other things, unfair impeachment by reading statements out of context. Accordingly, it is improper to read only part of a statement to create an unfair impression. For example, consider a statement that says: "The light was green. However, I only caught a glimpse of it and I may have been mistaken." The cross-examiner cannot use only the first sentence to impeach, because omitting the qualifying second sentence would be unfair. Although FRE 106 explicitly applies only to writings, some courts apply the same concept to oral statements when it is fair to do so.

Example (Statement Signed by Witness):

Q: Ms. Hart, you say that you had several thousand dollars missing from the store after the burglary, right?

A: Yes.

Q: After the burglary, you were interviewed by a police detective?

A: That's right.

Q: That was in the police station?

A: Yes.

Q: The same day as the burglary?

A: Yes, right after we discovered the burglary.

Q: The detective asked you questions and you answered them?

A: Yes.

Q: In fact, the detective typed your answers in a statement form, right?

A: Yes.

Q: He showed the statement to you?

A: Yes.

Q: And he asked you to sign it if the statement accurately contained what you had told him, right?

A: Yes.

Q: After reading it over, you signed the statement?

A: Yes.

Q: Ms. Hart, didn't you tell the detective that you couldn't find anything missing from your store after the burglary?

A: I'm not sure.

Q: Please mark this Defendant's Exhibit No. 10. [Hands exhibit to court clerk, who marks it as an exhibit.] I'm showing the exhibit to plaintiff's counsel. [Hands exhibit to lawyer, who examines it and hands it back.] I'm now showing Defendant's Exhibit No. 10 to Ms. Hart. Please take a look at it. [Hands exhibit to witness.] Is that the statement you made at the police station the day you discovered the burglary?

A: Yes, it is.

Q: It has the date of June 1, 2020, at the top [pointing]?

A: Yes.

Q: It has the title "Statement of Helen Hart" at the top?

A: Yes.

Q: At the bottom there's a signature. That's your signature, right?

A: Yes.

Q: Take a look at the middle of the page [pointing]. Make sure I read it accurately, word for word. "After I discovered the burglary I looked around the store but I couldn't see anything that was missing." Did I read that right?

A: Yes.

Q: Word for word?

A: Yes.

Finally, don't overlook pleadings and discovery responses as potential sources of impeaching written statements. For example, if a complaint or answer has been signed by a party (usually called a *verified* pleading, and permitted in some jurisdictions), or a discovery response has been signed by a party, it can be used to impeach. The most common situation involves impeachment using an interrogatory answer, because Fed. R. Civ. P. 33(b) requires that the answers be made "in writing under oath" and signed by the person making them. The impeachment procedure is like impeachment using a signed statement.

Example:

Q: Ms. Carter, you say today that you were not present at the board meeting on June 1, 2019?

A: That's right.

Q: [To court clerk] Please mark these interrogatory answers Defendant's Exhibit No. 5. [Show exhibit to opposing counsel.] Ms. Carter, I'm now showing you what has just been marked Defendant's Exhibit No. 5. [Holds exhibit in front of witness.] At the top it says "Plaintiff's Answers to Defendant's Interrogatories," right?

A: That's right.

Q: On the last page, it has a date and signature, right?

A: That's right.

Q: The date is May 1, 2020?

A: Yes.

Q: That's in your handwriting?
A: Yes.
Q: The signature here, that's your signature?
A: Yes.
Q: You signed these interrogatory answers on May 1, 2020?
A: Yes.
Q: Just above your signature, it says "I hereby swear that my answers to the above interrogatories are true and correct," right?
A: Yes.
Q: You then swore before a notary public that your answers were true and correct?
A: Yes.
Q: And over here, that's the notary's affidavit and seal?
A: Yes.
Q: Ms. Carter, let's take a look at interrogatory No. 12 and your answer to it. The interrogatory says: "State who was present at the board meeting of Ajax Corporation on June 1, 2019." Did I read that right?
A: Yes.
Q: Your sworn answer says: "Mr. Franklin, Mr. Williams, Ms. Henderson, Mr. Adams, and I were all present." Did I read your answer right, word for word?
A: Yes.

c. Sworn Transcripts

When a witness testifies under oath and a transcript of the testimony is prepared by a court reporter, the transcript becomes a potential source of impeachment if the witness testifies differently at trial. Common examples are transcripts of depositions, preliminary hearings, grand jury testimony, and other hearing or trial testimony.

Once again, use the 3 Cs—commit, credit, confront—when impeaching with sworn transcripts. Make sure you build up the circumstances under which the transcript of the witness's testimony was made. Be specific. Let the jurors know that the proceeding was important, that the witness was sworn to tell the truth, and (with depositions) was later given a transcript of her testimony to review, note any mistakes, and sign. Create a picture of the witness testifying at the deposition or hearing. As with any written statement, show or refer opposing counsel to the transcript page and line, and show it to the witness, before using it to impeach.

Example (Deposition):

Q: Mr. Hoffman, the Chevy was going more than 50 miles per hour, right?
A: No, I'd say more like 30.
Q: Let's turn back to December 1, 2020. You testified that day at what's called a deposition, right?
A: I don't remember the exact date, but I did have my deposition taken.
Q: That's when you came to my office?
A: Yes.
Q: We sat in a small conference room?
A: Yes.

Q: You were there, I was there, the other lawyer was there, and a court reporter was there?

A: Yes.

Q: The court reporter swore you in to tell the truth?

A: Yes.

Q: The same oath you took today?

A: Yes.

Q: Then I asked you questions about the collision?

A: Yes.

Q: And the other lawyer asked you questions?

A: Yes.

Q: You knew it was important to answer as accurately and truthfully as possible, didn't you?

A: Yes.

Q: And you did that—answered accurately and truthfully?

A: Yes.

Q: After the deposition, you received a booklet containing all the questions and answers?

A: Yes.

Q: You had a chance to review your answers to make sure they were accurate?

A: Yes.

Q: In fact, there was a correction sheet where you could make any corrections you felt needed to be made, right?

A: Yes.

Q: There was a signature page for you to sign, if the deposition transcript was accurate, right?

A: Yes.

Q: And you signed that signature page, didn't you?

A: Yes.

Q: Mr. Hoffman, I'm going to show you a page from your deposition in just a moment. It's already been marked Plaintiff's Exhibit No. 3. [Stands next to witness, and puts the deposition transcript before the witness.] But first, look at the first page of this exhibit. It says "Deposition of Henry Hoffman, taken on December 1, 2020," right?

A: Yes.

Q: Now look at the last page. It says "I hereby certify that the questions asked and answers given in this transcript are true and correct," right?

A: Yes.

Q: Right after that, there's a signature. That's your signature, Henry Hoffman, right?

A: Yes.

Q: Now look at page 42, line 15. I'm going to read from that page, beginning there [pointing]. "Question: Did you see the Chevy before the crash? Your answer: Yes, I did. Question: How fast was the Chevy going when it crashed into the other car? Your answer: At least 50 miles per hour." Did I read those questions and your answers right, word for word?

A: Yes.

This approach—reading the questions and answers and asking the witness to admit that you read them accurately—is the better approach. Many lawyers ask: "Is that what you said on that date?" However, that question form gives the witness a chance to say "I don't remember," "I'm not sure," or "I don't think so." Asking the witness if you read the questions and his answers word for word gives the witness no wiggle room.

Example (Preliminary Hearing):

Q: Mr. Williams, you say that you saw the defendant with a gun in his hand?

A: Yes.

Q: But actually you did not know if the defendant had a weapon, because it was too dark for you to see, right?

A: I'm not sure.

Q: Well, let's talk about the preliminary hearing in this case. That was held on September 1, 2020?

A: Around then.

Q: Right here in this courthouse?

A: Yes.

Q: You were a witness at that hearing?

A: Yes.

Q: You testified at that hearing under oath?

A: Yes.

Q: Just like you're under oath today?

A: Yes.

Q: You were in a courtroom?

A: Yes.

Q: Just like this courtroom?

A: Yes. Right down the hall.

Q: You testified from the witness stand?

A: Yes.

Q: Just like you're testifying today?

A: Yes.

Q: At that hearing, you testified about what you saw, heard, and did as you witnessed the robbery, right?

A: Sure.

Q: You told the truth at that hearing, didn't you?

A: Of course.

Q: Mr. Williams, I'm going to show you Defendant's Exhibit No. 10, a transcript of your testimony at that hearing. Counsel, it's page 12, beginning on line 15. [Shows transcript to witness and stands next to him.] Follow along to make sure I read it right. Weren't you asked this question and didn't you give this answer: "Question: Did you see the defendant with any weapon? Answer: I don't know. It was too dark to see." That's what the transcript of your testimony says, right?

A: Yes.

Make sure the other lawyer has a copy of the transcript you are using to impeach. If not, make sure you show her. Better yet, give her a copy of the transcript.

Note that in each of these examples of impeachment using a transcript of the witness's sworn testimony, the lawyer had the transcript marked as an exhibit, showed it to opposing counsel, then showed it to the witness and stood next to the witness while reading the impeaching part. As noted earlier, FRE 613 does not require showing the witness a "prior statement" before cross-examining the witness with the statement; it requires only that you show the statement to opposing counsel on request. However, showing the transcript to the witness is the more effective technique (it avoids responses like "I don't know; can I see that transcript?") and is perceived by the jurors as the fair thing to do.

d. Impeachment by Omission

Impeachment by omission is an important impeachment technique, but it must be used only in appropriate situations. When a witness has made a report or record of an event, and the witness failed to put in that report or record the fact that he is now testifying about, you might be able to impeach the witness by omission. However, such impeachment is effective only when it is used to expose important omissions, under circumstances in which the exposure is fair. The omission must be important, so that the jurors believe the omission cannot be explained by inadvertence or mistake. Always ask: If this fact actually existed, would the witness have recorded it in this report or record? The omission must also be fairly exposed. Always ask: Did the witness have control over the making of the report or record, so that the failure to put this fact in the report or record can fairly be attributed to the witness?

Example (Police Report):

Q: Officer Smith, you claim today that right after you got to the scene of the crash, Mr. Williams told you, "I'm sorry, it was my fault"?

A: That's what he said.

Q: Officer, Smith, you went through the police academy?

A: Yes.

Q: They trained you how to prepare police reports?

A: Yes.

Q: They told you to put the important facts in the report, didn't they?

A: Yes.

Q: And that's what you do when you write your reports—put in all the important facts?

A: I try to.

Q: Officer Smith, have you ever arrested someone for a crime?

A: Yes.

Q: And they've confessed?

A: Yes.

Q: When someone you've just arrested says, "I did it," that's important, isn't it?

A: Of course.

Q: You put his statement—"I did it"—in your report, don't you?

A: Yes.

Q: You've also been to the scenes of car crashes, right?

A: Yes.

Q: And sometimes one of the drivers will tell you that the accident was his fault, right?

A: That sometimes happens.

Q: When someone just involved in a car crash in which another person was seriously hurt says, "It's my fault," that's important, isn't it?

A: It can be, but it depends on the circumstances of the case.

Q: And if it's important, it goes in the report?

A: If it's important.

Q: Officer Smith, I'm showing you Plaintiff's Exhibit No. 10, which has already been marked. [Hands exhibit to witness.] Counsel, you have a copy of this exhibit. [Opposing counsel nods.] That's a copy of your accident report?

A: That's right.

Q: That's the report you prepared of the facts of this car crash?

A: Yes.

Q: Officer Smith, show me where your report contains Mr. Williams's words, "It's my fault."

A: It's not there.

You can heighten the omission by asking the witness to circle the nonexistent words with a Sharpie pen. That increases the tension and makes the omission even more prominent.

Example:

Q: Officer Smith, I'm handing you a red felt-tip pen. Look at the front page of your accident report. Please circle Mr. Williams's words—"It's my fault"—as they appear on that page.

A: I can't do that.

Q: Why not?

A: It's not in my report.

Q: Well, let's look at page two of your report, the narrative portion. Please circle Mr. Williams's words—"It's my fault"—as they appear on page two.

A: I can't do that.

Q: Is there a problem?

A: It's not in my report.

Example (Business Report):

Q: Ms. Dowd, your job as the secretary for the board is to record what happens during board meetings?

A: That's right.

Q: You record the board members who attended the meeting?

A: Of course.

Q: You take notes during the meeting?

A: Yes.

Q: Those notes include the topics under discussion?

A: Yes.

Q: The positions the board members in attendance take on those topics?

A: Yes, if they speak and take positions.

Q: Whether the board approved or disapproved some matter?

A: Yes.

Q: And the way the board members in attendance voted?

A: Yes, and if they abstained from voting.

Q: The reason you take notes is so that you can write an accurate account of what happened at the meeting?

A: Yes.

Q: The account of the meeting, those are called the minutes?

A: Yes, the minutes of the board meeting.

Q: Ms. Dowd, you say today that the board during its meeting on June 1, 2020, approved the contract with Jones Chemical Company?

A: Yes.

Q: Approving that contract was a big deal, wasn't it?

A: It was an important contract, yes.

Q: I'd like this document marked as an exhibit. [Hands exhibit to court clerk, who marks it as an exhibit.] I'm showing what has just been marked as Defendant's Exhibit No. 12 to plaintiff's counsel. [Hands exhibit to lawyer, who hands it back.] I'm now showing it to the witness. [Hands exhibit to witness.] That's the minutes of the board meeting of your company held on June 1, 2020, right?

A: Yes.

Q: In fact, that's your signature as secretary of the board at the bottom of the last page, isn't it?

A: Yes.

Q: Ms. Dowd, show us where the minutes of the board meeting say that the board approved the contract with Jones Chemical Company.

A: It's not in the minutes.

Q: In fact, the only notation in the minutes is on page two, where it says "The board discussed the proposed contract with Jones Chemical," right?

A: Yes.

Q: It says "discussed"?

A: Yes.

Q: It says "proposed contract," doesn't it?

A: Yes.

Q: It doesn't say "approved contract," does it?

A: No.

Remember that jurors will put weight on the omission only if it is fair to do so. This means that the witness must have control over the making of the report. Be careful about impeaching witnesses with "omissions" during depositions. If the witness never said something during the deposition that he now testifies about, it may be that the witness was never asked a question during the deposition that would have brought out that fact. In that situation, the omission is insignificant, and trying to make something of it fails, because the witness has no control over the questions the lawyers ask, or don't ask, during the deposition. In fact, the redirect examination can expose this effectively. For example, if the cross-examiner brings out that the witness in his deposition never said that "the defendant's car was going 50 miles per hour," on redirect the witness can say that "that lawyer never asked me how fast the defendant's car was going; if he had, I would have told him 50."

You can frequently combine impeachment with a prior inconsistent statement with impeachment by omission. This in effect impeaches the witness twice.

Example:

Q: Ms. Jackson, you say today that the light for Main Street was green when the two cars crashed?

A: That's right.

Q: You talked to Officer Jones right after the crash, right?

A: Yes.

Q: You told Officer Jones that the light for Main Street was red at the time of the crash, right?

A: Yes, I did.

Q: And you never told Officer Jones that the light for Main Street was green, did you?

A: No, I didn't.

Some lawyers like this "double impeachment," others think it complicates things unnecessarily. Sometimes it can be a useful technique, particularly if you are going to argue later that the witness is confused and doesn't really know what color the light was at the time of the crash.

For purposes of the collateral/noncollateral divide, prior inconsistent statements are taken on a case-by-case basis. If the witness denies or equivocates about making the statement, it may be proved up with extrinsic evidence if the statement is important (noncollateral).

3. Contradictory Facts

When a witness says something at trial that is inconsistent with a provable fact, the witness can be asked to admit the contradictory fact. For example, if the witness says he was 20 feet from the collision, he can be asked if he was in fact more than 100 feet away. Impeachment with contradictory facts, or impeachment by contradiction, is well recognized by the case law, although there is no specific rule governing it.

The good-faith requirement for impeachment is an important part of impeachment with contradictory facts. The cross-examiner cannot suggest a contradictory fact unless she has a good-faith basis to believe that the contradictory fact exists. Model Rule 3.3 prohibits a lawyer from knowingly offering false evidence, and Model Rule 3.4 prohibits a lawyer from alluding to any matter the lawyer does not reasonably believe will be supported by admissible evidence. For example, the witness cannot be asked to admit that he was in fact more than 100 feet away unless the cross-examiner has a good-faith basis to believe that this was so. The cross-examiner must have a factual basis for this belief, such as information from another eyewitness that this witness was more than 100 feet away. If the cross-examiner has no good-faith belief, she cannot ask the question suggesting this fact. Cross-examination is not an opportunity to throw unsubstantiated dirt at a witness.

If you have a good-faith basis for asking the witness to admit the contradictory fact, simply ask the question with the appropriate accompanying attitude. If the witness admits the contradictory fact, nothing more need be done. If the witness denies or equivocates, you should prove up the unadmitted impeachment with extrinsic evidence if it is important (noncollateral). Contradictory facts are treated on a case-by-case basis, like prior inconsistent statements; some are important, others are not.

Common sources of contradictory facts are facts that attack the witness's credibility, such as liquor or drug use that affected the witness's perception of the event.

Example:

> Q: Mr. Quigley, you say that you had been home all afternoon and had just gone outside when the crash happened?
> A: That's right.
> Q: Weren't you in fact at O'Brien's Tavern that afternoon?
> A: No.
> Q: Didn't you have several beers that afternoon before the crash happened?
> A: No.

If the witness denies or equivocates about the contradictory fact, the cross-examiner should prove it up if it is important (noncollateral). If this witness is an important eyewitness, whether he was home or had been in a bar drinking several beers obviously will affect his perception and credibility. This fact is important, and the cross-examiner should prove up the impeaching fact with extrinsic evidence, i.e., evidence other than the witness's testimony.

Note that it is the suggestion of facts during cross-examination that triggers the ethical requirements. Asking questions on cross-examination that do not suggest facts as true are proper. For example, asking "Do you wear prescription glasses?" followed by "Were you wearing them when you saw the accident?" is proper. If the witness says "no," that ends the matter. However, asking questions on cross-examination that suggest facts as true are proper only if both the good-faith basis to ask and the ability to prove up if required exist. For example, asking "You weren't wearing your prescription glasses when you saw the crash, were you?" is proper only if the lawyer has a good-faith factual basis to ask it, and can prove it up with extrinsic evidence if the witness does not admit it.

One common source of contradictory facts is testimony from your own witnesses. This is useful because you want to get your facts before the jurors immediately. Defense lawyers commonly use this approach during cross-examination of the plaintiff's witnesses, to get before the jurors the key defense facts and positions during the plaintiff's case.

Example (Cross-Examination of Prosecution Witness):

> Q: Mr. Jones, you claim that during the robbery at the convenience store, Mr. Franklin was one of the robbers?
> A: Yes.
> Q: And was inside the store?
> A: Yes.
> Q: And had a handgun?
> A: Yes.
> Q: Mr. Jones, isn't it true that Mr. Franklin was sitting in a blue Pontiac sedan parked around the side of the store when the store was robbed?
> A: No.

Q: Isn't it true that Mr. Franklin was never inside the store while all this was going on?

A: No.

Q: And isn't it true that Mr. Franklin never had a firearm of any kind while all this was going on?

A: No.

Because the witness has denied these facts, the cross-examiner should prove up the unadmitted facts with extrinsic evidence, as they are obviously important.

4. Prior Convictions

Prior convictions are commonly used for impeachment, particularly in criminal cases. Under FRE 609, when a witness testifies, his credibility can be attacked with a prior felony conviction, or any conviction, felony or misdemeanor, if a dishonest act or statement was an element of the crime. The conviction ordinarily must be less than ten years old (calculated from the time of sentencing or the release from confinement, whichever is later), although the court under FRE 609(b) may use a balancing test to admit older convictions. If the prior conviction is a non-dishonesty felony of the accused in a criminal case, there is a special balancing test under FRE 609(a) to determine admissibility—the probative value of a prior felony conviction must outweigh its prejudicial effect to the accused. Substantial case law has been developed over the admissibility of prior convictions, and research may be necessary in some situations. The safe approach is to raise admissibility issues in a pretrial motion and obtain a ruling before trial whenever possible.

If the prior conviction is properly admissible to impeach the witness's credibility, simply bring out the facts of the prior conviction and ask the witness to admit them. Most courts permit bringing out the crime on which the witness was convicted (whether by guilty plea or trial makes no difference), the date and place of the conviction, and the sentence imposed by the judge.

Example (Accused):

Q: Mr. Williams, you're a convicted felon, aren't you?

A: Yes.

Q: In fact, you were convicted of robbery on June 1, 2020?

A: Yes.

Q: Here in the Superior Court of Los Angeles?

A: Yes.

Q: Judge Watkins was the presiding judge?

A: I'm not sure.

Q: And the judge sentenced you to two years in the state penitentiary, isn't that true?

A: Yes.

Many defense lawyers in criminal cases will "volunteer" the prior conviction of a testifying defendant on direct examination, to draw the sting. In this way the prior conviction can be brought out more gently, as part of the witness's background. Keep in mind, however, that doing this will usually waive any error in a pretrial or other ruling permitting the prior conviction to be used to impeach.

Example (Direct Examination):

Q: Bobby, where did you grow up?
A: Right here in Phoenix.
Q: You went to school here?
A: Yes, Central High School.
Q: Did you graduate?
A: Yes, in 2010.
Q: What did you do after graduation?
A: I enlisted in the Army.
Q: For how long?
A: Three years.
Q: Where were you stationed?
A: After basic training, I spent almost all the time in Korea.
Q: When were you discharged?
A: In 2008.
Q: What kind of discharge?
A: An honorable discharge, as a private first class.
Q: What did you do after that?
A: I returned home, and started looking for work.
Q: Bobby, there was a time that you got in trouble with the law, right?
A: That's right.
Q: What happened?
A: It was after I got home. Some friends and I were using pot, and we got arrested.
Q: What happened?
A: I pleaded guilty to possession of marijuana, and was put on probation.
Q: Are you still on probation?
A: Yes.
Q: Any problems with the law since then?
A: No sir. I've been doing everything they tell me to do, and I've been working at the Food Giant for over a year now.

Under FRE 609, the trial judge must either permit a prior conviction to be used to impeach or exclude its use. However, some jurisdictions permit the judge to use a middle ground, usually called "sanitizing a prior conviction" or the "mere fact" approach, especially when the witness is also the defendant in a criminal case. When a prior conviction is the same as or similar to the charge in the case on trial, and the prior conviction is of the accused, there is always a danger that the jurors will misuse the prior conviction for an improper purpose; namely, as a prior bad act (usually inadmissible under FRE 404(b)) rather than for the proper limited purpose of assessing the credibility of the accused if he testifies. In this situation, judges may order that the prior conviction be admissible to impeach, but that it be referred to only as a "felony" rather than the specific charge. For example, if the accused is on trial for armed robbery, and his prior conviction is also for armed robbery, the judge may sanitize the prior conviction by barring any mention of what kind of charge it was, and only permitting references to a prior felony. Some jurisdictions allow this approach; others bar it.

Prior convictions are always deemed important (noncollateral). If the witness does not admit the prior conviction, you may prove it up with extrinsic evidence. The most common proof is a certified copy of the judgment of conviction.

5. Prior Dishonest Acts

Impeachment with a prior dishonest act is permitted under FRE 608(b). Some states do not allow this method. The prior bad act must "attack . . . the witness's character for truthfulness." Common examples include a witness misstating her assets and liabilities in a loan application or misstating her education and experience in a job application. FRE 608(b) expressly provides that a prior bad act cannot be proven with extrinsic evidence. This means that the prior bad act must be brought out while the witness is testifying—but if the witness denies the prior bad act, you are stuck with the witness's answer and cannot contradict it with other evidence.

Example:

> Q: Ms. Adams, you worked at Tyson Manufacturing in 2020?
> A: That's right.
> Q: You were a sales representative?
> A: That's right.
> Q: On July 1, 2020, you submitted a business expense reimbursement form to Tyson Manufacturing for $783 in expenses you had not actually incurred, right?
> A: Well, that's what they claimed.

Example:

> Q: Mr. Henderson, in August 2020 you submitted a loan application to the Wells Fargo Bank in San Francisco, right?
> A: Yes.
> Q: On that loan application, you were required to answer questions about your assets, liabilities, and financial history?
> A: Yes.
> Q: One of the questions on that loan application, Question 14, asked "Have you ever previously filed for bankruptcy?"
> A: That was one of the questions.
> Q: Mr. Henderson, didn't you answer "no" to that question, when in fact you had filed for bankruptcy in the United States Bankruptcy Court in Baltimore, Maryland, on June 1, 2020?
> A: Yes.

Note that if the witness had answered "No, that's not true," that would still be the end of the matter, and you would not be allowed to introduce extrinsic evidence to prove that the answer was false. For that reason, it is important to bring out the details of the prior bad act during the cross-examination, so that jurors will believe your question, rather than the false answer.

6. Character for Untruthfulness

Bad character for truthfulness is permitted as an impeachment technique, but it is not a cross-examination technique. Under FRE 608(a), any witness who has testified can have his character for truthfulness attacked by a character witness. Once a fact witness's character for truthfulness has been attacked, the party calling that fact witness can then present supporting character evidence. All such character testimony, whether attacking or supporting, must be in general reputation or personal opinion form, and is limited to the character for untruthfulness or truthfulness.

For example, the plaintiff calls a fact witness during the plaintiff's case-in-chief. Thereafter, the defendant, in the defendant's case-in-chief, calls a character witness who testifies (in the form of general reputation or personal opinion) that the fact witness's character for truthfulness is bad. Thereafter, the plaintiff, in the plaintiff's rebuttal case, may call a character witness who testifies (in the form of general reputation or personal opinion) that the fact witness's character for truthfulness is good.

A witness's character for truthfulness must be "attacked" before it can be supported. That is, evidence of bad character for truthfulness must come first, then rebutting evidence of good character for truthfulness. Mistakes about this order are common, particularly in criminal cases. For example, assume that the defendant testifies in the defendant's case-in-chief, and the cross-examination does little damage. The defense *cannot* call a witness to testify to the defendant's good character for truthfulness, because the defendant's character for truthfulness has not been attacked.

Note, however, that FRE 608(a) provides that evidence of good character for truthfulness evidence is allowed only after the witness's character for truthfulness "has been attacked." What does "attack" mean? The rule recognizes that sometimes, during cross-examination, a witness can be attacked in a way that directly suggests the witness is not a truthful person. If that happens, the witness can then be accredited with good character for truthfulness.

For example, suppose that a fact witness, a friend of the defendant, has testified in the defense case-in-chief that he was with the defendant in a bar at the same time the robbery the defendant is accused of committing happened. On cross-examination, the prosecutor asks: "You'd say anything to help your friend, the defendant, beat the rap, wouldn't you?" This kind of cross-examination suggests that the witness is not a truthful person, and it should open the door to permitting the defense to call a witness to testify (in reputation or opinion form) that the fact witness has a good character for truthfulness. Some case law holds that strong impeachment, such as with a significant prior inconsistent statement or a major felony conviction, can constitute an attack on the witness's character for truthfulness, thereby allowing submission of evidence of good character for truthfulness.

7. Treatises

Impeachment using learned treatises and other reliable authorities is discussed in Chapter 8, on expert witnesses.

8. Impeaching Out-of-Court Declarants

The impeachment methods are commonly used during cross-examination of "live" witnesses. However, jurors also hear evidence from out-of-court declarants whose statements are admissible because they are nonhearsay or fall within a hearsay exception. This frequently happens when the transcript of a deposition or preliminary hearing of a now unavailable witness is admitted as former testimony under FRE 804(b)(1). It happens when statements of employees or co-conspirators are admitted as party admissions under FRE 801(d)(2). It happens when an out-of-court statement is admitted under a hearsay exception, such as an excited utterance or a dying declaration. Whatever the evidentiary basis, jurors frequently hear from out-of-court declarants whose credibility is then in issue.

How can you impeach an out-of-court declarant if the declarant is not a live witness during the trial? FRE 806 provides that you can impeach an out-of-court declarant with any of the impeachment methods you could have used had the declarant appeared as a live witness during the trial. However, the procedure is different, because you can't actually cross-examine the declarant. Under FRE 806, you simply introduce the impeaching matter when and how you would have introduced it as extrinsic evidence had the witness denied it on cross-examination (you are then required to prove up the unadmitted impeachment when it is your next turn to introduce evidence).

For example, assume that the prosecution introduced the transcript of an eyewitness's preliminary hearing testimony as former testimony under FRE 804(b)(1)(A), because the witness has since died. In the defense case, the defendant may introduce evidence that the deceased eyewitness was a convicted felon. This is usually done by offering a certified copy of the record of conviction.

As another example, assume that the defendant has introduced the transcript of the deposition testimony of a doctor as former testimony, because the doctor lives out of state and cannot be subpoenaed for trial. In the plaintiff's rebuttal case, the plaintiff may introduce evidence that an authoritative treatise contradicts what the doctor said. This is usually done by having a plaintiff expert testify that the treatise is considered authoritative.

FRE 806 is an important and frequently overlooked rule, because it permits impeaching out-of-court declarants at trial (even if that witness could have been impeached when the witness testified at a preliminary hearing or deposition).

6.8 Planning and Preparing a Cross-Examination

Cross-examination involves more than learning to ask simple, clear, leading questions. It involves more than learning the technical impeachment requirements and skills. Effective cross-examination also requires a methodology for developing, organizing, and executing a cross-examination for every witness in every case. How do you do that?

First, always begin with the jurors' perspective. What do they expect and want cross-examination to be? They want it to be interesting and informative. They want it to grab their interest immediately, in the first minute, or else they will stop listening. They want it to be organized, so that they can easily follow and understand the points made. They want it to provide new information that will change their impressions about the witness, the facts, and the case as a whole.

A sound methodology is to ask a progressive series of questions:

1. What is my theory of the case?
2. What are my themes and labels?
3. What are my closing argument points about this witness?
4. What facts exist to support those points?

5. What order should I adopt to bring out those facts on cross?
6. What tone and attitude should I use during cross?
7. What questioning style should I use during cross?

Always start with your theory of the case. There's little point in cross-examining a witness unless that cross-examination supports your theory of the case. For example, if you are presenting a self-defense claim asserting that the alleged victim was actually the initial aggressor, there is nothing to be gained from impeaching a prosecution witness who only testified that your client was in the bar when the fight took place, because you are not contesting this fact.

Next, remember your themes, the words and short phrases that summarize your theory of the case. Remember your labels, the words and short phrases that characterize the parties, events, and other important things in the case. Incorporate those themes and labels into the cross-examinations.

Third, ask yourself: During closing arguments, what will I say to the jurors about this witness? If you're not going to mention it during closing arguments, it's probably not worth mentioning during cross-examination.

Next, ask: What facts exist, that you can bring out during the cross-examination of this witness, that will support your closing argument? The essence of cross-examination is getting witnesses to admit facts that will support your closing argument points. After that, focus on the order in which you will bring out these facts. The two strongest points should be brought out first and last during the cross-examination. Save other items for the middle, remembering that too many points only dilute the stronger points.

After that, decide on the tone and attitude you will display during the cross-examination, the attitude that you want the jurors to adopt about this witness. Always ask: Why is this witness testifying the way he is? Is the witness mistaken, confused, or forgetful? Is the witness slanting his testimony to help or hurt one side? Is the witness intentionally fabricating his testimony? Your attitude during the cross-examination must be consistent with your later explanation, during closing arguments, for why the witness said what he did.

Finally, remember your questioning style during cross-examination. Make your questions short, simple, and leading. Make sure your questions raise only one fact at a time. Make sure you use strong nouns and verbs. Avoid "quibble words," those adjectives and adverbs that characterize the testimony; and conclusions, the "one question too many" that summarizes the testimony. These characterizations and conclusions are better saved for closing argument.

Inexperienced lawyers frequently spend too much time on questioning style and form, and too little time on analyzing how the substance of the planned cross-examination supports their theory of the case, themes, and labels. The better approach is to progressively use the methodology just described.

Example:

This is an attempted burglary case. The defendant, Robert Jones, is charged with attempting to break into Webster Electronics, a repair store in an older part of town. The key witness is Detective Barlow, who was assigned to do a surveillance of the store on January 15, observed the defendant, and arrested him. The store had been previously burglarized through the rear door, and the police had received a tip that another burglary would be attempted that night.

Detective Barlow testified on direct examination that he drove to Webster Electronics about midnight, and parked in his unmarked vehicle across the street from the store, about 50 feet away. From that vantage point he could see the front of the store and, through a plate-glass window, the lighted customer area. Webster Electronics is in the middle of the block. Between Jones and the next store to the left is a narrow alley that leads to a larger alley behind Webster Electronics and the other stores on the block. Across the larger alley is a public housing project. For the next two hours nothing unusual happened.

About 2:00 a.m., a dark Ford sedan pulled up in front of the store. There were two persons in the car. After a short time, the passenger got out, walked to the front of the store, looked in, and then went down the narrow alley along the left side of the store and out of sight. About a minute later a burglar alarm went off. Moments later the passenger came running out of the alley and jumped into the car, whereupon the car quickly drove off.

Detective Barlow made a U-turn and caught up to the Ford sedan a few blocks later and put on his emergency lights. The Ford then sped up and tried to get away, going down various streets and alleys. Detective Barlow finally curbed the Ford, arrested and handcuffed the two occupants, and put them in his car. The passenger was the 18-year-old defendant. The back of the car had several empty beer cans, and both the car and the occupants smelled of beer.

Detective Barlow then returned to Webster Electronics, and examined the rear of the store. The window in the rear door had been broken, apparently setting off the burglar alarm.

How will you, the defense lawyer, cross-examine this witness? Work through the methodology.

1. What Is My Theory of the Case?

In this case, there are at least three possible defense theories: (1) mistaken identification; (2) the defendant was there, but was there for some other purpose; (3) the underage defendant was drinking beer, and stopped in the alley to urinate. The third theory is the strongest and has the most factual support (assuming that the defendant says that's what really happened).

2. What Are My Themes and Labels?

In this case, a good defense theme is "wrong place, wrong time," which will emphasize that the defendant happened to be in the alley urinating while someone else was trying to break into the rear of the store. Another good defense theme is "shoddy police work," which will emphasize that Barlow's surveillance was inadequate to determine what really happened in the rear alley. The defendant should be referred to as "Bobby" or "kid" to highlight his youth.

3. What Are My Closing Argument Points about This Witness?

If the themes are "wrong place, wrong time" and "shoddy police work," what arguments can you make during closing? Consider at least the following:

(1) no real proof of an attempted burglary; (2) if there was an attempted burglary, there's no proof that the defendant, as opposed to someone else, did it (because the store is in a high-crime area, many others could have done it); (3) the defendant had been drinking beer, and was only urinating in the alley; (4) Barlow was in a poor position to see what was going on, and he was the only police officer there. These are the conclusions you will argue during closing arguments.

4. What Facts Exist to Support Those Points?

The next step is to identify the facts, which the witness must or is likely to admit, that support those conclusions. For example, what facts support the conclusion that there is no proof of an attempted burglary? These include: The defendant was not carrying any burglary tools, such as a crowbar or large screwdriver; the car contained none of these things; the defendant was not seen with any fruits of a burglary, such as electronic devices or parts; Barlow never checked the rear door of the store when he first arrived to check the condition of the door and window; no fingerprints were found on the rear door belonging to the defendant.

What facts support the conclusion that Barlow did a shoddy job? These include: Barlow knew that previous burglaries had been committed through the rear door; Barlow positioned himself across the street from the front door; Barlow never checked the rear door when he first arrived; Barlow couldn't see down the narrow alley, and he couldn't see what was going on in the larger alley behind the store; Barlow never checked for evidence of urination. These are the facts you will bring out during cross-examination, bit by bit, that will support the conclusions you will argue in closing arguments.

5. In What Order Should I Bring Out Those Facts on Cross?

The two strongest points should be made first and last, when they grab the jurors' attention and make lasting impressions. Perhaps the two strongest points are: (1) Barlow was not in a position to see what actually happened in the two alleys; (2) Bobby was simply urinating in the narrow alley, and Barlow didn't even investigate this possibility. Using this order, the jurors will be shown that this witness can't say what was actually happening in the alleys, and the witness can't refute the defense that Bobby was merely urinating, nothing more.

6. What Tone and Attitude Should I Use on Cross?

Because the defense theory is that Barlow (and the police department) did a shoddy, inadequate job of surveillance, use a tone and attitude scorning that lack of professionalism. This is not a case of a lay witness being mistaken, yet it is not a case of a witness intentionally fabricating. A middle tone, which conveys the message "we expect more from an experienced burglary detective" and "if the police had done their job right, we'd know what really happened," is the proper tone here. That's the attitude you want the jurors to take, so you must project it during the cross-examination.

7. What Questioning Style Should I Use on Cross?

Finally, practice asking short, simple, leading questions that bring out the helpful facts, one fact at a time. Make sure the questions are leading, because experienced police officers will make speeches when you give them the opportunity. Make sure the questions are simple, for the same reason. Avoid quibble words, the characterizations and conclusions that should be saved for closing arguments.

Planning a cross-examination takes time. Good cross-examinations look simple, but that's only because they were progressively planned and executed using a sound methodology. Planning is the time-consuming but necessary hard part. It's 90 percent preparation, 10 percent execution.

6.9 Preparing Your Witnesses for Cross-Examination

It's not enough to prepare your own witnesses for direct examination; you must prepare them for cross-examination as well. Like direct examination, this involves both content and demeanor. First, review direct examination preparation, discussed in Section 5.6, because most of the considerations in preparing the witness for direct examination apply equally to cross-examination. In particular, keep in mind that the attorney-client privilege protects only your conversations with your client, and does not extend to your conversations with nonclient witnesses. Talk to your nonclient witnesses as if the jurors were listening to the conversation, because your conversations may be brought out when the witness testifies. Indeed, given the ubiquity of cellphones with recording capability, it is possible that the witness is recording your conversation. Do not say or do anything you don't want the jury to hear about.

Next, devote sufficient time to preparing for cross-examination. Most witnesses, particularly inexperienced ones, are nervous and anxious about cross-examination. They want to know: What's the other lawyer like, what's she going to ask me during cross-examination, and how should I respond? Witnesses do well on cross when they know what topics the cross-examiner is likely to explore; know how the cross-examiner is likely to ask questions; understand how best to answer those questions; and maintain an appropriate, consistent demeanor during the entire examination.

Like direct examination, cross-examination involves impressions. Impressions are created not just by the content of the witness's answers, but also by the witness's tone and demeanor while answering. Explain that he should have the same attitude, demeanor, and memory on cross as he had on direct, because jurors are sensitive to any changes.

He should keep the same body position, gestures, and eye contact he used on direct. He should look at the cross-examiner when the questions are asked and look at the cross-examiner when he gives his answers. Never look at the direct examiner, because that suggests the witness is uncertain or looking for help. Avoid looking at the jury all the time, because this usually appears artificial and awkward. The witness should project a consistent attitude: I'm here to tell what I know, regardless of who's asking the questions. Accordingly, the witness needs to understand that cross-examiners sometimes attempt to annoy and challenge witnesses to get them to lose their composure. The best antidote to such a cross-examination is consistency. The meaner the cross-examiner gets, the nicer the witness should remain.

Many lawyers review a short list of dos and don'ts, which might include the following:

1. Make sure you understand the question. If you don't, say so. Don't guess.
2. If you know the answer, give it. If you don't know, say so. Don't guess. If you can only approximate, say so. However, give simple, clear answers whenever possible.
3. Answer only what the question calls for. Don't volunteer additional information.
4. Answer questions only with what you personally saw, heard, or did.
5. Be calm and serious at all times. Avoid arguing or quibbling with the other lawyer or getting upset over the lawyer's questions or attitude. I will make any necessary objections if the other lawyer is acting improperly, and I will conduct a redirect examination if necessary to cover any matters that should be clarified or explained.
6. If there is an objection, wait until the court rules, and answer the question only if the court overrules the objection.

Review the topics the cross-examiner is likely to ask questions about. Review the questions the cross-examiner is likely to ask. You should know the strengths and weaknesses of the witness's testimony and should know what topics the cross-examiner will pursue and how she will pursue them. These should be discussed with the witness, so that the witness will be able to respond to them accurately and positively.

Finally, practice the actual anticipated cross-examination with your client. Really practice! *Practice* means practicing the cross-examination in a courtroom setting. Practice means asking the actual questions the cross-examiner is likely to ask and hearing the actual answers your client will give. It means practicing enough so that your client understands what is likely to happen during cross-examination; understands how to answer the expected questions confidently and accurately; and learns how to maintain a consistent, calm demeanor. Practice until the client becomes comfortable with what he is likely to be asked and becomes comfortable with his responses to the expected questions. In most cases, the enemy of effective handling of cross-examination is underpreparation, not overpreparation. A common approach is to have another lawyer do the practice cross-examinations, using the attitude and style the actual cross-examiner is likely to use during the trial.

With nonclient witnesses, remember that anything you do and say during witness preparation can be brought out when the witness testifies. Therefore, when talking to such witnesses, whether about direct or cross-examination, conduct yourself as if the jurors are listening. Emphasize to the witness that your job is to help the witness understand what testifying in court involves and to deal with the witness's concerns, by explaining the procedure, helping identify what parts of his testimony are important, and learning how the witness will answer expected questions. Remind the witness that it is perfectly proper to meet with you (and any other lawyer) so that you can determine what the witness's testimony will be. Always emphasize that the witness's job is to testify about what he saw, heard, and did as accurately as possible. In short, always tell the truth.

6.10 Problem Witnesses

If every witness fairly answered every question, cross-examination would be much easier. But life is not so easy. Some witnesses simply go off on their own, saying what they want to say. Some, like children or elderly witnesses, may do it unintentionally. Others, like adverse parties, police officers, experts, or other hostile witnesses, may do it intentionally. Some witnesses are evasive and nonresponsive, others like to make speeches. Some witnesses like to quibble over words or change the question, others constantly try to "explain" things. How do you control such problem witnesses?

Remember that to control the answers, you must control the questions, and to control the questions you must have total control of the facts. Witnesses will say what they want to say, rather than what you want them to say, if you give them the opportunity. The solution, then, is not to give the witness the opportunity, or at least not a fair opportunity. You do this by making your questions short, simple, and leading, one fact at a time, and avoiding quibble words, so there is only one reasonable short answer to each question. You do this by letting the witness know that you have total control of the facts and that you will catch the witness if she embellishes her answers. You also do this by watching the witness carefully as he answers, letting the witness know that you are listening closely.

> For a discussion of problem witnesses, please watch Video E.3., "Wyo STI: Adverse Witnesses and Controlling Witnesses on Cross-Examination."

Example:

A burglary detective has testified about a surveillance he did of a store during an attempted burglary. The lawyer is holding the detective's report, and lets the detective know he is holding it.

Q (by cross-examiner): You arrived at the store to begin your surveillance at 12:05 a.m.?

A: I'm not sure of the exact time.

Q: Detective Barlow, you wrote in your report that you arrived at the store at 12:05 a.m., isn't that right?

A: Yes.

Q: You were in an unmarked car directly across from the store on the far side of the street?

A: Yes.

Q: The street, Main Street, has four lanes of traffic and parking lanes on both sides?

A: That's right.

Q: A black Ford sedan pulled up in front of the store at 2:17 a.m., right?

A: Yes.

Q: The Ford was stopped between your car and the front of the store, right?

A: Yes.

Q: You couldn't see the license plate on the Ford at that time, could you?

A: No, I couldn't.

Q: The passenger then got out of the car?

A: Yes.

Q: Stood in front of the store?

A: That's right.

Q: The passenger then walked to the alley alongside the store?

A: Yes.

Q: And went in the alley?

A: Yes.

Q: From where you were parked, you couldn't see into the alley, could you?

A: That's right.

Q: You couldn't see what the passenger was doing?

A: That's right.

Q: And you couldn't see where the passenger went, could you?

A: That's right.

These short, simple, leading questions do not give the witness an opportunity to make speeches, and they let the witness know that you have total command of the facts. With most hostile witnesses, control is the name of the game. Always remember that to control the witness's answers, you must control your questions. Whenever you find yourself losing control, return to the basics of good cross-examination.

What should you do if you ask good questions, and the witness nevertheless gives unresponsive answers? Consider the following:

Example:

> Q (by cross-examiner): Mr. Bozza, you were standing on the corner of Main and Elm when the two cars collided?
>
> A: Yes, that's when the big Jaguar sports car went right through the red light.

When this happens and you get a bad answer, look at it from the jurors' point of view. The jurors don't care that most of the answer was unresponsive, because jurors don't care about the technical rules of evidence. Jurors are interested in information. The unresponsive part of the answer is a problem only for you, not the jurors.

Two things don't work well. First, trying to cut off the witness and drown out the answer by talking over the unresponsive answer is ineffective (e.g., A: "Yes, that's when . . ." Q: "Thank you Mr. Bozza, you've answered the question. My next question is . . ."). Jurors hate it when lawyers try to muzzle a witness and cut off his answers. Second, running to the judge for help is ineffective (e.g., "Your honor, I object to the unresponsive part of the witness's answer, ask that it be stricken, and ask that the jury be instructed to disregard the unresponsive part of the answer."). Jurors remember testimony better when they are instructed to disregard it and doing this merely points out that you are weak and unable to control the witness. Save this for situations in which you must do it to preserve an important point as error on appeal.

If these approaches don't work, what does? Remember that jurors are forming impressions about witnesses, and those impressions are created by more than the witnesses' verbal answers. How witnesses sound, look, and act are important, and that's the key to handling problem witnesses who won't obey the rules. You can't "unring the bell" and erase the bad answer, so do the next best thing: Show the jurors that the witness isn't playing fair and that the witness's answers should be ignored. The less fairly and reasonably the witness is acting, the more fair and reasonable you should be. The more the witness is a jerk, the nicer you must be. In short, don't join the witness; contrast and expose the witness. One method is to repeat the question until the witness answers just your question.

Example:

Q: Mr. Bozza, you were standing on the corner of Main and Elm when the two cars collided, right?

A: Yes, that's when the big Jaguar sports car went right through the red light.

Q: Mr. Bozza, maybe I didn't ask it clearly. You were standing on the corner when the two cars collided?

A: Yes, and that's when the Jag went through the light.

Q: Let me ask it one more time. You were standing on the corner when the two cars collided?

A: Yes.

If the witness continues to say what he wants to say, the jurors will quickly understand that your question is simple, clear, and fair, and will conclude that the witness just won't answer your question without volunteering what he wants to say. In addition, the judge will often jump in and admonish the witness when a witness repeatedly refuses to give responsive answers to simple questions (e.g., "Mr. Bozza, please listen to the question and answer only the question."). The important point is that the cross-examiner did not ask the judge for help in controlling the witness—the judge did it on her own.

Another method is to repeat the responsive part of the witness's answer and ask the witness to agree. This points out for the jurors that the witness was volunteering information that your question did not call for.

Example:

Q: Mr. Bozza, you were standing on the corner of Main and Elm when the two cars collided, right?

A: Yes, that's when the big Jaguar sports car went right through the red light and crashed into the other car.

Q: Mr. Bozza, your answer to my question is "yes"?

A: Yes.

Another method is to use "training questions" to see if the witness will give speeches. If he does, you then train the witness to obey.

Example:

Q: Mr. Bozza, you grew up in New York City, right?

A: Yes, in Queens, actually, and then I moved to Buffalo for college, and then I returned to Manhattan after I graduated.

This answer, of course, didn't hurt the cross-examiner, but it shows that the witness is likely to "take off" on questions. Now is the time to rein in the witness, train him to obey, and let him know that if he continues to give unrequested information you will expose it before the jury.

Example:

> Q: Mr. Bozza, let's take this one fact at a time. You were born in Queens, right?
> A: Yes.
> Q: You grew up in Queens?
> A: That's right.
> Q: When you went to college you moved to Buffalo?
> A: That's right, SUNY-Buffalo.
> Q: Mr. Bozza, my question was, you moved to Buffalo?
> A: Yes.
> Q: And you went to SUNY-Buffalo?
> A: Yes.
> Q: And after graduating, you moved back to Manhattan?
> A: Yes.

What do you do when a witness repeatedly answers with evasive responses such as "I don't know," "I'm not sure," and "I don't remember"? Again, keep in mind that cross-examination is about creating impressions. Jurors will quickly sense when a witness is unfairly avoiding answering reasonable questions, particularly when the witness had no difficulty answering the direct examiner's questions. Therefore, expose the witness as being unfair, rather than trying to get concrete answers.

Example:

> Q: Mr. Benson, you saw the collision?
> A: Yes.
> Q: The collision happened about 9:00 a.m.?
> A: I'm not sure of the exact time.
> Q: And you were about 25 feet from the cars when they crashed?
> A: I'm not sure of the exact distance.
> Q: But you were around 25 feet away?
> A: I'm not sure.
> Q: Well, were you less than 10 feet away?
> A: I'm not sure.
> Q: Were you more than 100 feet away?
> A: As I said, I'm not sure.
> Q: The only thing you're sure about is that you're not sure, is that it?

Regardless of what the witness answers, you have made your point that this witness, during cross-examination, is refusing to commit to facts he should be able to answer directly.

Problem witnesses must be shown to be what they are: acting unfairly and not playing by the rules. It's the unfairness that jurors react to and causes the jurors not to forget the bad answers, but to ignore them.

6.11 Recross-Examination

Many judges do not permit recross-examination, absent a compelling need. These judges regularly bar it under FRE 611(a). Most take the position that the direct, cross, and redirect examinations should bring out everything the witness has to say. Judges, and jurors, see recross-examination for what it usually is: an obvious attempt to get in the last word or emphasize something already covered during the cross-examination. If recross-examination is permitted, the usual rule is that only the cross-examiner, not another member of the trial team, can do the recross-examination.

If you feel that you need to recross a particular witness, ask the judge for the opportunity. Make a record. Tell the judge that you wish to go into a specific, limited area that the redirect examination went into for the first time, or which in fairness you should be allowed to address. Some judges sometimes permit a limited recross-examination. Other judges take the position that if the redirect examination went into a new area, you should have objected that it was "beyond the scope" at that time, rather than using the situation as an opportunity to request a recross-examination. These discretionary calls by the judge are based on considerations of fairness and courtroom efficiency.

6.12 Proving Up Unadmitted Impeachment

Most witnesses, when confronted with an impeaching matter, will admit it. When this happens, there is no need to prove it up, because the witness has already admitted the impeachment, and most jurisdictions do not allow further proof of an admitted prior inconsistent statement.

What happens when a witness is asked about an impeaching matter, but does not admit it? As discussed in Section 6.2, under the traditional analysis, if the impeaching matter is noncollateral and the witness denies it or equivocates, the cross-examiner should prove up the unadmitted impeachment with extrinsic evidence when the cross-examiner next has the opportunity to present evidence. If the unadmitted matter is collateral, it cannot be proved up with extrinsic evidence.

Today, however, judges are moving away from the traditional technical analysis and are focusing more on the importance of the unadmitted impeachment in determining whether it must be proved up. That's because the real concern is judicial efficiency, which is governed by the FRE 403 analysis. The key question is this: Is the unadmitted impeaching matter important enough, in the context of this case, that it makes sense to use court time to call another witness or introduce another exhibit to prove up the impeaching matter?

Four impeachment categories may be involved:

1. Bias, interest, and motive
2. Prior inconsistent statements
3. Contradictory facts
4. Prior convictions

Of these, bias, interest, and motive and prior convictions are always deemed important. Prior inconsistent statements and contradictory facts are taken on a case-by-case basis: some are important, others not.

1. Bias, Interest, and Motive

Proving up unadmitted impeachment showing bias or interest is usually simple. For example, suppose the following happens during the cross-examination of a plaintiff witness.

Example:

> Q: You were fired from your job by the defendant last year, right?
> A: No.

This fact, if true, shows that the witness is biased against the defendant. The cross-examiner, in the defendant's case-in-chief, should now prove that the witness was in fact fired by the defendant. This can be done by calling a witness with personal knowledge of the firing, or by introducing business records that record the firing.

Suppose the following happens during the cross-examination of a defense witness.

Example:

> Q: The defendant owes you $100,000, right?
> A: No, that's not true.

This fact, if true, shows that the witness has an interest in having the defendant win the lawsuit (making it more likely that the defendant will be able to repay the indebtedness). The cross-examiner, in the plaintiff's rebuttal case, should now prove that the defendant in fact owes the witness $100,000. This can be done by calling a witness who has personal knowledge of the indebtedness, or by introducing documents that prove the indebtedness.

More problematic is unadmitted impeachment showing motive. This most commonly arises in criminal cases, when the defense claims that a prosecution witness has a motive to testify falsely against the defendant. For example, suppose the following happens during cross-examination of a prosecution witness.

Example:

> Q: Mr. Lacy, you don't like the defendant, do you?
> A: I don't care about him one way or another.
> Q: You used to have a girlfriend named Marcy Jackson, right?
> A: Right.
> Q: But she's not your girlfriend anymore, is she?
> A: No.
> Q: In fact, she's now the defendant's girlfriend, right?
> A: That's what I hear.
> Q: And that made you angry?
> A: Not really.
> Q: And since then you've been looking for a way to get back at the defendant for stealing your girlfriend, isn't that true?
> A: No.

This cross-examination has directly suggested that the witness's testimony is motivated by a desire to retaliate against the defendant for stealing the witness's girlfriend. Because the witness has denied it, the cross-examiner should, during the defendant's case-in-chief, call a witness who can testify that the defendant was in fact angry about losing his girlfriend and was in fact looking for a way to get back at the defendant.

Judges and jurors will expect testimony from prove-up witnesses to be efficiently presented. Introduce the witness, get to the important information and bring it out quickly, and stop.

Example:

> Q: Mr. Roberts, do you know a Richard Lacy?
> A: Yes.
> Q: How did you get to know him?
> A: We're in the same class at Central High.
> Q: Do you know a Marcy Jackson?
> A: Yes.
> Q: How did you get to know her?
> A: She was his girlfriend until a few months ago. I used to see the two of them together all the time.
> Q: Is Marcy Jackson still Richard Lacy's girlfriend?
> A: No. She left him and started going with the defendant.
> Q: How did Richard Lacy react to that?
> A: He was really steamed. He kept saying he was going to find a way to get even.
> Q: When did he say that?
> A: It was shortly before the defendant got arrested.

2. Prior Inconsistent Statements

A prior inconsistent statement is the most commonly used impeachment method, and it is here that the prove-up requirement will apply most frequently. Any important (noncollateral) unadmitted prior inconsistent statement must be proved up. How this is done depends on the kind of prior inconsistent statement involved.

a. Oral Statements

Witnesses frequently deny making oral statements to another person. If the statement is important, it should be proved up. For example, consider a plaintiff witness who says on direct examination that the light for Main Street was red at the time of the crash. If the witness during cross-examination denies or equivocates about telling a police officer that the light was green at the time of the crash, that unadmitted impeaching statement must be proved up. You do this in the defense case-in-chief by calling any witness who personally heard the impeaching statement made (here, the police officer) to testify as to the statement.

Example:

> Q: Officer Jones, did you talk to a witness, a James Smith, after the collision?
> A: Yes, I did.

Q: Where was that?

A: Right at the accident scene. We were standing on the sidewalk.

Q: Was anyone else present?

A: No, it was just the two of us.

Q: What did Mr. Smith say?

A: He said: "The traffic light was green for Main Street at the time of the collision."

b. Written or Signed Statements

Witnesses are unlikely to deny making a written or signed statement, because the statement will be in the witness's handwriting or signed by the witness. Nevertheless, it sometimes happens and, if the statement is important, it must be proved up.

For example, consider a plaintiff witness who says on direct examination that the light for Main Street was red at the time of the crash. If the witness, during cross-examination, denies or equivocates about writing or signing a statement that the light was green at the time of the crash, that unadmitted impeaching statement must be proved up. You do this in the defense case-in-chief by calling a witness who either saw the statement when it was being made, or is familiar with the witness's handwriting or signature, to testify that the plaintiff's witness wrote or signed the statement. The impeaching part can then be read or shown to the jurors.

Example:

Q: Ms. Adams, you are an accident investigator?

A: Yes.

Q: As part of your investigation of this case, did you talk to a Mr. James Smith?

A: Yes.

Q: When and where was that?

A: It was two days after the accident, at his house.

Q: What happened during that talk?

A: I asked Mr. Smith if he would write out in his own handwriting what he saw that day, and he agreed.

Q: What did he do?

A: He took a plain sheet of paper I gave him, wrote on it while I watched, signed it, and gave it to me.

Q: I'm showing you what has already been marked Defendant's Exhibit No. 1 and shown to opposing counsel [hands exhibit to witness]. Do you recognize Defendant's Exhibit No. 1?

A: Yes.

Q: What do you recognize it to be?

A: That's the handwritten and signed statement Mr. Smith made.

Q: How do you know it's his statement?

A: I saw him write it and sign it, and then he gave it to me.

Q: Ms. Adams, please read the sentence that begins here [pointing].

A: "At the time of the crash, the light was green for Main Street."

Note that under FRE 801(d)(1)(A), the witness's prior statement was not made under oath at a judicial proceeding, so it is not substantive evidence.

Therefore, most judges will not allow such a statement to be formally admitted in evidence.

c. Transcripts of Sworn Testimony

Witnesses are unlikely to deny statements made while testifying under oath at a judicial proceeding, such as a deposition or hearing, where a court reporter was present and recorded everything that was said. However, witnesses sometimes deny or quibble over the accuracy of the transcript and claim that they "didn't say that" or "the court reporter got it wrong." If that happens, and the statement is important, it should be proved up.

For example, consider a defense witness who says on direct examination that the light for Main Street was red at the time of the crash. If the witness during cross-examination denies or equivocates about whether he said during his deposition that the light was green at the time of the crash, that unadmitted impeaching statement must be proved up. You do this by calling, in the plaintiff's rebuttal case, the court reporter who attended the deposition and prepared the transcript, to testify to the making of the deposition transcript and the accuracy of the questions asked of and answers given by the witness. Make sure that the court reporter brings the original stenographic notes in addition to the certified transcript of the testimony.

Example:

> Q: Ms. Holly, did you attend the deposition of a Mr. James Smith on June 1, 2020?
>
> A: Yes, I did.
>
> Q: Did you record the questions asked and answers given during that deposition?
>
> A: Yes.
>
> Q: How did you do that?
>
> A: I took the deposition first on my stenographic machine, which prints on a ribbon of paper the notes I type as the deposition is being held. I also make an audiotape, which I can use if I have trouble understanding any of the spoken words. Afterwards, I prepare a typed transcript of the deposition, check it for accuracy, and then certify that the transcript is accurate. The transcript contains all the questions asked and answers given during the deposition, word for word.
>
> Q: Do you have your stenographic notes and your deposition transcript with you today?
>
> A: Yes, I brought them here at your request.
>
> Q: How about the audiotape?
>
> A: I only keep the audiotape until I prepare the transcript, so that's no longer available.

[The notes and transcript should be marked as exhibits, shown to opposing counsel, and then given to the witness.]

> Q: Exhibit No. 1 is your original stenographic notes?
>
> A: Yes.
>
> Q: Exhibit No. 2 is the deposition transcript?
>
> A: Yes.
>
> Q: At my request, did you again compare the notes and the transcript?

A: I did. They're identical.

Q: I'm going to ask you to read from your original stenographic notes. Please turn to your notes where they record what is on page 32 of your transcript. Ms. Holly, please read the first question and answer on that page as they appear on your notes.

A: The first question is: "Q. What color was the light at the time of the crash?" Mr. Smith's answer is: "A. The light for Main Street was green."

Q: Does that accurately show the question asked, and Mr. Smith's answer, that day?

A: Yes, it does. It's word for word.

When faced with proving up a statement from a deposition or other judicial proceeding, the lawyers frequently stipulate to the accuracy of the transcript, so that the pertinent portions of the transcript can simply be read to the jury by the lawyer. This eliminates the need to call the court reporter as a witness.

Example:

LAWYER: Your honor, may I read a stipulation to the jury at this time?

JUDGE: You may.

LAWYER: Members of the jury, there is an agreement between the lawyers for the plaintiff and defendant that the transcript of Mr. James Smith's deposition taken on June 1, 2020, is an accurate, word-for-word transcript of the questions asked and the answers given during the deposition. In particular, Mr. Smith was asked this question and gave this answer during his deposition: "Q. What color was the light at the time of the crash?" Mr. Smith's answer was: "A. The light for Main Street was green."

Note that the witness's prior inconsistent statements that are contained in a deposition or other judicial proceeding are substantive evidence under FRE 801(d)(1)(A). That means the jurors can consider the truth of the statements. The entire transcript itself, however, is usually not offered in evidence or admitted as an exhibit.

d. Omissions

Whenever a witness has made a report or record of an event, and the witness failed to put in that report or record the fact that he is now testifying about, the witness can be impeached by that omission. This happens frequently with police officers and other investigators using their case reports. When confronted with the omission, the witnesses almost always admit the omission, particularly when they are shown the report or record.

In the rare event that the witness does not admit that the report or record omits a particular fact, consider asking the judge to permit the jurors to inspect the statement or record of that witness, or ask for permission to project it on a screen or monitor for the jurors. Although the report or record may not be admissible as substantive evidence, the jurors should be allowed to see it for this limited purpose.

3. Contradictory Facts

Witnesses are frequently asked during cross-examination to admit a fact inconsistent with what they testified to on direct examination. If the fact is important, and the witness denies it or equivocates about it, the fact must be proved up.

For example, consider a defense witness who says on direct examination that he had just left his office building and was walking to his car when he saw the crash. If the witness during cross-examination denies or equivocates about having had "three double scotches at the Corner Tavern in the hour before the crash," this contradictory fact is important and must be proved up. Plaintiff does this in the plaintiff's rebuttal case by calling anyone with personal knowledge of the fact.

Example:

Q: Ms. Baum, you're the owner of the Corner Tavern?
A: That's right.
Q: You also work there?
A: I own it, manage it, and work there as a bartender.
Q: Were you there on June 1, 2020?
A: Yes.
Q: Do you know a James Smith?
A: Sure, he's a regular. He lives a block away.
Q: Was he there on June 1?
A: Yes.
Q: What time?
A: He was there about an hour, from 4:00 to 5:00 p.m.
Q: What was he doing during that time?
A: He was sitting at the bar, watching the TV, and he had three double scotches.
Q: Are you sure about that?
A: You bet. I served him myself.
Q: What did he do after that?
A: Around 5:00 he walked out and went up the street toward his house.

4. Prior Convictions

Witnesses may be impeached with certain prior convictions, under FRE 609. When witnesses are asked about prior convictions, they will sometimes deny or equivocate. Because prior convictions as a category are always considered important (noncollateral), if the witness does not admit a prior conviction or equivocates about it, you must prove it up.

Consider a prosecution witness who is asked on cross-examination: "Weren't you convicted of burglary on June 1, 2020?" and denies it. In the defense case-in-chief, the defense must prove up the prior conviction. This is usually done by introducing a certified copy of the record of conviction as a public record under FRE 803(8).

Sometimes the witness, even when confronted with a certified copy of the record of conviction, will still deny that he is the same person as the person named on the record. This can be a problem when people have common names or use different names. When this happens, you should be prepared to prove that the witness is the same person named in the record of conviction. Probably the best proof is a certified copy of the witness's arrest record or prison record, including his photographs and fingerprints, that corresponds to the record of conviction. That record, which will prove the witness's identity, should also be admissible as a public record under FRE 803(8).

5. Failure to Prove Up When Required

What happens when a party is obligated to prove up important unadmitted impeachment, but fails to do so? There are three options. First, you can move to strike the unproved impeachment and instruct the jurors to disregarded it. For example, if a witness is cross-examined about drinking three scotches just before seeing the crash and denies it, and the cross-examiner never introduces extrinsic evidence of the drinking, you can move to strike the testimony and have the jury instructed to disregard the unproved matter. The problem, however, is that you can't unring the bell. Indeed, jury research suggests that instructions to disregard testimony have the opposite effect.

Second, you can move for a mistrial. If the unproved impeachment makes it impossible to have a fair trial, you must make the motion in timely fashion or else you will probably be deemed to have waived the issue on appeal. For example, if the defendant in a criminal case is cross-examined about a prior armed robbery conviction and denies it, and the prosecution in its rebuttal case fails to introduce evidence of the prior conviction, this should be a good ground for a mistrial. However, you need to make the motion promptly when the prosecution rests in rebuttal.

Third, you can elect not to move to strike and disregard. Instead, use the other side's failure to prove up important unadmitted impeachment during closing arguments. You can then point out what the other side did, why what it did is unfair, and why it did it. Many lawyers prefer to use the other side's failure during closing argument, because it can be an effective tool.

Example (Closing Argument):

> Remember when the defendant's lawyer cross-examined Mr. Johnson, the eyewitness who saw the whole thing from beginning to end? The lawyer asked him: "Didn't you have three scotches before you saw the crash?" Remember Mr. Johnson's answer: "No, that's not true." If that was true, wouldn't you think the first thing the lawyer would have done is present some evidence that Mr. Johnson had been drinking? But the lawyer never did! It makes you wonder: Why does their case depend on trying to smear a key eyewitness's integrity, and then never back it up with a single shred of evidence? What does that tell you about their case?

6.13 Trial Notebook

The cross-examination section of your trial notebook should contain the outlines of the planned cross-examinations of each witness who may be called by your opponents.

First, because you usually don't know the order in which your opponents will call their witnesses, put the cross-examination outlines in alphabetical order in your trial notebook, so you can find them quickly when a witness is called.

Second, create a witness folder for each witness. The folder will contain a copy of the cross-examination outline; a copy of each exhibit you may want the witness to qualify for admission in evidence or use in some way; and a copy of each statement the witness has made, whether deposition transcripts, written statements, or reports. The statements are potential impeachment material if the witness testifies inconsistently. The witness folder should contain everything you need to cross-examine each witness. Put the witness folders in alphabetical order so you can retrieve them quickly.

Third, prepare a cross-examination outline for each witness. The standard approach is to outline the cross-examination topics, in the order you intend to cover them. Note on the outline when you want to use exhibits, and note where you have impeachment on key facts if the witness testifies inconsistently.

Don't write out your expected cross-examination questions. This binds you to a script, which prevents you from watching and listening to the witness and spontaneously asking focused follow-up questions. Scripted cross-examinations rarely work well.[2]

> ◼◀ For a discussion about drafting cross-examination outlines, please watch the last half of Video D.2, "Wyo STI: Direct & Cross-Examination Outlines."

How do you actually outline the cross-examination? A common and effective method is to split the page down the middle. Put your cross-examination topics and notes on the left side. Leave the right side blank. During the direct examination of the witness, take only those notes that help your planned cross-examination. Put those notes on the blank right side of the page, next to the cross-examination topics to which the notes relate.

It is a serious mistake for the cross-examiner to take detailed notes during the direct examination. Have someone else do this if you feel it is necessary. You need to watch and listen intently during the direct examination so you can make timely and well-grounded objections, observe the witness's tone and body language, and make focused notes of particular things the witness says on your cross-examination outline.

Many lawyers put on the top of the outline a short summary of the expected direct testimony, each exhibit they may use with that witness, and all prior statements the witness made. Be sure to put exact quotes and page and line references to documents and transcripts so that impeachment material can be found quickly. Before you start your cross-examination, make sure you have all the exhibits at hand, in the order you plan to use them, and the witness's prior statements, in case you need to use them. This shows the jurors that you are organized, prepared, and know what you're doing.

---

2. Junior co-author Easton believes cross-examination questions, or more precisely the "guts" of the questions, should be written in advance whenever possible (though direct examination questions should not be written in advance). The guts of the questions are often small portions of prior statements by the witness, like "the car was going 50 m.p.h." Like Professor Mauet, Easton would not recommend writing out the full question, so he would omit the "right?" at the end of the factual statement that constitutes the cross-examination "question." But he believes in writing the guts of the question in advance, because the wording of cross-examination questions, which are really statements of fact, is critical. A small change in the wording might turn a solid cross-examination "question" into a dangerous one.

Junior co-author Easton also believes that every cross-examination question in the outline should be followed by a reference to the document, page, and line that supports the question. If you do this, you will know exactly where to go — usually to a portion of some prior statement by the witness — if the witness refuses to admit the fact in your "question." If there is nothing to support your question, you should remove it from your cross-examination outline.

Example:

DOUGLAS CANNON—CROSS-EXAMINATION

Purpose in trial:	Defendant is defense's key liability witness, will claim his lack of negl., and pl.'s contributory negl.
Exhibits:	1. intersection photos—Ex. #10
	2. intersection diagram—Ex. #9
Prior statements:	1. police report—Ex. #14, p. 3
	2. Def. deposition—Ex. #18, p. 40, line 6

Cross topics & references: *Direct notes*

1. Wife sick, to dr., appt. at 6:00, "late" (police report, Ex. #14, p. 3, third ¶). Dr. office 2 mi. from place of collision (map from internet, Ex. 72)

2. Wife nausea, lying back on front seat (police report, Ex. #14, p. 3, last ¶)

3. Sun at 6:00 p.m.: bright, low, in west (weather report, Ex. 62, second ¶)

4. Stopped in "middle" of intersection, waiting for light to change (deposition transcript, p. 28, line 6)

5. Only traffic light in intersection was over center of intersection (photo of intersection, Ex. 48)

6. Looking at light, up, left toward sun (police report, Ex. #14, p. 4, first ¶)

7. Didn't see Gable's oncoming car until "after began making turn" (deposition tr., p. 40, line 2)

8. "Didn't know where other car came from" (police report statement, p. 4, second ¶)

> 🌐 An example of a trial notebook, with shell forms and completed forms, is on the website that accompanies this book.

6.14 Common Problems

What are the recurring problems that inexperienced lawyers encounter during cross-examinations?

1. Weak Beginning

You have one or two minutes to let the jurors know that your cross-examination will be fresh and interesting and will bring out additional information to make them see this witness, and the case, differently. Start immediately with something important, something that has an impact, that makes the jurors think: This lawyer is worth listening to; I'll stayed tuned. Slow starts, particularly on cross-examination, do not work with today's jurors.

2. Weak Selection of Points

Cross-examination is in large part the art of identifying and focusing on a few key points that will make a difference in the jurors' perception of the witness and the case. Trying to cover everything, and spending time on marginal matters, only dilutes the key points. A good way to test yourself is to ask: Is this point important enough that I'm going to cover it in my closing argument? If not, it's usually not important enough to cover during cross-examination.

3. Losing Control

Cross-examination is frustrating, because the actual cross-examination rarely goes the way you had it planned. A common reaction, when things don't go as planned, is to begin arguing with the witness and forgetting your game plan. When this happens, the cross-examination degenerates, and jurors usually side with the witness. Losing control is often caused by having unrealistic expectations of what you can accomplish during the cross-examination of a particular witness.

4. Ineffective Impeachment Technique

Effective impeachment requires an effective technique. Many lawyers attempt to impeach witnesses, but have no impact on the jurors because there is no clean technique and accompanying attitude that grab the jurors' attention and drive home the point.

5. No Attitude Projection

Cross-examination consists in large part of creating impressions. Whenever you cross-examine, you need to decide what kind of attitude you want the jurors to adopt about this witness. Is the witness confused, mistaken, or forgetful? Unconsciously distorting because of bias, interest, or motive? Intentionally distorting or even fabricating facts? Unless you project the same attitude you want the jurors to have, it is unlikely they will adopt it.

6. Weak Ending

Cross-examinations frequently end when the cross-examiner runs out of questions to ask. This is a mistake, because jurors remember best what they hear first and last. Always ask: What's the most (or second most) important point I can make about this witness, that I am reasonably sure I can successfully make? Cross-examinations should always end on a high note.

CHAPTER 7

EXHIBITS AND VISUAL AIDS

7.1 Introduction

Ours is the age of visual media. Television, computers, and smart phones have become the dominant information-transmitting sources in our society. Printed and oral communications have taken a back seat to the visual media. A whole generation of Americans has been raised and educated primarily by seeing. Children learn by watching TV and using computers, not by reading. Critics complain that the art of clear speaking and clear writing is becoming lost.

Whether this change is desirable can be debated, but not its existence. Visual communications have grown by leaps and bounds. Advertising on TV, computers, magazines, and billboards is often predominantly nonverbal, influencing its viewers by subconscious appeals.

Social science research supports the shift from the oral and written to the visual. Studies show that learning and retention are significantly better if information is communicated visually. Studies confirm that if information is presented through multiple "channels"—oral, written, and visual—understanding and memory are again substantially improved. In short, visual exhibits are important not only in presenting new information in an attractive, memorable way but also in highlighting and summarizing information already presented through another medium. "Show and tell" works.

These changes have hardly gone unnoticed in the courtroom. Led by imaginative personal injury lawyers, other lawyers began to realize that, in the courtroom as well, a picture was indeed worth a thousand words. If a picture was so useful, so too could be a map, chart, diagram, model, movie, experiment, or in-court demonstration. Trial lawyers began using aerial photographs. Automobiles and machinery were reassembled in court. "A day in the life" movies portrayed personal injury plaintiffs. Elaborate models of buildings and accident sites appeared. In-court demonstrations became common. Computer-generated graphics and three-dimensional simulations were admissible. In short, exhibits assumed a new importance.

What can be an exhibit? In its broadest sense an exhibit can be anything, other than testimony, that can be perceived by the senses and be presented in the courtroom as evidence. Any trial lawyer who has ever been involved in a case that used exhibits creatively knows the impact they have on the jury.

The exhibits become the center of attention. They make an immediate and lasting impression on the jury. It sees the exhibits as not only more interesting, but also more reliable. Accordingly, any aspiring trial lawyer must learn more than how to establish the foundation for common as well as more dramatic exhibits. She must also learn when to use exhibits and other visual aids, and how to present them effectively at trial.

This chapter will discuss the proper procedures for having exhibits admitted in evidence, the foundation requirements of exhibits commonly encountered during trials, and how and when to use exhibits and other visual aids effectively during all the stages of a trial.

7.2 The Law

Evidence law regulates two distinct aspects of exhibits: the general procedural requirements for getting exhibits formally admitted in evidence, and the technical evidentiary foundations required for different kinds of exhibits. Evidence law does not specifically address the use of visual aids during the trial; this is largely controlled by the judge.

1. Foundation Procedure for Exhibits

Federal Rule of Evidence (FRE) 611(a) provides that the judge "should exercise reasonable control over the mode and order of . . . presenting evidence," but specific foundation procedures are based primarily on case law and local practices. Although the level of formality may differ among jurisdictions, and among judges within a jurisdiction, the purpose behind the procedures is the same: Create a clear record, establish the proper foundation for each exhibit, and give opposing parties a fair opportunity to challenge the admissibility of each exhibit.

Courtroom procedure usually includes the following steps:

1. Have the exhibit marked, if not already marked.
2. Show the exhibit to the opposing lawyer.
3. Ask permission to show the exhibit to the witness.
4. Give the exhibit to the witness.
5. Establish proper foundation for the exhibit.

6. Offer the exhibit in evidence.
7. Have the exhibit marked in evidence.
8. Have the witness use or mark the exhibit, if appropriate.
9. Ask permission to show or read the exhibit to the jurors.
10. Show or read the exhibit to the jurors.

Some judges still follow the traditional rule that exhibits can only be offered in evidence by the party currently presenting evidence. This means that only the plaintiff can introduce exhibits in evidence in the plaintiff's case-in-chief, and only the defendant in the defendant's case-in-chief. It also means that while the cross-examiner may use other exhibits during cross-examinations of the opponent's witnesses, the cross-examiner can only offer those exhibits in evidence when it is the cross-examiner's turn to present evidence. However, many judges now permit a cross-examiner to introduce exhibits in evidence during cross-examinations of an opponent's witnesses, provided that a proper foundation has been established. These procedures are governed by FRE 611(a) and are in the trial judge's discretion.

Your preliminary consideration is foundation witness selection. Many times, you will have more than one witness who is competent to qualify an exhibit for admission in evidence. When this is so, you will ordinarily select the witness who has the most knowledge of the exhibit and its required foundation and makes the best impression on the jury. Call the witness early in your case-in-chief, since it is usually advantageous to get your exhibits before the jury as soon as possible. Keep in mind that some exhibits may need more than one witness to establish a proper foundation. In such cases, do not offer the exhibit in evidence until the last necessary witness has testified.

The following steps for getting exhibits into evidence constitute the most complete procedure. Most courts have relaxed some of the requirements. For instance, many courts permit or require marking exhibits before trial. Many do not require asking permission to approach the witness. Nevertheless, you must be familiar with the most formal procedural requirements, then determine in advance of trial which ones have been relaxed or eliminated by your particular court. Be sure to make a good record of what you are doing in the courtroom by stating what you are doing as you do it, because court reporters record the words spoken in a courtroom, but not most of the nonverbal actions during trial.

Step 1. Have the exhibit marked, if not already marked

Every exhibit must be marked so it can be differentiated from all others. Exhibits are most commonly given sequential numbers or letters (e.g., 1, 2, 3). Where certain exhibits are part of a series, they can be marked 1A, 1B, 1C, or 1-1, 1-2, 1-3. Sets of exhibits that should remain together should be marked as group exhibits. Use any numbering system that logically marks the exhibits in your type of case. Exhibits are usually marked to show which party offered them (e.g., Plaintiff, Defendant, Government, Defendant Smith), although the practice in some jurisdictions is not to designate which side offered the exhibit. In that case, a common practice is to allocate certain numbers to the plaintiff, others to the defendant (e.g., plaintiff has #1-99, defendant has #100-199).

In most jurisdictions, exhibits are simply marked "Plaintiff's Exhibit #1," "Defendant's Exhibit #1," and so on. A few jurisdictions mark exhibits "for identification," as in "People's Exhibit #5 for identification." If the exhibits are not marked before trial, the court clerk or the court reporter, depending on local practice, usually marks them. In most jurisdictions exhibit labels are put on the exhibits, either on the front or the back of the exhibit. The exhibit labels, which are often color-coded, usually show which side offered the exhibit, the exhibit number, and when it was first introduced. Check with the judge's clerk before trial to learn how the judge wants exhibits to be marked.

Example:

> **LAWYER (to court clerk):** Please mark this Plaintiff's Exhibit No. 1.
>
> Hand the exhibit to the clerk, who will attach a label to the exhibit, mark it "Plaintiff's Exhibit No. 1," and return it to you.

If your jurisdiction permits or requires premarking exhibits, make sure your labels clearly designate which party's exhibits they are. If the exhibit has previously been used during the trial, it will already be marked, so this step is unnecessary.

When permitted by local practice, mark your exhibits before trial. This has become the common practice for exhibits that exist before trial, with mid-trial marking reserved for exhibits created during trial, such as an expert witness's written calculations. Indeed, the best practice is to provide notebooks containing copies of your exhibits, prenumbered, to opposing counsel, the judge, the court clerk, and sometimes even the jurors, at least for stipulated exhibits.

Step 2. Show the exhibit to the opposing lawyer

Fairness requires that the opposing lawyer see the exhibit so that she knows what kind of exhibit it is and what the proper foundation for that exhibit is, and so that she can make a timely objection if the foundation is not properly established or another evidentiary problem exists. Most jurisdictions require that the exhibit be shown to the opposing lawyer before the foundation is established (even if the opposing lawyer has already seen the exhibit as part of pretrial disclosures), and the common practice is to state what you are doing so that the trial record is clear.

Example:

> **LAWYER:** For the record, I am now showing Mr. Smith Plaintiff's Exhibit No. 1.
>
> Hand the exhibit to counsel, who should have a reasonable opportunity to inspect or read the exhibit, and get the exhibit back.

In a few jurisdictions the practice is to show the exhibit to the opposing counsel only when the exhibit is offered in evidence. This is not the preferred approach, however, since it does not give the opposing counsel a timely opportunity to examine the exhibit to determine what the proper foundation for that exhibit is, or to make an early objection.

In some jurisdictions, it is permissible to simply refer to the exhibit by number, if you have provided opposing counsel with a notebook containing copies of your exhibits.

Example

> **LAWYER:** Exhibit 17, counsel.

Step 3. Ask permission to show the exhibit to the witness

Example:

> LAWYER: Your honor, may I approach the witness?
> JUDGE: You may.

This formal requirement has been eliminated in many jurisdictions. In others, the judge expects you to request permission the first few times you approach witnesses, but loosens this requirement at the trial progresses.

In a few jurisdictions, including many military tribunals, the court clerk or bailiff hands exhibits to the witnesses.

Step 4. Give the exhibit to the witness

Example:

> LAWYER: Mr. Johnson, I am handing you Plaintiff's Exhibit No. 1.

> Walk to the witness and hand the exhibit to him or place it in front of him.

You should hand the exhibit to the witness so that the jury cannot see what the exhibit contains, since the jury should not see the exhibit unless it has been admitted in evidence. If the opposing lawyer has indicated that he has no objection to the exhibit, there is no problem. However, if you expect the opposing lawyer to object, this is important. Photographs, documents, and records can easily be handed to the witness without the jury seeing their contents. Physical objects and large diagrams, however, sometimes cannot be handled in the courtroom without the jury's seeing them. As the opponent, if you have a serious objection to the exhibit, ask the judge to require that the foundation for such an exhibit be first made out of the jury's presence and that you be permitted to cross-examine the witness. If the judge sustains your objection, the jury never sees the exhibit and cannot be improperly influenced by it. This is a useful procedure when potentially inflammatory or misleading exhibits are involved.

For smaller items, consider handing the exhibit to the witness in an opaque bag or box. Because the jurors cannot initially see the object, this can create a bit of mystery about the bag's or box's contents and thereby heighten juror interest in the exhibit.

Step 5. Establish proper foundation for the exhibit

You are now ready to establish the required foundation for the particular kind of exhibit you have. The next section of this chapter will cover the foundations necessary for different types of exhibits commonly introduced in trials.

Step 6. Offer the exhibit in evidence

Once you have established the proper foundation for the exhibit, offer it in evidence. The opposing lawyer may make an objection, briefly stating the evidentiary basis for it. Show the exhibit to the judge when you offer it in evidence, if the judge needs to see the exhibit to rule on any objections. Another option is to give the judge a "courtesy copy" of the exhibit.

Example:

> **LAWYER:** Your honor, we offer Plaintiff's Exhibit No. 1 in evidence.
> **JUDGE:** Any objections, counsel?
> **OPPOSING LAWYER:** Yes, your honor. It's hearsay.
> **JUDGE:** The objection is overruled. Plaintiff's Exhibit No. 1 is admitted.

If the objecting lawyer wants to make a lengthier argument on the objection, or the judge wants to hear further argument, this should be done at a "sidebar," out of the jury's hearing. This means that the lawyers will come to the front or side of the judge's bench and make their arguments in quiet voices so that the jurors cannot hear the legal arguments being made. The judge will then rule. On particularly important issues, the judge may excuse the jury from the courtroom or take the lawyers into the judge's chambers to hear the arguments. Regardless of the procedure, the important thing to remember is that legal arguments should not be heard by the jury, and it is improper for a lawyer to make an evidentiary objection in front of the jury in a way that is calculated to influence the jury.

Be careful, though, about being the attorney asking for a sidebar while the jurors are watching and listening. Jurors hate sidebars, just as all of us hate being excluded from important discussions, so they might resent you for asking for one. If possible, wait until the next break in the trial, then send word to the judge via a bailiff or clerk that you have an issue that requires the court's attention outside the hearing of the jury. In this way, you can get the opportunity to present a fuller and more nuanced argument without asking for that opportunity while the jury is present.

If you have a serious objection, or you think you can destroy the foundation for the exhibit, as the opposing counsel you can ask the judge for permission to examine the witness on the exhibit's foundation. This is sometimes, but not usually, done out of the jury's presence.

Example:

> **OPPOSING LAWYER:** Your honor, may I voir dire the witness on the exhibit?
> **JUDGE:** You may.
> **Q.** (By opposing lawyer) Officer Johnson, you didn't witness the accident, did you?
> **A.** That's right.
> **Q.** You arrived at the scene a few minutes later?
> **A.** Right.
> **Q.** The exhibit you've been shown, Plaintiff's Exhibit No. 2, is a photograph of the intersection of Main and Elm, right?
> **A.** Right.
> **Q.** Where the accident happened?
> **A.** Right.
> **Q.** This photo shows two cars in the intersection?
> **A.** Right.
> **Q.** The photo shows where the cars were when you got there?
> **A.** Right.
> **Q.** You don't know if the photo accurately shows where the cars were immediately after the accident, do you?
> **A.** No.

Q. That's because you didn't see the accident yourself?

A. Right.

LAWYER: Your honor, the defense renews its foundation and relevance objection to Plaintiff's Exhibit No. 2.

Whether a proper foundation can be established can only be determined at trial, since a witness is usually necessary to establish a proper foundation. However, other objections such as relevance or hearsay can often be ruled on in advance. Where this is the case, you should consider making a motion before trial to raise the objection. In civil cases, rulings on objections are sometimes made at the final pretrial conference, where the judge usually rules on the various objections raised in the joint pretrial memorandum.

Whenever you raise an evidentiary issue, you should obtain the court's ruling admitting or excluding the evidence. In the absence of a ruling, you have not preserved the evidentiary issue for appeal. It is surprisingly easy to move past the current dispute without first obtaining a ruling, so train yourself to avoid this mistake. Often the judge's oral ruling, if noted on the record, suffices, because the transcript will include the ruling.

Step 7. Have the exhibit marked in evidence

When the exhibit is admitted in evidence, a record must be made.

In some jurisdictions, the court clerk marks the exhibit "admitted" and notes the date and time the exhibit was admitted. This is usually marked on the exhibit label. In these jurisdictions you simply hand the exhibit to the clerk, who makes the appropriate notation. In other jurisdictions that still label exhibits "for identification," the clerk or court reporter shows that the exhibit is now in evidence by crossing out the "for identification" notation on the exhibit label. Whatever the procedure, make sure you follow it so that the record clearly shows that the exhibit is now in evidence. The exhibit now has a name, and you should thereafter refer to the exhibit by its official name (e.g., "Plaintiff Exhibit No. 4 in evidence" or simply "Plaintiff Exhibit 4").

Step 8. Have the witness use or mark the exhibit, if appropriate

Once the exhibit has been admitted in evidence, you should always consider how the exhibit can be used or marked to increase its usefulness. Tangible objects can be held to show how they were used. Diagrams and photographs can be marked to show locations and distances. Documents and records can have their significant sections underlined or highlighted. The various techniques for marking and using exhibits effectively are discussed in Section 7.6.

Keep in mind that some courts still do not allow documents and records to be marked, on the theory that underlining or circling important terms or sections alters exhibits. This presents no significant problem if you plan for this possibility in advance. If the already introduced evidence is Exhibit 4, simply have a copy of the exhibit marked as Exhibit 4-A. Then have the witness make notations on Exhibit 4-A. When the witness completes his marking of the new exhibit, offer Exhibit 4-A into evidence.

If the judge permits marking of an already admitted exhibit, she might require reoffering the exhibit in evidence after a witness has marked it. This is often the case when demonstrative exhibits are involved. As noted above, some courts bar any witness markings on an exhibit after the exhibit has been admitted in evidence. The moral is obvious: Know the judge's expectations.

Step 9. Ask permission to show or read the exhibit to the jurors

Example:

> LAWYER: Your honor, may we show Plaintiff's Exhibit No. 1 to the jury?
> JUDGE: You may.

This is a matter within the judge's discretion. The judge will usually allow the exhibit to be shown or read to the jury if it can be done efficiently. If the exhibit is a document several pages long, the judge may tell you to continue with your examination, as the jury will get a chance to see the exhibit during a break or other more convenient time.

Step 10. Show or read the exhibit to the jurors

"Publishing" an exhibit is simply the act of showing or reading an exhibit to the jury, but don't use that term when jurors are present because it is a legal term that might confuse them. How and when an exhibit should be published with maximum effectiveness will be discussed in detail in the next section. In general, however, how you publish the exhibit depends for the most part on what kind of exhibit it is. Many exhibits, such as photographs and tangible objects, are usually shown to the jury.

Example:

> LAWYER: Your honor, may we show Plaintiff's Exhibit No. 1 to the jury?
> JUDGE: You may.

> Hand the exhibit to the first juror (or hand the exhibit to the clerk, who will pass it to the first juror), who will look at it and pass it on to the next juror until all jurors have seen it. Then get the exhibit back after all the jurors have seen it, and give it to the court clerk.

Many courtrooms now have document cameras that can be used to show exhibits to jurors. Whenever possible, go to the courtroom in advance of trial to familiarize yourself with the available technology. Courtrooms, especially in state systems, vary widely on the technology front.

Other exhibits, principally documents and records, can be published either by showing or reading them to the jury. Where the documents are simple, such as with checks or promissory notes, the exhibit can easily be shown or read to the jury. If read, either the counsel or the witness can read it.

Example (Counsel):

> Counsel stands before the jury.

> LAWYER: Ladies and gentlemen, Plaintiff's Exhibit No. 1 reads as follows . . . [Reads the exhibit to the jury.]

Example (Witness):

> Q: Mr. Smith, please read Plaintiff's Exhibit No. 1 to the jury. [Witness reads the exhibit.]

Many records, however, are lengthy or complicated, and showing or reading them to the jury may be ineffective. The better technique is to ask the witness to read the important parts of the record to the jury. The jury can then look at the entire exhibit during a recess.

Example:

> Q: Mr. Smith, does that invoice, Plaintiff's Exhibit No. 1, show on what date the shipment was made?
> A: Yes, it was made on December 12, 2020.
> Q: Does it reflect the gross weight of the shipment?
> A: Yes, it was 1,936 lbs.
> Q: Does the invoice have a place where the addressee acknowledges receipt of the shipment?
> A: Yes.
> Q: What is contained in that place on the invoice?
> A: The place is captioned "Received the above shipment." It bears the signature R. Schwartz and the date of December 14, 2020.

Ask witnesses to point to relevant items on blowups or prepared images. Remember to make a good record of what you are asking the witness to do, so the transcript is understandable.

Be sure you give all of the exhibits to the clerk, court reporter, law clerk, judge, or whomever else is handling exhibits, whether they are admitted or not. This helps to make a record for appeal. In the midst of trial, it is easy to misplace exhibits, so it is wise to check with the exhibit handler regularly to see if she has all exhibits.

At the conclusion of your case-in-chief, it is always a sound procedure, before resting, to reoffer your exhibits in evidence or check with the judge or exhibit clerk that you have correctly recorded the admission of the exhibits. The judge or clerk will then usually run down his list of exhibits and report what his ruling was on each one. This creates a clear record and avoids possible confusion later in the trial or on appeal.

These steps are the most formal requirements for admitting exhibits in evidence. Most jurisdictions have eliminated some of the formalities. For instance, having the court reporter or clerk mark exhibits, marking them "for identification," or asking for permission to approach the witness are frequently no longer required. You should use the most efficient procedure allowed in your court, but you want to be familiar with all of the steps in the most formal process so you can go through them if necessary.

The following example illustrates the exhibits procedure usually followed in federal courts.

Example:

Exhibits have been marked before trial.

> Q: Your honor, may the record reflect that I am showing Plaintiff's Exhibit No. 1 to counsel? [Hands exhibit to opposing counsel, and gets it back.]
> JUDGE: It will.
> Q: [Hands exhibit to witness.] Mrs. White, I'm showing you Plaintiff's Exhibit No. 1. Do you recognize the scene in that photograph?
> A: Yes.
> Q: What scene does it show?

A: It shows the corner of Elm and Maple Streets where the accident happened.

Q: Does the photo fairly and accurately show how that intersection looked at the time of the collision?

A: Yes, it does.

Q: Your honor, we offer Plaintiff's Exhibit No. 1 in evidence.

JUDGE: Any objections, counsel?

LAWYER: No, your honor.

JUDGE: It's admitted.

Q: Mrs. White, does the photograph show where the two cars collided?

A: Yes.

Q: Using this red felt pen, please put an "X" where the cars collided. [Witness marks photograph.]

Q: Does the photograph show where you were standing when the cars collided?

A: Yes.

Q: Using this blue felt pen, please put a "W" in a circle where you were standing. [Witness marks photograph.]

Q: Your honor, may we show Plaintiff's Exhibit No. 1 to the jury?

JUDGE: You may. [Hands photograph to first juror.]

How do you handle exhibits that are already admitted by pretrial order or by stipulation of the parties? Keep in mind that although the exhibit is in evidence and therefore can be shown or read to the jury, the jury has not seen it before and does not know why it is reliable. Hence, it is best to use a witness to provide a quick introduction, although a formal foundation is unnecessary.

Example:

Get the exhibit from the court clerk.

Q: Ms. Johnson, I'm showing you Plaintiff's Exhibit No. 6, which has already been admitted in evidence. Do you know what this exhibit is?

A: Sure, it's one of my company's standard invoices, which we make each time we sell something to a customer.

Q: Let's talk about the information on the invoice. First, does it show who the customer is?

A: Yes, Robert Parker.

The same approach can be used when an exhibit is used again at trial, after it has already been admitted in evidence through an earlier witness. It is best to have the witness quickly identify the exhibit and acknowledge its accuracy, although you do not need or want to go through the formal foundation litany.

Example:

Q: Mr. Williams, I'm showing you a diagram, already admitted in evidence as Defendant's Exhibit No. 4. Do you recognize the intersection on the exhibit?

A: Yes, that's the corner of Main and Elm Streets.

Q: Please draw a "W" in a circle showing where you were standing when the two cars collided. [Witness marks the diagram.]

2. Foundation Requirements for Exhibits

Exhibits, like testimony, must be relevant, reliable, and right—the 3 Rs of evidence law. First, the exhibit must be *relevant*. Under FRE 401 to 402, the exhibit must have "any tendency" to make a fact "of consequence" to the case "more or less probable." If the exhibit proves or disproves something in issue in the case, it is logically relevant.

Second, the exhibit must be *reliable*. The reliability rules are FRE 801 to 807, which govern the admissibility of hearsay. If the exhibit contains an out-of-court statement, the exhibit must survive the scrutiny of the hearsay rules. The exhibit may be nonhearsay, because it is a statement made by a party-opponent, or a statement may have probative value by virtue of having been made (its probative value does not depend on the statement being true). Common examples of nonhearsay exhibits are contracts, promissory notes, checks, and notice letters. An exhibit may be hearsay (its probative value depends on its truth), but fall within a recognized hearsay exception. Common examples of materials within hearsay exceptions include business and public records; transcripts of former testimony; birth, death, and marriage records; and treatises. Finally, the exhibit may contain hearsay within hearsay, or double hearsay, in which case FRE 805 requires that each level of hearsay be satisfied with a hearsay exception before the exhibit can be admitted in its entirety.

Third, even if *relevant* and *reliable*, is it *right* to admit the exhibit? Several rules limit the admissibility of relevant and reliable evidence. These rules include FRE 403, which excludes relevant evidence if its "probative value is substantially outweighed by a danger of . . . unfair prejudice, confusing the issues, [or] misleading the jury," or for reasons of judicial economy. Special relevance rules include the character trait rules (FRE 404 to 405), the other acts rule (FRE 404(b)), the habit rule (FRE 406), policy exclusions (FRE 407 to 411), the sexual assault rules (FRE 412 to 415), and the privileges rule (FRE 501), all of which further regulate the admissibility of relevant evidence because of overriding policy considerations or political judgments.

Exhibits, if not self-authenticated through certification (such as business and private records), must be authenticated by a witness who has personal knowledge of the facts necessary to establish the proper foundation for that kind of exhibit. In trial lawyer language, a competent witness having firsthand knowledge of the necessary facts must "lay a foundation" for the exhibit.

The foundation requirements for particular kinds of exhibits establish that the exhibit is relevant and reliable. For example, identifying the gun in court as the same gun taken from the defendant when he was arrested establishes the relevance of the gun; showing that the record presented to the court is a business record of the company it comes from establishes the reliability of the record.

There are eight general kinds of exhibits:

1. Objects (FRE 901)
2. Demonstrative evidence (case law and custom)
3. Writings/instruments (FRE 901)
4. Business records (FRE 803(6))
5. Public records (FRE 803(8))
6. Summaries (FRE 1006)
7. Recorded recollections (FRE 803(5))
8. Transcripts of testimony (FRE 801(d)(1)(A) and 804(b)(1))

When the main concern is relevance (objects, demonstrative evidence, and writings), the law requires a showing that the exhibit is what it purports to be. When the main concern is reliability (business and public records, recorded recollection, summaries, and transcripts), the exhibit must be shown to be nonhearsay or to fall within a hearsay exception in FRE 803 to 807 or FRE 1006. The specific foundations for each of the eight types of exhibits are discussed in detail in Section 7.4.

In most civil and some criminal trials, many of the evidentiary issues surrounding the admissibility of exhibits are resolved before trial, either through a pretrial ruling or through stipulations between the lawyers. The judge will treat those exhibits as being formally admitted in evidence when the trial begins, so you need not present foundation evidence at trial. However, remember that foundations are important not just to the judge, but also to the jurors.

Although the exhibits are in evidence, the jurors have no way to assess the weight those exhibits should receive unless the jurors hear some foundation evidence to help them understand what the exhibit is, why it is relevant and reliable, and why they should give it substantial weight. With important exhibits, always consider presenting foundation testimony to enhance their weight. The other side may object on the ground that the exhibit is already in evidence, and the judge, in the interest of saving time and moving the trial along, may be receptive to that objection. When necessary, remind the judge that under FRE 104(e), a ruling on admissibility "does not limit a party's right to introduce before the jury evidence that is relevant to the weight or credibility of other evidence."

3. Visual Aids

Visual aids are not considered evidence, because they merely make visual what lawyers and witnesses say during the trial. Therefore, the formal evidentiary rules governing the admissibility of exhibits do not apply. For example, in opening statements and closing arguments, lawyers frequently make and use visual aids to supplement their oral presentations. As long as the lawyer can properly say it, the lawyer can show it through a visual aid. Common examples of aids used during opening statements include diagrams showing the relationship of corporate parties and employees, and chronologies showing the dates of key events. Common examples used during closing arguments include charts of damages calculations, bullet points of arguments, and legal elements of claims and defenses.

Lawyers also frequently use visual aids to supplement expert witness testimony. Common examples include charts showing the steps in a manufacturing process, steps in an accounting analysis, and steps in a surgical procedure. Again, such charts merely make visual what the witness says. As long as the expert can say it, the visual aid can show it. Commonly used visual aids are discussed in detail in Section 7.5.

Because visual aids are not considered evidence, judges usually do not admit them formally in evidence and usually do not let them go to the jury room during deliberations. No rule of evidence requires such restrictions, but most judges use their power under FRE 611(a) to make these rulings.

For a detailed discussion of the law on exhibits, *see* Mauet & Wolfson, *Trial Evidence* (7th ed., 2020).

7.3 The Jury's Perspective

This is the age of visual learning, and jurors expect trials to be visual as well. They want testimony to be made visual by showing, rather than only telling, what happened. Effective witness testimony uses sensory language that re-creates how an event happened so the jurors can, in addition to learning what happened, also emotionally connect with what the witness experienced and relive the event through the witness.

Jurors also want other information to be presented through exhibits and visual aids that use attention-capturing and memorable images. After all, jurors have been trained—by billboards, magazines, television, movies, and the internet—to expect professionally made graphics and eye-catching visual effects, and they now expect them during trials as well.

Most jurors, like most people, are right-brained (*affective*), focusing on the people in the story and making decisions quickly and impressionistically. For them, exhibits that grab them emotionally, such as graphic photographs and computer-generated simulations, are more effective. Other jurors are left-brained (*cognitive*), focusing on the issues in the case and making decisions methodically after assessing all the available information. For them, exhibits that are analytical, such as flowcharts and timelines, have the most impact. In a jury trial, most jurors will be right-brained, but some will be left-brained, so it is important to use exhibits and visual aids that appeal to both kinds of jurors.

Effective exhibits and visual aids grab and hold attention and send clear messages; more importantly, though, they significantly enhance memory. In a typical three-day trial, jurors will remember about 10 percent of the information they receive through witness testimony, but they will remember about 20 percent of the same information if it is presented visually. Retention will improve to better than 60 percent if the information is presented both through testimony and exhibits and visual aids. Information should always be presented through multiple channels whenever possible: hearing, seeing, and even touching and smelling.

Jurors want exhibits and visual aids to be big, colorful, and easy to understand, and to have a clear message. Large photographs, diagrams, and three-dimensional models, consistently color-coded and labeled, are effective. Computer-generated animations and simulations, projected on a screen or television monitor, are also effective. Enlargements of documents and records are effective, if key language is visually highlighted so the point of the document or record is immediately clear. All exhibits must be carefully planned, consistently designed, and logically marked, because professional-quality exhibits and visual aids send an important message: This lawyer cares enough about her case that she made sure everything important was presented visually.

How exhibits and visual aids are handled in the courtroom is also important to jurors. Lawyers who efficiently and consistently establish the necessary foundations for exhibits, and who effectively choreograph their use throughout the trial, are seen by jurors as competent, experienced professionals, and those lawyers will acquire more influence as the trial progresses. Witnesses who confidently explain their testimony using exhibits and visual aids are perceived as more credible and their testimony will be better remembered.

Effective trial lawyers understand that we live in the age of visual learning. Presenting information through witnesses alone—a parade of "talking heads"—is ineffective. It doesn't work on television news and it doesn't work in the courtroom.

7.4 Exhibit Foundations

Exhibits must have a proper foundation before they can be formally admitted in evidence and shared with the jury. The required foundation depends on the type of exhibit, and there are eight general types of exhibits. Knowing the proper foundations for each of these eight categories is more useful than trying to memorize the appropriate foundation for numerous specific exhibits.

1. Objects (FRE 901)
2. Demonstrative evidence (case law and custom)
3. Writings/instruments (FRE 901)
4. Business records (FRE 803(6))
5. Public records (FRE 803(8))
6. Summaries (FRE 1006)
7. Recorded recollections (FRE 803(5))
8. Transcripts of testimony (FRE 801(d)(1)(A) and 804(b)(1))

> ■◄ For a comprehensive discussion of exhibits, including foundation, please watch Video G.2, "Mauet on Exhibits."

When a proper foundation is presented, it demonstrates that the exhibit is relevant and reliable, and that it is right to admit the exhibit in evidence, absent FRE 403 or other rightness concerns. In other words, it meets the 3Rs of evidence law.

There are two interested parties when you establish the necessary foundation for each exhibit: the judge and the jury. The judge determines admissibility. The judge will be listening to make sure that the proper foundation is established, so that she can rule on any objections the opposing party may make. The judge is listening for the "buzz words," the key foundation litany for that kind of exhibit. Therefore, your first task is to satisfy the judge so the exhibit will be admitted into evidence.

What is the standard for admissibility? FRE 901(a) provides: "To satisfy the requirement of authenticating or identifying an item of evidence, the proponent must produce evidence sufficient to support a finding that the item is what the proponent claims it is." This is sometimes referred to as the *prima facie standard*, but it should not be confused with burdens of proof (preponderance, clear and convincing, and beyond a reasonable doubt). The standard is the same in civil and criminal cases. As long as the proponent presents some credible evidence that the exhibit is what the proponent claims it to be, the exhibit is properly admissible. Foundations for exhibits, then, require two basic things:

1. A competent foundation witness who has firsthand knowledge of the required foundation facts (unless the exhibit is self-authenticating).
2. Testimony from the foundation witness (or witnesses) that establishes the required foundation facts for that type of exhibit (unless the exhibit is self-authenticating).

The jury determines weight. The jury will be listening and watching to see how smoothly the procedure is followed and the foundation is established, and how persuasive that foundation is. The jurors are not particularly interested in the technical aspects of the foundation, but they are interested in getting a feel for how much weight this exhibit deserves.

These dual tasks—satisfy the judge and persuade the jury—should always guide your planning. Whenever you are dealing with a critical exhibit, always ask: In addition to the required foundation litany, what other information should I get from the foundation witness so that the jury will give the exhibit substantial weight?

As the opponent, you should do several things when an exhibit is offered in evidence. First, be prepared to object to any procedural mistakes, such as failing to show you the exhibit, or letting the jury see or hear the contents of the exhibit before the judge has ruled the exhibit admissible. Second, you can object to admission of the exhibit on the ground of lack of foundation, or any other appropriate evidentiary ground, such as relevance or hearsay. If you do not make a timely, well-founded objection, you waive error on appeal.

Third, you can ask the judge to permit you to conduct a *voir dire* of the witness on the foundation. This is discretionary with the court, but many judges will permit a cross-examination of the witness, limited to foundation matters, when an exhibit is offered in evidence, particularly if the admissibility question is a close one. You should ask for this only if there is a real possibility the judge may exclude the exhibit because of facts you can present during the voir dire.

In practice, some admissibility issues are resolved through pretrial motion, and the parties frequently reach stipulations on the admissibility of many exhibits. In criminal cases, the parties frequently fight over the admissibility of objects and demonstrative exhibits. In civil cases, the fight is more commonly over the admissibility of documents, records, and transcripts. Preparation, as always, is the key. Always assume that the other side will object to your exhibits. Always plan how you will respond to and overcome those objections. Add your opponent's likely objections and your responses to your direct and cross-examination outlines.

1. Objects

Objects, sometimes called *real evidence*, are admissible in evidence if they are shown to be the actual tangible thing involved in the case. Common examples in criminal cases are guns, knives, and other weapons; clothing; drugs; blood and other bodily fluids or tissues; and trace evidence such as fingerprints and firearms residue. Common examples in civil cases are car parts, such as brake components and fluids; consumer products, such as toaster ovens and power saws; and machinery, such as punch presses and farm implements.

Before an object can be admitted in evidence, the proponent must show two things through the testimony of a foundation witness who has firsthand knowledge of the necessary facts. First, the proponent must show that the object is what it purports to be: the actual thing. This "authenticates" the exhibit, as required by FRE 901, and establishes that the exhibit is relevant to the lawsuit. For example, if the gun in court is shown to be the actual gun taken from the defendant following his arrest, the gun

> 🎥◀ For a discussion of authentication, please watch the last portion of Video H.2, "Wyo STI: Best Evidence Rule and Authentication."

has been properly identified and is relevant. (If the gun in court is any other gun, it is probably not relevant to the lawsuit.) Second, the proponent ordinarily must show that the object is in the "same or substantially the same condition" now as it was on the relevant date. (If not, the exhibit may be misleading.)

For foundation purposes, there are three kinds of objects:

1. Objects that are uniquely identifiable through the senses as being the actual thing
2. Objects that are identifiable as the actual thing only through a chain of custody
3. Objects that cannot be uniquely identified as the actual thing, but can be admitted for the limited purpose of illustrating the real thing

Site visits are a form of real evidence, so they will also be discussed here.

a. Identifiable Through Sense Identification

An object is properly admissible if:

1. A foundation witness has personal knowledge of the required foundation facts.
2. The witness can identify the object through the senses.
3. The witness can state that the object is in the same or substantially the same condition now as it was on the relevant date.

Many objects can be identified through one or more of the five senses: sight, sound, smell, taste, or touch. The most common basis is sight identification. For example, people can identify their wallets, watches, purses, briefcases, and cars by sight (and perhaps also by smell and feel); they know what these items look like from experience. Whenever a witness, through personal contact with an object, knows what it looks like, that witness is a competent foundation witness who can identify the object and state that it is in the same or substantially the same condition as it was on the relevant date. For example, the police officer who arrested the defendant and removed a handgun from the defendant's coat can testify that the handgun in court is the handgun she took from the defendant following his arrest, and that the handgun is in the same condition now as it was at the time of the arrest. When establishing the foundation, always refer to the exhibit by its number; this creates a clear record.

The "substantially the same condition" element of foundation sometimes causes confusion, but it need not. If there has been a change in the object, the key question is whether that change is significant in this trial, so that it would be unfair to admit the changed object. If the change is not material to the issues in dispute at trial, the evidence is in substantially the same condition for that trial.

Example:

Have the exhibit marked, show it to opposing counsel, ask permission to approach the witness, and show the exhibit to the witness.

Q: Officer Smith, I'm showing you what has been marked Government Exhibit No. 6. Please examine it for a moment. [Witness inspects it.] Have you seen it before?
A: Yes, I have.

Q: When was the first time you saw Government Exhibit No. 6?

A: On June 1, 2020, when I arrested the defendant and searched his jacket pocket.

Q: Is Government Exhibit No. 6 in the same or substantially the same condition today as it was when you removed it from the defendant's jacket?

A: Yes. It looks exactly the same.

LAWYER: Your honor, we offer Government Exhibit No. 6 in evidence.

JUDGE: Any objection?

OPPOSING LAWYER: No, your honor.

JUDGE: Government Exhibit No. 6 is admitted.

That foundation is sufficient for the judge, who is concerned with whether the witness is competent to establish the foundation and whether the witness testifies to the required foundation. However, if the exhibit is particularly important, always consider asking the additional questions the jurors would likely ask if they could, because the answers may significantly add to the weight the jurors will give to the exhibit.

Example:

Q: Officer Smith, how can you be so sure that Government Exhibit No. 6 is in fact the same gun that you took from the defendant's jacket pocket?

A: Several reasons. First, I remember that gun; it has an unusual, distinctive wooden handle. Second, I recorded the serial number on my police report, and the number in my report matches the number on this gun. Third, I tied an evidence tag on the gun when I inventoried it, and that same tag is still attached to the trigger guard.

Example:

Have the exhibit marked, show it to opposing counsel, ask permission to approach the witness, and show the exhibit to the witness.

Q: Ms. Jackson, I'm showing you what has been marked State's Exhibit No. 2. Please take a look at it. [Witness inspects it.] Do you recognize it?

A: Yes.

Q: What is it?

A: That's my wristwatch that was taken during the robbery.

Q: Is it in the same or substantially the same condition now as it was at the time it was taken from you?

A: Yes, except for the evidence tag on it.

Q: Ms. Jackson, how is it that you can identify State's Exhibit No. 2 as being your wristwatch?

A: Well, my watch was a lady's Timex with a date window and a steel and gold band, just like this one has. I remember my watch had a scratch on the glass, and this one has the identical scratch. And I remember that the watch band had the gold worn off on the edges, just like this one. Oh yes, and the clasp was getting loose, just like this one. I know this is my watch.

LAWYER: Your honor, we offer State's Exhibit No. 2 in evidence.

JUDGE: Any objection?

OPPOSING LAWYER: No, your honor.
JUDGE: State's Exhibit No. 2 is admitted.

In some courts, the practice is that the object must be kept in a bag or box while the foundation is being established. This keeps the jurors from seeing the object before the foundation is established and before the court has ruled on admissibility. This avoids the problem created when jurors see an object that is never actually admitted in evidence.

What happens if the witness can say that the object "looks like" the object she is familiar with, but cannot be more certain? For example, what if a robbery victim testifies that the exhibit looks like the knife that was used during the robbery? Many judges will admit the exhibit with that foundation, on the basis that FRE 901 does not require more, and that the issue is then one of weight for the jury. But some will not, so think of ways you can strengthen the foundation, such as having a police officer establish that the exhibit was found in the defendant's apartment.

Example:

Have the exhibit marked, show it to opposing counsel, ask permission to approach the witness, and show the exhibit to the witness.

Q: Mr. Robinson, I'm showing you People's Exhibit No. 5. Please examine it for a moment. [Witness examines it.] Have you seen People's Exhibit No. 5 before?
A: Yes, I think so.
Q: When and where have you seen it?
A: That looks just like the knife the robber was holding when I got robbed on June 1.
Q: Does it look in the same condition now as it was at the time of the robbery?
A: It seems the same.
LAWYER: Your honor, we offer People's Exhibit No. 5.
OPPOSING LAWYER: We object, your honor. There has been no sufficient identification.
JUDGE: I'm sustaining the objection. If you have any additional foundational evidence, I'll hear it.

[Later the prosecutor calls the arresting officer as a witness.]

Q: Officer Roth, I'm showing you People's Exhibit No. 5. Please examine it for a moment and tell me if you have seen it before.
A: Yes, that's the knife I found in the defendant's bedroom on June 3, the day I arrested him and searched his apartment. I inventoried the knife.
Q: Is People's Exhibit No. 5 in the same or substantially the same condition now as it was on June 3?
A: Yes, except that today it has an evidence tag on it.
LAWYER: Your honor, we again offer People's Exhibit No. 5 in evidence.
OPPOSING LAWYER: Same objection, your honor. No foundation.
JUDGE: No, this testimony along with Mr. Robinson's is sufficient. The objection is overruled. People's Exhibit No. 5 is admitted.

What happens if the exhibit is not in the "same or substantially the same condition" now as it was on the relevant date? This depends on the exhibit and the reason it is being offered in evidence. For example, if a defendant has been charged with illegal possession of a deadly weapon, a handgun, it is important that the handgun be in operable condition (which makes it a deadly weapon). In this situation, the prosecutor must prove that the gun today is in operable condition and is in the same condition it was in when the gun was taken from the defendant. If the prosecutor cannot establish this, the gun may be excluded on FRE 403 grounds. In contrast, if a defendant has been charged with robbery, the victim's wallet, found on the defendant when arrested, need not be in the same condition. Here the relevance of the wallet is based on it being taken from the victim and being found on the defendant, regardless of whether the wallet has changed its appearance. As long as the victim can identify his wallet, it should be admitted. These are the kinds of issues that are frequently argued to the judge, out of the jury's hearing, when an exhibit is offered in evidence.

b. Chain of Custody

If objects cannot be authenticated through the senses, they must be authenticated by what is commonly called a *chain of custody*. Common examples in criminal cases are drugs, blood, and other bodily fluids that are sent to laboratories for testing. Common examples in civil cases are consumer products and automobile parts that are examined and tested by experts. Such things cannot be uniquely identified by the senses. For example, no witness can credibly say, simply by looking at a vial of blood, that this blood came from a particular person. No witness can credibly say, simply by looking at a hydraulic brake hose, that the brake hose came from a particular car.

A chain of custody is simply circumstantial evidence that is sufficient, under FRE 901, to show that the thing is what it purports to be. For example, before drugs and the lab results of drug testing are admissible in a criminal case, the prosecutor must first show that the drugs in court are the same drugs seized from the defendant and later tested. Establishing the chain of custody demonstrates the relevance of the exhibit and the later lab tests.

There are two ways a chain of custody is commonly demonstrated at trial: (1) continuous and exclusive possession by one or more persons, and (2) protective packaging to prevent the possibility of substitution or alteration.

Continuous and Exclusive Possession. If an object has been in the continuous possession of one or more persons, and safeguarded in a way that severely limits the possibility that any other persons had access to the object, a chain of custody is established if each, or in some instances many, of the persons in the chain testifies to that person's continuous and exclusive possession. For example, if a police officer took a mask from the defendant after an arrest, personally carried it to the police department and locked it in the officer's locker, to which only he has a key, and today took the mask from the locker and carried it to the courtroom, you have established that the mask in the courtroom is in fact the mask taken from the defendant. It has been in the continuous and exclusive possession of the police officer and there has been no realistic possibility of tampering or substitution.

Example:

Have the exhibit marked, show it to opposing counsel, ask permission to approach the witness, and show the exhibit to the witness.

Q: Officer Barlow, I'm showing you what has been marked State's Exhibit No. 3. Have you seen this exhibit before?

A: Yes, that's the mask I removed from my locker this morning and brought to the courtroom.

Q: When was the first time you saw State's Exhibit No. 3?

A: When I arrested the defendant on June 1, 2020, searched him, and found this mask in his pocket.

Q: What did you do with the mask?

A: I kept it in my jacket pocket until I got back to the police station, then I put it in a manila envelope and put it in my locker.

Q: Does your locker have a lock?

A: Yes, and I always keep it locked when I'm not there.

Q: Does anyone else have a key to your locker?

A: No, I have the only key.

Q: Officer Barlow, is State's Exhibit No. 3 in the same condition now as it was when you first saw it on June 1, 2020?

A: Yes.

LAWYER: Your honor, we offer State's Exhibit No. 3 in evidence.

JUDGE: Any objection?

OPPOSING LAWYER: Yes, your honor, no foundation.

JUDGE: Overruled. State's Exhibit No. 3 is admitted.

Take a more complicated but common case. A defendant was examined at the hospital and a blood sample was taken by a nurse, who gave it to a police officer, who delivered it to the police laboratory and gave it to a lab technician, who analyzed the sample for alcohol content. The sample and the results of the lab analysis are admissible if all three witnesses—nurse, police officer, and lab technician—testify.

Example:

Have the exhibit marked, show it to opposing counsel, ask permission to approach the witness, and show the exhibit to the witness.

[The first witness is the nurse.]

Q: Ms. Johnson, you're a registered nurse at University Hospital?

A: Yes.

Q: Were you on duty on June 1, 2020?

A: Yes, I was working in the emergency room.

Q: Did you see William Smith, the defendant, that day?

A: Yes, he was brought into the emergency room that evening.

Q: What did you do when he was brought in?

A: We examined him, and I took a blood sample from Mr. Smith.

Q: Ms. Johnson, I'm showing you what has been marked as State's Exhibit No. 7. [Hands witness the exhibit.] Have you seen that exhibit before?

A: Yes, that's the blood sample I took from Mr. Smith.

Q: How are you able to tell that is the same sample you took from Mr. Smith that day?

A: Because I placed the sample inside a glass tube and put a cap on the tube. I then prepared a hospital label by writing "William Smith, blood sample, 6/1/20, 1830 hr" in my handwriting and signed it, and I placed the label on the tube. That's our standard procedure.

I kept the tube in my possession until a police officer, Officer Sharon Edwards, came to the emergency room, and I gave Officer Edwards the tube.

Q: When you last saw State's Exhibit No. 7, what was its condition?

A: The sample was in the marked tube with the cap on it.

[The second witness is the police officer.]

Q: Officer Edwards, I'm showing you what has been marked as State's Exhibit No. 7. Please take a look at it, and tell us if you've seen it before.

A: Yes. I saw this exhibit on June 1, 2020, at around 9:00 in the evening, when I received it from Shirley Johnson, the nurse at University Hospital who was with the defendant, Mr. Smith.

Q: When you first received State's Exhibit No. 7, what was its condition?

A: It was in a labeled glass tube with a cap on it. It looked then the same as it does today.

Q: What did you do with the exhibit?

A: I personally took it to the police laboratory, which is in the police headquarters building, and delivered it to Myron Adams, a lab technician in the microanalysis section.

Q: What did Mr. Adams do with it?

A: He took it from me, and filled out a log book entry for the sample.

Q: What did you do after that?

A: I prepared a report summarizing what I had done with this sample.

Q: When you last saw State's Exhibit No. 7, what was its condition?

A: It was in the labeled glass tube with the cap on it. It looked just like it looks today.

[The third witness is the lab technician.]

Q: Mr. Adams, you're a microanalyst at the police crime lab?

A: That's right.

Q: I'm showing you what has been marked State's Exhibit No. 7. Take a look at it and tell us if you've seen that exhibit before.

A: Yes, I have.

Q: When did you first see it?

A: I first saw it on June 1, 2020, around 10:00 at night, when I received it from Officer Edwards.

Q: How is it that you remember that event?

A: I remember it because it was a sample in a DUI case, and I don't get many of those. I also remember it because I logged it in on our log book, which we do for every sample submitted to our lab.

Q: When you first received State's Exhibit No. 7, what was its condition?

A: It was in a glass tube with a cap on it, just like it is now.

Q: What did you do with that exhibit after you received it and logged it in?

A: I performed certain lab tests on the sample in the tube.

LAWYER: Your honor, we offer State's Exhibit No. 7 in evidence.

JUDGE: Any objections?

OPPOSING LAWYER: Yes, your honor. May I be heard at the bench?

JUDGE: Very well. Approach the bench. [Lawyers come to the bench.] What's the basis for your objection?

OPPOSING LAWYER: There's no testimony that the glass tube was sealed. The cap wasn't sealed, nor was the tube put into a sealed evidence bag. That's a flaw in the chain, because they haven't eliminated the possibility that the contents could have been substituted, altered, or tampered with.

LAWYER: All we have to do is meet the standard for admissibility in Rule 901. We don't have to eliminate all possibilities to get it in evidence.

JUDGE: The objection is overruled. There's been adequate testimony here on which a reasonable juror could find the exhibit in court is what it purports to be: a blood sample from the defendant. Any shortcomings in the chain go to weight, not admissibility. State's Exhibit No. 7 is admitted.

Note that a chain of custody need be shown only to the *prima facie* standard set forth in FRE 901(a). The chain need not to be proven beyond a reasonable doubt in a criminal case. Nonetheless, opposing lawyers sometimes make that argument, and sometimes judges are receptive to it. However, the burden of proof is an entirely different issue than the standard for admitting exhibits, and that argument should be rejected.

In the language of FRE 901, "the proponent must produce evidence sufficient to support a finding that the item is what the proponent claims it is." The proponent need not remove all doubt, or even a reasonable doubt, about whether the item is what she claims. But admissibility does not necessarily end the issue of the object's authenticity. When the judge admits the object into evidence, opposing counsel is allowed to attempt to convince the jury it is not what the proponent claims it is, by introducing contrary evidence or by arguing to the jury that the proponent did not adequately establish that the object is what she claims it is.

> ■◖ For a discussion of authentication, please watch the last portion of Video H.2, "Wyo STI: Best Evidence Rule and Authentication."

Note also that the laboratory's log book can be introduced as a business or public record. When the technician frequently handles such evidence, so that she has little or no personal memory of it, prosecutors usually call the technician and introduce the log book to prove the chain of custody.

Protective Packaging. The second way a chain of custody can be established is to show that the object was put in protective packaging that prevents the possibility of substitution, alteration, or tampering. This is a standard method in drug cases: The suspected drugs are placed in sealed evidence bags that remain sealed until the contents are removed and tested at a laboratory.

Example:

Have the exhibit marked, show it to opposing counsel, ask permission to approach the witness, and show the exhibit to the witness.

[First witness is the police officer.]

Q: Agent Henderson, what did you do with the brown powdery substance you took from the defendant on June 1, 2020?

A: I put it in a plastic evidence bag and kept it on my person. When I got back to the DEA office I labeled the bag and heat-sealed the opening.

Q: How did you label the bag?

A: The plastic bag has a label that is part of the bag, and I filled out in my handwriting all the information the label calls for: case number, location, date, time, suspect's name, my name, description and weight of contents, and so on.

Q: How did you heat-seal the bag?

A: The evidence bags are thick clear plastic bags that are open along one edge. After placing the brown powdery substance in the bag, I heat-sealed the opening by putting the opening into a device that heats the plastic until it melts together. It's like the heat sealers you sometimes see in kitchens to seal freezer bags. Once the opening is sealed, you can't open the bag unless you cut it open.

Q: Agent Henderson, I'm handing you what has been marked as Government Exhibit No. 1. Do you recognize it?

A: Yes.

Q: What do you recognize it to be?

A: That's the evidence bag in which I put the suspect drugs I took from the defendant.

Q: How do you know Government Exhibit No. 1 is the same bag?

A: Because I filled out the label in my own handwriting. It's right here [pointing].

Q: What did you do with Government Exhibit No. 1?

A: I shipped it to the DEA lab in Washington, D.C.

Q: How did you ship it?

A: In a box, by express mail.

Q: Agent Henderson, when you last saw Government Exhibit No. 1, what was its condition?

A: It was in a sealed condition.

Q: Please take a look at the exhibit as it appears today. Is there anything different about the exhibit today compared to how it looked when you shipped it to the DEA lab?

A: Yes. When I shipped it, the evidence bag was sealed on the opening side. The bag today has a second heat seal along the opposite edge.

Q: Other than that, is it in the same condition?

A: Yes.

[Second witness is the lab technician.]

Q: Ms. Donaldson, you're a technician at the DEA lab in Washington, D.C.?

A: Yes.

Q: What is your job with the DEA?

A: I work in the drug section. My job is to test suspect drugs that are sent to the lab and determine what illegal substances, if any, are present. I perform various chemical and other tests to make that determination.

Q: How does your lab get the suspect drugs for testing?

A: They are hand-delivered if the suspect drugs are seized locally. Otherwise, they are sent to us by express mail. Either way, suspect drugs are always put into standard evidence bags that are labeled and heat-sealed. When we get the bags, we make a record of the receipt. After we test them, we make a record of the results of our tests.

Q: I'm handing you Government Exhibit No. 1. Have you seen it before?

A: Yes.

Q: When and where did you first see it?

A: I first saw it on June 10, 2020, when one of our clerks delivered it to my work station.

Q: When you first saw Government Exhibit No. 1, what was its condition?

A: It was labeled, and the opening was heat-sealed. It looked like it should look.

Q: Did it have any sign of tampering?

A: No. The only way to tamper with it would be to cut it open to get at the contents, and you can immediately see that. That's why we use this kind of evidence bag with the heat seals.

Q: What did you do with the bag?

A: After I made a record that I had received it, I cut open the bag on the opposite side from where the heat-seal was, removed the contents, weighed the contents, and then took small samples from the contents. I then put the contents back into the evidence bag and heat-sealed the opening I had cut. That's right here [pointing]. I tested the samples I had taken and made a record of what my lab tests disclosed. Finally, I had one of our clerks return the resealed evidence bag to our storage room for safekeeping, in the event the bag would be needed for trial.

Q: When you last saw Government Exhibit No. 1, what was its condition?

A: Just the way it looks today. It had a heat-seal on the original opening, and a second heat-seal, the one I made, on the opposite edge.

LAWYER: Your honor, we offer Government Exhibit No. 1.

OPPOSING LAWYER: We object, your honor. They haven't called all the people who handled that exhibit.

JUDGE: Overruled. Government Exhibit No. 1 is admitted.

A chain of custody is usually thought of as applying to criminal cases, because that is where it is most frequently seen. However, a chain can be required in civil cases as well. This most commonly happens in product liability cases when a product is sent to a laboratory or expert for testing or examination. The results of lab tests or expert testimony will not be admissible unless the proponent first establishes that the actual product was tested or examined, and that it was in the same or substantially the same condition as on the relevant date. For example, if the hydraulic brake hoses from a car involved in a collision are sent to a laboratory to determine if the brake hoses were defective, an appropriate chain of custody must be established.

Example:

Have the exhibit marked, show it to opposing counsel, ask permission to approach the witness, and show the exhibit to the witness.

[The accident investigator is the first witness.]

Q: Mr. Appleton, tell us what you do for a living.

A: I'm an accident investigator. I specialize in vehicle accident investigations, and I have my own business.

Q: Mr. Appleton, did I ask you to investigate the collision that this case is concerned with?

A: Yes.

Q: When?

A: You contacted me on June 2, 2020, the day after the collision.

Q: Specifically, what did I ask you to do?

A: You asked me to go to the car involved in the collision, remove the rubber hydraulic brake hoses for each of the four wheels, preserve them so that their condition would not change, and then ship them to a laboratory for examination and testing.

Q: Were you able to do that?

A: Yes, I did it the same day you called.

Q: Let's take it step by step. What's the first thing you did?

A: I got from you the information about the car involved in the collision — its description, license number, and vehicle identification number — and the location where the car had been towed the previous day.

Q: And after that?

A: I went to the body shop where the car was being kept, got them to unlock the fenced area where the car was, and photographed the car, the wheel areas, and the rubber brake hoses going to each wheel. After that, I removed the brake hoses that go from the master cylinder to each of the four brakes, put them in separate large zip-lock bags, and labeled each of the four bags.

Q: Why did you put the brake hoses in zip-lock bags?

A: Two reasons. They were wet with brake fluid. Second, I wanted to make sure that the hoses were kept in the same condition for later examination and testing.

Q: What did you do with the four brake hoses now in the zip-lock bags?

A: I took them to my office, photographed them in the bags, and then wrapped up those four bags in plastic, taped the plastic with duct tape, wrapped that in bubble wrap, and put them in a FedEx box. I addressed the box to Dr. Mary Gomez at National Automotive Laboratory in Dallas, Texas. I called FedEx, told them I had a pickup, and they came in the afternoon and picked up the box. I then called Dr. Gomez and told her she would be getting the box the next morning. Finally, I wrote a report detailing what I did.

Q: From the time you first saw the car to the time you shipped the brake hoses to Dr. Gomez, did anyone else have access to the brake hoses?

A: No.

Q: I'm now showing you what has been marked Plaintiff's Exhibit No. 2. Have you seen it before?

A: Yes.

Q: What is it?

A: That's the FedEx box I used to ship the four brake hoses to Dr. Gomez.

Q: How can you tell that's the same box?

A: I filled out the shipping information on the FedEx label in my handwriting. I remember doing it and I recognize my handwriting.

Q: The last time you saw Plaintiff's Exhibit No. 2, what was its condition?

A: It was labeled and sealed, with the brake hoses inside, when I gave it to the FedEx driver.

Q: Mr. Appleton, let me show you what has been marked Plaintiff's Group Exhibit No. 3, consisting of four items. Do you recognize them?

A: Yes, they look like the four brake hoses and zip-lock bags I shipped to Dr. Gomez.

Q: Do they look any different than they looked when you shipped them to Dr. Gomez?

A: No, they look the same.

[The expert is the second witness.]

Q: Dr. Gomez, please introduce yourself.

A: My name is Mary Gomez. I'm a chemist at the National Automotive Laboratory in Dallas. My job as a chemist there is to inspect and test various automotive parts. I've been working there for over ten years.

Q: Dr. Gomez, let me show you what has been marked Plaintiff's Exhibit No. 2. Have you seen it before?

A: Yes.

Q: When did you first see it?

A: I got it on June 3, 2020. It was in my office mailbox in the morning.

Q: When you first saw Plaintiff's Exhibit No. 2, what was its condition?

A: It was sealed up. It looked normal.

Q: What did you do with the box?

A: I took it to my work station, pulled the tab to open the box, and removed the contents.

Q: What was inside the box?

A: First I had to unwrap the bubble wrap and the taped-up plastic, but then I found four zip-lock bags with one black rubber hose in each one.

Q: Were those bags zipped shut?

A: Yes, each was closed.

Q: Dr. Gomez, what did you do with the four black rubber hoses you received that day?

A: That day I carefully inspected and examined each of the hoses using a variety of equipment.

Q: Dr. Gomez, what did you do with the hoses after you inspected and examined them?

A: I put them back in their zip-lock bags, put the bags back in the FedEx box, and locked them up in my locker. Yesterday I removed them and brought them with me to the trial.

Q: Since you put the tubes back in the zip-lock bags and box, whose possession have they been in?

A: Mine. No one else has access to my storage locker.

Q: I'm now showing you what has been marked Plaintiff's Group Exhibit No. 3, consisting of four items. Do you recognize them?

A: Yes. Those are the brake hoses in their zip-lock bags I received in the FedEx package. I brought them here this morning.

Q: Are the brake hoses in this exhibit in the same or substantially the same condition they were in when you first received them and inspected and examined them?

A: Yes. My examination did not change the condition of the hoses. There may be slightly less residual brake fluid in them, because a few drops came out during my inspections, but the hoses themselves are in the same condition.

> **LAWYER:** Your honor, we offer Plaintiff's Exhibit No. 2 and 3.
> **OPPOSING LAWYER:** Objection, your honor. May we approach?
> **JUDGE:** Yes. [Lawyers come to the bench.]
> **OPPOSING LAWYER:** There's been no adequate chain proven here. In particular, there's been no showing that the FedEx box could not have been tampered with, and the zip-lock bags could have been tampered with and no one would ever know.
> **LAWYER:** Your honor, that objection goes to weight, not admissibility.
> **JUDGE:** I agree. Plaintiff's No. 2 and 3 are admitted.

In this example, a stronger objection would have been based on the fact that no witness testified that the condition of the brake hoses immediately following the accident was the same as the condition of the brake hoses when the investigator removed them, since things like weather and storage conditions may have altered the hoses. The greater the time period between the event and when the object is retrieved for examining and testing, the more significant this issue will be.

What happens if the object or substance was later consumed or destroyed during testing? For example, a small quantity of drugs may be entirely consumed during laboratory testing. This should not affect admissibility of the test results, so long as the testimony of the witnesses adequately establishes a chain of custody showing that what the lab tested (and consumed during the testing) came from the defendant. When destructive testing happens, it is a good practice to retain all the packaging and labels so that they can be used at trial to prove the chain.

What if there is a break in the chain of custody? For example, what happens if a blood sample is taken from a patient in a hospital emergency room, the sample lies on a counter for an hour without being labeled, and then is given to a police officer, who labels it and transports it to the police crime lab? The proponent should argue that the foundation, though hardly perfect, is sufficient under FRE 901(a), which only requires evidence sufficient to support a finding that the evidence is what it is claims to be: blood from the patient. The opponent will always argue that there has been a fatal flaw in the chain of custody because there is a real possibility that the blood sample came from someone else. In this gray area, judges can rule either way.

There is nothing magical about the concept of a chain of custody. The question is simply one of logic: Has the proponent presented enough credible evidence to show that the object or substance in court is what it claims to be?

In criminal cases the prosecution and defense frequently enter into stipulations on chain of custody evidence in drug or sexual assault cases. For example, they may stipulate that "State's Exhibit No. 3 was tested by Dr. Johnson at the Chicago Crime Lab on June 1, 2020." If there already has been evidence that the exhibit was seized from the defendant, Dr. Johnson will then be able to testify about the results of her tests performed on the exhibit. The stipulation eliminates the need to first call the other witnesses in the exhibit's chain of custody. Prosecutors like chain of custody stipulations because they eliminate the need to call the other witnesses in the chain, which can be time consuming and tedious. Some defense lawyers enter into chain of custody stipulations if they are not challenging the chain. Other defense lawyers never stipulate to anything in a criminal case, instead insisting that the prosecution formally prove everything it is required to prove.

c. Illustrative Objects

Sometimes an object may not be the actual thing, but may be helpful to illustrate the actual thing. In criminal cases, lawyers sometimes introduce a similar object to show the jurors what the actual object looked like, when the actual object cannot be found or has been destroyed. Common examples include weapons, such as a baseball bat or knife, and clothing, such as a ski mask or jacket. In civil cases, lawyers sometimes introduce a similar or identical object for the same reason. Common examples include consumer products, such as a toaster or power saw, and automotive and machine parts, such as a wheel brake assembly or punch press die. In these kinds of cases, there is no claim that the exhibit is the actual thing, only that it illustrates the actual thing.

An illustrative exhibit is admissible, in the court's discretion, if it fairly and accurately represents the actual object, and seeing the illustrative exhibit helps the jurors understand the actual object. When admitted, the jurors are usually given a limiting instruction that the exhibit is being admitted for the limited purpose of illustrating the real thing. Any objections are usually made on FRE 403 grounds, that the exhibit is misleading or unduly inflammatory.

Example:

[Cross-examination of victim]

Q: Mr. McGovern, the man who attacked you was wearing a ski mask, right?

A: Yes.

Q: The mask covered the man's head and face?

A: Yes.

Q: The mask had holes for the eyes, nose, and mouth?

A: Yes.

Q: It was black?

A: Either black, or a very dark color.

Have the exhibit marked, show it to opposing counsel, ask permission to approach the witness, and show the exhibit to the witness.

Q: I'm showing you what has just been marked as Defense Exhibit No. 2. Take a look at it for a moment. [Witness examines it.] Does that exhibit fairly and accurately illustrate the ski mask that the person who robbed you was wearing during the robbery?

A: As near as I can tell, yes.

LAWYER: Your honor, we offer Defense Exhibit No. 2 in evidence for illustrative purposes.

OPPOSING LAWYER: We object, your honor. There's been no showing that this is the mask used during the robbery.

JUDGE: Defense Exhibit No. 2 will be admitted for illustrative purposes only. Members of the jury, you may consider this exhibit only for the purpose of illustrating the mask the robber wore during the robbery. You should not consider this exhibit to be the actual mask.

Note that here the cross-examiner introduced an exhibit during the cross-examination. Some judges allow this, relying on FRE 611(a); others require that each side formally offer exhibits in evidence only during that side's case-in-chief.

Example:

> Q: Ms. Kessler, the toaster that caught on fire in your home, do you have it today?
> A: No. It was burned up in the fire and was completely destroyed.
> Q: What did it look like?
> A: It was a Sunburst toaster, two slots, plain chrome outside, with black controls on one end. I had it about a year.

Have the exhibit marked, show it to opposing counsel, ask permission to approach the witness, and show the exhibit to the witness.

> Q: I'm showing you Plaintiff's Exhibit No. 8. Have you seen it before?
> A: Not that toaster, but it looks exactly like the Sunburst toaster I had in my kitchen that caught on fire.
> Q: Is there anything different about this toaster from the one in your kitchen?
> A: Other than this one looking completely new, it looks identical.
> LAWYER: Your honor, we offer Plaintiff's Exhibit No. 8 in evidence for illustrative purposes.
> OPPOSING LAWYER: We object, your honor. It's not the actual toaster, and there's no need for an illustrative exhibit here.
> LAWYER: Your honor, we plan on using this exhibit with our expert to explain how the fire started.
> JUDGE: The objection is overruled. Plaintiff's Exhibit No. 8 is admitted for illustrative purposes. Members of the jury, this exhibit is being admitted for the limited purpose of showing what the actual toaster looked like.

Finally, offering an exhibit for illustrative purposes can be a backup argument when the foundation is inadequate to admit the exhibit as the actual thing. This is common in criminal cases, where there may not be a sufficient foundation to identify a weapon or article of clothing as the actual thing.

Example:

> Q: Ms. Hopkins, the knife the robber held in his hand, what did it look like?
> A: It was shining in the light, and the blade was maybe four or five inches long.
> Q: Did you notice anything else?
> A: No, nothing else about it that caught my eye.
> Q: Right after you were robbed, what happened?
> A: He ran out the alley toward the street and disappeared.
> Q: What did you do?
> A: I waited maybe a minute, then I walked slowly out of the alley, also toward the street.
> Q: As you walked out, did you notice anything?
> A: Yes. Just before I got to the street, I saw a knife lying in the alley.
> Q: What did you do?
> A: I picked it up, and gave it to the police after they arrived.

Have the exhibit marked, show it to opposing counsel, ask permission to approach the witness, and show the exhibit to the witness.

Q: I'm showing you People's Exhibit No. 2. Do you recognize this knife?
A: It looks like the knife I found in the alley.
Q: Ms. Hopkins, is that the knife the robber held when he robbed you?
A: It looks like it, but I can't be sure.
LAWYER: We offer People's Exhibit No. 2.
OPPOSING LAWYER: Objection, your honor. No adequate foundation.
JUDGE: Sustained.
LAWYER: Your honor, we offer People's Exhibit No. 2 only for illustrative purposes, not to say that it is the actual knife.
JUDGE: Very well. I'll allow it for that limited purpose. Members of the jury, this exhibit is being admitted for the limited purpose of showing what the actual knife looked like. You should not consider this exhibit to be the actual knife.

If an exhibit has been admitted for illustrative purposes only, judges permit the exhibit to be used during the testimony of witnesses and usually during closing arguments as well. However, some judges will not let illustrative exhibits go to the jury room during deliberations.

d. Site Visits

Every once in a while, but rarely, a party will ask the court to have the jury visit a scene that is important in the case. A site visit is essentially a form of real evidence, so the basic foundational issue is the same as for real evidence: Is the site in substantially the same condition as it was in at the time of the incident?

But site visits are time-consuming, costly (due to transportation expenses), and unwieldy. These are essentially FRE 403 issues that come down to a balancing of the probative value of visiting the site against the time to be used and the potential for confusion of the issues. Judges often urge attorneys who propose site visits to use other methods to inform the jury about the scene, especially photographs, maps, charts, and witness testimony.

2. Demonstrative Evidence

Demonstrative evidence is not the real thing involved in the case, but represents the real thing. Common examples in civil and criminal cases are photographs, movies, videotapes, x-rays, diagrams, models, maps, drawings, animations, and simulations.

Before demonstrative exhibits can be admitted in evidence, the proponent must show, through the testimony of a foundation witness who has firsthand knowledge of the necessary facts, that the demonstrative exhibit "fairly and accurately" represents the real thing at the relevant time. For example, before a photograph of an intersection is admissible, it must be shown to fairly and accurately portray how the intersection looked at the time of the collision. Before a diagram of a home is admissible, it must be shown to fairly and accurately show the layout of the home when it was burglarized. (If the exhibit does not fairly and accurately represent the real thing, it is not relevant, and will probably be misleading under FRE 403.) There is no requirement that the exhibit be to scale, only that it be fair and accurate so that it does not distort or mislead. If the exhibit is not to scale, that goes to weight, not admissibility.

Many courts also require testimony that the demonstrative exhibit is help-ful to the witness in explaining what happened. For example, when an eyewit-ness describes what happened using an intersection diagram, or an expert witness explains the plaintiff's injury using an anatomical model, the witness is asked whether the diagram or model will help the witness explain what happened. Some courts, however, do not require this, reasoning that a demonstrative exhibit should be admissible if it helps the jury understand what happened—and that is for the judge, not the witness, to decide.

For foundation purposes, it is useful to group demonstrative evidence into categories:

1. Photographs, movies, videotapes, sound recordings, and x-rays
2. Diagrams, models, maps, and drawings
3. Animations and simulations

a. Photographs, Movies, Videotapes, Sound Recordings, and X-rays

Photographs, movies, videotapes, sound recordings, and x-rays are properly admissible if: (1) a foundation witness has personal knowledge of how the real thing looked (or sounded) at the relevant time; and (2) the witness can state that the photograph, movie, videotape, sound recording, or x-ray "fairly and accu-rately" represents the real thing as it looked (or sounded) at the relevant time.

Whenever a witness knows how the real thing looked at the relevant time, that witness is a competent foundation witness who can identify the photograph or other demonstrative exhibit as fairly and accurately showing the real thing at the relevant time. For example, a person who witnessed a collision at an intersec-tion can testify that a photograph fairly and accurately shows how the intersection looked at the time of the crash.

The foundation witness need not be the person who took the photograph or witnessed the crash. The photograph need not have been taken near in time to the date of the crash. The photographer can be unknown. The only ques-tions are: Does this witness have firsthand knowledge of how the intersection looked at the time of the crash? Can the witness say that the photograph fairly and accurately shows how the intersection looked at the time of the crash? If the photograph, in addition to showing the intersection, also shows the location and condition of the vehicles immediately after the crash, the foundation wit-ness would have to be someone who actually saw the crash and can testify that the photograph accurately shows how the vehicles looked and where they were immediately after the crash.

Example:

Q: Mr. Andrews, did you see the crash that happened at Main and Elm Streets on June 1, 2020, at 4:30 in the afternoon?
A: Yes, I was right on the corner when it happened.
Q: Do you remember how that intersection looked on that day?
A: Oh yes, I know that intersection well. I live a block away.

Have the exhibit marked, show it to opposing counsel, ask permission to approach the witness, and show the exhibit to the witness.

Q: Mr. Andrews, I've just handed you Defendant's Exhibit No. 2. Do you recognize the scene shown in this exhibit?

A: Yes.

Q: What scene is shown in this exhibit?

A: It shows the intersection of Main and Elm.

Q: Does Defendant's Exhibit No. 2 fairly and accurately show how the intersection of Main and Elm looked on June 1, 2020?

A: Yes, it does.

LAWYER: Your honor, we offer Defendant's Exhibit No. 2 in evidence.

JUDGE: Any objections?

OPPOSING LAWYER: No, your honor.

JUDGE: Defendant's Exhibit No. 2 is admitted.

After the photograph is admitted in evidence, the jury can see it, and the witness can talk about the details of the photograph. Until it is admitted in evidence, however, the jury should not be permitted to see it, and the witness should not describe what is in the photograph. A common problem arises when the lawyer asks: "What is it?" and the witness responds: "That's a photograph of Main and Elm showing the two lanes of traffic and . . . ." That is improper, because the witness is divulging the contents of the photograph before it has been admitted in evidence. The better question to ask is: "What location or scene is shown in this photograph?" because the witness will usually say: "It shows the Main and Elm Street intersection," and nothing more.

Movies and videos are common exhibits. Lawyers frequently introduce videotapes showing the damage to a vehicle following a collision, movies showing the physical condition of an injured person, and tapes from surveillance cameras in banks and stores. They are admissible if a witness with firsthand knowledge of the facts testifies that the videotape fairly and accurately portrays the scene and what happened at the scene. This usually requires that the witness view the tape before coming to court, so that he can state that the videotape accurately portrays what it purports to show.

Example:

Have the exhibit marked, show it to opposing counsel, ask permission to approach the witness, and show the exhibit to the witness.

Q: Mrs. Wilson, I'm showing you a videotape that has been marked Plaintiff's Exhibit No. 6. Did I show you this videotape earlier today?

A: Yes, you played it for me in your office before we walked over to the courthouse.

Q: What scene is shown on that videotape?

A: It's a videotape of my car, taken right after the crash.

Q: Does this videotape, Plaintiff's Exhibit No. 6, fairly and accurately show the condition of your car after the collision?

A: Yes. My husband took that videotape right after my car had been towed to the body shop.

LAWYER: Your honor, we offer Plaintiff's Exhibit No. 6 in evidence.

JUDGE: Any objections?

OPPOSING LAWYER: No.

JUDGE: Plaintiff's Exhibit No. 6 is admitted.

Once the videotape is admitted, it can be played for the jury, and the witness can be asked about things on the video as it is playing.

Surveillance cameras are important, particularly in criminal cases, because they frequently capture a crime in progress. Some of the cameras take continuous motion pictures; others take freeze frames in short intervals. Regardless of the type, any witness who was present when the event happened can qualify the surveillance tape for admission in evidence. For example, a bank teller who was in the bank when it was robbed can testify that the tape fairly and accurately shows what happened during the robbery.

Example:

Q: Ms. Jones, where were you when the robbery happened?
A: I was at the first teller station.
Q: Could you see from your teller station what happened during the robbery?
A: I could see everything.

Have the exhibit marked, show it to opposing counsel, ask permission to approach the witness, and show the exhibit to the witness.

Q: I'm showing you what has been marked Government Exhibit No. 8. Have you seen it before?
A: Yes, I saw it about two days after the robbery and I saw it yesterday in your office.
Q: Does Government Exhibit No. 8 fairly and accurately show what happened during the time your bank was robbed?
A: It does.
LAWYER: We offer Government Exhibit No. 8, your honor.
JUDGE: Any objections?
OPPOSING LAWYER: We have no objections, your honor.
JUDGE: Government Exhibit No. 8 is admitted.

What happens if the surveillance tape records an event when no witness is present or, worse, the only witness is killed? For example, a warehouse is burglarized during the night and a surveillance camera records the burglary. The tape can still be admitted in evidence if a qualified witness testifies that the surveillance camera and system were on and in proper working order during that time. This is a proper foundation under FRE 901(b)(9).

Example:

Q: Mr. Glass, what's your position at Ace Warehouse?
A: I'm the director of security.
Q: As part of your job, are you in charge of the surveillance system at the warehouse?
A: Yes.
Q: What kind of system do you have?
A: We have surveillance cameras at three locations in the warehouse: the main door, the front office, and the loading dock area. Those cameras are connected to videotape machines that are locked in a secure area. The system is on a timer: It automatically turns on at 5:00 p.m.

and runs continuously until 9:00 a.m. when it shuts off. The date and time are shown continuously on the videotapes.

Q: Who makes sure the surveillance system is operating properly?

A: I do. Of course, if something is not working right, I call in the people who installed the system.

Q: Was the surveillance system working properly during the evening of June 1 and the morning of June 2, 2020?

A: Yes, it was.

Q: How do you know?

A: I always check the beginning and end of each night's tapes the next morning. In addition, since there was a break-in at the warehouse that night, I played back all of the videotapes to make sure they were recording properly and continuously, and they were. You can tell the tapes are running continuously by watching the counter at the bottom of the picture. We've had this system for about three years, and it's been real reliable.

Have the exhibit marked, show it to opposing counsel, ask permission to approach the witness, and show the exhibit to the witness.

Q: I'm showing you State's Exhibit No. 3. Have you seen it before?

A: Yes, that's our surveillance tape for the camera that covers the front office, for the evening of June 1 to the morning of June 2.

Q: How do you know the tape is for that time?

A: Because I pulled it during the morning of June 2, when we learned there had been a break-in. In addition, the tape has the date and running time appearing on the bottom of the taped image.

Q: Mr. Glass, does this exhibit, State's Exhibit No. 3, fairly and accurately show the front office area of Ace Warehouse between the hours of 5:00 p.m. on June 1, 2020, and 9:00 a.m. on June 2, 2020?

OPPOSING LAWYER: Objection, your honor. The witness wasn't there and has no personal knowledge of what happened in the front office.

JUDGE: Overruled. You may answer.

A: Yes it does.

LAWYER: We offer State's Exhibit No. 3 in evidence, your honor.

OPPOSING LAWYER: Same objection, your honor. No foundation.

JUDGE: Overruled. State's Exhibit No. 3 is admitted.

The videotape can then be played for the jury. Of course, because this is a long tape, you will need to start it shortly before the action begins to play only the relevant portion of the tape.

Photographs, movies, and videotapes frequently generate FRE 403 issues. A common objection is that the photograph or video is unduly inflammatory. This objection is often made to morgue photographs of homicide victims and "day in the life" videos showing the daily routine of severely injured plaintiffs. The issue is controlled by the balancing test of FRE 403: Is the probative value of the photograph or video substantially outweighed by the danger of unfair prejudice? For example, in a homicide case in which the only issue is identification, a color photograph of the victim in the morgue may have little probative value and may be excluded; when the issue is self-defense and the picture shows wounds on the victim's body, the same picture will have higher probative value and will usually be admitted. In a personal injury case, the plaintiff's physical condition is highly relevant, and a "day in the life" video will usually be admitted unless it is shown to be an unfair or misleading depiction of the plaintiff's daily routine.

Another common objection is that the photograph does not fairly and accurately show the lighting that existed at the time. For example, photographs taken in the daytime of crime scenes and accident locations obviously do not show the lighting conditions that existed when a nighttime crime or accident happened. When this situation exists, the party offering the photograph will usually ask that it be admitted for the limited purpose of showing the location of the crime or accident and not for any other purpose such as lighting.

Example:

LAWYER: Your honor, we offer Plaintiff's Exhibit No. 4 in evidence.

OPPOSING LAWYER: Objection, your honor. This is a daytime photo, but the accident happened at 11:00 at night. It does not fairly and accurately show the lighting; it misrepresents the lighting and is misleading.

LAWYER: Your honor, we're offering it for the limited purpose of showing the layout of the intersection. That's highly relevant. We have no objection to an appropriate limiting instruction.

JUDGE: Plaintiff's Exhibit No. 4 will be admitted for the limited purpose of showing how the intersection looked on the day of the accident. Members of the jury, you may not use this photo as evidence of the lighting conditions at the time of the accident. This is a daytime photograph, while the accident happened at night. You may consider this photo only for the physical layout of the intersection.

A related objection is that the photograph or video does not fairly show the scene because of changes that have happened. For example, if an accident happened in July, and the photograph was taken in November, it may not fairly or accurately show the leaves on trees and bushes as they were in July. If there is an issue about foliage affecting visibility or obstructing traffic signs, an objection may be sustained. If a crime happened in an alley in July, and a photograph was taken in September, and the alley has been cleaned up or changed in any important way, an objection may be sustained. Because of this, take photographs of accident and crime scenes as soon as possible to avoid or minimize such problems.

Another common objection is that the photograph or video distorts the perspective or is in some other way misleading, which is objectionable under FRE 403. For example, photographs, movies, and videos all use lenses, and a fish-eye or telephoto lens may unfairly distort the picture. Depending on the location and angle from which a photograph is taken, it may distort the relative sizes of objects and apparent distances. A fish-eye lens may distort perspective; a telephoto lens may make objects appear much closer together. Consider raising these issues before trial so that they can be fully examined and argued.

Finally, technology has created new uncertainty in this area. Images in digital photographs and videos are stored electronically, and those images can be altered with editing software in a way that is difficult to detect. For example, photographs can be altered to add, delete, or move objects. Videos can be edited. Although the foundation for admissibility remains the same—a witness with firsthand knowledge of the scene must testify that the photograph or video fairly and accurately shows the scene at the relevant date—foundation witnesses may not detect such changes, and it may be necessary to employ experts to uncover such misconduct.

Sound recordings are sometimes introduced as exhibits during trials. Common examples are tape recordings of face-to-face conversations and telephone conversations. These often are done secretly as part of criminal investigations. A sound recording is admissible if a competent witness who has firsthand knowledge of the facts can testify that the audiotape fairly and accurately recorded the conversation, and a competent witness can identify the persons whose voices are on the recording. Most commonly, the qualifying witness is one of the persons who engaged in the conversation, but any witness who overheard the conversation and can identify the voices can qualify the tape for admission in evidence.

Example:

Q: Special Agent Johnson, did you record the telephone conversation on June 1, 2020, between Mr. Woods and the defendant?

A: Yes.

Q: How did you do that?

A: Mr. Woods and I were in the FBI office in a small interview room. I connected the telephone in the room to a Sony audiotape recorder, and also connected the telephone to a transmitter and headphones so that I could overhear the conversation when it was happening.

Q: Were the recorder and transmitter in proper working order?

A: Yes. I tested both by calling our receptionist, then playing back the recording to make sure everything was working properly.

Q: Is that Sony audiotape recorder a reliable system?

A: Oh yes, we use the Sony because it's so reliable and the recording quality is high.

Q: Tell us how the telephone call was started.

A: I dialed the defendant's home telephone number—864-1234—gave the telephone to Mr. Woods, and listened in on my headphones so that I could hear both sides of the conversation.

Q: What happened after you dialed the number?

A: The phone rang a few times and then it was picked up and a voice answered.

Q: Did you recognize the voice on the other end?

A: Yes. I've heard that voice a number of times, both in person and over the telephone, and I recognized it immediately.

Q: Whose voice was it?

A: The person on the other end was Mr. Williams, the defendant.

Q: What happened during the call?

A: Mr. Woods and the defendant talked for a few minutes, then the call ended and Mr. Woods put the telephone down.

Q: What did you do after that?

A: I rewound the tape and played it back to make sure it had recorded the entire conversation accurately.

Q: Did it?

A: Yes.

Q: After that, what did you do?

A: I made a copy of the tape in a duplicating machine and then put the original tape into a plastic evidence bag, labeled the bag, and heat-sealed the bag to protect the original for later use at trial. I then locked the tape and bag in our evidence vault for safekeeping.

Q: Where is that tape now?

A: I brought it to the courtroom this morning. It's lying on the prosecution table.

Have the exhibit marked, show it to opposing counsel, ask permission to approach the witness, and show the exhibit to the witness.

Q: Agent Johnson, take a look at what has just been marked as Government Exhibit No. 8. Do you recognize it?

A: Yes.

Q: What do you recognize it to be?

A: That's the evidence bag containing the original tape recording of the telephone conversation made on June 1, 2020, between Mr. Woods and the defendant.

Q: How do you know that?

A: I can tell because of the label on the bag, which is in my handwriting. In addition, I labeled the tape itself and I can see my label on the tape.

Q: I'm now showing you a tape recorder that has been marked as Government Exhibit No. 9. Do you recognize this recorder?

A: Yes, it's a Sony tape recorder, the same recorder I used to make the sound recording. We have a number of them in the FBI office.

Q: Is this recorder in good working condition?

A: Yes. I tested it this morning before bringing it to court.

LAWYER: With the court's permission, may Agent Johnson remove the tape from Government Exhibit No. 8 and play it on the tape recorder for the jury?

JUDGE: Yes, based on my pretrial ruling.

Q: Agent Johnson, before you play the tape, please describe the voices so we can tell who the people are.

A: Sure. The first voice that answers the telephone and says "Hello?" is the defendant. He has the low voice. The other voice, the higher pitched voice that says "Hi Mr. Williams, this is Bob Woods" is Mr. Woods. They are the only two voices on the recording.

Q: Please play the tape for the jury. [Witness turns on tape.]

Foundational issues over the admissibility of tape recordings are usually raised before trial. As the proponent, even if the judge has ruled before trial that the tape is admissible, be sure the witness thoroughly describes how the recording was made and how the integrity of the tape was maintained until trial, because these matters will affect the weight the jurors give to the tape recording.

X-rays and other images are conceptually similar to photographs, movies, and videos. X-rays, CAT scans, sonograms, and other medical and scientific instruments show images invisible to the eye. These exhibits usually can be qualified for admission in either of two ways:

1. Testimony from a witness with firsthand knowledge of the necessary facts that the x-ray or other image fairly and accurately shows what it purports to show, or that the hospital procedure in taking x-rays produces an accurate result

2. Qualifying the x-ray or other image as a business record of the hospital or medical facility that created it

X-rays and other images can be admitted in evidence if a witness with first-hand knowledge of the facts testifies that the exhibit fairly and accurately shows what it purports to show. Because x-rays and many other imaging systems have become accepted by the medical and scientific communities and their reliability is not in doubt, no *Daubert* or *Frye* issues usually exist (*Daubert v. Merrell Dow Pharmaceuticals, Inc.*, 509 U.S. 579 (1993); *Frye v. United States*, 293 F. 1013 (D.C. Cir. 1923)). Therefore, there is no need to present expert testimony about how x-ray machines work or the science underlying the machines. All that is needed is someone who was present when the x-ray was taken, who can testify that the x-ray machine was working properly and that the exhibit is the x-ray of that particular patient. This foundation meets the requirements of FRE 901(a). If the witness testifies to the standard procedure under which the hospital takes and labels x-rays, this meets the requirements of FRE 901(b)(9).

Example:

Q: Dr. Williams, you're the doctor who treated Jane Curtis?
A: Yes.
Q: You did the surgery on her lower left leg?
A: Yes.
Q: As part of your treatment of Ms. Curtis, did you have x-rays taken?
A: Yes, both before and after the surgery.

Have the exhibit marked, show it to opposing counsel, ask permission to approach the witness, and show the exhibit to the witness.

Q: Dr. Williams, I'm handing you six x-rays marked Plaintiff's Group Exhibit No. 6A through 6F. Please examine them for a moment. [Doctor looks at x-rays.] Do you recognize them?
A: Yes, I do.
Q: What do you recognize them to be?
A: These are the x-rays I had taken of Ms. Curtis the day I performed the surgery on her lower left leg. 6A through 6C are the x-rays before the surgery, and 6D through 6F are the postsurgery x-rays.
Q: How is it you know that these are in fact the x-rays of Ms. Curtis taken on June 1, 2020?
A: I examined her. I know the condition of her leg and what fractures she had. I did the surgery and I know the pins and screws I used to repair the fractures.
Q: Was the x-ray machine in proper working order?
A: Yes.
Q: Do Exhibits 6A through 6C fairly and accurately show the condition of Ms. Curtis's leg before the surgery?
A: Yes.
Q: Do Exhibits 6D through 6F fairly and accurately show the condition of Ms. Curtis's leg after the surgery?
A: Yes.

LAWYER: Your honor, Plaintiff offers Group Exhibit 6A through 6F in evidence.

OPPOSING LAWYER: No objection, your honor.

JUDGE: Plaintiff's Group Exhibit 6A through 6F is admitted.

Once the x-rays are in evidence, they can be displayed to the jury and the doctor can explain what the x-rays show.

Today x-rays are almost always admitted in evidence as business records of the hospital or medical facility where they were taken. This makes sense because the process of labeling the x-rays—noting the date, patient name, patient number, and so on—is a regularly conducted business activity and meets the requirements of FRE 803(6). Indeed, in personal injury cases the hospital and doctor's records of the patient, including the x-rays, are almost always admitted as business records before trial and without opposition, because lawyers understand that they can easily be qualified as business records. If there are any evidentiary disputes, they will turn on other issues, not whether the medical records (including the x-rays) are business records.

b. Diagrams, Models, Maps, and Drawings

Diagrams, models, maps, and drawings are properly admissible in evidence if: (1) a foundation witness has personal knowledge of how the real thing looked at the relevant time; and (2) the witness can state that the diagram, model, map, or drawing "fairly and accurately" represents how the real thing looked at the relevant time.

In some jurisdictions, diagrams, models, maps, and drawings are considered to be "illustrative." That is, the exhibit is not the real thing but only represents or illustrates the real thing and is not considered to be substantive evidence. Therefore, the illustrative exhibit is only properly used to help a witness explain what happened but is not admitted as substantive evidence and does not go to the jury room during deliberations. In those jurisdictions the witness should be asked if the exhibit will help the witness explain what happened. Even if not required in your jurisdiction, this is a good question to ask, if you have prepared the witness to expect this question.

Whenever a witness knows how the real thing looked at the relevant time, the witness is a competent foundation witness who can identify the diagram or other demonstrative exhibit as fairly and accurately showing how the real thing looked at the relevant time. For example, the person who witnessed a robbery in a parking lot can testify that a diagram fairly and accurately shows the layout of the parking lot on the day (and time, if important) of the robbery.

The foundation witness need not be the person who made the diagram or who witnessed the robbery. The only questions are: Does this witness have firsthand knowledge of how the parking lot looked at the time of the robbery? Can the witness say that the diagram fairly and accurately shows how the parking lot looked at the time of the robbery? (Of course, if the diagram, in addition to showing the layout of the lot, also shows the location of cars on the lot at the time of the robbery, or shows where the robber

> ◀ For a demonstration involving a chart, please watch Video G.3, "Wyo STI: Demonstration of Problem 4.12."

and victim were, the foundation witness would have to be someone who actually saw the robbery.)

Example:

> Q: Mr. Smith, did you see the robbery that happened in the parking lot on the northeast corner of Main and Elm Streets on June 1, 2020, at 8:00 in the evening?
>
> A: I sure did. I was right in my attendant booth.
>
> Q: Do you remember how the lot looked at the time?
>
> A: Sure.

Have the exhibit marked, show it to opposing counsel, ask permission to approach the witness, and show the exhibit to the witness.

> Q: I'm showing you what was just marked State's Exhibit No. 2. Take a look at it for a moment. [Witness looks at it.] Does that diagram fairly and accurately show the layout of the parking lot as it looked on June 1, 2020?
>
> A: Yes.
>
> Q: Would using this diagram help you in explaining what you saw, heard, and did when the robbery happened?
>
> A: It sure would.
>
> LAWYER: Your honor, we offer State's Exhibit No. 2.
>
> OPPOSING LAWYER: No objection, your honor.
>
> JUDGE: State's Exhibit No. 2 is admitted.

The same foundation applies to models, which are the same thing as diagrams, only three-dimensional. The models can be plainly constructed, or they can be fully functional. For example, criminal cases sometimes use models of a home in which a crime occurred; the roof comes off so that the floor plan of the home can be seen. Civil cases sometimes use detailed models of a grade crossing where a collision between a car and train occurred; the model may have actual tracks and functional gates. Regardless of their sophistication, the basic question is the same: Does the model fairly and accurately represent the real thing? When the model is basic, any witness familiar with how the real thing looked at the relevant time can be a foundation witness. When the model is professionally made, it's usually best to use the person who made the model as the foundation witness.

Example:

> Q: Mr. Schwartz, did you make a model of the grade crossing where the collision between the car and the train happened?
>
> A: Yes.
>
> Q: How did you make it?
>
> A: I went to the grade crossing the day after the accident, observed it for some time, took a series of photographs, and then took detailed measurements of the important things I needed to make an accurate model.
>
> Q: Is the model you made a fair and accurate model of that grade crossing?
>
> A: Yes sir, it's as accurate as I could make it, and I've been a draftsman and model maker for a number of years now.

Q: Did you make the model to scale?

A: Yes.

Q: What scale did you use?

A: I used a scale of one inch on the model equaling two feet of the grade crossing. That allowed me to make the model about five feet long, so we could carry it to the courtroom.

Q: How did you color it?

A: I used the same colors on the model that are at the crossing.

Q: How about traffic controls, signs, lane markings, and other details like that?

A: I made them so that they look like the real ones, and are sized to scale on the model.

Have the exhibit marked, show it to opposing counsel, ask permission to approach the witness, and show the exhibit to the witness.

Q: Mr. Schwartz, I've just had wheeled into the courtroom what was previously marked Plaintiff's Exhibit No. 6. Is that the model you made of the grade crossing?

A: Yes.

Q: Does your model, Plaintiff's Exhibit No. 6, fairly and accurately show how the grade crossing looked on the day of the collision?

A: It does.

LAWYER: Your honor, we offer in evidence Plaintiff's Exhibit No. 6.

OPPOSING LAWYER: No objection, your honor.

JUDGE: Very well. Plaintiff's No. 6 is in evidence.

Many times, when a sophisticated diagram or model is made by a professional, the person will take detailed measurements of the location, but only weeks or months after the event happened. That person cannot say the diagram or model accurately shows the location on the date of the event because she did not witness the event. In those situations, you may need to call another witness to testify that the diagram or model accurately shows how the location looked at the time of the event. In practice, admissibility issues over sophisticated diagrams and models are usually resolved before trial.

Maps are frequently used in civil and criminal cases. For example, in a criminal case involving a car chase, the prosecutor may wish to introduce a map in evidence so that a police officer can mark the route of the chase. The foundation for maps is the same as for any demonstrative evidence: it is admissible if it fairly and accurately shows the real thing. Some courts may also admit maps issued by public agencies as self-authenticating under FRE 902(5).

Example:

Have the exhibit marked, show it to opposing counsel, ask permission to approach the witness, and show the exhibit to the witness.

Q: Officer Byrne, I'm showing you what is marked State's Exhibit No. 2. Please examine it for a moment. [Witness looks at exhibit.] Are you familiar with the area shown on this map?

A: Yes, that's the area I regularly patrol.

Q: What area is shown on this map?

A: This shows the north side of the city, from downtown to the city limits.

Q: Does State's Exhibit No. 2 fairly and accurately show the streets and avenues in that part of the city as they were on June 1, 2020, the day you were involved in this chase?

A: Yes.

Q: Does it show the streets and avenues you took during the chase?

A: Yes.

Q: Would this map help you in explaining where you went during the time you were involved in this chase?

A: Most definitely.

LAWYER: Your honor, we offer State's Exhibit No. 2.

JUDGE: Any objections?

OPPOSING LAWYER: No, your honor.

JUDGE: State's No. 2 is admitted.

Drawings by witnesses are no different from diagrams, models, or maps. A drawing represents the real thing, so the foundation is identical: A witness with firsthand knowledge of the real thing can make a drawing if the drawing fairly and accurately shows how the real thing looked at the relevant time. Witnesses are sometimes asked to make a drawing on butcher paper or a foam-core poster board during their testimony. For example, a witness to an accident or crime may be asked to make a drawing of the scene.

However, generally you should avoid asking witnesses to make drawings in the courtroom. The drawings rarely look clear and neat, and few witnesses can do it confidently and accurately. The better approach is to anticipate the need and have a diagram prepared before trial that the witness can use and mark if the need arises. Usually the only time a witness should make a drawing is when the need arises unexpectedly, which is most likely when you have a rebuttal witness on the stand.

c. Animations and Simulations

Computer-created animations and simulations are becoming increasingly common as software programs are making them easier and cheaper than ever to produce. Evidence law is slowly catching up to the technology, but court opinions are still frequently inconsistent in discussing the foundations necessary for these kinds of exhibits. Jurisdiction-specific research will be necessary in this area. Admissibility issues should be raised and ruled on well before trial.

What are animations and simulations? Although these terms are frequently used loosely and interchangeably and their definitions can vary, animations and simulations are conceptually different kinds of exhibits that have significantly different foundation requirements.

An *animation* is a visual illustration, usually a computer image, showing continuous motion or a freeze-frame sequence of an expert's opinion of how an event happened. If the expert is qualified, her opinion is helpful to the jury, and the testimony is relevant and reliable, the expert can give her opinion on how an event happened. The expert's testimony must, of course, meet the admissibility standards of FRE 702 (which incorporates the *Daubert-Joiner-Kumho Tire* analysis). If the expert meets these standards and is permitted to testify to her opinion, an animation that makes the expert's opinion visual and helps the expert explain that opinion will be admissible, provided that the animation fairly and accurately illustrates the opinion.

For example, if an accident reconstruction expert is permitted to testify that, in his opinion, the defendant's car had crossed over to the plaintiff's side of the road at the moment of impact, a computer animation (or, for that matter, any visual aid) illustrating that opinion should be admissible. The only foundation necessary is the expert's testimony that the animation fairly and accurately illustrates his opinion.

Example:

> Q: Dr. Stein, did you prepare a computer animation that illustrates your opinion of where the plaintiff's and defendant's cars were before and at the moment of impact?
> A: Yes.
>
> Have the exhibit marked, show it to opposing counsel, ask permission to approach the witness, and show the exhibit to the witness.
>
> Q: I'm showing you what has been marked Plaintiff's Exhibit No. 3. Is that a computer animation you prepared?
> A: Yes.
> Q: Does your animation fairly and accurately illustrate your professional opinion of where the plaintiff's and defendant's cars were before and at the moment of impact?
> A: Yes.
> LAWYER: Your honor, we offer Plaintiff's Exhibit No. 3 in evidence, ask permission to play the animation to the jury, and ask permission to have Dr. Stein explain the animation while it is being played.
> JUDGE: Any objection from the defense?
> OPPOSING LAWYER: None other than the matters we raised during the pretrial hearing, your honor.
> JUDGE: Plaintiff's Exhibit No. 3 will be admitted. You may play it for the jury, and Dr. Stein may explain the animation while it is being played.

When an animation is admitted in evidence, the jury is usually given a cautionary instruction that it should consider the animation only as a visual illustration of the expert's opinion, and not as a re-creation of how the collision actually happened. The animation, in other words, is only as good as the expert's opinion.

A *simulation* is a re-creation of an event based on scientific data of how the real event happened. A simulation must accurately re-create how the event happened. This means that the data used for the simulation—the input—must be reliable and sufficient, and the computer software program must be a program that can accurately and reliably create a simulation from the data, so that the simulation—the output—fairly and reliably shows what happened. This obviously requires foundation testimony from experts, usually the expert who accumulated the underlying data and the computer technician who used the data and software program to create the simulation. The software program is, in effect, the expert visually rendering an opinion on how the event happened. In short, a simulation must be shown to be relevant and reliable, and it should be subject to an FRE 702 (or, in some states, *Frye*) analysis.

For example, in airplane crash cases, plaintiffs frequently prepare a simulation of the last minute of an airplane flight before crashing. The simulation is usually a video image of the airplane in the air or the view from the cockpit through the windshield. It may include key instrument readings, such as compass direction, airspeed, altitude, and artificial horizon, and the audio of the radio communications between the pilots and ground control. The simulation will be admissible if it fairly and accurately shows the airplane's flight. This can be done if qualified experts testify that the flight data obtained from the airplane's "black box," air traffic control instruments, weather instruments, and other sources were reliable and sufficient to re-create what the airplane was doing during that last minute, that the data was entered into a computer software program that can reliably take flight and other data and convert it into a simulation of the airplane's flight, and that the resulting simulation fairly and accurately shows the airplane's flight.

The admissibility of simulations should be determined before trial in a *Daubert* hearing, where the witnesses involved in acquiring the data and creating the simulation testify. The usual issues center on the integrity and sufficiency of the data obtained and used (whether the simulation included all the necessary data, and whether it included any unreliable data), the reliability of the software program that crunched the data and generated the simulation, and any FRE 403 concerns. If flaws seriously affect the accuracy or reliability of the simulation, it should be excluded. If not, the simulation should be admitted and cross-examination can point out any matters that may affect the weight the jury should give it.

3. Writings/Instruments

Writings are written things that have legal significance because they were made. Common examples, which arise mostly in civil cases, are legal instruments such as contracts, checks, promissory notes, and wills; letters that contains the words of contract; and letters constituting notice, permission, and consent.

Before writings can be admitted in evidence, the proponent must show, through the testimony of a foundation witness who has firsthand knowledge of the necessary facts, that the writing was written or signed by the person it purports to be written or signed by. For example, a written contract is admissible if a witness testifies that she saw the plaintiff and defendant sign the contract. This authentication requirement is a protection against forgery and demonstrates the relevance of the writing. Under FRE 901(a), the foundation witness can be anyone who saw the person write or sign the writing, or is familiar with that person's handwriting or signature and can identify the handwriting or signature as being that of the person. Handwriting can also be proved through expert witness testimony based on a comparison between the writing and a known exemplar of the person's handwriting. Finally, handwriting can be proved circumstantially from surrounding events and conduct that identify the maker.

It is important to remember that writings are nonhearsay. This is because writings are not offered for their truth; they are being offered because they were made and substantive law gives legal significance to the fact that they were made. Because they are not hearsay, writings cannot be admitted in evidence merely by showing that they are business records. Although some writings, such as promissory notes, may also be business records, the business records foundation does not establish the essential foundation for admissibility: authenticating the handwriting or signature of the maker. Because writings are not hearsay, it necessarily follows that hearsay objections to their admission in evidence should be overruled.

While writings (i.e., documents that have legal significance because they were created) are nonhearsay, they sometimes contain hearsay. For example, a letter containing the words of a contract (e.g., "I accept your offer to sell me 1,000 tee shirts for $5 each") might also contain statements offered to prove the truths of the matters asserted (e.g., "you have really high-quality tee shirts," if offered to prove that the tee shirts were of high quality).

Ignoring possible hearsay issues, note again the *prima facie* standard in FRE 901(a): "evidence sufficient to support a finding that the item is what the proponent claims it is." It does not matter if the purported signer of the writing disputes his signature. A proper foundation for admission is established if a witness saw the writing being signed or is familiar with the person's handwriting and testifies that the signature is of that person. If the other side contests it, it simply becomes a disputed matter to be resolved by the jury.

For foundation purposes, it is useful to group writings into two categories:

1. Legal instruments, such as contracts, checks, promissory notes, and wills, that are nonhearsay because they have independent legal significance.
2. Letters and other written communications that are nonhearsay because they are party admissions or are offered for a nonhearsay purpose.

a. Legal Instruments

Contracts, checks, promissory notes, and wills are properly admissible if:

1. A foundation witness has personal knowledge of the required foundation facts.
2. The witness can state that he saw the person sign the writing; or that he is familiar with the handwriting of the person and that the signature on the writing is that person's; or that he has firsthand knowledge of other facts that circumstantially identify the maker of the writing; or there is expert handwriting comparison evidence.

Some courts also require testimony that the writing appears to be in the same condition now as when it was made, although as a practical matter a witness will not be able to say this unless the witness was present when the writing was signed. However, the primary concern with writings is that the words on them have not been altered or forged. Many courts take the better-reasoned position that it is up to the opponent to raise issues of alteration or forgery, which triggers application of the original documents rule, FRE 1001 to 1004. If your court requires this foundation, perhaps the safe question is to ask if the document "appears to be in the same condition now" or whether it "has any signs of alteration or changes." In most cases, a legal instrument can be easily and efficiently introduced by calling a witness who was present when it was signed.

Example (Contract):

Have the exhibit marked, show it to opposing counsel, ask permission to approach the witness, and show the exhibit to the witness.

Q: Ms. Adams, I'm showing you what has been marked as Plaintiff's Exhibit No. 7, a document consisting of five pages. Please examine

> it for a moment. [Witness does so.] Have you seen that document before?
>
> A: Yes.
>
> Q: When?
>
> A: On June 1, 2020, when Mr. Smith and I signed it.
>
> Q: Where were you when the two of you signed it?
>
> A: In my office.
>
> Q: Take a look at Plaintiff's Exhibit No. 7, at the bottom of page five. Do you recognize the signatures on that page?
>
> A: Yes.
>
> Q: Whose signatures are they?
>
> A: At the bottom, on the left side, is my signature. On the right side is Mr. Smith's signature. We both put our signatures on that page in my office on June 1, 2020.
>
> Q: Does Plaintiff's Exhibit No. 7 appear to be in the same condition now as it was on June 1, 2020?
>
> A: Yes.
>
> LAWYER: Your honor, we offer Plaintiff's Exhibit No. 7.
>
> OPPOSING LAWYER: No objection, your honor.
>
> JUDGE: Plaintiff's Exhibit No. 7 is in evidence.

After the exhibit has been admitted, you can read or show it to the jury.

Keep in mind that you are accomplishing two purposes with the foundation: You are satisfying the judge, who determines admissibility; and you are convincing the jury, which determines weight. If the exhibit is particularly important, ask the additional questions jurors would ask if they could.

Example:

> Q: Mr. White, do you know a person by the name of Samuel Johnson?
>
> A: Yes.
>
> Q: How long have you know him?
>
> A: About ten years.
>
> Q: Have you had business dealings with him during those years?
>
> A: Yes.
>
> Q: During those years, have you ever seen Mr. Johnson sign his name on things?
>
> A: Oh yes.
>
> Q: What kinds of things?
>
> A: Letters, checks, contracts, business documents.
>
> Q: Over the past ten years, how many times have you seen Mr. Johnson sign his name to things?
>
> A: I'd say around 50 or 60 times.
>
> Q: When you see Mr. Johnson's signature, can you recognize it?
>
> A: Oh yes, he has very distinctive handwriting.

Have the exhibit marked, show it to opposing counsel, ask permission to approach the witness, and show the exhibit to the witness.

> Q: I'm showing you Plaintiff's Exhibit No. 3. Take a look at the lower right-hand corner of that check. Do you see the signature?
>
> A: Yes.

Q: Do you recognize the signature?

A: Oh yes.

Q: How are you able to recognize that signature?

A: Because I've seen it at least 50 or 60 times. It's very distinctive.

Q: Whose signature appears on the lower right-hand corner of that check, Plaintiff's Exhibit No. 3?

A: That's Samuel Johnson's signature.

Note here that the witness can only authenticate the signature. Because he was not present when the check was made out and signed, the witness cannot say whether the check is in the same condition now as it was on the date it was made. Nevertheless, the witness can be asked: "Does this exhibit show any signs of alternation or change?" and the witness can truthfully answer that question.

Note also that only the portions of the check that constitute the legal instrument are nonhearsay. Other things on the check, such as a notation on the memo line that many checks have, the payee's endorsement signature on the back, and the various bank stamps that were placed there as the check went through the clearing process, are not a part of the check. The memo portion and the bank stamps are usually considered hearsay and must be shown to fall within a hearsay exception, and the endorsement signature must be authenticated before these things are admitted in evidence. This is a common mistake: lawyers thinking that if the check is authenticated, everything else on the front and back of the check is admissible without additional proof. That is not so. If the judge sustains objections to these parts of the check, you must prepare a copy of the check with the objectionable parts deleted (redacted), or call additional witnesses to get these parts admitted in evidence.

In most cases, you can introduce the original or a duplicate of the instrument. However, if "a genuine question is raised about the original's authenticity" (usually a claim that the signature on the instrument is a forgery or that the instrument has been altered), the original documents rule, FRE 1001 to 1004, requires that the original be produced unless the absence of the original is satisfactorily explained.

> ◼◀ For a discussion of the original documents rule, please watch the first portion of Video H.2, "Wyo STI: Best Evidence Rule and Authentication."

Example:

Q: Ms. Adams, let's turn now to June 1, 2020. Where were you around 9:00 in the morning?

A: I was in Mr. Smith's office.

Q: Why were you there?

A: We had set up a meeting to go over the contract and, if it was satisfactory, to sign it.

Have the exhibit marked, show it to opposing counsel ask, permission to approach the witness, and show the exhibit to the witness.

Q: I'm showing you Plaintiff's Exhibit No. 7. Do you recognize it?

A: Yes, that's the contract Mr. Smith and I signed on that date.

Q: How do you know that?

A: I remember the contract, and I signed it first and then Mr. Smith signed it as I watched.

Q: Is this the original or a copy?

A: It's the original. I kept the original after we signed it, and Mr. Smith kept a photocopy.

Q: On page five of the contract, whose signatures are at the bottom?

A: That's my signature and Mr. Smith's.

Q: Please turn to page four. Do you see the handwritten words near the middle of the page?

A: Yes.

Q: Whose handwriting is that?

A: Mine.

Q: How did your handwriting get on page four?

A: Before we signed the contract, we talked about adding a provision to Paragraph 14. I wanted a requirement of written notice of any claims of defective work, and he agreed to it, so I wrote those handwritten words at the end of Paragraph 14.

Q: Anything else?

A: Yes. After I wrote those words on the contract, I put my initials at the end of the handwritten words, and handed the contract to Mr. Smith. He then put his initials just below mine. They're right there [pointing].

Q: The photocopy of the contract that Mr. Smith got, when was that made?

A: I don't know. It was already there that morning with the original when I arrived.

Q: Did the photocopy contain the additional words you wrote on the contract and your and Mr. Smith's initials?

A: No. We only made the handwritten addition to the original.

LAWYER: Your honor, we offer the original of the contract, Plaintiff's Exhibit No. 7, in evidence.

OPPOSING LAWYER: Objection, your honor. The exhibit does not comply with the original documents rule.

JUDGE: Overruled. It will be admitted.

In this example, even though the plaintiff has gotten the original contract, with the handwritten additions, into evidence, it does not prevent the defendant from later introducing his photocopy of the contract in evidence or testifying that he never made or agreed to the claimed addition. Whether the contract was modified, and whether the defendant agreed to the modification, become disputed issues of fact, which are for the jury to resolve.

The identity of the signer of an instrument can also be proved through circumstantial evidence. FRE 901(a) does not limit the methods of proof. Sometimes conduct, either before or after the instrument was signed, will identify the signer. For example, it sometimes happens that when contracts are made through offer and acceptance letters, and the signature on the acceptance letter cannot be directly authenticated, there will be telephone calls that circumstantially prove the identity of the signature on the acceptance letter.

Example:

Have the exhibit marked, show it to opposing counsel, ask permission to approach the witness, and show the exhibit to the witness.

Q: Ms. Henderson, I'm showing you what's been marked Plaintiff's Exhibit No. 2. Have you seen this letter before?

A: Yes, I received it in the mail on June 8, 2020.

Q: Did you recognize the signature on the bottom of that letter?

A: No, I'd never seen that signature before.

Q: Ms. Henderson, do you know the defendant, Mr. Johnson?

A: Yes, I've known him for some time, but I never did any business with him before this deal.

Q: Are you familiar with his voice?

A: Yes. He has a distinctive voice.

Q: Were you familiar with his voice in June of 2020?

A: Yes.

Q: Let's go back to June 5, 2020. Did you get a telephone call from Mr. Johnson that day?

A: Yes.

Q: When and where?

A: It was in the morning, and I was in my office.

Q: How do you know the caller was Mr. Johnson?

A: I recognized his voice, and he introduced himself.

Q: Tell us what he said.

A: He said he had gotten my letter containing the offer and he said that he would be sending his acceptance and that I should get it in a couple of days.

LAWYER: Your honor, we offer Plaintiff's Exhibit No. 2.

OPPOSING LAWYER: We object, your honor. May we approach?

JUDGE: Yes. [Lawyers come to the bench.] What's the objection?

OPPOSING LAWYER: There's been no testimony identifying the signature on the letter as being Mr. Johnson's. The witness said she couldn't recognize it.

LAWYER: The maker of the letter has been identified through the earlier conversation Ms. Henderson had with Mr. Johnson. That's enough by itself, but there's more. The letter [showing judge the letter] says: "As I promised in our telephone call today, I am sending you this letter to confirm that we are accepting your offer."

JUDGE: The objection is overruled. There's been sufficient identification of the writer of the letter. Plaintiff's Exhibit No. 2 is admitted.

b. Letters and Other Written Communications

Letters and other written communications are admissible in evidence, provided that all the admissibility requirements are properly proven. The first step is to determine if the letter is hearsay or nonhearsay. Because letters are out-of-court statements, they are hearsay if offered for their truth, but nonhearsay if they have probative value because they were made. Common examples of nonhearsay letters are letters that have legal significance because they contain the words of contract or gift; contain words constituting notice, permission, authority, or consent; or contain the words of fraud, defamation, or threats. For example, a letter by plaintiff to defendant that contains an offer, and a reply letter from defendant that contains an acceptance, are both nonhearsay, because the two letters form a contract.

A letter that contains defamatory words, that puts the receiver on notice, or that contains a threat, is nonhearsay. A letter signed by a party (or agent or employee of a party) is admissible as a party admission under FRE 801(d)(2) if offered by the opposing party.

The second step is to authenticate the letter under FRE 901(a). A letter that is nonhearsay is properly authenticated if:

1. A foundation witness has personal knowledge of the required foundation facts.
2. The foundation witness can state that he saw the person sign the letter, or that he is familiar with the handwriting of that person and that the signature on the letter is that person's; or that he knows other circumstances identifying the maker of the letter as that person; or there is expert handwriting comparison evidence.

The third step is to prove, when necessary, that the addressee received the original letter. Most letters are relevant only if the addressees actually received them. For example, a letter containing the words of offer, and a letter containing words of notice, will be relevant only if the letters were sent to and received by the addressees. The proponent must show, either through direct or circumstantial evidence, that the addressee received the letter. This is usually shown through later statements of the addressee acknowledging receipt of the letter; later conduct of the addressee that is consistent with receiving the letter; or proof that the original of the letter was properly addressed, stamped, and mailed.

The fourth step is to prove, when necessary, that the letter in court is a true copy of the signed original. This is a requirement whenever the original was mailed and the only evidence of the letter is a photocopy or other duplicate.

There are two general types of foundations for letters: letters sent and letters received.

Letters Sent to a Person. When letters that are nonhearsay are sent to a person, the maker of the letter is usually the necessary foundation witness. The proponent of the letter must establish that:

1. The original letter was written and signed.
2. The original letter was sent to and received by the addressee. This can be shown through direct evidence, such as proof of hand delivery or an admission by the addressee that he received it, or through circumstantial evidence, most commonly proof that the letter was properly addressed, stamped, and deposited in a U.S. mailbox (this evidence triggers the presumption that the addressee actually received the letter).
3. The copy in court accurately shows the contents of the original letter.

Example:

Have the exhibit marked, show it to opposing counsel, ask permission to approach the witness, and show the exhibit to the witness.

Q: Ms. Gibbs, I'm handing you Plaintiff's Exhibit No. 1. Please review it for a moment. [Witness looks at exhibit.] Do you recognize this exhibit?

A: Yes, that's a photocopy of a letter I wrote and sent to Mr. Wolf.

Q: Where did you get this photocopy?

A: From my office file.

Q: What did you do with the original of the letter?

A: I signed it, put it in one of our company envelopes addressed to Mr. Wolf, stamped it for first-class mail with our postage meter, and put it in the mailbox in the lobby of my building.

Q: When did you do that?

A: The same date the letter bears, June 1, 2020.

Q: Did the postal service ever return that letter?

A: No.

Q: How do you know?

A: Whenever one of my letters is returned because of a bad address or other reason, my practice is to staple the letter and envelope to the photocopy and keep them in my file. I checked my file for this transaction. It had only this photocopy, which tells me the original was sent and was never returned.

Q: When did you make the photocopy of your original letter?

A: Right after my secretary typed the letter and envelope, she made the photocopy and gave them to me, and I put the copy in my office file. That's my standard office procedure.

Q: Is this exhibit, Plaintiff's Exhibit No. 1, an accurate copy of the original you signed and mailed to Mr. Wolf on June 1, 2020?

A: Yes. Except for the fact that this copy does not contain my signature, it's identical to the signed original.

LAWYER: Your honor, we offer Plaintiff's Exhibit No. 1.

OPPOSING LAWYER: We object, your honor. No foundation. There has been no evidence proving Mr. Wolf actually received that letter.

JUDGE: Overruled. Plaintiff's Exhibit No. 1 is admitted.

The letter can now be shown or read to the jury.

Letters sent to another person are commonly used, particularly in civil cases, and the requirements for admissibility are always the same: The letter must be nonhearsay or within an exception to the ban on hearsay, the signed original must be shown to have been received by the addressee, and the copy in court must be shown to accurately reflect the contents of the original.

The most common factual dispute centers on whether the addressee ever received the letter. Here, it is important that the proponent of the letter introduce evidence that not only satisfies the judge, who rules on admissibility, but also convinces the jurors, who determine weight. The usual way to prove that the addressee received the letter is through proof of mailing, as shown in the preceding example. Another common way is through discovery, such as the addressee admitting in a deposition that he received the letter, or a response to a request to admit facts, or by the addressee producing the original of the letter in response to a request to produce documents. But there are other ways, and FRE 901(a) does not limit how receipt of a letter can be circumstantially shown, as this is a question of logic.

For example, receipt of a letter can be shown by evidence that the addressee's reply letter is consistent with the terms of the letter. The *reply letter doctrine* provides that if the addressee in a reply letter refers to the contents of the original letter, it proves that the addressee received the letter. If a reply letter states: "I accept your offer contained in your letter of June 1, 2020," or makes other references to that first letter, it proves that the addressee received the letter. If the letter to the addressee asks that the addressee indicate his agreement with the terms of the offer by delivering the goods at a certain time and place, and the addressee makes the delivery, this proves that the addressee received the letter. If the addressee makes a telephone call to the sender of the letter and talks about the terms in the letter, it proves that the addressee got the letter. There are many ways to circumstantially prove that an addressee received a letter that meet the *prima facie* proof standard of FRE 901(a). If the addressee denies receipt, it becomes a disputed issue for the jury to resolve.

Remember that letters that are nonhearsay because they contain the words of contract (or defamation, misrepresentation, gift, permission, authority, consent, and so on) are nonhearsay only as to the actual words that constitute the contract. If the letter contains additional matters that are not the words of contract, they are probably hearsay and should be excluded, unless a hearsay exception applies.

Example:

> **LAWYER:** Your honor, we offer Defendant's Exhibit No. 2.
>
> **JUDGE:** Any objection, counsel?
>
> **OPPOSING LAWYER:** We have objections to parts of the letter, your honor. May we be heard at the bench?
>
> **JUDGE:** Yes. Please approach. [Lawyers come to the bench.] What's your objection? It looks like a standard offer letter.
>
> **OPPOSING LAWYER:** We have no objection to paragraphs one and two, your honor. They are the words of offer and the terms of the offer, and we agree those words are nonhearsay. But paragraph three is a different matter. That paragraph says: "I need not remind you that you failed to meet the terms and conditions of our last order. If that happens again with this order, we may be forced to deal with another vendor in the future." Those words are not part of the offer. They are hearsay, and no hearsay exception applies. Accordingly, we ask that paragraph three be excluded, and an exhibit with paragraph three deleted be allowed in evidence.
>
> **JUDGE:** Plaintiff, what's your position?
>
> **OPPOSING LAWYER:** We have no objection to deleting paragraph three and admitting a redacted copy of the letter. I'll do that over the next break.
>
> **JUDGE:** Very well. Defendant's Exhibit No. 2, with paragraph three redacted, is admitted. The defense will prepare an appropriate exhibit.

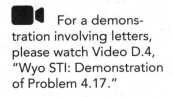 For a demonstration involving letters, please watch Video D.4, "Wyo STI: Demonstration of Problem 4.17."

Letters Received from a Person. When letters that are nonhearsay are received from a person, the proponent of the letter must establish that the person whose signature is on the letter in fact signed the letter. Because the letter offered is usually a signed original, there will be no need to qualify a copy. If the foundation witness is the person who received the letter, there will be no need to introduce circumstantial proof of receipt. If the court requires a showing that the exhibit is now in the same condition as when received, that can be easily shown.

A common example of this kind of letter is a letter containing an acceptance of an offer, thus making a contract. In this situation, the person who received the letter, if she can identify the signature on the letter, can quickly establish all the facts necessary for admission of the letter in evidence.

Example:

> Q: Ms. Roberts, please take a look at Plaintiff's Exhibit No. 2. Have you seen that exhibit before?
> A: Yes.
> Q: When was the first time you saw it?
> A: I received this letter in the mail about June 8, 2020.
> Q: Please look at the bottom of the letter. Are you familiar with the signature that appears on the letter?
> A: Yes, I've seen it lots of times.
> Q: Whose signature do you recognize it to be?
> A: That's Mr. Wolf's signature.
> Q: Is this letter, Plaintiff's Exhibit No. 2, in the same condition now as when you received it?
> A: Yes, I've kept it in my office file since I got it.
> LAWYER: Your honor, we offer Plaintiff's Exhibit No. 2.
> JUDGE: Any objection?
> OPPOSING LAWYER: No, your honor.
> JUDGE: Plaintiff's Exhibit No. 2 is admitted.

The letter can then be read or shown to the jurors.

What if the person who received the letter cannot identify the maker's signature? In this situation, one obvious solution is for the proponent to find a witness who can identify the maker's signature. If that fails, the proponent can use handwriting experts to prove that the letter in fact contains the signature of the maker. In addition, remember that under FRE 901(a), you can prove the identity of the person who made or signed the letter through any evidence that logically proves the fact. For example, consider a store owner who receives an extortion note that says, "Protecting your business will cost $100 each month, payable on the first of every month. If you don't, there will be dire consequences." The note is typed and unsigned. Subsequent conduct can identify who made the extortion note, even though the note has no signature.

Example:

> Q: Mr. Chavez, this typed note that you received, State's Exhibit No. 1, when did you get it?
> A: I found it in the mailbox at my store on June 25.
> Q: Did you see who put the note in your mailbox?
> A: No.
> Q: Let's turn to five days later, June 30. Did you see the defendant that day?
> A: I sure did.

Q: Where?

A: Right in my store.

Q: Did he say anything to you?

A: Yes.

Q: Tell us what he said.

A: He said, "Tomorrow is the first of the month. Are you going to pay, or do you want to see the dire consequences?"

LAWYER: Your honor, based on this testimony, we now offer State's Exhibit No. 1 in evidence and ask permission to show it to the jury.

OPPOSING LAWYER: Objection, your honor. There's been no evidence that the defendant typed that note, and there's no signature on it.

JUDGE: The objection is overruled. State's Exhibit No. 1 is in evidence, and may be shown to the jury.

The important thing to remember with letters is that you always need to determine if the letter is being offered for a nonhearsay purpose, and keep clear the different foundation requirements that apply to a letter sent to another person and a letter received from another person. Authentication of such letters can be done through direct testimony from witnesses, but it can also be done through any evidence that circumstantially proves the identity of the maker of the letter.

Finally, do not forget that letters may qualify as party admissions. Whenever a letter is written by a party-opponent (or an agent or employee of that party), you can introduce it in evidence if the letter is relevant and you authenticate the party-opponent's signature on it. It is much easier to have such letters admitted under FRE 801(d)(2), the party admission rule, than it is to argue that the letter is being offered for a proper nonhearsay purpose.

E-mails and Other Electronic Communications. Written communications, of course, are not limited to letters. In our computer world, e-mail and other electronic communications raise the same kinds of authentication and hearsay issues. You must always be prepared to prove that the e-mail you wrote was actually sent to and received by the intended recipient. You must always be prepared to prove that an e-mail you received actually came from the person it purports to be from. Under FRE 901(b)(9), this evidence can be electronic, such as testimony from electronics experts demonstrating that a particular e-mail was sent from one e-mail address to another. Under FRE 901(a), it can be circumstantial, such as evidence of a responsive e-mail or letter. Under FRE 901(b)(4), the evidence can establish that the sender used distinctive terms or markings.

The important thing to keep in mind is that the necessary foundation for letters, e-mails, and other communications must be determined and obtained well in advance of trial. Also remember that the proponent is not required to remove all doubt, or even a reasonable doubt, about the electronic communication's authenticity. FRE 901(a) requires only that "the proponent must produce evidence sufficient to support a finding that the [electronic communication] is what the proponent claims it is."

4. Business Records

Business records are records regularly made by any kind of business, or even by noncommercial entities. Common examples in both civil and criminal cases are medical records from hospitals, shipping records from trucking companies, sales records from retail stores, and employment records from manufacturers or nonprofit organizations.

Before business records can be admitted in evidence for their truth—to prove that an event or transaction happened—they must be shown to fall within a hearsay exception, usually the business records rule, FRE 803(6). The scope of the business records rule is best understood in steps.

First, what qualifies as a "business"? A *business*, which FRE 803(6) actually refers to as a "regularly conducted activity," is broadly defined as a "business, organization, occupation, or calling, whether or not for profit."

Second, what is a "record"? A *record* is "of an act, event, condition, opinion, or diagnosis if: (A) the record was made at or near the time by—or from information transmitted by—someone with knowledge; (B) the record was kept in the course of a regularly conducted activity of a business[; and] (C) making the record was the regular practice of that activity."

Third, what methods can be used to admit business records? Three basic methods are available:

1. Certification by a "custodian or another qualified person" under FRE 902(11). See also FRE 902(12), (13), and (14).
2. Testimony from a "custodian or another qualified witness" under FRE 803(6)(D).
3. Qualification as a party admission under FRE 801(d)(2), because the record is being offered by the opposing party.

Fourth, who is a qualified foundation witness? Whether the witness is the certification witness under FRE 902(11) or (12), or the custodian or other qualified witness under FRE 803(6)(D), the requirements are the same. The witness must be able to testify or certify that the business record is in fact a "record" of that business in accordance with the definition in FRE 803(6). The usual witness is either a "custodian" of the business's records, an employee who regularly makes that kind of record, or an employee who knows how that kind of record is regularly made. It is not necessary that the witness have any personal knowledge of this particular exhibit, event, or transaction, just that the witness know how this kind of record is regularly made and maintained by the business.

Although most foundation witnesses testify routinely and without objection, and courts are generally liberal in ruling that the witness is qualified to provide the foundation, two problems sometimes occur. These are the nonemployee and former employee problems. Many courts take the position that a nonemployee cannot be a qualified foundation witness, because a nonemployee by definition does not know the inner workings of the business that created the record. For example, just because someone regularly receives FedEx shipments, and always receives a shipping document with each shipment, does not mean that the person can qualify the shipping document as a business record of FedEx. Some courts take the position that a former employee of a business can be a qualified foundation witness only if that former employee was an employee during the time the particular record was created. The underlying question is the same: Does this witness really know how the business creates and maintains this kind of record? The safe approach is to use a current employee of the business as the foundation witness.

Fifth, what is the required foundation? FRE 803(6) is technical and requires the custodian or other qualified witness to testify or certify that the record:

1. was made by "someone with knowledge" of the facts or was made "from information transmitted" by a person with knowledge of the facts;
2. was "made at or near the time" of the acts and events recorded on it;
3. was made as part of the "regular practice of that activity"; and
4. was "kept in the course of a regularly conducted activity."

Because the foundation testimony must satisfy the judge, who determines admissibility, the safe approach is to have the witness testify in the language of the rule.

Example:

> Q: Ms. Hawkins, what's your position at Acme Corporation?
> A: I work in the records department.
> Q: How long?
> A: About eight years now.
> Q: Are you familiar with the business records your company regularly creates and maintains?
> A: Yes. That's my job.
> Q: In particular, are you familiar with how your company creates and maintains a record called a shipment confirmation?
> A: Yes, that's one of our standard records.

Have the exhibit marked, show it to opposing counsel, ask permission to approach the witness, and show the exhibit to the witness.

> Q: Ms. Hawkins, I'm showing you what is marked Defendant's Exhibit No. 2. Is that one of Acme Corporation's records?
> A: Yes, it's one of our shipment confirmations.
> Q: Was that record made by a person with knowledge of the facts?
> A: Yes. It's made by one of our shipping clerks.
> Q: Was that record made at or near the time of the acts and events appearing on it?
> A: Yes. The shipping clerk fills out the confirmation form when the shipment goes out.
> Q: Was that record made as part of the regular practice of Acme Corporation?
> A: Yes. We fill out the confirmation form every time a shipment goes out.
> Q: Was that record kept in the course of Acme Corporation's regularly conducted business activity?
> A: Yes. And we keep all confirmation forms in our computer system for seven years.
> LAWYER: Your honor, we offer Defendant's Exhibit No. 2.
> JUDGE: Any objection?
> OPPOSING LAWYER: No, your honor.
> JUDGE: Plaintiff's Exhibit No. 2 is admitted.

If the certification procedure under FRE 902(11) or (12) is used, the certification should contain the same language. Once the judge has ruled the record is admissible in evidence, it can be shown or read to the jury.

Note that business records can be created in numerous ways. The words of FRE 803(6) may not always comfortably fit the realities of how the particular exhibit was actually created. This should not matter because the underlying concern is reliability, and as long as the way in which the particular record was created and maintained is reliable, the record should qualify for admission. For example, today most business records are automatically generated by computer systems. A common example is retail stores that automatically generate daily sales and inventory records as sales are rung up on cash registers. This is possible because the sales clerk, when ringing up the sale, puts into the cash register both the inventory number and the sales price of the item sold, often by scanning a barcode. At the end of the day, the store's computer system has both a record of all sales from that particular cash register, and a record of total sales from all the registers, as well as an inventory record showing how many of each item were sold that day. These qualify as business records, and the printouts of these records are admissible.

Judges are principally concerned with whether the record has been properly qualified for admission under the business records exception, so the judge will be listening for the technical foundation buzzwords. The easiest way to satisfy the judge is to use the words of FRE 803(6) in the foundation questions, as the preceding example shows. That technical foundation, however, may not convince the jurors. Jurors want to know, in practical terms, how the record was actually made and whether they can trust it. With key business records, it is usually more persuasive to ask the foundation questions in language the jurors can better understand. As part of that foundation, ask whether the record is important to the operation of the business, and what would happen if the record were not carefully made and maintained. Those are the questions the jurors want answered.

Example:

> Q: Ms. Adams, how many years have you worked as a registered nurse in the emergency room at University Hospital?
>
> A: Over ten years.
>
> Q: Are you familiar with how the emergency room at the hospital makes and maintains emergency room reports?
>
> A: Of course.
>
> Q: When a patient comes to the ER, what's the first step?
>
> A: The patient is seen by a nurse, who examines the patient, talks to the patient if possible, takes vital signs such as blood pressure and pulse, and notes any medical conditions.
>
> Q: Does the nurse do anything with that information?
>
> A: Yes. He or she puts it into the ER report.
>
> Q: When?
>
> A: That's done as the nurse is examining the patient and getting the vital signs and other information from the patient.
>
> Q: After that, what happens?
>
> A: The patient is then seen by an emergency room doctor.
>
> Q: Does the doctor put any information on the ER report?
>
> A: Yes. Information based on the doctor's examination of the patient.
>
> Q: When does the doctor put this information in the report?
>
> A: Right after the examination. The doctor then electronically signs the ER report.

Q: What happens to the ER report after the nurse and doctor have filled it out?

A: It depends on what happens to the patient. If the patient is discharged, the patient gets a copy of the report and any instructions on what the patient should do next. If the patient is admitted, the patient is taken to a ward in the hospital and the ER report goes with him. Either way, when the patient is finally discharged, the ER report goes to the medical records department.

Q: Ms. Adams, is the ER report an important record for your hospital?

A: It's more than important. It's vital.

Q: What use does the hospital make of the ER report?

A: That's the key report that shows what the patient says happened to him, the patient's vital signs, the findings from the patient's examination, the tentative diagnosis, and the treatment plan. It's the blueprint of the patient's condition and how we plan to treat him.

Q: What happens if there's a mistake on the ER report?

A: Someone could die. We simply can't allow that to happen.

Q: What happens to the ER report when the patient is discharged?

A: All the records, which will include the ER report, are electronically filed by patient name and kept for at least ten years.

Have the exhibit marked, show it to opposing counsel, ask permission to approach the witness, and show the exhibit to the witness.

Q: I'm now handing you what's been marked Plaintiff's Exhibit No. 3. Is this one of the emergency room reports that you've been talking about?

A: Yes.

Q: Was this ER report, Plaintiff's Exhibit No. 3, made in the same way that you have been describing?

A: Yes.

LAWYER: Your honor, we offer Plaintiff's Exhibit No. 3.

OPPOSING LAWYER: We have no objection, your honor.

JUDGE: Plaintiff's No. 3 is admitted.

How do you handle a business record that has already been admitted in evidence before trial, either through a pretrial ruling, through a stipulation by the parties, or by the opposing lawyer stating that she has no opposition to its admission? Because the exhibit is already in evidence, there is no longer a legal need to provide a foundation, but there will still be a jury need. After all, the business records foundation demonstrates that the record is reliable, and reliability goes to weight. If the jurors hear no foundation at all, they will have no basis on which to give the exhibit the weight it deserves. Fortunately, you have a right to present such weight evidence, even if the exhibit is already in evidence. FRE 104(e) expressly provides: "This rule does not limit a party's right to introduce before the jury evidence relevant to the weight or credibility of other evidence." This is important because frequently the other side will not oppose the admission of an exhibit when they know that you can provide the appropriate foundation, because the real motivation of the other side is to keep you from providing that foundation for the jurors. Judges, who are always interested in moving the trial along, sometimes are receptive to objections to foundation testimony when the exhibit has already been admitted, and you may need to be forceful in asserting your right.

Example:

> Q: Ms. Adams, I'm showing you what's been marked Plaintiff's Exhibit No. 3.
> OPPOSING LAWYER: Your honor, in the interest of time, we have no objection to this exhibit being admitted in evidence.
> JUDGE: Very well. Plaintiff's Exhibit No. 3 is admitted. Continue.
> Q: Ms. Adams, explain for us how an emergency room report such as this one is made.
> OPPOSING LAWYER: Objection, your honor. The exhibit is already admitted in evidence.
> JUDGE: Counsel, why are you going into foundational matters, in light of the exhibit being in evidence?
> LAWYER: It goes to weight, your honor. The ER report is a critical report in this case, and under Rule 104, the jury is entitled to hear evidence that goes to weight. I'll be brief.
> JUDGE: Very well, but keep it brief.

You can then have the witness briefly, of course—tell how the record is created and why it is critical that the staff prepare it accurately and completely.

Remember that business records made by a party in the case can sometimes be admitted as party admissions. Records, after all, are statements by employees of the business, and if the opposing party wants to introduce them as statements of the party-opponent, they should qualify for admission under FRE 801(d)(2). The only requirement is that the record be shown to be made by an employee of the opposing party, and that the statement by the employee was "on a matter within the scope of that relationship and while it existed." Employees have inherent authority to speak about their jobs, so the employee's statement—the business record—is a statement attributable to the employer, the party.

Example:

> Have the exhibit marked, show it to opposing counsel, ask permission to approach the witness, and show the exhibit to the witness.
>
> LAWYER: Your honor, we offer Plaintiff's Exhibit No. 6. It's a record made by an employee of the defendant corporation. We offer it as a party admission.
> JUDGE: Any objection?
> OPPOSING LAWYER: Yes, your honor. There's been no business records foundation.
> JUDGE: Please approach. [Lawyers come to the bench.] Plaintiff, what's your response?
> LAWYER: Your honor, we are offering this record as a party admission. We obtained it from the defendant in response to our documents request. It's a shipping invoice, and you can see on its face that it was prepared by a Sam Jones, shipping clerk. He's an employee of the defendant company, and he has authority to speak about his job, which is shipping things. This record, which could be qualified as a business record, also qualifies as a party admission under Rule 801 since the defendant's employee made it and the plaintiff is offering it.
> JUDGE: I understand, and I agree. Plaintiff's Exhibit No. 6 is admitted.

The party admissions rule can also be used when the foundation for business records has been established through pretrial discovery in civil cases. For example, depositions frequently include questions to establish the business records foundation for exhibits a party intends to offer at trial. Requests for admissions, governed by Fed. R. Civ. P. 36, permit a request to the other party to admit the "genuineness of . . . documents." Lawyers frequently ask the responding party to admit that certain documents are in fact business records, as defined by FRE 803(6), of that business. Those deposition answers and responses to requests to admit can provide the business records foundation.

The business records rule can also be used as negative evidence. FRE 803(7) allows you to prove the nonoccurrence of an event by the absence of a business record that would have been created had the event occurred. Once again, remember that the foundation that the judge wants to hear (the admissibility foundation) may not be the same as what the jurors need to hear (the weight foundation). If the evidence is important, satisfy the judge and convince the jury. For example, if the plaintiff claims that the defendant never executed a stock purchase order the plaintiff made, the defendant can prove that the alleged order was never made by showing that a record of the claimed order was never generated. The proper foundation can be easily demonstrated.

Example:

Q: Mr. Johnson, what's your position at Sutton Securities?

A: I'm the general manager of the city office.

Q: As general manager, are you familiar with how Sutton Securities documents stock purchase orders?

A: Of course.

Q: What kind of document does Sutton create when a stock purchase order is placed by a customer?

A: We always prepare a stock transaction form showing who placed the order, what date, what security was ordered, how many shares, what price, and so on.

Q: Do you keep those transaction forms after preparing them?

A: Yes, we keep them for at least seven years.

Q: Mr. Johnson, did you search your records for a stock transaction form showing a purchase order the plaintiff, Mr. Atkinson, claims he placed on June 1, 2020, for 500 shares of General Electric common stock?

A: Yes.

Q: Did you find any record for that claimed order?

A: No, I didn't.

Q: If Mr. Atkinson had actually placed that order, would you have a record of that purchase?

A: Of course.

This foundation may be adequate for the judge, but it may not be enough to convince the jury. Every juror knows of instances in which records were lost, misfiled, misplaced, or destroyed, so not finding a record where you expect to find it if it exists may not be convincing testimony. If the evidence is important, convince the jurors.

Example:

Q: Mr. Johnson, let's talk about that stock transaction form. What is it?

A: It's a computer form that the stockbroker fills out when taking an order from a customer. It's filled in on the computer screen and then saved to the computer. The broker then prints out two copies, one of which gets mailed to the customer to confirm the transaction; the other the broker keeps as a paper record of the transaction so the broker can verify the transaction and keep track of his commissions. We keep the paper record for two years. The computer system saves the record, of course, and you can retrieve it by date, customer, stock, and so on. The computer gets backed up daily, and there's a backup record in our main office. The computer records we keep for at least seven years.

Q: When you looked for this claimed order by Mr. Atkinson on June 1, 2020, how did you go about it?

A: I first got on the computer and called it up by Mr. Atkinson's name and date, and there was no record of any order by him on that date. Next I searched under Mr. Atkinson's name for 30 days on either side of June 1, in case the date was off, and I found nothing. I then looked under common misspellings of Mr. Atkinson's name, and again found nothing. I then called up all purchases of GE common stock within 30 days of June 1, and found no orders by Mr. Atkinson or anyone with a similar name. After that, I looked in the brokers' paper copies of stock transaction forms to see if I could find any evidence of this order, and again I found nothing. Finally, I had one of our technical people repeat the search and check our backup tapes at the main office. We found no paperwork or computer record for this claimed order.

Finally, what kinds of issues commonly arise when business records are offered as exhibits? Several stand out, and they are important. Too many lawyers stop thinking of other objections that can still be made, even though the record is qualified as a business record. Some should, of course, be thought through and raised before trial whenever possible. As both the proponent and opponent, always consider, in addition to relevance issues, the following objections:

- Not part of the business record
- Not trustworthy
- Not a regularly made record
- Contains double hearsay, and no exception applies
- Contains expert opinions, without adequate foundation
- A summary, not a business record

A *business record* is a record that records the activities of the business, if the record was made by an employee at or near the time of the event or transaction it records. Things added later should not qualify as part of the record. For example, if a typed business record has handwritten comments in the margins or on the back side, or has things crossed out and handwritten changes added, those should not be admitted as part of the record.

Example:

> **LAWYER:** We offer Defendant's Exhibit No. 6, your honor.
>
> **OPPOSING LAWYER:** We object, your honor, and would like to be heard at the bench.
>
> **JUDGE:** Well, we'll take our morning break now. [Jurors leave the courtroom.] Counsel, what's your objection?
>
> **LAWYER:** We have no objection to the record in general, your honor. However, someone has written by hand on the right margin the words: "Agreed delivery date was actually July 1." There's been no testimony of who made this, when it was made, or how it got there. That's not properly a part of the business record, and we ask that this be redacted from the record.
>
> **JUDGE:** Defense?
>
> **LAWYER:** When we pulled the transaction file, your honor, this was the state of the record. It's obvious that someone from the company wrote this on the record. As such, it's a record by an employee, and should qualify as a business record.
>
> **JUDGE:** That's not enough to qualify the handwritten addition as a business record. The objection is sustained. The defense will prepare a redacted version of the record that complies with my ruling.

FRE 803(6)(E) provides that a record, shown to be a business record, can still be excluded if "the source of information" or "the method or circumstances of preparation indicate lack of trustworthiness." This issue sometimes arises when a business, thinking that litigation may soon follow, conducts an investigation and prepares a record that appears to be little more than a self-serving memorandum. If the record is obviously self-serving—if it fails the "smell test"—the judge can exclude it. For example, after an accident involving a forklift, the forklift manufacturer sends its investigator to the scene, and the investigator writes a report finding that the forklift was not the problem and putting the blame on the employee or employer. Some judges will rule that this report, obviously written with litigation in mind, is not sufficiently trustworthy and should be excluded.

If the record is not made in the FRE 803(6)(C) "regular practice of that activity," it may not qualify as a business record. Records need not be made with any particular frequency, but they do have to be made as part of the regular practice of that business. For example, if a business, after a warehouse theft, takes inventory and creates a list of the stolen items, that list is not a regularly made record, if this is the first time the business ever created such a list. In contrast, if the business always makes such a stolen-item list every time a theft occurs, many judges will admit it as a business record, even though thefts occur infrequently and irregularly.

Double hearsay issues are common in business record use, but are frequently overlooked. Just because a record qualifies as a business record does not mean that everything on the face of the record is automatically admissible. As long as the information contained on the record came from employees (who have a business duty to report, transmit, and record information accurately), there might be no double hearsay issues. However, if the record contains information or statements from nonemployees (who have no business duty to report, transmit, and record accurately), that information or those statements are hearsay and inadmissible unless, under FRE 805, they qualify under a hearsay exception. In other words, the business record is one level of hearsay (which falls within the business records hearsay exception); information and statements from nonemployees constitute a second level of hearsay (which may fall within a hearsay exception, such as an excited utterance; or may be nonhearsay, such as a party admission).

When offering or opposing the admission or business records, always look for potential double hearsay problems. See if the record contains information or statements from nonemployees. If so, see if a hearsay exception or a nonhearsay rationale applies. This problem arises frequently with accident reports that contain statements by the participants and witnesses.

Example:

> LAWYER: Your honor, we offer Plaintiff's Exhibit No. 2 in evidence.
>
> OPPOSING LAWYER: Your honor, may we approach? We have an objection that is better heard at the bench.
>
> JUDGE: Yes. [Lawyers come to the bench.]
>
> OPPOSING LAWYER: We have no objection to this accident investigation report, your honor, insofar as it is a business record that records facts observed by the investigator who wrote the report. However, that report also contains statements taken from the plaintiff, defendant, and a bystander. Those statements are hearsay within hearsay. We object to them and ask that these statements be deleted from the record.
>
> JUDGE: Plaintiff, any response?
>
> LAWYER: Since plaintiff is introducing the record, the statement of the defendant contained in the record is a statement of the party-opponent and is not hearsay. The statements of the plaintiff and bystander, we agree they are double hearsay and no hearsay exception applies.
>
> JUDGE: The statements of the plaintiff and bystander are excluded. The defendant's statement is a party admission and properly admissible. Plaintiff will prepare a redacted copy of the report that reflects my ruling.

Next, look for inadmissible expert opinions on business records. Just because a record qualifies under the business records exception does not mean that it can avoid the requirements of the expert witness rules in FRE 702 to 704. Always ask: If the person who stated the opinion were testifying in court, would that person qualify as an expert, and would there be a proper foundation for that opinion? For example, an emergency room report commonly contains the treating doctor's diagnosis, and the report is usually signed by the doctor. In this situation, the treating doctor is qualified to give opinions about the patient's medical condition. Therefore, the report, containing the doctor's expert opinions, is properly admissible. But consider another example. An accident report contains the factual observations of the investigator who was at the scene of the accident, and it also contains the notation that "This accident appears to be caused by Car #2 going around the curve too fast given the road and weather conditions." Unless the investigator is qualified to give such an opinion, and there is an adequate foundation for it, the opinion is inadmissible under the expert witness rules. If the maker of the report would not be allowed to testify to his opinion, the part of the business record containing the opinion should be inadmissible as well.

Finally, look for exhibits that are not business records, but rather are summaries of records, which are admissible only if the requirements of FRE 1006 are met. This problem comes up frequently when information retrieved from computer databases is involved. Computer records, of course, are business records if the requirements of FRE 803(6) are met. Most courts take the position that computerized records are business records if the output from the computer is in the same form as the original input. In other words, if you merely ask the computer to print out records that are already in the computer's database, the printouts qualify as business records. However, if the computer database is searched, and only selected information is retrieved, so that the printout is a new form, most courts hold that the printout is a summary, not a business record.

For example, suppose the database of a department store is searched for sales to a particular person over a certain period of time, and a printout of those sales is made. That printout is a new form that was not previously stored in the computer. That printout is a summary, not a business record, and the requirements of FRE 1006 must be met before it is properly admissible.

5. Public Records

Public records are records regularly made by any kind of local, state, or federal governmental agency. Common examples in both civil and criminal cases are driver's licenses and vehicle registrations from motor vehicle departments, death certificates and autopsy reports from medical examiners' offices, and employment records from public schools and agencies. Before public records can be admitted for their truth—to prove that an event or transaction happened—they must be shown to fall within a hearsay exception, usually the public records rule, FRE 803(8).

FRE 803(8) makes admissible "[a] record or statement of a public office if (A) it sets out:

(i) the office's activities;
(ii) a matter observed while under a legal duty to report, but not including, in a criminal case, a matter observed by law enforcement personnel; or
(iii) in a civil case or against the government in a criminal case, factual findings from a legally authorized investigation."

The (i) subsection governs the admissibility of routine activities of the public agency. For example, records of the state fish and wildlife department recording how many hunting licenses were issued on a particular day, or records of the county highway department recording how many cars traveled on a particular section of a highway during a particular week, are admissible under this rule in any kind of case.

The (ii) subsection governs the admissibility of observations by public agencies in civil cases. For instance, accident reports of the city police department are admissible in civil cases. Note the express exclusion in this section of police reports in criminal cases. This rule forces police officers to testify in person about their observations, because their police reports are inadmissible in criminal cases.

The (iii) subsection governs the admissibility of "factual findings from a legally authorized investigation." This section applies to civil cases, and against the government in criminal cases. The term *factual findings* has been interpreted broadly to include opinions and conclusions of the agency making the investigation.

The effect of this subsection is limited, however, because few public agencies are directed by law to make such factual findings. For example, police accident reports containing conclusions of how the accident happened and who was at fault are not admissible under this subsection because police departments are not statutorily directed to investigate vehicle accidents and make such findings, although they commonly do. In contrast, the National Transportation Safety Board is statutorily directed to determine the cause of airplane accidents, and the Equal Employment Opportunity Commission is statutorily directed to determine if employees were improperly terminated because of race, sex, or age.

If a public record is properly admissible under this rule, FRE 902 and 1005 permit the introduction of a certified copy of the public record. Because a certified copy is self-authenticating, no live foundation witness is needed. There are different rules for certifying domestic public records under seal and not under seal, and foreign public documents require double certification, so always check the wording of the requirements for certifying a particular kind of public record.

In routine situations, the procedure is simple. Order from the public agency a certified copy of the record you need. There is usually a fee for this service. The agency will then make a photocopy or microfilm copy of the record and attach a statement from an authorized employee certifying that the attached record is a correct copy of a record of the agency. The statement will be signed by the employee and will usually carry the seal of the agency; it may also have a red or blue ribbon attached. This certified copy can then be marked as an exhibit, shown to opposing counsel, and offered in evidence.

In practice, admissibility issues surrounding public records are usually raised and decided before trial. The most common issues are whether the record contains double hearsay, and whether the record contains inadmissible opinions and conclusions. These issues are similar to the issues in the context of business records under FRE 803(6).

For example, if a police accident report is offered in evidence in a civil case, the report may be generally admissible as a public record, but that does not mean that statements of the drivers and bystanders to the accident are admissible. These statements are hearsay within hearsay and are inadmissible unless a hearsay exception or a nonhearsay rationale applies. In addition, the report may contain inadmissible opinions and conclusions that are not properly admissible because the maker of the report is not qualified to make such expert opinions and conclusions. The analysis is essentially the same as for double hearsay and expert opinions contained in business records, as discussed earlier.

FRE 803(10) permits the introduction of evidence of the absence of a public record to prove the nonoccurence of an event or the nonexistence of some matter. Probably the most common uses are to prove that the driver of a car was not licensed at the time of a collision, or that a business failed to obtain a required license or permit. For example, if you request a certified copy of a driver's license for a particular person for a particular date, and there is no such license on record, the motor vehicle department will provide a certified statement from an authorized employee that the records of the agency were searched for that record, but that no driver's license for the person was found.

Note that nothing in the rule prevents you from calling a live witness from a public agency to qualify the public record for admission in evidence. Though this is rarely done, if the public record is not self-explanatory it may make sense to have a live witness present to qualify the record for admission in evidence and then explain things contained on the record.

6. Summaries

FRE 1006 permits the admission of a "summary, chart, or calculation to prove the content of voluminous writings, recordings, or photographs that cannot be conveniently examined in court." The rule recognizes that jurors are unlikely to go through lengthy records, so a summary or other compilation of such records helps the jurors.

The party intending to use a summary at trial must make the underlying records and documents available for examination and copying under reasonable circumstances before trial. This notice provision gives the opposing party a fair opportunity to compare the summary against the underlying records and documents to make sure that the summary is accurate and complete. In practice, this is usually done during the pretrial discovery phase of the litigation. The rule does not prevent the underlying records and documents from being introduced in evidence in addition to the summary, and the rule specifically provides that the judge can order production of the underlying records in court.

This rule is frequently used in commercial, products liability, and other document-intensive cases. Indeed, judges sometimes order the parties to present their evidence in summary form as a way to streamline the presentation of each side's case.

Although FRE 1006 is silent on the point, it is clear that the underlying records and documents must themselves be admissible before the summary can be admissible. This means that the foundation witness at trial must establish several things:

- The summary is based on underlying records that are business or public records under FRE 803(6) or (8), or the underlying documents fall within another hearsay exception or a nonhearsay rationale such as a contract.
- The witness has examined the underlying records.
- The witness is qualified to make the summary.
- The summary completely and accurately summarizes the underlying records.

The foundation witness, then, must be a person who can identify the underlying records as records of that business, and can also testify that she reviewed those records and made a summary of those records that is complete and accurate. Sometimes two witnesses may be necessary to establish the proper foundation.

Example:

Q: Ms. Williams, what's your job with Acme Motors?

A: I'm a bookkeeper and I work in the records department.

Q: How long have you done that?

A: Almost eight years.

Q: Are you familiar with the purchase records Acme Motors generates and maintains when it buys automobiles from the manufacturers?

A: Yes. There's standard documentation we create for each purchase, and we keep those records for several years.

Q: Ms. Williams, were you asked to collect the records for all automobiles purchased by Acme Motors from American Motors for the years 2018, 2019, and 2020?

A: Yes. And I did so.

Q: How many documents were there?

A: Well, there were several hundred purchases, and we generated thousands of documents. It's enough to fill a file cabinet.

Q: Were you also asked to review those records to determine which of those purchases included a Model 14 automatic transmission?

A: Yes.

Q: Did you do that?

A: Yes, I did.

Q: Finally, Ms. Williams, were you asked to prepare a summary chart of the purchases of automobiles from American Motors for the years 2018 through 2020 that included a Model 14 automatic transmission?

A: Yes, I was asked to do that several months ago.

Q: Did you do that?

A: Yes.

Have the exhibit marked, show it to opposing counsel, ask permission to approach the witness, and show the exhibit to the witness.

Q: I'm showing you what has been marked Plaintiff's Exhibit No. 6. Do you recognize this exhibit?

A: Yes, that's the summary I made.

Q: Does this summary, Plaintiff's Exhibit No. 6, accurately and completely summarize the purchases of automobiles from American Motors with a Model 14 automatic transmission for the years 2018 through 2020?

A: Yes.

Q: Does it accurately and completely summarize the business records of Acme Motors for these purchases?

A: Yes. I double-checked everything on the summary against our records.

LAWYER: Your honor, we offer Plaintiff's Exhibit No. 6.

JUDGE: Defense, any objection?

OPPOSING LAWYER: No, your honor.

JUDGE: Plaintiff's Exhibit No. 6 is admitted.

The summary can now be shown to the jury, and the foundation witness can explain what is on the summary and how she obtained the various dates and figures.

Summary charts can also be created to show calculations based on records admitted in evidence. Although such charts may not strictly fall under FRE 1006, courts commonly permit testimony of experts based on exhibits admitted during trial and permit the experts to prepare and use summary charts to explain their testimony. For example, this is routinely done in criminal tax prosecutions. After the prosecution has introduced its documentary and other evidence, a forensic accountant then uses that admitted evidence to do the tax calculations and prepare a summary chart to show the gross income, the taxable income, and the tax that should have been paid on that income. The accountant is usually the last witness called in the prosecution's case-in-chief.

7. Recorded Recollections

FRE 803(5) governs the admissibility of recorded recollection. When a witness forgets an event, or some details of an event, but made or adopted a memorandum or record of the event when the event was fresh in the witness's mind, the rule permits the memorandum or record to be presented to the jury as a substitute for the witness's forgotten memory.

FRE 803(5) makes admissible a record that: "(A) is on a matter the witness once knew about but now cannot recall well enough to testify fully and accurately; (B) was made or adopted by the witness when the matter was fresh in the witness's memory; and (C) accurately reflects the witness's knowledge." If the record is admitted under this rule, "the record may be read into evidence but may be received as an exhibit only when offered by an adverse party."

The foundation, then, requires showing that:

■ The witness once had personal knowledge of the facts.
■ The witness now has forgotten some or all of the facts.
■ The witness made an accurate record of the facts when those facts were fresh in the witness's mind.
■ The exhibit in court is that record.

The part of the record that contains the forgotten facts may be read to the jury, but only the adverse party may introduce the record as an exhibit.

Example:

Q: Mr. Quigley, tell us who else attended the board meeting on June 1, 2020.
A: Well, I was there, and I remember Jack Johnson was there, but I'm not sure of the others.
Q: Would anything help you remember?
A: Not really. We have a board meeting at least every three months, and I just don't have a memory of everyone who attended board meetings that long ago.
Q: Did you make a record of who attended that meeting?
A: Yes, I wrote a memo and put it in my personal files.

Have the exhibit marked, show it to opposing counsel, ask permission to approach the witness, and show the exhibit to the witness.

Q: I'm showing you what has just been marked as Defendant's Exhibit No. 8. Have you seen this document before?
A: Yes, that's the memo I wrote at the time of that board meeting.
Q: At the time you wrote the memo, were the facts fresh in your mind?
A: Sure. I wrote the memo during the meeting.
Q: Does this memo, Defendant's Exhibit No. 8, correctly reflect who attended that board meeting?
A: Yes, I'm sure of it.
LAWYER: Your honor, we ask permission to read Defendant's Exhibit No. 8 to the jury.
JUDGE: Any objection?
OPPOSING LAWYER: No, your honor.
JUDGE: Counsel, you or the witness may read that part of the memo that reflects who attended the meeting.

The recorded recollection rule is infrequently used for two reasons. First, the record often will also qualify as a business record, which gets the record formally admitted in evidence. Once admitted, you can show and read the record to the jury. For example, businesses routinely record minutes of board meetings, and the minutes ordinarily will be admissible as business records, so there will be no reason to use other memoranda to prove who attended a particular meeting. Second, frequently the witness will, after being shown the record, say that the record refreshes his memory. Under FRE 612, the witness can then testify directly about the now-remembered facts. For example, if in the preceding example the witness said that the record jogs his memory of who attended the meeting, the witness can then name the persons who attended. The record itself, however, cannot be offered in evidence by the proponent of the testimony.

8. Transcripts of Testimony

Transcripts of witness testimony are presented frequently during trials, and two rules usually provide the basis for overcoming hearsay objections. First, the testimony of a party will, when offered by the opposing party, be admissible as a party admission. For example, if the plaintiff at trial wants to introduce the defendant's deposition testimony, it will be admissible as a party admission under FRE 801(d)(2). Second, the deposition, preliminary hearing, or other hearing testimony of any witness (including parties) who is unavailable at the time of trial will usually be admissible as former testimony under FRE 804(b)(1). For example, if an eyewitness to a vehicle collision is deposed and later moves out of the country, the transcript of the witness's testimony at a deposition will be admissible. If an eyewitness to a crime testifies at a preliminary hearing and later dies, the transcript of the witness's testimony will be admissible. (See also Fed. R. Civ. P. 32, which further governs the use of deposition transcripts in civil proceedings.)

If transcripts are admissible, usually because they qualify as party admissions or former testimony, other concerns must be addressed. First, how much of the transcript will be offered? Second, how will the judge rule on objections that were made during the deposition? Third, how do you actually present the transcript at trial?

Transcripts of testimony are boring. This is usually also true of videotaped testimony. The first order of business, then, is to determine what parts of the transcript you and your opponent will want to present at trial. Whatever it is, you should pare it down to just a few minutes of key testimony, because after that the boredom factor will take over and many jurors will stop listening.

What you can present, and what the other side can also present, depends in large part on whether the transcript is a party admission, or is the former testimony of a witness. When the testimony is admissible as a party admission, the party offering the transcript can designate whatever portions it wishes. The other side can only designate additional portions to be included under FRE 106 so that the testimony is not taken unfairly out of context: This is because a transcript offered by the opposing party is a party admission under FRE 801(d)(2); when offered by the deposed party, the transcript is hearsay and generally inadmissible.

When the transcript of a witness's testimony qualifies as former testimony under FRE 804(b)(1), the entire transcript will qualify as an exception to the hearsay rule, regardless of which side initially offers the transcript. However, FRE 804(b)(1)(B) only applies to testimony "offered against a party who had—or, in a civil case, whose predecessor in interest had—an opportunity and similar motive to develop it by direct, cross-, or redirect examination." If this qualification is met, either party would have a right to offer any portions of the transcript they choose to designate.

Next, how will the judge rule on pending objections? This will not be a concern if the transcript is of a preliminary hearing or other hearing where a judge was present and ruled on any objections. However, depositions are taken without a judge present, and objections made during the deposition have not been ruled on. During the deposition, the witness is usually required to answer questions despite objections (Fed. R. Civ. P. 30(c)(2) provides that the witness's testimony shall be "taken subject to any objection," in most instances). Those pending objections have to be ruled on, and additional objections that the lawyers can still make must be ruled on as well.

Judges usually have standard pretrial orders on how each side should designate additional objections to the portions of a transcript the other side wants to introduce at trial. These orders usually require the party offering the transcript to identify the portions it intends to offer; the opposing party will then identify the portions it objects to and state the bases for the objections. After that, the objecting party will identify additional portions it intends to offer, and the offering party will in turn identify the portions it objects to.

7.5 Visual Aids

Visual aids are permitted during trials because they make visual what witnesses say during their testimony or lawyers say during their opening statements and closing arguments. Visual aids are not considered evidence. Judges usually do not admit visual aids formally in evidence, so they do not go into the jury room during the jury's deliberations. This means that the jurors usually see the visual aid only once, when it is used during a witness's testimony or a lawyer's opening or closing.

Despite these limitations, trial lawyers frequently use visual aids, because they have a significant impact on the jurors. Visual aids make the spoken word more immediate, make complex information understandable, and substantially enhance juror memory.

Procedurally, no formal foundation is required for visual aids, as they are not formally admitted in evidence. However, whenever a visual aid is used during the trial, particularly during the examinations of witnesses, it should be marked with an exhibit number, because it should become part of the trial record. When lawyers display a visual aid during their opening statements or closing arguments, they simply state what they are doing. If a visual aid is used during the direct examination of an expert, the expert states that she has a visual aid that is accurate and will help explain her testimony. Sometimes it is appropriate to let the judge and your opponent know that you are going to use a visual aid, so any objections can be handled beforehand.

Trial lawyers commonly use several kinds of visual aids during a jury trial.

1. Opening Statements

Visual aids can support the storytelling purpose of an opening statement, by helping jurors understand the characters, learn what happened and why, create a story in their minds of what happened, and realize that an injustice has happened that must be set right. Good visual aids do more than that: They also tell the jurors, right from the beginning of the trial, that you care about the case and care that the jurors fully understand what happened and why.

Lawyers commonly use several kinds of visual aids during opening statements. In cases involving multiple parties, an organizational chart can be helpful or even essential. For example, a foam-core poster board showing who the plaintiffs and defendants are (Figure 7.1) and listing or containing photographs of the key witnesses from those parties (Figure 7.2) who will testify during the trial, will help clarify the parties and witnesses central to the case.

In personal injury and criminal cases, lawyers commonly use demonstrative exhibits, such as large photographs or diagrams, during opening statement, because they create a vivid and clear picture of where the action happened, making it much easier to understand what happened and how it happened (Figures 7.3 and 7.4). As long as the photograph or diagram is properly admissible or is already in evidence

> ⊕ The figures in this chapter are also on the accompanying website in full color and motion.

by pretrial order, and makes visual what the lawyer is saying (and which will later be proven), it can be used during the opening statement.

Many civil commercial cases and criminal white-collar cases involve conduct over an extended period of time. A well-designed timeline can make these sequential events clear for the jurors. Commercial software is available so that timelines can be made easily and inexpensively (Figures 7.5 and 7.6).

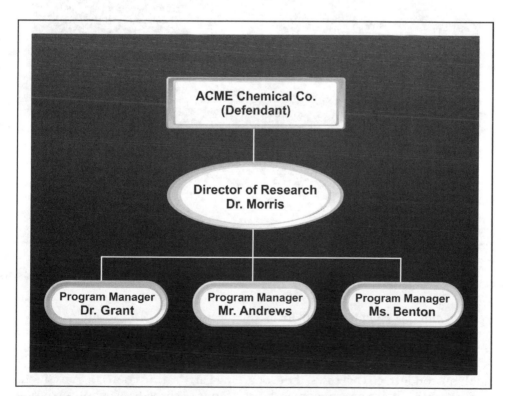

Fig. 7.1 Corporate Personnel. Courtesy of inData Corporation ©

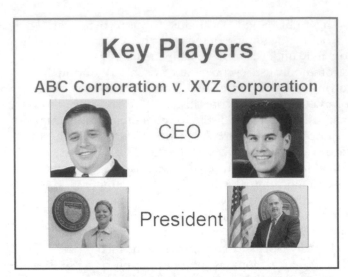

Fig. 7.2 Key Players. Courtesy of inData Corporation ©

Fig. 7.3 Photo of Intersection. Courtesy of inData Corporation ©

Opening statements should focus on the other side's misconduct, so the jurors form a clear picture of the bad things the other side did. An effective way to do that is to put up on an easel a large photograph of the other party, or the key employee of the other party, as the opening statement talks about the other side's misconduct. In civil cases, if the opposing party's deposition contains significant admissions, lawyers sometimes show excerpts of the video deposition during

Fig. 7.4 Photo of Alley. Courtesy of inData Corporation ©

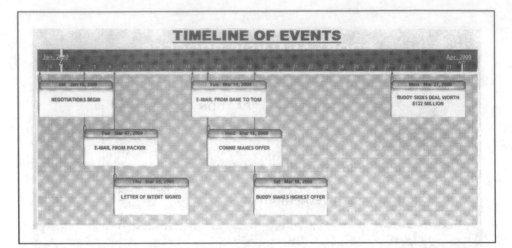

Fig. 7.5 Civil Timeline. Courtesy of inData Corporation ©

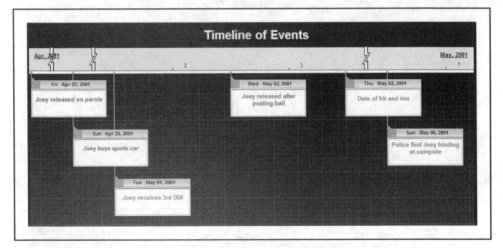

Fig. 7.6 Criminal Timeline. Courtesy of inData Corporation ©

opening statements, so that the jurors hear of the misconduct directly from the opposing party.

A caveat is in order. Once used, a visual aid or exhibit is no longer new. It is important to give the jurors new visual aids and exhibits as the trial progresses, so you need to decide whether to use a particular visual aid in the opening statement, during your case-in-chief, or during the closing argument.

2. Direct Examinations of Experts

Visual aids are frequently used during the direct examinations of experts, because experts are used to explain complex matters outside the common experience of the jurors. Indeed, expert testimony is frequently not understandable unless visual aids are used for clarification.

Experts frequently explain steps in a process, such as a chemical reaction (Figure 7.7) or surgical procedure (Figure 7.8). Visual aids that show the steps make juror understanding easier.

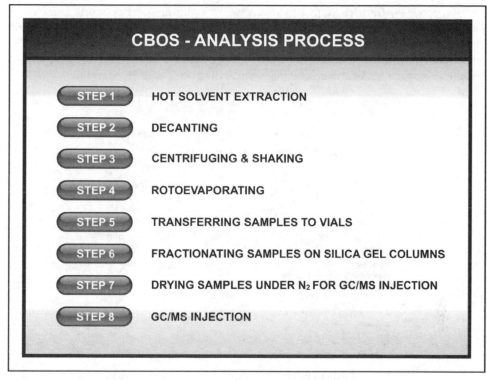

Fig. 7.7 Chemical Process. Courtesy of inData Corporation ©

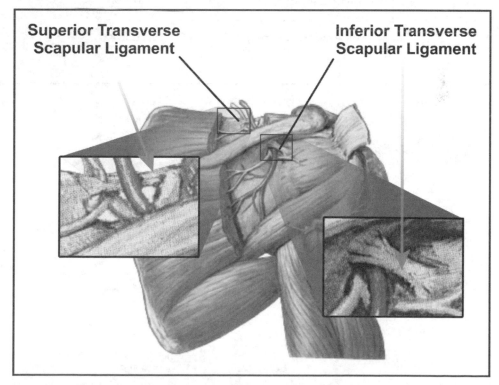

Fig. 7.8 Shoulder Surgery. Courtesy of inData Corporation ©

Experts also frequently testify about a particular analysis or study the expert made. A visual aid that shows the sequence of the analysis makes the testimony clearer. Finally, experts are often asked to make damages calculations (Figure 7.9) or other economic projections or discuss components of equipment (Figure 7.10). Visual aids again make the calculations and components understandable.

Lost Profits Analysis

Cost Description	Fixed Costs ($)
Inventory or Materials	$ 2,785
Direct labor (includes payroll taxes)	1,232
Other expenses	500
Other expenses	500
Salaries (includes payroll taxes)	23,435
Supplies	200
Repairs & maintenance	2,000
Advertising	1,300
Car, delivery and travel	1,900
Accounting and legal	850
Rent	10,125
Telephone	1,850
Utilities	3,200
Insurance	895
Taxes (Real estate, etc.)	750
Total Fixed Expenses	$ 51,522

Fig. 7.9 Lost Profits. Courtesy of inData Corporation ©

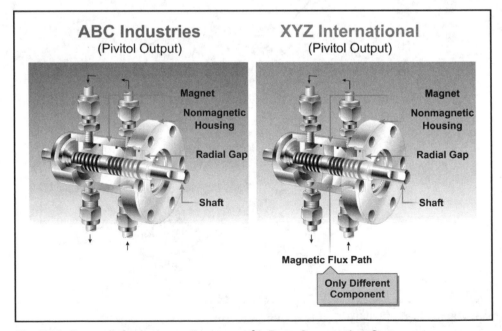

Fig. 7.10 Patent Infringement. Courtesy of inData Corporation ©

3. Cross-Examinations of Lay and Expert Witnesses

Visual aids are frequently used during the cross-examinations of both lay and expert witnesses. Some judges permit lawyers to write, on butcher paper or a blank poster board, things the witness says during the cross-examination. As long as what is written down fairly and accurately shows what the witness said, some judges permit this as merely making visual what the witness has just said. (Judges who do not permit this usually feel that the visual aid puts undue emphasis on those parts of the cross-examination and is more properly a part of closing argument.) More commonly, visual aids are used while impeaching a witness. Many judges now permit lawyers to write down what a witness says today and what the witness said previously. While the witness is being impeached with a prior inconsistent statement, the lawyer makes a "today" and "before" chart that makes visual the inconsistency (Figure 7.11).

Most judges permit the impeaching source to be displayed before the jury while the impeachment occurs. For example, judges usually allow cross-examiners to project on a screen or monitor the portion of the deposition videotape or transcript that contains the impeaching questions and answers (Figures 7.12 to 7.14).

Keith Packer Testimony

	Trial Testimony	Deposition Testimony
Distance from Hotel	"14 feet"	"26 feet"
Distance from Car	"11 feet"	"32 feet"
Amount of Water	"Heavy Rain"	"Light Drizzle"
Time of Report	"12:15 am"	"11:43 pm"

Fig. 7.11 Impeachment. Courtesy of inData Corporation ©

Fig. 7.12 Taped Deposition. Courtesy of inData Corporation ©

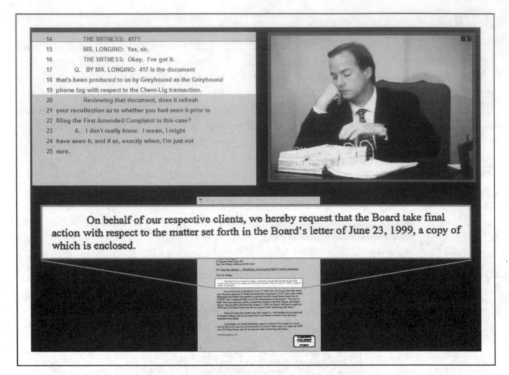

Fig. 7.13 Taped Deposition with Exhibit. Courtesy of inData Corporation ©

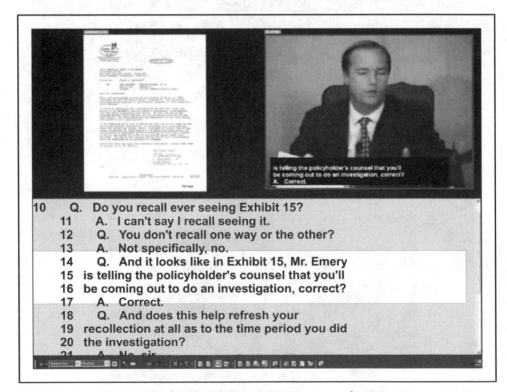

Fig. 7.14 Taped Deposition with Scrolling Text. Courtesy of inData Corporation ©

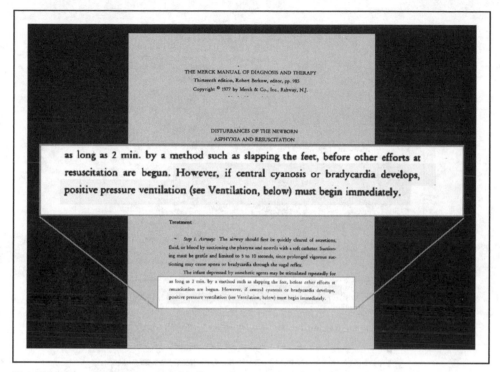

Fig. 7.15 Treatise. Courtesy of inData Corporation ©

Many judges permit the impeaching part of a treatise to be displayed before the jury when an expert is being impeached with an authoritative treatise (Figure 7.15). Although FRE 803(18) expressly provides that a treatise used to impeach "may be read into evidence but not received as an exhibit," many judges permit the jury to read along on a screen, monitor, or poster board as the lawyer reads the impeaching part.

After the cross-examination is over, the visual aid is taken down and is not used again. Because visual aids are not considered evidence, and they are not formally admitted in evidence, their use is limited to making the cross-examination visual.

4. Closing Arguments

Visual aids are also commonly used during closing arguments. Indeed, it is rare for a lawyer not to use a visual aid to supplement the closing argument. For example, lawyers frequently create a chart of bullet points on a PowerPoint slide or poster board to itemize the main points of the argument (Figure 7.16). As long as the lawyer can say it, judges allow a visual aid to make the same points visually. The bullet points should be revealed one at a time by using the "build" feature in PowerPoint or magnetic overlays on a poster board.

Lawyers frequently create a chart showing the legal elements of a claim or defense (Figure 7.17) and the permitted elements of damages (Figure 7.18), and then show how the evidence has proved (or failed to prove) those elements. As long as the visual aid fairly and accurately summarizes the elements of the claims,

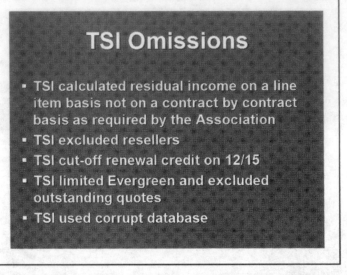

Fig. 7.16 Closing Argument Bullet Points. Courtesy of inData Corporation ©

Fraud

Plaintiff claims that defendant defrauded plaintiff. To establish this claim, plaintiff must prove by clear and convincing evidence:

(1) Defendant made a representation to plaintiff;

(2) The representation was false;

(3) The representation was material, which means that it was sufficiently important to influence a reasonable person's actions;

(4) Defendant knew that the representation was false;

(5) Defendant intended that plaintiff would act upon the representation in the manner reasonably contemplated by defendant;

(6) Plaintiff did not know that the representation was false;

(7) Plaintiff relied on the truth of the representation;

(8) Plaintiff's reliance was reasonable and justified under the circumstances; and

(9) As a result, plaintiff was damaged.

Fig. 7.17 Fraud Elements. Courtesy of inData Corporation ©

defenses, and damages set out in the jury instructions, judges permit it. Plaintiff's lawyers in personal injury and commercial cases almost always use a damages chart on which to suggest or compute dollar amounts for each permitted kind of damages.

Many judges permit lawyers to highlight key language in a jury instruction by enlarging the instruction and highlighting the key language (Figure 7.19). Their feeling is that if the lawyer can discuss that key language, the lawyer ought to be able to put that language on a board or screen while it is being discussed. (Judges who do not permit this usually feel that jurors should take the instructions as a whole and not just read parts of them.)

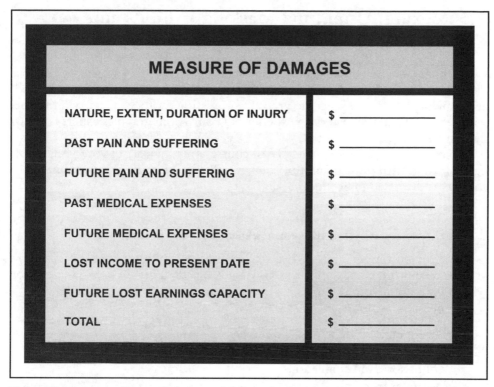

Fig. 7.18 Damages Chart. Courtesy of inData Corporation ©

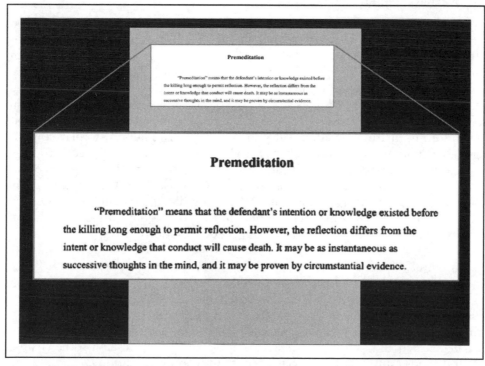

Fig. 7.19 Premeditation Definition. Courtesy of inData Corporation ©

7.6 Making, Using, and Marking Exhibits and Visual Aids

Exhibits and visual aids should be made early, well in advance of the trial date. This avoids last-minute crises and ensures that the exhibits and visual aids are available when you schedule preparation sessions with your party and other witnesses. Getting the help of an experienced courtroom graphics expert is always helpful and frequently essential.

Selecting exhibits and visual aids, of course, must be part of your visual strategy, which in turn must be part of your overall trial strategy. Developing a visual strategy is discussed in Section 11.13.

1. Making Exhibits and Visual Aids Before Trial

Start by putting exhibits and visual aids into several categories, because how you make and prepare exhibits and visual aids before trial will depend largely on which kinds are involved:

- Objects
- Photographs, videotapes, and movies
- Diagrams, models, and maps
- Animations and simulations
- Documents, records, and summaries
- Charts
- Transcripts and videotapes

Computers and specialized software programs have made it much easier to create, save, and retrieve exhibits and visual aids. However, keep in mind a key distinction: Will this visual aid be seen only in the courtroom (during the opening statement, plaintiff's or defendant's case, or closing argument), or will it also be an exhibit that will go to the jury room during deliberations? The clear trend, particularly in document-intensive cases, is to put all records and documents into computer databases. This usually means that the jurors will not see those exhibits again during their deliberations. Jury rooms are rarely equipped to play computerized exhibits and judges are reluctant to have jurors return to the courtroom to review evidence once their deliberations begin. In contrast, objects, paper exhibits, and large exhibits on foam-core poster boards usually go to the jury room. A wise strategy, then, is to coordinate the kinds of exhibits and visual aids you make and use so that some are seen only in the courtroom during the trial, but key exhibits also go to the jury room during deliberations.

a. Objects

Objects first must be obtained. Once in your or another appropriate person's or entity's possession, they must be secured and kept in the same condition for trial. If the object can be authenticated by sight, nothing else need be done. If the object can only be authenticated through a chain of custody, make sure that it is safeguarded and that witnesses will be available who can establish the chain of custody and testify that the object remains in the same condition.

More can be done, however. An object can be photographed and enlarged to poster-board size, if the enlargement will make important details more visible.

Fig. 7.20 Watch Animation. Courtesy of inData Corporation ©

Sometimes a series of photographs of the object from different angles is important. Sometimes the object can be photographed, digitized, and put into a computer software program so that the object can be viewed from any side and rotated in any direction (Figure 7.20).

If the object is too large to bring into the courtroom, as is frequently the case in products liability cases involving vehicles, machines, and equipment, photograph and videotape the object so that the jurors will gain a clear understanding of what the object looks like and how it functions. If the actual object is unavailable, introduce an identical object as an illustrative exhibit that shows how the actual object looked.

If the scene cannot be adequately shown with a photograph or diagram, consider using a video of the scene that accurately shows the scene at the time of the accident or crime (Figure 7.21).

b. Photographs, Videotapes, and Movies

Photographs, videotapes, and movies often have high psychological impact, and you should always think of creative ways to use them. Photographs are frequently used to show places, things, and people. Photographs of accident and crime scenes can include aerial or bird's-eye views, the view from the locations where witnesses stood, and the perspectives of the drivers (Figure 7.22). Photographic sequences and videotapes can show the view from several perspectives, such as from a car traveling down a winding road.

Photographs can show the location of skid marks, car parts, blood stains, bullet holes, and other forensic evidence. They can show the condition of vehicles,

Fig. 7.21 Accident Scene Video. Courtesy of inData
Corporation ©

Fig. 7.22 Driver Point of View. Courtesy of inData Corporation ©

equipment, and machinery. They can show the physical and emotional condition of accident and crime victims. Photographs can show the physical condition of an injured person before, immediately after the injury, and at various times during the recovery period. A "day in the life" videotape of a permanently injured plaintiff (Figure 7.23) can dramatically show how difficult life and its daily routines are for that plaintiff. The videotape is usually made by an experienced videographer hired by the plaintiff, and is frequently narrated by a family member, therapist, or doctor.

c. Diagrams, Models, and Maps

Diagrams and maps of intersections can make the scene of a collision understandable (Figure 7.24). Diagrams of the street, alley, or apartment where a crime happened can make that scene more understandable. Diagrams (Figure 7.25) and maps can show the route vehicles and people took. Three-dimensional models can re-create a scene even more effectively, especially when the vertical dimension is important (Figure 7.26). Working models of vehicles and other machinery can re-create both the appearance of the scene and how an accident happened.

Most of the time you will want to have an experienced courtroom graphics expert make these demonstrative exhibits. You will certainly need an expert if you want to create three-dimensional models.

d. Animations and Simulations

Animations and simulations are used in conjunction with expert testimony. Animations (Figure 7.27) illustrate the expert's opinions; simulations re-create an event based on technical data from the event. Making animations and simulations takes time and money, but they can be effective in making visual the expert's opinions and converting event data into a visual re-creation. If you plan to use animations, simulations, or other exhibits with a testifying expert, you will need to get your expert, as well as technical experts, involved early in the pretrial phase. Remember that in civil cases, Fed. R. Civ. P. 26(a)(2)(B)(iii) requires that parties disclose, 90 days before trial, all exhibits that retained and specially employed testifying experts will use to "summarize or support" their opinions. Other jurisdictions may have similar requirements.

e. Documents, Records, and Summaries

Documents and records are frequently the principal evidence in commercial cases, but they are also important in other cases, so how you present them is important. First, be selective. No jury will look at hundreds of documents or records to make sense of them. Put them in a computer database so that you can retrieve them quickly should the need arise during trial. However, do not even think about showing all of them to the jurors during a trial. For trial, select the most important dozen or less that are at the heart of your case. Most "paper" cases can be distilled down to a small number of essential documents. Consider creating individual notebooks for the jurors containing these exhibits, particularly if witnesses are going to refer to them repeatedly.

Second, determine how you can make your key exhibits stand out. Think of a document or record as an image, which must convey the significance of the document or record in only a few seconds. One way is to project the exhibit on a large screen. The advantage of the projection is that you can use software

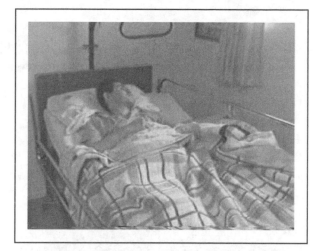

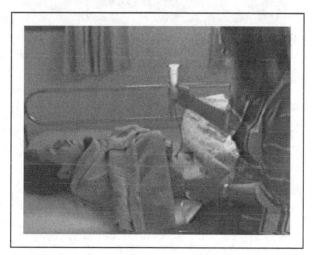

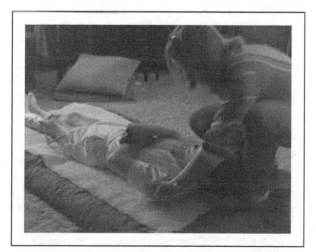

Fig. 7.23 A Day in the Life video.

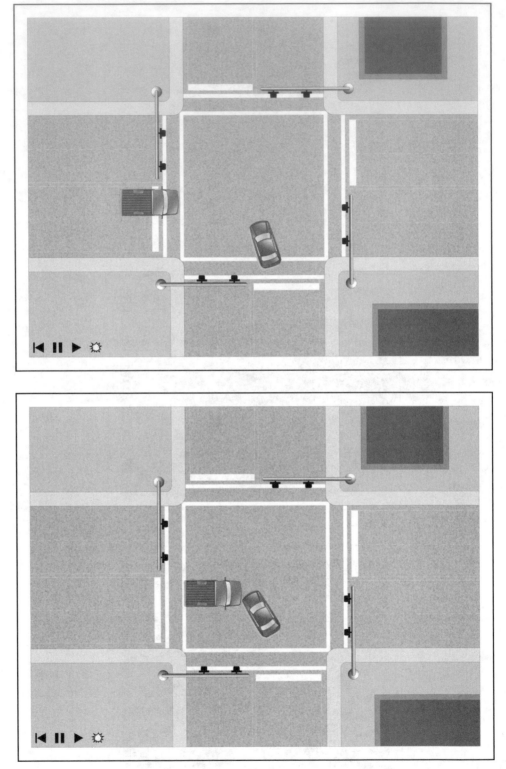

Fig. 7.24 Intersection Animation. Courtesy of inData Corporation ©

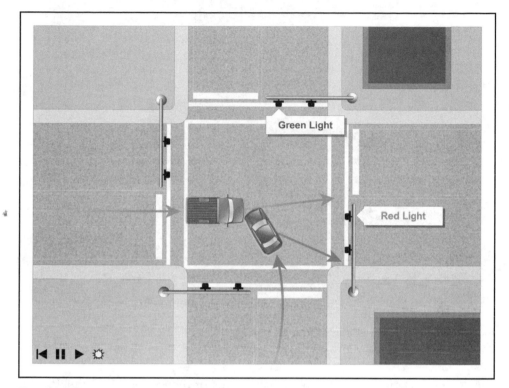

Fig. 7.24 (Continued)

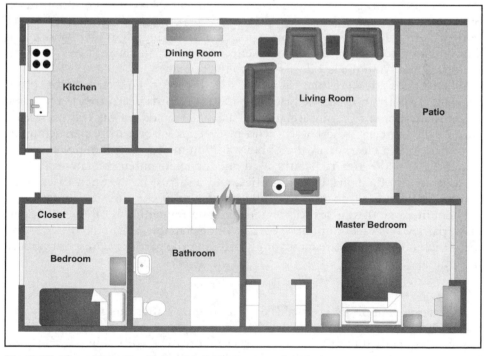

Fig. 7.25 Floor Plan. Courtesy of inData Corporation ©

Fig. 7.26 Model. Courtesy of inData Corporation ©

such as PowerPoint to highlight the key words of the exhibit with underlining, color, callouts, and zoom features (Figures 7.28, 7.29, and 7.30). When the key words of an exhibit are blown up, the jurors' attention is immediately focused on those words. Another way is to enlarge a document or record and mount it on 30" × 40" or 40" × 60" foam-core poster board. You can enlarge the key words, sentences, or paragraphs on a separate poster board or highlight them with color. Consider how to present several documents in a coordinated way, such as creating a timeline and tying the key documents to the timeline.

Third, consider creating summaries and data compilations that distill important information gleaned from numerous records down to a manageable amount and present that information in an understandable way (Figure 7.31). Jurors will appreciate the lawyers who made extra efforts to present complex information in a clear, easily digestible way. Summaries of voluminous records under FRE 1006 are frequently used in document-intensive lawsuits, such as contract, products liability, securities, and antitrust cases. Such cases often involve thousands of documents and records, and presenting the information in them in a way that jurors will understand and remember is often the biggest task trial lawyers face. Summaries are an indispensable aid in such cases, and judges in complex cases are increasingly ordering the parties to present evidence in summary form.

f. Charts

Charts are important visual aids during opening statements and closing arguments and are often essential exhibits in commercial cases. In opening statements, lawyers frequently use organization charts to show the relationship of parties and witnesses, and chronological charts to explain a sequence of events. In closing

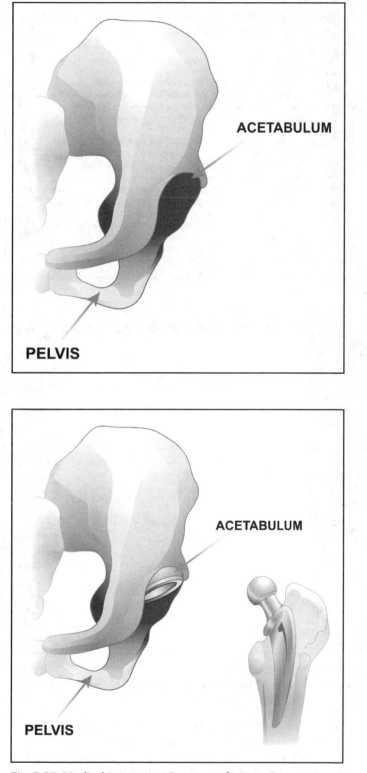

Fig. 7.27 Medical Animation. Courtesy of inData Corporation ©

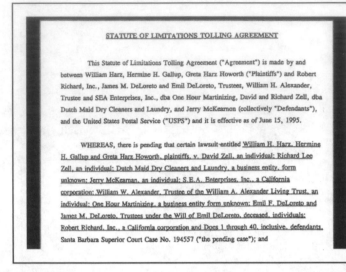

Fig. 7.28 Business Record. Courtesy of inData Corporation ©

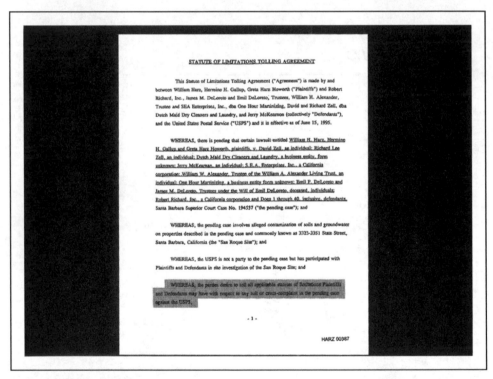

Fig. 7.29 Business Record Highlight. Courtesy of inData Corporation ©

arguments, lawyers frequently use charts summarizing the elements of claims and defenses and damages charts showing the proper elements of damages. A common approach is to use the "import" feature of PowerPoint to add each element to the chart, discuss that element, and then add the next one. In this way the jurors focus only on the element being discussed.

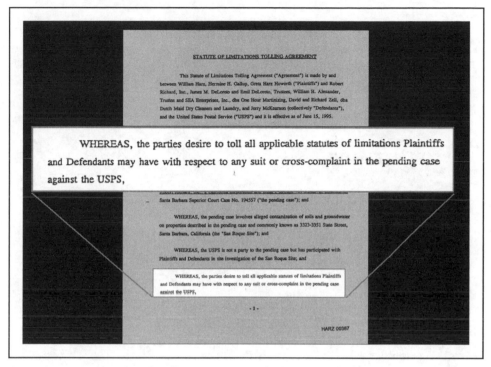

Fig. 7.30 Business Record Callout. Courtesy of inData Corporation ©

In commercial cases, charts are frequently used to make financial and technical data more easily understandable. Such charts summarize business records and require the same foundation as summaries under FRE 1006. There are four basic kinds of charts: fever charts, bar charts, pie charts, and tables. Each is particularly useful to present certain kinds of data and highlight particular relationships.

Fever charts (Figure 7.32) are useful for showing quantities over time, such as increasing annual sales over several years. *Bar charts* (Figure 7.33) are useful for showing comparative quantities, such as annual sales in several states. *Pie charts* (Figure 7.34) are useful for showing percentages of a whole, such as the relative percentages of sales to several purchasers. Finally, *tables* (Figure 7.35) are useful for organizing and comparing more detailed information, such as the mileage between a number of cities. The purpose of all charts is the same: Distill complex information into a quickly and easily understood visual display. However, don't get carried away by the possibilities. For example, if you decide that bar charts will be effective, use only bar charts during the trial, and design and color them the same. Simplicity and consistency are important to the jurors.

The purpose of making large courtroom exhibits and visual aids is to create attractive exhibits—images—that grab attention and quickly convey clear messages, so jurors will remember and rely on your exhibits, rather than the other side's, when they decide the case. With photographs, make sure they are large and cropped to eliminate unnecessary information. Minimize labels in the photographs. Photographs are most effective when they have a clear image that sends an obvious, immediate message. With maps and diagrams, put north at the top, and again minimize the labeling. With documents and records, pare them down to the smallest possible number, and use blow-ups of the key language to draw the jurors' attention.

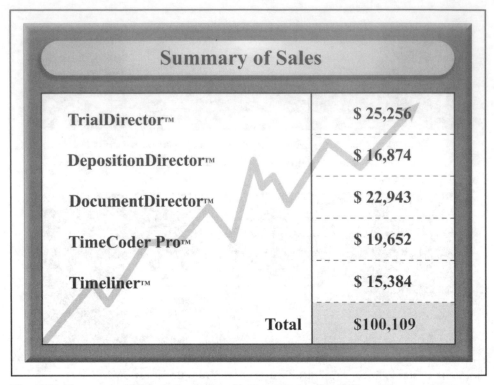

Fig. 7.31 Summary of Sales. Courtesy of inData Corporation ©

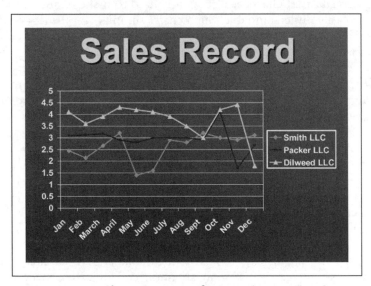

Fig. 7.32 Fever Chart. Courtesy of inData Corporation ©

When creating charts, diagrams, and summaries, as well as when preparing other exhibits, keep in mind the following composition rules, which apply to poster boards and to any exhibits and visual aids that are projected on screens and monitors.

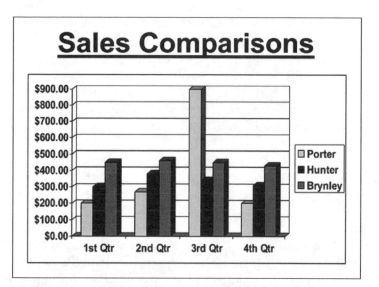

Fig. 7.33 Bar Chart. Courtesy of inData Corporation ©

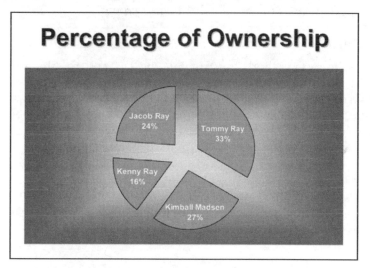

Fig. 7.34 Pie Chart. Courtesy of inData Corporation ©

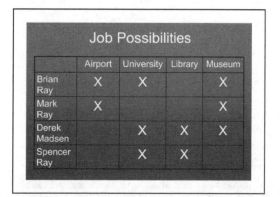

Fig. 7.35 Table Chart. Courtesy of inData Corporation ©

BASIC RULES FOR MAKING CHARTS, DIAGRAMS, AND SUMMARIES

1. **Board**
   - ■ Use standard 30" × 40" to 40"× 60" foam-core poster board.
   - ■ Use poster board with 10 to 15 percent color, preferably light gray, blue, tan, or beige color. Avoid a plain white board, as this creates too stark a contrast, particularly with black lettering. Use a dull matte finish to minimize glare.
   - ■ Another possibility is to reverse the colors: Use light lettering, such as gold, on a dark background, such as navy blue or burgundy. Whatever you choose, remain consistent, so that jurors identify the charts and diagrams as yours.

2. **Lettering**
   - ■ Use lettering that is at least one inch high so that the diagram can be read easily by all the jurors. Many graphics experts suggest using sans serif lettering.
   - ■ *Weight* refers to the thickness of the lettering. Use medium-weight lettering for the heading and light-weight lettering for the body. This will give the appearance of the heading being in bold type.[1]

3. **Color**
   Color is important, both for catching the eye and for the associations it implies. Use black for the basic parts of the diagram, and use color for the key parts. Avoid using pale colors, particularly pale green, pink, or lavender, as these are difficult to see for persons with perception weaknesses. Use vibrant colors, particularly red and yellow, to attract attention. Use no more than two or three colors. Use the same colors from diagram to diagram.

4. **Movement**
   Make the diagram appear to have movement; this draws attention. Use arrows and dotted lines to represent movement and jagged lines to represent changes. Mark vehicles with a 1, 2, and 3 to show their location at key times.

5. **Symbols**
   Select effective symbols to represent vehicles, pedestrians, and other important objects that will be marked on the diagram. Use the same symbols from diagram to diagram.

6. **Composition**
   There are no strict rules for creating charts and diagrams. The only rule is that each diagram or chart must draw and hold attention, and communicate its intended message quickly and clearly. However, the following suggestions usually help, particularly in making informational charts and diagrams such as a summary chart or damages calculation chart:

---

1. Junior co-author Easton believes that all type should be in bold, because many judges and jurors have vision challenges. He uses larger bold type for headings. He also uses colored text for emphasis, where appropriate.

- Don't use all capital letters. They are harder to read, especially for people with poor reading skills. Use a capital letter to start a line.
- Headings should use medium-weight type and be centered on the board. The body should use light-weight type. Both heading and body should use the same style and size of type.
- Margins should be justified on the left, ragged on the right.
- Use numbers or bullets on the left margin to signal new points.
- Use about two inches of white space as a border on the top, bottom, and sides of the diagram. Avoid using a framed border, because it draws attention to the border and away from the important information.
- Spacing between the letters and between the lines should be sufficient to avoid a cramped appearance. Spacing between the heading and the body of a diagram should be about twice the spacing between the lines of the diagram.

Remember the "billboard test": if the message you intend to send is not sent and received in a few seconds, the diagram is too busy. If the diagram sends more than one message, it is too complicated. If there is unnecessary information, remove it. If there is too much detail on any one diagram, jurors will not understand and retain the message. Avoid displaying too many words or numbers at the same time, because jurors will not absorb large quantities of information presented simultaneously. Always keep it simple, focused, and consistent.

g. Transcripts and Videotapes

Deposition and other hearing testimony of parties, admissible as party admissions, and of any unavailable witnesses, admissible as former testimony, are frequently presented at trial. As discussed earlier, before trial the lawyers need to designate the portions of transcripts they want presented and obtain rulings on any objections. Once the judge has ruled on what portions of the testimony are admissible, the offering party must determine how best to present that testimony.

If the testimony was videotaped, which is increasingly the case with depositions, the videotape must be edited so that it contains only the portions that the parties have designated and the judge has ruled are admissible. This means that you must get a videographer to edit the videotape so that it accurately reflects the judge's rulings, and makes smooth transitions from segment to segment. Judges sometimes rule on admissibility issues shortly before or even during trial, so you may need to have a videographer ready to do the editing quickly and on short notice. Once the edited videotape is prepared and admitted in evidence, it can be played in court and projected on a screen or monitor.

Consider preparing a videotape that also contains the transcript of the questions and answers in the lower portion of the picture. The technology exists to coordinate the videotape with the scrolling transcript. Most judges permit this because it helps the jurors hear and understand the testimony. You will need to have a witness available to testify that the scrolling transcript is a verbatim transcript of the questions and answers on the videotape, in case there is a dispute over its accuracy. Adding the scrolling transcript is an effective approach when you want the jurors to focus on the content of the witness's testimony. If you want the jurors to focus on the witness's demeanor, it's probably more effective to show the videotape without the scrolling transcript.

If the testimony was only taken by a court reporter and made into a written transcript, how can you present the testimony effectively? The standard way lawyers present the testimony at trial is to reenact the deposition or hearing. A witness, often someone from the lawyer's office, is selected to role-play the deposition witness. Select a witness whose age, gender, ethnicity, and other characteristics reasonably reflect the deponent's actual characteristics, but it is also important for the reader to be someone the jury will like. In court, the judge will usually explain that a deposition of a party or witness was taken some time ago, and that a portion of that testimony will now be presented. The role-playing witness then takes the stand. The lawyer asks the questions asked during the deposition and the witness answers them, essentially reenacting the deposition. Both the lawyer and witness have a transcript of the deposition marked to show which questions and answers will be presented. The lawyer and witness should strive for realism. Melodramatic readings are unrealistic and may draw objections from the other side. When depositions and other testimony are presented this way, some judges also allow the edited transcript to be admitted as an exhibit. This can be useful, if you intend to read key questions and answers again during your closing argument.

2. Using Exhibits and Visual Aids During Trial

In opening statements, many judges allow lawyers to use exhibits that they, in good faith, believe will be admissible during the trial. They may use visual aids to present facts that they, in good faith, believe will be proved during the trial. In closing arguments, lawyers may use exhibits that have been admitted in evidence during the trial, and may use visual aids to highlight points that they are entitled to argue. For example, lawyers frequently use organization charts, timelines, and photographs in opening statements, and frequently use documents, diagrams, and charts with bullet points of key facts during closing arguments. Such aids can be used at any time during the opening and closing. Lawyers usually put them on an easel, screen, or monitor when they want to use them and take them down when done. It is a mistake to let jurors see exhibits and visual aids before you want to use them, or to leave them up after you have finished using them, because jurors will look at the exhibits and visual aids rather than focusing on what you are saying.

Exhibits and visual aids are commonly used during the direct examinations of lay and expert witnesses, and here you have choices and decisions to make. Once an exhibit is admitted in evidence, you can show or read it to the jurors; jurors are always eager to hear and see exhibits at the first opportunity. When is it best to do that?

Remember that exhibits attract attention, so they also take attention away from the witness. The minute a large courtroom exhibit is put on an easel or projected on a screen or monitor, jurors stop looking at the witness and focus on the exhibit. The exhibit will win the war for the jurors' attention every time. Always ask: Where do I want the jury's attention to be focused, on the witness or on the exhibit?

Key occurrence witnesses, such as the plaintiff and defendant in a civil case, the victim and defendant in a criminal case, and critical eyewitnesses, ordinarily should be the center of attention. It is usually better to have the witness first tell the story of what happened without having exhibits interrupt the storytelling, particularly if the story is dramatic or traumatic. After the witness has told the story, exhibits such as objects, photographs, and diagrams can be introduced and used to highlight and repeat key facts.[2] This basic approach—tell the story first, then use exhibits at the end of the direct examination to highlight and repeat—keeps things simple for the witness. It also works well for the jurors, who focus first on the witness and can connect with the witness on an emotional level. Then they can focus on the exhibits, which reinforce the testimony.

With experienced witnesses, such as police officers and experts, you can usually have the witness testify and use exhibits at the same time. For example, police officers who arrived at the scene after a collision or crime frequently testify while standing next to a large photograph or diagram, and point out things on the exhibit as they testify. Expert witnesses frequently testify and use exhibits and visual aids as they explain the bases for their opinions. Experienced witnesses are much more capable of doing this comfortably and effectively.

Direct examinations of records witnesses in commercial cases are often organized differently. In these cases, the story is in the documents and records, and the witness explains the story contained therein by providing any necessary foundation for the exhibits and, after they are admitted, explaining what the documents and records show. Therefore, the spotlight should be on the documents and records, not the witness. For example, consider a breach of contract case in which the plaintiff sues the defendant for nonpayment on a delivery of goods. The plaintiff's documentation—order form, shipping record, billing invoice, and the like—tells the story of what happened. Those records can be enlarged on poster boards or projected on a screen, and the witness can walk the jurors through the events, pointing to the records that show the events and explaining anything on the records that may require explanation.

The choreography of witness testimony and exhibits during the direct examinations is important. It should be planned in advance and executed smoothly. Too many lawyers reflexively introduce exhibits at the first opportunity during the direct examination, when that is frequently not the best way to organize the examination. Always remember that exhibits attract attention to themselves and detract attention from the witness. Always ask: Where do I want the spotlight to be now, on the witness or on the exhibit?

3. Marking Exhibits and Visual Aids During Trial

Finally, how do you mark exhibits and visual aids during trial? Once the exhibit is admitted in evidence, almost all courts permit the marking of photographs, diagrams, maps, documents, and records. The most common way is to put the exhibit on an easel, directly in front of the jurors but a few feet away. Give the jurors a few seconds to take in the exhibit before talking or having the witness talk. Jurors will not listen if they are actively processing a new exhibit.

There are many ways you can and should mark exhibits to enhance their persuasiveness. For example, key language in documents and records can be highlighted by using yellow color behind that language, or by having a witness circle or underline that language on the enlarged exhibit or a copy of it. Diagrams, photographs, and maps can be marked to show where witnesses were standing; where vehicles were positioned; the path vehicles and people took; and distances,

---

2. For junior co-author Easton's different view, please see Chapter 5, note 1, page 119.

speeds, and times. As long as the markings fairly and accurately show the admitted facts and are not misleading or inflammatory, they are proper.

There are two approaches: Have the exhibits marked before trial, and have witnesses mark the exhibits during trial. There are advantages and disadvantages to each approach.

The advantage of completing and marking exhibits and visual aids before trial is that they can be professionally done. For example, an intersection diagram can show the location of the two cars at the moment of impact. An eyewitness can then testify that the diagram, including the location of the cars, is accurate. The diagram will look neat and professional. The downside is that the jurors all know that the lawyer had the diagram prepared the way he wanted it to look. In short, the credibility of the diagram is suspect.

The advantage of marking exhibits and visual aids during trial is that the jurors know the markings come directly from the eyewitness. For example, when an eyewitness marks a diagram to show where the two cars were at the moment of impact, jurors will, if they believe the witness, also believe the diagram. In short, the diagram may not look as professional, but it will be credible.

Trial lawyers differ on this issue. Some lawyers always like to complete exhibits before trial, because they are nervous about whether witnesses can mark them clearly and accurately. Other lawyers always want witnesses to mark exhibits during trial while the jurors are watching. The best approach is probably a compromise: If the exhibit shows facts that are not seriously in dispute, it is safer to have the exhibit completed beforehand. If the exhibit will show disputed facts, it is probably more persuasive to have witnesses mark exhibits in front of the jurors. Most witnesses, with a little practice before trial, can effectively mark diagrams and other exhibits in court.

Whether you mark exhibits before trial or have witnesses mark them during trial, you need to decide what should be marked. Consider what to mark, what colors and symbols to use, and who will do the marking.

First, what can you mark? In commercial cases, documents and records are frequently highlighted and labeled to draw attention to key language (Figure 7.36). In criminal cases, photographs and diagrams are commonly marked to show the locations of witnesses, victim, and defendant, and, if a night-time crime, the light sources. In personal injury cases, diagrams are routinely marked to show where the accident happened and important locations, distances, and speeds.

Remember what you are trying to accomplish. With documents and records, you are drawing the jurors' attention to key words, sentences, and paragraphs. Highlight by using a yellow highlighter, drawing lines under the key words, or circling them (Figure 7.37). Show what abbreviations, terms, and other entries on business forms mean by labeling them. With a live witness, you can simply ask the witness the appropriate questions and ask the witness to do the appropriate highlighting or labeling.

With photographs, diagrams, and maps, you are drawing the jurors' attention to key facts that witnesses have testified about. In civil and criminal cases, these usually include the locations of vehicles and people; paths the vehicles and people took; and distances, speeds, times, and lighting. If it's important to your case, always see if you can get a witness to mark it on a large demonstrative exhibit (Figures 7.38 and 7.39).

Proprietary Information

(a)   Confidential Restrictions. I, Mandy Ray, agree to hold in strict confidence and in trust for the sole benefit of the Company all Proprietary Information (as defined below) that I may have access to during the course of my relationship with the Company and will not disclose any Proprietary Information, directly or indirectly, to anyone outside of the Company, or use, copy, publish, summarize, or remove from Company premises such information (or remove from the premises any other property of the Company) except (i) during my relationship to the extent necessary to carry out my responsibilities as an employee of the Company or (ii) after termination of the relationship, as **specifically authorized by the President of the Company**. I further understand that the publication of any Proprietary Information through literature or speeches must be approved in advance in writing by the President of the Company.

Fig. 7.36 Annotation of Document. Courtesy of inData Corporation ©

Proprietary Information

(a)   Confidential Restrictions. I, **Mandy Ray**, agree to hold in strict confidence and in trust for the sole benefit of the Company all Proprietary Information (as defined below) that I may have access to during the course of my relationship with the Company and will not disclose any Proprietary Information, directly or indirectly, to anyone outside of the Company, or use, copy, publish, summarize, or remove from Company premises such information (or remove from the premises any other property of the Company) except (i) during my relationship to the extent necessary to carry out my responsibilities as an employee of the Company or (ii) after termination of the relationship, as specifically authorized by the President of the Company. I further understand that the publication of any Proprietary Information through literature or speeches must be approved in advance in writing by the President of the Company.

Fig. 7.37 Highlighting of Document. Courtesy of inData Corporation ©

Decide next what colors to use for the various things that will be marked on the exhibit. Colors stimulate associations and emotions. For example, in an accident case, you may decide to use a red car figure for the defendant's car, a green car figure for the plaintiff's car, and blue circles around a "W" to mark the locations of witnesses. If you are going to use more than one demonstrative exhibit, use the same colors consistently on each exhibit.

Decide what symbols to use. Symbols also convey associations and emotions. For example, you can use an X to mark the location of a person on the ground, but a stick figure may be better. You can use a rectangular box to represent a vehicle, but a car or truck figure may be better. You can use three car figures, and

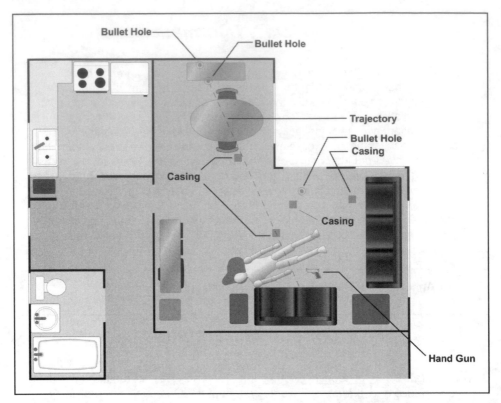

Fig. 7.38 Criminal Case Diagram. Courtesy of inData Corporation ©

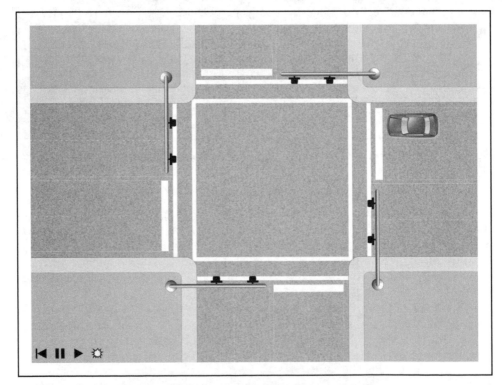

Fig. 7.39 Civil Case Diagram. Courtesy of inData Corporation ©

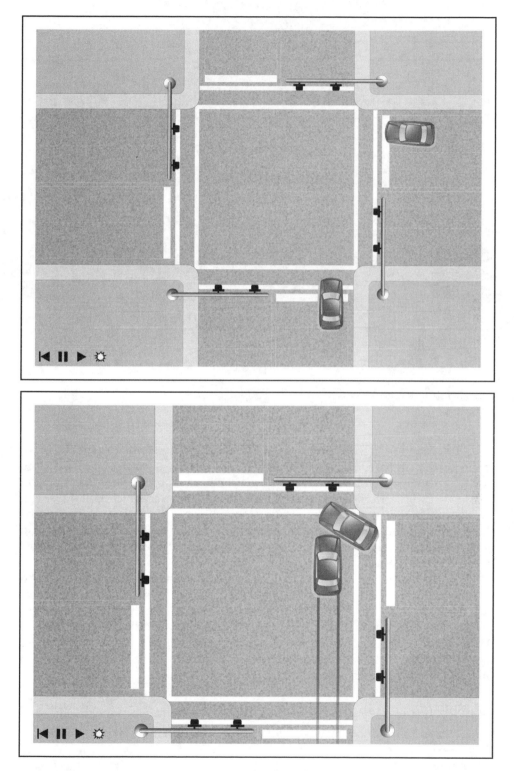

Fig. 7.39 (Continued)

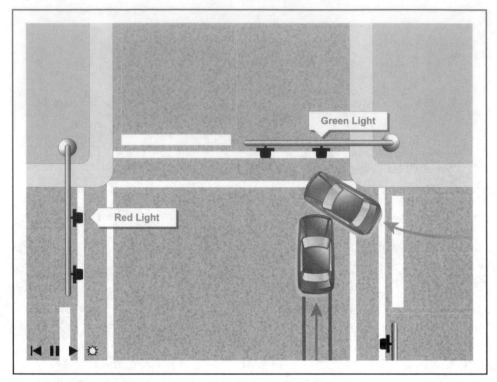

Fig. 7.39 (Continued)

place a 1, 2, and 3 on them, to represent the location of a car before the collision, at the point of impact, and where it came to rest. You can use arrows to show the direction of movement. You can use dotted lines to represent the path a person took. You can use a yellow marker to circle the locations of street lights. You can use lines to label distances between two points. You can label cars with the speeds they were traveling. In short, put on the exhibit the key facts that prove what you need to prove. Once those facts are marked on a big demonstrative exhibit, jurors will not forget them.

Last, decide which witness or witnesses can most persuasively mark each exhibit, and then practice with those witnesses. Tell the witnesses during preparation sessions exactly what you will be asking them to do and how you want them to do it, and then practice it. Don't just ask the witness to "mark," "show," or "indicate" something. Give the witness specific directions on where to go, where to stand, and how to mark. Train the witness to face the jury when talking, then turn to the exhibit when asked to mark it.

Example (Civil Case):

> LAWYER: Your honor, may Ms. Johnson continue her testimony by the exhibit?
>
> JUDGE: Yes.
>
> LAWYER: Ms. Johnson, please step down from the witness stand and walk over to where I've set up the easel in front of the jury. Please stand to the left of the easel and face the jury. [Witness does so.]

Q: Does this diagram, Plaintiff's Exhibit No. 3 in evidence, show the location where the two cars collided?

A: Yes, it does.

Q: Using this adhesive red car figure, please place it where the Chevy was when it collided with the Ford.

A: It was right here. [Witness puts figure on diagram.]

Q: Using this adhesive green car figure, please place it where the Ford was when it collided with the Chevy.

A: It was right here. [Witness puts figure on diagram.]

Q: How fast was the Chevy going at the time of the collision?

A: About 30 miles an hour.

Q: Using this red marker, please write "30 mph" by the Chevy. [Witness does so.]

Q: How fast was the Ford going at the time of the collision?

A: Almost nothing. Maybe two or three miles an hour.

Q: Using this green marker, please write "2–3 mph" by the Ford. [Witness does so.]

Q: Finally, at the time of the collision, what color was the traffic light for Flm Street?

A: It was red.

Q: Using the red marker, please label the traffic light in the middle of the intersection "red." [Witness does so.]

Q: Thank you, Ms. Johnson. Please return to the witness stand.

Note that when you tell the witness exactly what to do and what to use, you make a clear record at the same time. This makes everything clearer and more efficient, because there is usually no need to make statements for the record (e.g., "Your honor, for the record the witness has just written the word 'red' next to the traffic signal on the diagram.").

Example (Criminal Case):

Q: Officer Williams, please step down and stand to the left of State's Exhibit No. 5, already in evidence, which I'm putting on the easel. Have you seen this photographic blow-up before?

A: Yes.

Q: What scene is shown in State's Exhibit No. 5?

A: This shows the alley outside the bar where the shooting took place.

Q: When you got there, did you see the defendant?

A: Yes, he was standing over here, by the wall.

Q: Using this yellow marker, please draw a stick figure and label it "Defendant" to show where the defendant was standing. [Witness does so.]

Q: When you got there, did you see Mr. Smith?

A: Yes, he was lying on the ground by the back door to the bar.

Q: Using this red marker, please draw a stick figure and label it "Smith" to show where he was lying. [Witness does so.]

Q: How far apart were the defendant and Mr. Smith when you first saw them?

A: About 20 feet.

Q: Using this blue marker, please draw a pointed line between the defendant and Mr. Smith and write "20 feet" on the line. [Witness does so.]

Q: Thank you, officer. Please return to the stand.

Your large demonstrative exhibits (e.g., a blow-up of a key document or record, an intersection or crime scene diagram) are the exhibits that contain the key facts supporting your position on liability and damages. These are the exhibits you want in the jury room during deliberation, so that the jurors will be looking at your key exhibits as they discuss liability and damages.

Finally, plan how you can protect the integrity of your exhibits, particularly the large demonstrative charts and diagrams. You spent time planning how they should look and money to make them look right, and you don't want the other side to mark them up and dilute their impact. Can you keep the other side from asking witnesses, either during the cross-examination of your witnesses or the direct examination of their witnesses, to mark additional things?

It is clear that lawyers can use any admitted exhibits during cross-examination. Less clear is whether the cross-examiner can have the witness mark additional things on the exhibits. Judges commonly permit this under FRE 611(a), as long as the lawyer is having legitimate things marked, rather than simply trying to clutter up the diagram to make it confusing. However, the better approach is to avoid the problem altogether. Provide a copy of the diagram and ask the judge to have the cross-examiner mark what he wants on the copy, or provide a plastic overlay and ask the judge to have the cross-examiner mark only on the overlay. Most judges will be sensitive to your right to protect the integrity of your exhibits, particularly if you provide reasonable alternatives. However the judge rules, the ruling will apply to you as well as your opponent.

7.7 Trial Notebook

Your trial notebook should contain an exhibit list for your exhibits and an exhibit list for every other party. The lists help you keep track of the admissibility status of each exhibit as the trial progresses. Exhibit lists are usually organized as follows:

EXHIBIT LIST—PLAINTIFF

Ex.#:	Exhibit description:	Sponsoring witness:	Status:	Notes:
1	Police accident report	Officer Johnson	reserved ruling	remember to demand ruling
2a-d	Hospital x-rays	Dr. Robinson	admitted, no objection	have copy for witness to mark
3	Hospital records	Blutowski certificate of authentication	admitted over objection	
4	Intersection diagram	Wendy Wilson		

In civil cases, the parties are usually required to list the exhibits they intend to offer during the trial in the final pretrial statement. It is usually convenient for both sides to have the court clerk use the same numbers you used to list your exhibits in the pretrial statement, and have your exhibit list reflect the same numbers. Give the court clerk your exhibit list when the trial begins. In criminal cases, the exhibits are usually marked by the court clerk as the trial progresses. However it is done, your exhibit list must be marked appropriately as new exhibits are offered and their admissibility ruled on.

> ▶ For a discussion of effective use of trial notebooks, including exhibit lists, please watch Video A.5, "Wyo STI: Trial Notebooks."

7.8 Common Problems

What are the recurring problems that inexperienced lawyers encounter when using exhibits?

> ⊕ An example of a trial notebook, with shell forms and completed forms, is on the website that accompanies this book.

1. No Overall Visual Strategy

There is more to exhibits than merely getting them in evidence. You need an overall visual strategy for exhibits and visual aids that covers the trial from opening statements through closing arguments, that tells the story of your case visually, that presents information consistently, and that integrates smoothly with witness testimony. This strategy obviously has to be thought through well before trial.

> ▶ For a discussion of the mechanics of exhibits, please watch Video G.1, "Wyo STI: Exhibits and Laying a Foundation."

2. Exhibits and Visual Aids Fail the "Billboard Test"

A common problem in trials is exhibits that have too much information, are too cluttered, and fail to send a clear message in a few seconds. Always remember the billboard test: Does this exhibit or visual aid immediately send a clear message to the jurors?

3. Too Many Exhibits

Simplicity and clarity win trials. In document-intensive commercial cases, resist the urge to introduce every paper that is admissible. Instead, focus on the dozen or less documents that are the key to your case, and decide how you can best present these documents so that they grab and hold the jurors' attention.

4. Not Providing Smooth Judge and Jury Foundations

Foundations make a difference. Judges are impressed by lawyers who know how to get any kind of exhibit into evidence smoothly and efficiently. Jurors use the foundation procedure to assess which lawyer is more competent. Establishing foundations for exhibits should never be seen as a boring but necessary ritual. It's an opportunity to impress both judge and jury.

5. Not Anticipating Objections and Raising Issues Early

Anticipate that the opposing side will object to each exhibit and visual aid, and prepare your responses. If an objection has merit, concede the point and find another way to prove what you want to prove. If the objection has no merit, be prepared to show the judge why the evidentiary rules have been satisfied.

Raise anticipated evidentiary issues before trial. It gives the judge notice of possible disputes and time to make a considered ruling. Raising evidentiary issues early, both as proponent and opponent, shows the judge that you are prepared and confident of your positions—messages that are always important to send early in any case.

EXPERTS

8.1 Introduction

Most civil and criminal trials today involve expert witnesses. In civil cases, juries hear testimony from treating and nontreating physicians, design engineers, and accountants. In criminal cases, juries hear from pathologists, chemists, and gang experts. In both types of cases, experts are regularly called to testify about matters that are beyond the jurors' personal experience.

To present effective direct and cross-examinations of experts, trial lawyers must know the applicable law, in both federal and state courts, and the jury's perspective. They must understand that jurors have attitudes and expectations about experts and expert testimony, as well as limited interest and attention spans. The best experts are good communicators who make their testimony interesting, brief, and easy to understand. Done well, experts explain reality by helping jurors understand complex and technical evidence. Done poorly, experts only bore, overwhelm, and confuse jurors.

8.2 The Law

Expert witnesses must pass three sets of evidentiary and procedural barriers. They must comply with the rules that govern direct and cross-examinations of any witness, which are discussed in Sections 5.2 and 6.2. They must comply with the special rules that govern the testimony of experts in Federal Rules of Evidence (FRE) 701 to 706 and Fed. R. Civ. P. 26. Finally, in federal and most state courts, they must comply with the case law since 1993 that has substantially altered the admissibility requirements for expert testimony.

1. Direct Examination

The evidence law governing expert witness testimony is best understood by asking a series of questions.

a. Is the Subject Appropriate for Expert Testimony?

Under FRE 702(a), an expert witness may testify only if his testimony will "help the trier of fact to understand the evidence or to determine a fact in issue." If expert testimony is not helpful, it should be excluded. Testimony is not helpful if the expert proposes to testify about something that is already within the common knowledge of the jurors or is just speculative. Such testimony is not helpful and is a waste of time under FRE 403. For example, many jurisdictions permit experts to testify about factors that affect the accuracy of eyewitness identifications, because such expert testimony will help the jury assess the eyewitness testimony. Other jurisdictions bar such expert testimony on the ground that things that affect the accuracy of eyewitness testimony are already within the common knowledge of jurors.

b. Is the Expert Properly Qualified?

FRE 702 mandates that an expert witness be "qualified as an expert by knowledge, skill, experience, training, or education." The rule is silent on how well qualified the expert must be. In federal courts, the standard has been generous, with most judges willing to accept any expert who has knowledge superior to that of the jurors. In recent years, however, many judges have become more demanding and require that the expert have actual expertise on the specific subject in issue to which the testimony is directed. If the expert is qualified to testify, the issue then becomes one of the appropriate weight to assign to the testimony, which is a question for the jury. For example, in a medical malpractice case, most courts will allow a doctor, retained as an expert, to testify about the applicable standard of care, even though the doctor is not board certified (unless a statute provides otherwise). Courts usually hold that the doctor has enough expertise so that his testimony assists the jury, and that board certification or lack of it goes to the weight the jury should give the doctor's testimony.

c. Is the Expert's Testimony Relevant and Reliable?

For decades, the admissibility of expert testimony, in both federal and state courts, was governed by *Frye v. United States*, 293 F. 1013 (D.C. Cir. 1923). That changed in 1993, when the Supreme Court decided *Daubert v. Merrell Dow Pharmaceuticals*, 509 U.S. 579 (1993). *Daubert* was followed by *General Electric v.*

Joiner, 522 U.S. 136 (1997), and *Kumho Tire v. Carmichael*, 526 U.S. 137 (1999). The *Daubert-Joiner-Kumho Tire* trilogy has significantly changed the way federal courts (and those state courts that follow the federal courts) analyze the admissibility of expert testimony. In 2000, FRE 702 was amended to incorporate the holdings in these cases.

Whenever there is an issue about the admissibility of expert testimony, you must ask: Is the case in federal or state court? Is the witness a "scientific expert" or a "training and experience" expert? What admissibility analysis applies to that expert in that jurisdiction?

In federal courts, the judge as "gatekeeper" must determine if the proposed testimony of any expert is relevant and sufficiently reliable for the jury to hear. This gatekeeping function applies to both "scientific experts" (those who base their testimony on scientific tests and methods) and "training and experience experts" (those who base their testimony on personal observation and experience). Under FRE 702, the judge must determine if "(b) the testimony is based on sufficient facts or data; (c) the testimony is the product of reliable principles and methods; and (d) the expert has reliably applied the principles and methods to the facts of the case."

The judge makes this admissibility determination (often after a pretrial *Daubert* hearing) by applying the so-called *Daubert* factors: (1) whether the theory or technique has been tested; (2) whether the theory or technique has been published and peer-reviewed; (3) the known or potential error rate; and (4) whether the theory or technique has been generally accepted by the scientific community. These factors obviously apply to scientific experts. The judge has flexibility in deciding what additional factors apply to scientific experts and what pertinent factors should be applied to assess the reliability of training and experience experts.

Most state courts have adopted *Daubert*. A minority continue to follow *Frye* and its "general acceptance" rule, but several of these are large population states, so *Frye* remains significant. Under *Frye*, an expert may testify if the tests or principles underlying the expert's testimony "have gained general acceptance in the particular field in which it belongs." Under *Frye*, the relevant scientific community, not the judge, controls admissibility.

d. Were Underlying Tests Properly Done?

In many cases, the reliability of underlying tests and methods is well established and is not in issue. However, the proponent must still show that the tests done in this case were properly done by competent persons using reliable equipment. For example, in a drunk-driving case, the prosecutor need not show that the Breathalyzer test is reliable, because that is an established fact, but the prosecutor must still show that the results in *this* case are reliable because the unit used was reliable, in proper working order, properly calibrated, and operated by a competent technician.

e. Are the Sources of Facts and Data Relied on Proper?

Under FRE 703, the expert may base her testimony on facts or data "the expert has been made aware of or personally observed. If experts in the particular field would reasonably rely on those kinds of facts or data in forming an opinion on the subject, they need not be admissible for the opinion to be admitted." This means that the expert can give her opinions without the underlying data first being admitted in evidence, as long as experts in this field reasonably rely on that kind of data. For example, a doctor can testify to her diagnosis of the patient without first having admitted in evidence the x-rays and lab tests on which the testimony is based.

f. When Must the Sources Be Disclosed?

FRE 705 provides that an expert may state his opinions and reasons for them "without first testifying to the underlying facts or data," unless the court requires otherwise. This means that the direct examiner has flexibility in structuring and developing the expert's testimony, and can bring out the expert's opinions before going into the underlying data.

g. Are the Sources Themselves Admissible?

FRE 703 provides: "But if the facts or data would otherwise be inadmissible, the proponent of the opinion may disclose them to the jury only if their probative value in helping the jury evaluate the opinion substantially outweighs their prejudicial effect." This is an important rule. It means that the underlying data on which the expert bases his opinion is presumptively inadmissible unless the judge rules otherwise or there is an independent evidentiary basis for admitting the underlying data in evidence.

In federal courts, the proponent should attempt to get the underlying data independently admitted whenever possible, such as through a business records foundation. If that is impossible, the proponent should request that the jury be allowed to hear the underlying data because it is necessary for the jury to properly understand and evaluate the expert's testimony. If that fails, you will need to tell the expert that FRE 703 prevents him from testifying to the underlying data, and the direct examination will have to be modified appropriately.

However, what is inadmissible during the expert's direct examination under FRE 703 might be admissible during redirect examination. The Advisory Committee Notes accompanying the 2000 amendment that added the language quoted above to FRE 703 state, "Of course, an adversary's attack on an expert's basis will often open the door to a proponent's rebuttal with information that was reasonably relied upon by the expert, even if that information would not have been disclosable initially under the balancing test provided by this amendment."

Some states that have adopted the Federal Rules of Evidence have not adopted the present FRE 703. Thus, the old FRE 703 still controls; it arguably allows the expert to testify about the data underlying her testimony, even if that data is not in evidence, as long as the data is the kind of information such experts rely on in making evaluations. Because some states still follow the old FRE 703, state courts are a more predictable forum for trial lawyers to try cases that are heavily based on expert witnesses.

Note that FRE 803(18) permits using learned treatises to support an expert's testimony on direct examination if the expert "relied on" the treatise. Because this rule permits reading the pertinent portions of the treatises into evidence, FRE 703 does not affect the treatise rule.

h. Are the Forms of the Expert's Testimony Proper?

FRE 702 permits an expert to testify "in the form of an opinion or otherwise." Although experts commonly testify to their opinions (and usually "to a reasonable degree of medical or scientific certainty"), nothing in the rules requires it. Experts can testify to their "conclusions," "determinations," or "results of their evaluations," as long as they do not cross the line into guesswork or speculation. Experts can still answer hypothetical questions.

Indeed, your expert's testimony will be more persuasive if you call it a "conclusion." Refer to the opposing expert's testimony as an "opinion," because opinions are not as persuasive as conclusions. Labels are important.

Note also that the expert's testimony is admissible only if the party calling the expert has complied with the disclosure requirements of the discovery rules. Fed. R. Civ. P. 26(a)(2) requires that the retained or specially employed testifying expert prepare a written and signed report that "must contain . . . a complete statement of all opinions the witness will express and the basis and reasons for them" as well as other information. If this is not done in a proper and timely way before trial, Rule 37(c) might bar the expert from testifying at trial.

i. Can the Expert Testify About Ultimate Issues?

FRE 704 provides that "[a]n opinion is not objectionable just because it embraces an ultimate issue." However, FRE 702 requires that expert testimony "help the trier of fact to understand the evidence or to determine a fact in issue." Putting the two rules together produces the correct result: An expert may testify to "ultimate issues" if "helpful" to the jury. The expert may testify about the ultimate factual or legal issue in the case, as long as the testimony helps the jury understand the issues and resolve them. For example, a qualified accident reconstruction expert can testify that, at the moment of impact, the defendant's car was on the plaintiff's side of the road. However, the expert cannot say that the collision was the defendant's fault or that the defendant was negligent. Such testimony is not helpful, because the jury can reach the decision of fault or negligence as well as the expert, once the jury has heard the expert's testimony about the location of the cars.

In criminal cases, FRE 704(b) excludes ultimate issues testimony involving the mental state or condition of the defendant. An expert "must not state an opinion about whether the defendant did or did not have a mental state or condition that constitutes an element of the crime charged or of a defense." For example, a defense psychiatrist may testify that the defendant is a paranoid schizophrenic (the clinical diagnosis), but may not testify that the defendant could not, as a result of a severe mental disease or defect, understand that what he did was wrong (the legal test of insanity).

2. Cross-Examination

Cross-examinations of experts must comply with the evidence rules that apply to the cross-examinations of any witness (see Chapter 6). However, there is one special cross-examination rule that applies only to experts: impeachment with learned treatises.

FRE 803(18) provides that "[a] statement contained in a treatise, periodical, or pamphlet . . . established as a reliable authority" may be used to impeach an expert witness. The statements may be read into evidence, but the treatise itself is not admitted as an exhibit. Treatises can be shown to be reliable through an admission by the witness, other expert testimony, or judicial notice.

For detailed discussions of the law on experts, *see* Mauet & Wolfson, *Trial Evidence* (7th ed., 2020), and Stephen D. Easton, *Opposing the Adverse Expert* (2d ed., 2018).

8.3 The Jury's Perspective

Jurors ask the same questions of experts as of any witness: Who is he? Why is he here? Can I believe him? With experts, however, jurors have additional concerns. Many jurors are suspicious of experts, particularly if the expert was specifically retained to testify in this case. Their suspicions are based on several concerns: Why is it necessary to hire an expert to prove the party's case? Will the expert be boring? Will the expert's testimony be unintelligible? Will the expert be arrogant and condescending? Is the expert biased because he always testifies for one side or because he earns his living being a professional witness? Does the expert have real expertise, or is he willing to testify about anything and say anything for money? And why is this expert being paid so much?

> ◼◀ For an overview of effective jury presentations of expert testimony, please watch Video F.4, "Mauet on Experts."

Effective trial lawyers understand the jurors' concerns about experts, respond to them, and turn those concerns around by making the expert a friendly teacher and guide who explains what the evidence means.

8.4 Finding and Preparing Experts

1. Good Experts

Find a good expert. In many cases, of course, your experts are already chosen. The physicians who treated the plaintiff, the engineers who designed the motorcycle helmet, and the chemists who analyzed the drugs will be your expert witnesses, and you have no choice in the matter. However, if you need nontreating physicians or other testifying experts, you have choices.

What makes a good expert? Good experts have four principal characteristics: They are knowledgeable, well prepared, impartial, and dynamic. First, good experts are knowledgeable, not just in their field in general, but in the specific issues involved in the case. Their expertise comes not just from formal education and training, but also from firsthand experience with the specific issues involved. For example, if the issue in the trial is the rehabilitation and prognosis of a plaintiff who suffered a ruptured Achilles tendon, find an orthopedic specialist with specific training and experience with that kind of injury. The more specific the education, training, and experience of your expert—the more it matches the issues in the case—the more persuasive your expert will be.

Second, good experts are well prepared. Preparation always takes time. Make sure your expert sets aside the necessary time to educate you, and herself, about the case; writes a thorough expert report that meets the requirements of Fed.

R. Civ. P. 26(a)(2); and adequately prepares for her deposition and trial testimony. If your expert appears unwilling to set aside the time you believe it will take for the expert and you to become well prepared, and to make herself reasonably accessible to accomplish this, it's time to look for another expert.

Third, good experts are impartial. They don't reflexively favor one side or the other, or have a preconceived view of things. Beware the expert who testifies frequently, who always testifies for the plaintiff or the defendant, or who always comes to the same conclusion on a particular subject. Jurors are sensitive to obvious bias and interest.

Fourth, good experts must be good communicators. They are dynamic, confident, and communicate clearly. Lawyers often put too much emphasis on impressive-sounding credentials, and too little emphasis on finding experts who are good communicators. Jurors, by contrast, put more weight on good communication skills than on paper credentials. Think of the great teachers you had in school. They were likeable and made learning fun. They made complex information simple. They motivated you so that you wanted to learn new things. If an expert has everything else, but is not an effective communicator, that expert should not become your testifying expert. The more complex and unfamiliar the subjects on which the experts testify, the more jurors decide which expert to believe through circumstantial cues such as which expert is more likeable, testifies in a simple, straightforward manner, and has no apparent bias or interest.

2. Finding Good Experts

Where do you find good experts? Start with your own experience. If you have used an effective expert in the past, and he is the right kind of expert for this case, consider using him again. If the expert is local, this is often better, because jurors usually prefer local experts to those from out of town, and the local experts will be more readily available. Ask other lawyers in your firm, or other lawyers you have confidence in who have similar kinds of practices, for their experiences and recommendations. Good experts quickly become known in trial circles. Experienced litigators and trial lawyers all create lists of experts who have been good witnesses on particular issues in the past. Check with local colleges and universities for persons with the proper expertise, experience, and communication skills. Research jury verdict reporters for similar kinds of cases, because the reporters frequently identify the testifying experts used by the parties. Finally, be wary of experts who advertise in legal periodicals or other media. Jurors are rightly suspicious of experts who advertise their availability and who appear eager to be experts for money.

3. Preparing the Expert

Prepare the expert to be a persuasive teacher. Preparation takes time. At the pretrial stage, this means interviewing the expert, providing the expert with all information necessary for the expert's evaluation, assisting the expert in complying with the Fed. R. Civ. P. 26(a)(2) expert report requirements, and preparing the expert for deposition. At the trial stage, it means preparing the expert to be a persuasive communicator before the jury. This includes all the usual things involved in witness preparation, discussed in Section 5.6.

Keep in mind that your conversations with your testifying expert may not be privileged and may be admissible at trial. Fed. R. Civ. P. 26(b)(4)(C) governs this issue, providing that some communications are protected, others not. States may have different rules.

First, get the expert to think of herself not as an expert, but as a teacher, helper, and guide. The expert must teach the jurors about the subject and help guide them through complex information to reach the goal: understanding what happened and why it happened. The expert does not make the case; the expert explains the case that you have already proven. This means that you need to limit the expert's function. The expert's job is not to tell the jurors everything she knows about the subject, but to tell the jurors what they need to know to understand what happened in *this* case.

Second, simplify the expert's presentation. Get the expert to use plain English. Jurors find experts more persuasive when they replace their specialized vocabulary with plain English. Get the expert to answer most questions in sound bites, which are easier for the jurors to understand and digest than long-winded discussions. If the expert needs to give a longer answer, have the expert break down the answer into parts and number them (e.g., "Three reasons; first . . ."), so that each part is a sound bite. Get the expert to understand and accept that your direct examination will be in the 20- to 30-minute range, if possible, not hours, because juror attention spans are limited.

Third, simplify the expert's explanations. Get the expert to use visual aids to illustrate and supplement his answers. Jurors love seeing visual aids that explain what the expert did, how he did it, and why he did it. Prepare the expert to use examples and analogies from everyday life to explain the concepts and principles he is talking about. Visual aids and real-life examples make complex information much easier to understand and accept.

Fourth, get the expert to be assertive and positive. Experts usually choose their words carefully and frequently become tentative in the process (particularly because they know they will be cross-examined later). This erodes the expert's credibility and influence. This is particularly important when the expert explains what really happened and why it happened (which is your theory of the case), and why he rejects the other side's theory of what happened. How the expert says it is as important as what he says. Jurors will believe and follow the expert they like, understand, and trust, and that comes primarily from how the expert testifies. Training experts to be persuasive communicators takes time, even with experienced experts. There simply are no shortcuts.

Finally, train yourself. It is easy to forget that the expert should be the center of attention, not you. Lawyers frequently fall into the trap of trying to show jurors that they also know the subject matter. This is not the time to show off. Let the expert be the expert. Your job on direct examination is to ask the questions the jurors want answered, and ask those questions the way the jurors want them asked.

8.5 General Structure of Expert Direct Examinations

Direct examinations of experts, like all direct examinations, should be structured in a way that makes the witness's testimony clear and meets the jurors' needs. A typical structure for direct examinations is:

1. Introduction
2. Professional education, training, and experience
3. What the expert did and why
4. The expert's conclusions
5. The expert's bases and explanations

Note that this structure is not required. The expert witness rules, FRE 702 to 706, permit flexibility. However, this structure works well in most situations.

1. Introduction

Whenever an expert enters the courtroom, the jurors are asking three questions: Who is he? What did he do? Why did he do it? A good introduction has both verbal and nonverbal components.

a. Nonverbal Beginning

Work on the nonverbal aspects of the first minute, particularly if your expert has had little experience testifying during a jury trial. Make sure the expert dresses appropriately. For most experts this means either a suit, sport jacket and slacks, or a lab jacket if that is what the expert wears at work. Make sure the expert knows how to enter the courtroom, where to walk, who will administer the oath and how that should be done, and how the expert should sit and conduct himself on the witness stand. Finally, decide what the expert should carry with him. The expert will need a copy of his expert report and perhaps the exhibits and visual aids he will use while explaining his testimony.

b. Verbal Beginning

The verbal introduction should immediately address the juror's questions: Who is she, what did she do, and why did she do it? Unfortunately, the traditional start simply does not address the jurors' questions.

Example (Ineffective Traditional Start):

Q: Tell us your name.
A: I'm Sharon Jones.
Q: What is your occupation?
A: I'm a chemist.
Q: Where are you employed?
A: I work at Ace Chemicals.
Q: How did you become a chemist?

And so on. However, these traditional questions do not address the jurors' needs and interests. The better way is to ask introductory questions that immediately tell the jurors who the expert is, how she became involved in the case, and what she did.

Example (Modern Start):

Q: Dr. Wilson, are you the orthopedic specialist who treated Mr. Mason when he was brought to the emergency room on June 1, 2020?
A: Yes.

Q: Did you do the surgery on Mr. Mason's leg?
A: Yes.
Q: Did you supervise Mr. Mason's rehabilitation?
A: Yes.

Example:

Q: Professor Johnson, please introduce yourself.
A: My name is Lars Johnson. I'm a mechanical engineer. I'm a professor at the university's engineering school.
Q: Did I ask you to study the motorcycle helmet involved in this crash?
A: Yes, you did.
Q: Were you able to determine if the design of the helmet is a reasonably safe design?
A: Yes.

These introductory questions efficiently orient the jurors by showing who the expert is, what he did, and why he's here. They are more conversational and engaging. Are they leading? Of course. However, because introductory questions are on preliminary matters not in dispute, leading questions are proper under FRE 611(c). Few lawyers object to them, and few judges will sustain such objections if made. Leading questions are simply an efficient, sensible way to establish these uncontested matters.

Sometimes you will want to let the jurors know what the expert did *not* do, so they won't be disappointed later.

Example:

Q: Dr. Smith, did I ask you to examine Mr. Jackson to determine if he is able to return to work?
A: Yes, you asked me a few months ago.
Q: You didn't treat Mr. Jackson when he was taken to the emergency room, did you?
A: No, Dr. Wilson did that. I became involved after that time.
Q: Dr. Smith, did you do what was necessary to evaluate Mr. Jackson to determine if he would be able to return to work?
A: Yes, I did.
Q: Are you prepared today to tell us what you did, why you did it, and what conclusions you reached?
A: I am.

2. Professional Education, Training, and Experience

Once the expert has been introduced, qualifying the expert is the usual next step. The judge needs the information to determine if the expert should be permitted to testify, and the jurors need it to determine the expert's credibility. The judge answers the threshold questions: Is this expert sufficiently qualified? Will his testimony be helpful to the jury? The jurors answer the ultimate questions: Is this expert believable? Is she more believable than the opposing expert?

What impresses lawyers and judges may not be what impresses jurors. Lawyers put a great deal of weight on an expert's paper credentials, especially the expert's formal education and training. Jurors, by contrast, usually put more emphasis on the expert's practical credentials, the expert's specific hands-on experience. After all, most jurors got good at what they do for a living by repeatedly doing it; shouldn't the same hold true for experts? You need to meet both the judge's and the jurors' interests and expectations.

a. Education and Training

What counts in the expert's formal education and training? Judges, like lawyers, are impressed by résumés that reflect prestigious universities and institutions for degrees and postgraduate training, academic and professional honors, memberships in honorary societies and other professional associations, and a lengthy publication history. Jurors are less easily impressed by these things, and may even react negatively to some of them, such as memberships in professional associations and publications that have little to do with the issues in the case. How do you reconcile this conflict?

A common approach is to bring out in testimony only the core credentials that establish the expert's qualifications. These credentials usually include:

- Education and degrees received
- Professional licenses and certifications
- Teaching experience
- Publications, if directly related to testimony
- Important positions held in professional organizations

The other details will be on the expert's résumé, which you can offer as an exhibit later in the direct examination. Judges routinely admit an expert's résumé as a business record under FRE 803(6) or as otherwise reliable hearsay under FRE 807, because doing so saves time. This makes the qualifications testimony more efficient, while still providing, through the résumé, the details of the expert's credentials. Make sure the expert's résumé is accurate, complete, and up to date.

Under this approach, the expert's core credentials can be brought out quickly. As always, use a transition question to get started on the new topic.

Example:

> Q: Dr. Wilson, let's begin by learning about the education and training you received to become a specialist in orthopedic surgery. Where did you attend medical school?

Example:

> Q: Professor Johnson, let's turn now to how you became a professor in mechanical engineering at the university. What did you study in college?

Sometimes an introductory statement helps orient the jurors to how the rest of the direct examination will be organized.

Example:

> Q: Dr. Adams, we're going to turn next to your education, training, and experience as a doctor. After that we'll turn to how you evaluated Mrs. Griggs, the conclusions you reached, and the reasons for those conclusions.

It is easy to bring out an expert's credentials, but difficult to do so without making the expert sound pompous. After all, you are asking the expert to tell the jurors why he's such an impressive expert. How do you bring out the expert's education and training and still keep the expert from sounding pompous?

Many lawyers mix leading with nonleading questions. Bring out the expert's most impressive credentials through leading questions, then follow them up with nonleading questions. This keeps the expert sounding modest about her accomplishments and goes over better with the jurors. Have the expert translate any specialized terms into plain English. Look for ways to personalize the expert, to show that underneath the expertise there's a normal person who's much like the jurors. And do it all efficiently. Qualifying the expert should take only a few minutes, because that's all the jurors will tolerate.

Example:

Q: Dr. Wilson, you're a doctor specializing in orthopedic surgery?
A: That's right.
Q: You're licensed in this state?
A: Yes.
Q: Where did you go to college?
A: At the University of Connecticut.
Q: You then attended Harvard Medical School?
A: That's right.
Q: After graduation, what did you decide to specialize in?
A: I decided to do my residency in orthopedic surgery.
Q: What's a residency?
A: That's a program where you work in a hospital studying a particular field of medicine under experts in that field. For orthopedic surgery, it's a four-year program.
Q: Dr. Wilson, you're what's called board certified in orthopedic surgery?
A: Yes.
Q: What's board certification, and how do you get it?
A: Every specialty in medicine is controlled by a board. In my field, it's the American Board of Orthopedics. When you complete your residency program, you are eligible to take the board examination. It's a combination of written and oral tests.
Q: Did you take and pass those tests?
A: Yes, in 2000.
Q: You've been a board-certified specialist since then?
A: Yes.
Q: Is board certification the highest level of certification in orthopedic surgery?
A: Yes, there's nothing beyond that.

Look for ways to personalize the expert. Jurors are always curious about other people, and one of the things they like to know is how others chose their line of work. Satisfy the jurors' curiosity and humanize your expert.

Example:

Q: What made you decide to be a meteorologist?

A: I've always been fascinated by the weather, especially big storms. We grew up on the coast, and I always loved to watch the big storms when they hit the beach.

Look for other credentials that will have an impact on the jurors. A common one is teaching in a particular field. Jurors are impressed by experts who are good enough to be hired to teach their field to others, whether it's in professional and graduate programs, undergraduate colleges, or technical schools.

Example:

Q: Dr. Henderson, in addition to your practice, I understand you teach?
A: Yes, I'm an assistant clinical professor of medicine at the medical college.
Q: What's that mean?
A: It means I teach part-time. I teach young doctors in the orthopedics residency program.
Q: How long have you been doing that?
A: For five years.
Q: Do you like teaching?
A: I love it. Teaching young doctors to be specialists in orthopedic medicine is very rewarding.

Another credential jurors might put weight on is publications, provided they are directly relevant to the issues in the case.

Example:

Q: Dr. Adams, have you written and published any articles that have a direct bearing on what you did in this case?
A: Yes. In this case I was asked to examine and evaluate Mrs. Morgan to see if she could return to work as a secretary at her company. Five years ago, I wrote an article called "Evaluating the Injured for Disability Assessments." It was published in the *Journal of Orthopedics*, which is the monthly journal of the American College of Orthopedics.

Finally, consider bringing out any other impressive qualifications or honors, again using leading questions so the expert does not appear pompous.

Example:

Q: Dr. Tudor, I understand that you are on the certification board of the American Board of Psychiatry.
A: Yes.
Q: What does that involve?
A: The certification board is the group that creates and administers the tests that determine who will receive board certification in psychiatry each year in the United States.
Q: And I understand you have been the chair of that board?
A: Yes, from 2015 to 2020.

b. Experience

Hands-on experience is what impresses most jurors. After all, that's how they got to be experts at their own jobs. Hands-on experience is particularly important with training and experience experts, although it also applies to scientific experts. Accordingly, spending time to show the expert's work experience relevant to the issues is important. Bring out the expert's length of experience, the focus of that experience, and end up with impressive numbers whenever possible. As always, use an introductory or transition question to get started.

Example:

> Q: Dr. Gantz, let's turn to your actual experience treating patients. How many years have you practiced as an orthopedic specialist?
> A: 30 years.
> Q: During that time, have you ever treated patients with joint injuries?
> A: Of course.
> Q: How often?
> A: Almost every day.
> Q: Have you ever treated patients with elbow dislocations?
> A: Yes.
> Q: How often?
> A: Probably once a week.
> Q: We've learned in this case that Mr. Wilson suffered a posterior dislocation of his right elbow. Before you saw Mr. Wilson in the emergency room, had you ever treated other patients for the same kind of elbow dislocation?
> A: Yes. Posterior elbow dislocations are common, particularly with children, but they also happen in adults. I see that kind of dislocation at least once a month.
> Q: Over the past 30 years, about how many times have you treated patients with posterior elbow dislocations?
> A: Probably over 300 times.

Example:

> Q: Ms. Spiegel, let's talk about your company, the Spiegel Gallery. What does your company do?
> A: We buy and sell paintings. We specialize in American landscape artists of the nineteenth and twentieth centuries.
> Q: How long have you had your own company?
> A: I started the gallery 12 years ago.
> Q: Before that, had you been in the art business?
> A: Yes. I worked at two other galleries in New York for a total of almost 10 years.
> Q: During the 22 years you've been in the business, have you done appraisals of paintings?
> A: Yes. That's the main part of my work. I have to appraise paintings to determine what we're willing to pay if we buy them. I also need to appraise paintings when we show paintings owned by individuals who want us to sell their paintings for them on a commission basis.

> Q: How many paintings have you appraised to determine their market value over the past 22 years?
> A: I usually do two or three appraisals a week, so over the past 22 years that probably adds up to 2,000 to 3,000 appraisals.
> Q: In this case we're concerned about the value of a Thomas Moran landscape. Over those 22 years, have you ever appraised other landscape paintings by Moran?
> A: Oh, yes. Moran is a well-known artist whose work is in high demand.
> Q: How many Moran landscapes have you appraised over the years?
> A: I probably sell one a year, so I've probably appraised 20 to 25 over the years I've been in the art business.

Notice how the hands-on experience starts with general experience, then focuses on experience directly relevant to the issues in the case, and ends up with impressive numbers whenever possible. It's the numbers that impress most jurors and stick in their minds.

Finally, consider bringing out the expert's previous experience testifying in court. Most judges permit this testimony, although some consider it irrelevant and hearsay. Jurors might be impressed by that experience, as long as the numbers are not so large that they suggest the expert makes his living being a professional witness.

Example:

> Q: Dr. Barnes, have you previously testified as an expert in courts in the United States?
> A: Yes.
> Q: For how many years, and how many times?
> A: Since 2010. I think I've testified as an expert witness during trials about 15 times since then.

c. Voir Dire, Tendering Witness as Expert, and Stipulations

When you have brought out the expert's education, training, and experience, the witness should be qualified to testify as an expert. If the opposing side wishes to object on the ground that the witness is not sufficiently qualified, this is the time to make the objection, or else it will be waived.

The opposing side may ask to "voir dire the witness on his qualifications"; that is, to conduct a cross-examination limited to the expert's professional background.

Example:

> Q (BY CROSS-EXAMINER): Your honor, may I voir dire Dr. Adams on her qualifications?

The purpose of such a limited cross-examination is to demonstrate that the expert is not qualified, so that the judge will bar the expert from further testifying. Though judges usually grant the request, such cross-examinations almost never succeed in disqualifying the expert. Judges typically rule that the matters brought out go to weight, not admissibility, and the jurors then get the impression that the cross-examiner tried but failed to discredit the expert.

Accordingly, most trial lawyers don't ask to voir dire the witness on her qualifications unless they have a realistic chance of disqualifying the expert. These matters are usually better brought out during the expert's normal cross-examination. If, however, the expert has significant problems with credentials or experience, some trial lawyers will sometimes ask to voir dire the expert to expose those problems, even though they know the judge will probably deny the motion to bar the expert from testifying.

The opposing side may also offer to "stipulate to the expert's qualifications"; that is, to agree that the expert is sufficiently qualified to testify as an expert.

Example:

> **OPPOSING LAWYER:** Your honor, in the interest of saving time, we'll stipulate that Professor Higgins is competent to testify as an expert in this case.

The cross-examiner's purpose in offering the stipulation is usually to prevent the direct examiner from bringing out the expert's impressive credentials and experience, particularly if this expert has a more impressive background than his own expert. For that reason, you will usually want to refuse the stipulation, particularly if the judge will then use the fact of the stipulation to bar you from further developing your expert's qualifications. A good approach is to refuse the offer but propose a counteroffer.

Example:

> **DIRECT EXAMINER:** Your honor, we're willing to stipulate that Professor Higgins is better qualified than their expert. Otherwise, we believe the jurors are entitled to hear the backgrounds of both experts so they can decide who to believe.

The other side, of course, will hardly agree, and you have made your point.

In some state courts, the practice is to tender the witness as an expert in a particular field. The judge then hears any objections and rules on whether the expert may continue to testify as an expert.

Example:

> **DIRECT EXAMINER:** Your honor, we tender Dr. Williams as an expert in orthopedics, and in particular an expert in the treatment of posterior elbow dislocations.
> **JUDGE:** Counsel, any objection?
> **OPPOSING LAWYER:** No, your honor.
> **JUDGE:** Very well. Counsel, you may continue your direct examination.

Federal courts and many state courts, however, disapprove of this procedure and some bar it. This is because the act of tendering an expert puts the judge in the position of appearing to ratify the expert. The jury's function is to determine the credibility of the expert and the weight to be given to the expert's testimony, so judges do not want to give the impression that their rulings should in any way be interpreted by the jurors as approving or disapproving of an expert or the expert's testimony.

Finally, note that in civil cases the admissibility of expert testimony frequently is resolved at the pretrial stage. For example, most judges require, as part of the final pretrial statement, that each side list its testifying experts with summaries of their expected testimony and list any objections to the opposing party's experts' qualifications and opinions. If you state that you have no objections to the opposing party's experts' qualifications, you have waived any later objections on this point. In practice, lawyers rarely object to expert testimony on the ground that the expert is not qualified to testify, because almost all testifying experts will meet the standards of FRE 702.

A difficulty sometimes occurs at trial when the judge or the opposing party attempts to bar or limit your development of an expert's education, training, and experience before the jury. The usual ground is that because there is no dispute over whether the expert is qualified, there is no need to do this. Once again, point out that the jurors need some background to make an informed assessment of witness credibility, which is a critical jury function. Point out that FRE 104(e) expressly confers this right. Most judges will overrule the objection, yet urge you to be efficient.

Example:

> Q: Dr. Wheeler, let's talk next about your education, training, and actual experience.
>
> OPPOSING LAWYER: Your honor, we object under Rule 403. We already agreed before trial that Dr. Wheeler is qualified to testify. This simply wastes court time.
>
> DIRECT EXAMINER: Your honor, the jury's job is to determine which expert to believe, and it can hardly do that unless it learns about the backgrounds of both side's experts. I will bring out Dr. Wheeler's background quickly.
>
> JUDGE: The objection is overruled.

After the expert highlights his education, training, and experience, now is the time to introduce the expert's résumé, which will provide the details.

Example:

> DIRECT EXAMINER: Your honor, at this time we offer Dr. Wheeler's résumé as Plaintiff's Exhibit No. 8.
>
> JUDGE: Any objection?
>
> OPPOSING LAWYER: No, your honor.
>
> JUDGE: Very well. Plaintiff's Exhibit No. 8 is admitted.

3. What the Expert Did and Why

The next logical step is to bring out what the expert did. A few experts will not testify about their conclusions, such as treating physicians who will only testify to what they did. However, most experts will also provide their conclusions, and describing what they did sets the stage for those later conclusions. Therefore, you need to answer the jurors' questions about experts: What did he do? How did he do it? Why did he do it?

a. What the Expert Did

Bringing out what the expert did, how, and why, can be done efficiently. Try to break up the witness's testimony so that most of the answers are 10- to 15-second sound bites. As always, use a transition question to get started.

Example:

> Q: Ms. Jackson, let's turn next to what you did, why you did it, and how you did it. First, what did you do in this case?
>
> A: I made an appraisal of the vacant lot at Main and Elm Streets to determine its fair market value as of June 1, 2020.
>
> Q: Why did you do that?
>
> A: You asked me to appraise that lot.
>
> Q: How did you do the appraisal?
>
> A: There's an accepted method used in real estate appraisal, and I followed it.
>
> Q: Describe that method.
>
> A: To find the fair market value of a vacant parcel of real estate, the accepted method is to look for what are called "comparables." That is, the appraiser looks at similar parcels that have been sold in the past few months in similar locations and uses that information to determine the fair market value.
>
> Q: Did you use that method?
>
> A: Yes. The parcel at Main and Elm was a vacant corner lot with commercial zoning that would allow construction of a retail store. I researched the public records to find other corner lots with the same zoning in the same part of town, located on corners of commercial streets, that were about the same size. The selling price of those comparables will give you the price range for which similar lots have been sold recently.
>
> Q: How many comparables did you find?
>
> A: I found seven lots that were similar enough to be useful.
>
> Q: How do you go from finding those comparables to determining the fair market value of the parcel at Main and Elm?
>
> A: That's the second step. The problem with real estate is that no two parcels are identical. I had to evaluate the strengths and weaknesses of the comparable lots, evaluate the strengths and weaknesses of the parcel at Main and Elm, and make a judgment of where the Main and Elm parcel would fit in the price range. In addition, the market changes over time. I had to factor in whether the real estate market during this time—in particular the market for vacant commercial zoned lots—was stable, rising, or falling.
>
> Q: Did you do those things?
>
> A: Yes, I did.
>
> Q: Were you able to determine the fair market value of the lot at Main and Elm as of June 1, 2020?
>
> A: Yes, I was.

This can be a good time to use visual aids. Jurors always like visual aids, because they show the information graphically and provide a change from ordinary witness testimony. Visual aids are particularly useful when the expert is talking about a process that involves several steps.

Example:

Q: Professor James, did you bring with you a visual aid that explains the process by which raw iron is made into car doors?
A: Yes. That's the visual aid marked Exhibit No. 3.
Q: Would that exhibit help you in explaining that process?
A: It certainly would.

If the expert is only going to testify about what he saw and did, and not give opinions, this is the core part of the expert's testimony, and it should receive appropriate detail. Make sure the expert uses plain English, and have the expert define any technical terms. Jurors strongly prefer experts who use plain English while testifying. Make what the expert did into a story that jurors can follow easily.

Example (Treating Orthopedist):

Q: Dr. Gibson, let's turn now to what you did when you saw Jim White in the emergency room at the hospital. Where was he when you first saw him?
A: He was lying on a cart and had just been wheeled from the emergency entrance into one of the examining rooms.
Q: What was happening when you got there?
A: He was being examined by nurses and a resident. They were checking his vital signs and examining him for obvious signs of injury.
Q: Was he talking?
A: No. He kept going in and out of consciousness.
Q: What did you do first?
A: I talked to the ambulance attendant.
Q: What did the attendant tell you?
A: He said that Mr. White had been involved in a car accident at an intersection, and that he had been struck on his driver's side door by another car, commonly called a T-bone collision.
Q: What did you do next?
A: I checked his vital signs—blood pressure, pulse, and respiration—which were stable and within normal limits. I then examined his known injuries, which the nurses and resident had already identified.
Q: What were those injuries?
A: There were two. He had a large bruise on his forehead and a cut near his scalp line, which was bleeding. In addition, his left arm looked injured, and I suspected a fracture in the upper arm.
Q: What did you do next?
A: I had a portable x-ray unit brought into the examining room, and took x-rays of his head, neck, and arm.
Q: Why x-rays of his head?
A: I was concerned that he might have suffered a fracture of his skull or was hemorrhaging blood into his brain.
Q: What did the x-rays show?
A: The x-rays of his skull and neck were negative, that is, showed no fractures or other abnormalities. The x-rays of his left arm showed a fracture in the humerus, the bone between the elbow and shoulder. The fracture was completely through the humerus near the elbow.

Q: After you determined the location and extent of his injuries, what did you do next?

A: I had the patient taken to an operating room and followed him there. The plan was to stitch up the cut on his forehead and to reduce and set the fracture.

Q: How did you do that?

A: A nurse anesthetist administered anesthesia through a drip IV, that is, a needle and tube attached to the patient's right arm, which is connected to a container of a water solution. After that I cleaned the cut on his forehead and used sutures to close the cut. I then set the fracture.

Q: How did you do that?

A: When the patient is unconscious and his muscles are relaxed, it is usually possible to manipulate the humerus to make sure that the bones on either side of the fracture are in their proper positions so that the bones will grow together and heal properly. You can usually put the bones back in place manually, which is preferable to surgery. I was able to do that in this case. I then took x-rays to make sure that the bones in the humerus were positioned properly, and then put a plaster cast on the arm, from the shoulder to the wrist, and then taped the arm to the chest. This immobilizes the arm.

Q: What happened after that?

A: The patient was wheeled into a recovery room. We needed to make sure his vital signs remained stable as he came out of the anesthesia, and we needed to monitor his mental state. He did come out about 30 minutes later, and shortly after that started speaking clearly. He then was transferred to a ward for further observation.

Q: Did you see him after that?

A: No, his care was taken over by the staff of the internal medicine department.

In this example, the treating physician, though testifying as an expert, is not expressing opinions on issues such as causation or prognosis. Therefore, the story of what the doctor did will be the last part of his direct examination.

b. Expert Compensation

Why the expert did what he did is frequently simple: The expert was paid to do it. Experts who have been retained to study the issues and give opinions on those issues commonly testify during trials, and you must always be ready to deal with the fact that your experts, as well as the other side's experts, are being paid. The concern is that the experts, who frequently bill at an impressive rate and have already been paid substantial amounts, will be seen as willing to say anything for money. There are different approaches to dealing with this situation.

First, you and opposing counsel can agree before trial not to go into the issue of compensation with any of the experts. When both side's experts are being compensated at similar rates and have already received similar compensation for their work, there is little point in going into the opposing experts' compensation, as the opposing lawyer can make the same point with your experts. Make sure you put such an agreement on the record, so the judge is aware of it. The agreement has the same effect as a stipulation between the parties.

Example:

> **LAWYER:** Your honor, before we call our first expert witness, I want to put on the record that the defense and I have agreed that neither side will go into the issue of expert compensation during the examinations of any of the experts who will testify during the trial.
>
> **JUDGE:** Defense, does that correctly state your agreement?
>
> **OPPOSING LAWYER:** It does, your honor.
>
> **JUDGE:** Very well. Neither side will raise any matter dealing with expert compensation during the direct or cross-examinations of any testifying experts.

Second, you can bring out the fact of compensation during the direct examination. This draws the sting before the opposing side can make something of it during cross-examination. Make sure your expert is not defensive about the fact of compensation. Jurors expect experts to be compensated, as long as the basis and amount of compensation are reasonable.

Example (Physician):

> **Q:** Dr. Wilkinson, are you being compensated for your work in this case?
> **A:** Of course.
> **Q:** How are you being compensated?
> **A:** I'm being paid at my usual hourly rate for the time I spent studying this matter, writing my report, and testifying.
> **Q:** What's your hourly rate?
> **A:** It's $500 per hour.
> **Q:** Why that rate?
> **A:** When I see patients in my office, that's about what I charge per hour. Since being a witness takes me away from the office, I've always charged the same hourly rate as my office work.
> **Q:** How much time have you spent on this matter so far?
> **A:** About 25 hours. That includes reviewing all the medical records, writing my report, and appearing for my deposition.
> **Q:** Have you been paid for that time?
> **A:** Yes.

Jurors are always interested in learning if the witness is a "professional witness" who makes a living testifying for money, or always testifies for plaintiffs or defendants. Show the jurors that your witness has no such bias or interest.

Example (Engineer):

> **Q:** Professor Weiss, how frequently do you agree to be an expert witness?
> **A:** Not very often. I'm a professor in the engineering department, and that's my full-time job. I'll agree to be an expert witness if I find the issues interesting, and the case does not require out-of-state travel. I only agree to be a witness on product safety issues, because that's my area of interest.
> **Q:** How often do you agree to be an expert witness each year?
> **A:** It probably averages out to once per year in recent years.
> **Q:** Which side usually hires you to evaluate a case?

A: It varies. Some years it's the plaintiff, some years the defendant. Over the years it's been fairly even.

If the witness is usually called as an expert by plaintiffs or defendants, and there is an easy explanation for this, bring it out.

Example:

Q: Dr. Kelliher, who typically calls you as a witness in criminal cases?
A: It's almost always the prosecution.
Q: Why is that?
A: As a county pathologist in the medical examiner's office, I determine causes of death, and if the cause of death was through homicidal means—typically gunshot and stabbing injuries—I regularly testify in a later trial. Since the prosecution has to prove that the victim died through homicidal means, it's the prosecution that usually calls me as an expert witness.

Third, you can simply leave any discussion of fees out of the direct examination and prepare the witness for possible cross-examination on that point. This often works well if the expert is experienced and her fees are reasonable. After all, jurors assume that experts are being paid for their work, and having this fact confirmed during cross-examination usually accomplishes little.

4. The Expert's Conclusions

Most experts, of course, are called as witnesses to testify about their conclusions and the reasons for those conclusions. The next logical step, then, is to bring out those opinions (followed later by the explanations and bases for the opinions). The traditional, formulaic way is as follows:

Example (Traditional Formula):

Q: Dr. Wilson, do you have an opinion, to a reasonable degree of medical [or scientific] certainty, whether Mary Smith's injuries are permanent?
A: I do.
Q: What is your opinion?

This traditional way has shortcomings. First, the word *opinion* is weak. To jurors, everyone has opinions, and many of those opinions don't amount to much. If one person has an opinion, it usually means that someone else has a contrary opinion. FRE 702 allows flexibility by permitting the expert to testify "in the form of an opinion or otherwise." For that reason, use stronger, more assertive phrases whenever possible. Ask the expert: "What did you conclude?," "What were you able to determine?," or "What were the results of your examination?"

Second, the commonly used language—"to a reasonable degree of medical or scientific certainty"—adds nothing of significance and is not required by the evidence rules or case law. All that is required is that the expert not guess or speculate. It is the jury's function to determine certainty and weight. Of course, some trial judges are comfortable with the traditional language, but case law recognizes that it means little to jurors. Unless the judge insists that you use the traditional language, it's best to avoid it.

Example:

> Q: Dr. Atkins, were you able to determine if Mary Johnson will ever be able to return to competitive gymnastics?
> A: Yes, I was.
> Q: What did you determine?

Example:

> Q: Ms. Pointer, after you studied Mr. Johnson's life and job history, were you able to calculate his economic losses caused by this collision?
> A: Yes.
> Q: What are Mr. Johnson's economic losses?

These kinds of questions are simple, yet forceful and assertive, and give the expert's testimony greater impact. Of course, if the expert feels more comfortable, or insists on, using the traditional opinion language, you should accommodate his preferences.

If the expert will be testifying about several conclusions, consider using a visual aid, such as a poster-board exhibit or a PowerPoint slide projected on a screen, that itemizes each of the opinions.

5. The Expert's Bases and Explanations

The final logical step in the expert's direct examination is to have the expert explain the reasons for her conclusions. Once the jurors have heard what the expert's conclusions are, they want to know why and how the expert reached them. This explanation can be started through a simple question.

Examples:

> Q: Dr. Atkins, what are the reasons for your conclusion?
> Q: Please explain how you calculated Mr. Johnson's economic losses.

If the expert has testified in the form of an opinion, you can still ask a simple follow-up question.

Example:

> Q: How did you reach that opinion?

The bases for the expert's conclusions are a critically important part of the expert's testimony, because the bases give the expert an opportunity to explain and support his conclusions; that is, his (and your) theory of what really happened and why. Now is the time to have the expert assume the teacher role, by giving simple, concise explanations of the bases for and reasoning underlying the conclusions. This explanation should be organized carefully and integrated with visual aids, admitted exhibits, unadmitted sources if permitted, and treatises. Remember, the expert only needs to explain how he came to his conclusions; he should *not* tell the jurors everything he knows on the subject! This explanation should take a few minutes. Any more, and the jurors lose interest.

a. Rule 703

You must keep in mind the significant differences between federal and state courts. Federal courts follow FRE 703, which provides in part: "But if the facts or data [on which the expert bases his conclusions] would otherwise be inadmissible, the proponent of the opinion may disclose them to the jury only if their probative value in helping the jury evaluate the opinion substantially outweighs their prejudicial effect." This is an important limitation in federal courts, and you must determine before trial how the judge will apply it.

FRE 703 makes the bases for an expert's opinions presumptively *inadmissible*, unless the judge rules otherwise or the bases are admissible on independent evidentiary grounds. As a practical matter, you will know the bases for an expert's opinions because the expert will have previously submitted the expert report required under Fed. R. Civ. P. 26(a)(2). The report should disclose if the expert relied on information that is otherwise inadmissible under the evidence rules.

In federal court, you would like to know, before trial whenever possible, if your expert will be allowed to state these otherwise inadmissible bases for her conclusions when she testifies. Frequently, you will know this in advance if the judge requires that any objections to expert testimony be set forth in the final pretrial statement, or the opposing party has filed a motion in limine to limit your expert's testimony and the court has ruled on the issue. However, you should consider raising the issue before trial and getting a ruling on what limits, if any, will be imposed on your expert's testimony in light of FRE 703. As the proponent, you should argue to the court that the jury needs to hear all the bases for the expert's conclusions in order to understand the expert's testimony, and that the bases for your expert's conclusions are reliable and trustworthy sources.

Consider the typical kinds of sources experts commonly use to evaluate issues and come to conclusions:

1. Personal examination and study
2. Tests
3. Records
4. Testimony and statements of witnesses
5. Consultation with other experts
6. Treatises

For example, the plaintiff's treating physician in a personal injury case is frequently asked to give opinions on the extent and permanence of the plaintiff's injuries. A treating physician might use the following sources on which to base those opinions: his own examinations, x-rays and lab tests; hospital and other doctors' medical records; medical treatises; conversations with the plaintiff's family members; and consultation with other doctors. Under FRE 703, which bases will the doctor be able to disclose and reveal the contents of? The short answer is none, unless the judge permits otherwise, or unless those bases have an independent ground for being admitted in evidence. You should consider raising the issue, if it has not already been raised, so you will know if there will be any limitations on the expert's testimony, and so you can advise your expert and organize your direct examination to comply with the judge's ruling.

In the preceding doctor example, the judge will probably permit the expert to disclose the contents of x-rays and lab reports, hospital records, other doctors' medical records, and treatises. However, the judge may prohibit the expert from disclosing the contents of conversations with the plaintiff's family members and other doctors on the basis that those are otherwise inadmissible hearsay and are unnecessary for the jury to understand the expert's testimony. Once the judge has ruled, you will need to inform the doctor and modify your planned direct examination accordingly.

b. Expert as Teacher

How the expert discloses the bases for his conclusions and explains how they led to his conclusions is important. This is when you want the expert to become the teacher, helper, and guide who makes it all simple, clear, and easy to understand. Have the expert use visual aids and exhibits. Have him demonstrate things. Have him step down from the witness stand and give his explanations before the jurors.

Before the expert testifies, get the underlying exhibits the expert relied on formally admitted in evidence, whenever possible. Don't use the expert as a foundation witness for exhibits such as medical records and lab reports; these can usually be admitted beforehand through other witnesses, by certification, or by stipulations. Use the expert to qualify only those visual aids that the expert prepared herself, or exhibits, such as treatises, that only the expert can qualify. Note that visual aids that the expert uses to explain the bases for her conclusion can be shown to the jury while the expert testifies. However, visual aids that are not formally admitted in evidence might not be usable during closing argument or sent to the jury room during deliberations.

In addition, don't have the expert read extensively from records and other documents. This is invariably dull. Instead, find the key entries and statements in those records and documents that the expert relied on in reaching her conclusions and have blow-ups (poster boards or PowerPoint slides) of those entries and statements ready so that the expert can refer to them during her testimony.

Example:

> Q: Dr. Smith, did you determine if Mary Ames will be able to resume her career as a professional skater?
>
> A: Yes.
>
> Q: What did you determine?
>
> A: Unfortunately, Mary will never be able to compete at the professional level again.
>
> Q: Are you prepared to explain how you reached that conclusion?
>
> A: Yes, I am.
>
> Q: Your honor, may Dr. Smith continue his testimony before the jury? We've placed certain exhibits and equipment on a table for his use.
>
> JUDGE: Certainly. Please step down, Dr. Smith. [Witness leaves the witness stand and walks to the table in front of the jury box.]
>
> Q: First, tell us why Mary will never be able to compete as a professional skater again.
>
> A: Mary fractured two vertebrae in her back during the collision. Those vertebrae had to be fused to the adjoining vertebrae. Once those vertebrae are fused, they can't move. This means that Mary's back can't bend nearly as much as it could before. Being able to bend your

back is essential to do many of the moves and spins involved in figure skating.

Q: Did you bring any exhibits and visual aids with you today to illustrate how Mary's back was fused?

A: Yes, I have three exhibits here that do this; Exhibits 5 and 6, two x-rays of Mary's back taken just before and after the surgery, and Exhibit 7, a model of the lumbar region of the back—that's the part of the back we call the small of the back, where it curves inward.

Q: Your honor, Exhibits 5, 6, and 7 have already been admitted in evidence. Dr. Smith, using Exhibits 5 and 6, please explain how Mary's back was fused.

A: I'm putting those two x-rays on the shadow box so we can all see them [puts x-rays on back-lighted shadow box positioned so all jurors can see]. The first x-ray, Exhibit 5, was taken before the surgery. When you look here, at the two lumbar vertebrae that are called L-2 and L-3, you can see [pointing] that the bones have been cracked in several places. The cracks are these darker lines. That happened because those vertebrae were crushed together, what doctors call compression fractures. Now look at the second x-ray, Exhibit 6. This was taken right after the surgery. You can see here [pointing] that several screws and bands have been put in those two vertebrae to hold the broken bones in place. The screws and bands are made of stainless steel, and they appear bright. In addition, you can see here [pointing] the larger pins that hold those two vertebrae to the vertebrae directly above and below.

Q: What do those pins have to do with flexibility?

A: They mean that four vertebrae, from L-1 to L-4, are now rigid and can't bend any more.

Q: Is that a permanent condition?

A: Oh, yes. Once you fuse those bones, they can't move.

Q: Dr. Smith, how does that affect Mary's skating?

A: I can best show that by using Exhibit 7, a model of the five lumbar vertebrae. You can see that the vertebrae are numbered from top to bottom, L-1 to L-5, and there is a disc between each one. The discs in this model are blue [pointing]. In a normal spine, like Mary had before the collision, these vertebrae have some flexibility, like this [demonstrating], because the discs are flexible. That's what allows us to move our backs forward and backward [demonstrating], side to side [demonstrating], and to rotate [demonstrating]. In Mary's back, four of these vertebrae, L-1 to L-4, are fused together, so Mary can't bend there at all. That significantly limits her ability to bend and rotate.

Q: Is that significant in skating?

A: It's critical.

Q: Dr. Smith, one last question. In terms of Mary's career as a professional skater, what does all this mean?

A: It means that her career is over.

If the expert has made assumptions that form part of the basis for the expert's testimony, it is better to bring them out as part of the direct examination and explain why the expert made those assumptions and why they are reasonable.

This anticipates and defuses the cross-examination. This is commonly done when economists testify in personal injury and wrongful death cases.

Example:

> Q: Professor Andrews, did you make any assumptions about the rate of inflation over the next 30 years?
> A: Yes, I did.
> Q: What assumptions did you make?
> A: I assumed that inflation rates would vary over the next 30 years, but that the inflation rate for that time period would average out to be 3 percent per year.
> Q: How did you come to decide on 3 percent per year?
> A: Several reasons. First . . .

c. Treatises

Consider using treatises during the direct examination of experts. FRE 803(18) provides that an expert may read statements from published treatises, if the treatise was "relied on by the expert on direct examination" and the treatise is "established as a reliable authority." When you first retain an expert, ask your expert to review the established treatises and incorporate key statements from those treatises in her report. The expert should be allowed to read any statements that support the expert's opinions and explanations during the direct examination.

Example:

> Q: Dr. Spencer, as part of your evaluation of this case, did you rely on any treatises—books—in your field?
> A: Yes.
> Q: Which one?
> A: I relied in part on a standard treatise, *Williams on Obstetrics*.
> Q: Is *Williams on Obstetrics* recognized as a reliable authority in your field?
> A: Absolutely. It's probably the most-used treatise in obstetrics today.
> Q: Did you rely on any statements in *Williams on Obstetrics* during your evaluation of this case?
> A: Yes.
> Q: Do you have that treatise with you?
> A: Yes [holds up treatise], it's been marked as Plaintiff's Exhibit No. 3. I relied particularly on page 353, the section called "Disturbances in the Newborn—Asphyxia." That's the section I found particularly useful.
> Q: Your honor, at this time we ask that Dr. Spencer be allowed to read those statements from the treatise that he relied on in reaching his conclusions.
> JUDGE: He may. Proceed.
> Q: Dr. Spencer, please read those statements.
> A: On page 353 of the treatise, it says: "If an infant does not breathe spontaneously at birth, and the infant is depressed by anesthetic

agents, the infant may be stimulated repeatedly for as long as two minutes by methods such as slapping the feet, before other resuscitation methods are started. However, if central cyanosis develops, positive pressure ventilation must be started immediately."

Many judges also permit projecting the statements from the treatise on a screen or monitor so the jurors can read along with the witness. The treatise itself is not admissible as an exhibit under FRE 803(18).

d. Take Issue with the Other Expert

When an expert testifies, the other side usually will put on an opposing expert with different conclusions, opinions, and reasoning. This is the "dueling experts" situation. Jurors naturally want to get an answer to the obvious question: If this expert is right, why is the other expert wrong? Because the defense expert testifies later, the defense expert is often asked that question. This gives the expert the opportunity to contrast the two evaluations, and show why his conclusions, opinions, and reasoning are more sensible than the other expert's.

Example:

> Q: Mr. Wilshire, are you aware that the plaintiff's expert, Professor Adams, is of the opinion that this all-terrain vehicle has an unreasonably dangerous design?
> A: Yes, I read her report and her deposition, and was told that she testified the same way earlier in this trial.
> Q: Do you agree with her opinion?
> A: No, I certainly don't.
> Q: Tell us why you disagree.
> A: Several reasons. First . . .

This question then gives the defense expert the opportunity to explain why his theory—his conclusions, opinions, and the bases for them—is better reasoned, and has more supporting data, than the other expert's.

Plaintiffs, of course, can also anticipate the defense experts, and they commonly do this in two ways. First, plaintiff's experts are sometimes asked directly if they agree or disagree with the defense expert's approach and conclusions (obtained from that expert's report and deposition testimony). The expert can then testify why he rejects the defense expert's approach. This, of course, anticipates the defense expert's testimony, and gives the jurors reasons to reject the other side's testimony before they hear it. It also anticipates the defense's likely cross-examination of the expert. This is a common inoculation or forewarning technique. Second, plaintiff's experts are sometimes recalled as witnesses in the plaintiff's rebuttal case to explain why they disagree with the experts who testified in the defense case.

e. End Big

Finally, as with any direct examination, end big. What's the most important thing the expert says that helps your case? Try to end on that point, and let the jurors know, through your phrasing, voice, and body language, that you are asking a key question.

Example:

> Q: Professor Wilson, one final question: The design of this toaster-oven, in particular the design of its wiring, is that a reasonably safe design?
> A: No, it's not. The wiring design of that toaster-oven makes it unreasonably dangerous.

Example:

> Q: Dr. Smith, we need the answer to one last question. Will Mr. Jones ever be able to work again as an automotive mechanic?
> A: No, I'm afraid not. The damage to his back is simply too severe. He's going to have to find another line of work.

6. Other Organization

The structure outlined here—introduction, professional qualifications, what expert did, the opinions, and the bases for the opinions—is the most common way to organize expert direct examinations, but it is not the only way. The expert witness rules, FRE 702 to 705, allow flexibility.

a. Opinion Quickly

Remember that jurors today have limited attention spans. That holds true as to expert witnesses, and it is particularly true for successive experts. Jurors want you to get to the bottom line quickly. For that reason, more lawyers are using the flexibility of the rules, particularly FRE 705, to get to the expert's opinions quickly, then loop back for the details. This works particularly well when you know there will be no objections to your expert's qualifications.

Example:

> Q: Professor Adams, did I ask you to examine the electric heater involved in this fire?
> A: Yes, you did.
> Q: What did I ask you to do?
> A: You asked me to examine the design of the heater to determine whether or not the design is unreasonably dangerous.
> Q: Did you do that?
> A: Yes, I completed my study a few months ago.
> Q: Professor Adams, is the design of that electric heater unreasonably dangerous?
> A: Yes, it is.
> Q: Before we get to what you did and how you did it, let's first learn a little about you. You're an electrical engineer?
> A: That's right.

And so on. Some lawyers feel it is more effective to have the expert state his opinions quickly, when all the jurors are listening, then loop back to qualifications and the other direct examination testimony.

b. Hypothetical Question

Finally, the expert witness rules, particularly FRE 702, 703, and 705, have eliminated the need for hypothetical questions. However, the rules still permit you to use them. Some lawyers use hypothetical questions as a vehicle to sum up the key points of their case by calling the expert as the last witness in the case-in-chief.

If you plan to use a hypothetical question, prepare it in advance. Make sure it includes all the undisputed important facts and your side's version of important disputed facts that have been presented during the trial. Make sure your expert is comfortable with the contents of the hypothetical and how it is worded. Consider raising the hypothetical beforehand with the judge, so that any objections to it can be ruled on before the expert testifies before the jury.

Example:

Q: Dr. Young, I'm going to ask you to assume certain facts as true. After that I'm going to ask you some questions based on those facts. Assume:
  1. A female professional figure skater is 24 years old.
  2. On June 1, 2020, she is in perfect health.
  3. On June 2, 2020, she is involved in a vehicle collision.
  4. Among the injuries she received during that collision were compression fractures of the L-2 and L-3 vertebrae.
  5. Doctors at Mercy Hospital operated on her back that day and fused her lumbar vertebrae between the L-1 and L-4 vertebrae.
  6. She made a normal recovery from her injuries and the surgery.
  7. Because of the surgery, she is unable to move her back between the L-1 and L-4 vertebrae.
  8. The limitations to her back are permanent.
  Dr. Young, based on these facts, are you able to determine if she will ever be able to resume her career as a competitive figure skater?
A: Yes, I can.
Q: What is your determination?
A: This woman will never be able to compete again as a competitive figure skater.

8.6 Example of Direct Examination

The following direct examination is from a case where the trial judge had already ruled that the bases of the expert's conclusions and opinions were admissible under FRE 703. It involves an orthopedist who testifies to her treatment of the plaintiff following an automobile accident in a personal injury case. The witness is testifying in the plaintiff's case.

Introduction.

Q: Dr. Klein, please introduce yourself to the jury.

This is a modern introduction that immediately lets the jurors know what the witness will testify about.

A: My name is Michelle Klein. I'm a doctor specializing in orthopedics.
Q: Dr. Klein, you treated Mr. Gable at the Mercy Hospital emergency room on June 1, 2020?
A: Yes.
Q: And you supervised his recovery and therapy afterwards?
A: That's right.
Q: Dr. Klein, are you prepared today to tell us about Mr. Gable's elbow and what the future holds for him?
A: Yes, I am.

Background — Education and Training.

Q: Dr. Klein, let's start by learning a little about you. You went to Stanford University?
A: Yes.
Q: And medical school at Yale?
A: That's right.
Q: When did you graduate from Yale Medical School?
A: In 1985.
Q: Where did you do your residency?
A: At Massachusetts General Hospital in Boston.

Note the transition question to the new topic.

Q: Please tell us about your residency training.
A: My residency was in orthopedics, which is the area of medicine that deals with injuries and diseases of the bones, muscles, and joints. It's a four-year program. What you do is treat patients with orthopedic problems under the supervision of recognized specialists, so you become experienced in diagnosing and treating the conditions that patients have. I completed the residency in 1989.
Q: Dr. Klein, you're licensed to practice medicine in this state?
A: Yes, since 1990.

Board certification is an impressive credential and should always be brought out.

Q: You're also board certified as a specialist in orthopedics?
A: Yes.
Q: Aren't all orthopedists board certified?
A: No.
Q: How does a doctor become board certified in orthopedics?
A: Each medical specialty is controlled by a board. In orthopedics, it's the American Board of Orthopedics. You are eligible to take the exam, which is a two-day exam, after completing your residency. I took the exam, passed it, and became board certified in 1991.
Q: Is being board certified the highest level of certification recognized in your field?
A: Yes.

Note what was *not* brought out: memberships in professional organizations and publications history.

Q: Dr. Klein, you also teach?
A: Yes, I'm a clinical assistant professor at the state university medical school.
Q: What do you teach?
A: I teach in the orthopedics residency program, helping doctors become specialists in orthopedics.
Q: How long have you been teaching there?
A: Eight years.

Background—Experience.

Another transition question.

Q: Dr. Klein, let's turn now to your actual experience treating patients. You have your own practice in orthopedics?
A: Yes.
Q: Tell us about your practice.
A: I've had my own office here since 1994. My practice is full time, and is limited to patients with orthopedic problems.
Q: Have you ever treated patients with joint problems?
A: Of course.
Q: Have you treated patients with joint dislocations?
A: Yes. I probably see a dislocation two or three times a week in my office.
Q: Dr. Klein, in this case Mr. Gable suffered a dislocation of his right elbow. Have you ever treated patients with that particular condition before?

For most jurors, this is the most impressive credential: actual hands-on experience.

A: Many times. Elbow dislocations are quite common. You see them often in athletes and children.
Q: Since 1994, about how many patients have you treated for elbow dislocations?
A: I can only estimate. I see that two or three times a month, so I've treated a few hundred elbow dislocations over the years.

This would be a good place to introduce the expert's résumé, which details his education, training, and experience.

What Expert Did—Hospital.

Q: Dr. Klein, let's turn now to June 1, 2020, when you treated Mr. Gable at the Mercy Hospital emergency room. How did you come to treat him there?
A: I was the orthopedist on call that day. I was called when Mr. Gable was being brought by ambulance to the emergency room.
Q: Tell us what happened in the emergency room.

A: I met Mr. Gable in the ER shortly after he arrived. He was on a stretcher in one of the examining rooms. He was in pain, but he was coherent and I found out from him what happened.

Q: What was that?

This patient statement is properly admissible under FRE 803(4).

Note how the doctor gives simple explanations.

A: He said he was in an automobile collision. He had braced himself before the crash, and the force of the crash threw him forward. He thought his arm was broken.

Q: What did you do?

A: Two basic things. I gave him a physical examination. He seemed to have no injuries other than an elbow dislocation in his right elbow. It was rather obvious, because of the bone displacement, that his elbow was out of alignment. I then had x-rays taken of his right arm with a portable x-ray unit. The x-rays showed that no bones in the arm were broken, but that Mr. Gable had a posterior dislocation of the elbow joint.

Q: What's a posterior dislocation?

A: That's when the bones of the lower arm, the ulna and radius, are pushed back and behind the bone of the upper arm, the humerus. This often happens when people fall and instinctively put their arm out to break the fall. The elbow can't take that kind of stress, so it dislocates at the joint.

A visual aid is always a good idea.

Q: Dr. Klein, I'm showing you a model of an elbow joint, marked Plaintiff's Exhibit No. 6 [Figure 8.1]. Using the model, please explain what happens to the elbow joint in a dislocation.

Analogies are also useful.

A: Sure. In a posterior dislocation, the lower arm is pushed back, behind the upper arm, like this [demonstrating]. The joint is normally held together by several ligaments, which are colored blue on this model. The ligaments are like nylon straps. They are flexible, but only for the normal range of motion of the joint. A dislocation stretches and sometimes tears the ligaments, since the bones in a dislocation are separated beyond the normal range of motion of the joint [demonstrating]. There may also be other damage, most commonly bleeding into the joint and soft tissue damage.

Q: How did you treat Mr. Gable?

A: I used the standard treatment for this type of injury. He was taken up to surgery and given a general anesthetic. I then set his arm while he was unconscious, took another series of x-rays to make sure the bones were in proper alignment at the elbow joint, and then applied a plaster cast on the arm, which held the arm in a right angle.

Q: How did you set the arm?

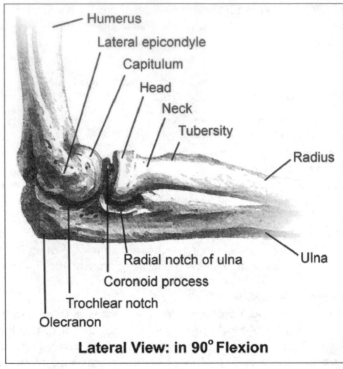

Fig. 8.1 Model of Elbow Joint

Describing how the joint was actually set is important.

A: It's a standard procedure. When the patient is unconscious, the muscles relax. With the help of the surgical staff, you steadily pull on the lower arm until it slides back into its proper location. Most of the time, you can pop the lower arm back in place without surgery. That in fact happened with Mr. Gable.

Q: Did Mr. Gable get any medication following your setting the elbow?

A: Yes, he was prescribed a pain killer and an anti-inflammatory drug to keep down the swelling. Again, that's standard treatment.

Q: How long did Mr. Gable remain at the hospital?

A: He was discharged a few hours later. Like all surgical patients, he spent some time in the recovery room to make sure his vital signs were normal. After he woke up, I talked to him, gave him the prescriptions for the medications, and made arrangements to see him in my office in four weeks. Later that day his wife took him home.

What Expert Did — Therapy.

Q: Dr. Klein, let's turn next to the time you removed Mr. Gable's cast and therapy began. When did that happen?

A: One month later. I saw Mr. Gable in my office. I sawed off the cast using a vibrating saw and examined the arm. It was in the condition you would expect.

Q: What condition was that?

This testimony corroborates the plaintiff's earlier testimony.

A: The arm was smaller, because the muscles shrink when not used. The range of motion was approximately 10 degrees to either side of a right angle, like this [demonstrating].

Q: Why couldn't the arm move more?

A: In an injury like this, the ligaments are damaged. Putting the arm in a cast gives the ligaments time to begin healing. Unfortunately, the ligaments also shrink and quickly lose their ability to stretch, limiting the range of motion.

Q: So you were expecting it?

A: Yes, it always happens in injuries like this.

The therapy program.

Q: Dr. Klein, tell us about the therapy program you put Mr. Gable on.

A: It was the standard therapy. To regain the normal range of motion, the patient soaks his elbow in hot water for 10 to 15 minutes, then slowly stretches the arm back and forth. This stretches the ligaments. This needs to be done three or four times a day. If all goes well, most patients regain full range of motion in a few weeks.

Q: Is this painful?

A: Sure. It's painful for everyone, and the amount of pain is related to the amount of damage to the ligaments and soft tissue.

This is an important point, as the defense will argue that the plaintiff did not do his therapy fully.

Q: Did Mr. Gable do the therapy?

A: Yes.

Q: How do you know?

A: Because the range of motion got much better. The next time I saw him, about four weeks after removing the cast, he had regained most of the normal range of motion. This would not happen unless he did the therapy.

Q: How much motion had he regained?

A: He could flex his arm like this [demonstrating] all the way up. He could extend his arm like this [demonstrating] most of the way, but was still missing the last 20 to 30 degrees of full extension [demonstrating].

Q: Did you discuss this with him?

A: Yes, I told him to keep doing the therapy to try to get full extension.

Q: Did he ever regain full extension of the right arm?

A: No. He kept doing the therapy for several more weeks, but never regained the last 20 to 30 degrees of extension.

Q: Why was that?

This explanation is essential to the plaintiff's case.

A: Not all patients with elbow dislocations regain full range of motion, no matter how hard they work at the therapy. The reason is that the ligaments, after being stretched and torn in a dislocation, lose some of their flexibility. They just never flex as well again. In addition, torn ligaments develop scar tissue when they heal. Scar tissue does not flex well, and the scar tissue can interfere with the joint itself. The scar tissue acts like a wood shim in the hinge of a door, that keeps it from opening or closing completely.

Q: Have you had other patients with an elbow injury like Mr. Gable who have also not regained full range of motion afterwards?

One of plaintiff's case themes is "15 percent."

A: Yes. I'd say about 15 percent never regain it completely, based on my experience and the medical literature.

Q: Even though they do the therapy program?

A: That's right.

Expert's Conclusions.

(1) Permanent condition

Q: Dr. Klein, is Mr. Gable's limited range of motion in his right elbow a permanent condition?

A: Yes. Given the length of time he did the therapy, the time since the injury, and his age, in all likelihood that's the way his arm is going to be for the rest of his life.

(2) Work as a mechanic

Q: Let's turn finally to what all this means to Mr. Gable. You know he worked as an automobile mechanic, right?

A: Yes, he told me about his job.

Q: Will Mr. Gable ever be able to work again as an automobile mechanic?

A: No, I don't think so.

Q: Why not?

Bases for Conclusions.

This is where the expert assumes the teacher role. Many lawyers will have the expert step down from the witness stand and use exhibits and visual aids when the explanations are relatively complicated.

A: Two basic reasons. First, he does not have full range of motion in the elbow joint. His job as a mechanic requires that he have full range of motion in both arms. Second, and just as important, his right elbow joint is not as strong as it once was. The ligaments have been damaged, and have lost strength. Again, his job requires full strength in both arms. In short, his elbow is simply not up to taking the kind of repetitive strain that is put on the arm in mechanic work.

Ending.

Q: Dr. Klein, isn't there something you, or other orthopedic specialists, can do to get Mr. Gable's right elbow back to normal so he can return to his job?

A: Unfortunately, no. Doctors can't perform miracles. I'm afraid Mr. Gable's elbow is as good now as it's ever going to get. That's the way it's going to be for the rest of his life.

Q: Nothing further on direct, your honor.

8.7 Cross-Examination

There is a maxim all doctors learn in their first days in medical school: "First, do no harm." That maxim applies equally to cross-examination, and in particular to cross-examination of experts. Experts know more about the subject matter than you do. Most are experienced courtroom witnesses. Some will be dangerous advocates for a position and will hurt you whenever they can. What does this mean for cross-examiners?

> ⊕ For additional examples of expert direct and cross-examinations, see Chapter 8 on the accompanying website.

First, don't show off. Resist the urge to throw around technical terms or ask fancy questions that only show you also know something about the subject matter. Jurors don't care, and you will never be as knowledgeable as the expert. Second, keep your expectations reasonable. Rarely will you be able to destroy the other side's expert. Cross-examination of experts, like cross-examination in general, is your opportunity to create doubts about the opposing expert and his testimony. Third, remember that in trials there are usually opposing experts. They have theirs, and you have yours. Do you need to make this point during cross-examination of the opposing expert, or can you establish the same point, more safely, with your own expert? In short, keep your cross-examinations of experts short, simple, and safe.

> ◼◣ For a discussion of both friendly and adverse expert witnesses that emphasizes the challenges and opportunities of cross-examination, please watch Video F.1, "Wyo STI: Expert Witnesses."

1. Preparation

Preparation, of course, is the key to cross-examination, and that's particularly true with experts. First, learn everything you can about the subject matter. Get the leading treatises, textbooks, and articles; read them, and make sure you understand them. Your own expert can help you here. Though you will not become as knowledgeable as the expert, you must become knowledgeable about the specific subject matter involved in your case.

Second, learn everything you can about the opposing expert's background. Research her résumé. Make sure she has all the credentials she claims to have. Look for gaps in the résumé; these may indicate that the expert is hiding part of her history. Obtain copies of every book and article the expert has ever written and read them. Internet searches can be productive.

Third, learn everything you can about the opposing expert's involvement in litigation, both in this case and in previous cases. In civil cases, review the expert's report (required under the disclosure obligations of Fed. R. Civ. P. 26) and the expert's deposition transcript. Just as important, get copies of the expert's reports, deposition testimony, and trial testimony in all previous cases. Rule 26 requires disclosure of the expert's litigation history for the previous four years, but go back as far as you can. Certain organizations, including the American Association for Justice and the Defense Research Institute, have databases on experts that list all the cases in which that expert has previously testified. E-mail members of your firm and other trial lawyer friends to learn if any has had experience with this expert.

In criminal cases, disclosure requirements and discovery rights are frequently minimal, so you may need to do your own investigation to uncover this information. For example, Fed. R. Crim. P. 16 permits discovery only of "results or reports of physical or mental examinations, and of any scientific tests or experiment," and a "written summary of testimony" of experts each side intends to use at trial.

Fourth, use your own consulting expert to prepare the cross-examination of the opposing expert. Your expert can help review the opposing expert's résumé, report, and deposition transcript to find fertile areas for cross-examination. Your own expert can be your sounding board as you develop your cross-examination. Keep in mind that Rule 26(b)(4) provides for trial preparation protection for some, but not all, communications between the lawyer and the testifying expert in civil cases. Therefore, if your client can afford to allow you to do so, it is beneficial to hire a consulting expert who is not expected to testify to help you prepare for cross-examination of the opposing expert.

2. Specific Topics

You are now ready to focus on the actual planned cross-examination of the opposing expert. Always ask the key questions: Do I need to cross this expert? Did the expert say anything that hurts me? Is the expert's background vulnerable? Did the expert do, or fail to do, something that makes him vulnerable? Are the expert's opinions vulnerable? Are the bases of the expert's opinions vulnerable? Always consider the following topics for cross-examining any expert.

a. Expert's Qualifications

An easy attack on an expert's qualifications is to point out that the expert has not yet attained the highest degree or certification attainable in that field. However, this kind of cross-examination will be effective only if your own expert has credentials superior to those of the expert you are cross-examining.

Example:

> Q: Dr. Wilson, board certification by the American Board of Internal Medicine is the highest level of certification in your specialty?
> A: Yes.
> Q: You said earlier that you were board eligible?
> A: Yes.
> Q: Board eligible is not the same thing as board certified, is it?
> A: No.
> Q: To become board certified, you need to take and pass the board examinations?
> A: Yes.
> Q: And you haven't done that, right?
> A: Not yet.

Another common attack is to show that the expert has little or no hands-on experience in the field. This can be effective when cross-examining professors and other academics, especially if your expert has significant work experience, because jurors put substantial weight on such experience.

Example:

> Q: Professor Andrews, you received your doctorate degree in electrical engineering in 2000?
> A: That's right.
> Q: The year you graduated, you were hired as an assistant professor at the university?
> A: Yes.
> Q: And you've been at the university ever since?
> A: Yes.
> Q: You teach, research, and write?
> A: Yes.
> Q: Professor Andrews, have you ever worked for a company that makes toaster-ovens?
> A: No.
> Q: Have you ever worked for a company that makes any kind of electrical consumer product?
> A: No.
> Q: Have you ever designed a toaster-oven?
> A: No.
> Q: Have you ever designed any kind of electrical consumer product?
> A: No.

Another common, and subtler, cross-examination is to show that although the expert has expertise, the focus of that expertise is in a different area than the one involved in the trial. This cross-examination builds up the expert's real expertise, then points out that it has no real bearing on the trial issues.

Example:

> Q: Dr. Kelliher, you've written numerous articles on psychiatry over the past 30 years, right?
> A: Yes.
> Q: In fact, your résumé lists over 30 articles?
> A: Yes.
> Q: Almost all of those articles deal with mental conditions of elderly patients?
> A: Yes.
> Q: And they deal with mental conditions such as Alzheimer's disease?
> A: Yes.
> Q: Short-term memory loss?
> A: Yes.
> Q: And depression?
> A: Yes.
> Q: Dr. Kelliher, in this criminal case, the issue is whether the defendant was insane at the time he killed the victim, right?
> A: Yes.
> Q: Of your 30 articles, how many of them deal with the mental state of criminal defendants, right?
> A: None.

Q: Of your 30 articles, none of them deals with paranoid schizophrenia, right?

A: That's true.

b. Bias and Interest

Evidence of bias and interest is important to jurors, who expect experts to be impartial and not wedded to a particular point of view. A common cross-examination approach is to show that the expert is a professional witness who widely advertises his services.

Example:

Q: Mr. Erickson, you like being hired as an expert witness, don't you?

A: I'm willing to be a witness if someone wants to engage me.

Q: You advertise your services in *Trial* magazine?

A: I have a professional announcement there, yes.

Q: That's the magazine published for plaintiffs' lawyers?

A: Yes.

Q: You also advertise your services in *DRI*, right?

A: Yes.

Q: That's the magazine published for defense lawyers?

A: Yes.

Q: You also advertise your services in state bar journals?

A: Yes.

Q: And you advertise your services in the *ABA Journal*?

A: Yes.

Q: That's the journal published by the American Bar Association?

A: Yes.

Q: That's the journal that gets mailed to about 400,000 lawyers every month?

A: I don't know how many lawyers receive it.

A related approach is to demonstrate how much money the expert derives from testifying. Again, this kind of cross-examination is effective only if you can contrast it with your own expert.

Example:

Q: Mr. Higgins, you're self-employed?

A: At present, yes.

Q: You work out of your home?

A: My office is at home, yes.

Q: Over the past 4 years you've testified in depositions and trials in 23 cases, correct?

A: I'm not sure of the exact number.

Q: You listed 23 cases in your expert report, correct?

A: If you say so.

Q: Would you like to take another look at your report to see how many cases you said you've testified in during the past 4 years?

A: No.

Q: In each of those cases you were paid?

A: Yes.

> Q: And in this case you're being paid?
> A: Yes.
> Q: In this case you're charging $600 per hour?
> A: Yes.
> Q: And you've billed for over $18,000 in this case so far?
> A: Yes.
> Q: That's $18,000 so far, in 1 of 24 cases, in the past 4 years?
> A: Yes.

Another related approach is to expose the expert who holds himself out as a "jack of all trades." See if the expert claims, on his résumé or in advertisements, to have expertise in many areas. Check the other cases in which he has submitted an expert report or testified, to see the issues on which he claims expertise.

Example:

> Q: Mr. Jackson, you say you are an expert in engineering safety issues?
> A: Yes.
> Q: You advertise yourself like that, right?
> A: I have a professional announcement where I set out my areas of expertise.
> Q: You have what you call a professional announcement in the June 2020 issue of the *ABA Journal?*
> A: Yes.
> Q: In that issue you call yourself an expert in "forensic engineering," right?
> A: Yes.
> Q: You say you are an expert in accident reconstruction?
> A: Yes.
> Q: In construction defects?
> A: Yes.
> Q: Machine guards?
> A: Yes.
> Q: Motorcycle helmets?
> A: Yes.
> Q: Traffic safety?
> A: Yes.
> Q: Boat safety?
> A: Yes.
> Q: Did I miss anything?
> A: I'm not sure.

If the witness testifies exclusively or predominantly for plaintiffs or defendants, or has testified repeatedly for a particular lawyer or law firm, this is a fertile area for cross-examination.

Example:

> Q: Dr. Adams, you've been retained as an economics expert 16 times over the past 4 years?
> A: Yes.
> Q: Almost all of those 16 times involved the issue of the economic loss to the surviving spouse and children in wrongful death cases?
> A: Yes, that's my area.

Q: In those 16 cases, you were always retained by the plaintiff's lawyer?
A: Yes.
Q: Not once by the defense, right?
A: Yes.

Example:

Q: Ms. Smith, you've known the defense lawyer, Mr. Campbell, for several years?
A: Yes.
Q: Mr. Campbell hired you as a defense expert in this case?
A: He retained me, yes.
Q: Mr. Campbell has hired you in other cases?
A: Yes.
Q: In fact, this is the sixth case in which you have been hired as an expert witness by Mr. Campbell, right?
A: Yes.
Q: And in those 5 other cases, you were paid over $90,000 for your work, right?
A: I'm not sure, but that sounds about right.

c. Data Relied on

If the expert relied on information or data from secondhand sources, and made no attempt to verify their accuracy, this can be a fertile topic for cross-examination, if you have evidence that the information was inaccurate. It may also create an opportunity to get the expert to criticize his own party or the party's lawyer for not supplying all the data that could have been provided.

Example:

Q: Dr. Barnes, in reaching your opinions, you relied on the accident reports prepared by the police, correct?
A: In part, yes.
Q: Those reports contained interviews of witnesses to the accident?
A: Yes.
Q: Those were the reports that the plaintiff's lawyer sent to you?
A: That's right.
Q: You assumed that the plaintiff's lawyer sent you all the police reports?
A: Yes.
Q: You assumed that the reports accurately recorded what the witnesses said?
A: Yes, I had no reason to believe otherwise.
Q: You assumed that the witnesses accurately reported what they saw?
A: Yes.
Q: You didn't interview those witnesses yourself, did you?
A: No, I didn't.
Q: Your opinion assumes that the information from the witnesses contained in the police reports is accurate, right?
A: Yes.

If the expert relied on biased sources of information, this can easily be exposed. This is frequently the basis for attacks on the testimony of psychiatric experts, who rely on interviews of the patient and family members.

Example:

> Q: Dr. McCarthy, as part of your evaluation of the defendant's state of mind, you talked to his family members?
>
> A: Yes, that's part of every evaluation.
>
> Q: You talked to his mother?
>
> A: Yes.
>
> Q: His father?
>
> A: Yes.
>
> Q: And his sister?
>
> A: Yes.
>
> Q: All of them claimed that the defendant had experienced various psychiatric episodes during the past few years?
>
> A: That's right.
>
> Q: Dr. McCarthy, what efforts did you make to verify the accuracy of the information the defendant's mother, father, and sister gave you?
>
> A: I didn't, other than comparing them with other interviews and medical records.
>
> Q: What efforts did you take to determine if that information was exaggerated?
>
> A: I didn't.
>
> Q: Your opinion relies significantly on that information, right?
>
> A: Not entirely, but the family members were an important source.
>
> Q: You also interviewed the defendant?
>
> A: Of course.
>
> Q: When you interviewed him, he had been charged with murder?
>
> A: Yes.
>
> Q: His lawyer asked you to evaluate him to determine if he could raise an insanity defense?
>
> A: He asked me to evaluate his mental state, yes.
>
> Q: And the defendant knew why you were interviewing him, right?
>
> A: Yes.

d. Assumptions

If the expert made assumptions that are either wrong or cannot be verified, cross-examination should bring this out. This is frequently the basis for attacks on the testimony of economic experts.

Example:

> Q: Mr. Higgins, your calculations of the future economic loss to Mrs. Adams, caused by the loss of her husband, are based on certain assumptions, right?
>
> A: Of course.
>
> Q: You assumed that Mr. Adams would have worked for 30 more years?

A: Yes.

Q: You don't know if Mr. Adams in fact would have worked for 30 more years had he lived, do you?

A: Not with total certainty, no.

Q: You assumed that the rate of return for safe investments in the future would be 4 percent?

A: Yes.

Q: You don't know in fact if it will be 4 percent, do you?

A: No, that's my best estimate of what will happen in the future.

Q: Mr. Higgins, if any of your assumptions about the future are wrong, then your calculations will also be wrong, isn't that so?

A: It would affect my calculations, yes.

Cross-examination can go a step further: Change the assumptions and show how such a change would affect the conclusion. For example, even a small change in investment rates would have a significant effect on the final yield if a sum of money is invested over a substantial period of time.

Example:

Q: Professor Higgins, if the interest rate of safe investments over the next 30 years is actually 3 percent, not the 4 percent you estimate, that would change your calculations of the present value of lost future income, right?

A: Yes.

Q: In this case, your calculations of the present value of lost future income would then be about $100,000 too high, right?

A: I don't know the exact amount, but it would be in that range.

Q: If the interest rate is actually 2 percent, not 4 percent, your calculations would be off by another $100,000?

A: If the rate is actually 2 percent, yes.

e. **What Expert Did Not Do**

If an expert did not do all the things that could or should have been done under the circumstances, this will affect the weight of the expert's testimony.

Example:

Q: Officer Smith, as a member of the DUI squad, you've received specialized training to determine if a driver is under the influence of alcohol, right?

A: That's right.

Q: And you've had experience in administering those tests?

A: That's right.

Q: Those tests are called field tests?

A: Yes.

Q: One of the field tests is walking a straight line?

A: Yes.

Q: Another is touching the finger to the nose?

A: Yes.

Q: Another is writing the alphabet?

A: Yes.

Q: And another is counting backwards?
A: Yes.
Q: In this case, you had Mr. Johnson do the walking test?
A: That's right.
Q: You never had him do the finger-to-nose?
A: No, I didn't.
Q: Or writing the alphabet?
A: No, I didn't.
Q: Or counting backwards?
A: No, I didn't.

This approach is a common way to cross-examine medical experts in failure-to-diagnose cases. You can identify all the procedures and tests that can be done to diagnose a particular disease or condition, and then show that some of these were never done.

Example:

Q: Dr. Zimmerman, there are several ways to determine whether a patient has breast cancer, right?
A: Certainly.
Q: The doctor can do a breast exam for the presence of any lumps?
A: Yes.
Q: The doctor can order a mammogram?
A: Yes.
Q: The doctor can do a needle biopsy of any lumps?
A: Yes.
Q: The doctor can do an incisional biopsy of any lumps?
A: Yes.
Q: The doctor can examine the biopsy specimen under a microscope?
A: Yes.
Q: The doctor can test the biopsy specimen for estrogen levels?
A: Yes.
Q: The doctor can test for liver function?
A: Yes.
Q: And there are a number of other procedures and tests available to help diagnose whether a patient has breast cancer?
A: That's true.
Q: In this case, Dr. Zimmerman, you did a physical exam for lumps?
A: That's right.
Q: You had a mammogram taken?
A: That's right.
Q: But you never did a biopsy, did you?
A: That's true.
Q: Never examined any biopsy specimen, did you?
A: That's true.
Q: Never tested any biopsy specimen?
A: That's true.
Q: You never did those other procedures or tests to determine if Mrs. Hayes had breast cancer, right?
A: That's right.

f. Prior Inconsistent Statements

One of the most effective cross-examinations is to show that, in the past, the expert said something substantially different from what she is now saying. Common sources of impeaching statements are the expert's report, deposition transcript, transcripts of the expert's testimony in other depositions and trials, and the expert's publications. All of these are fertile sources of prior inconsistent statements.

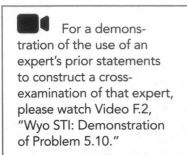 For a demonstration of the use of an expert's prior statements to construct a cross-examination of that expert, please watch Video F.2, "Wyo STI: Demonstration of Problem 5.10."

Effective impeachment with prior inconsistent statements requires both technique and attitude. Remember the 3Cs technique—commit, credit, and confront—discussed in Section 6.7. Commit the expert to her testimony, credit the impeaching source, confront the expert with the prior statement, and *stop*. Project the attitude you want the jurors to adopt about this expert as you impeach: Is this inconsistency a mistake, or is the expert intentionally changing her positions? Your tone and body language have to signal the appropriate attitude.

Example (Expert Report):

Q: Dr. Burns, you say today it is highly unlikely that Ms. Erickson will ever be able to return to her job as a customer service representative?
A: That's right.
Q: That's your opinion today?
A: That's right.
Q: Dr. Burns, you prepared a written report in this case?
A: Yes.
Q: You signed it?
A: Yes.
Q: You have a copy of your report, marked Defendant's Exhibit No. 4, with you?
A: Yes.
Q: Turn to page 6 of your report, the second full paragraph. Your report says. "It is difficult to determine whether the surgery on Ms. Erickson's back will preclude her from returning to her previous job, or whether it will cause any limitations in her daily activities." Did I read it right?
A: That's what it says.
Q: That's what you wrote six months ago?
A: Yes.

Example (Deposition):

Q: Professor Winter, this isn't the first time you've testified in this case, is it?
A: No.
Q: You testified about three months ago when you had your deposition taken, right?
A: That's right.
Q: That's when I asked you questions and you answered them under oath?

A: Yes.

Q: Later on you had a chance to look at a booklet, called the deposition transcript, that had all the questions and answers from your deposition?

A: Yes, I saw it.

Q: You had a chance to make any corrections?

A: Yes.

Q: And you signed it to show that the questions and answers were accurately recorded, right?

A: Yes, I signed it.

Q: Professor Winter, today you take the position that the design of this motorcycle helmet with a three-inch brim is an unreasonably dangerous design, right?

A: That's right.

Q: And that's because any brim three inches long is always unreasonably dangerous?

A: That's right.

Q: [Have deposition transcript marked as an exhibit, show it to opposing counsel, and then the witness.] Let's turn to page 66 of your deposition transcript, beginning at line 4. I'm going to read a question asked and the answer you gave that day. Please follow along to make sure I read it word for word:

"Q: Professor, is it your contention that all motorcycle helmets with a brim three inches long are unreasonably dangerous?

A: Yes, but only if the brim is a fixed brim. A brim that snaps on and off could be different."

Professor, did I read that right, word for word?

A: Yes.

g. Treatises

Impeachment with an authoritative treatise can be powerful. In the jurors' minds, a treatise represents the collective wisdom in a particular field and would not have been published if it were not authoritative. If an expert's testimony conflicts with a treatise, jurors will usually believe the treatise, unless the expert presents a compelling reason why he disagrees with it. A sound procedure is to ask every expert during his deposition what treatises he considers to be reliable authorities in his field, and then review those treatises for any conflicts with the expert's report and deposition testimony. These conflicts will be the basis for the impeachment during trial.

Impeachment with treatises is controlled by FRE 803(18), which requires that the treatise must be published, brought to the "attention of the expert witness on cross-examination," and established as a "reliable authority" through the testimony or admission of the witness or by other expert testimony or by judicial notice. The treatise can then be used to impeach, which is done by reading statements in the treatise "into evidence." The treatise itself is not admissible as an exhibit. Most judges permit the statements from the treatise to be projected on a screen or monitor so jurors can follow along as the lawyer reads them. Give the court clerk a copy of the page so that it can be marked as an exhibit and included in the trial record.

Example (Doctor):

Q: Doctor, your view is that if a patient does the prescribed physical therapy, every patient should return to a full range of motion in the elbow joint?

A: Yes, that's what the therapy is intended to accomplish.

Q: And your view is that if the patient does that therapy, he should always be able to have full range of motion?

A: Yes.

Q: Doctor, you're familiar with Goldstein's medical treatise called *Orthopedics and Trauma?*

A: Yes.

Q: In fact, that treatise is recognized as a reliable authority in the field of orthopedics, right?

A: I think that's probably true.

Q: It's a frequently used text in medical schools?

A: Yes.

Q: It's a frequently used reference by orthopedists?

A: Yes.

Q: You've probably referred to it from time to time?

A: Probably.

Q: In fact, you have a copy of the treatise in your office, don't you?

A: Yes.

Q: Doctor, I'm going to read from page 734 of Goldstein's treatise, *Orthopedics and Trauma,* which the court clerk has already marked as Defendant's Exhibit No. 42, and counsel has already seen. I've put that page on the screen and highlighted the first two sentences of the second paragraph. Please follow along to make sure I read those two sentences word for word. They read: "When elbow dislocations cause enough damage to soft tissues in the joint, therapy alone may not result in the return of full range of motion. Medical studies have shown that 10% to 20% of such patients experience an incomplete recovery." Doctor, did I read that right?

A: Yes.

Example (Fingerprint Expert):

Q: Sergeant, you say that there is a match between a latent print, taken from the robbery scene, and Mr. Johnson's known right index fingerprint?

A: That's right.

Q: You say that because you found eight identical characteristics between the latent print and the known print?

A: Yes.

Q: You say eight matches is enough to make a positive identification?

A: In this case, eight was enough.

Q: Sergeant, you're familiar with the reference book *Scientific Evidence in Civil and Criminal Cases?*

A: I've heard of it.

Q: [Have book marked as an exhibit, show it to opposing counsel, and show it to the witness.] This book, which has just been marked

Defendant's Exhibit No. 6, is a reliable authority in the field of finger-print identification, isn't it?

A: I can't say that. That's not the reference work our crime lab uses.

DIRECT EXAMINER: Your honor, we will establish the reliability of the reference book when we call Mr. Adams in our case-in-chief.

JUDGE: On that representation, you may continue your cross-examination.

Q: Sergeant, I'm going to read from page 514 in *Scientific Evidence in Civil and Criminal Cases*. Follow along with me [standing next to witness and pointing to the page]. It says: "By tradition, but not by empirical studies, latent print examiners in the United States have required a matching of at least six to eight characteristics in both prints for identity, though most experts prefer at least 10–12 concordances." That's what it says, right?

A: That's what it says there.

As the direct examiner, make sure that the cross-examiner uses the treatise fairly. Under FRE 106, whenever part of a writing is introduced during the trial, an adverse party can require that other parts of the writing be introduced at that time if those other parts "in fairness ought to be considered at the same time." The rule prevents reading parts of a writing to create an unfair or misleading impression. If the cross-examiner is reading only part of a treatise and is leaving out other parts that change the tenor of the impeachment, make the objection.

Example:

LAWYER: Objection, your honor. Counsel is reading only the first part of the statement. Under Rule 106, I would like to read the rest of the statement.

h. Using Opposing Expert to Build Up Your Expert

Consider using the expert to ratify what your expert did. When this happens, you can later argue that even the opposing expert agreed with your expert's performance. This is a common approach when your expert is a treating physician and the opposing expert never treated the patient. It is a safe technique to use when you have no direct ammunition to deploy against the other expert.

Example:

Q: Dr. Torres, you didn't treat the plaintiff, did you?

A: No.

Q: You became involved much later?

A: Yes.

Q: Dr. Klein's examination of the plaintiff in the emergency room, that's what you would do?

A: On the whole, yes.

Q: Dr. Klein's reduction of the fracture, that was done in a medically sound way?

A: Yes.

Q: The therapy program that Dr. Klein structured for the plaintiff, that was a sound program?

A: Yes, the therapy was the standard one orthopedists prescribe.

Q: The medication Dr. Klein prescribed to deal with the swelling and pain, those were good choices?

A: Yes.

i. Experts Disagree

Consider "neutralizing" the experts. This is another safe technique if you have no real ammunition against the opposing expert. If the expert will agree that experts in her field sometimes disagree and can have different opinions, the experts will cancel each other out in the jurors' eyes. The "experts sometimes disagree" routine is a good one to use when sympathies or common sense support your side. You can later argue that when even the experts can't agree, it's up to the jurors to resolve the issue and do what's right.

Example:

Q: Dr. Mason, psychiatrists don't always agree on everything, do they?

A: Not always.

Q: That's because psychiatry is not a precise science?

A: Well, I'd say it's an interpretative field.

Q: And interpretations can differ?

A: Yes.

Q: Just because one psychiatrist has a professional disagreement with another psychiatrist doesn't necessarily mean that one is right and the other one is wrong?

A: Not necessarily.

Q: Even good psychiatrists can disagree with each other?

A: Yes.

Q: You know the defense psychiatrist, Dr. Gladstone?

A: Yes.

Q: You respect each other, don't you?

A: I hope so.

Q: Even if from time to time you may disagree over something?

A: Yes.

Q: Dr. Mason, when two experts disagree, it's up to the jury to decide which one to believe, isn't it?

A: I suppose so.

j. Order of Cross-Examination Points

Finally, decide which of these cross-examination points are good enough to use with each expert, and decide on the order of your points. The best two points should be the beginning and end of your cross-examination. Starting big is important. Jurors will give you little time to demonstrate that your cross-examination is worth listening to before they tune out.

Ending big is also important. Your last point should hang in the air, so that jurors know you have established something important and you can end on a note of triumph. Have a safe harbor, though. If your planned ending does not go well, have an alternative ending that is completely safe. Too many expert cross-examinations end on a negative note because the expert did not agree with what you had intended to be your final point.

8.8 Example of Cross-Examination

The witness being cross-examined is Dr. Klein, whose direct examination appears in Section 8.6.

Q: Dr. Klein, you've heard the saying: "Patient, heal thyself"?
A: Certainly.
Q: That's a phrase all doctors learn in medical school?
A: Yes.
Q: That's because every patient has to take responsibility for his own recovery, right?
A: That's certainly part of it.
Q: Doctors can't force patients to get better, can they?
A: No, the patient needs to cooperate with the doctor.
Q: A well-motivated patient is more likely to have a full recovery?
A: That's usually true.
Q: It's true when the patient needs to go through a physical therapy program, right?
A: Yes.
Q: Dr. Klein, let's turn now to medications, and in particular painkillers. Mr. Gable was prescribed Tylenol No. 3 with codeine when he was discharged from the hospital?
A: Yes.
Q: He stopped taking it two weeks later when the prescription ran out?
A: Yes, that's what he said.
Q: He said it made him feel groggy and out of it?
A: Yes.
Q: Tylenol No. 3 with codeine isn't the only painkiller doctors can prescribe, is it?
A: No, there are many painkillers.
Q: Probably dozens?
A: At least.
Q: Doctors have a book, the *Physician's Desk Reference*, that describes all the medications that are available?
A: Yes.
Q: In fact, you have that book in your office?
A: Yes.
Q: If Mr. Gable had asked you for another prescription painkiller, you could have given him one?
A: Yes.
Q: And if he didn't like how the ones with codeine made him feel, you could have tried another one?
A: Yes.
Q: Until you found one that worked and didn't make him feel groggy or out of it?
A: Probably.
Q: But Mr. Gable never asked you for another prescription painkiller, did he?
A: No.
Q: So he did the therapy without painkillers?

A: Without prescription medication. I understand he was taking over-the-counter medication, such as aspirin.

Q: Dr. Klein, let's turn next to Mr. Gable's physical therapy program. That therapy is designed to regain full range of motion in the elbow joint, right?

A: Yes, that's the hope.

Q: This involves applying heat to the elbow, stretching the arm back and forth, and gradually increasing the range of motion until full range of motion returns, right?

A: Yes, that's what we hope to achieve.

Q: He was to do that three or four times a day?

A: Yes.

Q: When patients do that therapy, the great majority of them regain full motion in the elbow, right?

A: Most, but not all.

Q: In fact, 80 to 90 percent regain full range of motion?

A: Yes, that's what the studies show.

Q: To get 100 percent range of motion back, you need to do the therapy?

A: Yes.

Q: Every day, three or four times a day?

A: Yes.

Q: If the patient doesn't do the therapy, the patient can't expect to recover fully, can he?

A: That's right.

Q: That physical therapy can be painful?

A: It's usually painful.

Q: If the pain is too severe, it can prevent patients from doing the therapy?

A: Sometimes.

Q: When that happens, when the pain is too severe, taking a prescription pain medication can block the pain?

A: It can help, although no pain medication can totally block the pain. In fact, that could be dangerous.

Q: Mr. Gable told you that the therapy was painful, didn't he?

A: Yes.

Q: But he never asked you for any prescription painkillers, did he?

A: No, he never did.

Q: If he had asked for help, you certainly would have helped him with the pain, right?

A: Yes.

Q: But he never asked?

A: He never asked.

Q: Dr. Klein, you know that another doctor, Dr. Bradsky, also evaluated Mr. Gable and his right elbow?

A: Yes, I've read his report.

Q: Dr. Bradsky has an opinion that is different from yours?

A: Yes.

Q: Dr. Bradsky feels that Mr. Gable should have regained full range of motion in his elbow joint, and that he didn't because he failed to do the therapy he was directed to do, right?

A: Yes, that's what his report says.

Q: You know Dr. Bradsky, don't you?

A: Yes.

Q: You consider him to be a good doctor?

A: Yes.

Q: You respect his opinions?

A: Yes, although I disagree with him here.

Q: That sometimes happens in the world of medicine, doesn't it?

A: Yes.

Q: Two competent experts can disagree over
something?

A: Yes.

Q: When that happens, the jury decides who to
believe?

A: I guess so.

> ◼◀ For a demon-
> stration of the direct
> and cross-examination
> of a doctor who did not
> actually treat the plaintiff,
> please watch Video F.3,
> "Wyo STI: Demonstration
> of Problem 6.12."

8.9 Redirect and Recross-Examinations

The discussions of redirect examinations, in Section 5.16, and recross-examinations, in Section 6.11, apply with equal force to expert witnesses.

There is one topic that is peculiar to expert witnesses: impeachment with treatises, governed by FRE 803(18). Under FRE 106, the rule of completeness, a lawyer during cross-examination cannot impeach by selectively reading from a treatise (or any other writing) to create an unfair impression. You can and should object at that time and insist that the lawyer read the entire section that puts things fairly in context. Second, if your expert is impeached by a statement from a treatise, on redirect consider asking the expert if he agrees with the treatise, and why he did things differently than the treatise prescribes. This is a common approach with doctors who treated a patient differently than the procedures recommended in the treatise.

Example:

Q: Dr. Kaye, when the baby you had just delivered showed signs of difficulty breathing, what's the first thing you did?

A: I used a bulb syringe to clear out the baby's mouth and throat,
observed her to make sure she was breathing, and then put a mask
on her face to administer pure oxygen.

Q: The other lawyer read from a treatise that says that when a newborn
shows signs of respiratory distress, you should immediately use a bag
to provide positive pressure ventilation to the lungs. Remember that
passage from the treatise?

A: I do.

Q: Did you do that in this case?

A: No.

Q: Do you agree with the treatise?

A: In general, yes.

Q: Why didn't you use a bag to provide positive pressure ventilation in this case?

Q: For one important reason. That treatise describes a generally accepted procedure when the baby is a full-term baby. I was delivering an underweight, premature baby. Using a bag to provide positive pressure to the lungs is a risky procedure, because it is easy to damage or rupture the lungs of a premature baby. When that happens, it is often fatal. Since the baby appeared to be breathing on her own, I chose administering pure oxygen by mask as the much safer procedure.

8.10 Trial Notebook

An example of a trial notebook, with shell forms and completed forms, is on the website that accompanies this book.

The discussions of outlining your direct examinations, in Section 5.17, and your cross-examinations, in Section 6.13, apply with equal force to expert witnesses. However, with experts, some lawyers write out the key questions fully on the outline, so those questions can be asked correctly during the trial. This is particularly important if you will be asking hypothetical questions.

8.11 Common Problems

What are the recurring problems that lawyers encounter during expert direct and cross-examinations?

1. Too Much, Too Long

Jurors have limited attention spans, particularly when they are confronted with complex, technical information. Jurors don't want all the details. They want just enough information to understand the issues and the expert's positions on them. On direct examination, make your expert the 20- to 30-minute expert who gives the jurors an overview of what he did, why he did it, and why his positions make sense.

2. Not Enough Visual Aids

Persuasive experts are good teachers, and good teachers know that learning today is largely visual. Put your expert in the teacher mode. Create visual aids that show what the expert did, what she concluded, and how she came to her conclusions. Get the expert off the witness stand so she can "teach" in front of the jurors. Too many experts are merely "talking heads" in the courtroom, and today's jurors quickly lose interest in them.

3. Weak Beginning

Direct and cross-examinations need to grab the jurors' attention immediately, because you have only one or two minutes to show the jurors that this direct or cross is going to be interesting. Slow starts just don't work today. The direct examination beginning must answer the jurors' questions: Who is he, why is he here, and can we trust him? What did he do? Why did he do it? The cross-examination beginning must send an immediate signal: This is going to be interesting and shed new light on the case. Anything less, and jurors will quickly tune out.

4. Weak Ending

Direct and cross-examinations should always end on a high note, because jurors remember best what they hear last. Always ask: What's the most important point of the direct examination, and how can I end on that point? What's my strongest point for cross-examination, and how can I end on that point? Too many direct and cross-examinations simply end because the lawyer has run out of questions.

5. Not Enough Witness Preparation

Getting expert witnesses to spend enough time preparing to testify is frequently a problem. Too many experts think that they don't need to spend time preparing for direct examination because they know the issues and have testified as experts in other trials. Too many experts think they can handle anything the cross-examiner raises. However, becoming a persuasive witness takes time, even for experts, and there is simply no substitute for adequate preparation.

6. Showing Off

Both lawyer and expert need to resist the urge to show off. For experts, this means being simple and clear, using plain English, and becoming the friendly teacher, helper, and guide. For lawyers, it means resisting the temptation to show that you also know about the field by using technical jargon.

CHAPTER 9

CLOSING ARGUMENTS

9.1 Introduction

The closing argument is each side's last opportunity to remind the jury of its themes, what the case is all about from its point of view, why that side's version of reality is both accurate and preferable, and why fairness and justice require a favorable verdict. By the end of the trial, the jurors know the evidence, and most have an opinion about what the right verdict should be. Many are tired and resistant to arguments from the lawyers. Closing arguments are the last opportunity to give the favorable jurors the strongest arguments for that side, so that those jurors will be better advocates during the actual jury deliberations.

To make effective closing arguments, trial lawyers must know the applicable law and the jury's perspective. They must repeat the themes and labels they have used throughout the trial to send compelling emotional messages. They must know the tools of persuasive argumentation and the kinds of arguments that are effective for commonly litigated issues. As plaintiff, they must know how to allocate resources between the plaintiff's closing and rebuttal arguments. Done well, a closing argument makes the favorable jurors stronger advocates for that side during deliberations. Done poorly, the closing argument only bores, confuses, or alienates the jury.

9.2 The Law

There are no federal rules or statutes governing closing arguments except Fed. R. Crim. P. 29.1, which governs criminal cases. The state statutes are largely silent as well, or supply only general rules. The real rules governing closing arguments are found in federal and state case law. Custom also plays a major role.

1. Procedure

Federal civil rules are silent on the right to make a closing argument. Fed. R. Crim. P. 29.1 sets forth the procedure in criminal cases: The prosecution argues first, followed by the defense, with the prosecution having the right of rebuttal. State rules are largely silent or general. Nevertheless, trial judges invariably allow closing arguments in jury trials, recognizing that closing arguments give the jury a last opportunity to hear the positions of the parties; review the evidence; and relate the evidence to the elements of the claims, damages, defenses, and the burdens of proof.

Jurisdictions vary as to the procedure and order of closing arguments. In federal and most state courts, the plaintiff has the right to argue first, followed by the defense, with the plaintiff having the right to make a rebuttal argument. This is the usual procedure in both civil and criminal cases.

The plaintiff's right to argue first and last is a function of the plaintiff having the burden of proof on its claims. In cases in which all the plaintiff's claims have been admitted, and the only contested issues are the defendant's affirmative defenses or counterclaims on which the defense has the burden of proof, most courts give the defense the right to argue first and last.

In a few states, each side only has the right to argue once; and in criminal cases, a few states provide that the defense argues first, followed by the prosecution.

Some judges routinely impose time limitations on closing arguments. Other judges impose time limitations only when they think limitations are needed. When judges impose time limitations, they frequently limit each side to between 30 and 60 minutes; in complex or lengthy cases more time may be given.

Judges may also impose limitations on the plaintiff's right of rebuttal. For example, if plaintiff has a total of 60 minutes for argument, the judge may decide that plaintiff can reserve not more than 15 minutes of the allotted time for rebuttal. This prevents the plaintiff from giving a short closing argument and saving most of its time for rebuttal, which would be unfair to the defense.

2. Content

Closing arguments can review and discuss the evidence actually admitted during the trial. Reasonable inferences from the evidence can be argued. However, lawyers cannot mention evidence that was not admitted. Rule 3.4 of the Model Rules of Professional Conduct makes this clear.

Most judges permit lawyers to refer to matters within the common knowledge of the jurors, such as important historical and current events, and weave them into the arguments. Many judges permit references to the Constitution, the Bible, Shakespearean plays, and other well-known literary works. Some permit references to current cultural events, such as movies, television commercials, and the like. Some judges permit lawyers to mention personal experiences in their lives to make a point, but many do not.

Most judges also permit lawyers to use the jury instructions and verdict forms during their arguments, including the actual language of key instructions, to show the instructions to the jury, and paraphrase the instructions, as long as this is done accurately and fairly. Most judges permit lawyers to make visual aids summarizing the language of key instructions.

Lawyers may use exhibits that have been admitted in evidence. Lawyers are also commonly permitted to create visual aids to supplement their arguments, provided that the visual aids contain only things the lawyers could state orally.

3. Improper Closing Arguments

What is improper in closing arguments? Case law has identified several areas:

- Mentioning unadmitted evidence
- Misstating or mischaracterizing evidence
- Improperly commenting on missing evidence
- Stating personal opinions
- Appealing to sympathy or prejudice
- Improperly arguing the law
- Improperly arguing damages
- Arguing the consequences of verdict
- Improperly arguing on rebuttal

a. Mentioning Unadmitted Evidence

Closing arguments must be based on admitted evidence. Therefore, mentioning unadmitted evidence is improper. In egregious cases, this may cause a mistrial and, if intentionally done, may bar a retrial. Model Rule 3.4(e) provides that a lawyer shall not "allude to any matter that [is] not be supported by admissible evidence." If an argument mentions evidence that the judge has ruled inadmissible, the violation of the judge's order is obviously a violation of the rule as well.

The most common errors involve mentioning background information about parties and witnesses when there was no proof of the background; mentioning exhibits that were not admitted in evidence; commenting on evidence, admitted for a limited purpose, for an improper purpose; commenting on a defendant's prior bad acts or prior criminal convictions, when such evidence was not admitted under FRE 404(b), 608(b), or 609; and commenting on a defendant's exercise of the constitutional right to silence. Improper comments on the defendant's silence in criminal cases are particularly serious and often cause a mistrial.

Sometimes a lawyer innocently, but clumsily, refers to "evidence" that was never admitted during the trial, especially in civil cases. Due to the extensive discovery in civil cases, there are almost always items of "evidence" that a lawyer knows about that did not get admitted at trial, for assorted reasons. Before you give your closing, flush that "evidence" from your mind. A closing argument should only discuss evidence that was actually admitted, not unproven facts.

Courts commonly permit closing arguments to mention matters within the common knowledge of the jurors, but the line between common knowledge and unadmitted evidence is unclear. For example, lawyers frequently refer to

well-known historical events, such as Pearl Harbor, President Kennedy's assas-
sination, and the attack on the World Trade Center. They frequently refer to
well-known facts in their locale, such as that during rush hour the traffic on the
Kennedy Expressway in Chicago is horrendous. In this area, it is important to
know the attitude of the trial judge.

b. Misstating or Mischaracterizing Evidence

Closing arguments must be based on admitted evidence, although the lawyers may argue "reasonable inferences" from that evidence.

The line between what is a reasonable inference from the evidence and what
is a misstatement or mischaracterization of the evidence is blurry. Except in clear
cases, judges are reluctant to substitute their judgement for that of the jury, and
will frequently overrule an objection and instruct the jury that it must determine
if the lawyer is fairly and accurately stating the evidence.

c. Improperly Commenting on Missing Evidence

Lawyers frequently argue the significance of missing witnesses and evidence.
Such an argument is proper if the witness or evidence is in the control of the other
party, and that party did not call the witness or introduce the evidence. In some
jurisdictions, the judge may give the jury a "missing witness" instruction, which
permits the jury to draw a negative inference from a party's failure to present a
witness or exhibit in that party's control. However, if the witness or exhibit is
accessible to both parties, such an argument is improper.

Lawyers may never comment on missing evidence if that evidence was
excluded by a pretrial order or a trial ruling.

d. Stating Personal Opinions

A lawyer may not state personal opinions at any time. This includes vouching for the credibility, or lack of credibility, of any witness, and includes stating
personal knowledge of facts. "I believe," "I know," and "I think" are phrases best
deleted from a trial lawyer's vocabulary. Personal attacks on parties, witnesses, and
opposing lawyers are also improper, because they are neither evidence nor reasonable inferences from the evidence. Model Rule 3.4(e) provides that a lawyer "shall
not . . . assert personal knowledge of facts in issue . . . or state a personal opinion
as to the justness of a cause, the credibility of a witness, the culpability of a civil
litigant or the guilt or innocence of an accused."

e. Appealing to Sympathy or Prejudice

Direct appeals to sympathy, prejudice, or other passions are improper because
such arguments ask the jury to base its verdict on something other than the evidence and law. These misdeeds most commonly occur in criminal cases, where
some jurisdictions permit, but others bar, prosecutors from arguing that the jury
has a duty to deter crime and protect the community. Asking the jury to base its
verdict on some personal characteristic of a party, such as race, sex, or citizenship,
is obviously improper, and arguing a party's poverty or wealth (unless punitive
damages are in issue) is also improper.

Of course, emotion is a major factor in many trials, especially criminal and personal injury civil trials. Lawyers are not required to ignore the emotional aspects
of a case, but they cannot suggest that the jury should decide the case based on
emotion rather than the evidence.

f. Improperly Arguing the Law

Closing arguments may discuss the law on which the court will instruct the jury, and may refer to and use the instructions the court will give to the jury. After all, the jury's job is to relate the evidence to the applicable law, and good closing arguments do that.

Lawyers may not, however, misstate, mischaracterize, or distort the applicable law. They cannot attempt to shift the burden of proof from the side that bears it. In almost all jurisdictions, the lawyers may not ask the jury to ignore or reject the law, commonly called *a jury nullification* argument.

May the lawyers define elements or terms in a jury instruction beyond what the instruction itself contains? This question arises frequently in criminal cases over the definition of "beyond a reasonable doubt." In jurisdictions in which the court defines it, judges usually bar lawyers from defining it further. Even many jurisdictions that do not define it bar attorney definition.

g. Improperly Arguing Damages

In civil cases, the jury must follow the applicable law that defines the proper measure of damages. In doing this, the jury should assess damages fairly and reasonably, and not base its decision on sympathy, prejudice, personal feelings, or personal interests.

The most common improper argument is the *golden rule* argument, which asks the jury to step into the shoes of a party, usually the injured plaintiff, and decide what damages would be appropriate if the jury were in that party's position. On the defense side, lawyers may not argue the effect of a particular verdict on the community, taxes, or a person's or business's reputation. Unless the case involves punitive damages, lawyers may not ask the jury to return a verdict to punish the defendant.

Finally, jurisdictions vary widely as to the propriety of using a "per diem" or "unit of time" argument. Such an argument asks the jurors to award a certain dollar amount for each day, or smaller unit of time, of the plaintiff's pain and suffering, and then multiply it by the plaintiff's expected lifespan. Some jurisdictions allow such arguments; others expressly prohibit them. Some also hold that the golden rule applies to liability arguments as well. A few jurisdictions bar asking for a specific dollar amount for pain and suffering damages.

h. Arguing the Consequences of a Verdict

Lawyers may not argue the consequences of a verdict in civil or criminal cases, because that is not a proper jury function. In civil cases, for example, the defense may not argue that if the jury finds against the county it will cause county taxes to increase. This problem arises most commonly in criminal cases, when prosecutors argue the consequences to the victim and community if the defendant is acquitted, or the defense lawyers argue the consequences to the defendant and his family if the defendant is convicted. Common improper comments are directed to possible sentences, parole, or appeals, if the defendant is convicted. All are improper, because all of them ask the jury to base its verdict on matters other than the evidence and the law.

i. Improperly Arguing on Rebuttal

In most jurisdictions, the party with the burden of proof has the right to argue first, and also to make a rebuttal argument after the other side argues.

The plaintiff usually has that right, because the plaintiff usually bears the burden of proof.

Plaintiff's right of rebuttal is obviously an advantage, but it cannot be misused, and most issues in this area deal with the proper scope of the rebuttal argument. The plaintiff's rebuttal is restricted to responding to arguments made by the defense. The plaintiff may not raise a completely new argument for the first time, as this would deprive the defendant of any meaningful opportunity to counter the argument. For example, if plaintiff did not argue for punitive damages in the closing argument, it may not argue punitive damages in the rebuttal argument, unless the defendant argued the issue in its final argument. If plaintiff did not disclose the dollar amounts of damages it is seeking in the closing argument, most judges will, if an objection is made, bar plaintiff from asking for specific dollar amounts for the first time in rebuttal. The line between what is proper rebuttal and what constitutes a new argument is blurry. It is based on fairness, but it is driven in part by the attitude of the trial judge. In rare cases, judges have given the defense a surrebuttal to respond to new arguments first made in the plaintiff's rebuttal.

For a detailed discussion of the law on closing arguments, *see* Mauet & Wolfson, *Trial Evidence* (7th ed., 2020).

9.3 The Jury's Perspective

What are jurors feeling and thinking as the lawyers give their closing arguments? First, many jurors are tired—physically, mentally, and emotionally. They now know that being a juror is a demanding job, and that little in a real trial is as exciting or dramatic as the drama portrayed on television. Most are looking forward to the end of the trial so they can return to their normal lives. Second, jurors are now knowledgeable about the facts. They heard and saw the witnesses and exhibits from both sides, and most feel that they have more than enough information to understand what happened. Third, most jurors are now opinionated. They know the facts, understand the issues, and know what the right verdict should be. Most feel that they don't need to hear from the lawyers again to decide the case correctly. Fourth, most jurors are now resistant to arguments—especially from the lawyers—that clash with the positions and views they now have about the case. Despite the court's admonition to "keep an open mind" and "not decide the case until you have heard the arguments of counsel," most jurors now believe they know what the verdict should be, and usually assume that the other jurors will see the case as they do. Finally, jurors want to feel good about the decision they are about to make. They need to feel that their verdict will achieve justice and be fair to the parties.

Closing arguments must meet the jurors' needs, rather than the lawyers' wants. They must be efficient and focused, because jurors will not tolerate long arguments. They must be helpful: not simply reviewing what the witnesses have said and exhibits have shown, but explaining what the evidence *means* and how it proves or disproves the required elements of the claims, damages, and defenses. They must recognize that most jurors don't change their minds during the closing arguments. Closing arguments must be directed both to the few jurors who are undecided or uncertain, to persuade them to vote your way, and to the favorable jurors who already plan to vote your way, to provide them with stronger arguments that they can adopt and use during the deliberations. Finally, closing arguments must appeal to the jurors' sense of fairness and justice and show that a favorable verdict is consistent with those higher goals.

Effective trial lawyers understand the jurors' needs, interests, and expectations at this late stage of the trial. They respond by delivering closing arguments that are efficient, get to the core issues quickly, focus on what the evidence means, address the jurors' concerns candidly, empower the jurors to do justice, and show that fairness and justice in this case require a favorable verdict. Effective closing arguments persuade through both content and delivery.

9.4. Jury Instructions and Instructions Conference

Before the closing arguments can begin, you must know the instructions the judge will give to the jurors because you should use those instructions during your closing argument. While the practice in many jurisdictions is for the judge to instruct the jury on the law immediately following the lawyers' closing arguments, some courts instruct the jury immediately before the closing arguments. In federal courts, Rule 51 of the Federal Rules of Civil Procedure, and Rule 30 of the Federal Rules of Criminal Procedure, govern the instruction process, but do so only in general terms. Hence, you must know when to draft requested instructions and submit them to the judge and other lawyers, how to draft instructions and verdict forms, and how to argue and preserve the record at the instructions conference.

1. When to Draft Jury Instructions and Submit Them to the Judge

In civil cases, most judges require the parties to submit their requested jury instructions, and state any objections to the other side's instructions, as part of the pretrial memorandum. During the final pretrial conference, the judge may rule on objections to the requested instructions. Many judges have standing orders in civil cases on how requested jury instructions should be prepared and submitted.

> For overviews of the jury instruction drafting process, please watch Video I.1, "Wyo STI: Civil Jury Instructions" and Video I.2, "Wyo STI: Criminal Jury Instructions."

In many criminal cases and some civil cases, judges want the requested jury instructions at, or a few days before, the beginning of the trial. Most judges set a specific deadline for the submission of requested jury instructions (although most also permit later additional requested instructions if warranted by the evidence presented during the trial). In these cases, the judge will usually rule on which instructions will be given at the instructions conference, which is most commonly held just before closing arguments. Even if the judge only wants the instructions at the beginning of the trial, prepare them well in advance. Doing this is critically important, and doing it properly takes time. On the eve of trial, you should be preparing your key witnesses and polishing your planned opening statement and direct and cross-examinations, not drafting jury instructions. Also, knowing the jury instructions, especially those outlining the elements of claims, crimes, and defenses, will help you organize your opening statement, presentation of evidence, and closing argument.

2. How to Draft Jury Instructions and Verdict Forms

There are several categories of instructions: preliminary and general instructions, burden of proof instructions, elements instructions, instructions defining claims and defenses, witness credibility instructions, measure of damages instructions, and verdict forms. Your job is to draft each of them in a way that correctly states the law applicable to the case.

Many jurisdictions have approved "pattern" or "uniform" instructions and verdict forms for frequently tried cases, such as common criminal, torts, and contract cases. In these jurisdictions, preparing jury instructions is relatively easy. You simply select the appropriate instructions and tailor them to the specifics of your case. Many jurisdictions have their pattern instructions available electronically so that completing and printing the appropriate instructions is even easier.

The instructions are usually numbered, marked to reflect which side requested them, and cited to the sources of the instructions. For example, plaintiff's first instruction might be marked "Plaintiff's Instruction #1; Pattern Jury Instruction #14." The judge then gets one set of marked and unmarked instructions from each party. Each party gets a marked set of the requested instructions from every other party. (The unmarked instructions are the actual instructions that will be given to the jury during deliberations, in those jurisdictions where the instructions are both read and given to the jury.)

If your jurisdiction has no applicable pattern jury instructions, you must draft them. The authority for the instructions is usually a statute, case law, or a pattern instruction adapted from another jurisdiction. Most judges again want an unmarked set as well as a marked set of instructions from each party. The marked instructions should be numbered, indicate which side requested the instruction, and state the source of the instruction. For example, defendant's first instruction might be marked "Defendant's Instruction No. 1; Based on Arizona Revised Statutes Ch. 4, Sec. 13."

You must also draft the verdict forms. There are two basic types of verdict forms, the general verdict and the special verdict (sometimes called a "special interrogatory"). Most jurisdictions use general verdict forms for most cases. A general verdict form simply asks the jury to announce which side won and, where appropriate, the amount of damages awarded.

Example:

> (Choose one)
> We the jury find in favor of plaintiff Johnson and against defendant Smith.
> We find plaintiff Johnson has proven damages in the amount of $__.
> *Or*
> We the jury find in favor of defendant Smith and against plaintiff Johnson.

Example:

> (Choose one)
> We the jury find the defendant, John Williams
> _____ Not Guilty
> _____ Guilty

If there are multiple parties or claims, the verdict forms must be drafted accordingly.

The special verdict form, sometimes used in civil cases, asks the jury to answer sequential questions. In federal courts special verdicts are discretionary with the judge. Some states make special verdicts discretionary, while a few require them.

Example:

> 1. Did plaintiff prove that defendant was negligent?
>   Yes or No (Circle your answer)
>   If "No," stop.
>   If "Yes," answer the next question.
> 2. Did plaintiff prove that defendant's negligence caused the accident?
>   Yes or No (Circle your answer)
>   If "No," stop.
>   If "Yes," answer the next question.
> 3. What amount of money did plaintiff prove is necessary to compensate plaintiff for her damages?
> $__.

If given a choice, what type of verdict should you seek? Although this needs to be assessed by both sides in each case, plaintiffs usually prefer a general verdict for its simplicity. Defendants frequently favor a special verdict, particularly where the claims and defenses are complex and the possibility of inconsistent verdicts arises. In addition, where the exposure of a particular defendant in a multi-defendant case is low, that defendant may want special verdicts directed to its involvement in the case.

3. How to Argue and Preserve the Record at the Instructions Conference

The instructions conference, sometimes called the "charge conference," held to "settle instructions," decides on the wording of the instructions and verdict forms and whether they will be submitted to the jury. Instructions conferences are frequently held in the judge's chambers.

The judge will usually go over the requested instructions, first plaintiff's, then defendant's, one by one, and rule on any objections. While this is going on, make sure that a record is being made! The better practice is to have the court reporter present during

For additional insight regarding the drafting of jury instructions and the jury instructions conference, please watch Video I.3, "Wyo STI: Jury Instruction Feedback and Questions Panel."

the conference. In some jurisdictions, however, the court reporter is sometimes excused during the conference, and afterwards the judge and lawyers summarize what happened on the record. If the latter occurs, make sure that the court reporter takes down all your objections and reasons.

If claimed error occurs during the instructions conference, it is your duty to make sure that the trial record adequately shows that error. First, make sure your objections to instructions are specific. Most jurisdictions require that you state specific reasons why your instruction should be given and why your opponent's should not be. Second, make sure that the judge rules on all your proposed instructions. Most jurisdictions do not allow you to claim error based on the judge's failure to consider your instructions unless the record is clear that you submitted them, expressly asked the judge to rule on them, and obtained a ruling. Third, make sure that your instructions, which the judge denied, are submitted to the court clerk for inclusion in the trial record. (If your instructions were filed with the clerk before trial, they will be part of the trial record.) Most jurisdictions require that the denied instructions be physically preserved in the trial record for appeal.

Finally, learn your jurisdiction's waiver rules. Some require only that the record clearly show your objections at the instructions conference in order to raise error on appeal. Others require that you renew your objections before and after the instructions are read to the jury. Many require that you raise any claimed error in a motion for a new trial.

9.5 Content of Effective Closing Arguments

An effective closing argument accomplishes several goals. It grabs the jurors' attention; incorporates the same themes and labels used in the opening statement; shows the jurors what the evidence means and what it adds up to; explains what the key persons did and why they did it; uses logic and emotion to reach the jurors' minds and hearts to empower them to reach the right verdict; and arms the favorable jurors so they become stronger advocates for your side during deliberations. It answers the fundamental question: Why should we win? And it does all these things quickly and efficiently.

The essence of effective closing arguments is argumentation. Reviewing the evidence is not argumentation. An uninspired recitation of what witnesses said and what exhibits contained is the last thing jurors want to hear now. Instead, jurors want to know how that evidence has proved, or failed to prove, what the parties are required to prove: the elements of their claims, damages, and defenses. They want the evidence to be put together to form a clear picture of what happened and why it happened.

Effective closing arguments must integrate your theory of the case, your themes, the admitted evidence, and the jury instructions the judge will give. Experienced trial lawyers outline their expected closing arguments early, well before trial, and modify them as needed to discuss new evidence and delete evidence that is not admitted, as the trial progresses.

Planning an effective closing argument is a creative process in which lawyers have great freedom. Remember that you, an advocate, are like the director of a play. Though limited to the admitted evidence, reasonable inferences, and the applicable law, you have great flexibility in organizing the argument. You must be consistent with your theory of the case, themes, and labels, but you have numerous ways of presenting them during the argument. At this last stage of the trial the test is: Does this argument persuade?

1. Impact Beginning

You have one or two minutes at best to capture the jury's interest. That's the reality of closing arguments. The jurors are now informed, many are opinionated, and some are tired. Most know what the right verdict should be and are anxious to start deliberating. Most are thinking: Since I now know the facts, why should I continue to listen, to you or any other lawyer? Therefore, the first few seconds must send one strong message: I'm worth listening to, because I'll make my points and discuss the evidence and law in an interesting and helpful way.

This means that the traditional way of starting a closing argument—thanking the jurors for their service, reminding them that they're in the home stretch, and telling them what the purpose of a closing argument is—doesn't work anymore. Jurors will quit listening before you get to anything important. How do you grab their attention by making an immediate impact?

a. Start with Your Themes

A common approach is to start immediately by forcefully stating the key themes you have used throughout the trial.

Example (Plaintiff):

> JUDGE: Counsel, you may proceed with your closing argument.
> LAWYER: Thank you, your honor. One second—that's all it takes to ruin a life. One second of carelessness, and a man's career is over. One second of carelessness, and a man's family is devastated. One second of carelessness, and a man's dreams for the future are destroyed. Now we need to answer one last question: What will make it right?

Example (Defendant):

> Members of the jury, any product can be dangerous if the directions are not followed. Any product can be dangerous if the warnings are ignored. And any product can be dangerous if it is used for an unintended and improper purpose. In this case, the plaintiff managed to do all three. But when he hurt himself, instead of taking responsibility for what he did, he tried to blame us, and that's not right.

Example (Prosecution):

> This is a case about revenge. It's been about revenge ever since the card game, the card game where that defendant lost money and claimed Bobby Jackson cheated him. Since that day, that's been the only thing on the defendant's mind: revenge. Three weeks later, he got revenge, by robbing Bobby Jackson in the alley. And today's the day when that defendant—finally—has to face up to what he did.

Example (Defense):

> It's a rule of nature: Everyone is entitled to defend himself. It's also a rule of law: When faced with the imminent use of deadly force, a person is entitled to defend himself with deadly force. That's all this case is about, and that's all it's ever been about. Frank Johnson was faced with immediate deadly force that night, and he did exactly what the law allows: He used deadly force to defend himself. That's not only lawful, that's reasonable. If he hadn't, he'd have died that night.

b. Re-create the Event

Another common start is to re-create the key event from your point of view. This is effective when the case involves a memorable or traumatic event.

Example (Plaintiff):

> This is a case about trust, because Mary trusted Mr. Johnson. How do we know? It begins on June 1, 2020. Let's go back to the board room at Acme Manufacturing. They've reached a deal, and the meeting is wrapping up. Mary Jones and Acme's president, William Johnson, get up from opposite sides of the conference table. Johnson extends his hand to Mary and says: "Mary, this is going to be a wonderful relationship." Mary was on cloud nine: her biggest contract ever, with the biggest company ever, a company she could trust. She didn't know that within six months, what seemed to be the perfect dream would turn into an endless nightmare.

Example (Defendant):

> When Mr. Cannon saw the plaintiff's car run the red light and come directly at him, he thought he was going to die. He reacted by instinct: slammed on his brakes, as hard as he could, and yanked the wheel to one side, as fast as he could. There's nothing else he could do. That car, the plaintiff's car, didn't slow down. It raced right through the red light, and smashed into the side of Mr. Cannon's car. In just one or two seconds, it was over, and Mr. Cannon was thinking one thing: I'm lucky to be alive. Little did he know that the plaintiff, who ran that red light, who caused this collision, would file a lawsuit claiming that he had the right of way.

Example (Prosecution):

> Members of the jury, she'll always see his face. The face that was on top of her, almost touching her. The face that smirked as he was assaulting her. If there's anything in Mary Smith's life that she will always see, always remember, and always know, it's the face of the man who raped her on June 1, 2020: the man sitting right over there, that defendant. And she'll see that face, and know who it is, every day for the rest of her life.

Example (Defense):

> Let's go back to June 1, 2020, around 9:00 p.m. Mike Adams is sitting at the bar of the Hog's Breath Tavern. He's minding his own business, nursing a beer. That's when Vinny Johnson, who had been drinking for

hours, who had downed more beers than he could count, who was flat-out drunk, stumbles over to Mike and says: "Hey, buy me a beer." Mike says: "No thanks," but Johnson was in no mood to take no for an answer. Johnson says: "I said, buy me a beer," and Mike again says: "No thanks." That's when Johnson says: "Buy me a beer, or it'll be the last thing you don't do." Johnson reaches into his pocket and pulls out a knife. Mike reacts instantly, grabs a beer bottle, smashes it on Johnson's head, and Johnson goes down. It happens that fast, and that's exactly what happens, nothing more, nothing less. That's self-defense.

c. Show Dramatic Evidence

Sometimes a case will have a "smoking gun" piece of evidence. A good way to start is to produce that evidence immediately and say that it proves what you've been saying all along.

Example:

Members of the jury, it's all right here, right on the store's surveillance tape. Here's the frame that we had blown up, State's Exhibit No. 1 [puts enlargement on easel]. That's the defendant right there [pointing]. You can plainly see him, and it's obviously him. It's as simple as that.

Example:

Here it is [holding up document]! Here's the document they didn't want you to see. That insurance company's own memorandum, from its vice president, says: "Because of our continuing losses since the last quarter, claims agents should question all claims made, particularly the high-dollar claims." That's how you know that company never gave Mrs. Hill's claim a fair hearing. That's why they denied her claim for no reason. And that's how you know they acted in bad faith.

d. Empower the Jury

Sometimes lawyers like to begin by stressing the jury's collective wisdom and power to decide. This can be an effective start when you are asking the jury to do something that isn't easy or popular.

Example:

Justice isn't about doing the easy thing. Justice isn't about doing the popular thing. Justice is about doing the right thing. That's why there are 12 of you, and that's why you have been called to decide this case. The 12 of you have more collective wisdom, and more collective experience, than anyone in this courtroom. That's why the law puts in your hands the most important power that exists: the power to do justice, the power to do what's right.

Example:

Who's telling the truth? They can't both be. One is telling the truth, the other one isn't, that's clear. So how do you decide? You do it the way we do it in our daily lives: by looking at the two witnesses and seeing which one doesn't look or sound right. You do it by seeing if their testimony squares with what you know about people and about how real life works. You do it by seeing which one is supported by the other witnesses and exhibits. That's why you, the jurors, are trusted with making the ultimate decision: Who's telling the truth?

e. Tell a Story

Telling a well-known story can sometimes effectively make a central point in your case. You can then loop back to the point of the story and tie it to the facts of your case. Make sure the story is short and ties in clearly to the point you are making.

Example:

We all know the story of Robinson Crusoe. Robinson Crusoe had been on the island alone, year after year. Yet every day he kept looking for a sign that someone else was there. And then one day he saw it, and he knew: I am not alone. What Robinson Crusoe saw in the wet sand was a human footprint, and he knew someone else was on the island. Knew for sure, although he hadn't seen him yet. That, members of the jury, is the power of circumstantial evidence. Let's look at the "footprints" in this case and see what they tell us.

Example:

We've learned since we were little that we shouldn't be greedy. In fact, in Aesop's Fables, there's the story about a little boy who sees a large clay pitcher in a courtyard. The opening in the pitcher is just large enough to put his hand in it. When he reaches in, he finds out it's full of hazelnuts, which he loves to eat. He grabs as big a handful as he can, and pulls his arm back out. When his hand gets to the opening in the pitcher, he finds he can't get his hand back out, not without letting go of the nuts. Now he's stuck—he can't get his hand out, and he's not going to let go of the nuts. He starts to cry, and a grownup stops to see what's the matter. She tells him what we all know: Take only a few hazelnuts at a time, and don't be greedy. Unfortunately, that's a lesson the defendant hasn't learned yet. That's why this is a case about greed.

Are these the only ways to start a closing argument? Of course not. Just use your imagination. The only rule is that every closing argument must have an impact beginning. It must grab the jurors' attention, and send a strong message: I'm worth listening to; stay tuned.

2. Arguing

Jurors want to know how the evidence has proved, or failed to prove, the required elements of the parties' claims, damages, and defenses. They want the evidence to be put together to form a clear picture of what happened, why it happened, and what motivated the people to do what they did. They want to have their questions answered and concerns addressed. They also need to feel good about their verdict, confident that it's the fair and right outcome. These juror needs are at the core of every closing argument. The way to start is to ask yourself four questions.

a. What to Argue

First, what are the key disputes in the case? In almost every case, most elements of the claims, damages, and defenses are not in dispute, and it usually does little good to spend much time talking about them. Instead, identify and zero in on the key disputes. For example, in a personal injury case, the defense may concede liability, and the only dispute is whether the plaintiff was also negligent, or what the proper amount of noneconomic damages is. In a commercial case, the parties may agree on the economic losses the plaintiff incurred, but dispute whether the defendant is responsible for any of those losses. In a criminal case, the parties may agree that an armed robbery occurred, and the only dispute is over the identity of the robber. In most cases, only one or two elements of the claims, damages, or defenses are at the heart of the dispute. That's where the fight is. You might as well get right to it. In addition, remember that most cases involve one or more of three common issues: witness credibility (Who do you believe?); inferences (Has the evidence circumstantially proved an element?); and burdens of proof (Has an element been proven to the required degree?).

Second, what are your strongest and weakest points? Effective closing arguments not only argue the strongest favorable evidence, they also address and blunt the opponent's strongest points. Good arguments turn the other side's arguments around, so that apparent weaknesses become your strengths. It is a serious mistake to argue only your strengths and avoid your weaknesses. Research has shown that two-sided arguments—those that also raise the opponent's strongest points and refute them—are more effective in cases in which the issues are close.

Third, what are the jurors' main questions and concerns? Closing arguments are your last opportunity to deal with what the jurors are thinking and feeling. If jurors could ask questions now, what would their questions be? If jurors could say what troubles them about the case, what would they say? Lawyers who directly acknowledge the jurors' questions and concerns and deal with them candidly have a distinct advantage during closing arguments.

Fourth, where is the emotional core of the case? Remember that most jurors decide cases on emotion, then justify their decisions with what they see as logic. Jurors like to find in favor of people they like and trust, and against people they dislike and distrust. Where's the emotional connection that gets jurors to feel that your side is the good side, the side that should win? That connection must be expressed through an emotional theme. For example, "not playing by the rules," "greed," and "David versus Goliath," all reflect emotional responses to the underlying facts of the case.

Addressing these four questions will show you where to focus your closing arguments in any case.

b. How to Argue

How, then, do you argue? Remember that argument is not reciting or reviewing the evidence. Argument is making a point—a conclusion—and supporting it with all available ammunition. First, make a point. Be assertive and confident when you make it.

Examples:

> That defendant was going too fast around the curve.
>
> She couldn't see well enough to be sure what she saw.
>
> He was desperate, and time was running out.
>
> That company put profits ahead of safety.
>
> That toaster oven was a time bomb waiting to explode.

Second, back it up. Why is that point true? How do we know? How has it been proven? Show how your point—your conclusion—is supported by a number of sources. Sometimes the sources will be direct evidence that proves your point; sometimes they will support inferences you want the jurors to draw. Always consider the following.

Testimony of Witnesses. Witness testimony, of course, will usually be part of the support for any point. Show why your witnesses are credible (and you opponent's witnesses are not). But don't just refer vaguely to the testimony. Make the witness's testimony come alive by reenacting what the witness said and did, or by quoting directly from the witness's testimony. Make it vivid. Show what the witnesses actually said, rather than just summarizing their testimony in conclusory fashion. If the testimony is corroborated by other witnesses, point that out.

Example:

> Members of the jury, Mr. Hummels sat here [walking to the witness stand], he was under oath, he looked right at the defendant, and he pointed his finger at the defendant [demonstrating] and said: "That's the man who robbed me. I'm positive."

Example:

> What Ms. English said was so important, I wrote it down to make sure I got it right [picks up paper]. I asked her: "How much would it have cost your company to make a valve on the top of that lighter that couldn't leak?" And she said: "We estimated it would have cost $2.00 more per lighter." Two dollars per lighter.

Admitted Exhibits. Any exhibit formally admitted in evidence can be used during closing argument. In personal injury and criminal cases, use of photographs and diagrams is common. In commercial cases, documents and records will often be key sources of proof. Again, don't just refer vaguely to the exhibit. Show the jurors the actual exhibit, point out that it was admitted in evidence, and point to and read the key information.

Example:

> Here's the photograph that shows exactly what happened [picks up exhibit and walks over to jury box]. It's Exhibit No. 3, which her honor admitted in evidence. Now look over here [pointing]. You can see the skid marks on the road, leading right to the defendant's car. You can see where those skid marks start and where they end. That photograph proves that the defendant never put on his brakes until he was already past the crosswalk.

Example:

> Folks, here are the words they don't want you to see. It's on the contract, the contract they wrote, the contract they signed, which has been admitted in evidence as Plaintiff's Exhibit No. 6. Take a look on page six, right in the middle of the page. [Page six is projected on a screen or monitor.] I've highlighted the key sentence. It says: "However, if weather conditions at the construction site prevent working on any day, that day will not count in determining the completion date required under this contract." It's right there, in black and white.

Jury Instructions. Jury instructions should always be used during closing arguments. Almost all judges allow you to quote from the instructions and make visual aids that accurately summarize them. Instructions that lawyers commonly use during closing arguments discuss elements of claims and defenses, witness credibility, measure of damages, and burdens of proof. Many attorneys also use verdict forms.

Embrace the instructions. Let the jurors know that the instructions are your friend. Show how they can use the elements instructions as a blueprint to analyze the evidence. Show how the credibility instruction helps to assess the believability of a particular witness. Show how the measure of damages instruction is a roadmap for properly determining compensation. If an instruction is unfavorable, show how that instruction is not really applicable to the case.

Example:

> Members of the jury, his honor will instruct you that we must prove four things in a contract case. First, the parties entered into a valid contract; second, the plaintiff performed each of his obligations under that contract; third, the defendant failed to perform what he was obligated to perform under that contract; and fourth, the plaintiff was damaged as a result of the defendant's breach. I've put those four things on a poster-board [puts poster board on easel]. Let's see how we've proved each of these things.

Example:

> When you have direct conflicts between two eyewitnesses, they can't both be right. So who do you believe? Let's again look to the law for guidance. Her honor will instruct you that when you decide on the credibility of the witnesses, you should consider: the witnesses' ability and opportunity to observe; their manner and memory while testifying; any bias, interest, or motive they may have; and any inconsistent statements they may have made. With that as a guide, let's look at what Frank Jones told us, and see if what he says is believable.

Common Sense and Life Experiences. Tying the evidence to common sense and the jurors' life experiences is a common and often effective technique. After all, if the evidence is consistent with the jurors' life experiences, it makes sense and will be believable.

Example:

> The prosecution wants you to believe that Frank ran when the police arrived, and that somehow proves he had a guilty mind. But that doesn't

make any sense. When you're a 17-year-old kid living in that part of town, and a police car comes around a corner with its lights flashing, every 17-year-old reacts by instinct, even if he's done absolutely nothing wrong. In this case, Frank's running means absolutely nothing.

Example:

When a businessman cashes a payment check without recording the check on that day's receipts, what's that prove? If he does it once or twice, it might be just a mistake. But when he does it again and again, dozens of times in a single year, it proves something else. Our experiences in life tell us loud and clear what he's doing: That businessman is cheating on his taxes, by failing to record and report thousands of dollars of income. That's the only reasonable explanation, and that's exactly what happened here.

Stories and Analogies. Stories and analogies can provide powerful support for arguments, particularly if they are well-known stories and analogies we learned as children.

Example:

The plaintiff's alarm had gone off for no reason so many times, no wonder the alarm company did nothing when it went off this time. It's just like the story about the shepherd crying wolf. Remember that one? A young shepherd is out in the fields watching the sheep. Because he's young and bored, he yells, "Wolf, wolf," and the villagers run out to help, but discover there's no wolf—it's a false alarm. The next day he does it again, and the same thing happens. But when the shepherd does it a third time, the villagers are tired of the false alarms, and nobody runs out to help; he's cried "wolf" once too often. That's exactly what we have here.

Example:

The real winners in life are the people who simply go about the business of life, work hard, work steadily, and eventually succeed. There's an old story we all remember about the tortoise and the hare. They agree to race, and the hare is so confident he'll win that he races ahead, and then decides to take a nap. Of course, while he's napping the tortoise plods by, slowly but steadily, and reaches the finish line ahead of the hare. Folks, Frank Smith may be a tortoise, but over the long haul, in life, he's a winner, and he always reaches the finish line.

Can a lawyer recount a personal experience to make a point during closing arguments? For example, can a lawyer say, "When I was in the Army in Viet Nam . . ."? Courts often rule that personal experiences are improper because they are actually personal opinions or appeals to sympathy. Many courts only allow discussing universal experiences common to all of us. For example, "We've all had the experience of walking up to someone thinking that person was someone you know, and you find out you were mistaken."

Rhetorical Questions. Among the most powerful tools are rhetorical questions. They actively engage the jurors. They address the jurors' questions and concerns. They can put the other side on the defensive by challenging it to answer difficult questions. Rhetorical questions should be sprinkled throughout closing arguments. A word of caution, however: Make sure the rhetorical question doesn't have an easy answer that the other side can provide and turn the point around on you.

Example:

> When you heard Bobby Adams testify, and you heard that he had been involved in the armed robbery with the defendant, many of you were probably thinking: He was involved in this crime. Why would the government enter into an agreement with him and allow him to plead guilty to plain robbery? Is that right? And can we believe what he says? Those are good questions, and there are good answers to them. First, sometimes you have to use the little fish to catch the big fish.

Example:

> When the plaintiff's lawyer gets up to argue again, see if he addresses the questions all of us have about his client. Why didn't that plaintiff report this collision to the police? If he was so seriously hurt, why didn't he go to the hospital? Or call a doctor? Why did he wait one whole week? The fact is, he didn't do any of these things because this accident was his fault, and he wasn't seriously hurt.

Visual Aids. Visual aids, in addition to admitted exhibits, are an important part of closing arguments, because they stimulate interest and involve the jurors at a time when they are tired and impatient. Every closing argument should have exhibits and visual aids interspersed periodically, so that you are never just a talking head for more than a few minutes. As discussed previously, you can use any exhibit that was formally admitted in evidence. You also can create and use any visual aid that "says" anything that you can say during closing arguments.

Example:

> When the plaintiff rode down that dirt path, was he acting reasonably? Absolutely not. Why not? Several reasons, and I'm going to put them on this board [put poster board on easel, or use a PowerPoint slide with progressive bullet points; the poster board or slide is entitled "Plaintiff Acted Unreasonably"]. First [writing], that dirt path was bumpy. Second [writing], it was dark. Third [writing], there were no street lights. Fourth [writing], his bicycle had no lights. Fifth [writing], he was not wearing a helmet. And sixth [writing], he was holding two shopping bags while trying to steer. That's six different ways that plaintiff was acting unreasonably. No wonder he had an accident. No wonder his own negligence caused his own injuries.

Example:

> So where did the plaintiff really fall down? Did he really fall down in the street because of a pothole, or was it somewhere else? For the answer, we only need to look at the emergency room report. When the plaintiff told

the nurse what really happened, that was before he was thinking about suing anyone. And the nurse wrote down what he said. It's so important I had that part of the emergency room report blown up. You've seen it—it's Defendant's Exhibit No. 7. We had to introduce it in evidence. Here's the blow-up of page 2 [put enlargement on easel]. I highlighted his words in yellow. He said: "I tripped on the curb and fell down." It's right there. His words, in black and white.

Two-Sided Arguments. Most cases that go to trial will involve some close issues. Persuasion research shows that when issues are close, two-sided arguments are stronger. That is, you should not only argue your strengths, but also deal candidly with your weaknesses (the other side's strengths). The jurors will talk about them during deliberations anyway, so avoiding or ignoring the problems is hardly a solution.

Example:

Throughout this trial, the defense has said, over and over, that the defendant is insane and not responsible for killing his boss. The defense says that the defendant's history of seeing psychiatrists over the past several years somehow proves that he's insane. But does that argument hold up? Not when you actually look at why he was seeing those psychiatrists. Let's start with his seeing Dr. Phillips eight years ago. What was that for? Mild depression. He was worried about his job. He had trouble sleeping. Perhaps good reasons to see a psychiatrist, but hardly evidence that the defendant was insane.

Example:

The defendant claims that delays on the job site were caused by bad weather, and that's something the defendant is not responsible for under the contract. Well, they're right about one thing—if bad weather actually caused the delay, they're not responsible. It's easy to make that claim, but proving it is another thing. Let's look at their own records, the daily reports from the job site, and you can see that their claim doesn't hold up.

Turn the Facts and Arguments Around. Often the best way to deal with apparent weaknesses is to turn them around, whenever possible. That is, turn the weakness into a strength by showing that the apparent weakness actually proves something entirely different. In short, turn the other side's arguments around. That's what good trial lawyers instinctively do.

Example:

Did Mary Smith pick the defendant out of the photo spread? No. But what does that prove? She told us she did that because she wanted to see the defendant in person, so she could be sure. And at the lineup, she immediately knew he was the one, and immediately told Detective O'Connor: "That's the man who robbed me. I'm sure." Isn't that exactly what you want a careful eyewitness to do? That's exactly what Mary Smith did.

Example:

> Everyone sees things slightly differently. That's what makes us human. So when two people see the same thing, they're going to describe it in their own way, using their own words. When they do, and they describe things a little differently, it doesn't mean one person is right, the other wrong. When you go into the jury room and talk about the evidence, each of you will remember a particular witness slightly differently. It doesn't mean one of you is right, another is wrong. It means you're human. It's when you hear two witnesses with perfectly identical testimony that you have to start wondering what's going on, and that didn't happen here.

Comment on Unkept Promises. Finally, lawyers commonly make promises during opening statements. Experienced lawyers take notes on the other side's opening statement. In particular, they write down what the other side promised the jury it would present proof of during the trial. If the party fails to present such proof, you can argue that the other side has failed to do what it promised to do.

Example:

> Remember when the defense, in their opening statement, promised that they would present written proof that the defendant was at his job when this robbery happened? That's what the defense promised: "written proof." But what did we get? Just the expected self-serving testimony of the defendant that he was at work that morning. Absolutely nothing else. Did they present any time cards? No. Did they present any attendance records? No. Did they present any memos of meetings showing the defendant was there? No. That speaks volumes.

3. Ending

The ending, the last minute or two of the closing argument, must end on a high note and accomplish several things. It should repeat the themes one last time. It should summarize the basis for liability or nonliability, or guilt or innocence. It should tell the jurors what you want them to do through their verdict. If the verdict forms and choices in civil cases are complicated, it should explain how you want the jurors to fill out the verdict forms and answer any special questions. Finally, it should empower and motivate the jurors to see that fairness is served and justice is done. In content, the ending often will be much like the ending of the opening statement, but in delivery, it must convey more passion and conviction.

Example (Prosecution):

> In short, what that defendant did was motivated by one thing: revenge. He decided to kill James Marshall, he planned how he would do it, and he carried it out just as he had planned it. Now it's time for you, the jury, to find that defendant guilty of premeditated murder. The facts demand it, and justice demands it.

Example (Defense):

We said it when this trial started, and we'll say it again one last time. This case is about shoddy police work. It's about mistaken identification. And it's about a rush to judgment. When the police cut corners, when the police decide to charge someone before they gather the facts, a horrible mistake can be made. You've seen how that's happened in this case. It's got to stop now, and only you have the power to stop it. Only you can keep a horrible mistake from becoming a horrible injustice. Your verdict can only say, loud and clear, not guilty. Frank is not guilty of murder.

Example (Plaintiff in Products Liability Case):

That cigarette lighter was unreasonably dangerous. That defendant knew it was unreasonably dangerous when they sold it to the unsuspecting public. Mrs. Harte was fatally injured because of it. And the worst part? They could have prevented it, and they should have prevented it. For two dollars, they could have made a safe lighter, made it in a way that the lighter could never flare up and kill someone. Because that defendant decided to put those two dollars into its pocket, instead of putting those two dollars into the lighter, a tragedy happened. Because that defendant put profits over safety, a life has been lost. Through your verdict, tell that defendant: Lives are more important than profits. Mrs. Harte's life is more important than your profits.

Example (Defendant in Products Liability Case):

We end up, then, where we began when this case started. We said then, and we say again, that you can't force people to be safe. You can give them instructions, but you can't force them to read the instructions. You can give them warnings, but you can't force them to heed the warnings. You can tell them how to use a product, but you can't force them to use it the right way. If people want to misuse a product, you can't stop them. At some point in time you have to say: Act responsibly, and use common sense. The plain fact is, the plaintiff didn't read those instructions, didn't heed that warning, and didn't act responsibly. That's the reason, the only reason, this tragedy happened. And that's simply not our fault. Your verdict needs to say that, loud and clear: Don't blame someone else when you don't act responsibly yourself.

In criminal cases, the verdict forms merely ask the jurors to decide if the defendant is guilty or not guilty of each charge. In civil cases, jurors are usually given a general verdict form, which asks the jurors to find for the plaintiff or defendant on each count and, if they find for the plaintiff, the amount of damages plaintiff should receive. In some civil cases, however, jurors are given special verdict forms (sometimes called *special interrogatories*) that ask them to make a series of sequential factual determinations. For example, the verdict form may read: "Do you find that the defendant was negligent? If 'yes,' go to the next question; if 'no,' stop." Do you find that the plaintiff was also negligent? If 'yes,' go to the next question; if 'no,' stop." And so on. These special verdicts are more commonly used in commercial cases and other cases with technical or complicated claims and defenses. In such cases it is important to go over the verdict forms and explain what you want the jurors to do.

Example:

> Members of the jury, her honor will give you a special verdict form that you must answer. Here's a blow-up of that form [put blow-up of verdict form on easel]. Notice that there are four questions you will have to answer. The first question is: "Do you find that the defendant was negligent?" That one's easy. The evidence has overwhelmingly shown that the defendant ran a red light and caused this collision. Therefore, the only answer to that question is "yes." The next question is . . .

9.6 Delivery

The delivery of the closing argument is at least as important as its content. As with the opening statement, the jurors are always asking: Are you saying this because you've been hired to say it, or do you really believe it? The jurors will be looking for any verbal and nonverbal cues that suggest you are anything less than totally sincere.

For a discussion of effective delivery of closing arguments, please watch Video C.3, "Wyo STI: Closing Arguments."

Effective closing arguments need to reach the jurors' hearts as well as their minds. This means you need to show passion and commitment for your side. Some lawyers are naturally forceful and emotional, whereas others have a calmer, more controlled demeanor. Both can be effective styles. Regardless of your personality and speaking style, your passion and commitment must be on display immediately. When the judge says: "Counsel, you may proceed with your closing argument," get up immediately, thank the judge, walk confidently and assertively to a spot a few feet away from the middle of the jury box, plant your feet, make eye contact with the jurors, and start. From that moment on, everything you say and do must convey that you are sincere, committed to your side, and expect to win this case.

Avoid using a podium, unless required by the court. A podium is a physical barrier between you and the jurors. You won't use reinforcing body language, gestures, and eye contact if you are standing behind a podium. If you are required to use a podium, try to stand to one side, so the jurors can see your whole body.

Keep your vocabulary simple and your sentence structure clear. Get rid of the legalese! Closing argument is not a speech. It's a passionate conversation on a subject you feel strongly about, to convince others to join your side. Don't worry about fracturing a sentence or mispronouncing words. It's passion and commitment that count now, not the technical niceties of the English language. A common mistake inexperienced lawyers make is to write out the planned closing argument, then practice delivering it. This rarely works, because written language is more formal, uses a more sophisticated vocabulary, and uses more complex sentence structure. It doesn't work in opening statements, and it doesn't work in closing arguments. Instead, outline your closing argument, then practice giving it, using the words and phrases you naturally use when you are talking with others on a subject you feel strongly about.

Practice giving your closing argument with as few notes as possible, usually a one- or two-page outline and perhaps a few other notes you've taken during the trial. Practice as many times as you need to give your actual closing without notes. Notes are a serious impediment to persuasive communication. They keep you from focusing on *how* to deliver the closing argument, prevent you from making eye contact with each of the jurors, and inhibit the natural body language that reinforces what you are saying. Notes remind the jurors that what you are saying has all been planned and written out in advance, rather than coming from the heart. Also, when jurors see a lawyer using notes, they think "she's just reading a script," so you won't convey that you believe passionately in your argument if you use them. In short, though extensive notes may serve as a comfort blanket for inexperienced lawyers, they almost always formalize the content, deaden the delivery, and detract from your credibility. That's too high a price to pay during closing arguments, where passion and commitment count.

Finally, learn and practice all the verbal and nonverbal components of effective communication. Effective delivery begins with your physical presence. Wear a suit or outfit that conveys confidence and authority. Stand still, facing the jurors, a few feet away from the middle of the jury rail (unless you are forced to use a podium). Put your feet about a foot apart and lean forward slightly. Avoid wandering around or rocking in place, because these are distracting mannerisms. Instead, change your location and body position to signal that you are moving from one topic to another.

Use deep breathing to make sure you have enough air to speak forcefully and confidently. Vary your volume, pitch, speech rate, articulation, pauses, and silences to maintain jurors' interest.

Use hand, arm, and facial gestures to punctuate your speech. Have your hands ready to talk by holding them about waist level (rather than in your pockets, clasped in front, or held behind your back), so they will be ready when you want to make reinforcing gestures. When your arms, hands, and face are all involved, these upper-body gestures draw attention to your face and make you a much more interesting and emphatic speaker.

Maintain eye contact with each juror. Look at one juror, direct a thought to that juror, then look at another juror and direct another thought to that juror. This way you will be talking to all the jurors, neither singling out nor ignoring any particular juror, and maintaining eye contact for a few seconds with successive jurors. In our culture, looking people in the eye is important.

9.7 Common Issues in Closing Arguments

Trial lawyers repeatedly encounter a number of the same issues in both civil and criminal cases. Over time, they develop effective arguments for those issues. Trial lawyers are shameless borrowers. When they hear or read an effective argument, they put it in a memory bank for future use.

Start collecting effective arguments and modify them to fit your personality and style. Over time you will collect arguments that you can use with common recurring issues. The following will give you a good start.

1. General Issues

a. Length of Closing Arguments

How long should an effective closing argument be? Some judges set time limits on closing arguments; others leave it to the lawyers. In typical cases, those civil and criminal cases that last between 2 and 4 days, lawyers usually use between 20 and 40 minutes per side. That's enough time to make an effective argument, yet not so long that jurors tune out and become bored. In other cases, depending on the length of the trial, the complexity of issues, and the high-profile nature of the case, judges may allow more time, such as 60 minutes for each side.

Lawyers usually use most of their allotted time, but that is not always wise. Sometimes lawyers make short closing arguments to emphasize that their clients are only peripherally involved parties. For example, in criminal cases involving multiple defendants, the lawyer for the defendant with the least amount of proof against her may make a short closing argument emphasizing a "why are we here?" theme.

b. Allocation of Time Between Liability and Damages

In civil cases involving both liability and damages, the parties must decide how to apportion their time between the two issues. Lawyers usually allocate their time based on the relative significance and complexity of these issues in each case. In personal injury cases, however, plaintiff's lawyers usually emphasize liability in opening statements and damages in closing arguments. Their view usually is that if they haven't proven liability by now, closing arguments won't change things. Instead, though they spend some time on liability, they use most of their time discussing the permissible elements of damages and justifying the dollar amounts they are asking the jurors to award for each element.

c. Allocation of Time Between Plaintiff's Closing and Rebuttal

In most jurisdictions, the plaintiff, having the burden of proof, has the right to open and close. That is, the plaintiff makes the first closing argument, followed by the defendant's closing argument, and then the plaintiff has the right to make a rebuttal argument. How much time should be allocated to rebuttal?

Many lawyers use too much time for rebuttal and fail to use that time effectively. A good rebuttal argument is short, focused, and positive. A good rule of thumb is that the rebuttal should be no longer than half of the closing argument, and preferably less. For instance, if plaintiff will have a total of 30 minutes to argue, plaintiff should use about 20 to 25 minutes for the closing argument and save 5 to 10 minutes for rebuttal. Judges who impose time limitations may also limit the time the plaintiff can reserve for rebuttal.

d. Arguing Liability Only, or Liability and Damages

One of the hardest decisions defendants in civil cases have to make, in both personal injury and commercial cases, is whether to argue liability only, or to argue both liability and damages. There is no easy answer to this question. Defendants always prefer to win on liability, but failing that they want to minimize damages, particularly when the plaintiff's damages request will be high. They also know that if they argue only liability, the plaintiff in rebuttal must limit its argument to the liability issue. Defendants fear that if they argue both liability and damages, it will weaken their liability argument (the jurors are likely to think that you don't believe your own liability argument, since you're also talking about damages), and give plaintiff a second opportunity to argue damages. However, if they argue liability only, and the jury finds for the plaintiff on that issue, defendants will not have addressed damages at all (the jurors are likely to think that you're not disputing the plaintiff's suggested dollar amounts for the various elements of damages). These decisions, of course, are influenced by the strengths and weaknesses of the liability and damages issues and the amount of money realistically at risk. In a perfect world, defendants would like to argue that they are not liable, but also "buy insurance" by arguing that the plaintiff's damages claims are excessive and unreasonable. Can defendants do that credibly?

Views differ. Some defense lawyers believe that you cannot credibly argue both liability and damages and that if you do, you essentially concede liability. Other defense lawyers believe that you can credibly argue both issues if you set it up carefully. There are two basic ways they do this. One way is to argue liability first, then damages, and tell the jurors what you are doing and why.

Example (Defendant):

> That's why, members of the jury, this accident was not our fault. It's the plaintiff who caused this accident, and he has no one to blame but himself.
>
> Let's turn for a moment to their damages claims, what they've spent so much time talking about. Now, some of you are thinking: "Wait a minute. If the defendant's not liable for this accident, why are you talking about damages at all?" That's a fair question, and it deserves a straight answer. We believe the evidence has shown this accident was the plaintiff's fault, and therefore you should return a verdict for the defense. We think you'll agree with us. I could stop right here. But my duty to my client requires me to discuss every issue raised by the plaintiff. So let's spend a few minutes looking at what they've asked for, and see if it holds up, see if it's sensible and reasonable.

The other way is to structure the defense argument so that you argue damages first, then end up with liability.

Example (Defendant):

> Members of the jury, having just heard the plaintiff's argument, two things jump out: They haven't proven that we're responsible for this accident, and what they've asked for in damages is unreasonable and unsupported.
>
> Let's deal with their damages claims first. We're not responsible for any damages, since this accident was not our fault, but you know, they spent so much time talking about all the money they'd like to get, I'm obligated to respond to what they've said. [Argues that plaintiff's damages are inflated and not supported by evidence.] That's why, folks, if the plaintiff were entitled to get anything, which he's not, the most he should ever receive is $46,000.
>
> Now let's turn to the real issue here: Has the plaintiff proven that we're responsible for this accident? The obvious answer is no. They haven't come close. If anything, the evidence has shown that the plaintiff himself was careless, and his carelessness caused this accident. How do we know? First, . . .

e. Anticipating Defense Argument, or Waiting for Rebuttal

Because the plaintiff gets to argue first and last, the plaintiff has a choice to make: Should she anticipate the defense's likely arguments and deal with them in plaintiff's closing argument, or hold off and respond to them in plaintiff's rebuttal argument?

Many plaintiffs and prosecutors use their closing argument to argue their case forcefully and use rebuttal to answer any defense arguments that have to be addressed. They feel that there is little point in trying to anticipate defense arguments, because you have rebuttal to mount a counterattack.

Some lawyers, however, feel that it can be effective to anticipate some defense arguments. Persuasion research has shown that when the issues are close, two-sided arguments are stronger. That is, it is more persuasive to both argue your strengths and provide counterarguments for your weaknesses, those things the other side is likely to argue. This being so, sometimes as plaintiff you can anticipate a defense argument and destroy it in your closing argument. If the defense makes the argument, the jurors will already know what it is and will have heard effective responses to it.

Finally, some plaintiffs sometimes save a strong argument for rebuttal, on the theory that a strong counterattack during rebuttal is a more effective strategy. The risk, of course, is that the defense may not raise the issue in the defense argument and will object (as being beyond the scope) if the plaintiff raises the argument for the first time in rebuttal.

f. Anticipating Plaintiff's Rebuttal

Because the defense only argues once, it must anticipate the plaintiff's rebuttal argument. First, learn how the plaintiff's attorney frequently makes rebuttal arguments. Every lawyer develops favorite routines, and plaintiff's lawyers often save those routines for rebuttal. Second, your preparation for closing argument will identify the plaintiff's strongest arguments. If any of those routines and arguments were not used in the plaintiff's first closing argument (sometimes called *sandbagging*), there is a good chance that the plaintiff is saving them for rebuttal. Those are the arguments you need to raise and answer in the defense closing argument. A common approach is to remind the jurors that the defense does not have a second argument and that all you can do is try to anticipate the arguments plaintiff will make in rebuttal and trust the jurors to find answers to the rest.

Example (Defendant):

> Members of the jury, we're at a disadvantage. You see, we only get to argue once. After I sit down, plaintiff gets to make a second argument, and I don't get a chance to respond. So all I can do is try to anticipate now what they'll say and answer them. For the rest, just look to the evidence, because that's where all the answers are.

Example (Defendant):

> They haven't argued it yet, so they're obviously saving it for rebuttal, knowing I don't have a chance to respond. If they argue . . . , all you need to do is remember Mrs. Johnson's testimony, where she said. . . . That's where the answer to that argument is.

It is also important for the defense to be alert to improper rebuttal arguments. Plaintiff's rebuttal argument is just that: a chance to rebut the defense closing argument. It is not intended to give the plaintiff an opportunity to make entirely new arguments for the first time, because that would be unfair. For example, if the defense did not discuss damages in its closing, the plaintiff may not discuss damages in rebuttal.

g. Multiple Parties and Claims

A common dilemma in both civil and criminal cases is how to deal with multiple parties, most commonly multiple defendants. The plaintiff wants the jurors to see the defendants as a group, so that if one defendant is liable or guilty, the others must be as well. The defendants, of course, want to be considered individually, particularly the defendant against whom the plaintiff has the least evidence. That defendant will want to isolate himself from the other defendants and argue that although the plaintiff has presented evidence, there was little credible evidence against that defendant. In criminal cases, with the high burden of proof, this argument is commonly made by the more peripheral defendants. Co-defendants usually hate this argument, because it usually implies that, though the evidence against this defendant is weak, the evidence against the other defendants is strong. Nonetheless, if you represent a peripheral defendant, you should consider making the argument.

Example (Defendant):

> His honor will tell you that you must consider each defendant separately, and that you cannot find any defendant guilty unless the evidence against that defendant proves his guilt beyond a reasonable doubt. That's particularly important when you consider the evidence the prosecution presented against Bobby Jackson—or, more importantly, what they didn't present. The prosecution brought no witnesses who said Bobby robbed the bank. They brought no witnesses who said Bobby was even near the bank when it was robbed. They brought no witnesses who said Bobby helped plan or carry out the robbery. So how can they even claim that they've proven Bobby guilty of anything beyond a reasonable doubt? They want you to find him guilty by association, that because he's a friend of the other defendants, he must be involved. That's not right, and it's not the law.

The same kind of dilemma arises with multiple claims. Plaintiffs (and prosecutors) often bring multiple claims (or charges), hoping that the jurors will find that at least one of them has been proven. The defense must argue that the claims have to be assessed individually, or that what the plaintiff has done is raise multiple claims in the hope that the jurors will assume that at least some of the claims must be true, when in fact there's a common defense to all of them. In short, the defense needs to warn the jurors about that kind of tactic and argue that this tactic by itself proves the weakness of the plaintiff's case.

Example (Defendant):

> You know, the prosecution filed all kinds of charges here. They've charged robbery, burglary, assault, theft, and the list goes on. They obviously think

that if they charge Bobby with all kinds of things, you're going to think that at least one of them must be true. But you're too smart for that. You know that since the prosecution has failed to prove, beyond a reasonable doubt, that Bobby was even there, or involved in any way, all their charges—no matter how many they filed—must fail as well. And that's the fatal flaw in their entire case: They failed to prove Bobby was involved in any crime.

h. Eyewitness Credibility and Conflicts

Perhaps the most common witness issues in trials involve eyewitness credibility and conflicts. In a personal injury case, one witness testifies that a collision happened one way, another witness testifies it happened differently. In a commercial case, two witnesses differ as to what was said during a key meeting. In criminal cases, there are frequently conflicts between the prosecution's eyewitnesses and the defendant's testimony. In these situations, jurors need to resolve the credibility issue, and lawyers need to argue how they should resolve it.

A good way to begin is to ask: Why is this witness saying what he's saying? People do and say things for a reason. Is he mistaken? Confused? Doesn't remember? Has he made prior inconsistent statements about the event or conversation? If so, what accounts for them? Is he biased or interested? Does he have a motive to distort or lie? Are there things in his background that suggest he can't be trusted? Good cross-examinations bring out these facts, and good witness credibility arguments focus on them.

> For a discussion of the challenges of discussing witness credibility in final argument, see Video C.4, "Wyo STI: Professors Irving Younger and Steve Easton on 'The Ten Commandments of Cross-Examination,' Part 3 (Arguing Witness Credibility in Closing)."

Example:

Folks, in this case we have two parties, Mr. Gable and Mr. Cannon, who say two different things. Mr. Gable says the light was yellow when he entered the intersection. Mr. Cannon says it had already turned to red. Well, they can't both be right, so who do you believe?

One way to decide that is to ask: Who was in a better position to see what they say they saw? Who was that? Mr. Gable. He was in a perfect position to see what was happening. He was going straight down the street, with the traffic light directly in front of him. Compare that with Mr. Cannon, who was stopped in the middle of the intersection, under the light, trying to make a left-hand turn. He couldn't possibly see the color of the light at the same time he says he was watching the oncoming traffic. If this case was just about whether to believe Mr. Gable or Mr. Cannon, you'd have to go with Mr. Gable, because he was in a better position to see everything, including that light.

But there's more. Remember what the bystander, Mr. Bozza, said? He was standing on the corner when it happened. He told us that when the two cars crashed, the light was still yellow for Main Street. His testimony backs up Mr. Gable, and Mr. Bozza doesn't care who wins this lawsuit. That's how we know this collision happened just the way Mr. Gable said it did.

Example:

Members of the jury, the issue that decides this case is clear. At the key meeting on June 1, did Mr. Thompson tell Mr. Jacobs that the apartment building under construction would have six inches of fiberglass insulation in the ceiling? Mr. Thompson says that's exactly what he said, but Mr. Jacobs denies it. Both have reasons to testify as they did. So who's telling the truth?

Her honor will instruct you that you should consider: Who has a better memory of the meeting? Whose version of the meeting makes more sense? And whose version is supported by the other evidence? Remember that for Mr. Thompson, this was the most important meeting of his life, and he'll remember it all his life. For Mr. Jacobs, it was just another meeting, just like several others that week alone. It shouldn't surprise us, then, that Mr. Thompson had a much better memory of that meeting than Mr. Jacobs, a much better memory of exactly what happened during the meeting, and a much better memory of the words they spoke that day.

And doesn't it make sense that Mr. Thompson would tell Mr. Jacobs that his building had six inches of insulation in the ceiling? That's what the blueprints and specifications said. Those blueprints and specs were right on the table for anyone to look at. Why on earth would Mr. Thompson say anything different than what his own plans and specs said?

Example:

Mr. Golden didn't expect to be a witness to a shooting that morning. He was simply sitting at the bus stop, waiting for the downtown express. And then, suddenly, without warning, a shot rang out, one man fell to the pavement a few feet away, and another man, holding a gun, ran past him going north on Maple Street. Before Mr. Golden even realized what had happened, it was over, and the man was out of sight. That's the prosecution's case in a nutshell—the testimony of Mr. Golden, their only eyewitness, who now claims that Bobby Smith was the man with the gun.

But is that a credible identification? Mr. Golden saw that man's face for, according to his own testimony, about three seconds. It was already dark, and there was very little street lighting. Remember when I asked Mr. Golden: What kind of clothing was that man wearing? He couldn't say, other than dark pants and a sweatshirt. Did he have any unusual hair style? Facial hair? Facial features? Tattoos? He didn't remember any. What about the gun? Was it a revolver or an automatic? Blue steel or chrome plated? He couldn't say.

The best we can say for Mr. Golden is that it was too unexpected, and happened too fast, that Mr. Golden couldn't get a good look at that man, certainly not the kind of look you need to be sure of what you saw. That's not the kind of identification you can rely on, not when the question is whether the prosecution has proved its case beyond a reasonable doubt.

Example:

You heard Bobby Dalton testify. Dalton was originally charged with bank robbery along with the defendant. He then entered into a plea agreement with the government, pleaded guilty to reduced charges, and will be sentenced after this trial is over. The defense says: You can't believe the prosecution's case because it depends on the word of a former co-conspirator, who cut a deal with the government to save his own neck. That sounds good at first, but it just doesn't hold up.

First of all, we didn't pick Dalton to be a witness; the defendant did, by getting Dalton involved in this conspiracy. Dalton gave you a unique insider's account of how this conspiracy was formed, what it did, and who its leader was. Second, we're not saying believe Dalton just because he testified under oath. Don't take just his word for it. Instead, see if what he said is corroborated by the other evidence. When you do, you'll see that everything he said fits with all the other evidence. That's how you know Bobby Dalton told us the truth.

i. Expert Credibility and Conflicts

Another common area for witness credibility and conflict issues is the battle of the experts. Whenever the sides present conflicting expert testimony, jurors will ask, and lawyers must answer: Why should the jurors believe one expert over another?

Again, look at the testimony of the competing experts. Does your expert have better education and training? Better hands-on experience? Does the opposing expert always testify for the plaintiff or defendant or regularly work for the opposing lawyer? Does their expert actively solicit consulting work? Make his living as an expert witness? Did their expert use unreliable data? Make questionable assumptions? Did the expert fail to do all the tests and analyses she should have done? Did she make inconsistent statements in her deposition or in other testimony? Was she impeached by a treatise? These are the things you brought out on cross-examination. Closing argument is the time to explain their significance.

Example:

Let's turn next to the doctors who testified. Dr. Klein, Mr. Gable's treating doctor, told us that Mr. Gable will never be able to work as a mechanic again, because of the damage to his elbow. The joint's too weak, and has limited range of motion. Dr. Klein says that's a permanent condition. The defense doctor, Dr. Bradsky, claims there's nothing permanently wrong with Mr. Gable's elbow, and that with a little more therapy he should be able to go back to his job. The question you need to answer is: Who do you believe, Dr. Klein or Dr. Bradsky?

Let's take a look at what each did. Dr. Klein, an orthopedic specialist with over 20 years of experience, treated Mr. Gable at the hospital and supervised his therapy. Dr. Klein was there from the beginning. If anyone knows Mr. Gable and his elbow, it's Dr. Klein. And another thing: Dr. Klein wasn't hired to be a witness. She came here as Mr. Gable's treating physician, with no axe to grind. Contrast that with Dr. Bradsky. How did he get involved? The defense lawyers hired him. When did he get involved? Over a year after Mr. Gable was injured. How many times did he examine Mr. Gable? Once. And who has Dr. Bradsky testified for the last six times he's been hired as an expert? You got it; always hired by the defense.

Example:

> Members of the jury, was the defendant insane at the time he shot his girlfriend to death? The defendant's expert, Dr. Rubin, says yes. The court psychiatrist, Dr. Kelliher, says no. Which one makes more sense?
>
> Dr. Rubin has a private practice and has seen lots of patients with psychiatric conditions over the years, but he has almost no experience in evaluating whether defendants were legally insane when they committed their crimes.
>
> Dr. Kelliher, on the other hand, deals with criminal defendants every day. That's his job as the court psychiatrist. He spends close to half of his time specifically evaluating whether defendants charged with crimes are insane. He's done that hundreds of times over the years. And Dr. Kelliher says that one of the most difficult things is to determine if defendants are faking symptoms—*malingering*, he called it—and merely pretending to be insane. That's where experience counts, and only Dr. Kelliher has that kind of experience.

j. Exhibit Management

Both plaintiff and defendant can, and should, use admitted exhibits and visual aids during their closing arguments. When plaintiff's closing argument is over, the plaintiff should have two or three large exhibits on easels, positioned for maximum visual effect. For example, the plaintiff may have a large intersection diagram summarizing the liability facts, and a large damages chart summarizing the dollar amounts requested for the various elements of damages.

What should the defendant do when the defense begins its closing argument? One approach is to simply take down plaintiff's exhibits and put them by plaintiff's counsel table. Another way is to keep one plaintiff's exhibit up and attack it at the beginning of the defense argument. For example, if the defense is not going to discuss damages at all, it's best to remove the plaintiff's damages chart before beginning the argument. If the defense is going to discuss damages, it's sometimes useful to keep the plaintiff's damages chart and immediately point to numbers that are unreasonable and unsupported and explain why.

2. Civil Issues

a. Negligence

Of all civil cases, the most common jury trial is a personal injury case based on a vehicle collision. In these cases, the jury must first determine whether the defendant was negligent. A standard negligence instruction provides: "Negligence is the failure to act as a reasonably careful person would act under the circumstances." Good closing arguments use the admitted facts to show that the legal standard has, or has not, been met.

Example:

> So was the defendant negligent? The defense wants you to believe that because the defendant was driving at the speed limit, that somehow proves he was not negligent. But we know better than that. His honor will tell you that negligence is the failure to act as a reasonably careful person

would act under the circumstances. Was the defendant driving the way a reasonably careful person would have driven that night? Remember that the road was dark. It had snowed earlier in the day, and the road surface was wet. The temperature had fallen after the sun went down, and the wet surface was now frozen. Everyone knows that when you've got a frozen road surface, you can't just drive at the speed limit. You've got to slow down, way down, in case you hit ice. That's what the defendant should have done, if he'd acted carefully. But he didn't, and that's negligence.

b. Causation

Even if negligence is proven, there is no liability unless the negligence caused the injury. A standard causation instruction provides: "Negligence causes an injury if it helps produce it and if the injury would not have happened without the negligence." A standard violation-of-statute instruction provides: "If you find that a person has violated any of these traffic laws, that person is negligent, and you must then determine if that negligence was a cause of the injury to the plaintiff." Good closing arguments use the admitted facts to show how the legal standard has, or has not, been met.

Example:

Did Mr. Wilkins have a drink that night? Yes. He told you that he was driving home after dinner with his wife, where he had two glasses of wine, one before, and one during, dinner. But what does that prove? The plaintiff wants you to believe that simply because Mr. Wilkins had wine with dinner, that means he's responsible for this accident happening. But that's not right, and it's not the law. The court will tell you that negligence causes an injury if it helps produce it, and *if*—here's the key part—the injury would not have happened without the negligence. The plain truth of the matter is that this accident had nothing to do with Mr. Wilkins having wine with dinner, because this accident would have happened anyway. It was caused by the plaintiff making a left-hand turn in front of Mr. Wilkins's car, and there's simply no way Mr. Wilkins—or anyone else—could possibly have reacted in time.

c. Comparative Fault

In many negligence cases, the issue is whether, in addition to the defendant's fault, another person was also at fault. Two situations commonly arise. First, defendant frequently claims that plaintiff was solely or partially at fault. If the jury finds both plaintiff and defendant at fault, it must then apportion damages between them. Second, defendant sometimes claims that a third party (usually called a *nonparty at fault*) is also responsible.

If the jury finds that plaintiff, defendant, and the nonparty at fault are all responsible, it must then apportion damages among them. In these cases, plaintiff will usually argue that his fault and that of the nonparty are minimal and that the named defendant is principally at fault. Defendant will usually argue that his fault is minimal and that plaintiff or the nonparty is principally at fault. Both sides frequently accuse the other side of secretly wanting a compromise verdict splitting liability. Both sides frequently use a visual aid or the verdict form to suggest percentages for how the jury should apportion fault (which totals 0 or 100 percent).

Example (Plaintiff):

> We've proven that the defendant failed to yield to Mr. Gable's oncoming car, and we've proven that the defendant's illegal left-hand turn caused the collision with Mr. Gable's car. The rules of the road are simple: You can't make a left-hand turn unless it's safe. You have to wait for oncoming traffic to pass before you make that turn.
>
> So what's the defendant's argument? It's that, although the defendant made an illegal left-hand turn, Mr. Gable should have reacted more quickly and slammed on his brakes faster, and this somehow makes it partly Mr. Gable's fault. What they really want you to do is shift the blame for this collision from the defendant, where it belongs, and put some of the blame on Mr. Gable.
>
> Folks, reject that argument. It's not supported by the facts, it's not supported by the law, and it's not supported by common sense. Here's the verdict form (holding up verdict form) his honor will give you. Where it says "Plaintiff's percentage of fault," write in "0." Where it says "Defendant's percentage of fault," write in "100." That's the only verdict that's fair, that shows what really happened here.

Example (Plaintiff):

> Members of the jury, her honor will give you a verdict form that asks you to decide the relative degrees of fault in this case. She will tell you that you may consider the fault, if any, of three people: The plaintiff, Ms. Adams; the defendant, Mr. Smith; and a third person, the driver of the sports car who was never identified.
>
> What happened here is simple. Mr. Smith rear-ended Ms. Adams's car. We all agree on that. Why it happened is also simple. The driver of the sports car backed out of an alley directly in front of Ms. Adams, causing her to slam on her brakes, and Mr. Smith failed to brake in time and ran into the back of Ms. Adams's car. After that happened, the driver of the sports car left the scene, and we don't know who he is.
>
> What should we do about this? The defendant would have you believe that this collision was totally the fault of the driver of the sports car, because he backed out of the alley in front of Ms. Adams's car. The defense wants you to put 100 percent of the fault on that man, and none on himself. But that's not the right thing to do here. The defendant had a responsibility to keep a safe distance between his car and the car in front of him—Ms. Adams's car. That's to give yourself time to brake in case the car in front of you, for whatever reason, also brakes. Because Mr. Smith was tailgating, he couldn't react in time, and that's his fault.
>
> What the defense really wants you to do is put 50 percent of the blame on the sports car driver, so the defendant only has to bear 50 percent of the blame. But that's not the right verdict here. This collision happened for one simple reason: The defendant was tailgating, and that's why he bears 100 percent of the responsibility for this collision.

d. Compensatory Damages

Plaintiffs should always spend time in the closing argument discussing damages, suggesting damages amounts, and explaining why the amounts requested are both reasonable and supported by the evidence. This is particularly so in personal injury cases in which noneconomic damages are significant. A common damages instruction in many states in personal injury cases provides for several damages "elements": the nature, extent, and duration of the injury; pain, suffering, disfigurement, disability, and mental anguish; present and future medical expenses; present and future lost income; and losses to marital and family relationships. Plaintiffs usually use a poster board listing these elements, discuss each of the elements and fill in the dollar amount they request, then total the amounts for a final damages figure. (In a few jurisdictions, parties cannot suggest specific dollar amounts for noneconomic damages.)

Plaintiffs spend most of their time discussing the noneconomic losses and explaining why those losses require damages in a certain amount. In particular, plaintiffs need to deal with three damages elements: the present value of lost future income, compensation for pain and suffering, and compensation for the loss of a relationship. If defendants decide to discuss plaintiff's damages claims, they usually attack plaintiff's requested damages for the noneconomic loss elements and suggest that, even if plaintiff proves liability, damages should not be more than a certain amount.

How high should plaintiff's requested damages be? How low should defendant's alternative suggested damages be? There has been substantial jury research on these questions (psychologists call them "anchoring effects"), and three things stand out. First, most verdicts will be within the range of the plaintiff's requested and defendant's suggested damages. These usually provide the high and low figures (the anchors) for the jury's thinking, and its verdict is usually a compromise somewhere between the two figures. Second, the higher the plaintiff's request, the higher the jury's verdict is likely to be, provided that the plaintiff's request is credible. Third, the lower the defendant's suggested alternative, the lower the jury's verdict is likely to be, again provided that the defendant's alternative is credible. Therefore, both plaintiff and defendant must ask the same question: How high, or low, can my damages figure be and still be credible? Too high or too low, and the risk is that jurors will ignore it, and it will have no influence on their decision or will influence their decision negatively.

Whatever that suggested amount, you need to explain how you reached that figure and why that amount is reasonable. Those are the questions jurors always have: Why that amount? How did you determine it? Why not half that? Or double? Effective plaintiff's lawyers translate what happened to the plaintiff into money damages and explain to the jurors how they determined those damages and why that's the least the jurors should award in this case. Effective defense lawyers explain that damages must be reasonable and based on proof rather than speculation or sympathy, and they then translate that reasonableness into an alternative damages recommendation.

Some jurisdictions allow so called "per diem" or "unit of time" arguments, so long as the unit of time is not too small. For example, a plaintiff's attorney might argue that the plaintiff should be compensated for pain and suffering with $25,000 for each of the next 20 years. However, a plaintiff's attorney may not ask for a dollar for every minute or hour other small unit of time.

Example (Plaintiff's Damages):

Members of the jury, let's turn now to compensation. We need to discuss it, because Ms. Adams has suffered serious injuries and losses, and because the defendant is clearly responsible for those losses. What will it take to make Ms. Adams whole? What will it take to give back to her what the defendant's negligence took from her? His honor will tell you that you should consider several things, and I've put them on this poster board [puts board on easel].

The first thing we need to consider is medical expenses. That's easy. Ms. Adams's hospital bill was $4,280, and her doctors' bills were $3,682. There's no dispute over that. So her medical expenses are $7,962 [writes figure on board].

The next thing we need to consider is lost income. Again, that's easy. Ms. Adams was out of work for six weeks, and she makes $1,000 a week at her company. This means she lost $6,000 when she was off work on medical leave [writes figure on board].

The third thing we need to consider is the nature, extent, and duration of Ms. Adams's injuries . . . .

Finally, we need to consider the pain, suffering, and mental anguish Ms. Adams went through and will continue to go through in the coming years . . . .

What, then, is the least we need to do to compensate Helen Adams fully for her injuries, medical expenses, lost income, and for what she went through? We suggest that the least we should do, the least amount that will even begin to compensate her, is the amount of $75,962. If you don't think that's fair and adequate compensation, it's up to you to decide what that amount should be. And if the defense thinks that amount is too high, when they get to argue let them tell you why that amount is too high. If they don't, you know they don't have any issue with it.

Example (Lost Future Income):

Let's turn now to the next thing we need to consider: lost future income. Some things are not disputed. Bob Clark worked as a carpenter. Since high school, that's what he's done, what he's become skilled at. Because of his back injury, which the doctors all agree is permanent, he'll never work as a carpenter again.

What's that mean for Mr. Clark's future? You heard Ms. Willis, the employment specialist, tell us that Mr. Clark's earning potential dropped from $40,000 a year, what he was earning as a carpenter, down to $20,000, what he can expect to earn as a high school graduate in today's job market. Mr. Clark has lost $20,000 a year in income, and he's only 40 years old. Ms. Willis told us that Mr. Clark would be expected to work at least until age 60, and perhaps more. This means that he's going to lose $20,000 a year for at least 20 years, which is at least $400,000. So should we compensate Mr. Clark for that amount, to cover his lost future income? No. Remember Dr. Johnson, the economist who teaches at the university? He calculated how much money it will take to put in the bank today, so that Mr. Clark can draw out $20,000 a year over the next 20 years, and the account will then be completely spent. He said that if we put $243,000 in a safe bank account today, it should, because of interest, pay that $20,000 for the next 20 years. So that amount, $243,000, is the least we should award to compensate Mr. Clark for his future lost income.

Example (Noneconomic Losses):

Now we turn to the last two items [pointing]. First, there's the nature, extent, and duration of the injury. How can we compensate Mr. Clark for the fact that he has a permanent back injury, an injury that not only affects his income, which we've already talked about, but affects the rest of his life? He can't do many of the things he used to be able to do: work around the house doing the odd jobs, playing with his young children, playing golf at the municipal course. These are the kinds of things we take for granted in our lives, and we never realize how much they mean until we lose them. That's what's happened to Mr. Clark. And these are permanent losses, for a man who's only 40 years old, in the prime of his life. We know that Mr. Clark is likely to live for 38 more years, according to those life statistics we heard. We suggest that Mr. Clark be compensated $5,000 each year for the disability that forever affects his quality of life. That's a total of $190,000. That's the least we should do. If the defense thinks that's too high, have them explain why Mr. Clark's injuries and losses to his quality of life don't deserve to be compensated fully.

Second, there's the last item: pain, suffering, disfigurement, and mental anguish. That's the hardest one to come to grips with, isn't it? How do we compensate Mr. Clark for all the pain, suffering, and mental anguish he's gone through since his back was broken? How do we compensate him for what he'll go through for the rest of his life? We all, like Mr. Clark, would prefer that this never happened, but it has, and we need to deal with it. Pain is probably the thing people fear the most, isn't it? Everyone wants their lives to be free of pain, so they can truly live their lives. Folks, Mr. Clark has been in constant pain for the past two years, and the doctors have told us that he'll always experience some pain. That's because he has stainless steel pins holding three of his vertebrae together.

We suggest he be compensated in the amount of $50,000 for what he's gone through since this collision. And for the rest of his life—what's likely to be another 38 years—we suggest another $380,000. That totals $430,000. Now, some of you may ask: Why that amount? Good question. No one can say for sure what that amount should be, and I can't tell you what it should be. The most I can do is make a reasonable suggestion, and that's $430,000. If you feel that amount isn't enough to compensate Mr. Clark for what he'll live with for the rest of his life, for what's likely to be 38 years, it's your duty as jurors to decide what that amount should be. That's why we put this issue in your hands. The 12 of you together, given your collective wisdom and experience in life, you understand what Mr. Clark has lost, and you'll know what's right.

Example (Loss of Relationship in Wrongful Death):

What should we do to compensate Mary Harte for the loss of her mother? For the loss of that special relationship? Some of you may feel that one or two million dollars is the right amount. Others of you may feel that the right amount is four or five million dollars. That's for you to decide. I can't tell you what's right, and neither can the other side. What I can do is this: Trust the 12 of you to put your heads together, put your collective experiences in life together, and you will know what's fair, full, reasonable compensation.

Example (Pain and Suffering—Defendant):

Members of the jury, the plaintiff's lawyer has asked you to give the plaintiff $200,000 for pain and suffering. One thing is clear from his argument: They'd really like that money. But this is a court of law, and you are jurors charged with upholding the law. We need to decide what's reasonable, not just what they'd like to get.

Let's look at what happened since the collision. We agree that the plaintiff went through a tough period. We agree that a broken leg is painful and that the rehabilitation can be difficult. However, we know from the doctors that the plaintiff was essentially back to normal six months later. We know that his leg has recovered fully. And we know that he's pain-free today. Given that he made a complete recovery in about six months, and that's he's been pain-free since, does it make sense to give him $200,000? That's simply not reasonable. We suggest that if he's entitled to anything, the sum of $20,000 will be more than adequate compensation for his recovery period.

In commercial cases, the issue of consequential damages in contract claims frequently arises. Plaintiffs naturally want to have all their losses attributed to defendant's breach. Defendants usually argue that plaintiffs are guilty of overreaching, and that most of their damages claims are neither covered in the contracts nor were within the contemplation of the parties when they signed the contracts. Plaintiff cannot recover for consequential damages unless those damages were foreseeable to the parties when they entered into the contract.

Example (Commercial Case—Defendant):

Let's talk next about the plaintiff's damages claims. Even if they prove—which they haven't—that the problems with the heating system we installed are our fault, where are the damages? Plaintiff is the one that didn't notify us of any problems. And then, instead of calling us to fix our system, they called someone else, who charged much more than we would have charged, and took much longer than we would have taken. We're not responsible for that decision, and we're not responsible for that delay.

But that's not all. Plaintiff claims that they lost profits during those three weeks the store was without heat. First, there's been no proof that they lost sales, or profits, because of the heating problem. Second, that's not something we're responsible for. No one ever contemplated that we would be responsible for any lost profits if there was a heating problem. They never talked about that, and there's nothing about that in our contract.

e. Punitive Damages

Plaintiff's lawyers love, and defense lawyers abhor, the prospect of arguing punitive damages in tort cases, particularly when the defendant is a sizeable corporation. Those jurisdictions that allow punitive damages usually require that the plaintiff prove the defendant intentionally caused the injury, was motivated by ill will, or consciously disregarded a risk that the injury would occur. Most jurisdictions require that this be proved by clear and convincing evidence, although some follow the preponderance standard. If punitive damages are proved, the jury may award an amount that will punish the defendant for the misconduct and deter the defendant and others from engaging in the same or similar conduct in the future. A common measuring stick has been the defendant's economic worth.

However, the Supreme Court has decided several cases that involve due process limitations on punitive damages awards. The most important of these are *BMW v. Gore*, 517 U.S. 559 (1996), and *State Farm v. Campbell*, 538 U.S. 408 (2003). Two points are notable. First, to be properly admissible under FRE 404(b) on the issue of punitive damages, other acts evidence must have a nexus—be substantially similar—to the specific harm suffered by the plaintiff, and those other acts cannot have been legal conduct where they occurred. Second, a ratio of punitive damages to compensatory damages of greater than 9:1 will probably not be upheld on appeal unless the "reprehensibility" and other factors in the defendant's conduct are unusually high.

Make sure your arguments track the jury instructions on punitive damages (which in turn reflect the *BMW* and *Campbell* holdings). Make sure that the other acts evidence you use to show culpability has a direct relationship to the plaintiff's harm. Be reasonable in your punitive damages requests, because a ratio greater than 9:1 will be judicially scrutinized.

Where punitive damages are allowed, plaintiffs usually argue that defendant's misconduct is outrageous; that it has happened before; and that only a hard hit in the wallet will get defendant's attention and keep defendant and others like it from doing the same thing again. Defendants usually argue that the situation does not call for punitive damages at all, because the defendant's conduct did not rise to the level of intentional conduct and was an isolated event.

Example (Plaintiff):

> What will it take to get that corporation's attention? What will it take to make it stop? It's bad enough that the defendant's cigarette lighter flared up and seriously injured Mrs. Harte. It's worse when it knew the lighter could flare up and hurt someone else, because it already had heard from other people that the lighter had flared up when they used it. But it's the worst thing of all when that corporation could have fixed it, knew how to fix it, and should have fixed it.
>
> It didn't fix that lighter, because fixing it would have cost two dollars per lighter, and that two dollars would cut into profits. Folks, that corporation designed, built, and sold a time bomb it knew was waiting to explode. It put profits over safety. It decided to put those two dollars in its pocket instead of into its lighter. That corporation consciously disregarded a risk that people would be injured by that lighter, and that's why you need to return what's called punitive damages.

What will make it stop? A corporation knows only one thing: money. Hit the corporation where it counts, in the pocketbook. Take its profit away. You heard that corporation has earned over $1,000,000 selling that lighter. It has a net worth of over $20,000,000. So what will get that corporation's attention? We suggest you return a verdict for punitive damages in the amount of at least $1,000,000. That will get their attention. That will send them a clear message: Never, never, sell a time bomb that you know can hurt innocent people. Never, never, put profits over safety.

f. Burdens of Proof

Finally, lawyers frequently argue the burden of proof in civil cases. Plaintiffs in particular need to point out that a civil case is not a criminal case—that the standards are entirely different—and illustrate what the "preponderance" or "more likely than not" standard means. Plaintiffs often make these points in the rebuttal argument. Defendants in fraud and punitive damages cases usually argue that the burden of proof, usually a clear and convincing standard, is a high standard that plaintiff's evidence has not come close to meeting.

Example (Plaintiff Rebuttal):

Members of the jury, this isn't a criminal case. You're not going to be asked whether anyone is guilty of anything. His honor in his instructions is not even going to use the word "guilty." So why does the defense keep using that word? There's only one reason: They want to confuse you into thinking this is a criminal case with a higher burden of proof.

Listen when his honor tells you that what we have to prove, and the only thing we have to prove, is that the defendant's negligence caused this collision, and we only have to prove that by a preponderance of the evidence, showing it's more likely than not. All we have to do is tip the scale [using arms to show a balance scale], no matter how slightly. Any tipping will do. If there's just slightly more evidence showing the defendant negligent than not, we've met our burden of proof. In this case, of course, we've proved that and then some.

3. Criminal Issues

a. Circumstantial Evidence

Circumstantial evidence issues arise in both civil and criminal cases, but they are more common and significant in criminal cases. This is probably because mental states are important issues in criminal cases, and they are frequently proven through circumstantial evidence. In addition, the high burden of proof in criminal cases makes the quality of the circumstantial evidence important.

Prosecutors usually argue that the law does not distinguish between direct and circumstantial evidence, and that circumstantial evidence is sometimes as strong as, or stronger than, direct evidence. Prosecutors also frequently use time-honored analogies to show how strong such evidence can be. Defense lawyers usually argue that the circumstantial evidence in this case proves little or nothing and remind the jurors how little direct eyewitness testimony they heard during the trial.

Example (Prosecution):

The victim, Mary Wells, testified that the defendant assaulted her when she went to the defendant's employment agency to interview for a modeling job. At first the defendant denied she had even been there. The defendant in his second statement to the police claimed the victim propositioned him during the interview. How do we know the defendant's story is a lie? Look to the circumstantial evidence, because that evidence proves he had a guilty mind, and the person with the guilty mind is guilty of the crime.

Circumstantial evidence is like snow falling during the night. You may not have seen it falling, but if there was no snow the day before when you went to sleep, and then there's snow on the ground the next morning, you know to a certainty that it snowed during the night.

What's the circumstantial evidence in this case? When the defendant was interviewed at his home that evening by the police, he at first denied that the victim had even been at his agency earlier that day for an interview. He didn't know that the police had already searched his agency and found the burned application form, the form the victim had filled out, the form the defendant burned in the wastebasket afterwards. Only when he was confronted with the truth did he change his story.

That's the power of circumstantial evidence, folks. If the defendant had nothing to hide, why would he deny she had been there? Why would he try to destroy the only document that proves she had been at his agency? There's only one conclusion: He did exactly what the victim said he did.

Example (Defense):

The prosecution usually talks about how reliable eyewitnesses are. Of course, when the prosecution has no eyewitnesses, they always talk about how wonderful circumstantial evidence is. That explains their argument here. They want you to believe that simply because Bobby's palm print was found on the checkout counter that somehow proves he's guilty of burglary. But you're too smart to buy that. Bobby lives a block away. He's been in that hardware store lots of times. The palm print is on the checkout counter. How many of us have ever put our hands on the checkout counter when we were making a purchase?

Most important of all, the prosecution can't tell you how old that palm print is. Their own expert told us that you can't date a print. All you can do is determine whose print it is. For all we know, Bobby left that print on the counter a month earlier. So much for circumstantial evidence proving anything here.

b. Lesser Included Offenses

Unique to criminal cases is the concept of lesser included offenses. For example, in many states, if the defendant is charged with first-degree (premeditated) murder, that charge includes the lesser offenses of second-degree (unpremeditated) murder, and manslaughter, and perhaps other offenses. If there is evidence to support a jury finding on any lesser included offense, the jury will be instructed accordingly.

This can create a problem for both sides, because the lawyers did not refer to any lesser included offenses in their opening statements, and the judge usually instructs the jury on the applicable law only before or after the closing arguments. Inexperienced lawyers often simply avoid talking about lesser included offenses. That is a mistake, because jurors want guidance. The prosecutor needs to deal candidly with the fact that the court will instruct the jury on lesser included charges, and show the jury why it should find the defendant guilty of the highest charge. The defense usually argues that the evidence has not proved the highest charge, nor has it proved any of the lesser charges, so the only possible verdict is not guilty.

The jury's tendency to compromise is important here and must be assessed carefully. In a close case, when the prosecutor argues for a guilty-of-murder verdict, and the defense argues for a not-guilty verdict, the jury may well decide to reject both extremes and compromise by returning a verdict on a lesser included offense such as manslaughter. Both sides need to assess whether this is an acceptable verdict. If so, the argument must acknowledge this possibility and recognize it as a verdict reasonable jurors might reach. If not, the argument has to explain why, given the evidence, a compromise verdict on some middle ground would not be right or fair.

Example (Prosecution):

The defendant has been charged with first-degree murder. As his honor will instruct you in a few minutes, first-degree murder includes what's called the lesser included crimes of second-degree murder and manslaughter. In other words, you will have four verdict choices: first-degree murder, second-degree murder, manslaughter, and not guilty. You will all have to agree on one of them. In this case, however, the evidence clearly points to only one choice: guilty of first-degree murder.

Let's look at what we know. We know the defendant and victim had been arguing inside the tavern. We know that first the victim, then the defendant, left the tavern, and the argument continued on the street. We know that about two minutes later the defendant shot and killed the victim. Most important of all, we know that the victim was standing on the street, unarmed, about ten feet away, doing nothing other than arguing, when the defendant pulled a gun and shot him through the heart. After killing him, the defendant tried to run away but was caught by the other patrons of the tavern who had gone outside when they heard the shot.

What the evidence proves is that the defendant deliberately took his .38 caliber revolver, aimed it at the unarmed victim, and pulled the trigger. Folks, that's not self-defense, that's not manslaughter, and that's not second-degree murder. What that defendant did was a premeditated killing, and that's first-degree murder.

Example (Defense):

At most, this was an argument that spiraled out of control. Nobody premeditated anything, and nobody intended anything. The best the prosecution can hope for under the facts is that you compromise by finding him guilty of manslaughter, but that wouldn't be the right verdict here. The simple truth is, Mr. Rausch thought that Johnson was packing a knife, since he usually does, and when Johnson lunged at him, Mr. Rausch thought he was going to get stabbed.

Was that a reasonable thing to believe? Sure, knowing what we know about Johnson, the kind of violent person he was, and how he was known to carry a knife. That's what Mr. Rausch also knew, so of course he reasonably believed he was about to get stabbed. Under these circumstances, who wouldn't?

That's why this is a case of self-defense, and why the prosecution has failed to prove Mr. Rausch guilty beyond a reasonable doubt of anything. Not murder, not manslaughter. That's why the only verdict in this case has to be not guilty.

c. Mental States

In criminal cases, the prosecution must always prove the required mental state of the offense charged, such as intent, knowledge, or recklessness. This must be proved beyond a reasonable doubt, and that proof often involves circumstantial evidence. Prosecutors usually argue that the defendant's mental state is amply proved by his conduct before, during, and after the crime, or that defendant had a motive to commit the crime that proves his state of mind. Defendants usually argue that such evidence is insufficient to prove the required mental state beyond a reasonable doubt.

Example (Prosecution):

Did the defendant intend to defraud Dr. Smith, or is this just a big mistake, as the defense wants you to believe? Well, let's look at the facts. That defendant conned Dr. Smith out of $50,000 on the pretense that he would use that money to start a direct sales real estate business in which he and Dr. Smith were supposed to be equal partners.

Over nine months passed before Dr. Smith called the police and said she'd been conned. And over those nine months, what did the defendant do? Essentially nothing. Did he rent office space? No. Did he develop a marketing plan? No. Did he try to get sellers to list their homes with him? No. Did he prepare any monthly listings brochures? No. Did he ever incorporate the business as he said he'd do? No. The only thing the defendant tried to do during those nine months is con other persons into "investing" in his "business."

Folks, you weren't born yesterday. You know that these facts prove only one thing: That defendant never intended to start a business. That was simply the carrot, to talk Dr. Smith out of $50,000. He intended to defraud Dr. Smith, and he succeeded.

Example (Defense):

Bill Martin is guilty of only one thing: Not understanding how difficult it is to start up a new business, not understanding how much time it takes. If this were a real fraud, the first thing a real con artist would have done is to take off with Dr. Smith's money the minute he got his hands on it. But Bill didn't. He was in touch with Dr. Smith regularly. He explained to Dr. Smith that things were taking more time than expected. He explained that he could only spend so much time on it, since he was still holding down a full-time job.

Bill's guilty only of getting in over his head. He's hardly the first person with an idea, a good idea, that didn't get off the ground. But that's not fraud. That's simply an honest, innocent mistake.

d. Defenses

Affirmative defenses frequently play a critical role in criminal trials. The defense frequently takes the approach of agreeing that the defendant committed certain acts but argues that the defendant's conduct was completely justified or explained by a defense. The most common affirmative defense is self-defense. (Generally, the absence of consent is an element of the crime of sexual assault, so the prosecution carries the burden on that issue, though it otherwise operates like an affirmative defense. Similarly, although an alibi defense is not an affirmative defense, it, too, operates like one when the defense says that the defendant was misidentified and wrongfully accused and introduces evidence that the defendant was somewhere else when the crime was committed.)

Burdens of proof are important issues in affirmative defenses, because jurisdictions differ on what they are and on which party they will be imposed. In some jurisdictions, the burden is on the defense to prove an affirmative defense, usually by a preponderance of the evidence. In others, the burden is on the prosecution to *disprove* the affirmative defense beyond a reasonable doubt. You need to know who has the burden of proof and what the standard is and be sensitive to subtle attempts by your opponent to shift the burden or state the standard incorrectly.

Example (Prosecution):

> Members of the jury, we've proven that the defendant, Frank Jones, intentionally stabbed the victim, Elmer Smith, in the Tap Root Pub, and that Mr. Smith died within two hours. We've proven the defendant committed murder, and we've done that beyond a reasonable doubt. There's only one question remaining: Did the defendant prove it was self-defense? Since the defendant raised self-defense, it's up to him to prove self-defense by a preponderance of the evidence.
>
> Did he prove this was self-defense? No. How do we know? The only evidence of self-defense came out of the defendant's own mouth, when he testified that Mr. Smith had grabbed a beer bottle and was about to hit him over the head with it. Well, consider the source. The defendant's got every reason in the world to testify the way he did. He wants to beat the rap more than anything, and he's obviously willing to say anything.
>
> The problem is, there were other witnesses in the bar. We called three of them, and none of them supported the defendant's story. Three eyewitnesses saw the victim without a beer bottle in his hand. Three eyewitnesses saw the victim make no attempt to strike the defendant. Three eyewitnesses said all they saw and heard was some argument between the two, and then the defendant suddenly stabbed Mr. Smith in the chest. That's not self-defense. That's murder.

Example (Defense):

> What did those three witnesses, that the prosecution talks about so much, actually prove? Nothing that contradicts what Frank said happened.

What the prosecution didn't mention is that those three witnesses were sitting at a nearby table, having a few beers, having a good time. They weren't paying any attention to what was going on at the bar between Frank and Mr. Smith. None of them paid any attention until someone screamed, and by that time it was pretty much over. Of course they didn't see the events that led up to the stabbing, so of course they didn't see what Frank saw: Mr. Smith holding a beer bottle, about to hit Frank over the head with it.

In short, not one prosecution witness has contradicted what Frank told you about what happened. Truth is, under those facts Frank was completely justified in defending himself. He resisted deadly force with deadly force, nothing more. That's self-defense.

e. Burden of Proof

In all criminal cases, the prosecution must prove the defendant's guilt beyond a reasonable doubt. More specifically, the prosecution must prove each element of each charge (which includes proving the identity of the defendant) beyond a reasonable doubt. In federal and many state courts, the jury is given a definition of *beyond a reasonable doubt*, and lawyers are usually barred from further defining it. However, lawyers may, and commonly do, give examples of the kinds of doubts we have in events that happen in our lives, and argue that those are reasonable or unreasonable doubts. In some jurisdictions, *beyond a reasonable doubt* is not defined further. In these jurisdictions, it is for the jury to determine what it means, and lawyers again frequently use examples from real life to give it meaning.

The permissible extent of arguments attempting to define *beyond a reasonable doubt* or to illustrate its meaning often depends on the law in specific jurisdictions and on the attitude of the trial judge. Hence, you must always learn these before making a reasonable doubt argument.

Example (Defense):

Her honor will tell you that you cannot vote to convict unless all of you decide that the prosecution has proved every element of its charge beyond a reasonable doubt. That's the law. That's what our Constitution has said for over 200 years. Beyond a reasonable doubt doesn't mean you think he might be guilty. It doesn't mean you think he could be guilty. It doesn't even mean you think he's probably guilty. It's much more than that. As her honor will tell you, beyond a reasonable doubt means that the evidence in this case must leave you *firmly convinced* that he's guilty. Firmly convinced. In this case, the prosecution's evidence hasn't come close to firmly convincing anyone.

Example: (Defense):

Did I lock the back door? Did I set the alarm? How many of us have gone to bed at night and then had those doubts? We've all had them. Were those reasonable doubts? If we thought about the door or alarm for a moment, then confidently fell asleep, we know we had no reasonable doubts. But if we tossed and turned, unable to sleep, still wondering if we had, that tells us we had reasonable doubts—we just weren't sure. Members of the jury, this case is full of those reasonable doubts.

The prosecution usually addresses the reasonable doubt issue in its rebuttal argument.

Example (Prosecution):

We're human. We think. Part of thinking is to question things. As her honor will instruct you, we have to prove the defendant's guilt beyond a reasonable doubt. That is a good and decent standard, and we accept it without question or hesitation. But it doesn't mean all doubt or any doubt. There are few things in this world that we know with absolute certainty. In a criminal case, we're not required to overcome every conceivable doubt someone can come up with. We're only required to overcome every *reasonable* doubt. That's the same standard of proof juries accept every time they convict someone of a crime in the courts of this country. We accept that burden, we've met that burden, and we've gone beyond that burden.

9.8 Plaintiff's Rebuttal

Everyone likes to have the last word. That's what makes the rebuttal argument such a potent weapon. Almost all jurisdictions give the side with the burden of proof, ordinarily the plaintiff, the right to make a rebuttal argument. How should the plaintiff best use this advantage?

First, make sure your rebuttal argument is proper. A rebuttal argument should do just that: rebut things brought out in the defense closing argument. Rebuttal is not intended to give the plaintiff an opportunity to raise completely new matters. That would be unfair, because the defense then would have no reasonable opportunity to respond to the new argument. If this happens, the defense needs to object promptly to the improper rebuttal. For example, if the defense closing argued only liability and did not discuss damages, the plaintiff in rebuttal may not argue damages. Whether something is improper rebuttal is often a judgment call, and judges vary on how strictly they enforce the bar to improper rebuttal.

This does not mean that you should write your rebuttal while you are listening to the defense closing. Rather, your rebuttal should be written and practiced in advance, just like your initial closing argument. If you know the case well enough to try it effectively, you know what the defendant is likely to argue in closing. Write a rebuttal that responds to that likely argument. Then adjust it as necessary to respond to the actual closing. But usually your adjustments should be minor.

Second, start big. By the time of rebuttal, jurors have already heard two closing arguments and they are ready to start their deliberations. If you do not say something quickly that grabs the jurors' attention, most jurors will tune out.

Example:

How dare they? How dare they say this is all Mr. Johnson's fault? When all the evidence tells us that he did everything he could to avoid this collision? When he did all he could possibly do to recover from his injuries? What the defense has done is what it always does when it has no defense: Blame the victim.

Example:

There's an old saying: If you don't have the facts, argue the law. If you don't have the law, argue the facts. And if you don't have the facts or the law, just argue. That's exactly what the defense just did, isn't it?

Example:

For 20 minutes the defense argued and argued, and they talked about everything except the one thing that counts: the evidence. They can talk about the Constitution, they can talk about the defendant's rights, but when they won't talk about the evidence, that speaks volumes.

Third, be brief. The best rebuttal arguments are the ones that efficiently make strong points, then end. Keep your rebuttal in typical cases down to five or ten minutes. The points you make will stand out more, and jurors will appreciate the brevity.

Fourth, maintain a positive, assertive, confident tone. Perhaps the most difficult part of rebuttal is to use it properly—to rebut the defense arguments—without sounding defensive in the process. This is largely a matter of tone and attitude. If you sound as if you are merely responding to the defense arguments, you will sound defensive. Instead, act confident, hammer away with your strongest points, and show the jurors that those points completely refute the defense's argument.

Example:

What color was the light when the two cars collided? Yellow. How do we know? Because Mr. Able saw the collision and said so. Because Ms. Birch saw the collision and said so. The defendant, of course, claims the light was red. It's what you'd expect him to say. It's what you'd expect the defense to talk about in their argument. But saying it doesn't make it true. What you need to decide is: Whose testimony is more believable, the testimony of Mr. Able and Ms. Birch, or that story from the defendant? The answer to that is obvious.

Example:

Three eyewitnesses during this trial pointed at the defendant and said: "That's the man who robbed the store." Three eyewitnesses, and all were positive. Despite that, the defense wants you to believe that somehow their identifications don't mean much, because the robbery happened so quickly. If that's the case, how come all three of those eyewitnesses attended a lineup, one after another, and after seeing that lineup with seven similar-looking men in it, all three pointed at the defendant and said: "That's the man." That happens only when the eyewitnesses know who robbed the store, and they know the robber is in the lineup.

Finally, end strong. Most good endings remind the jurors of the plaintiff's themes, and stress that the evidence, fairness, and justice demand a verdict for the plaintiff.

Example:

> Members of the jury, it's time to end the denials. It's time for that defendant to take responsibility for what he did on June 1, 2020. It's time to make things right. You have that power. You have the power to achieve justice. You have the power to tell that defendant: Take responsibility for your actions. You have the power to return a verdict that will fairly and fully compensate Bob Martin for what happened to him, his career, and his family. We know you will do that.

Example:

> Members of the jury, we've brought you the evidence that proves the defendant committed this crime, and we've proved it beyond a reasonable doubt. Find the defendant guilty of the crime he committed on June 1, 2020—the crime of murder. That's justice for the victim, and justice for that defendant. That's the verdict justice demands.

9.9 Example of Closing Argument

Gable v. Cannon (Personal Injury):

This *Gable v. Cannon* case is the one for which the opening statements were analyzed (Section 4.6).

PLAINTIFF'S CLOSING ARGUMENT

> [■◀] For additional examples of closing arguments (and opening statements), see Video C.5, "Wyo STI: Demonstration of Problem 9.4."

The modern way to start a closing argument: Immediately make an important point.

> Members of the jury, one thing here is perfectly clear: That defendant, Douglas Cannon, made a big mistake. He made an illegal left-hand turn right in front of Jim Gable's oncoming car. When you do that and you cause a collision, it's the fault of the person who made the left-hand turn. We all know that, and we've all known it since we began learning to drive. The car going straight has the right of way. The car turning left has to yield the right of way to oncoming traffic. But that's what the defendant failed to do, and today's the day where he finally has to take responsibility for what he did.

Whenever possible, show multiple witnesses and exhibits proving your point.

> How do we know it happened that way? There are three reasons why we know. One is Mr. Gable's testimony. Who had the best view of what was going on? It had to be Mr. Gable. He's driving south on Main, straight down the road, crawling along at 20 to 25 miles per hour. He's alone in his car, no distractions. He sees the traffic light directly ahead, and everything unfolds right in front of him. Contrast that with where that defendant was. He was driving his sick wife to the doctor's office at the

hospital. He admits he had inched out well into the intersection, so he was practically under the light—the only light. Notice what that means. The defendant says he was looking up at the traffic light, so he's got to be looking almost straight up at it. He can't be looking at that light and at the same time looking at oncoming traffic. So if you ask who was in a better position to see what was going on, where the cars were when the light first turned yellow, and what color the light was when the two cars collided, it's Mr. Gable.

"Who had the better view" is an effective argument.
Always point out when a witness is neutral.

But there's more. There's also Mr. Bozza, the one eyewitness with no axe to grind. He doesn't know either side, and doesn't care which way your verdict goes. What does he tell us? He said he was on the southeast corner, about to cross Main Street. He said that as he stepped off the curb to cross Main, he saw the crash, and the light for Elm was still red at the time of the crash. Well, if the light was red for Elm at the time of the crash, it had to be green or yellow for Main, just like Mr. Gable has been saying for two years. But what about that statement Mr. Bozza made to their investigator? Two days after the crash they sent an investigator out to his house and got him to sign a statement. That statement was written by their investigator, and it says "The light was green for Elm at the time." When Mr. Bozza signed their statement, he didn't catch that mistake at the time, but he told us about it. He told us that statement was incorrect. The fact still remains that the only witness with no axe to grind here, Mr. Bozza, tells us that at the time of the crash the light was red for Elm Street. Mr. Bozza's testimony backs up Mr. Gable's testimony that the light for Main Street was yellow when the crash happened.

An interesting label for a circumstantial evidence argument.

That's two reasons. What's the third? It's the witness they don't want you to think about. It's the witness they don't want you to see in court. But it came to court. It's the law of physics. The law of physics has no axe to grind, doesn't care who wins, and never forgets. Why is the law of physics so important? Remember when Mr. Gable said he was going, tops, 25 miles per hour? No one disagreed with him. And remember when I asked Sergeant Tracy that odd question: Sergeant Tracy, a car going 25 miles per hour, how far does it go in one second? He said that's easy; there's a formula. It's 37½ feet per second. How long, Sergeant Tracy, is the yellow light at Main and Elm? Three seconds. So for a car to be going 25 miles per hour and run a red light, how far away from the intersection must it have been when the light first turned yellow? He said that's simple, 3 times 37½ feet, which is 112½ feet.

The argument now rejects the principal defense claim.

Members of the jury, the defense's whole case depends on the Main Street light turning red before Mr. Gable got to the intersection. And for that to be true, Mr. Gable's car would have to have been more than 112½ feet away when the light first turned yellow. Their problem is, and it's a fatal problem: No one says that's what happened. Mr. Gable says it didn't happen that way. Mr. Bozza, the independent, disinterested eyewitness, says it didn't happen that way. And the law of physics says it didn't happen that way. And even the defendant couldn't say where Mr. Gable's car was when the light first turned yellow. That's how we know that when the two cars collided, the light was yellow for Main Street, and that defendant made an illegal left-hand turn. Because that defendant failed to yield to Mr. Gable's oncoming car, that collision is the defendant's fault. He was negligent, plain and simple.

These rhetorical questions are a challenge to the defense.
Either explanation shows the defendant was negligent.

Remember I asked at the beginning of the trial: Why didn't the defendant just wait? Why didn't he wait, not just until the light had turned to yellow, but three seconds of yellow had passed, and the oncoming traffic had stopped? Then he could have made his left-hand turn, legally and safely. What was he doing? What was he thinking? Where was he looking? They still haven't answered that, but there are only two possibilities. One is, the defendant was busy looking up at the traffic light because there is only one right in the middle of the intersection, and as he looks up it turns yellow and he makes a left turn without first looking at oncoming traffic. Well, if he did that, that's his fault. You can't assume there are no oncoming cars. The other possibility is, the defendant is under the light, it turns yellow, he glances down the street and assumes Mr. Gable's car is going to stop. Well, if he did that, that's also his fault. You can't assume oncoming cars are going to stop. You have to wait and make sure. So whether he looked up and turned left without looking, or he turned left after assuming the oncoming car was going to stop, it makes no difference. That defendant made an illegal, dangerous, left-hand turn when Mr. Gable had the right of way. That's negligence, and that makes this collision his fault.

Notice that plaintiff keeps emphasizing that this is a case about failure to yield the right of way, not a yellow light–red light dispute.

You already know the rules of the road. You already know the law that applies here. Her honor will go over it again, but it's what you know because you are all drivers. And the bottom line is: Don't go making a left-hand turn until you know you can make it safely. Look and make sure the oncoming cars have stopped. Don't guess. Just keep your foot on your brake until it's safe to make that turn.

Folks, when you sign the verdict form, put the blame where it belongs. Tell Mr. Cannon two years of denial is enough. There comes a time when you have to take responsibility for what you did, and yes, pay for what you did. That time is now.

The damages issue is now addressed.
A visual aid.

Let's turn to what happened to Mr. Gable, and what we need to do about it, because that's the real issue in this case. What happened to Mr. Gable, and what will make it right? What happened is clear. Mr. Gable had his right elbow joint torn out of its socket from the force of the collision. You can see it clearly right here on the x-ray [holds up x-ray]. Dr. Klein had to take Mr. Gable to the surgery room, put him under a general anesthetic, and set the arm back in its socket. Four weeks later, Dr. Klein removed the cast and Mr. Gable started the therapy program.

Did Mr. Gable do the therapy? You bet. You heard Dr. Klein say that she knows he did the therapy, because his range of motion got much better. Did the therapy work? You bet. Mr. Gable's arm got better, and it got better quickly. But then it stopped getting better. When it got to this point [demonstrating], it stopped getting better. No matter how much he kept doing the therapy, he could never straighten out that arm. Now, if this were something that happened in Mr. Gable's case and no one else in the history of medicine, we wouldn't be here today. The fact is, however, that not everyone recovers completely from such a severe injury. Remember what Dr. Klein said? She said about 15 to 20 percent of patients never recover full range of motion after such an injury, even though they do the therapy. Even Dr. Bradsky, the doctor the defense hired, had to agree with that. So this case is not about whether Mr. Gable did the therapy. We know he did. And it has nothing to do with whether Mr. Gable took prescription pain medication. That's a patient choice issue, as Dr. Klein told us, and Mr. Gable was perfectly capable, like lots of other patients, of doing the therapy without painkillers.

One of plaintiff's themes.
This defuses an expected defense argument.

The simple fact of the matter is that Mr. Gable is one of those 15 to 20 percent of patients who never recover fully, and it's not his fault. The real tragedy here is that Mr. Gable can't work as a mechanic any more. His elbow doesn't have the range of motion he needs to do that kind of work, and the joint isn't strong enough to take that kind of strain. He's lost the only job he's ever had, the only job he's ever been trained for, the only job he knows how to do. What are we going to do about that, and about his other losses?

Almost all plaintiffs will use a damages chart at this point.
Plaintiffs will usually begin with out-of-pocket expenses, and end with pain and suffering.

Her honor will tell you that, when you decide how to compensate Mr. Gable for his losses, you should consider the following, which I've put up on this board [puts board on easel]. First, Mr. Gable's medical expenses are clear, you've seen the bills, and there's no dispute over them. The hospital bill, Dr. Klein's bill, and the therapist's bill, total $8,450 [writes figure on board].

Lost income and future lost income are a big part of damages in this case.

Next, Mr. Gable's been out of work for two years, ever since this happened to him. Jim, as you heard from his boss, was earning $40,000 a year as a mechanic. He's lost $80,000 just for the past two years, and there's no dispute over that [writes figure on board].

Next, there's Mr. Gable's future lost income. He's 38 years old. He'll never work as a mechanic again, because of that arm. You heard the economist, Professor Becker, tell us that Mr. Gable, with a high school education, will probably not earn over $20,000 a year in the future. That's the way the job market is for high school graduates these days. This means that he's lost $20,000 a year of earnings capacity, and that will be the case for 24 more years, since he probably would have worked as a mechanic until age 62, if his arm hadn't been damaged. You then heard a lot of technical stuff from Dr. Becker, but the key question he answered was: How much money do we need to put in a safe investment now, earning interest, so that Mr. Gable can draw out $20,000 a year for the next 24 years, before the money runs out? And the answer is: $220,000. That's not in dispute either. The defense didn't even call an economist to challenge Dr. Becker's testimony. To compensate Mr. Gable for the loss of his career, that's what we need to do [writes figure on board].

This explains the economist's testimony on the present value of future earnings.

Next, her honor will tell you that you need to consider the nature and extent of Mr. Gable's injury. Before June 1, 2020, he was a completely healthy man, who had a good job, and was active in all the ways a 38-year-old man is active. Mr. Gable used to do all the things we like to do, and can do: play with the kids, work around the house, and in his spare time play golf, go fishing, do things like that. Those are the kinds of things that make life complete, and Mr. Gable, who's a hands-on kind of guy, can't do them anymore. What does it mean to have that taken away from you and how do we begin to compensate for that? Mr. Gable's 38 years old, and, as her honor told us, he's likely to live for 40 more years. He's got more living ahead of him than he has behind him. We suggest you compensate Mr. Gable $10,000 a year for the rest of his life. That's $400,000 [writes figure on board]. If that's not enough, it's your duty to decide what's right. If the defense says that's too much, let them get up and explain to you why that's too much.

This puts the loss in human terms.
Most plaintiffs will "suggest" a figure, then show how it was calculated.
Pain and suffering is usually the last damages element.

Finally, there's the question of pain, suffering, and disfigurement [pointing]. Mr. Gable was in pain from the moment of that collision, through the therapy, and only recently has the pain eased. Whenever he moves that arm the wrong way, it hurts. Whenever he forgets and tries to straighten out that arm, the way it used to, it hurts. Folks, pain is the kind of thing we don't even think about when we don't have it, and pain's the kind of thing that's on our mind constantly when we do have it. Jim's had that pain almost every hour over the past two years, and when he uses his arm the wrong way, it's back. What should we do about that? We suggest that $50,000 is the least that will compensate Mr. Gable for what he's gone through, and what he still lives with [writes figure on board]. Again, if that's too low, it's your duty to decide what's right. If the defense says it's too much, let them get up and explain why that's too much.

Again, a "suggestion."

The ending, with a request for a specific verdict amount.

Plaintiffs always want the jurors to end up thinking about compensation and damages.

> Members of the jury, that defendant made an illegal left-hand turn in front of Mr. Gable's car, causing a collision that ruined his elbow, ruined his career, and shattered his life. For two years, that defendant has denied responsibility. At the beginning of this trial, we said we would ask you to tell that defendant through your verdict: Two years of denial is enough. Today's the day you finally take responsibility for what you did, and today's the day you pay for what you did. The only verdict that makes sense here, the only verdict that is supported by the evidence, the only verdict that fully compensates Mr. Gable for the devastation to his life, is a verdict in favor of Mr. Gable in this amount: $758,450 [writes figure on board]. Thank you.

DEFENDANT'S CLOSING ARGUMENT

The defense liability argument is that the plaintiff entered the intersection after the light turned red. This introduction sets up that argument.

> May it please the court, counsel, members of the jury. Sometimes a case in court reminds us of ourselves. Something we've done. And we've all done this, haven't we? Sometimes in the past we've all succumbed to that temptation. We've all kept that foot on the accelerator when that light turns from green to yellow. We know what yellow means. Yellow means to take your foot off the gas, be careful, and slow down, because you can't, as her honor is going to tell you, you can't go into an intersection on a yellow light unless you know you can do it safely. But we've all done it, haven't we? Keep the foot on the gas and go through the intersection.
>
> Folks, what's the first thing we do when we go through that intersection? When we know we shouldn't have gone through, what is the first thing we do? We look in the mirror and say, whew, glad Sergeant Tracy wasn't here today. Why do we feel that? Because we know right here [pointing to chest] it is not right. We know right here [pointing] we've taken a chance. We've taken a chance with a two- or three- or four- or five-thousand-pound car, and we've gone through a light that we know darn well we should have slowed up and stopped for.
>
> That's particularly important in this case. You know why? Because this case is not just about a false charge of negligent driving against Doug Cannon. This case is about safety on the highway. This case is about taking your foot off the gas when you get to an intersection so you don't risk somebody's life. That's what this case is about.

A good argument, showing defendant had no reason to make a late left-hand turn.

> But they tried to turn you around in this case. They've tried to change a light from red back to yellow. Let me show you the evidence that shows that the plaintiff ran a red light. First of all, there's Doug himself. Why, for

no reason, would he risk his life, his wife Marsha's life, and their unborn child, to make a left turn when he is not in a hurry to go anywhere? In rush hour traffic, with people crossing the street, with the plaintiff's black Jaguar coming down on him just 15 or 20 feet away? Why would he do that? Doug saw the light, he had a good view of the light, and he knows that light was red.

A corroboration witness.

Second of all, there's Marsha. She had a good view of the light, because she was sitting right next to Doug. She said the light was red before Doug started to make his turn.

This argument at least tries to neutralize the witness's trial testimony.

And there's Mr. Bozza. In his written statement, made two days after the accident, remember what he said? It's right here on his signed statement [holds up statement]: "I had seen the light before I stepped off the curb—*before*—and it was green for Elm Street." The light had turned green for him, which means it was red for the Jaguar. And that was *before* the collision.

The hospital record contains the plaintiff's impeaching words, so the defense makes a big deal of it.

And then, of course, there's the medical record. Now you know why I worked so hard to get the plaintiff's hospital emergency records into evidence. Members of the jury, I put this record in your hands so you can read it, you can read the words from the plaintiff's mouth when he was waiting to be treated. Sure, he was in pain, but he had no reason to say anything except the truth. See right there [pointing to record]? It says: "Other driver ran red light." Red. He said the light was red.

Another visual.
This is a "last clear chance" argument.

There's more. Look at the photograph that Sergeant Tracy took [holds up photograph]. It shows that the big black Jaguar ran into the right rear quarter panel of Doug's Chevy. Why is that so important? Who could have kept this accident from ever happening? Even if Doug turned in front of the plaintiff's Jaguar, who had the chance to stop it? The answer is the plaintiff. Why is that? Because if just for one second Mr. Gable took his foot off that powerful Jaguar's accelerator, this accident would never have happened. So Mr. Gable could have stopped it too.

More impeachment of the plaintiff.

Let's turn now to excuses. Today the plaintiff tells us the reason his dislocated right elbow didn't get any better was because the stretching exercises—his therapy program—stopped working. That's what he says now, when he's in court looking for money. But look at what he told Dr. Klein, his own doctor. He told Dr. Klein that he stopped doing the therapy after a while because it wasn't working, and she had to tell him to keep doing the exercises. What does that tell you about his motivation, about his failing to follow his own doctor's orders?

No prescription pain medication is an important point when linked to the therapy argument.

> And what did he tell Dr. Bradsky, the doctor we asked to examine him? He told Dr. Bradsky that he stopped doing the therapy because it was too painful. Yet did the plaintiff ever ask his own doctor for prescription pain medication? Something to take care of the pain, so he could do the therapy the way he was supposed to? All Dr. Klein told him to do was: Soak your right elbow in hot water, then stretch the joint back and forth for 15 minutes. Do that three times a day until you get back full range of motion. It's no different than trying to touch your toes. If you keep doing it, after a while you'll be able to touch them. Maybe not the first week, but if you keep at it, it will happen. And if your muscles get sore while you're doing that, take some pain medication. Did the plaintiff do the therapy the way he should have? No. Did the plaintiff ever ask Dr. Klein for some medication to deal with the pain he says he had? No. Yet the plaintiff comes to court saying his arm never recovered fully, and it's someone else's fault. That's not right, and it has to stop now.

Defendant ends by summarizing the liability argument.

> Members of the jury, this is a case about safety, and it's a case about excuses. If that plaintiff had just taken his foot off that accelerator for just one second, just slowed down a bit, just thought about the safety of others for a moment, this accident would not have happened. If that plaintiff had just done the therapy—really done it—his arm would be back to normal. Instead, this is a case about a man who's trying to blame someone else for what he didn't do. That's just not right.

Notice that the defendant has made a "no liability" argument, rather than suggesting that both parties may share the blame. This is the usual defense approach, even in comparative negligence jurisdictions.

> Doug and Marsha Cannon ask one thing: Make it stop. Stop the blame. Stop the excuses. When you deliberate, sign the verdict that says: Doug, this was not your fault. Sign the verdict that says: "We, the jury, find in favor of the defendant, Douglas Cannon." And tell that plaintiff, through that verdict: Don't ever come into a court of law when you could have prevented this from ever happening. Don't come into a court of law when all you have to offer is excuses. Thank you.

PLAINTIFF'S REBUTTAL ARGUMENT

Effective rebuttals must start quickly and be assertive.
"Blame the victim" is a common argument in both civil and criminal cases.

> Members of the jury, blame the victim. It's the oldest defense around. When you have no defense, you simply blame the victim.
> Blame the victim by accusing him of driving a Jaguar. Notice how many times the defense reminded you of Mr. Gable's car? As if that has anything to with this case. Blame the victim for not anticipating that the defendant would make an illegal left-hand turn. As if Mr. Gable, or any other motorist, is required to do that. Her honor will read you no instruction that says that. And blame the victim for not reacting faster when the

defendant made that illegal turn. What the defense has been arguing is like the driver who hits a pedestrian in a crosswalk and then says: "If that pedestrian had been more nimble, if that pedestrian had only reacted and jumped out of the way faster, I wouldn't have hit him. Guess that makes it the pedestrian's fault." Folks, that argument doesn't hold water, and it doesn't hold water here.

But the blame game continues. The defense also wants to blame the victim for not recovering fully, and blame him for losing his career as a mechanic. Blame Mr. Gable by claiming he didn't do the therapy. Blame Mr. Gable for not taking prescription painkillers. Folks, we know Mr. Gable did the therapy. Dr. Klein told us he did. She knows. And he didn't need painkillers to do the therapy. Mr. Gable was plenty motivated. He had to get back to work, back to supporting his family. What's happened here is exactly what Dr. Klein said happened. Mr. Gable's one of those 15 to 20 percent of people who have an injury this severe and never recover fully. Never regain full range of motion. Never regain the strength the joint used to have. In Mr. Gable's case, it ended his career as a mechanic, and destroyed the life he's worked so hard to build.

"Empowering the jury" to do justice is a frequently used ending.

Members of the jury, it's time to stop the denials. It's time to tell that defendant: Take responsibility for your illegal left-hand turn. Take responsibility for your negligence. Take responsibility for what your negligence did to Mr. Gable and his family. That's where you, the jury, come in. Only you have the power to do that. Only you have the power to make it right. Thank you.

9.10 Trial Notebook

Persuasive closing arguments don't just happen. They require preparation—lots of it. The preparation starts, of course, when you first get the case and begin thinking about how to present your side to a jury at trial. It continues as you select your theory of the case, themes, and labels. It continues during trial as you give your opening statement, present evidence in your case-in-chief, and cross-examine the other side's witnesses. It continues as you make short notes of ideas that come to you during the trial and the key answers witnesses gave during their testimony. Now it's time to refine your closing arguments outline and add the finishing touches.

The closing arguments section of your trial notebook should have everything you need to complete your closing argument preparation and deliver it at the end of the trial. First, keep some blank sheets of paper in this section. Use them to take notes on ideas that come to you during the trial. These will include catchy phrases that come to mind, key witness answers, visual aids, particular arguments, and any other ideas that occur to you as the trial progresses. By the end of the trial you will probably have a few pages of notes. These notes, with the notes you made on the other side's opening statement, will be important when you put the finishing touches on your planned closing argument.

Second, put the outline of your planned closing argument in this section. It should be a one- or two-page outline that you can refer to if the need arises as you give your closing argument. The outline should be in large print, so that you can glance at it quickly. However, keep the outline out of your line of sight as you give the closing argument. If the outline is too close, you will constantly look at it even if you don't need to, and this will seriously detract from your delivery. The outline is there if you lose your train of thought and need to glance at it to get back on track.

At the top of your outline, note the things you need on hand and will refer to as you give the closing argument. These include:

- Admitted exhibits
- Notes (or excerpts from the trial transcript if available) on key questions and answers witnesses gave
- Jury instructions the court will give
- Visual aids you have created and will use during the argument

Before you begin your closing argument, you need to make sure these things are immediately available. Put them neatly on your counsel table, in the order in which you plan to use them.

Example (Plaintiff in Automobile Collision):

CLOSING ARGUMENT

Exhibits:

1. intersection diagram (P#6)
2. x-rays (P#2a-c)
3. elbow diagram (P#11)

Notes:

1. Gable testimony re: distance
2. Dr. Bradsky cross re: rehab

Instructions:

1. right of way (#8)
2. left turn must yield (#9)
3. measure of damages (#17)

Visual aids:

1. bullet points re: liability
2. bullet points re: damages elements

Introduction

2 seconds, failure to yield, 15-20% (themes)

Collision

Def. fail to yield right of way/yellow light

How do we know it happened that way?

1. Gable testimony (Q&A from direct)
2. Bozza bystander testimony
3. physics—3 sec yellow, 25 mph, 50' away (P#6)

Defendant's version doesn't hold up

1. preoccupied with sick spouse
2. under the light
3. sun in face
4. didn't look, or looked and guessed car would stop

Damages

What will make it right?
Arm damaged, career over (P#2, P#11)
Dr. Klein & 15-20% v. Dr. Bradsky testimony (cross Q&A)
What has Gable lost? (Bullet points on damages)
Meds—$8,450
Lost income—economist—present value—$220,000
Quality of life losses—$400,000 & $50,000

Conclusion

Justice, take responsibility, fairness
You have the power to make it right

Should you take notes on your opponent's closing argument? Certainly, if you have an opportunity to respond and plan to respond directly to that argument. How should you take notes on your opponent's closing argument? Lawyers do this in either of two ways. One way is to use a yellow pad that is already three-hole punched; take notes on the pad and then insert the notes in the trial notebook. The other, and probably the more useful, way is to take notes directly on your closing argument outline. For example, the defendant's notes on the plaintiff's closing argument are put on the defendant's closing argument outline. The plaintiff's notes on the defendant's closing argument are put on the plaintiff's rebuttal argument outline. This way your outline will have the notes directly where you want them.

Whichever method you use, make your notes brief. Inexperienced lawyers spend too much time on note taking. Remember that the court reporter is making a complete record of what is being said. The only reason to take notes now is so you will not forget something you need to respond to when you get up to argue. Too much note taking interferes with active listening, interferes with your thinking, and interferes with your making timely objections to improper arguments. Too much note taking also interferes with your watching the jurors' body language as they react to the other side's arguments.

If you represent the plaintiff, you should also plan and outline your rebuttal argument.

Example (Plaintiff Rebuttal):

REBUTTAL ARGUMENT

Introduction

How dare they claim Mr. Gable didn't do rehab!

Defense arguments

1. Gable didn't do rehab
2. Mrs. Cannon says light red
3. Dr. Bradsky—should be able to return to work

Ending

After two years, they're still not taking responsibility

🌐 An example of a trial notebook, with shell forms and completed forms, is on the website that accompanies this book.

9.11 Common Problems

1. Boring

A boring closing argument turns jurors off just as they're getting ready to deliberate. This must be avoided at all costs. Watch the jurors. Are they still listening and watching? Do they appear interested? By the time of the closing arguments, jurors are tired and want to start deliberating. Jurors will let you know through their body language whether your argument is making points or is wasting their time.

2. Weak First Minute

The first minute must grab the jurors' attention. It must say: I'm still worth listening to, so stay tuned. The slow, traditional start—thanking the jurors, telling them we're in the home stretch, and so on—will not work today. Strong beginnings are carefully planned, given without notes, and delivered with good eye contact, confident voice, and reinforcing body language.

3. Not Using Opening Statement's Themes and Labels

Jurors are sensitive to inconsistency. They notice if your theory of the case has changed, and they notice if you are using different themes and labels than the ones you used during opening statements. This problem also arises when different lawyers do the opening statement and closing argument. When this must be done, both lawyers must make sure that the opening and closing are consistent with each other, and must agree to themes and labels that both lawyers feel comfortable with.

4. Not Arguing

The heart of closing argument is argumentation. *Arguing* is making a point, then backing it up with testimony, exhibits, law, and common sense. Inexperienced lawyers frequently just review the evidence or go over what the witnesses said. The jurors don't want you to summarize the evidence. They heard it as well as you did and, in those jurisdictions that permit it, some took notes. The jurors want you to explain what the evidence means, what it proves or fails to prove. When arguing, the party with the burden of proof must be positive and show why its evidence has met its burden of proof. It is a mistake to spend too much time arguing that your opponent's case is weak when your opponent does not have the burden of proof. Especially in criminal cases, the prosecution must show how it has proved each element of the charges beyond a reasonable doubt.

◼️ For a discussion of both opening statements and closing arguments, please watch Video C.1, "Mauet on Opening Statements and Closing Arguments."

5. Not Using Exhibits and Visual Aids

This is the age of visual learning, and the ramifications of that fact apply just as much to closing arguments as to anything else. Always consider ways to use admitted exhibits, actual witness testimony, summaries of key jury instructions, and visual aids containing bullet points of key arguments. Consider using a combination of poster boards, PowerPoint projections, and other presentation media. Use butcher paper to write things down as you talk. Weave these visual aids throughout your closing argument, so that you are never a talking head for more than three or four minutes without giving the jurors something new and visual to focus their attention.

6. Too Much Law

Good closing arguments use the law. The jurors want to know how the evidence fits the law and proves, or fails to prove, the claims and defenses. However, inexperienced lawyers frequently read long jury instructions verbatim or spend substantial time discussing the law. This is rarely useful. Instead, summarize the key instructions orally or, better yet, make a poster board containing only the key words or short phrases from the instructions. This is much more efficient and focuses the jurors' thinking.

7. Not Dealing with Weaknesses Candidly

An important part of closing argument is addressing juror concerns and apparent weaknesses. Inexperienced lawyers frequently ignore the weaknesses, hoping that the jurors will forget them. This never works. Jurors don't forget, nor will the other lawyer, who will enjoy pointing out that you are avoiding the unfavorable evidence. Good lawyers always deal candidly with the jurors' concerns and look for ways to turn apparent weaknesses into strengths.

8. Weak Ending

Like the first minute, the last minute must be strong. The last minute must be carefully planned, delivered without notes, and done with good eye contact, confident voice, and reinforcing body language. The last things you say must convey that you have the winning side.

9. Inadequate Preparation

Your closing must be outlined, rehearsed, and practiced out loud well in advance of trial. Most of your practice sessions will have to occur before the trial itself takes place, because you will have little or no chance to practice during the trial. As the trial progresses, you can adjust your planned closing to discuss evidence that was unexpectedly introduced and to ignore evidence that was surprisingly excluded. But you need to practice before the trial takes place.

10. Too Many Notes

Inexperienced lawyers frequently write out their planned closing argument and then deliver it. This rarely works well. First, written language does not sound like spoken language. You can always tell when a lawyer is reciting a previously written closing argument, and so can the jurors. Second, extensive notes interfere with maintaining eye contact and using your voice and body to reinforce your words. If you are constantly looking at your notes, the jurors get the impression that you are giving a canned speech, that your argument is not coming from the heart. Instead, put your key ideas and phrases on a one- or two-page outline where they will be available if you lose your train of thought.

11. No Passion

During closing arguments jurors are thinking: Who sounds like a winner? Are you just saying this because you've been paid to say it, or do you really believe it? In short, jurors are looking between the lines, because delivery is at least as important as content. Lawyers are different, of course, and passion comes in different packages. In closing arguments, jurors can still be influenced by the lawyer who makes strong points and delivers them with total conviction.

CHAPTER 10

EVIDENTIARY OBJECTIONS

10.1 Introduction

Witness testimony and exhibits introduced during a trial must survive screening by the law of evidence. That law, however, is not self-executing. Evidence will ordinarily be admitted unless the opposing party makes an objection at the right time, with the right rule, and for the right reason. Good trial lawyers are prepared to make proper evidentiary objections to the other side's evidence. Good trial lawyers anticipate that the opposing lawyer may object to everything and are always prepared to respond to those objections.

To make proper, timely objections, lawyers need to know evidence law and the judge and jury's attitudes about trial objections. They need to know when and how to make objections, what rules to base their objections on, and what arguments will be effective in persuading the judge. They must understand how the law of evidence is structured and how good judges apply it to achieve a fair trial for both sides. However, because evidentiary objections are frequently made while jurors are watching, trial lawyers must also understand how jurors react to lawyers' objections and how they react to the judge's rulings. These considerations strongly influence whether an objection should be made and when and how it should be made. Done well, objections that are carefully prepared, timed, and argued keep improper evidence from being presented to the jury, earn the

For a comprehensive discussion of matters related to objections, please watch Video H.1, "Wyo STI: Objections Panel (Including Common Objections, Anticipating Opponents' Objections, Questions to Ask Before Objecting, and Raising Evidentiary Issues at Trial)."

respect of the judge, and impress the jury. Done poorly, evidentiary objections fail to exclude such evidence, irritate the judge and jury, and decrease the objecting lawyer's influence in the courtroom.

10.2 The Law

Trial lawyers need to be evidence advocates. It is not enough to know the applicable jurisdiction's law of evidence, although that is obviously required. They need to know when to make objections; how to argue objections; and, when necessary, how to make a record for appeal. They need to organize and structure evidence law so that evidentiary issues can be spotted, raised, and argued quickly.

1. Procedure

The starting point is Federal Rule of Evidence (FRE) 103, which governs objection procedure. Objections must be made at the right time, with the right rule, and for the right reason.

a. Right Time

First, objections must be timely. Unless a lawyer objects in a timely way, the objection is usually waived and cannot be raised on appeal. As a general rule, raise the issue as early as possible, either before trial (in a motion in limine) or, if during trial, before a particular witness is called or a particular exhibit is introduced. Raising an objection early, out of the presence of the jury, will be appreciated by the trial judge, who will have more time to hear the lawyers' arguments and reach a considered ruling.

If the judge "rules definitively on the record," either before or at trial, under FRE 103(b) the objection need not be renewed to preserve an appeal when the evidence is actually offered during the trial. However, you should not take comfort in this provision of FRE 103 when your pretrial or other early objection is overruled, because circumstances might have changed between the making of the early ruling and the time the issue arises later at trial. When in doubt as to whether the judge's ruling is definitive, you must renew the objection when the evidence is offered. Keep in mind that many states still require that you renew your objection when the evidence is actually offered during trial to preserve error for appeal. One way to ensure preservation of an evidentiary issue for appeal without raising the ire of the judge and jury is to state, "We object on the grounds previously discussed, Your Honor," when the issue arises during trial.

During trial, objections must be made in a timely way as well. When a question is improper, an objection should be made before the witness answers the question. When an answer is improper, an objection should be made as soon as the improper answer becomes apparent, followed by a request to strike the improper answer and to instruct the jury to disregard the answer. When an exhibit is improper, an objection should be made when the exhibit is offered in evidence and before the exhibit is read or shown to the jurors.

b. Right Rule

Second, objections must be based on the right rule. Making a general objection—"Objection, your honor"—raises only relevance. Lawyers should state a specific evidentiary reason for objecting. Put another way, the judge only needs to rule on the evidentiary ground that the objecting party specifically raises. If that ground is wrong, the objection should be overruled, even though there was another proper ground that could have been raised. If the judge sustains your objection without asking for the basis of the objection, that is the best of all worlds, because the judge's ruling will be correct if there is any proper basis for sustaining your objection.

c. Right Reason

Third, objections must be based on the right reason. This is where evidence advocacy becomes important. Many evidentiary rulings are judgment calls, particularly in the relevance area, so good lawyers argue why a particular ruling is the right one. When objections are raised before trial, the lawyers will have a better opportunity to explain their positions on the disputed evidence and argue why the judge should rule in their favor. By contrast, if objections are raised in the presence of the jury, lawyers may state only a succinct evidentiary ground for the objection—"Objection, your honor. That calls for hearsay"—and they may not extensively argue their positions. The lawyers can ask for a bench conference to argue the objection, but that is discretionary with the judge.

d. Record for Appeal

Lawyers need to understand and remember that evidentiary battles are largely won or lost in the trial courtroom, because appellate reversal of trial court evidentiary rulings is highly unlikely. Of course, on critical evidentiary issues the lawyers need to make a clear record for appeal, or else the issue will be waived and the appellate court will not consider it. Making a clear record involves making a timely objection; basing the objection on a specific evidentiary rule; and, if the jury heard or saw improper evidence, making a timely motion to strike and disregard and, if necessary, a motion for mistrial. If the objection is sustained, the lawyer offering the evidence must make an offer of proof under FRE 103(a)(2) to preserve any error for appeal.

> █◀ For a discussion of the importance of making an adequate record at trial to preserve potential appellate issues, please watch Video A.10, "Wyo STI: Relationship Between Trial and Appeal."

e. Ethics

There are two situations in which evidentiary objections raise ethical considerations. First, it is improper to make an objection without a good-faith evidentiary basis merely to disrupt the other side's presentation of evidence. Second, it is improper to make an objection and then extensively argue the objection in the presence of the jury (called a *speaking objection*) merely to get before the jury information that otherwise it would not have received. Both kinds of conduct may violate Model Rule 3.4; they unquestionably do when the judge has previously ordered a lawyer to refrain from such conduct.

2. The 3Rs Approach to Evidence Advocacy

Trial lawyers must learn how to become evidence advocates. FRE 103(a) creates formidable barriers to appellate reversal, and trial judges have broad discretion that appellate courts are loathe to override. For trial lawyers, the challenge is to win disputed evidentiary issues in the trial court, and to do that lawyers must win the battle to "move the mind" of the trial judge. Trial lawyers do so in part by knowing the procedure through which evidentiary issues are raised and ruled on in the trial courts. But there is more to it than that. Lawyers also need to understand the logic and structure of the Federal Rules of Evidence and their state counterparts, and translate that knowledge into an effective methodology that quickly identifies and analyzes all important evidentiary problems.

Evidentiary issues are best seen through the filtration process of the *3Rs*. All offered evidence must successfully pass through three evidentiary filters: It must be relevant, reliable, and right. Evidentiary issues are best analyzed through three sequential questions.

a. Is the Evidence Relevant for the Offered Purpose?

Evidence is not admissible unless it is *relevant*. Relevance analysis should begin with a statement of purpose. Why does the proponent want the jury to hear or see the evidence? The party offering the evidence should be required to explain the issue to which the evidence is directed. Once that happens, the opposing party can respond, and the judge can rule.

Under FRE 401, evidence is *relevant* if it has "any tendency" to make a fact that is "of consequence" to the action "more or less probable than it would be without the evidence." This involves two tests. First, the evidence must be directed to a matter "of consequence." This is controlled by the pleadings and the applicable substantive law and will be reflected in the jury instructions for the elements of the claims and defenses.

Second, the evidence must be probative. It must have "any tendency" to make something of consequence "more or less probable." The matter of consequence does not have to be in dispute. Whether offered evidence is probative is controlled by logic and human experience. If the evidence is both of consequence and probative, it is relevant, and is admissible unless other rules exclude it.

b. Is the Evidence Reliable for the Offered Purpose?

Evidence is not admissible unless it is *reliable*. The jury should not, as a general rule, receive evidence that is secondhand information, because trials are too important. Juries should be given the most reliable available information from witnesses and exhibits, and that information should be tested. We have learned from experience that effective cross-examination of witnesses is important to test the reliability of their testimony, and the hearsay rules generally implement the right to cross-examine.

The hearsay rules in FRE 801 to 807 are part of this reliability analysis. If offered evidence, whether from witnesses or exhibits, involves an out-of-court statement that is now being repeated in court to establish the truth of these words, FRE 802 excludes the evidence unless the statement either is nonhearsay (FRE 801) or falls within a hearsay exception (FRE 803 to 805 and 807).

In addition, witnesses must be competent (FRE 601 to 606), they must have firsthand knowledge of the facts they are testifying about (FRE 602), they must comply with the lay and expert witness opinion rules (FRE 701 to 705), and their testimony must comply with the rules that control the manner and scope of direct and cross-examinations (FRE 607 to 615). Exhibits must be properly identified and authenticated by competent witnesses, or be self-authenticating (FRE 901 to 902), and writings must comply with the original documents rule (FRE 1001 to 1004).

Finally, in limited circumstances information may be presented to the jury without formal proof. These circumstances are covered in the rules governing judicial notice (FRE 201), presumptions in civil cases (FRE 301 to 302), and stipulations between the parties that certain facts are true.

c. Is It Right to Admit the Evidence for the Offered Purpose?

Third, evidence is not admissible unless it is shown to be *right*. That is, even though evidence is both relevant and reliable, that evidence may be further limited or excluded for fairness and efficiency reasons or for overriding social and political reasons.

The integrity of decision making and considerations of judicial efficiency fall within FRE 403, which excludes relevant evidence "if its probative value is substantially outweighed by a danger of one or more of the following: unfair prejudice, confusing the issues, misleading the jury, wasting time, or needlessly presenting cumulative evidence."

The social and political judgment rules govern character traits (FRE 404 to 405), other acts (FRE 404(b)), habit (FRE 406), policy exclusions (FRE 407 to 411), sexual assault (FRE 412 to 415), and privileges (FRE 501 and 502).

Only evidence that successfully passes through the three filters—relevant, reliable, and right—can be submitted to the jury, which then can decide what weight, if any, it should be given. In short, the judge determines admissibility and the jury determines weight.

For a detailed discussion of the law on evidentiary objections and the 3Rs approach to evidence advocacy, *see* Mauet & Wolfson, *Trial Evidence* (7th ed., 2020).

10.3 The Jury's Perspective

How do jurors react to evidentiary objections and rulings? On the one hand, jurors resent constant objections and the lawyers who make them, because information is being kept from them and constant interruptions become annoying. Whenever an objection is made, jurors understand that a lawyer is trying to keep them from hearing or seeing something. Excluded evidence is the forbidden fruit, tantalizing because they can't have it. Jurors will assume that the evidence—whether the objection was sustained or overruled—is important. Why else would a lawyer have objected to it? On the other hand, jurors have seen enough television to understand that lawyers make and judges rule on objections, so they expect some objections to be made during the trial.

When an objection is overruled, jurors will naturally pay more attention to the testimony or exhibit. When an objection is sustained, jurors will naturally speculate on what the evidence would have been had they been allowed to receive it. In some situations, letting the jurors speculate on what the denied evidence was may be worse than allowing them to receive it. Certainly, when an objection to testimony is sustained and the jury is instructed to disregard it, the jurors can hardly "unremember" what they just heard (although they might not discuss it openly during their deliberations).

Evidentiary objections have another aspect. Jurors notice which lawyer makes objections confidently, they notice which lawyer seems to be winning most of the objections, and they notice how the judge reacts to the objections and how the judge rules on them. This is part of what jurors use to form impressions of who the better lawyer is. That lawyer will gain influence as the trial progresses.

Effective trial lawyers understand the jurors' attitudes about, and reactions to, evidentiary objections. They raise objections before trial and out of the jury's presence whenever it is possible and wise to do so. They make objections in the jury's presence only when the issue is important, when they have a well-founded evidentiary basis for the objection, and when they expect it to be sustained. At all times, they project professionalism: respect for the judge, opposing counsel, and the rules of ethics.

10.4 Objections Strategy

Successful evidentiary objections do not simply happen. They require a sound approach and solid execution. An effective objections strategy includes the following considerations.

1. Help the Judge Get It Right

Evidentiary objections involve a measure of trust. Judges naturally trust those lawyers whose attitude is that they want to help the judge reach the right ruling. Conversely, judges soon learn to distrust those lawyers who seem intent on catching the judge in a mistake so that they can raise error on appeal. In the real world of trials, the close calls often go to the lawyer the judge trusts. Hence, everything you do should send positive signals to the trial judge: I'm prepared to try this case, I know evidence law, and I want to help you analyze the evidentiary issues that are raised and reach the right rulings.

2. Raise It Early

Early is better. Whenever possible, make all substantive objections before trial. Early objections give the trial judge time to understand the objection, hear arguments from the lawyers, research the issue if necessary, and make a considered ruling. Early objections help the judge get it right. Early objections are also an expression of confidence by the lawyer: I'm raising this issue now, because I'm confident that when the judge considers it thoroughly, he'll rule in my favor. Although the judge may not be able to rule on all objections when they are made, and may defer some rulings until the trial, the judge will still appreciate the early notice of the objections.

There's an important flip side. Late objections raise unwelcome concerns in the mind of the judge: Why did the lawyer wait until now to raise this issue? If he didn't know about it until now, he's probably unprepared. If he's known about it for some time, why didn't he raise it earlier? Was it because he thought if I had time to think and reflect I would probably rule against him? Is he trying to rush me so that I'll get it wrong? These are not thoughts you want the judge to have about you.

3. Raise as Proponent and Opponent

There is no evidentiary rule that permits only opponents of offered evidence to raise evidentiary issues. Proponents of offered evidence can also bring anticipated issues to the judge's attention. If you anticipate the opposing side will raise objections to some of your evidence, a good strategy is to raise the issues first. Doing this again sends positive signals to the judge: I'm confident enough of my positions on these issues that I'm raising them early. If the opposing side's objections have merit, don't fight them and concede the point. This strengthens your credibility with the trial judge.

Raising anticipated objections to your evidence early has another benefit. It helps you plan for the trial. If you already know that certain evidence will be admissible at trial, you can confidently incorporate that evidence into your opening statement, direct examinations of your witnesses, and cross-examinations of your opponent's witnesses. If the judge rules that certain evidence is inadmissible, you benefit as well. As the saying goes, knowledge is power, and knowing the judge's rulings on your evidence well before trial helps you plan and prepare.

4. Multiple or Focused Reasons

Should you raise multiple reasons for evidentiary objections, or should you raise only your best argument? This depends in part on timing. When you raise evidentiary objections before trial, or at least out of the presence of the jury, you can consider raising multiple alternative reasons. The judge will not be rushed and can consider all the reasons you raise why the offered evidence should not be admitted. The judge will not be put off by multiple reasons, as long as each reason has an arguable evidentiary basis.

Evidentiary objections in the presence of the jury are another matter. First, the judge will not appreciate the late objection (unless the objection could not have been made earlier) and may view multiple alternative objections as a sign of surprise or desperation. Second, the jurors may react the same way. For those reasons, it is often better to make concise objections, stating only your strongest reason, in the presence of the jury. Remember, though, that most objections that are not timely raised do not preserve issues for appeal.

5. Is It Important, and Should I Win It?

Having a good-faith basis for making an evidentiary objection is hardly sufficient. You need to ask two additional questions. First, is this important? Judges and jurors quickly become annoyed when lawyers constantly make objections, valid or not, during the trial. Objections interrupt the presentation of evidence. They interrupt the jurors' concentration and break the courtroom mood. We don't like people who constantly interrupt us when we are talking, and jurors don't like it during trials. Even worse, some technical objections, such as to the form of questions, often succeed only in forcing the other side to ask better questions and enhance its direct and cross-examinations.

In the courtroom, each side has a limited number of objections that it can use before the judge's and jury's patience are exhausted. Accordingly, use your objections wisely. Save them for the important things, the things that can make a difference in the trial, the things that further your trial strategy. Trials involve reciprocity. If you constantly badger the other side with trivial objections, the other side can do the same thing to you, and you will get little sympathy from the judge or jurors.

Second, should I win this objection? There's little point in making an objection unless you have a realistic chance of getting your objection sustained. Losing evidentiary disputes has consequences. Every time you make and lose an objection, your stock falls. Conversely, every time you make and win an objection, your stock rises. If you consistently win the evidentiary disputes, the judge will come to trust you, and the jurors will see you as the better lawyer. Unfortunately, though, jurors sometimes view a series of sustained objections as a vigorous attempt to hide evidence from them.

There's one exception to this generalization. In criminal cases, defense lawyers frequently object to evidence, knowing that the judge will probably overrule their objection. Nevertheless, they feel compelled to make the objection, to make sure that they have not waived any error on appeal, and to avoid later issues as to competency of counsel.

6. How Do I Get Around a Sustained Objection?

Don't be intimidated when the judge sustains your opponent's objection. An objection sustained is just that, nothing more. It doesn't necessarily mean that you cannot get the evidence properly admitted. Keep trying, if that evidence is important to your case. If the objection is based on hearsay, is there a way you can offer the evidence so that it does not run afoul of the hearsay rules? If the objection is based on lack of foundation, can you establish a proper foundation? If the objection is to the form of a question, can you rephrase the question so it is in proper form? Experienced lawyers view the opposing lawyer's objections as a challenge, not a roadblock.

7. If I Cannot Get Around It, How Do I Make a Record for Appeal?

If the judge sustains an objection to your offered evidence, make sure you preserve any error for appeal if that evidence is important. If the judge sustained an objection to an exhibit, make sure the exhibit is marked and the court clerk gets it so that the exhibit is included in the trial court record. If the judge sustained an objection to a question or a witness's answer, you need to make an offer of proof.

An *offer of proof*, governed by FRE 103(a)(2), is simply the way in which the offering lawyer shows what the excluded evidence would have been. This should be done as soon as possible, and out of the jury's presence. An offer of proof gives the trial judge an opportunity to change her ruling, and it gives the appellate court the information necessary to review the trial judge's ruling. With excluded witness testimony, one way lawyers can make an offer of proof is to make a narrative statement of the proposed questions and witness answers. That statement can be made orally or in writing. Make sure that the offer of proof itself complies with the evidence rules—that is, that your question and the witness's answer are not objectionable for any reason.

Example:

> **LAWYER:** Your honor, may we approach the bench?
> **JUDGE:** Yes. [Lawyers come up to the judge's bench.]
> **LAWYER:** Your honor, I'd like to make an offer of proof.
> **JUDGE:** Very well.
> **LAWYER:** My question, to which an objection was sustained, was: "Tell us what the driver of the truck said right after the crash." If the witness were allowed to answer that question, he would have said: "The driver jumped out, walked over to my car, and said 'I'm sorry, I shouldn't have been out here with the company truck.'" That statement is a statement by an employee of the party-opponent, and is admissible under Rule 801.
> **JUDGE:** Do you agree, counsel?
> **OPPOSING COUNSEL:** I agree that the witness would probably testify as counsel has indicated. I don't agree that this is admissible.
> **JUDGE:** My ruling stands. Continue with your examination.

Another, and better way, if the witness is in court, is to ask the proposed questions and get the witness's answers, out of the presence of the jurors. The court reporter's trial transcript will then contain the actual excluded testimony.

Example:

> **LAWYER:** Your honor, now that the jurors are out of the courtroom, may I make an offer of proof, since the witness is still on the stand?
> **JUDGE:** Proceed.
> **Q:** (BY LAWYER): Mr. Jackson, what did the driver of the truck do after the crash?
> **A:** He got out of his truck and walked over to my car.
> **Q:** Did he say anything?
> **A:** Yes.
> **Q:** Tell us what he said.
> **A:** He said: "I'm sorry. I shouldn't have been out here with the company truck."
> **LAWYER:** Your honor, in light of the witness's answers, we ask that you reconsider your ruling.
> **JUDGE:** I have, and my ruling remains the same. The objection is sustained.

If an objection has been overruled—to a question, a witness's answer, or an exhibit—there is no need to do anything further to preserve error. The trial transcript will contain the question and answer, and the trial court record will include the admitted exhibit. This is sufficient for the appellate court to assess whether the trial judge's ruling was correct.

Finally, make sure the judge rules and make sure the ruling, whether sustaining or overruling an objection, is a definitive ruling. This is particularly important with pretrial rulings. Under FRE 103(b), if the judge makes a definitive ruling on the record, it means that you need not renew your objection during trial, when the evidence is actually offered, to preserve error on appeal. If the ruling was not definitive—the judge reserved ruling, made a preliminary ruling, or stated that she would reconsider the ruling at trial—the objection must be renewed when the evidence is offered. When in doubt over whether a ruling is definitive, renew the objection at trial. The judge's ruling should be in a written order or minute entry or stated on the record with a court reporter present, because disputes over what the judge actually ruled can arise later.

8. Watch the Judge

Throughout the trial, watch the judge and notice where the judge is looking. When a judge looks over at you while a witness is testifying, it is often because the judge is anticipating your objection to a question or answer and will sustain an objection if you make it. These nonverbal cues can be important during the course of a trial.

10.5 Objections Procedure

Making effective evidentiary objections, and arguments in support of or in response to the objections, involves three things. First, how do you make and respond to objections before or during trial? Second, which objections should be raised before trial, and which should await the trial? Third, what are the common evidentiary objections that arise before and during trial?

1. How to Make and Argue Evidentiary Objections

How do you make effective evidentiary objections and respond to them? Remember that early is good, and both early and in writing is even better. How objections are raised depends largely on when they are made.

a. Before Trial

Before trial, evidentiary issues are raised in two basic ways. First, parties frequently file written pretrial motions to preclude evidence under FRE 104(a) (also called *motions in limine*) and file written responses to the motions. This is commonly done in both civil and criminal cases.

Drafting the motion carefully is important. It tells the judge and the opposing side that this motion is important, you have researched it thoroughly, and you expect to win it.

As the proponent of evidence, start with a positive statement of why you are offering the evidence and why it is properly admissible for that purpose. After that, state that the evidence is not being offered for an improper purpose. This approach is more effective with judges, who respond better to positive statements of proper purpose. For example, if you are offering evidence as other acts evidence under FRE 404(b), explain that the evidence is properly admissible to prove a proper purpose, such as motive, and that it is not being offered for an improper purpose, such as propensity or bad character.

Second, evidentiary issues arise before trial when the judge schedules a hearing on the parties' pretrial statement. In civil cases, in both federal and state courts, most judges require, under Fed. R. Civ. P. 16(d), that the parties prepare a joint final pretrial statement that, among other things, identifies what objections each side has to the witnesses and exhibits that the other side intends to present at trial. Many judges also require that each party submit a trial brief setting out their positions on these disputed issues. Before trial, the judge may hold a hearing on the pretrial statement and the trial briefs to hear arguments and rule on the evidentiary and other issues.

Regardless of how the evidentiary disputes arise before trial, the judge may rule without a hearing. Because of this, it is important that your motions, pretrial statement, and trial brief clearly state your positions on these issues and fully set forth the applicable facts and evidentiary law. In most cases, the judge will want to hear arguments on some or all of the issues and will set a time for that hearing. Some judges like to hold the hearing in advance of the trial, because the rulings may streamline the trial and may promote settlement. Other judges prefer to hold the hearing immediately before the trial begins.

b. During Breaks in the Trial

The second way evidentiary issues are presented is by the lawyers raising them during breaks in the trial. The issues can be raised by a written or oral motion.

Example:

> **LAWYER:** Your honor, before the jury is brought out, we have a motion to preclude the plaintiff's next witness, Helen Johnson, from testifying to certain matters.
>
> **JUDGE:** Very well. What is it?
>
> **LAWYER:** We believe that plaintiff will ask Ms. Johnson, who is a neighbor of the defendant, her opinion on whether the defendant is a careful driver. She was asked that question during her deposition. Such testimony is character trait evidence, and it is inadmissible in civil cases under Rule 404.
>
> **JUDGE:** Plaintiff, any response?
>
> **PLAINTIFF'S LAWYER:** Yes, your honor. We are just going to ask Ms. Johnson if she has ever seen the defendant drive in excess of the speed limit. We expect her to say she did on several occasions. We're not going to ask her to characterize the defendant's driving in a general way.
>
> **LAWYER:** If that's the case, your honor, the testimony violates Rule 404(b), because it is evidence of other acts that proves only propensity or bad character, which is improper under that rule.
>
> **JUDGE:** The motion is granted. Ms. Johnson will not be permitted to describe the defendant's driving characteristics or give her opinion on them.

c. During Trial in Presence of Jury

The third way evidentiary issues are raised is by lawyers making evidentiary objections during trial and in the presence of the jury. In this situation, the lawyer should stand up (this draws the judge's attention and shows you are serious), state the objection ("Objection, your honor"), state the evidentiary ground succinctly ("The question calls for hearsay"), and wait for the judge's ruling. The judge may rule immediately, or may ask the opposing lawyer to make a concise response. However, neither lawyer should be able to make speeches with the jury listening ("speaking objections"), particularly if the speech is intended to influence the jurors rather than persuade the judge. Most judges will quickly reprimand lawyers who attempt to extensively argue in the jury's presence.

Example:

> Q (PLAINTIFF'S LAWYER): Mr. Jones, what did the defendant say when he got out of his car?
>
> DEFENSE LAWYER: [Stands up.] Objection, your honor. That calls for hearsay.
>
> JUDGE: Plaintiff, any response?
>
> PLAINTIFF'S LAWYER: It's the statement of a party opponent, your honor.
>
> JUDGE: The objection is overruled. The witness may answer.

If the judge wants to hear further arguments, he will direct the lawyers to approach the bench or, if the issue is particularly important, excuse the jury from the courtroom and then hear the arguments. If the lawyers want to argue further, they should ask to approach the bench for a "sidebar," a hearing out of the presence of the jury. Do this before the judge rules, because once the judge has ruled, particularly with the jury watching, it is unlikely that the judge will change his ruling. Some judges freely allow such conferences; others rarely allow them. Regardless of the judge's attitude, do not ask for a sidebar unless the evidentiary issue is substantial. If the judge does allow a bench conference, direct your comments and arguments to the judge, not the other lawyer.

Example:

> Q (DEFENDANT'S LAWYER): Ms. Smith, how long have you known the plaintiff?
>
> A: About 10 years.
>
> Q: Do you know what kind of driver he is?
>
> PLAINTIFF'S LAWYER: [Stands up.] Your honor, we object. This is improper character trait evidence.
>
> DEFENDANT'S LAWYER: Your honor, may we be heard at the bench?
>
> JUDGE: Yes. Please come to the bench. [Lawyers come up to the bench.]
>
> DEFENDANT'S LAWYER: On direct, the witness testified she commutes every day with the plaintiff, and she was allowed to testify that the plaintiff always stops at the stop sign at Main and Elm, where this accident happened. Your honor previously ruled that this was proper habit evidence under Rule 406. All I'm trying to do on cross is to elicit testimony that contradicts this habit testimony.
>
> JUDGE: Plaintiff?
>
> PLAINTIFF'S LAWYER: Your honor, what the defense is trying to do is get into character trait evidence, which is explicitly inadmissible in civil cases under Rule 404(a). Just because we were allowed to bring out

proper habit evidence under the habit rule doesn't open the door to character trait evidence under the character rule.

JUDGE: The objection is sustained.

Before you ask for a bench conference, think about the downside of such a request. First, if you make this request too often, the judge will be upset that you are slowing down the trial. Second, and more importantly, jurors often resent bench conferences. It is human nature to want to be included in important discussions. When you ask for a sidebar, you are asking for permission to exclude the jurors from an important discussion. Consider whether there is an alternative to a bench conference. Can you raise the issue outside the jury's hearing before trial or, for mid-trial matters, at a time when the jury is not in the room when you ask the judge to consider the matter? Can you wait until the next break in the trial and, during the break, tell the clerk or the bailiff that you have a matter for the court's consideration outside the presence of the jury? In these ways, you get the hearing outside the jury's presence that you need, but you do not ask the judge to exclude them when they are listening.

Make sure you get a ruling on each of your objections. Unfortunately, judges sometimes do not make an explicit ruling, leaving the record unclear. If it is important, expressly ask the judge for a ruling.

Example:

Q: Officer Smith, what did the bystander indicate to you when you arrived at the scene?

OPPOSING LAWYER: [Standing] Objection, your honor. That calls for hearsay.

JUDGE: Counsel, perhaps you can rephrase the question.

OPPOSING LAWYER: Your honor, may I have a ruling on my objection?

JUDGE: The objection is sustained.

Evidence is frequently admitted for a limited purpose. For example, an statement of a party-opponent is admissible only as to that party; a prior inconsistent statement not made under oath and used to impeach is not admissible as substantive evidence; and a statement admitted for the limited purpose of showing notice or knowledge is not admissible for its truth. In these situations, the jury should be instructed on the limited proper purpose of that evidence. Under FRE 105, you must ask the judge to give the jury an appropriate limiting instruction when the evidence is admitted. If you do not, you waive error on appeal.

Example:

Q: Mr. Adams, what did you tell the defendant after he brought his car to your service station?

A: I told him: "Your brakes don't work. Don't drive that car."

OPPOSING LAWYER: Your honor, may we have an instruction on the proper limited use of this evidence?

JUDGE: Yes. Members of the jury, this testimony is being admitted only on the issue of whether the defendant had notice of a problem with his brakes. It should not be considered by you for any other purpose.

Finally, there is no need to keep objecting to the same thing if the judge's attitude is clear and repeating your objection in the presence of the jury will only aggravate the situation and prejudice the jury. Ask the judge for a *continuing objection*, which will preserve error as to that particular evidence so that you do not have to renew your objection each time the witness is asked about that topic. Make sure you state exactly what evidence you are objecting to, so that the record for appellate purposes is clear.

Example:

> Q: Mr. Clark, you were also present at the second board meeting on June 1, 2020, right?
>
> OPPOSING LAWYER: [standing] Objection, your honor. That's beyond the scope of the direct examination. We didn't go into that board meeting on direct.
>
> JUDGE: Overruled. The witness will answer.
>
> A: Yes, I was present at the second meeting.
>
> Q: Who else was present at the second meeting?
>
> OPPOSING LAWYER: [standing] Your honor, may we have a continuing objection to all questions that ask about the second board meeting?
>
> JUDGE: Yes. The record will show that counsel has a continuing objection to the cross-examination going into the second board meeting.

2. What Evidentiary Issues Can Be Raised Before Trial?

What issues can be raised before trial? The easy answer is: Consider raising all important evidentiary issues you are aware of before trial. This shows the judge and your opponent that you are prepared and confident of your positions. The judge will be able to rule on some of the issues before trial, and early rulings benefit everyone. Even if the judge cannot rule on some issues, the judge is at least alerted to the issues and will be better able to deal with them later.

Avoid raising trivial issues before trial. These merely divert the judge's attention from the important issues that make a real difference in how the case is tried, and the judge may begin looking for ways to avoid trying a "problem case." The better approach is to raise all the *important* issues early, so that the judge will focus on them and give them the attention they deserve.

What kinds of issues are important? Which ones raise significant relevance and hearsay issues? Which ones are thorny and complex? Issues involving FRE 403 concerns with unduly inflammatory evidence can usually be raised early. The admissibility of character trait, other acts, or habit evidence (FRE 404 to 406), policy exclusions (FRE 407 to 411), sexual assault evidence (FRE 412 to 415), and privileges exclusions (FRE 501) usually can be raised early. Issues involving out of court statements can often be raised early, particularly if the dispute centers, as it often does, on whether the offered testimony or exhibit is admissible under a nonhearsay (FRE 801) analysis, whether a hearsay exception (FRE 803 to 807) applies, or whether there is a double hearsay (FRE 805) problem. Issues involving the admissibility of expert testimony often should be raised through a pretrial *Daubert* motion.[1]

---

1. Junior co-author Easton believes it can sometimes be better to wait until trial to raise issues regarding the admissibility of expert testimony. In his view, raising issues regarding an expert's weaknesses before trial gives your opponent and her expert a roadmap of your trial cross (if you lose your motion to exclude, which is probable) that they will use to shore up the expert's trial testimony.

Finally, pay attention to issues that may take time to resolve. In particular, raise any admissibility issues involving transcripts of testimony that are generally admissible as statements of a party opponent (FRE 801(d)(2)) or former testimony (FRE 804(b)(1)). Just because a transcript (the most common are deposition transcripts in civil cases and preliminary hearing transcripts in criminal cases) may be generally admissible as nonhearsay or under a hearsay exception does not mean that the entire transcript is admissible. There still may be relevance and other hearsay issues. There may be objections to the form of questions and to improper opinion testimony. These issues should be raised well before trial.

10.6 Evidentiary Objections to Witness Testimony

The following are the evidentiary objections to witness testimony that lawyers frequently make before and during trial. Additional objections applicable only to expert witnesses are discussed in Chapter 8, and objections directed to opening statements and closing arguments are in Chapters 4 and 9.

Note that the order of the following list reflects substantive objections, followed by form and procedural objections. The substantive objections (1 through 10) often can be anticipated and raised before trial; the form and procedural objections (11 through 32) usually must be made during the trial.

1. Irrelevant (FRE 401, 402)

Under FRE 401, evidence is relevant if it meets two tests. First, the evidence must be "of consequence" to the action, which is determined by the pleadings and the underlying substantive law. A good way to assess if evidence is of consequence is to look at the jury instructions for the elements of the claims, damages, and defenses. These elements form the framework for analyzing whether offered evidence is of consequence to the action.

Relevance objections frequently have to be argued, because the judge needs to know the purpose of the offered evidence before he can make an informed ruling. For that reason, many relevance objections are argued at a sidebar conference, if they were not raised and ruled on before trial.

Example:

Q (PLAINTIFF'S LAWYER): Mr. Wilson, are you familiar with the financial condition of the defendant corporation?

DEFENSE LAWYER: Objection, your honor. That is irrelevant.

JUDGE: Approach the bench. [Lawyers come to the bench.] Why is this irrelevant?

DEFENSE LAWYER: In this case, plaintiff is seeking only compensatory damages. Evidence of the defendant's size, wealth, or financial condition may be relevant to the issue of punitive damages, but plaintiff is not seeking punitive damages in this case.

JUDGE: I understand. The objection is sustained.

The second test under FRE 401 is that the offered evidence must be probative, meaning that it has "any tendency" to prove or disprove a fact of consequence to the action. Because the any tendency standard is so low, objections on this basis alone are rarely sustained. When such objections are made, they usually involve circumstantial evidence for which the connection to issues in the case is not obvious.

Example:

> Q (PROSECUTOR): Mrs. Higgins, were you at the bank on June 1, one week before the robbery?
>
> A: Yes.
>
> Q: Did you see the defendant that day?
>
> DEFENSE LAWYER: Your honor, we object on relevance grounds. May we approach?
>
> JUDGE: Yes. [Lawyers come to the bench.] Prosecution, where's this testimony going?
>
> PROSECUTOR: The witness will testify that she saw the defendant outside the bank that day, that he was looking at the bank, but never came inside.
>
> JUDGE: What's that prove?
>
> PROSECUTOR: It shows the defendant was already planning the robbery and casing the bank.
>
> DEFENSE LAWYER: The fact that he's outside the bank hardly proves he was planning to rob it.
>
> JUDGE: The objection is overruled. The witness may answer.

If the offered evidence is admissible under the general relevance analysis, the next step is to determine if any of the special relevance rules, which are based on social policy and political judgments, apply and exclude the offered evidence. These are contained in FRE 404 to 415 and 501.

2. Violates Character Trait Rules (FRE 404, 405)

FRE 404(a) and 405 govern the admissibility of character trait evidence, and they are highly technical rules. Under certain circumstances, in certain cases, evidence law permits introducing relevant character traits of certain persons. There are two branches: the *essential element* rule and the *circumstantial evidence* rule.

a. Essential Element Rule

A character trait is sometimes, though infrequently, an "essential element" of a claim, charge, or defense. In these circumstances, character trait evidence is admissible under FRE 405(b) in both civil and criminal cases when offered by a proper party at a proper time. Look at the statutory definitions or elements instructions for the claims, charges, or defenses. If any requires proving someone's character trait to establish a *prima facie* claim, charge, or defense, the essential element rule applies, and the person's relevant character trait can be proven in the plaintiff's or defendant's case-in-chief by reputation, personal opinion, and specific instances of conduct.

Common examples of the essential element rule are negligent hiring cases, in which plaintiff claims the defendant trucking company negligently hired a driver it knew to be a reckless driver; child custody cases, in which one parent charges that the other parent is a violent person; wrongful termination cases, in which the defense claims the plaintiff was terminated for being dishonest; and defamation cases, in which the defense claims the affirmative defense of truth (e.g., that the plaintiff is in fact violent).

Example:

> JUDGE: This is defendant's motion to preclude the introduction of character trait evidence. The complaint claims that the defendant nursing home hired an employee, Smith, who the nursing home knew was a violent person, and that Smith assaulted the plaintiff, a patient in the defendant's facility. Defendant's motion seeks to preclude evidence of specific instances of conduct—that Smith assaulted several other patients of another nursing home where he was employed over the three years before he was hired by the defendant nursing home. I have read the motion, response, and attached memoranda, and heard the arguments of counsel. My ruling is that this evidence is properly admissible under the essential element rule in Rule 405(b), which permits proving a relevant character trait—in this case Smith's violent character—through evidence of reputation, personal opinion, and specific instances of conduct. Accordingly, defendant's motion is denied.

b. Circumstantial Evidence Rule

The circumstantial evidence rule, FRE 404(a)(2), is much more frequently used. It permits, in limited situations in criminal cases, evidence of a person's character trait as circumstantial proof that the person acted consistently with his character at a particular time. In general, the defendant in a criminal case has the option to introduce evidence of a relevant character trait of himself and, sometimes, of the victim. If that happens, the prosecution then can rebut with contrary character trait evidence. Under the circumstantial evidence rule, a character trait can only be proved through reputation and personal opinion (not with specific instances of conduct).

Common character traits include peacefulness, honesty, and truthfulness. Common examples of use of the circumstantial evidence rule arise in homicide and assault cases, where the defense introduces evidence of the defendant's good character for peacefulness; homicide and assault cases involving self-defense, where the defense introduces evidence of the victim's character for violence; burglary, theft, and fraud cases, where the defense introduces evidence of the defendant's good character for honesty; and perjury and false statement cases, where the defense introduces evidence of the defendant's good character for truthfulness.

There are two important exceptions to the general procedural rule in FRE 404 (the defense initiates, the prosecution then may rebut). First, when the defendant introduces proof of self-defense (that the victim was the first aggressor) in a homicide case, the prosecution can rebut with evidence of the victim's good character for peacefulness (FRE 404(a)(2)(C)). Second, when the defense attacks the character of the victim, the prosecution can then attack the defendant's character for the same character trait (FRE 404(a)(2)(B)(ii)).

Character trait rules are technical and must be thoroughly understood and researched, because appellate reversal is common. Issues should be raised before trial whenever possible.

Example (Assault—Self-Defense Case):

> Q (DEFENSE LAWYER): Mr. Quigley, do you have a personal opinion of the victim's character for peacefulness?
> A: Yes. I've known him for a long time.
> Q: What is your personal opinion of his character?
> PROSECUTOR: Objection. Improper character evidence.
> JUDGE: Overruled. The witness may answer.
> A: In my opinion, he's an extremely violent person.
> Q: Can you give us examples of times he has been violent?
> PROSECUTOR: Objection, your honor. Now they're trying to go into specific instances of conduct. That's improper under Rule 405(a).
> JUDGE: Sustained.

Under FRE 608(a), there is a third way character trait evidence can be introduced in trials. Whenever any witness testifies, the witness's credibility is in issue, so the witness can be attacked by evidence that the witness has a bad character for truthfulness. That character can be shown through reputation and personal opinion. Once the witness has been attacked with evidence of his bad character for truthfulness, the other side can rebut with evidence of his good character for truthfulness.

This kind of evidence is commonly introduced in criminal cases, where the defense introduces evidence that the victim (who testified) is an untruthful person, or the prosecution introduces evidence that the defendant (who testified) is an untruthful person.

Example:

> Q (PROSECUTOR): Ms. Quigley, do you know the reputation for truthfulness of John Barnes, who testified earlier in this trial?
> DEFENSE LAWYER: Objection, your honor. We didn't open the door to this.
> JUDGE: Overruled. Ms. Quigley, you may answer the question.
> A: Yes.
> Q: How have you come to know his reputation?
> A: I've known him for years. He lives in my neighborhood, and the neighbors talk about him regularly.
> Q: What is his reputation for truthfulness?
> A: It's bad. He's known as someone whose word can't be trusted.
> Q: Why do the neighbors feel that way?
> DEFENSE LAWYER: Objection. They're trying to get into specific instances.
> JUDGE: Sustained. Ask another question.

Finally, under FRE 405(a) and 608(b), the cross-examination rules that apply to character trait witnesses are important. Whenever a witness testifies about someone else's character, in reputation or personal opinion form, that witness may be cross-examined about specific instances of conduct inconsistent with the claimed character (so long as there is a good-faith ethical basis for asking about them).

Example:

> Q (PROSECUTOR): You say the defendant's reputation for peacefulness in our community is good?
> A: That's right.

Q: Mr. Adams, did you hear that the defendant assaulted another man at the City Tavern last year?

DEFENSE: Objection, your honor. They're trying to go into specific instances of conduct.

JUDGE: Overruled. This is cross-examination. The witness may answer.

A: No, I didn't hear anything about that.

> ◼◀ For a discussion of the law of evidence regarding character, credibility, and habit, please watch Video H.5, "Wyo STI: Profs. Younger and Easton, plus Mackey, on Character and Credibility."

3. Violates Other Acts Rules (FRE 404(b), 608(b))

FRE 404(b)(2) permits the introduction of other crimes, wrongs, and acts in limited circumstances in both civil and criminal cases. Such evidence is also called *extrinsic evidence* and *uncharged misconduct*. Other acts evidence is not admissible when its only probative value is to show "on a particular occasion the person acted in accordance with the character" (FRE 404(b)(1)), meaning that it only proves the person has a bad character or a propensity to commit such acts. Rather, such evidence is properly admissible only when it is probative of something actually in issue, such as, but not limited to, motive (FRE 404(b)(2)). This rule no longer lists other examples of relevant matters, but they still exist.

The balancing test under FRE 403 frequently is an important consideration. In many cases, the offered other acts evidence may have some probative value to prove identity, intent, knowledge, or other proper purpose, but it is also prejudicial because it shows the person to be a bad character or to have a propensity to commit other crimes or bad acts. When opposing the introduction of other acts evidence, you should always argue that the probative value of the evidence for a proper purpose is low, and that the probative value is substantially outweighed by the danger of unfair prejudice.

Disputes usually center on whether the offered evidence is actually probative of something in issue, how probative that evidence is, and whether that probative value is substantially outweighed by the FRE 403 considerations. The other acts rule must be thoroughly researched and understood, because appellate reversal is common in this area, particularly in criminal cases. The issue should be raised before trial whenever possible, because the judge may need time to assess the evidence in light of the overall issues to make a considered ruling.

Example:

JUDGE: Defense, this is your pretrial motion to preclude evidence.

DEFENSE LAWYER: Your honor, we made this motion to preclude the plaintiff from introducing evidence that the defendant was previously cited for running the stop sign at Main and Elm, the same stop sign involved in this accident. That's exactly the kind of evidence prohibited by Rule 404(b), because its only probative value is to show propensity, namely that if the defendant failed to stop at that stop sign before, he probably failed to stop at the stop sign this time.

JUDGE: Plaintiff?

PLAINTIFF LAWYER: Your honor, that evidence not only is circumstantial evidence making it more likely he failed to stop at the time of the collision, it also proves he knew that there was a stop sign at that intersection and that he was required to stop there.

DEFENSE LAWYER: That's propensity evidence, and improper. Not only that, there's no issue of knowledge in this case. They can't invent an issue and then claim their offered evidence proves that nonexistent issue.

JUDGE: Defendant's motion is granted. The only probative value of this evidence is to show the defendant is a bad driver, which is barred by Rule 404(b).

Example:

DEFENSE LAWYER: Your honor, this is our motion to preclude the prosecution from introducing evidence that one month before the burglary of the fast-food restaurant — the charge that we are going to start trying today — the defendant committed a burglary of a house in another neighborhood. That's improper under Rule 404(b), and we ask that evidence be precluded.

PROSECUTOR: This evidence shows identity and a common plan and scheme. He was caught burgling a residential home, one month before. That home is only two miles from the fast-food restaurant he is charged with burgling. That evidence makes it much more likely he's the burglar of the fast-food restaurant. It's highly relevant on an issue in this case — identity.

DEFENSE LAWYER: This is not similar M.O. evidence, your honor. There's nothing common about these two events, other than they are both burglaries. The real probative point of this evidence is to show that once a burglar, always a burglar. That's exactly what the jury will take that evidence for, and that's improper under both Rules 404(b) and 403.

JUDGE: The defense motion is granted. There's no similar *modus operandi* between the two burglaries that would make this evidence highly probative on the identity issue, and there's a substantial risk that a jury would misuse this evidence and use it as proof of propensity, regardless of any limiting instruction I could give.

Under FRE 608(b), other acts evidence "to attack or support the witness's character of truthfulness," also may be inquired about during cross-examination to attack the credibility of a testifying witness. Common examples are showing that a testifying witness previously submitted an employment application falsely showing he has a college degree, or submitted a loan application falsely stating his assets and liabilities. Such evidence is brought out during the witness's cross-examination. Of course, the cross-examiner must have a good-faith ethical basis for believing these other acts exist.

Example:

Q (DEFENSE LAWYER): Mr. Jackson, you used to work at the ABC Manufacturing Company, right?

A: That's right.

Q: Weren't you fired last year?

A: Yes.

Q: That's because you submitted false expense reimbursement forms to the company, right?
PLAINTIFF: Objection, your honor. Violates Rule 404(b).
JUDGE: No, this is cross-examination. The witness will answer.
A: That's what they claimed.

4. Violates Habit Rule (FRE 406)

FRE 406 governs the admission of habit and routine practice evidence. Such evidence is circumstantial evidence of conduct at a particular time. The rule does not define those terms, but the Advisory Committee Notes make clear that "habit" is how someone regularly, almost automatically, responds to a specific recurring situation. "Routine practice" is habit evidence in a business or industry setting. For example, you always lock your front door when leaving your house; your assistant always mails the outgoing mail in the lobby mail drop when she leaves the office.

Habit evidence is different from character trait evidence. Habit is a reflexive, recurring, situation-specific behavior. A character trait is a general personality characteristic that is not situation-specific. For example, evidence that you are a "careful" person is a character trait; evidence that you "always lock your office door" is habit. This distinction is important, because character trait evidence is inadmissible as circumstantial proof of conduct in civil cases under FRE 404(a). Lawyers in negligence cases frequently attempt to offer such evidence as habit evidence under FRE 406. Routine practice evidence is frequently offered in commercial and products liability cases.

Example:

Q: Ms. Adams, let's talk about your driving for a moment. Are you a careful driver?
PLAINTIFF'S LAWYER: Objection, your honor. Improper character trait evidence.
JUDGE: Sustained.
Q: Do you make it a habit of obeying the traffic laws?
PLAINTIFF'S LAWYER: Objection. Same basis.
JUDGE: Sustained.
Q: Well, do you make it a habit of stopping at stop signs?
PLAINTIFF'S LAWYER: Objection. Same basis.
JUDGE: Sustained. Counsel, move on to another topic.

Example:

Q: Mr. King, what's your job at ABC Manufacturing?
A: I'm the quality control inspector.
Q: What's that involve?
A: I check every box as it comes down the assembly line. I make sure that each box has the product, the instructions for use, and safety warnings. If it does, I close the box and send it to the machine that shrink wraps the box so it is sealed. If it doesn't, I pull the box off the line and send it back.

Q: Were you working in April 2020, when the toaster involved in this case was shipped from your plant?

A: Yes sir, I worked every day that month.

5. Violates Policy Exclusion Rules (FRE 407–411)

FRE 407 to 411 make certain kinds of evidence generally inadmissible, not because such evidence is not relevant, but because there is a danger that the jury might use such evidence as proof of fault, or because exclusion serves higher social goals. FRE 407 generally excludes evidence of subsequent remedial measures; FRE 409 generally excludes evidence of payment of medical expenses; FRE 411 generally excludes evidence of liability insurance; FRE 408 generally excludes evidence of settlements or offers of settlement in civil cases; and FRE 410 generally excludes plea negotiations and discussions in criminal cases.

These rules follow the approach of FRE 404(b): Evidence of these things is generally inadmissible, but it may be admissible if probative of something actually in issue in the trial, such as ownership and control or bias and interest. When evidence is properly admissible for these limited purposes, the jury should be given a limiting instruction under FRE 105 on the proper limited purpose of the evidence.

Issues in the policy exclusions area can, and should, be anticipated before trial. Parties usually make pretrial motions to determine the admissibility of particular evidence, and judges can usually rule on these issues before trial. Most issues involve whether an exception to the general rule of exclusion applies.

Example:

JUDGE: This is a slip-and-fall case in which plaintiff claims she slipped on a wet spot at the entry to defendant's store in a shopping mall. This is the defendant's motion in limine to preclude evidence that the defendant carries insurance and subsequently mopped the area where plaintiff was injured. Defense, anything in addition to your written motion?

DEFENSE LAWYER: Yes, your honor. We have asserted, in our answer to the complaint and since, that the slip and fall occurred outside the doors to our store, and that maintaining that area is the responsibility of the mall owners. The fact that we, as careful businessmen, carry insurance on the entrance to our store, or that our manager had someone mop up the area outside our store, does not change the fact that what happens outside our store is not our legal responsibility, and there's a grave danger that the jury will misuse that evidence.

JUDGE: Plaintiff?

PLAINTIFF'S LAWYER: The issue in this case is whether the defendant is responsible for the area outside their doors where this injury occurred. The defense says no, and still says no, so it's an actual disputed issue. Evidence of defendant's insurance and mopping up the area is exactly the kind of evidence Rules 407 and 411 make admissible. The defense can't have it both ways. They can't deny legal responsibility for that area, and then complain about our evidence showing they have responsibility.

JUDGE: The evidence is admissible. I'll give a limiting instruction on the proper use of this evidence.

6. Violates Sexual Assault Rules (FRE 412–415)

FRE 412 is often referred to as the *rape shield rule*, although it is broader than that. The rule protects the privacy interests of victims of sexual misconduct by generally barring all evidence of the victim's sexual history. The only exceptions to the general rule of inadmissibility in criminal cases are in FRE 412(b)(1): (A) to prove that someone else was the source of semen, injury, or other physical evidence; (B) sexual conduct with the accused to prove the defense of consent; and (C) if exclusion would violate the defendant's constitutional rights. The rule requires a party offering sexual conduct evidence to give notice in writing before trial, and the court must conduct a hearing in camera.

FRE 413 to 415 govern the admissibility of other acts evidence relating to the accused in both criminal and civil cases. Under FRE 413, evidence that the accused committed other offenses of sexual assault is admissible in sexual assault cases for any relevant purpose. FRE 414 allows such evidence in child molestation cases, and FRE 415 allows such evidence in civil cases based on allegations of sexual assault or child molestation. In short, propensity evidence regarding the alleged assailant is now admissible in these cases.

Because these rules now broadly permit the admission of other acts evidence as to the accused in both criminal and civil sexual assault and child molestation cases, the only argument against admission is for the defense to argue that the evidence should still be excluded under FRE 403's balancing test.

Example:

> **DEFENSE LAWYER:** Your honor, this is our motion to preclude the prosecution from introducing any evidence of the defendant's prior sexual assault three years ago in the present sexual assault case. We understand that Rule 413 permits such evidence for any relevant purpose. However, Rule 413 does not trump Rule 403. The defendant in the present case is charged with sexually assaulting a stranger on the street. The sexual assault three years ago involved what's sometimes called a date rape situation, where the defendant and victim had known each other for some time. The two situations are obviously quite different. Even if the earlier incident has some probative value, that value is low, and it is highly prejudicial to the defendant's ability to receive a fair trial here.
>
> **PROSECUTOR:** Your honor, Rule 413 makes such evidence explicitly admissible. The probative value is clearly high: Proof that the defendant sexually assaulted someone on a date makes it much more likely that he would sexually assault someone else in the future. That's simply common sense. Since it has such high probative value, Rule 403 does not operate to bar its admission.
>
> **JUDGE:** The motion is denied.

7. Violates Privilege Rules (FRE 501, 502)

Policy reasons underlie the privilege exclusions. Under certain circumstances, it is more important to foster candid communications between certain persons even if it comes at the expense of a jury not receiving relevant evidence. Privileges were initially a creation of the common law, but in recent years development of privileges law has also been statutory. In federal courts, privileges have always been based on case law, and FRE 501 and 502 maintain that approach, though FRE 502 itself was created by statute.

There are always several issues you must address when you are facing a privilege issue. First, determine which jurisdiction's privilege law applies. In federal courts, federal privilege law applies in criminal cases and civil cases based on federal question jurisdiction. However, in federal civil cases based on diversity jurisdiction, FRE 501 applies the *Erie* doctrine, which means that the forum state's privilege law applies. In state courts, that state's privilege law usually applies.

Second, determine what the recognized privileges are in that jurisdiction. The privileges generally recognized by federal courts are set forth in the deleted FRE 501 to 513. The various states differ substantially in the privileges they recognize and in their definitions of a particular privilege. The most frequent nonconstitutional privileges issues usually involve the attorney-client, spousal bar, interspousal communications, and doctor-patient privileges.

Third, who is the holder of the privilege? Privileges are considered personal to the holder. Only the holder can assert or waive a privilege (except that a lawyer can assert a privilege on behalf of a client).

Fourth, has there been a waiver of the privilege? The holder can waive the benefit of the privilege by disclosing, or not objecting to the disclosure of, privileged information, or by engaging in speech or conduct inconsistent with the privilege. (FRE 502 significantly changes the law on advertent and inadvertent waivers in federal and state proceedings.) In addition, most jurisdictions also hold that a privilege will not operate in certain situations, primarily those in which eliciting privileged information is necessary to accurately resolve litigation between the parties to the privilege, or circumstances in which asserting the privilege would constitute an abuse of the privilege.

Finally, has there been a termination of the privilege? Most privileges never terminate, even though the relationship on which the privilege was based has ended. However, some privileges do not survive termination of the relationship.

Privilege issues can be thorny, and jurisdiction-specific research will always be necessary. These issues should be raised well before trial so that the judge will have time to consider them carefully and reach a proper ruling.

Example:

> **JUDGE:** This is a hearing on defendants' joint motion to preclude evidence of a conversation between the two co-defendants in this case, who are husband and wife. Defense, any additional arguments?
>
> **DEFENDANT'S LAWYER:** Yes, your honor. The only remaining issue is whether this secret recording of a telephone conversation between the two defendants is protected by the interspousal communications privilege. There is no dispute that the two defendants were, and are, husband and wife. There is no dispute that they, as holders of the privilege, have asserted it in a timely way. The government says that since the secret recording of their telephone conversation was lawfully done, that constituted a breach of confidentiality, and the privilege falls. However, here they had a reasonable expectation that their conversation would be confidential, and they took reasonable

steps to ensure confidentiality. That's more than enough to protect the privilege.

JUDGE: Prosecution?

PROSECUTOR: Not only was the privilege broken, your honor, but the tape clearly shows that they were planning a fraud, the very fraud with which they are charged in this indictment. Under the law, the privilege does not apply to joint crimes.

JUDGE: I have reviewed the tape recording of the conversation, and it is clear from the tape that the conversation falls within the joint crimes exception to the interspousal communications privilege. Accordingly, the motion is denied.

8. Unfairly Prejudicial/Waste of Time (FRE 403)

Even if evidence has "any tendency" to prove or disprove a fact "of consequence" (FRE 401), that is not enough. Under FRE 403, the offered evidence's "probative value" cannot be "substantially outweighed" by "a danger of . . . unfair prejudice, confusing the issues, misleading the jury, undue delay, wasting time, or needlessly presenting cumulative evidence."

When objecting under this rule, it is particularly important to use the wording of the rule to support your objection and argument. Judges quickly become jaded by objections that merely claim in conclusory fashion that the offered evidence is "prejudicial." Instead, show how the offered evidence has low probative value, and how it creates a substantial danger of unfair prejudice, confusion, or misleading the jury. That's the balancing test the rule requires the judge to apply. For that reason, Rule 403 objections are best made out of the jury's hearing.

Example:

DEFENSE LAWYER: Your honor, before the jury comes back, we have an evidentiary matter that should be heard before the prosecution calls the victim's mother as its next witness.

JUDGE: Very well. What is it?

DEFENSE LAWYER: We believe the prosecution will try to introduce a color photograph of the victim lying in a body pan at the morgue following the autopsy. The only thing the photograph can possibly show that's in any way relevant is that it's a photo of the victim, and he's dead. That's not in dispute, and there are other ways to identify the victim and prove he's dead. What the prosecution really wants to do is show the mother a gory photo of her son to stimulate an emotional response from the mother and inflame the jury. That's improper under Rule 403. Any probative value this photo may have is substantially outweighed by the danger of unfair prejudice.

PROSECUTOR: Your honor, we're entitled to prove our case, and we have to prove the identity of the victim and the fact that he's dead. The photograph clearly does that.

JUDGE: If the physical condition or appearance of the victim were relevant here, I would let it in for that purpose. However, no one has suggested that to be the case. Therefore, the objection is sustained.

9. Hearsay (FRE 801–807)

Under FRE 801(c), *hearsay* is "a statement that: (1) the declarant does not make while testifying at the current trial or hearing, and (2) a party offers in evidence to prove the truth of the matter asserted in the statement." If something is hearsay, it is inadmissible unless a hearsay exception or exclusion applies.

The hearsay definition has three parts. First, there must be a "statement." A statement must be an "assertion" of some matter (FRE 801(a)), and an assertion can be made in three ways: oral assertion, written assertion, and nonverbal conduct intended as an assertion.

Second, the statement must have been made out-of-court, to use dated but still almost universal language, and is now being repeated in court (FRE 801(c)(1), which actually refers to a statement that "the declarant does not make while testifying at the current trial or hearing"). It does not matter that the witness on the stand is the same person as the out-of-court declarant. All that matters is that an out-of-court statement might be repeated in court.

Third, the statement must be offered "to prove the truth of the matter asserted" in the statement (FRE 801(c)(2)). If the statement is offered for its truth, it is hearsay. If the statement is offered because it was said, it is not hearsay. Put another way, if the out-of-court statement's probative value depends on it being true, it is hearsay; if its probative value is based on the statement being said, it is not hearsay.

A good way to test this third requirement is to ask: As the opponent, who do I want to cross-examine? If the statement is offered for its truth, you want to cross-examine the out-of-court declarant (because only the out-of-court declarant has firsthand knowledge of the facts); if the statement is being offered merely because it was said, you want to cross-examine the witness on the stand (because the in-court witness has firsthand knowledge that the out-of-court statement was said).

Example:

> Q: Tell us what you said to Mr. Jackson after you looked at his car.
> OPPOSING LAWYER: Objection, your honor.
> JUDGE: Approach. [Lawyers come to the bench.] What's the witness going to say?
> LAWYER: He will say he told Mr. Jackson: "Don't drive your car. The brakes don't work."
> OPPOSING LAWYER: That's hearsay, your honor.
> LAWYER: Those are the actual words of notice, your honor, and are not hearsay for that limited purpose.
> JUDGE: The objection is overruled. The witness may answer, and I will give a limiting instruction under Rule 105 on the proper use of this evidence.

Disputes about whether words or conduct constituted an assertion are unusual and, when they do arise, usually esoteric and philosophical. There is rarely a dispute over whether the offered statement was made out of court. Thus, hearsay issues usually center on the third requirement, which requires understanding the purpose for which the out-of-court statement is now being offered.

As the party offering an out-of-court statement, you must deal with trial court realities. The opposing lawyer, and probably most judges, will assume that any out-of-court statement is being offered for a hearsay purpose: its truth. That's why it is important, as the proponent of such evidence, that you raise anticipated hearsay objections before trial, when you have an adequate opportunity to show, in your written motion and during the hearing, why the statement is properly admissible.

As the proponent, you must show that the out-of-court statement falls into one of three possible categories. First, the statement is nonhearsay because it is being offered because it was said, and not for its truth. Common examples are statements that have independent legal significance, such as the words of contract, misrepresentation, defamation, gift, and permission; statements that are prior inconsistent statements and are used to impeach a testifying witness; and statements that are offered to show their effect on the listener's state of mind, such as statements that put the listener on notice, impart knowledge, or induce fear. In these situations, what matters is that the statements were made, not whether the statements are true.

Second, the out-of-court statement is not hearsay because it falls within an exclusion to the hearsay rule found in FRE 801(d). Under that rule, five kinds of statements are outside the hearsay definition: (1) a prior inconsistent statement, if made under oath at a trial or other proceeding; (2) a prior consistent statement offered to rebut a charge of recent fabrication, improper influence, or motive; (3) a prior consistent statement offered to rehabilitate the declarant's credibility when attacked on another ground; (4) a statement of identification made at a lineup, show up, or other identification procedure; and (5) a statement by a party-opponent (made by the party, or by an authorized person, or an agent or employee if within the scope of the agency or employment and made during the existence of the relationship, or by a co-conspirator if made during the course of the conspiracy and in furtherance of it).

Third, the out-of-court statement is hearsay, but a hearsay exception applies. The hearsay exceptions are contained in FRE 803, 804, and 807. The more commonly used hearsay exceptions are:

- Present sense impressions (803(1))
- Excited utterances (803(2))
- Then-existing mental or physical condition (803(3))
- Statements made for medical diagnosis or treatment (803(4))
- Former testimony (804(b)(1))
- Statements against interest (804(b)(3))
- Dying declarations (804(b)(2))
- Business records (803(6), (7))
- Public and similar records (803(8)–(17))
- Recorded recollection (803(5))
- Reputation (803(19)–(21))
- Treatises (803(18))
- Residual exception (807)

Finally, don't forget the double hearsay or hearsay-within-hearsay issue governed by FRE 805. This concept applies most commonly to business and public records that may contain statements of persons who are not employees of the business or agency and have no business duty to report and record information accurately. Those statements of nonemployees, if offered for their truth, are

analytically hearsay, and are not admissible in evidence unless a nonhearsay rationale or a hearsay exception applies.

As the proponent of any out-of-court statement, oral or written, you need to
anticipate that your opponent may object to each statement on hearsay grounds.
The safe and better approach is to raise these anticipated issues before trial and get
a ruling whenever possible. Most judges will be happy to make as many pretrial
rulings as possible, knowing that the trial will run more smoothly and the jury will
have fewer interruptions. Even if the judge reserves ruling on some issues until
the trial, you have alerted the judge to the issues.

Example:

> JUDGE: This is a pretrial hearing on defendant's motion to preclude plain-
> tiff from introducing at trial certain statements contained in the police
> accident report. Defense?
>
> DEFENDANT'S LAWYER: Your honor, there are two statements contained in
> the police accident report our motion is directed to. First, there are
> statements of bystanders about how this accident happened. Those
> statements are hearsay, and no hearsay exception applies. We ask
> that if the accident report is admissible as a public record, that the
> bystander statements be excluded. Second, there is a statement
> by the plaintiff about how this accident happened. If offered by the
> plaintiff, that statement is also hearsay, no exception applies, and we
> ask that statement be excluded.
>
> JUDGE: Plaintiff?
>
> PLAINTIFF'S LAWYER: We agree that the statements by the bystanders and
> the statement by the plaintiff should be deleted from the report if we
> offer the report in evidence.
>
> JUDGE: Very well. Those statements will be deleted from the report if
> the accident report is offered by the plaintiff at trial. If that happens,
> plaintiff will prepare a redacted copy of the report.

At trial you must still remain alert to hearsay issues. Most of the time these
will involve witnesses attempting to say what other persons have said or what they
themselves have previously said.

Example:

> Q: Mr. Barber, after you saw the collision, what did you do?
> A: I waited around until the police arrived.
> Q: Did they arrive?
> A: Yes, several minutes later.
> Q: Did you talk to them?
> A: Yes.
> Q: When?
> A: Probably about 30 minutes later.
> Q: What did you tell the police?
> OPPOSING LAWYER: Objection. That calls for hearsay.
> JUDGE: Sustained.
> Q: Did you tell the police the same thing you've said today?

OPPOSING LAWYER: Objection. Same basis.
JUDGE: Sustained. Counsel, move on.

10. Violates Original Documents Rule (FRE 1001–1004)

The original documents rule (sometimes still con-fusingly referred to as the *best evidence rule*) deter-mines how the contents of writings, recordings, and photographs can be proven during trial. FRE 1002 provides, "An original writing, recording, or photo-graph is required in order to prove its content unless these rules or a federal statute provides otherwise." There are four such exceptions.

> ◼◧ For a discussion of the Original Documents Rule, please watch the first portion of Video H.2, "Wyo STI: Best Evidence Rule and Authentication."

First, "duplicates" are generally admissible to the same extent as "originals" (FRE 1003). This rule recognizes that in the age of photocopiers, it is unnecessary in most cases to present originals for trial. For example, in a breach of contract case, in which the only issue is whether defendant performed its obligations under the contract, plaintiff may introduce a duplicate of the original contract the parties signed.

Second, the original is still required if a "genuine question is raised about the original's authenticity" or it would be "unfair" to admit a duplicate (FRE 1003). For example, if the defendant claims that his signature on the contract is a forgery, or that terms on the contract have been altered, the original must be produced, because it is easier to determine from the original if there has in fact been a forg-ery or alteration. If plaintiff claims that a product warning is inadequate, it would be unfair to introduce a black-and-white photocopy of the warning sheet if the original had the product warning printed in red ink.

Third, the production of the original is excused if (1) all originals have been lost or destroyed in good faith; (2) no original can be obtained through any judi-cial process; or (3) the original was in the control of the opponent who was put on notice that the contents of the original would be required, and the opponent does not produce the original (FRE 1104(a)-(c)). If the production of the original is excused, the proponent can offer other evidence of its contents. For example, if the original has been lost in a fire or flood, or is in a foreign country, or was in the possession of the opponent, the production of the original is excused and the proponent can introduce other evidence of the contents, such as a photocopy of the original or oral testimony.

Fourth, the original documents rule applies only when the writing, record-ing, or photograph is "closely related to a controlling issue" (FRE 1004(d)). For example, it applies to the contract involved in a contract dispute (a duplicate or original must be introduced in evidence to prove the contract terms); it does not apply to an expert witness's medical license in a personal injury case (the doctor can testify that he is a physician licensed to practice medicine in this state).

11. Violates Court's Pretrial Order

Many evidentiary issues are raised and ruled on before trial. When the judge, under FRE 103(b), "rules definitively on the record" admitting or excluding evidence, the parties are bound by the ruling. If the other party at trial attempts to present evidence that was previously ruled inadmissible, you must object. This issue most commonly arises when the judge made a number of oral pretrial rulings, and there is no written order recording the rulings. Good practice dictates that you get a written order whenever possible, or at least obtain a transcript of the judge's oral rulings.

12. Witness Incompetent (FRE 601)

Witnesses must be competent to testify. The Federal Rules have eliminated the common law incompetency rules, and every witness who takes the oath is competent to testify. However, not all states have eliminated all the traditional incompetency rules. For example, some states still retain minimum age requirements for witnesses, and a number of states still follow different versions of the Dead Man's Act. Under FRE 601, in federal civil cases based on diversity jurisdiction, the *Erie* doctrine applies, and the forum state's witness competency law applies.

What happens if a witness is very young, senile, or has a significant mental disability? Under FRE 601, such witnesses are competent, yet it may be a waste of time to attempt to examine them at trial. In practice, most judges assess this situation under FRE 403, and determine if the witness can comprehend the duty to tell the truth and has a minimal ability to testify usefully about past events. If not, the witness is precluded under FRE 403, because trying to elicit meaningful testimony would be a waste of time. However, the preference is to have the witness testify whenever possible. Judges often ask some preliminary questions to make this determination.

Example:

> Q **(BY JUDGE):** Mary, how old are you?
> A: Four.
> Q: Do you know what it means to tell a lie?
> A: [Nods her head.]
> Q: What is a lie?
> A: When you make up something.
> Q: Mary, do you remember what happened the day your mommy's car crashed with another car?
> A: Yes.
> Q: Can you tell us about that, and not make something up?
> A: Yes.
> Q: Mary, what happened that day, when the car crashed?
> A: My mom and I got hurt, and we went to the hospital.
> **JUDGE:** Counsel, I've heard enough. You may begin your direct examination.

13. No Firsthand Knowledge (FRE 602)

FRE 602 requires that a witness have firsthand knowledge of the matters about which the witness is testifying. This ensures reliability of the testimony. This is routinely done by having the witness first testify that he saw or heard something, then the witness can describe what he saw or heard. The firsthand knowledge requirement does not apply to expert witnesses, who are governed by FRE 702 to 706.

Example:

> Q: Mr. Barnes, what color was the light when the two cars collided?
> OPPOSING LAWYER: Objection. No showing of firsthand knowledge.
> JUDGE: Sustained.
> Q: Were you at the intersection of Main and Elm when the two cars collided?
> A: Yes, I was standing on the southeast corner.
> Q: Did you see the traffic light at that time?
> A: Yes, I was looking right at it.
> Q: What color was that light when the two cars collided?
> A: It was red for the Main Street traffic.

Note that the objection only forced the direct examiner to develop the witness's testimony in more detail. For that reason, experienced lawyers rarely object on this basis.

It sometimes becomes apparent only after the fact that a witness has testified to something about which he has no firsthand knowledge. When that happens, you should object and move to strike the answer and instruct the jury to disregard the answer. Of course, the jurors cannot "unremember" the answer, but it does point out to the jurors that the witness doesn't personally know that fact.

Example:

> Q: What color was the light at Main and Elm when the two cars collided?
> A: It was red for the Main Street traffic.
> Q: How do you know?
> A: Because Mary Smith saw the crash and she told me.
> OPPOSING LAWYER: Objection, your honor. No personal knowledge.
> JUDGE: Sustained.
> OPPOSING LAWYER: We move to strike and instruct the jury to disregard the answer.
> JUDGE: Very well. Members of the jury, you are to disregard the witness's answer regarding the color of the light, since that information is not within the personal knowledge of this witness.

14. Improper Lay Witness Opinion (FRE 701)

FRE 701 requires that lay witness opinions or inferences be limited to those that are "rationally based on the witness's perception" and are "helpful to clearly understanding the witness's testimony or to determining a fact in issue." If the witness has firsthand knowledge (also required by FRE 602), and the testimony is "helpful," the witness may give an opinion or testify to an inference.

Common examples of proper lay witness opinion testimony are testimony that a car was going a certain speed, someone appeared intoxicated, or that someone looked frightened. As long as the witness personally saw the event, and has some life experience with that kind of event or behavior, the testimony is proper.

Common examples of improper lay witness opinion testimony are testimony that an accident was unavoidable, a person had to shoot his gun in self-defense, or that a driver was taking evasive action. These are conclusions for the jury to draw, not for the witness to opine or speculate about.

Example:

Q: At that time, did you hear anything?
A: Yes, I heard a loud crunch.
Q: How fast was the black car going?
OPPOSING LAWYER: Objection. No foundation.
JUDGE: Sustained.
Q: Did you see the cars in the crash?
A: Yes, there was a white car and a black car.
Q: When did you first see them?
A: A few seconds before the crash.
Q: How fast was the black car going?
A: At least 50 miles per hour.

Note that this objection, while proper, only succeeded in forcing the direct examiner to prepare a better foundation for the witness's opinion on speed. For that reason, experienced lawyers think carefully before objecting on this basis.

A witness may not be asked to comment on the truth of another witness's testimony, as this is a jury function.

Example:

Q: Officer Jones, did the defendant lie when he said that you hit him with your handgun at the time he was arrested?
OPPOSING LAWYER: Objection, your honor.
JUDGE: Sustained. Witness credibility is for the jury to determine.

15. Misstates or Mischaracterizes Evidence

The general rule (though not specifically codified) is that a question cannot misstate or mischaracterize evidence already admitted. This usually happens when a question picks up on a previous answer but twists it enough to misstate it.

Example:

Q: What's the next thing the defendant did?
A: He pushed the victim back with his hands.
Q: After the defendant attacked the victim, what happened?
OPPOSING LAWYER: Objection. Counsel is misstating the witness's testimony.
JUDGE: Sustained. Rephrase your question.

16. Assumes Facts Not in Evidence

A question cannot assume facts not in evidence. This usually happens when a question refers to evidence that may be introduced at a later time but has not yet been introduced.

Example:

> Q: What was the man holding the gun doing at that time?
> OPPOSING LAWYER: Objection. There's been no evidence of a man holding a gun.
> JUDGE: Sustained.

17. Leading (FRE 611(c))

FRE 611(c) governs the use of leading questions in direct and cross-examination. A leading question is a question that suggests the desired answer. For example, asking: "You fled from the scene, right?" suggests that the desired answer is yes. Adding "did you or did you not" or "if anything" may not cure the defect. For example, asking: "Did you take your gun, cock it, and point it at his head, or not?" still suggests that the desired answer is yes.

During direct examination, leading questions "should not be used . . . except as necessary to develop the witness's testimony." The rule is one of preference, and the trial judge has broad discretion here. If the witness is very young, senile, has a significant mental disability, or has limited understanding of English, and eliciting information with nonleading questions is difficult or impossible, the judge will, upon request, permit leading questions on direct.

Leading questions are broadly permitted to elicit information on preliminary matters and matters not in dispute, such as a witness's background. Leading on these matters is simply an efficient means of bringing out this uncontested information. Leading questions are permitted when establishing the foundations for exhibits, since this is often a practical necessity.

Good lawyers, of course, do not try to lead on direct, at least when they get to important testimony, because doing so detracts from the witness's credibility. Good lawyers also do not object to most leading on direct, understanding that the objection usually only forces the direct examiner to improve the questions and answers. Save the leading objection for when the direct examiner is blatantly spoon-feeding the desired answers on important matters, or when it appears the witness would never provide that testimony but for the leading questions.

Example:

> Q: Mr. Williams, you didn't drive your car over the 55 miles per hour speed limit, did you?
> OPPOSING LAWYER: Objection. Counsel is leading the witness.
> JUDGE: Sustained.

Example:

> Q: Ms. Anderson, were you at the corner of Main and Elm Street on June 1, 2020, at 3:00 in the afternoon?
> OPPOSING LAWYER: Objection. Leading.
> JUDGE: Overruled. The witness may answer.
> A: Yes, I was.

Example:

> Q: Dr. Abrams, you're a doctor specializing in orthopedics, right?

OPPOSING LAWYER: Objection, your honor, to the leading question.
JUDGE: No, this is background. Go ahead and answer.
A: Yes.

FRE 611(c) provides that, on cross-examination, leading questions are "[o]rdinarily" permitted. The rule also expressly provides that when a party calls "a hostile witness, an adverse party, or a witness identified with an adverse party," such as an employee or family member, the witness can be examined with leading questions.

Example:

Q (PLAINTIFF'S LAWYER): You're the chief financial officer of the defendant corporation, right?
A: That's right.
Q: You signed the contract that's at the center of this dispute, right?
OPPOSING LAWYER: Objection. He's leading his own witness.
JUDGE: Overruled. He's an adverse witness. Leading questions will be permitted.

18. Calls for a Narrative

A question that is so general that it calls for a broad and lengthy answer is improper, as such an answer may contain inadmissible evidence. The trial judge has the discretion to require more specific questions. This rule is probably enforced more in criminal cases.

Good lawyers do not ask questions that call for a narrative answer, because such questions do not persuasively break up the witness's testimony into easily digestible pieces. Good lawyers often do not object to such questions, recognizing that narrative answers are frequently rambling and confusing, and objecting only forces the direct examiner to ask better, more focused questions. They save the narrative objection for when there is a serious danger that the witness will testify about something important that is inadmissible.

Example:

Q: Tell us everything you saw, heard, and did during that meeting.
OPPOSING LAWYER: Objection. Calls for a narrative.
JUDGE: Sustained.

19. Asked and Answered/Repetitive/Cumulative (FRE 403)

If a witness has answered a specific question once, it should not be asked again during that examination. Repeating the question is just an attempt to repeat and emphasize the answer. The "asked and answered" objection prevents this from happening.

Example:

Q: Who was present at the meeting?
A: Mr. Hopkins, Ms. Johnson, and myself.

Q: Let me go over that again. The meeting was attended by Hopkins, Johnson, and you?
OPPOSING LAWYER: Objection. Asked and answered.
JUDGE: Sustained.

The objection applies to questions already asked and answered in the direct examination or the cross-examination. Of course, the cross-examination can go into matters already brought out during the direct, and the redirect examination can go into matters already brought out on cross.

The most common problems occur when a lawyer asks the same question again, but rephrases it slightly, with the purpose of having the witness repeat a favorable answer. The issue is: Is the lawyer constantly using this technique to repeat favorable information already established by the lawyer during this examination? If so, consider making the objection.

Closely related is the "cumulative" objection. This deals with the situation where the examiner is beating a point to death by calling numerous witnesses to make the same point. This objection is regulated by FRE 611(a) and 403, which give the judge power to control the examinations and limit evidence if it causes undue delay, waste of time, or needless presentation of cumulative evidence. Good lawyers make these objections when they see the opposing lawyer wasting court time by calling successive witnesses who repeat the same testimony to the point where the jurors are getting bored.

Example:

LAWYER: Your honor, we call John Smith as our next witness.
OPPOSING LAWYER: Objection, your honor. May we approach?
JUDGE: Yes. [Lawyers come to the bench.]
OPPOSING LAWYER: Mr. Smith is another character witness for the defense. They've already called five witnesses to testify that the defendant is an honest person. This is getting unnecessarily cumulative and repetitive.
JUDGE: Counsel, is Mr. Smith going to say anything other than that the defendant has a good reputation for honesty?
LAWYER: No, your honor, but this is an important point in our case.
JUDGE: That may be, but you've established it through several witnesses already. The objection is sustained.

20. Speculative

A question that asks the witness to speculate or guess about some event or condition is improper. These questions often begin with "Isn't it possible that . . ." or "Why . . ." Such questions are improper because speculation from lay witnesses is not probative and does not help the jury resolve any issues.

Example:

Q: Why did the driver of the black car suddenly speed up?
OPPOSING LAWYER: Objection. Calls for speculation.
JUDGE: Sustained.

21. Confusing/Misleading/Vague/Ambiguous

A question that is confusing, misleading, or unintelligible is improper. Such questions do not assist the jury, and no witness should be forced to answer them. These occur most commonly during cross-examination.

Example:

> Q: Did you know that if the facts were not as you perceived them to be, that you could have been mistaken about the things you say you previously perceived?
> **OPPOSING LAWYER:** Objection, your honor. Confusing and unintelligible.
> **JUDGE:** Sustained. Ask another question.

22. Compound

A compound question is objectionable because a simple answer is inherently ambiguous. Regardless of whether the witness says yes or no, a single response may not accurately answer both questions. Compound questions occur most commonly during cross-examination.

Example:

> Q: You immediately ran from the scene when the shots were fired and then hid in your car, didn't you?
> **OPPOSING LAWYER:** Objection, that's a compound question.
> **JUDGE:** Sustained. Counsel, ask those questions one at a time.

23. Argumentative

An argumentative question is improper because its real purpose is not to elicit information, but rather to make an argument to the jury. Arguments should be made during the closing arguments, not during witness examinations. These questions usually occur during cross-examination.

Example:

> Q: You wouldn't know the truth if it was staring you in the face, would you?
> **OPPOSING LAWYER:** Objection. He's arguing with the witness.
> **JUDGE:** Sustained.

24. Embarrassing/Harassing (FRE 611(a)(3))

FRE 611(a)(3) directs trial judges to "protect witnesses from harassment or undue embarrassment." This objection is frequently called *badgering the witness.* This objection occurs principally during cross-examination. Whether the cross-examination is appropriate or excessive depends largely on the witness. What is inappropriate during the cross-examination of an eyewitness to a collision may be appropriate during the cross-examination of a co-defendant who has cut a deal with the government and is now testifying as a prosecution witness. Judges vary on how much leeway they will give cross-examiners.

Example:

> Q: Mr. Williams, you've been singing like a canary ever since you cut a deal with the prosecution, haven't you?
> OPPOSING LAWYER: Objection, your honor. Harassing the witness.
> JUDGE: Sustained.

25. Unresponsive Answer

A question may be proper, but the witness's response may not answer the question. If the answer is unresponsive, it is improper. Some judges take the view that this objection can only be made by the lawyer asking the question, because only the questioner has a right to have a responsive answer. If the objection is sustained, move to strike and have the jury instructed to disregard the answer. If the answer violates another rule of evidence, the opposing lawyer can, of course, object to the answer on that basis. This objection is made most commonly when lawyers examine adverse and hostile witnesses.

Example:

> Q: Didn't you pull a gun from your pocket at that time?
> A: Well, he was trying to kill me.
> LAWYER: Objection to the answer, your honor. It's unresponsive.
> JUDGE: Sustained.
> LAWYER: Move to strike and instruct the jury to disregard the answer.
> JUDGE: Members of the jury, you will disregard the witness's last answer.

26. No Question Pending

A witness may answer a question, and then, before another question is asked, suddenly start talking again. This is improper, because the question has been answered and there is no question that the witness needs to answer. This happens most commonly with witnesses who are eager to give lengthy answers and explain everything.

Example:

> Q: Mr. Adams, where were you when the cars collided?
> A: I was right on the southwest corner of Main and Elm Streets. You see, I had been to the store earlier, and then I . . .
> OPPOSING LAWYER: Objection. There's no question pending.
> JUDGE: Sustained. Mr. Adams, please wait until your lawyer asks you another question.

27. Improperly Refreshing Recollection (FRE 612)

FRE 612 governs refreshing a witness's recollection. Witnesses frequently forget things when they testify. When they do, the examiner can use anything, but most commonly a report or statement, to jog the witness's memory. The report, statement, or other thing need not have been made by the witness. Although FRE 612 explicitly refers only to writings used to refresh memory, in practice judges usually allow anything else, such as physical objects, photographs, and diagrams, to do the same thing.

The procedural requirements must be kept clear. First, the witness's memory must be shown to need jogging. This is usually accomplished when the witness says she "doesn't remember" or "doesn't recall" something. Second, the report or statement used to jog memory must be marked as an exhibit, shown to opposing counsel, then shown to the witness. Third, the witness should be asked to read the report or statement to herself. Fourth, the witness should be asked if that report or statement jogs her memory. If the witness says yes, the report or statement should be taken from the witness. Finally, the witness should be asked about the fact about which she now has had her memory jogged.

The opposing lawyer has the right to see the report or statement used to refresh memory while testifying, cross-examine the witness on it, and introduce in evidence those portions that related to the witness's testimony. If the writing was used to refresh the witness's memory *before* testifying, the judge may order that it be produced so that the opposing lawyer can use it.

Problems frequently occur during refreshing recollection. First, lawyers ask witnesses to read a record or statement before they show that the witness needs her memory refreshed. Second, lawyers ask the witness to read the report or statement, and the witness begins to read it aloud. This is improper, unless the record or statement is already admitted in evidence. Third, lawyers offer the report or statement in evidence after using it to jog memory. This is improper, because under FRE 612 only the opposing lawyer has the option to introduce the relevant portions of the report or statement in evidence. Fourth, lawyers fail to take the report or statement from the witness after it jogs the witness's memory—the result being that the witness continues her testimony but is actually reading from the report. When this happens, it is apparent that the witness's memory has in fact not been jogged. Judges usually enforce this rule with lay witnesses, but often relax it for police officers and experts who have prepared detailed reports, as it is unrealistic that they would remember all those details.

Example:

Q: Mr. Williams, does your statement, which I've just handed to you, refresh your memory?

A: Yes.

Q: Who were the other people attending the meeting?

A: Well, there was Mr. Jones [looking at report], there was Ms. Williamson . . . .

OPPOSING LAWYER: Your honor, we object. The witness is reading from his statement.

JUDGE: Sustained. Mr. Williams, please hand the statement back to your lawyer.

The flip side of FRE 612 is FRE 803(5), the recorded recollection rule. If a record or statement actually jogs memory, FRE 612 governs. If the witness says the report or statement does not jog memory, and the report or statement was made or adopted by the witness, usually it can be qualified as recorded recollection under FRE 803(5) and the pertinent parts of the report or statement then can be read to the jury.

28. Improper Impeachment

Impeachment is a complex, technical area. First, make sure that the impeachment itself is a proper method, and that it complies with the requirements of the governing rule or case law. Seven impeachment methods are recognized under the Federal Rules of Evidence and case law:

- Bias, interest, and motive (case law)
- Prior inconsistent statements (FRE 613)
- Contradictory facts (case law)
- Prior convictions (FRE 609)
- Character for untruthfulness (FRE 608(a))
- Conduct probative of untruthfulness (FRE 608(b))
- Treatises (FRE 803(18))

Second, make sure the cross-examiner is impeaching in good faith. Model Rule 3.4(e) provides that a lawyer cannot "allude to any matter that the lawyer does not reasonably believe is relevant or that will not be supported by admissible evidence." A lawyer cannot suggest a fact to be true unless the lawyer has a good-faith basis for believing that the fact exists. For example, asking a witness: "Didn't you have three double martinis at the Tap Root Pub just before you witnessed the crash?" is improper unless the lawyer has credible information showing this to be the case. If you believe opposing counsel is making up facts to smear the witness, object, ask to approach the bench, tell the judge you have no information about these facts, and ask about the factual basis for asking those questions. If the cross-examiner cannot provide a factual basis for the questions, they are highly improper.

Third, make sure the impeachment procedure is proper. Although the Federal Rules are largely silent on procedure, most judges follow the common law approach, which requires a "confrontation" or "warning question" during cross-examination (or during the direct, if the lawyer is impeaching his own witness), as this is a fair and efficient procedure. If the witness must be asked about the impeaching matter during cross-examination, it gives the witness a fair opportunity to admit, deny, or (on redirect) explain the impeaching matter. If the cross-examiner fails to raise an impeaching matter during cross-examination of the witness, and later tries to introduce evidence of that impeaching matter through another witness or exhibit, most judges will sustain an objection to the improper impeachment procedure.

In addition, make sure the cross-examiner obeys FRE 106, the rule of completeness. It requires, "If a party introduces all or part of a writing or recorded statement, an adverse party may require the introduction, at that time, of any other part—or any other writing or recorded statement—that in fairness ought to be considered at the same time." This prevents the cross-examiner from reading an impeaching statement out of context to create an unfair or misleading impression.

Fourth, make sure the procedure after the impeachment is proper and actually followed. If the witness admits the impeaching matter, nothing further need be done. If the witness denies or equivocates, the cross-examiner must "prove up" the impeaching matter with "extrinsic evidence" if the unadmitted impeachment is "noncollateral." This means that if the witness has not admitted the impeaching matter, and the matter is noncollateral (important), the cross-examiner must later introduce other evidence—"extrinsic evidence"—to prove the impeaching matter. For example, if a plaintiff's witness is asked: "Didn't you have three double martinis at the Tap Root Pub just before you witnessed the crash?" and the witness denies it, the cross-examiner must, sometime during the defense case-in-chief, introduce evidence of the drinking by calling a witness, such as the bartender who served the drinks, to prove the unadmitted matter.

Under case law, bias, interest, motive, and prior convictions are always important and must be proved up if the witness does not admit them. Prior inconsistent statements and contradictory facts are taken on a case-by-case basis; some are important, some not. Only the important unadmitted ones must be proved up. Finally, prior bad acts probative of untruthfulness cannot be proven with extrinsic evidence, as there is an express bar in FRE 608(b).[2]

The most frequently used impeachment method is prior inconsistent statements. Despite FRE 613(a), many judges require that the witness be confronted with the prior statement on cross-examination, and that the impeaching statement be read verbatim. This prevents the cross-examiner from paraphrasing the prior statement and making it sound more impeaching than it really is. If the lawyer is not reading verbatim from the prior statement, object.

Example:

Q: Ms. Abrams, you say that the black car was going 50 miles per hour?
A: That's right.
Q: Ms. Abrams, you had your deposition taken, right?
A: Yes.
Q: Didn't you say in your deposition that the black car might have been going 70 miles per hour?
OPPOSING LAWYER: I object. Counsel is not reading the witness's deposition answer verbatim.
JUDGE: Sustained. Please read the actual question and answer.
Q: On page 33 of your deposition, line 6, were you asked this question and did you give this answer: "Q. How fast was the black car going? A. It seemed to be going 50 miles per hour, but it's possible it may have gone as fast as 70 miles per hour." Did I read it right?
A: Yes, that's what I said.

Finally, make sure that the prior inconsistent statement is in fact contradictory. Many judges will sustain objections to prior inconsistent statements that are only marginally inconsistent, using FRE 403 as the basis.

Example:

Q: You say today that the car was going 50 miles per hour?
A: Yes.

---

2. Junior co-author Easton believes that, in modern practice, the issue is not so much whether the attorney attempting to impeach the witness must prove up the impeachment if the witness denies the impeaching fact, but instead whether impeaching counsel will be permitted to do so. It is unwise for an attorney to attempt to impeach, but then leave the witness's denial of a fact unchallenged.

If the impeachment is considered collateral, impeaching counsel will be stuck with the witness's answer. If it is important, counsel will be allowed to prove the impeaching fact with extrinsic evidence, i.e., evidence other than the witness's testimony.

Q: Didn't you tell the police officer that the car was going about 45 to 50 miles per hour?

OPPOSING LAWYER: Objection, your honor. That is not impeaching.

JUDGE: Sustained. Counsel, move on to something else.

29. Beyond the Scope (FRE 611(b))

Under FRE 611(b), "Cross-examination should not go beyond the subject matter of the direct examination and matters affecting the witness's credibility. The court may allow inquiry into additional matters as if on direct examination." Examination "as if on direct examination" usually means that leading questions will be forbidden.

This is the so-called restricted scope of cross rule. It is followed in most, but not all, of the states. If the cross-examiner goes into entirely new topics that were not gone into during the direct, make the objection.

Example:

Q (BY CROSS-EXAMINER): Let's now turn to the events after the board meeting on June 1, and specifically to the meeting on June 15. At that next meeting, didn't you . . .

OPPOSING LAWYER: Objection. Beyond the scope. We didn't go into that meeting on direct.

JUDGE: Sustained. Counsel, I'll give you leeway to go into that meeting, but you'll have to do it as if on direct.

There is no express rule governing the scope of the redirect examination, but most judges, using the principle of FRE 611(a), rule that the redirect examination must be limited to matters brought out on cross-examination. If the redirect examination goes into entirely new matters, make the objection.

30. Improper Rehabilitation

After a witness has been cross-examined and impeached, the redirect examination can rehabilitate the witness. Rehabilitation could consist of four things. First, if the witness has been impeached with a prior inconsistent statement, under FRE 613 the witness must be given an opportunity to "explain," to reduce the impact of the impeachment, and this is usually done on redirect. For example, if the witness has been impeached with a prior statement to the police in which he says he didn't see the shooting (and on direct he testified that he had seen the shooting), on redirect the witness can be asked: "Why did you tell the police that you didn't see the shooting?" This gives the witness an opportunity to explain why he made the statement at that time.

Second, redirect can bring out other parts of statements, writings, events, or transactions to put things fairly in context and alter undue impressions that may have been created during the cross-examination. For example, if the cross-examiner has suggested that a meeting between the defendant and another individual was suspicious, redirect can bring out that the defendant and other individual are social friends and meet regularly.

Third, under FRE 801(d)(1)(B)(i), if the cross-examination has suggested that the witness's testimony is the product of recent fabrication or improper influence or motive, the redirect examination can bring out a prior consistent statement if that consistent statement was made before the time of the event triggering the claim of recent fabrication, improper influence, or motive. For example, if the cross-examiner has suggested that the witness's testimony, which favored the defendant, is a product of the witness having been recently hired by the defendant, redirect examination can now bring out a prior consistent statement if it was made before the witness was hired by the defendant.

Example (Cross):

Q: You say today that the defendant's truck had the green light?
A: That's right.
Q: One month ago you were hired by the defendant?
A: That's right.
Q: So now you're telling us that the defendant's truck had the green light?
A: Yes.

On redirect, the following is now proper:

Q: Let's talk about what happened right after the accident. Did you talk to the police?
A: Yes.
Q: What did you tell the police about the light?
A: I told them the truck had the green light.
Q: The same thing you're saying today?
A: Yes.
Q: That statement to the police, did that happen before you were hired by the defendant?
A: That happened almost a year before I got hired.

Fourth, a new rehabilitation rule, FRE 801(d)(1)(B)(ii), permits using a prior consistent statement to "rehabilitate the declarant's credibility as a witness when attacked on another ground." The scope of this new subsection is still unclear.

31. Improper Rebuttal

Rebuttal evidence is evidence that rebuts, refutes, contradicts, or diminishes evidence presented by the other party. The admissibility of rebuttal evidence is regulated by the trial judge under FRE 611(a). In general, rebuttal evidence is proper when the defendant has introduced significant new evidence in the defendant's case-in-chief, and fairness requires that the plaintiff be given a reasonable opportunity to respond to that evidence. For example, if the defendant, charged with theft, testifies that he did not have a motive to steal because he owns a successful business, the prosecution can prove in rebuttal that the business is deeply in debt.

Rebuttal is not simply an opportunity to have the last word. A plaintiff cannot recall witnesses, already called in the plaintiff's case-in-chief, as rebuttal witnesses merely to repeat their testimony. Some judges also hold that a rebuttal witness is not proper if that witness could have testified in the plaintiff's case-in-chief, and the plaintiff is "sandbagging" by withholding the witness for later use in rebuttal. These are fairness issues, and they are addressed to the sound discretion of the judge.

32. Miscellaneous Fairness Objections (FRE 102, 611(a))

Finally, remember that trials are intended to be fair. If the opposing lawyer is doing anything that is unfair to a witness or opposing counsel, the judge has the power to stop it. For example, if an examining lawyer is intentionally blocking your view of the witness or is whispering to a witness on the stand so that you cannot hear what is being said, make an objection.

10.7 Evidentiary Objections to Exhibits

The following are the evidentiary objections that lawyers frequently make before and during trial that are directed to the admissibility and handling of exhibits.

1. Improper Foundation Witness

Every exhibit must have a proper foundation established before it is admissible in evidence. For exhibits that are not self-authenticating, this means calling a live witness who has firsthand knowledge of the facts required to establish a proper foundation. For example, a foundation witness for business records must be a "custodian or another qualified person" (FRE 902(11)). A foundation witness for authenticating the signature on a contract must have seen the signature put on the contract or be familiar with the handwriting and recognize the signature as being made by that person. A foundation witness for a photograph or diagram of an intersection must be familiar with how the intersection looked at the time of the collision and say that the photograph or diagram accurately shows the intersection at that time.

2. Improper Foundation Procedure

Although the practice varies somewhat among jurisdictions, most require a certain foundation procedure: Mark the exhibit; show it to opposing counsel; ask permission to approach the witness; give the exhibit to the witness; establish the proper foundation; offer the exhibit in evidence; (perhaps) have it marked in evidence; and show or read the exhibit to the jury.

Common foundation errors include failing to show the exhibit to the opposing counsel, handling the exhibit so that jurors see the content before it is admitted in evidence, and having the witness read from the exhibit before it is admitted in evidence.

3. No Foundation

There are seven basic exhibit types: objects, demonstrative evidence, writings and instruments, business records, public records, recorded recollections, and summaries. Each type requires a particular foundation, and the foundation establishes that the exhibit is relevant and reliable.

FRE 901 to 903, 1005, and 1006 contain the general authentication requirements for most exhibits. The exhibit must be shown to be what it purports to be, either through the testimony of a qualified foundation witness or through the self-authentication process. For example, objects are admissible if the foundation witness says it is the actual thing and it is in substantially the same condition as it was on the relevant date; demonstrative evidence is admissible if the foundation witness says it fairly and accurately represents the real thing as it appeared on the relevant date; business records are admissible if a qualified witness or a certification provides the proper business records foundation; and public records are admissible if a properly certified copy is presented in court.

If an element of the necessary foundation for that particular type of exhibit is missing, you can object: "Objection, your honor. No foundation." If the objection is sustained, some judges may require the objecting party to state what part of the necessary foundation has not been established. This gives the offering party an opportunity to cure the defect if it can.

Remember the standard for admission of exhibits, sometimes called the *prima facie standard*. Under FRE 901, an exhibit is admissible if the proponent presents evidence "sufficient to support a finding" that the exhibit is what its proponent claims it to be. For example, if a witness who is familiar with the defendant's handwriting says the signature on a check is the defendant's, the check is admissible, even though the defendant may later testify and say he never signed that check.

4. Record Not Trustworthy

Business records are not admissible under FRE 803(6)(E) if the opponent shows "that the source of information or the method or circumstances of preparation indicate a lack of trustworthiness." This means that if the record is clearly written to be self-serving, particularly when litigation becomes a distinct possibility, the judge may exclude it on this ground. The public records rule, FRE 803(8), contains a similar provision.

5. Record Contains Double Hearsay/Hearsay Within Hearsay

When a business or public record is offered in evidence, look for double hearsay. FRE 805 permits the admission of hearsay within hearsay only if each level of hearsay conforms to an exception to the hearsay rule. Even if the record is qualified as a business or public record under FRE 803(6) or 803(8), this does not mean that everything on the record is properly admissible. Always look for statements made and information obtained from nonemployees that appear on the records, because there may be hearsay within hearsay.

For example, a hospital emergency room record may contain statements of the patient; a police accident report may contain statements by the drivers and other eyewitnesses. Those statements are a second level of hearsay, and they are not admissible unless a hearsay exception or a nonhearsay use applies. The statements of the patient might be admissible under FRE 803(4) as a statement made for the purpose of diagnosis or treatment; the statements of the defendant driver are admissible if the police report is offered by the plaintiff, because the defendant's statement then qualifies under FRE 801(d)(2)(A) as a statement by a party opponent. In contrast, the statements of the other eyewitnesses to the accident probably do not fall within any hearsay exception. When your opponent offers the accident report, you must object and ask that the eyewitness statements be redacted from the report before it is admitted in evidence.

6. Record Contains Inadmissible Expert Opinions and Conclusions

Many business and public records contain opinions and other evaluative and conclusory statements. The admissibility of those records can then conflict with the expert witness rules, FRE 702 to 704. Those rules require that only witnesses properly qualified as experts, who demonstrate an adequate foundation for their evaluations, can testify to their opinions at trial.

For example, a hospital emergency room report contains the treating doctor's notation that "Patient has a compound fracture of the left tibia." The report is a business record, and the doctor's diagnosis contained in the report is admissible. There is no requirement that the doctor be first qualified as an expert; his qualifications are assumed under the circumstances, particularly if the report is signed by the doctor and shows him to be an M.D. However, consider a police accident report that contains the officer's notation that "This accident was caused by car #2 going around the curve too fast under existing road conditions." If the officer were testifying at trial, he ordinarily would not qualify as an accident reconstruction expert, and he would not be able to give his opinions on what caused the accident. In that case, the officer's opinion on the accident report must be deleted before the factual portions of the report will be admissible as a public record. Put another way, the business and public records rules cannot be used to do an end run around the requirements of the expert witness rules.

7. Violates Original Documents Rule

FRE 1001 to 1004 contain the original documents rule and provide that it applies if a "writing, recording, or photograph" is "closely related to a controlling issue." The rule has four parts: (1) in general, duplicates are admissible to the same extent as the original; (2) originals are required if a "genuine question is raised as to the original's authenticity" or it would be "unfair to admit the duplicate"; (3) the production of the original is excused if it was lost or destroyed in good faith, its production cannot be compelled by judicial process, or the original was in the possession or control of the opposing party and that party did not produce it although the party was on notice that the contents of the original would be the subject of proof at trial; and (4) if the production of the original is excused, the proponent may offer any other evidence of the contents of the writing, recording, or photograph.

The original documents rule rarely comes into play. When it does, it is usually because a party claims that a writing, such as a contract, is a forgery or has been altered or tampered with. In that event, the original must be produced or its absence must be explained.

8. Reading from/Showing Exhibit Not in Evidence

The point of requiring a proper foundation for exhibits is that if the foundation cannot be established, the jury should not see or read the content of the exhibit. It follows that exhibits should be handled in a way that jurors cannot see them or read their contents before they have been admitted in evidence. For example, lawyers and witnesses should handle photographs so that jurors do not see their contents before they have been formally admitted.

Another common problem is that, during the foundation procedure, witnesses begin to describe or read the contents of the exhibit before it has been admitted. For example, after handing an exhibit to the witness and being asked: "What is it?," the witness replies: "That's the letter I sent to Mr. Smith where I said that I would . . . ." The latter portion of the testimony is improper, because the exhibit is not yet in evidence.

9. Improper Marking of Exhibit

Almost all jurisdictions permit witnesses to mark exhibits after they have been admitted in evidence. For example, a key paragraph in a contract can be highlighted or circled, and a photograph or diagram of an intersection can be marked to show the locations of cars and witnesses.

Marking exhibits must be fair and supported by witness testimony. For example, if a witness says a car was at a certain spot, the diagram can be marked to show this fact. If there is no evidence to support this fact, the diagram cannot be marked. The markings cannot be pejorative or argumentative. For example, a witness cannot mark "murderer" or "reckless driver." The markings also cannot distort or mislead. For example, a stick figure drawn to show where the defendant was standing cannot be several times too large. All in all, however, the parties are free to mark exhibits so long as there is evidence to support the markings, the markings are fair, and the markings do not distort or mislead.

Some judges, though, believe that once an exhibit has been admitted, it cannot be marked. This presents no real barrier if you are prepared for this possibility. Simply bring a copy of Exhibit 16, labelled Exhibit 16-A, ask the witness to mark on the copy, then offer Exhibit 16-A into evidence.

10.8 Trial Notebook

Your trial notebook should have a "Law" section. This section should contain several things that can be reviewed before every trial and are instantly accessible when a need arises. First, it should have a copy of the Federal Rules of Evidence (although many lawyers keep a pamphlet version with their trial notebook). Second, it should have checklists for the common objections to witness testimony, expert testimony, exhibits, opening statements, and closing arguments. Third, it should have a foundations checklist setting forth the required foundation for common kinds of exhibits. Finally, it should have a copy of the trial brief that you previously filed with the court or briefs on pretrial motions in limine.

> 🌐 A copy of these checklists is found under Chapter 2 on the website that accompanies this book.

10.9 Common Problems

What are the recurring problems lawyers encounter in making, arguing, and responding to evidentiary objections?

1. Not Making an "Objection"

Objections start by telling the judge you have an objection. Stand up and say "Objection, your honor," "I object," or simply "Objection." Inexperienced lawyers frequently start by asking a question — "Your honor, isn't that hearsay?" — or making a statement — "I don't see how this is relevant." This does not start the objection process, and the judge may well ignore you. Always make it clear that you are objecting, and look and sound assertive when doing so.

2. Not Stating Reason for Objections

Objections are not self-executing. They need a reason, a specific evidentiary ground on which the objection is based, and that ground needs to be stated clearly. Saying "Objection" and nothing else raises only relevance (unless the ground is apparent from the context) and does little to persuade the judge to rule in your favor. Always support your objections with a specific, brief evidentiary ground — "hearsay," "no foundation," "improper character evidence," and so on — and sound confident when you state it.

3. Making "Speaking" Objections

You cannot argue the evidence or make a speech, either to support or respond to an objection, in the presence of the jury. This rule is frequently violated in the heat of battle by both inexperienced and experienced lawyers. Making a speaking objection with the jury listening is by itself improper, and the judge may reprimand you. Instead, consider asking the judge for a sidebar conference so you can argue the objection more fully out of the hearing of the jury. If the opposing lawyer starts a long-winded argument in the presence of the jury, object and consider asking for a sidebar conference.

4. Not Raising Objections Earlier

Judges like hearing objections earlier rather than later, and it's the judge you want to keep happy. Even better, put your objections in writing whenever possible, so that your objections, reasons, and arguments are part of the trial record and the judge has time to reach a considered ruling. There is rarely a strategic or tactical benefit arising from raising evidentiary issues at the last minute.

5. Not Making Timely Objections

An objection must be timely. It should be made when the grounds first become apparent, which is usually before the jury hears the testimony or sees the exhibit. Inexperienced lawyers frequently hesitate to make an objection quickly, the result being that the witness answers the question or the exhibit is shown or read to the jury. Any later objection will usually be untimely, and you have probably waived error on appeal.

When the grounds for an objection do not become apparent until after the jury has heard or seen the evidence, you still must make a prompt objection. In addition, you must ask the judge to strike the evidence and instruct the jury to disregard it. If critical evidence is involved, making a fair trial impossible, ask for a mistrial.

6. Not Getting a Ruling

Make sure the judge makes a ruling on your objection. If there is no ruling, there is almost no possibility of preserving error for appeal. If the judge does not make an express or clear ruling on your pretrial motion, it is your job to ask the judge for a ruling. If the judge has reserved ruling or made a conditional ruling, be sure to renew your objection and ask for a definitive ruling when the evidence is later offered during the trial.

7. Not Making an Offer of Proof

When the other side's objection to your evidence is sustained, be sure to make an offer of proof as soon as possible. If you do not make an offer of proof, neither the trial judge nor the appellate court will know what the excluded evidence was, and you will probably have waived error on appeal.

8. Not Establishing Yourself as the Evidence Expert

Close calls often go to the lawyer who establishes herself as the evidence "expert" the judge learns to trust. Evidence experts raise the known important issues early and in writing. They make objections only when they have solid evidentiary reasons for them. They concede the point when the other side has a proper objection. Establishing that you are the evidence expert in the courtroom is a process that begins early in the litigation and continues throughout the trial.

CHAPTER 11

TRIAL PREPARATION AND STRATEGY

11.1 Introduction

The "secret" to effective trial advocacy is no secret at all. It's preparation, preparation, and more preparation! It's 90 percent perspiration, 10 percent inspiration. It's preparing sooner, not later. Hence, the trial lawyer who starts preparing for trial early, does it systematically and thoroughly, and incorporates an understanding of psychology into that preparation is more likely to achieve a successful result at trial.

11.2 Trial Preparation Timetable

When should you take the numerous steps that are necessary to be fully prepared to try a case to a jury? The easy answer is earlier rather than later. Time pressures intensify as a trial date approaches, and unexpected emergencies are an inevitable part of trial work.

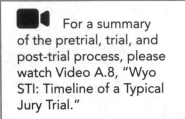 For a summary of the pretrial, trial, and post-trial process, please watch Video A.8, "Wyo STI: Timeline of a Typical Jury Trial."

How early is early? In busy trial practices, such as municipal and state prosecutors and public defenders, trial lawyers frequently have a few days at best to prepare for trial. In major cases, trial lawyers may need months to prepare for trial. The following chronology of events should be a useful guide for most cases.

Early in work on case (initial preparation)

Draft key proposed jury instructions
Begin construction of direct and cross-examination outlines
Identify key exhibits

4–8 weeks before trial (review of litigation file)

Identify your trial team
Review pleadings
File amended pleadings if necessary (and still permitted)
Review discovery
Amend and supplement discovery if necessary (and permitted)
File trial memo or motions in limine on anticipated evidentiary and other issues
Designate deposition excerpts and objections
Obtain rulings on pending motions if possible
Serve trial subpoenas
Learn how the judge conducts the trial
Visit the courtroom and check the setup and technology

3–4 weeks before trial (preparation of trial notebook)

Organize trial notebook
Prepare jury instructions
Prepare exhibit folders
Prepare witness folders
Order courtroom exhibits and visual aids (large charts, photo enlargements)
Order courtroom equipment (projectors, screens, video monitors, etc.)
Obtain rulings on motions if possible
Check on service of trial subpoenas
File proposed jury instructions with the court

2–3 weeks before trial (trial preparation)

Brainstorm: refine theory of the case, themes, and labels
Brainstorm: focus on the people, storytelling, and key disputes
Prepare proposed jury selection strategy
Prepare jury voir dire questions
Prepare opening statement outline and begin practicing opening statement out loud
Prepare closing argument outline and begin practicing final argument out loud
Refine direct examination outlines
Refine cross-examination outlines
Call or meet with key witnesses and check on availability of all witnesses
Schedule witnesses for final trial preparation

1–2 weeks before trial (focused trial preparation)

Discuss possible stipulations with opponent
Prepare client for testimony and courtroom presence
Prepare witnesses for testifying at trial
Check on availability of your witnesses
Check with court on trial date

Week before trial (final trial preparation)

Keep in touch with your witnesses
Advise witnesses when they will probably be needed
Keep preparing client
Keep preparing witnesses
Refine order of witnesses
Refine exhibits list
Finalize cross-examination outlines
Continue rehearsing opening statement and closing argument
Check with court on trial date, starting time, and schedule

Should you blindly follow this chronology? Of course not. Every case has its own pulse. The underlying purpose of the chronology, however, is sound: Do as much as you can early to minimize the emergencies and unexpected demands on your time that inevitably arise as the trial date approaches. This allows you to focus your time in the final days on key tasks, such as delivering an effective opening statement, having well-prepared witnesses ready to testify, and refining your planned cross-examinations. The more time you have to think, rehearse, and refine, because other tasks are completed, the better your trial performance will be.

11.3 Organization of Litigation Files and Trial Notebook

Ours is an age of records, and the field of law is no exception. Everything is routinely recorded and duplicated. Even a simple case can, and invariably will, generate substantial paperwork. Consequently, litigation files must be organized, divided, and indexed to provide immediate and accurate access to their contents at any time. Trial notebooks must be organized to provide an outline and quick reference for the actual trial. The lawyer who is organized will appear prepared, confident, and professional to the jury, judge, client, and opponent.

1. Litigation Files

There is no magic in organizing litigation files. Most law firms have systems for the types of cases the firms routinely handle. The important point is that your system must be logical, clearly indexed, and bound whenever possible. It should be in place when litigation starts, not just when a trial seems likely.

Litigation files are usually divided into several categories. The files should have tabbed dividers for each category. In larger cases, categories may be further divided. For example, discovery could be further divided into initial disclosures, interrogatories, documents requests, depositions, and requests to admit facts. Correspondence could be divided into correspondence with client, lawyers, and others. Whenever possible, the divider contents should be bound in chronological order.

The following file organization and categories are commonly used:

1. *Court documents*
   a. pleadings
   b. discovery
   c. motions
   d. orders
   e. subpoenas
2. *Attorney's records*
   a. chronological litigation history
   b. retainer contract, bills, costs
   c. correspondence
   d. legal research
   e. miscellaneous
3. *Evidence*
   Documents and records that may become exhibits at trial should be placed in clear plastic document protectors whenever practical. (This prevents them from being marked up during the litigation process.) Make copies. While the exhibits will depend on the specific case, the following are commonly involved:
   a. bills, invoices, statements, receipts
   b. correspondence between parties and with nonparties
   c. business records and public records
   d. photographs, diagrams, maps, charts

(These exhibits will later be placed into a separate exhibits folder.) Other exhibits, such as physical objects and large diagrams and models, should be protected and safeguarded in a secure location.

2. Trial Notebook

Organizing materials for trial differs from organizing litigation files. Litigation files are designed to be all-inclusive. Trial materials, by contrast, include only those materials that will actually be used during the trial; they need to be organized in a way that parallels how they will be used at trial. The standard way trial lawyers organize their trial materials is through a trial notebook. (Many trial lawyers use portable computers or electronic notebooks in the courtroom to store materials, such as pleadings, discovery, depositions, and business records, for easier access and quicker retrieval. Litigation and courtroom software is being constantly refined and improved so that substantial parts of a trial notebook can be effectively computerized.)

> ◼◀ For a discussion of effective use of trial notebooks, please watch Video A.5, "Wyo STI: Trial Notebooks."

A trial notebook is simply a three-ring notebook containing appropriately tabbed sections that parallel the trial process. The notebook itself should be a three-ring notebook, 1½ to 2 inches thick, which will hold standard letter-sized (8½ × 11) paper. A notebook with a locking mechanism for the rings, a label slot on the binding, and a pocket inside the front cover for "do lists" is the most useful. If your case is too large to fit into one notebook, simply use two or more notebooks and divide the materials accordingly. For example, you might have your facts, pleadings, discovery, and motions in one notebook (or computer file), and the remaining sections in another.

The three-ring notebook should have a series of color-coded tabbed dividers, made of stiff paper, plastic covered, with reinforced holes and tabs.

How the trial notebook is divided and organized is up to the individual trial lawyer, and various systems exist. Commercial trial notebooks and forms are available, although their designs are generally inflexible. The important point is that you can and should organize your trial notebook to be useful for *you*.

A common organizational system is the following:

1. facts
2. pleadings
3. discovery
4. motions
5. charts
6. jury
7. openings
8. plaintiff
9. defendant
10. closings
11. instructions
12. law

These trial notebook sections should contain the following:

1. *Facts*
   a. summary sheet containing the parties, lawyers, addresses, telephone numbers and other contact information, and a summary of the pleadings, if useful
   b. reports such as police reports, investigator's reports, and other fact summaries
   c. chronology of events, if useful

2. *Pleadings*
   a. amended pleadings, in order
   b. pretrial order, if it amends pleadings
   c. copies of statutes applicable to claims and defenses

3. *Discovery*
   a. initial disclosures
   b. interrogatories and answers
   c. requests to produce documents and responses
   d. deposition summaries
   e. requests to admit facts and responses

4. *Motions*
   a. motions, responses, and orders, in order
   b. pretrial memorandum and order
   c. anticipated trial motions

5. *Charts*
   a. trial chart (elements of claims, defenses, and proof)
   b. witness list (your witnesses, addresses, email addresses, phone numbers, and other contact information)
   c. exhibit list (for each party)
   d. opponent's witness list

6. *Jury*
   a. jury chart form
   b. juror profile outline
   c. requested voir dire questions to submit to judge
   d. checklist of your voir dire questions
   e. copies of applicable jury selection statutes and rules

7. *Openings*
   a. outline of your planned opening statement
   b. blank pages for notes on opponent's opening statement

8. *Plaintiff*
   a. if plaintiff, an outline of each direct examination
   b. if defendant, an outline of each anticipated cross

9. *Defendant*
   a. if plaintiff, an outline of each anticipated cross
   b. if defendant, an outline of each direct examination

10. *Closings*
    a. blank pages to note ideas during trial for closings
    b. outline of your planned closing argument
    c. blank pages for notes on opponent's closing argument
    d. outline of your planned rebuttal argument, if plaintiff

11. *Instructions*
    a. your proposed jury instructions
    b. opponent's proposed jury instructions
    c. court's instructions

12. *Law*
    a. rules of evidence—federal and state
    b. your trial memorandum
    c. opponent's trial memorandum
    d. copies of key statutes
    e. copies of key cases

The trial notebook will then organize and contain everything you need to conduct the entire trial, except for the following.

a. Exhibits

Exhibits should be placed in a separate notebook or file folder, inside plastic document protectors if necessary, and premarked as exhibits whenever permitted by local rules. You should also have additional copies ("courtesy copies") of these exhibits for your own reference, and for the judge, jury, opponent, and witness. A useful system is to have the original and several copies of each exhibit in a separate file divider.

b. Witness Folders

There should be a separate file divider or notebook tab for each witness expected to testify at trial. Each divider should contain a copy of each statement the witness has made, such as deposition transcripts, reports, and statements to police and investigators. It should also contain a copy of each exhibit the witness will use or qualify for admission during the examination. These folders are essential both during the preparation of witnesses before trial and during trial to refresh recollection on direct or impeach during cross-examination.

c. Transcripts

Complete transcripts of depositions, hearings, and other proceedings should be in a separate file folder.

d. Jury Instructions

If jury instructions have not been submitted to the judge before trial, the originals and required copies should be kept in a separate file folder. If they are submitted in advance, copies should be in your file folder.

e. Notepads

You should have letter-sized notepads, three-hole punched, with a stiff back for note-taking during the trial. Such notes can then easily be placed in the appropriate sections of the trial notebook. Some lawyers use laptop computers or tablets for note taking.

The trial notebook, exhibits, witness folders, transcripts, jury instructions, and notepads can be kept secure in a catalog case, which every trial lawyer should have.

🌐 A completed trial
notebook and forms
can be found on the
website that accompanies
this book.

Finally, learn how your trial judge conducts a trial, and examine the courtroom in which the case will be tried. Every judge has personal preferences on how a trial should be run, and these can influence your presentation. Courtroom layouts, sound systems, lighting, technology, and computer systems vary significantly, and these can have an important influence on how witnesses testify and what exhibits you can use persuasively during the trial.

11.4 Elements of Claims and Defenses

Trials involve two basic concepts. First, evidence at trial must be legally sufficient. It must meet the burden of proof on each element of each claim or defense raised in the pleadings. This concept is legal and is directed to the judge. Second, evidence at trial must be persuasive. It must be understood, absorbed, remembered, and accepted by the trier of fact. This concept is psychological and is directed to the jury.

The easy way to prepare for the legal sufficiency of your case (and the legal insufficiency of your opponent's case) is to organize a trial chart. A trial chart is simply a visual way of outlining your trial evidence. Using the jury instructions, which itemize the elements of the claims and defenses involved in your case, the trial chart should list each required element for each claim and defense. The trial chart should then show the proof for each element, whether by witnesses, exhibits, pleadings, admissions in discovery, judicial notice, stipulations, or other source.

Example (Plaintiff):

Trial Chart

Elements of claim: (Count I—Contract)	*Proof:*
1. Contract terms	1. Contract (Pl. Ex. #1)

2. Contract executed	2. a. Answer to complaint
	   b. Def. admission in deposition
	   c. Def. interrogatory answer

3. Pl. performed	3. a. Pl. testimony
	   b. Pl. letter to def. (P#2)
	   c. Pl. records (P#5)

4. Def. breached	4. a. Pl. testimony
	   b. Def. records (P#3)
	   c. Contractor who completed job

5. Pl. damages	5. a. Pl. testimony
	   b. Contractor who completed job
	   c. Pl. checks (P#8)
	   d. Contractor's records (P#9)

The trial chart should be continued for each element of your required proof and your opponent's anticipated proof.

When completed, the chart is an effective method for identifying areas where your (and your opponent's) proof is strong and where it is weak. It will identify the areas where you should strengthen the proof if possible, where your opponent's attack is likely to come, and where the critical issues at trial will be. Finally, the chart is useful during trial when making and opposing motions for directed verdicts.

When your legal analysis, through your trial chart, is completed, preparation can then focus on the psychological aspects of the upcoming trial.

11.5 Psychological Principles of Jury Persuasion

Reflect back on the psychological principles discussed in Chapter 2. How do jurors make individual decisions? Jurors are mostly affective thinkers who use deductive reasoning to make decisions. They care more about the people than the legal issues. They use their attitudes and beliefs to filter information and decide what to believe. They reach decisions quickly, based on relatively little information. After reaching decisions they believe are fair, they selectively accept, reject, or distort new information so that it "fits" their already reached decisions. Jury selection is primarily concerned with learning jurors' likely attitudes about issues important to the case, and determining which jurors will be receptive, and which ones resistant, to each side's party, theory of the case, themes, and labels.

How do jurors reach group decisions? When jurors begin deliberating, group dynamics become important. Whether a juror is a persuader, participant, or nonparticipant largely determines how much influence that juror will have with the other jurors in reaching a group decision—the verdict. Jury selection is also concerned with determining how "strong" each juror is likely to be during deliberations, so that peremptory challenges can be used against persuaders likely to be hostile to that side.

What influences these jurors? Credible witnesses, who testify clearly, simply, and dynamically, are important. So are visual aids and exhibits, because seeing has more impact than hearing. Jurors like stories that focus on the people, not the legal issues. Vivid, visceral, and visual evidence makes a difference. Efficiency in presenting information is important, since jurors have limited attention spans, and limited interest in learning new things. Using themes, labels, and repetition, and ordering the information advantageously, has much to do with whether the jury accepts and remembers it.

These psychological principles can be distilled into six key concepts that should influence trial preparation and the trial itself. They are:

1. Prepare from the jury's point of view
2. Develop a theory of the case
3. Select themes and labels
4. Emphasize the people
5. Use storytelling techniques
6. Focus on the key facts and issues

For a panel discussion of presenting your client's case persuasively, please watch Video A.3, "Wyo STI: Overall Trial Strategy and Persuasion Panel."

Let's apply these concepts to trial preparation, beginning with the theory of the case.

11.6 Theory of the Case

What is the "theory of the case"? Your theory of the case is simply a logical, persuasive story of "what really happened." It must be consistent with the credible evidence and with the jury's perception of how life works. Your theory of the case must combine your undisputed evidence and your version of the disputed evidence that you will present in storytelling form at trial.

When do you develop your theory of the case? Your version of what really happened is a process that begins when your case starts and steadily develops as the discovery in the case progresses. When discovery is completed, you should have a good grasp of the undisputed evidence, where the evidence is in dispute, and what the key factual disputes are. By this time, and *before* you begin other trial preparation, you must decide on what your theory of the case will be, because your trial preparation needs to focus on proving your theory and discrediting your opponent's theory.

How do you go about developing a theory of the case? This requires several steps. First, review the elements of each claim (or defense) in the case and prepare the jury instructions if you have not already submitted them to the court. Second, analyze how you intend to prove (or disprove) each of those elements through admissible testimony and exhibits. Third, analyze the contradictory facts that your opponent has available to determine the key issues that will be disputed at trial, and what witnesses and exhibits your opponent will probably use to prove his side of those issues at trial. These steps should already have been completed by preparing your trial chart. Fourth, research all possible evidentiary issues that may arise to all of the likely proof so that you can realistically determine what will be admissible at trial. Finally, review all the admissible evidence you and your opponent have on the key issues to identify each side's strengths and weaknesses. This is where the critical contests during the trial will be. You must then plan how you can bolster any weaknesses you have and how you can persuasively attack your opponent's weaknesses.

Trials are in large part a contest to see which party's version of disputed events the jury will accept as true and which party's version of "what really happened" is more plausible and appealing. This ongoing process of developing logical, consistent positions on disputed facts and integrating them harmoniously with the undisputed facts to create a persuasive story of what really happened is what trial lawyers call developing a theory of the case.

Consider the following:

Example:

> In an automobile negligence case, the plaintiff pedestrian was struck by defendant's car at an intersection. Some evidence will place the plaintiff within the crosswalk with the walk light green. Other testimony will place the plaintiff outside the crosswalk, jaywalking across the intersection.

As plaintiff, your theory could be one of the following:

a. Plaintiff was in the crosswalk and had the right of way (ordinary negligence).
b. Plaintiff may have been outside the crosswalk but was injured because the defendant could have stopped his car but didn't (last clear chance).
c. Both plaintiff and defendant may have been negligent, but defendant bears most of the fault (comparative negligence).

Example:

In a murder case, the prosecution's evidence will show that after a violent argument the victim was shot by a man some witnesses will identify as the defendant.

As defendant, your theory could be one of the following:

a. Defendant did not do the shooting (identification).
b. Defendant did the shooting, but was justified in defending himself (self-defense).
c. Defendant did the shooting, but the circumstances do not make the shooting a murder (manslaughter or lesser charge).

As you can see, your position on the facts, both disputed and undisputed, must be developed well in advance of trial. Each disputed fact must be analyzed and a position taken on it that is consistent with your theory of the case. Only then can you move on to the next stages of your trial preparation.

Most trials, where the issues are close, are decided on a few pivotal points. It may be an admissibility issue on a critical exhibit or a key witness's testimony. It may be the impression a crucial witness makes on the jury. It may involve how effective your cross-examination of a key witness is. Whatever the issues, thorough trial preparation must include determining what those issues will be at trial. In short, you must find out what the crucial issues will be, how you want to articulate those issues to the jury, and how to prepare for the critical issues more thoroughly and convincingly than your opponent so that the jury will resolve these issues in your favor. All these considerations must come together in deciding on your theory of the case.

11.7 Themes and Labels

Jurors cannot absorb all the information that a trial produces, so they use subconscious strategies to deal with sensory overload. One strategy is to identify key points or themes that help jurors process information more quickly. A theme is simply a memorable word or phrase that summarizes your position on a critical issue. A trial lawyer must identify the critical issues involved in the case, develop themes for them, and state them in memorable ways so that the jurors will use *your* themes in processing the contested facts and resolving the disputed issues.

Themes should be morally and emotionally compelling. They should incorporate the jurors' sense of fairness and universal truths. They should be simple and have immediate meaning. They should focus on people, not legal issues. In short, themes must translate legalese into simple, compelling, human propositions that are consistent with the attitudes jurors already hold about people, events, and life in general.

Consider, for example, a breach of contract case. If plaintiff's case is based on proof that defendant defrauded her, the theme might be "this is a case about trust" or "two people made promises to each other, and now one doesn't want to live up to his word."

Consider a personal injury case. If plaintiff's case is based on proof that defendant ran a red light, the liability theme might be "people who take chances hurt others" or "this is a case about breaking the rules of the road." The damages theme might be "Mary Smith's only companion is her pain."

Consider a wrongful death case. If plaintiff wishes to emphasize damages, the theme for the plaintiff spouse might be "this is a case about loneliness" or "as we grow older, the thing we fear most is being alone."

In every case, you can, and should, develop themes for the key issues on liability and damages. These will, if they are carefully chosen and expressed, become focal points for the jurors' thinking. If the jurors use *your* themes as a reference point during deliberations, you have a much better chance of getting a favorable verdict.

Both sides, of course, need to consider the themes the other side is likely to use and plan accordingly. You need themes that not only summarize your side, but are also effective antidotes to your opponent's likely themes.

The same careful planning should also go into your selection of labels. What are "labels"? Labels are simply the ways you will refer to the people and events during the trial. Labels convey meanings and values to the jury, since how we characterize things influences how others perceive them.

Consider how language can affect perception. Calling two cars hitting each other a "collision," "crash," "impact," or "smash" conveys a different impression than calling it an "accident" or "two cars hit each other." Asking a witness "how slowly was the car moving" conveys a different image than asking "how fast was the sports car traveling." Referring to a witness as "Bobby" conveys a different stature than "Mr. Williams." Referring to a party as "the defendant" sends different signals to the jury than "Mr. Smith." "That corporation" says something different than "Grandma's Cookies." However, be careful about using pejorative labels. For example, some courts bar lawyers from using labels such as "victim" or "rape" when there is a factual dispute over whether someone was a victim (as in a self-defense case) or whether a rape occurred (as in a consent defense case).

The careful trial lawyer selects labels for parties, events, things, and actions that send signals to the jury on how it should perceive those parties, events, things, and actions. Once selected, those labels must be used consistently throughout each stage of the trial.

11.8 Dramatize, Humanize, and Visualize Using People Stories

Jurors, like everyone else, are a product of their environment. Many people stop consciously and actively learning when they finish their formal schooling, and most of what they learn later comes through television and computers. Therefore, they have been trained to expect drama, an emphasis on personalities, and sophisticated visual effects. They expect everything quickly, in simple, digestible sound bites. They expect interesting visual aids. And they want it all to be easy and enjoyable. Anything less and you've violated the "boring rule," and jurors will quickly change channels.

The lesson for trial lawyers is obvious. First, use storytelling techniques. Search for interesting, dramatic, and different ways to present your case. Jurors expect a certain energy level from lawyers and witnesses. Try to re-create what happened through "word pictures," rather than merely telling the jury what happened. Put the jurors in the picture so they can feel, not just see, what happened. Second, focus on the people, not just on the events. People do things for a reason. Jurors want to know not just what happened but also what motivated the people behind the events. Jurors want to know about the key players so they can decide whom to silently cheer for. Third, use visual aids as much as possible. Watch how news programs integrate visuals with narration. Notice how highway billboards attract attention and send simple messages quickly. These are the techniques that are effective with the public. Why not bring that knowledge into the courtroom? Carefully prepared exhibits can persuasively summarize your liability and damages cases, and the exhibits will keep persuading the jury during its deliberations. Finally, do it simply and quickly. Jurors expect information in five- to ten-minute segments (that TV training again). Focus on your themes and key facts and repeat them. A courtroom is no different than a classroom. People learn better when a few key ideas are repeated from time to time.

> For a discussion of the importance of investigation, the impact of emotion in trial, and other ways in which mock trials do not precisely duplicate real trials, please watch Video A.9, "Wyo STI: Limitations of a Trial Practice Course."

11.9 Focus on the Key Disputed Facts and Issues

Finally, focus on the key disputes in the case and gather the evidence that will convince the jury to accept your version of the disputed facts. If that evidence is testimony, prepare the witnesses so that they are dynamic, confident, detailed, and vivid, particularly on the key disputes. If the evidence is exhibits, make sure they are more visually appealing than your opponent's. Wars are often won or lost because of a key battle. The same holds true for trials.

For example, the outcome of a personal injury case may depend on which side's version of an intersection collision the jury will accept. The outcome of a contract case may depend on which side's version of a critical meeting and the conversation held during that meeting the jury will accept. In both cases, you need to prepare the witnesses and exhibits so that they are more convincing—dynamic, confident, detailed, and vivid—on the key disputed facts than the other side.

You are now ready to use your organizational system and your understanding of the psychology of persuasion to actually plan and implement the various tasks that make up preparing for a jury trial.

11.10 Opening Statement and Closing Argument Preparation

Work backward. Plan your closing argument first. Everything else then follows. This advice is given by many experienced trial lawyers, and there's a good reason for it: It works.

Why? Because the backward approach makes you think about the elements of the claims and defenses, the jury instructions, your theory of the case, themes and labels, undisputed evidence, and key areas where the evidence is in dispute. It makes you think about integrating these concerns into a persuasive whole—your closing argument. It makes you think about what is important and what is merely interesting or peripheral. Your closing argument must do two basic things: It must win the war over the high ground—whose themes will be more appealing to the jury—and win the war over the disputed facts—whose version of the disputed events the jury will accept as true. In short, planning the closing argument first will tell you what to emphasize and what to cover lightly, or not at all, in the other stages of the trial. If it's not important enough to mention during closing arguments, it's probably not important enough to mention during the other stages either.

If you plan your closing first, you will then know what needs to be in your opening statement. Your opening should do several things. First, it should state your themes and theory of the case. This should be done quickly, in the first minute or two. The themes should then be repeated periodically during the opening statement, so that if the jury retains one idea, it should be your themes. Second, it should describe what happened in storytelling form. Decide on the visual aids and exhibits to use during the opening statement that will supplement your storytelling, and that are part of an overall visual strategy. Third, it should anticipate problems and weaknesses by weaving them into your storytelling. Finally, it must be delivered forcefully, with few or no notes at all. The opening statement must show that you have a winning case, and that you, through your conduct and attitude, believe in it.

How do you outline your opening once you've decided what will be in it? One thing you should *not* do (although many inexperienced trial lawyers do) is write out what you will say and use it verbatim during your opening statement. The reason becomes clear once you've seen it done this way. People write differently from how they speak, and a written opening doesn't sound right when delivered to a jury. If you must write out your opening (security blankets are sometimes a necessity), be sure to reduce it to an outline before you give it, and don't memorize what you've written.

An opening statement outline should be on one page whenever possible (and it's possible in almost every case). It should be in large print, noting the "buzz words" that will trigger recall if needed. Some lawyers also put down key dates, names, and events as a protection against a memory block in the middle of the opening statement. The outline can then be put on counsel table or a podium for reference if necessary. When you give the opening statement, however, it is absolutely essential that you get away from notes, look squarely at the jurors, and tell them about the case from your point of view.

Example (Plaintiff in an Intersection Collision):

Opening statement

1. Themes: people in a hurry; hurting others;
        taking chances;
        little injury can end a career
2. Bob Johnson's background—self-made man
                family man
3. Intersection—where Bob's life changed forever
4. How it happened on 6/1/15—Bob's eyes
                witnesses
                crash, crushed, snapped, and so on
5. Aftermath—hospital—excruciating pain
                head injury, no pain killers
6. Aftermath—rehabilitation—Bob learned reality
            doctor—never return to normal
7. Today—Bob's situation—learning to cope
            Bob's family—lost what taken for granted
8. Request for verdict—do the right thing

How do you prepare your closing argument? As suggested earlier, organize your main points, based on your theory of the case, themes and labels, undisputed evidence, and your version of the disputed facts. These will tell you what you need to argue at the end of the case (as well as what to emphasize in your opening and witness examinations).

Reserve several blank pages at the front of the closing arguments section of your trial notebook. During the trial, as you hear key testimony from witnesses, statements by lawyers, and questions (if permitted) from jurors, see key exhibits, and have periodic brainstorms, write them down on the blank pages. These add up during a trial. These specific references to witness testimony and other sources become the details that provide the support and substance of your arguments. Your final preparation for closing arguments, therefore, consists of selecting from these notes the points you want to add to the closing arguments you organized and rehearsed before the trial started.

Your outline will be organized much like your opening statement. Since a persuasive argument must come from the heart and cannot be read, your outline should be that and nothing more—one or two pages of notes, in large print, containing the key points you want to argue, in the order you want to argue them, with the references to your themes, exhibits, and testimony. The only reading you should do will be reading from key exhibits and jury instructions or quoting from key testimony.

11.11 Jury Selection Preparation

If you know your theory of the case and your themes and labels, have your closing argument outlined and your opening statement prepared, know what your client and key witnesses are like and what they will say, you can plan your jury selection strategy. This involves two basic tasks: developing a profile of favorable and unfavorable jurors, and outlining proposed voir dire topics and drafting requested voir dire questions for the judge.

What's a jury profile? This is simply a description of juror backgrounds and experiences that you believe are likely to favor, and disfavor, your side. How do you do this? In large cases, lawyers can afford the luxuries of hiring jury psychologists to survey the community to determine its attitudes about issues pertinent to the trial and hiring mock juries to test their theories and themes. In most cases, however, trial lawyers must rely on their experience, knowledge of the community, and perhaps intuition to do the same thing—determine if certain types of jurors, based on their backgrounds and experiences, are likely to be attitudinally disposed toward or against your side. Putting these demographics and experiences on a profile makes them easier to apply during the jury selection process when you exercise your peremptory challenges.

Example:

> Plaintiff has sued a trucking company for personal injuries arising from a collision between her car and defendant's truck. Plaintiff is a homemaker with two small children. Defendant is a large national corporation.

Juror Profile—defendant

Unfavorable:	*Favorable:*
Homemakers	Professionals
Young women	Middle-aged jurors
Blue collar	Managerial-level employees
Low income	Middle/white-collar incomes
Previous plaintiffs	Insurance industry employees
Independent	Company people

In some civil cases, jurors who are favorable on liability may be unfavorable on damages. Consequently, you must refine your juror profile thinking to account for how strong you are on these two areas. For example, if plaintiff is strong on liability but marginal on damages, plaintiff's juror profile should emphasize the jurors that will be favorable and unfavorable on damages.

Once you have identified the backgrounds and experiences of likely unfavorable jurors (an admittedly inexact task), you will know what kinds of questions to ask during voir dire. If lawyers will do the voir dire questioning, you need only make a checklist of the topics you must cover during your questioning. If the judge will do all or some of the questioning, you will need to draft proposed voir dire questions and submit them to the judge. This is usually done by filing a request, using the formality of a motion, with the court before trial.

Example:

Plaintiff's Requested Voir Dire Questions

Plaintiff requests that the following questions be asked of the jury during the court's voir dire:

1. Have you ever been a plaintiff in a lawsuit?
2. Have you ever . . .? If so, . . .?
3. Are you . . .?

Finally, your trial notebook should have a jury chart to record the basic information about each juror obtained during the voir dire examination so that you can review it before deciding which jurors to challenge.

The type of diagram or chart depends on how jury selection will be conducted. If the strike system is used, all jurors in the venire will be questioned before any challenges are made. Under this system, you can use a legal pad to record the basic information about each juror. (Some lawyers use a form to record the background information of each juror; this allows you to do less writing to record the information and spend more time watching the jurors. Better yet, have someone else write down the information so you can concentrate on the jurors.)

If the panel system is used, jurors will usually be called into the jury box and only those jurors will be initially questioned. As challenges are exercised and jurors are excused, new jurors replace the excused jurors and are also questioned. Under this system it is necessary to develop a way to keep track of jurors in the box. Most lawyers use a jury box diagram on legal-sized paper to record juror names and backgrounds. When a challenge is exercised, the juror is crossed off and a new box created. (Small yellow Post-it notes work exceptionally well here.)

Example (Jury Chart):

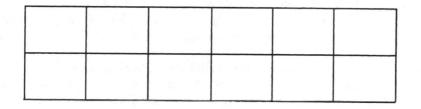

The diagram will cover most of a page. In each of the squares you then simply record in abbreviated form the basic information obtained during the questioning, as demonstrated below.

> **John Doe** — 40 — carpenter — self-emp. 10 yrs. — 3C in grade school — W part-time bookkeeper 15 yrs. — owns home Chicago, N. side — 2 yrs. army

11.12 Witness Selection and Preparation

1. Witness Selection

Your case-in-chief will be presented principally through the witnesses you call and the exhibits you introduce. With witnesses you must decide three basic things: whom you will call as witnesses, what you will have these witnesses say, and how you will organize all this in your trial notebook.

Whom you call as witnesses to prove your case is sometimes not an issue. You simply must call the witnesses you know of to establish a *prima facie* case, and there is no room for choices. Most of the time, however, you will have choices. For example, of the several occurrence witnesses available, which ones will you call? Which witnesses will you call to introduce and explain business records to the jury? Which of the police officers who responded to the scene of the accident or crime should you call? In deciding whether to call certain available witnesses, remember the following considerations:

1. Do not overprove your case. Many lawyers call far too many witnesses, thereby boring the jury or, even worse, creating the impression that the lawyer doesn't have confidence in her own witnesses or in the jurors' ability to absorb information. In general, calling a primary witness and one or two corroboration witnesses on any key point is enough. It's usually best to make your case-in-chief simple and fast, then quit while ahead.

2. Use strong witnesses. Stick with strong, likeable witnesses and avoid marginal or weak witnesses who can be damaged by cross-examination, unless such witnesses are essential to establishing a *prima facie* case.

3. Don't try to prove everything. You are required only to prove the elements of your claims and defenses or to refute the other side's. Avoid calling witnesses merely because they have something interesting to say. Stick to your game plan and prove only your claims and theory of the case. Every added witness gives your opponent an opportunity to hurt your case. Don't provide extra opportunities.

4. Don't sandbag. Do not fail to call a strong witness in your case-in-chief because you plan to call that witness in rebuttal. First, it's a psychologically bad strategy to save a strong witness for late in the trial. Jurors listen to and are persuaded by witnesses while their minds are still open and undecided. By the rebuttal stage, jurors have usually made their minds up about the case, and the strong witness will have little impact. Second, your opponent may surprise you by resting or by presenting evidence in an area not related to your witness's testimony, thereby preventing you from calling him in rebuttal. The court may also rule that since the witness could have been called in your case-in-chief, the witness is an improper rebuttal witness.

FRE 615, which governs excluding witnesses during the trial (so witnesses cannot hear each other testify), makes exceptions for parties who are natural persons, for designated representatives of a party not a natural person, and for a person whose presence is essential to a party.

Therefore, when representing a governmental entity, a corporation, or other artificial entity, you must decide who, if anyone, will sit with you at counsel table during the trial. In criminal cases, the prosecution commonly designates the case agent or lead detective. In commercial cases, a corporate party frequently designates an employee who was involved in the events and transactions at the center of the case. Another common selection is a senior employee or officer who knows the facts of the case (and will be a good witness if the other side calls him as an adverse witness during the trial). These persons show that you, and the corporation, are serious about the trial. For the jury, the designated person becomes the face of the corporation and shows that the trial involves real people.

2. Witness Preparation

Preparing witnesses for trial is not the same as preparing witnesses for depositions. This is not the time to learn what the case is all about or to obtain interesting information. You should know from interviews and formal discovery what the witnesses can contribute to your case. You also know, from your preparations so far, what you are legally required to prove, what your theory of the case is, and what your themes and labels will be for the trial.

Preparation for trial involves culling out of what each witness *can* say those things the witness *will* say that will prove your case, and preparing each witness to do this persuasively. Witness preparation involves both testimony selection and testimony preparation. Keep the following in mind:

1. Witnesses should be prepared for trial individually by the lawyer who will do the direct examination of that witness. Having an "associate" prepare witnesses rarely works well. Only when you have personally prepared a witness, know precisely what he will testify about, have a feel for the kind of witness he is, and understand how to ask questions that trigger the good responses can you effectively present that witness at trial. Remind the witness that it is perfectly proper to get together to prepare the witness for testifying at trial (and the jury might be told this in an instruction).

2. Review with the witness everything where the witness is "down on paper." This includes depositions, other sworn testimony, oral and written statements, interrogatory answers, and any reports the witness made. These are the sources for refreshing recollection on direct examination and impeachment on cross-examination. These should all be in the witness folder that you have already prepared. Have the witness read these, or read them to the witness, if necessary. Point out particularly important areas and any areas where the statements differ with each other. Determine if the witness's current memory differs from these statements. If so, and the witness insists that his present recollection, not the earlier statement, is accurate, explain how the opposing lawyer may impeach him with the statement and show how this is done. (Do not show the witness your direct examination outline or other work product, because you might be waiving work product protection by doing so.)

3. Review with the witness all exhibits he will identify or authenticate. Explain how you will need to "lay the foundation" for exhibits and show how this is done.

4. Review the probable testimony of other witnesses to see if any inconsistencies exist between any of the witnesses. If so, see if there are any explanations for important inconsistencies that can be brought out through the witnesses at trial if opposing counsel makes an issue of them.

5. Prepare the direct examination of the witness and review it with the witness. Make sure the witness can actually testify to what you anticipate he can. Make sure he can lay the proper foundation for all necessary exhibits. Once the organization of the direct examination is settled, practice the direct examination with the witness. Lawyers, however, differ on how this should be done. Some lawyers practice the actual questions and answers with the witness, and do this repeatedly, until both the lawyer and witness are comfortable with the direct examination. These lawyers feel that this is the only way to adequately prepare witnesses for their direct examination. On the other hand, some lawyers feel that repeatedly

practicing the actual questions and answers with the witness has drawbacks. These lawyers feel that too much practice makes the testimony at trial sound canned, not spontaneous. These lawyers go over with the witness what will be covered by the direct examination, but they avoid practicing the actual questions and answers.

6. Prepare for the cross-examination of the witness. Review the areas that you anticipate the cross-examination will cover. Review any anticipated impeachment. Have another lawyer conduct practice cross-examinations using the same tone and attitude as the cross-examiner is likely to use at trial. Above all, *practice the actual cross-examination with the witness.* Talking about the cross-examination can only go so far. The witness needs the experience of actually being cross-examined in a realistic environment.

7. Prepare the witness for his courtroom appearance. Decide on what he should wear. Jurors expect neat, conservatively dressed witnesses, with clothes appropriate to the witness's background. For most males, this means a suit or jacket and tie. For witnesses who wear uniforms, work attire may be effective. Explain how the courtroom is arranged and where the judge, lawyers, court reporter, court clerk, bailiff, and spectators sit. Explain how the witness will enter the courtroom, where and how he will take the oath, where he will sit while giving his testimony, how he should sit and appear while there, and how he will leave the courtroom. If the witness is a party that will sit with you at counsel table, remind him that the jury will be watching and assessing him, even when he is not testifying. Instruct him not to whisper or interrupt you when court is in session. Instead, have him write on a notepad anything he wants to tell you when you are occupied with witness testimony or other critical matters.

> ◼️📹 For a discussion of witness preparation, please watch Video D.3, "Wyo STI: Direct Examination, Including Witness Preparation."

8. Prepare the witness for the procedural and evidentiary rules that govern his testimony. Some lawyers have printed instructions they give each witness.

Example:

Instructions for Witnesses

a. Listen, think, then answer. Listen carefully to each question. Answer only that question. Do not ramble on or volunteer information. Look at the jury when answering key questions. Speak loudly and clearly so that the last juror can hear you easily. Do not look at the judge or at me for help if asked difficult questions during cross-examination.

b. If you do not understand a question, say so, and the lawyer will probably rephrase it. If you do not *know* an answer to a question, say so. If you do not *remember* an answer, say, "I don't recall" or "I don't remember." The lawyer may show you your previous statements to jog your memory. If you can only approximate dates, times, and distances, give only your best approximations. If you cannot answer a question with "yes" or "no," say so. Either the lawyer will ask another question or you will be allowed to explain your answer. Give positive, clear, and direct answers to every question whenever possible.

c. Use your own vocabulary. Use the words you normally use and feel comfortable with. Don't use someone else's vocabulary, "police talk," or other stilted, artificial speech.

d. Be serious and polite at all times. Do not exaggerate or understate facts. Don't give cute or clever answers. Never argue with the lawyers or judge. The lawyer on cross-examination may attempt to confuse you, have you argue with him, or have you lose your temper. Resist these temptations. Never argue. Never lose your temper.

e. You will be allowed to testify only to what you personally saw, heard, and did. You generally cannot testify to what others know, or to opinions, conclusions, and speculations.

f. If an objection is made by either lawyer to any question or answer, stop. (The lawyers will usually stand up when they object.) Wait for the judge to rule. If she overrules the objection, answer the question. If she sustains the objection, simply wait for the next question. Never try to squeeze an answer in when an objection has been made. Never talk while the judge is talking.

g. After the cross-examination, the direct examiner may ask more questions; this is called "redirect examination." The cross-examiner may also ask more questions; this is called "recross-examination." On direct and redirect examination, leading questions are usually not permitted. On cross- and recross-examination, leading questions are proper.

h. Above all, *always tell the complete truth according to your best memory of the events and transactions involved.*

3. Direct Examination Outline

How do you create an outline of your planned direct examination in your trial notebook? There are two common methods.

a. *The Q & A method.* Under this approach, every question you intend to ask the witness (and a summary of the expected answer) is written out. This is the method frequently employed by inexperienced lawyers during their first few trials. Its advantage is that you can draft your questions in proper form in advance. The disadvantages are that, unless you are a great actor, your questions will invariably sound as though they are being read from a script—hardly the impression you want to convey. This approach also weds you to the script and hinders your flexibility in asking logical follow-up questions. If you do use this method for your first few trials, never show your questions and answers to your witness, since they may then be discoverable (the other side may argue that they were used by the witness to prepare for testifying, possibly making them discoverable at trial under FRE 612).[1]

b. *The witness summary method.* Under this approach, used by most experienced trial lawyers, you outline the key things the witness will testify about on direct. You then simply follow the outline, asking the questions that elicit the desired answers. The advantages are that your questions will sound fresh and spontaneous, and you retain flexibility to ask follow-up and clarifying questions. A convenient way to organize the direct under this approach is to note at the top of the outline the exhibits the witness will work with or qualify and the witness's

---

1. Junior co-author Easton believes the Q & A outline method leads to bad habits and ineffective direct examinations. In his view, even new trial attorneys should not use it.

prior statements (which will be in the witness's file folder). The rest of the page is then split into three columns: dates and times, witness testimony, and exhibits. This makes it visually simple to know where you are and what you should do next. As the examination progresses, you simply check off what has been done as it occurs.

Example (John Doe—Direct Examination):

Exhibits: 1. wallet (P#2)
2. building photo
3. lineup photo (P#6) (P#1)

Statements: 1. grand jury transcript of 6/20/20, pp. 1-8

2. statement to police in report, p. 7

1.	Background	Brad Smithers; 1242 12th Ave.; there 8 years; homeowner; wife and three children	
2.	5/20/20	three-bedroom home; ranch style; doors, locks, lights	
3.	2:00 a.m.	in home, TV, beer, lights	
4.	What happened	two men break in door; mid twenties, about 5' 10" and 6' 10"; white; take wallet; search home; take watch and computers; make threats; run out	*ID def.*
5.	Aftermath	called police; officers arrived; spoke to them	
6.	Lineup	9:00 a.m. call to station; talked to police; viewed lineup; ID def.; shown wallet; ID'd it	*ID photo*—P#1 *ID photo*—P#6 *ID wallet*—P#2[2]

---

2. Junior co-author Easton prefers to organize his outlines as bullet point lists under headings. For example:

What Happened Inside Home

- two men break in door
  - mid twenties
  - about 5' 10" and 6' 10"
  - white
    - [Point to defendants]
- they have guns
- they take
  - wallet
  - watch
  - computers
- they make threats
- they run out

Junior co-author Easton finds this format easier to use during trial, because he can keep track of which information (i.e., which bullet points) the witness has provided. He can then ask follow-up questions to elicit the facts not yet established.

All the direct examination outlines should be put in your trial notebook (under plaintiff or defendant, depending on whom you represent) in the order you plan to call them in your case-in-chief.

4. Witness List

Finally, you need to keep a list of witnesses in the charts section of your trial notebook. The witness list will show each witness's name, home address and telephone, work address and telephone, cell phone and email address, any other contact information useful for locating and scheduling him during the trial, and a one-sentence synopsis of the witness's role at trial. Some lawyers put the list in alphabetical order. Others put the list in the order in which the witnesses are expected to testify at trial. The witness list is critical for keeping in touch with the witnesses as the trial date approaches and during the trial.

Example (Witness List — Plaintiff):

Frank Miller	accountant who prepared defendant's tax returns
123 North, Chicago (works at home), fmiller@xmail.com	
H (312) 888-1123 W (same) cell: (312) 499-1234	

Mrs. Sharon Jones	bookkeeper at defendant's company
2300 N. Clark, Chicago (works 8-12), ShariJ@worldnet.com	
H (312) 888-9876 W (312) 726-8231 cell: (312) 994-4321	
H ( ) W ( )	

11.13 Developing a Visual Strategy

You need a visual strategy. Getting exhibits in evidence is not a strategy. Using technology, or a particular technology such as PowerPoint, is not a strategy. A visual strategy must clearly present your key information and send key messages to the jurors. It must determine what exhibits and visual aids you will use during the trial, when you will use them, and how you will present them. It also has to meet your budget limitations.

Think about how you develop a trial strategy for witness testimony. You review your theory of the case, themes, and labels. Then you decide what witnesses to call in your case-in-chief, what each witness will testify about, how each witness's direct examination will be structured, and in what order you will call those witnesses. You spend a considerable amount of time creating a strategy for the witnesses in your case-in-chief, the testimonial part of your case. You need to do the same kind of planning for the visual part.

Imagine, for a moment, that you had no live witnesses—that your entire case had to be presented through exhibits and visual aids. You would have to tell the story of your case through a progressive series of memorable images, much like a photographic exhibition or silent movie tells a story. How do you do that?

First, create a series of memorable pictures. Think of exhibits and visual aids as creating pictures that the jurors will imprint in their memories. For example, a large color photograph or a "day in the life" videotape of an accident victim will trigger a lasting image.

Second, move the story of your case forward chronologically, because that is how we are used to hearing stories told. For example, in a breach of contract case, the documents tell the story of what happened when the contract was first signed, when and how the defendant breached the contract, what efforts the plaintiff made to get the work done, and the losses the plaintiff incurred because of the breach.

Third, keep the exhibits and visual aids fresh and new. Jurors tire of seeing the same thing over and over again, so you need to present key information in different ways. For example, in a vehicle collision case, you can use photographs of the intersection, diagrams of the intersection showing how the collision happened, and photographs of the intersection and cars after the collision. This keeps the visuals new and interesting, while highlighting and repeating the key information.

Fourth, keep it simple. In criminal and personal injury cases, decide on the five to ten key images that will highlight your liability and damages evidence. As plaintiff, allocate your key exhibits evenly between liability and damages to let the jurors know that both are equally important. As defendant, have your key exhibits reflect whether you will defend on both liability and damages. In commercial cases that are document-intensive, identify the core dozen or less documents and records that tell the story of the transaction that went bad. Then decide how you can effectively present those documents to the jurors so that they tell your story of what happened.

Will jurors be allowed to take notes during the trial? When jurors cannot take notes, there may be a greater need to use exhibits and visual aids to highlight and repeat key information. In addition, keep in mind that judges usually allow formally admitted exhibits to go to the jury room during deliberations, but usually do not allow visual aids to go to the jury room (because visual aids are not considered evidence). You usually want a key exhibit to summarize your case on liability and damages. Make that exhibit big, colorful, and attractive, so that the jurors will use that exhibit as a reference point when they discuss liability and damages. Jurors often put a large exhibit on the chalk rail in the jury room, where they can constantly refer to it during deliberations. Make sure that this exhibit is one of yours. For example, a large diagram of an intersection, showing the locations of the vehicles, speeds, and distances, can be your key liability exhibit that goes to the jury room during deliberation.

Once you have thought through your visual strategy, you need to incorporate it into your overall trial strategy. In particular, you need to decide which exhibits and visual aids you will use in each stage of the trial: opening statement, eyewitness and expert direct examinations in the case-in-chief, cross-examinations of the opponent's witnesses, and closing arguments.

The last step in the process is deciding, for each exhibit and visual aid, what visual medium to use to present your information and messages. This is where technology comes into play, and where a thorough understanding of technology (or hiring a litigation support firm early in the process) is essential. Remember that technology is a tool to implement your strategy. The earlier in the process you get professional help, the better you will be able to create and implement a visual strategy that effectively highlights key information and sends key messages. However, remain in charge.

Check the courtroom logistics early. These include the location of any windows, and whether they can be draped; the courtroom lighting, and whether it can be turned off or dimmed; power source locations; floor, wall, and table space; and lines of sight for the jurors, witness, lawyers, and judge. Check the existing courtroom technology. Does the room have a document camera, video projector, screen, monitors, and the like? Does the courtroom computer system have presentation software?

Find out early what the judge wants and allows. Must all paper exhibits be downloaded into courtroom computers? Can the jurors be given exhibits notebooks? Will the judge place limitations on what hardware and software you can use in the courtroom, and where you can station it? Popular presentation software programs include PowerPoint, Adobe Acrobat, Summation, Harvard Graphics, and Trial Director. Make sure that the ones you use will be compatible with the courtroom system, or that you can use your own hardware and software in the courtroom.

Determine early what you can spend to present your case visually. There are four broad categories you should consider: (1) graphic exhibits and visual aids, (2) scanned documents, (3) deposition transcripts, and (4) computer animations and simulations. Large graphic exhibits and visual aids, such as foam-core poster board enlargements (30″ × 40″ to 40″ × 60″) of documents, records, photographs, diagrams, maps, and charts, may cost anywhere from $50 to $1,000 or more, depending on their sophistication. Two- and three-dimensional models, depending again on their sophistication, may range considerably in cost. Scanning documents and business records into a computer and coding them for easy retrieval during trial might be costly, but it is often well worth the expenditure in a document-intensive case. Similarly, it might be wise to invest the funds required to take a videotaped deposition with a scrolling transcript. Preparing a computer animation that illustrates an expert's testimony, or preparing a computer simulation of how an event happened, will probably be quite expensive.

The media you use to implement your visual strategy will be significantly affected by your budget. Take this up with the client early, then let your litigation support firm know your cost limitations. For a typical three-day personal injury case, in which the plaintiff uses several foam-core poster boards, a PowerPoint presentation as part of the closing argument, and the videotaped deposition of the defendant, costs may be in the $10,000 to $20,000 range. In larger and more complex cases, it is not uncommon for a party to spend 10 percent of its trial budget on exhibits and visual aids.

For example, consider a personal injury case. Plaintiff might use the following exhibits and visual aids: photographs of the plaintiff before and after the collision; intersection photographs; an intersection diagram to be marked by witnesses; emergency room reports, x-rays, hospital reports, and doctor reports; defendant's videotaped deposition; car repair bills; medical bills; a summary chart of plaintiff's past and future medical expenses; employment records; a summary chart of plaintiff's lost future income; a checklist of key arguments; a damages chart; and key language from jury instructions.

Once plaintiff has an inventory of all the exhibits and visual aids, plaintiff's counsel must decide when to use them: in the opening statement, during the direct examinations of eyewitnesses and experts, during the cross-examinations of defense witnesses, or in the closing argument. Finally, plaintiff must decide how to present them: in their original state, as enlargements mounted on foam-core poster boards, as computer projections on a screen or monitor, or even as handwritten points on butcher paper.

Determine the necessary foundation for each exhibit and who the best witness is to provide it. Plan when in the direct examination of that witness the exhibit should be first used and qualified for admission. If the exhibit can be marked or highlighted, plan how this can be done most effectively and train the witness to do this during the direct examination.

Finally, you need to keep a list of exhibits in your trial notebook. The exhibit list will show, for each party, the exhibit number, exhibit description, and boxes to check showing the evidentiary status of the exhibit—if offered, admitted, refused, reserved, or withdrawn. The exhibit list is essential for you to keep track of the admissibility status of your, and your opponent's, exhibits during trial.

Example (Exhibits List—Plaintiff):

#	Exhibits marked for identification	Offered	Admitted	Refused	Reserved	Withdrawn
1	Construction contract	x	x			
2	Final payment check	x			x	
3a-g	Monthly progress reports (7)	x	x			

11.14 Order of Proof

The last step in preparing your case-in-chief is deciding the order in which you will present your evidence. Your proof will come from four possible sources: witnesses, exhibits, stipulations, and judicial notice. You have control over the order in which you will present your evidence, and you are limited only by the availability of your witnesses. Hence, the principal question is: What order of proof will present my case most effectively?

There are several considerations you should keep in mind in deciding on the order of proof. These include the following:

a. Present your case in chronological order or some other logical progression, as viewed from the jury's perspective. Jurors follow testimony most easily when it is ordered chronologically, particularly when occurrence evidence is involved.

Since jurors are familiar with chronological storytelling, use the same approach with your case unless there is a compelling reason to alter your approach. This is probably the most important consideration in determining your order of proof. It will usually override competing and conflicting considerations.

b. Start with a strong, important witness to give the jury a good initial impression of your case. The first plaintiff witness should give an overview of the case, be credible, focus on the defendant's misconduct, and be safe on cross-examination.

c. Finish with a strong witness. Jurors generally remember what they hear and see first and last. These are the psychological principles of primacy and recency. Use them to your advantage.

d. Begin each morning and afternoon session with a strong and interesting witness whenever possible. Jurors are fresh and retain information better at the beginning of court sessions.

e. If you must call your opposing party or another adverse witness during your case-in-chief, it is usually safer to call him during the middle of your case. If the witness does more damage than he helps, he will not have started your case-in-chief on a bad note, and you can immediately follow him with favorable testimony. On the other hand, lawyers sometimes prefer to take a risk and begin their case-in-chief by calling the opposing party as an adverse witness. This can work well if the witness is unprepared or will make a bad impression on the jury, but it can also backfire.

f. Call important corroboration witnesses immediately after the primary witness has testified. This usually has the effect of driving home important points that the jury will then accept as true. On the other hand, jurors are easily bored. Avoid calling several corroboration witnesses to the same point. Overkill adds nothing, and boring the jury is costly. Sometimes a corroboration witness can be called later so that the jury does not repeatedly hear the same evidence.

g. Several witnesses are sometimes necessary to establish technical elements of proof. These can be boring witnesses. Unless doing so will interrupt the logical progression of your case, these witnesses can sometimes be interspersed with more interesting witnesses. In any event, these technical witnesses should be efficiently presented. Keep in mind, however, that technical witnesses may be necessary both to provide foundations for critical exhibits you want to introduce at a certain time and as predicate witnesses for other witnesses, unless the court will allow you to call witnesses out of turn on your representation that you will "connect it up." (For example, chain-of-custody witnesses are necessary predicate witnesses before an expert can testify to the results of laboratory tests on the evidence involved.)

h. Reading depositions, stipulations, and documentary evidence is inherently less interesting and usually boring. See how you can make this come alive. Choose a good witness for reading in deposition testimony. Consider using short parts of video depositions. Enlarge key documents to make them more appealing. Intersperse this kind of evidence with more interesting proof, unless it will disrupt the orderly presentation of your case. Keep it short—only introduce the truly important portions.

i. Get your exhibits in evidence and show them to the jury as soon as possible. Jurors understand and retain what they see much better than what they hear. Use photographs, diagrams, models, maps, and summary charts (particularly if enlarged), and recordings, movies, and in-court demonstrations whenever possible. Jurors remember dramatic visual presentations. Work particularly on having such exhibits summarize your liability and damages proof. If, for example, the jury will use your intersection diagram during deliberations as their reference exhibit when they discuss liability, this will be a powerful influence.

j. Alternate lay witnesses and expert witnesses to keep the jury's attention.

k. An expert often is a good final witness because he can effectively summarize the evidence in your case. This will capsulize your case just before you rest.

1. Finally, remember that your planned order of proof must remain flexible. Witnesses, particularly experts, have busy schedules and can be available only at certain times. Last minute problems invariably arise, requiring you to adjust your expected order. Remember also that the above considerations can and often will compete with each other so that there is no one way in which your proof should be ordered. As usual, there is no simple solution to these conflicts. Each case must be analyzed, and the advantages and disadvantages of each order considered, to arrive at an order that appears reasonable — one that presents your case in a logical, progressive way that is easy for the jury to follow and understand.

The following examples are simple illustrations of one way in which the proof could be organized in common civil and criminal cases.

Example (Plaintiff in Collision Case):

1. plaintiff
2. eyewitness
3. police officer at scene
4. ambulance driver
5. doctor at emergency room
6. treating physician
7. former employer on damages
8. spouse on damages

Example (Prosecution in Murder Case):

1. eyewitness to shooting
2. first police officer at scene
3. ambulance driver
4. doctor at emergency room
5. pathologist on cause of death
6. second eyewitness
7. arresting police officer
8. detective on defendant's admissions

11.15 Cross-Examination Preparation

Your final trial preparation task is to prepare the cross-examination of your opponent's witnesses. This has been saved for last for a reason. Cross-examination preparation cannot be focused until you know exactly what your theory of the case is, what themes and labels you will use, and what the key factual disputes will be during the trial.

Effective cross-examinations require preparation. Discovery, in civil and most criminal cases, makes it possible to determine what your opponent's witnesses will probably say at trial. Since you know what the direct testimony of these witnesses will be, you can and should prepare your cross-examinations in advance as well.

Preparation for cross-examinations should include the following:

a. Outline each witness's probable testimony on direct examination, including the exhibits she is likely to identify and qualify for admission.

b. Review all depositions, statements, and reports the witness made. For parties, review the amended pleadings and interrogatory answers as well.

c. Ask yourself the key question: What will I say about this witness during closing argument? Your cross-examination should elicit only enough facts to support your closing argument, and nothing more. Many, perhaps most, cross-examinations fail because they are unrealistic and attempt too much.

d. What must the witness admit that is favorable to your side? What exhibits of yours can she identify and qualify? What facts can she testify to that help you? Where has she made previous statements that "lock her in" on testimony that will help your side?

e. What is the witness reasonably likely to admit that is favorable to your side? What testimony is she likely to give that sounds improbable? What testimony is in conflict with other witnesses? What testimony contradicts common sense and the jurors' experiences in life? What testimony conflicts with the exhibits?

f. What impeachment do you have of the witness's probable testimony? Will her testimony conflict with any of her previous statements and reports? Do her previous statements conflict with each other?

g. When you have reviewed the available materials and have collected possible cross-examination ideas into three basic categories—favorable testimony, likely admissions, and impeachment—you need to arrange your cross-examination into specific points. The fewer good points you have, the more likely the jury is to remember them. The jury will never remember ten specific things you cover on cross. Try to keep your major points to a handful, and make sure that they all contribute to your theory of the case, themes, and closing argument. Avoid unimportant points entirely, since they only dilute your strong points.

h. Arrange the points you have decided to cover on cross-examination in an intelligent order. Obtain favorable admissions before you attempt to impeach.

i. Start crisply on a strong point and end crisply on another strong point. Your best points should come first and last, because jurors remember best the things they hear first and last (the principles of primacy and recency).

Successful cross-examinations are almost entirely the product of hard work, thorough preparation and planning, and an understanding of what you can realistically accomplish. There's simply no other way to do it.

When you've completed the cross-examination preparation for each witness, you still need to organize your planned cross-examination and put it in your trial notebook. A common problem of inexperienced trial lawyers here is a lack of organization. During the direct examination they feverishly take notes, and this rarely does anything worthwhile. The better approach is to *take only those notes that will help your planned cross-examination*. This is easily accomplished if you organize your cross notes so that you can integrate anything useful the witness says on direct into your notes.

A common system is to outline the planned cross-examination on one side of a sheet of paper, by specific topics. The other half of the sheet is blank; this is where you will note anything specific the witness says on direct that you can use on cross. This will limit your note-taking during the direct, giving you more time to watch the witness testify, which is usually more useful anyway. Some lawyers put a short synopsis of the witness's expected direct testimony, and a list of prior statements, at the top of the page.

Example (John Smith—Cross-Examination):

DIRECT: Witness will probably testify he was walking down the street late at night, was accosted by a man he claims was the defendant, who claimed he had a gun, and was robbed of $35, and later identified def. in lineup.

STATEMENTS: statement to police (pp. 6-8 of reports)
                        grand jury transcript of 6/20/20

Cross-examination	Direct examination
1. late at night dark, no lights near	1.
2. happened suddenly, not expecting trouble	2.
3. worried about being hurt, looking for gun	3.
4. never saw gun (GJ transcript, p. 7) (statement, p. 8)	4.
5. description to police, general never noted scar on face	5.[3]

Under this system, the only notes you will make during the direct examination are on any specific facts the witness makes that help you on the points you have planned to make on cross. These notes can be made on your cross outline

---

3. Junior co-author Easton believes that you should draft the key parts of your cross-examination questions in advance when possible, in part because a small change in the wording might change your solid cross-examination question, which is really a statement of fact, into one that could get you into trouble. Each "question," which is really a statement of fact, should be followed by an annotation that tells you what document you will use to prove up your "question" if the witness refuses to admit the fact in your question. Thus, a portion of an Easton cross-examination outline would look like the following example:

Poor Lighting Conditions

- The accident occurred at "11:15 p.m."
  o Ex. 32, Officer Anderson Report, p. 1, third line
- It "was dark that night."
  o "Q: What was the lighting like?
  A: It was dark that night."
  Wilson deposition, p. 44, lines 4 to 5
- You "could barely see."
  o "Q: How good a look did you get?
  A: I could barely see."
     Wilson deposition, p. 46, lines 12 to 13

next to the topic involved. In this way, your direct examination notes are useful because they are immediately correlated to your planned cross-examination.

All the cross-examination outlines should be put in your trial notebook (under plaintiff or defendant, depending on whom you represent) in either alphabetical order or in the order you anticipate your opponent will call the witnesses at trial.

11.16 Examples of Trial Strategy

1. The Case— *Robert Johnson v. Mary Smith*

On June 1, 2020, at approximately 5:30 p.m., Robert Johnson's and Mary Smith's cars collided in the intersection of Main and Broadway. Johnson was driving southbound on Main Street toward the intersection with Broadway. Smith had been driving northbound on Main Street and had stopped in the intersection, waiting to make a left turn to go west on Broadway. Johnson was alone in his car, a six-year-old Jaguar sports car. Smith's husband was a passenger in her car, a one-year-old Buick sedan.

Johnson was on his way home from the shop where he worked as an automobile mechanic. Smith was driving her husband, who had been feeling nauseated most of the day, to their doctor's office.

According to Johnson, as he was driving southbound on Main, the light turned yellow when he was about three car lengths from the intersection. It was too late to stop, so he continued into the intersection on the yellow light. He was still traveling about 25 mph, the same speed as the other rush-hour traffic in front of and behind him. Just as he entered the intersection, a car (Smith's car) that had been stopped in the intersection, facing northbound and waiting to make a left turn, suddenly made the left turn in front of him while the light for Main was still yellow. Johnson slammed on his brakes, but it was too late. Johnson's car slammed into the right side of Smith's car.

According to Smith, she was stopped in the northbound lane of Main, waiting to make a left turn on Broadway. The oncoming stream of cars prevented her from making the turn. The light turned yellow, she waited until the light turned red for Main, and then made her left turn. As she was making her left turn, a car, coming southbound on Main, ran the red light and crashed into the right side of her car.

The force of the crash threw Johnson forward. He braced himself by instinctively locking his arms on the steering wheel, but the force of the collision broke his right upper arm and dislocated his right elbow. He also received a classic whiplash injury to his neck. Smith and her husband were shaken up by the collision but did not require medical attention. Both cars were extensively damaged.

Other than Johnson and Smith, the collision was witnessed by a pedestrian at the corner, Ben Jones, and Smith's husband, Robert Smith. Jones's testimony will be consistent with Johnson's. Robert Smith's testimony will be consistent with his wife's.

Police soon arrived. They noted that Johnson's car had about 10 feet of tire skid marks behind it. Main and Broadway Streets are both two-lane roads with parking on both sides of the streets. The single traffic light hanging over the center of the intersection has a three-second yellow light.

Johnson was taken by ambulance to a local hospital. His arm was examined, x-rayed, diagnosed as an elbow dislocation, and put in a cast. His neck was examined, x-rays showed no fractures, and he was diagnosed as having a moderate whiplash injury. Johnson was discharged the next day.

During the month following his injuries, Johnson stayed at home recuperating. His whiplash injury slowly got better, but he still was in substantial pain from the neck and arm injuries. He took prescription medication for the pain.

A month later, Johnson's orthopedic specialist removed the cast. (Johnson had seen this specialist two years earlier for neck pain caused by a mild arthritis, which had responded to heat and medication treatment.) The rehabilitation program began. It consisted of heat treatment and arm-stretching exercises to regain full, pain-free motion and strength in the arm. Johnson stopped doing the exercises after several weeks, claiming that the pain, despite his medication, was too severe, and that it stopped improving his arm by the time he stopped. His doctor instructed him to resume therapy. Johnson did, but stopped after a few weeks for the same reasons. Today his elbow remains tender, especially when used extensively, and the range of motion has still not returned to normal.

Johnson was recently examined by a defense orthopedic specialist. That doctor's opinion is that Johnson should be able to regain full, pain-free use of the arm if Johnson would only continue with the therapy program.

Johnson, 35 years old and married with two children, worked as an automotive mechanic. He tried to return to work since the collision, but the pain and loss of motion prevented him from doing the physical work required of a mechanic. His boss reluctantly laid him off. Johnson has been living on unemployment benefits and savings, and his wife works to make ends meet. Johnson has lived in this town his entire life.

Smith is 60 years old, married with grown children. She and her husband are retired. They sold a small retail store they had owned and managed and moved to this town last year.

The case is scheduled for trial in a few weeks. Plaintiff's complaint alleges common law negligence and violation of statutory driving rules. The case will be tried under the state's comparative negligence law.

2. Plaintiff's Strategy

(Step into the mind of plaintiff's lawyer as he thinks through his approach to the upcoming trial.)

It's now four weeks from the trial date. I've done some of the basic trial preparation. I've reviewed the litigation file, filed all amendments and supplemental responses to discovery, had trial subpoenas issued, and set up my trial notebook. I've already prepared my trial chart, witness list, exhibit list, and proposed jury instructions. (Most of these were already submitted to the court in the joint pretrial memorandum.) I've organized witness folders for the expected witnesses and collected my exhibits in an exhibits folder.

It looks as if this one is really going to trial. My latest demand and the defense's last offer are still miles apart. They just don't see the issues, particularly damages, the way I do. It's time to get serious about putting this case together.

a. Theory of the Case

What's my theory of the case on liability? One thing to avoid is calling this a "who had the red light" case. The jury will probably think a 35-year-old mechanic is more likely to have run a red light than a 60-year-old woman. The better approach is to pick another theory that avoids "red light" issues.

How about calling this a "failure to yield" case? After all, my plaintiff was driving straight through an intersection, and the defendant, trying to make a left turn, turned directly in front of the plaintiff. The defendant had a legal duty to yield to oncoming traffic. Under this theory, it doesn't really matter what color the traffic light was when the cars were both in the intersection. Plaintiff still had the right of way, and defendant still had the duty to yield until it was safe to make the left turn. It seems that this is also a better way to realistically impose 100 percent responsibility on the defendant.

What's my theory of the case on damages? This is my major concern. What I need to avoid is a verdict in the $50,000 range. This would merely be compensation for plaintiff's medical expenses, a year's lost wages, and a little pain and suffering. I need to sell to the jury the fact that plaintiff's elbow condition is permanent, through no fault of his own, that it has reduced his lifetime earning capacity by approximately 50 percent, and that it seriously affects the quality of his life. I'd like to get a verdict in the $400,000 range. This is going to be very difficult.

My theory on damages needs to do three things. First, I'm going to avoid the whiplash injury as the basis for damages. It's a red herring. The arthritis in plaintiff's neck was a preexisting condition and is as likely a reason for his continuing pain as is the whiplash injury. I can't ask the jury to give serious money for this. The better tack is to buy credibility with the jury by taking this position.

Second, I need to sell the idea that a "seemingly minor injury can sometimes have devastating, career-ending consequences." If the jury accepts this idea, they will at least be willing to consider compensating plaintiff for his loss of earnings capacity. (Maybe some references to athletes who have had minor injuries, which were nevertheless career-ending, will work with sports-minded jurors.)

Third, I need to sell the fact that plaintiff truly tried to do the rehabilitation, but couldn't because of the pain, which was caused by the damage to the elbow structures. I need to sell the fact that people sometimes don't come back 100 percent from an injury of this kind. "He made a real effort" is going to be an important part of this case. I need to sell the fact that plaintiff hates not being able to work and has every motivation in the world to recover completely.

b. Themes and Labels

How do I create themes that will focus the jury's attention on my theory of the case? My themes must be easy to remember, must be based on universal truths, and must explain why things happened as they did.

On the liability issue, my factual argument is going to be that the defendant, who was taking her nauseated husband to the doctor, was in a hurry and took a chance by guessing or assuming that the oncoming car would stop when the light turned yellow. I'm going to be careful not to suggest that she is a bad driver, only that the situation that day let her take a chance she might not otherwise have taken. A theme that captures this idea might be "people in a hurry take chances" or "people in a hurry can hurt others," or "it's dangerous to assume what other people will do."

On the damages issue, my themes are pretty clear. I'm going to argue that "common injuries can sometimes have devastating consequences" to explain how the elbow dislocation ended plaintiff's career as an auto mechanic or any other job that requires physical arm strength. I'm also going to argue that "not everyone bounces back 100 percent from an injury" to explain why the rehabilitation program did not restore the arm enough to return successfully to work.

What about labels for people, places, things, and events? I need to dignify the plaintiff; "Mr. Johnson" is appropriate. I need to watch attacking the defendant, who looks and sounds like everyone's model grandmother; "Mrs. Smith" sounds right. However, the Smiths owned a business before retiring. I'll want to mention that they "owned a business" whenever possible, to offset the jurors' possible fears that a plaintiff verdict may ruin the Smith's retirement years.

For the collision, I'll need to create "impact" word pictures. Words like "collision," "impact," "crash," "crunch," "smashed," and so on should draw the picture. For the injury to plaintiff, words like "thrown forward," "felt arm snap," and "arm dangled by his side" will picture what the injury was. For the rehabilitation period, words like "he tried to," "stretching the damaged ligaments," and "despite the pain" should create images of how painful the program was.

The key, then, is to work these themes into my opening statement and closing argument and to work the labels into my entire presentation of the case.

c. Dramatize, Humanize, Visualize

I need to both "re-create" this collision for the jurors so that they can experience what the plaintiff experienced, and show that the collision was sufficiently traumatic to account for his injuries and permanent effects on his life. I also need to make the plaintiff come alive as Robert Johnson, a human being and family man, one the jury can identify with, feel sorry for, and want to help. Only if I get the jurors in a frame of mind where they want to help will plaintiff get substantial damages. Graphic exhibits and "visual" testimony are going to be very important in this case.

d. Opening Statement and Closing Argument

From my theory of the case and themes and labels, and the importance of dramatic, visual evidence, I already know the basics of my closing argument. I'll outline the basics now, and use notes I take during trial to provide the specifics that flesh out the argument. (In closing, I'll need to emphasize damages more than in my opening, since the last impression I want the jury to have is that the real question is what an adequate damages award is, not whether liability has been proved. I'll probably use a damages elements chart, based on the damages jury instruction, to thoroughly review them.)

These basic concepts—theories and themes and labels—must be carried into the opening statement as well. I could start out my opening statement with "this is a case where someone failed to yield the right of way to oncoming traffic, and it ruined Mr. Johnson's life." Whatever it is, I want to get my themes on liability and damages before the jury right away, and mention them several times during my opening.

However, I'll want to focus on liability in my opening. Even though my most difficult trial task is to sell my damages to the jury, I don't want to come across at the beginning of the trial as someone who's interested only in money. Instead,

I'm going to concentrate on how the collision happened, and then describe what happened to the plaintiff's life and what the future holds for him, but avoid talking about dollars. I'll only ask for "substantial damages" or "compensation for what happened" to the plaintiff, but not mention dollar amounts. This will take the emphasis off money and instead focus on the plaintiff as a human being who now needs help.

Finally, I need to make what happened come alive. Standard chronological storytelling—through the *plaintiff's* eyes—to "re-create" how the collision happened, and what happened to the plaintiff afterward, should work well.

Will I want to use visual exhibits in the opening? While this is helpful in some cases, I'm going to avoid them here. A left-turn collision is easy to explain, so there's no necessity for using exhibits. Besides, I want to concentrate on the picture of the plaintiff as a human being, and exhibits won't do much for me there.

e. Jury Selection

What kind of jury am I looking for? I obviously want a jury that will return a favorable verdict, but that's too general to be helpful. What are my strengths and weaknesses? I think I'm in pretty good shape on the liability issue—failure to yield. It's damages I'm worried about. What kind of jurors will award $400,000 to help Bob Johnson rebuild his life? In short, it's time to develop a profile of favorable and unfavorable jurors.

On liability, favorable jurors are likely to be drivers, people who are familiar with the rules of the road and what it's like to drive in rush-hour conditions. I'm going to avoid jurors who have never driven, no longer drive, drive rarely, or are primarily rural drivers.

On damages, I want jurors who can understand mathematics and will follow my lost-future-income proof, particularly from my economic expert. I want jurors who are physically active, both in their jobs and in their leisure interests. I want jurors who are familiar with handling large sums of money who won't be turned off by the prospect of giving a substantial award of money. I'm going to avoid jurors who have desk jobs and are physically inactive. I'm also going to avoid jurors with medical backgrounds who have seen seriously injured persons and will not see the plaintiff's situation as serious. Finally, I'm going to avoid jurors who have had pain in their own lives, particularly older jurors who might see pain as an inevitable part of life. I'm also going to avoid jurors who have started new careers after age 35 (or know of people who have).

What specific voir dire questions do I want asked? I need to know the jurors' socioeconomic levels, since I'm looking for jurors who will be willing to award perhaps $400,000 in damages if the facts warrant it. Therefore, I'll need to ask about residence, education, and jobs to identify jurors used to handling substantial sums of money. I also need to identify persons with sedentary lifestyles who would probably be unsympathetic to the plaintiff. Therefore, I'll need to learn about their interests, hobbies, and spare-time activities. I definitely need to discover if any jurors or their spouses or immediate family have medical backgrounds or employment, since jurors who have seen major physical handicaps will probably not see the plaintiff's condition as significant. Finally, I need to know if any jurors have been injured seriously or were plaintiffs in personal injury lawsuits, since I doubt such jurors will be sympathetic to the plaintiff.

f. Witnesses

I don't have much selectivity with witnesses. Possible witnesses include:

(liability)	plaintiff
	police officers at scene
	bystander/eyewitness
(damages)	emergency room doctor
	emergency room nurses
	ambulance attendants
	treating orthopedic specialist
	plaintiff's employer
	economic expert on lost future income
	occupational expert on future employment
	automobile repair witness on bills
	plaintiff's spouse
	plaintiff's children

Of these, I probably won't call the emergency room nurses, ambulance attendants, automobile repair witness, and plaintiff's children. I won't do anything dangerous, like call the defendant or her husband as adverse witnesses. I plan to keep my case clean and simple.

What do I need to focus on in my case-in-chief? Several things. First, I need to make the jurors like my plaintiff so that they will *want* to help him. I'll do this by showing he's an all-American guy who's held a good job for years and has a stable family life. I'll definitely *avoid* talking about money or financial damages during his direct examination. He'll talk only about his background, the collision, and particularly his motivation and attempts to rehabilitate his arm.

Second, I'll focus on the bystander/eyewitness to support the plaintiff's testimony on how the collision happened. The bystander is the only independent eyewitness, and he supports us.

Third, I'll use witnesses *other* than the plaintiff to prove damages. These will include the employer, spouse, occupational expert, and economist.

Finally, I'll need to prove that the plaintiff genuinely tried to regain full use of his arm, that his condition is probably permanent, and that it prevents him from ever working as a mechanic or in another labor-intensive job. The hospital physician and the orthopedic specialist will be the key witnesses.

g. Exhibits

Several exhibits will be important in my case. On liability, I'll have photographs of the intersection enlarged to 30" × 40" or larger and mounted on foam-core poster boards. I'll probably use one aerial photo and two photos taken from the north and south showing the drivers' views of the intersection. I'll also want one looking north, taken *in* the intersection, to show the defendant's view (this should show how unlikely it is that defendant could watch the only overhead traffic light and oncoming traffic at the same time). I'll also need photos of the two damaged cars. Finally, and most important, I'll have several copies of a large, attractive intersection diagram on which witnesses will mark the key facts that summarize my liability case.

On damages, my main concern is proving permanence of injury. The x-rays will be useful to visualize the displacement of the bones and explain the soft-tissue damage that must have occurred in the joint capsule. The doctors will need large color diagrams of the elbow joint and a working model of an elbow to explain where ligament damage and scarring probably occurred and why some patients never recover fully from this type of dislocation. The jury needs to see *inside* the plaintiff's arm to understand why his injury is a permanent, career-ending one. Finally, whatever visual aids the economist can provide to show plaintiff's lost future income, reduced to present case value, may be helpful (but I'll need to see them first).

h. Order of Proof

In what order will I call these witnesses? My basic plan is to prove liability first, then damages. On liability, the logical choice is to call the plaintiff first, followed by the bystander, and the best police officer at the scene (the one who made the diagram of the intersection and prepared a report about the scene).

On damages, I have a choice. Should I present the medical evidence first or the economic-loss evidence first? The medical evidence should be first because I want to show the jury why the injury ended the plaintiff's ability to work as a mechanic before I start talking about money. This approach also will end my case-in chief on damages, usually a sound order.

My order of proof will probably be as follows:

1. plaintiff
2. bystander/eyewitness
3. police officer at scene
4. emergency room physician
5. orthopedic specialist
6. plaintiff's spouse
7. repair records witness (unless stipulated)
8. plaintiff's employer
9. occupational expert
10. economic expert

i. Cross-Examinations

Through the pretrial memorandum I know that the defense may call only three witnesses: the defendant, her husband (the passenger in her car), and an orthopedic specialist.

This alone tells me a great deal. First, it appears that the defense will attack my case on liability by challenging my version of what happened. I don't think the defense will win on liability, but since this is a comparative negligence jurisdiction, the defense may argue that plaintiff was also at fault and suggest that liability should be apportioned accordingly. Second, the defense will attack my claim of permanent injury through its orthopedic expert (who examined the plaintiff recently). Finally, it looks as if the defense will not contest, and perhaps even ignore, my economic proof on the theory that it's irrelevant because the injury is not permanent, but I will be prepared in case this is incorrect.

What will I need to do during my cross-examinations of these witnesses? My approach to the defendant and her husband will be similar. I need to bring out *facts* supporting my argument that defendant was in a hurry to get to the doctor and that her attention was on her husband. I also want to show that defendant could not watch the overhead traffic light and oncoming traffic at the same time.

With the defendant's husband, I'll simply point out that he was feeling nauseated and couldn't have been paying much attention to the lights or traffic. I'll need to do this gently because the defendant and her husband seem to be nice people.

The cross of the orthopedic specialist will be important since his opinion is that plaintiff should even today be able to rehabilitate his arm fully if he tried. The most I can get out of him is probably two points, but they're important. First, he didn't treat the plaintiff and monitor his progress during the rehabilitation period. Second, not all patients with elbow dislocations recover completely, despite their best efforts. If I can get these points out, I'll stop, because I have enough for my closing argument.

Well, that's about it so far. Now I've got to start preparing my witnesses to implement my trial strategy. At the same time, I've got to keep thinking my strategy through, again and again, refining and shaping it the way I want, and working with my witnesses repeatedly so that what I bring out during their examinations serves my strategy. Time for a fresh pot of coffee.

3. Defendant's Strategy

(Step into the mind of defendant's lawyer as she thinks through her approach to the upcoming trial.)

We offered $70,000 to settle this case (based principally on two years' lost wages, repair bills, and medical expenses); plaintiff rejected it. We're not going to raise our offer, and the insurance company says I should try it. I will. I've got all the preliminary work done, my files are set up, and my trial notebook is organized. Time to start thinking through my trial strategy.

a. Theory of the Case

What's my theory on liability? It's unrealistic to expect an outright win on liability; getting a 50-50 split would be great, although the jury will probably put most of the liability on the defendant. I can't concede liability, however, and I need an approach that may put some of the blame on the plaintiff. If I can show that the plaintiff *may* have entered the intersection on the red light or without appropriate caution, the jury might split liability. After all, it was rush hour traffic, and plaintiff was driving a Jaguar sports car, an expensive adult toy. This image may help me.

What's my theory on damages? I'm much stronger here. Plaintiff wants to retire on this case, and I don't think the jury will let him do so. This is a case where a plaintiff suffers a common dislocation and won't do the therapy or take the pain medication necessary to rehabilitate the arm. Plaintiff wants to be able to sit around his house for the rest of his life and have the defendant pay for it. I can also show that plaintiff didn't follow doctors' orders. If plaintiff had done what the doctors told him, he would be back on the job and his damages would be minimal.

b. Themes and Labels

My themes are going to be important. I need something that will take the focus off the defendant and put it on the plaintiff, if the jury is going to apportion liability. My liability theme needs to suggest that plaintiff was careless.

The short 10-foot skid marks give me a start. They suggest that plaintiff kept his foot on the gas and only applied the brakes just before the impact. If plaintiff had simply braked even one second earlier, or had his foot ready to brake, this collision would never have happened. How about "plaintiff did not give Mr. and Mrs. Smith even one second of caution" or "one second of caution—that's what this case is all about." This then lets me argue that plaintiff shares responsibility for what happened.

On damages, my themes are obvious. "This is a case about a man who won't follow doctor's orders" and "the plaintiff won't try, and wants you to reward him for it." These themes strongly suggest that what the plaintiff is asking for is simply unfair.

Some labels I can use during the trial will create images that help me. Plaintiff was driving a "Jaguar" or a "fancy sports car." This will generate popular images of the typical speeding sports car driver. "Doctor's orders" is another label all jurors will instantly understand. In addition, plaintiff is just "lying around" and "not even trying," additional images that will help me on damages.

c. Dramatize, Humanize, Visualize

I have one clear advantage. Mr. and Mrs. Smith come across as everyone's favorite grandparents. I'll need to personalize them, show the jury what kind of people they are, and make it difficult to return a large verdict against such nice people.

I also need to show that what happened could just as easily have seriously injured Mr. Smith and that he had good reason to be shaken up by the accident.

Most of all, I need to capture the jury's perspective of how this accident happened. I need to have the Smiths tell what *they* saw from *their* perspective. If I can get the jury to visualize what they saw—a sports car zooming through the intersection late—I have a good chance of putting a good portion of the liability on the plaintiff.

d. Opening Statement and Closing Argument

From my theory of the case and themes and labels, I already have the basics of my closing argument. What do I need to accomplish during my opening statement? As defendant, I go second. I need to jar the jury's thinking away from the plaintiff's perspective. I need to get the jury mentally in the back seat of my car and watch the accident happen. To do that I need to tell a clear but attention-getting story of what the Smiths saw at Main and Broadway, and how they were lucky not to be seriously injured.

I also need to suggest, but subtly, that plaintiff wants to retire on this case without any serious efforts on his part to rehabilitate his arm. I need to suggest overreaching and unfairness in what plaintiff is asking. However, I need to give the jury good reasons for reaching these conclusions. Therefore, I need to spell out how plaintiff failed to follow doctor's orders and do his therapy.

Do I need exhibits in my opening? Probably not; I can tell my case without them. If plaintiff uses a large intersection diagram in his opening, I'll make sure that his exhibits are removed before I begin.

e. Jury Selection

What am I looking for in the jury? I'd like jurors who will at least consider my liability case and can find both drivers contributed to the accident. However, my principal job is to keep damages down. I can live with a $70,000 verdict; it's a verdict in the $400,000 range (what I know the plaintiff is shooting for) that scares me to death! What kind of jurors could return such a verdict, and hence are jurors to avoid?

I want the "Buick set"—solid middle-class values, workers, middle-aged or older, property owners. I want jurors who have earned what they have through hard work, who live in modest homes and drive modest cars. I'd love jurors with medical backgrounds, people who accept the idea that pain and physical discomfort are just part of everybody's life from time to time. I prefer desk workers who are physically inactive. Jurors to avoid, then, are the young, low socioeconomic level, manual laborers, athletic, outdoor-oriented. These are probably the dangerous jurors who are capable of giving plaintiff what he wants. My voir dire questions, then, will focus on learning about the backgrounds and experiences that fit my profile of dangerous jurors.

f. Witnesses

The three witnesses I have are no secret: the defendant, her husband, and my orthopedic expert. (I've decided not to call witnesses to contradict the plaintiff's occupational and economic experts. My attitude is that their opinions are based on false premises: that plaintiff's arm is permanently injured, so there's no reason to present contrary evidence. I'll handle these points on cross and in closing argument.)

My direct examinations of Mary Smith and her husband will focus on several points. First, I need to show they're nice people, have worked hard all their lives, and earned the right to retire. Second, I need to show that Mrs. Smith is a careful driver and that she was being *particularly* careful that day, since she had a nauseated husband in her car and she needed to drive smoothly. Finally, I need to show how the accident really happened, through *their* eyes, and how lucky they were to avoid serious injury.

My orthopedics expert is crucial. I need to accomplish two things. First, I need to have the doctor come across as a nice person, not some cold, unfeeling, arrogant doctor. Second, the doctor needs to show how the plaintiff could have, and should have, rehabilitated his arm. He needs to explain that there are two common reasons why rehabilitation fails: lack of motivation, and a medical problem with the arm. If the former, it's the patient's problem. If the latter, surgery can usually correct a physical reason for restricted range of motion in the joint. He needs to show that an otherwise healthy 35-year-old man should generally recover completely from such a dislocation, and in the plaintiff's case he found after examination of the arm that there is no apparent reason that rehabilitation, if actually carried through, would not succeed and get him back on his former job.

I need to prepare the doctor for cross-examination. I know that plaintiff's biggest point is that not everyone recovers completely from such an injury (and he will argue in closings that plaintiff is just one who can't recover completely and that this is not his fault). The doctor needs to point out that if there is an incomplete recovery, the reasons are either motivational or physical.

g. Exhibits

I need a good exhibit to offset plaintiff's intersection diagram. I'll use the same kind of diagram and put the key defense facts on it. If my exhibit looks as good as the plaintiff's diagram, it will support my closing argument that both parties bear responsibility for the accident.

On damages, I need to be sure my doctor has charts and models so he can use them to explain his testimony and keep the jury's attention at the end of my case.

h. Order of Proof

This one's easy. I'll put the defendant and her husband on first, and end up with the doctor. He's my key witness on damages, so he should be my last witness.

i. Cross-Examinations

My cross of the plaintiff will be important on liability as well as damages. If plaintiff's version goes unchallenged, the danger is that the jury will accept it and tune out before I get a chance to put my case on. Therefore, I need to get *my* theory of the case before the jury during the cross-examination.

On liability, my cross of the plaintiff will focus on one idea: When the light turned yellow, he didn't exhibit the kind of caution called for under the circumstances. I know (from the deposition) that when the light turned yellow, plaintiff never took his foot off the gas and held it near the brake; instead, he simply kept going. My argument will be that this is not the kind of caution a yellow light calls for. In addition, I need to suggest that his estimation that he was three car lengths from the intersection is just that—an estimation, and he's not really sure.

The bystander needs to be handled differently. I need to suggest on cross that he wasn't expecting an accident, wasn't paying close attention to the cars since he wasn't driving, and really only noticed what happened *after* it all happened.

The police officer represents an opportunity. I think the 10-foot skid marks he can testify about will help me. I should be able to get him to state that entering an intersection on a yellow light creates a potentially dangerous environment and that a prudent driver is always ready to brake quickly.

What about my cross-examinations of the occupational expert and economist? My closing argument will be that these witnesses are irrelevant because no permanent injury is involved. If I cross the occupational expert at all, it will be brief, perhaps suggesting that a 35-year-old could easily be retrained for other work, if that were necessary. My cross of the economist should also be short. Economists usually compute lost future income based on certain assumptions about future rates of inflation and prudent investment yields. The usual result of their calculations is that lost future income, when adjusted for inflation and reduced to present cash value, creates a sum that in the first year will generate more interest income than plaintiff ever earned in any year. (This usually sounds like an excessive amount to the jury.) I'll also need to stress that he assumed plaintiff's arm injury is permanent, and his entire calculations are based on that assumption. This should give me enough ammunition to argue that the economist's testimony rests on a false assumption, is excessive in any event, and should be ignored.

Plaintiff's spouse is one witness I'll go easy on, or perhaps avoid cross-examining entirely. There's nothing she's likely to say that will help my case. Better to get her off the stand quickly.

The two treating doctors are the last witnesses I need to plan. My direct examination of my orthopedic specialist will provide the points of my cross-examination of plaintiff's doctors. I'll try to get them to admit that a complete recovery after a common dislocation is expected; career-ending injuries are rare, and when they do occur there is usually a medical complication involved; patients unwilling to follow a prescribed therapy program often cause their own failure to recover completely; if pain is serious, a variety of medications can be tried to assist the therapy program; and surgery can usually correct physical conditions that impede a full recovery. They will have to admit that plaintiff's x-rays show no physical problem with the elbow joint.

What do I do next? I need to kick all these ideas around in my mind, refine them, and run them past someone with more trial experience. Then I'll start working with my witnesses. If all goes well at trial, the jury will put at least some of the liability on the plaintiff and will keep damages in the $70,000 range. I think that would be a successful trial result. Better set the alarm clock extra early tomorrow.

11.17 Trial Lawyer's Self-Evaluation Guide

When a trial is over, trial lawyers are only human. They bask in the warm glow of victory or sink into the despair of defeat. Once the trial is over, however, every trial lawyer should ultimately ask: What did I learn from this trial, what did I do well and not so well, and how can I get better?

Good trial lawyers get better because they learn from their experiences. They don't avoid critical self-analysis because "the jury was too stupid to understand my case" or other defensive attitudes. Good trial lawyers review their performances dispassionately and learn from their mistakes.

The following self-evaluation guide may help you review your trial performances in the future.

1. Strategy

Did I develop a persuasive theory of the case?
Did I develop persuasive themes?
Did I develop persuasive labels for people, places, and events?
Did I develop people stories?
Did I identify the key disputed issues?
Did I develop my important facts on the disputed issues?
Did I pursue only what I could realistically accomplish?
Did I anticipate my opponent's strategy?
Did I anticipate problems and weaknesses?
Did I brainstorm my case with others?

2. Execution

a. *Opening*
   Did I present my theory of the case?
   Did I present my themes?
   Did I use my labels for people, places, and events?
   Did I use storytelling to present facts and my case?
   Did I use persuasive exhibits?
   Did I realistically deal with my weaknesses?
   Did I accomplish my purposes efficiently?

b. *Witnesses*
   Did my examinations serve my overall strategy?
   Did I use simple, factual, nonleading questions on direct?

Did I elicit "word pictures" on direct?
Did I present people stories on direct?
Did I use simple, factual, leading questions (i.e., statements of fact) on cross?
Did I "save" my conclusions during cross for closing?
Did I accomplish my purposes efficiently?

c. *Exhibits*

Did I make and use persuasive exhibits and visual aids?
Did I use exhibits in openings, closings, and witness examinations?
Did I provide legally sufficient and persuasive foundations?
Did I effectively manage my own and my opponent's exhibits throughout the trial?

d. *Closing*

Did I argue my theory of the case?
Did I consistently use my themes?
Did I consistently use my labels for people, places, and events?
Did I develop the important facts and logical inferences to support my version of the key disputed issues?
Did I use exhibits, instructions, analogies, and rhetorical questions?
Did I use both logic and emotion?
Did I accomplish my purposes efficiently?

3. Delivery

a. *Verbal*

Did my witnesses and I create "word pictures"?
Did my witnesses and I use "plain English"?
Did I effectively modulate my voice to maintain the jury's interest and emphasize key points?
Did I effectively use pacing and pauses?
Did I have any distracting verbal mannerisms?

b. *Nonverbal*

Did I avoid using notes during my opening and closing?
Did I maintain eye contact with witnesses and jurors?
Did I use reinforcing movement and gestures?
Did I project appropriate attitudes?
Did I have any distracting nonverbal mannerisms?

CHAPTER 12

BENCH TRIALS AND OTHER CONTESTED HEARINGS

12.1 Introduction

"What you say about jury trials is all very interesting, but what if it's not a jury trial? How much of what we know about the psychology of persuasion in jury trials is applicable to bench trials and other contested hearings?" A good question, and often asked. The question is important because "bench trials," also called "court trials" and "trials to the court," are common and becoming more common.

There are two reasons why cases are not tried to a jury and instead become bench trials in which the judge is the trier of the facts. First, the case may involve claims to which there is no right to trial by jury. The claims may involve only equitable remedies, such as injunctions or specific performance. They may involve areas such as probate, domestic relations, juveniles, bankruptcy, or admiralty, in which state and federal law generally do not permit jury trials. The claims may be based on specific statutes, such as the Federal Tort Claims Act, that confer no such right. Second, the parties may either have made no timely demand for a jury trial or have waived their rights to a jury before the case proceeded to trial.

How often do bench trials occur? While complete national statistics are elusive, the following are good approximations. In criminal cases, about 10 to 15 percent of all trials are bench trials, although the percentages can vary significantly among state and federal jurisdictions. In civil cases, about 30 to 35 percent of all trials are bench trials. These percentages rise if the definition of a bench trial includes contested dispositive hearings, such as hearings on petitions for preliminary injunctions, and proceedings before quasi-judicial bodies, such as arbitrations and administrative hearings. Unless you are trying personal injury, employment (where plaintiffs usually demand a jury), or criminal cases (where defendants usually demand a jury), your next trial probably will be a bench trial.

The conclusion is clear: Bench trials are everyday occurrences in civil and criminal cases, in federal and state courts. Every competent trial lawyer needs to know how things are done differently in a bench trial.

12.2 The Law of Bench Trials

The law of bench trials differs from that of jury trials in four basic respects: Trial procedures may differ; evidentiary issues may be handled differently; findings of fact and conclusions of law may be required; and standards of review on appeal are different.

First, trial procedures may differ. FRE 611(a) gives the trial judge substantial power to control trial procedures, and some judges freely use that power. For example, a judge may decide to try the case in bits and pieces, hear witnesses out of turn, hear all the liability evidence first and the damages evidence second, restrict opening statements and closing arguments, receive the direct examinations of experts in statement form, and impose time limitations on each side's presentation of its case. Although a judge may impose these special procedures in jury trials, he is more likely to impose them in bench trials.

Trial procedure may differ in another way. In bench trials, the judge is likely to participate actively throughout the trial, from asking questions during opening statements and closing arguments, to questioning witnesses during their direct and cross-examinations, to telling lawyers about his concerns and interests as the trial proceeds.

Second, evidentiary issues may be handled differently. In jury trials, judges prefer to rule on evidentiary objections before trial (and out of the jury's presence) whenever possible. During bench trials, most judges hear and rule on evidentiary issues as they occur during the trial. Since judges have to hear the offered evidence to rule on the objections, usually little is gained by hearing the objections separately. Keep in mind too that although jurors may dislike frequent objections, judges are used to objections and may actually welcome them if they are directed at significant matters, are well founded, and simplify the case.

However, there is a clear preference for admissibility in bench trials. Judges frequently "let it in for what it's worth," knowing that this is generally a safe ruling. An appellate court is more concerned with whether the trial judge failed to consider proper evidence than whether the judge heard improper evidence. The appellate court often presumes that the trial judge is not improperly influenced by any erroneously admitted evidence.

Third, procedural rules frequently require the trial judge to make findings of fact and conclusions of law at the end of a bench trial. For example, in federal courts, Fed. R. Civ. P. 52(a) requires findings and conclusions in civil cases, while Fed. R. Crim. P. 23(c) permits them in criminal cases. Some states follow the federal approach, while others permit the trial judge to make general findings that dispose of the case. The rules requiring specific findings of fact and conclusions of law are designed to engender care by trial judges and promote meaningful appellate review, since written findings and conclusions detail how the judge evaluated the evidence and reached her legal conclusions. The trial judge can request that the parties submit proposed findings and conclusions, but she should ultimately prepare her own. A memorandum opinion or an oral decision made on the record may be adequate under the federal rules, but these are not favored methods.

Finally, appellate standards make reversing a bench trial because of evidentiary error particularly difficult. Appellate courts presume the trial judge considered only evidence that was properly admitted for a proper purpose, presume the prejudicial impact of erroneously admitted evidence was slight, and presume the judge was not influenced by offered evidence that was properly excluded. If evidence was received over objection, and later the judge determines that the evidence was improperly admitted, appellate courts presume the trial judge was not improperly influenced by that evidence. Good trial judges know this and quickly learn how to keep objectionable matters out of their findings of fact and conclusions of law.

In addition, the trial judge's evidentiary rulings are reviewed by an "abuse of discretion" standard, and findings of fact are reviewed by a "clearly erroneous" standard. Only conclusions of law are reviewed by a "de novo" standard. Coupled with the harmless error rule in FRE 103, these standards are a formidable barrier to appellate reversal. There are only two areas where appellate reversals of bench trials frequently occur: where the record shows that the trial judge misunderstood the required elements of claims, damages, and defenses under the applicable substantive law, and where the record affirmatively shows that the trial judge relied on improperly admitted material evidence in reaching her decision.

These barriers to appellate reversal do not mean, however, that you should not make objections and procedural motions during a bench trial if you believe they have merit. Avoid making technical "form" objections that accomplish little other than to annoy the judge. However, you must make timely and well-founded objections on important substantive matters. If you do not object, the judge can consider the admitted evidence for any proper purpose. And evidentiary objections should always be forcefully argued so that you win them in the trial court.

Make sure the trial judge rules on your objections. Without a ruling, there is no possibility of appeal on that basis. When an objection to offered evidence is sustained, be sure to make a timely and sufficient offer of proof. This is necessary not only to preserve error for appeal, but also to let the judge know what the rejected evidence is so that she has an opportunity to change her ruling. All too often, lawyers think about offers of proof in jury trials but not during bench trials. This is a mistake.

12.3 Know Your Judge

How does your judge conduct bench trials? If you do not know, and he does not say, find out. During the final pretrial conference, ask the judge how he intends to try the case, if he wants to streamline the presentation of witnesses and exhibits, and whether he has any scheduling concerns that may cause the case to be tried in bits and pieces rather than in one block of time. If the judge expresses interest or concern about particular aspects of the case, take note and plan how to address these matters during the trial. Ask the judge if he intends to rule on anticipated evidentiary issues before or during the trial. Some judges have standing orders on how they want trials conducted in their courtrooms.

Ask members of your firm and other lawyers about their experiences with the judge in your kind of case. Ask the judge's former law clerks and court personnel about their observations. Watch the judge during a bench trial or a contested motion hearing for clues on how he acts, thinks, and likes to receive information. Does the judge prefer to get information visually or aurally? If you cannot watch the judge, read a transcript of a bench trial or hearing to determine whether the judge prefers to listen or to receive information visually, for instance, through court papers, exhibits, and other visual aids. How actively does the judge question the lawyers during opening statements and closing arguments? How actively does the judge question the witnesses during direct and cross-examinations? How does the judge handle objections? This knowledge can influence how you present your case and how you and your witnesses can communicate with the judge most effectively.

What is your judge's practice background and judicial track record? People's life experiences influence their views. Judges are no different. They are not legal automatons who dispassionately dispense justice. Judges are human beings with attitudes about people, events, and life in general. Bench directories are a good source of information. *The American Bench* and *Almanac of the Federal Judiciary* are two directories that provide background information on state and federal judges. Many larger jurisdictions have directories that list the backgrounds and procedures of their judges.

For insight about both bench and jury trials from judges' perspectives, please watch Video A.7, "Wyo STI: Judges and Court Reporters Panel."

How well does your judge know your kind of case? Remember that a judge may try several cases each year. As the years go by, that judge develops both expertise and attitudes. A computer search of the judge's name should turn up his published articles, books, and trial court opinions, as well as reported appellate decisions of his cases. Those experiences strongly influence a judge's thinking, because he uses past case experiences to assess evidence.

How much does the judge already know about your case? Here, local trial procedure helps provide the answer. In the federal system, the judge will have lived with your case since it was filed, probably will have ruled on motions during that time, and probably will have held pretrial conferences with the lawyers. If the judge has heard and ruled on important motions, such as a motion for summary judgement or a motion to preclude expert testimony, the judge already will know most of the important facts of the case. In civil (but sometimes not in criminal) cases, the judge will have the final pretrial statement detailing the claims and defenses, uncontested and contested facts, witness lists and a summary of their expected testimony, and exhibits lists. In civil (but usually not in criminal) cases, the judge may want each party to submit a trial memorandum detailing anticipated evidentiary and procedural issues and the party's position on them. A trial memorandum always helps the judge prepare for the trial, but it is particularly important in a bench trial. Influencing the judge about anticipated issues is always more important than educating your opponent.

Procedures vary in state courts. In smaller jurisdictions, the court organization is usually like the federal system in that judges are assigned the case when it is first filed in the clerk's office; the case then stays with that judge for the duration of the process. However, many highly populated jurisdictions use a central assignment system in which some judges only rule on pretrial matters and other judges only try cases. When discovery is complete and the case is ready for trial, the presiding judge will assign the case to one of the trial judges for trial. That trial judge will not have seen the case file before and will know nothing about it. You need to educate that judge quickly and professionally. Court files may be incomplete or unorganized, so give him a bound, tabbed, and indexed set of pleadings, key motions, and orders. Give the judge (and opposing counsel) a trial memorandum detailing the claims, defenses, expected evidence, and anticipated evidentiary disputes. Ask the judge or his law clerk what else he needs to become familiar with the case.

What is the judge's history with the lawyers? The judge may not know about the case but may well know something about the lawyers from prior professional or personal contact and from courthouse gossip. Always remember that the legal profession has a long memory, and professionalism and reputation are important. The judge's impressions about the lawyers will largely be created during the first meeting with the judge after he has been assigned the case. Your conduct during that meeting (and all others) should always send the same message: I am competent, professional, well prepared, and eager to try this case. Trials involve a measure of trust, and lawyers who demonstrate they are trustworthy throughout the litigation process have a distinct advantage when the case is actually tried.

What is the judge's history with the testifying experts? Judges become familiar with the experts that plaintiffs and defendants regularly call as witnesses in commonly tried cases. Judges develop attitudes about them and learn who the good experts and the not-so-good experts are. (Trial lawyers do this; why wouldn't judges?) This history should influence who you retain as experts at the beginning of the case and which experts you choose to have testify at trial.

Finally, what is the judge's history with the parties? Some parties, such as local, state, and federal governments, and large corporations with a major local presence, are regularly involved in civil and criminal cases (and are often represented by the same lawyers). Judges become familiar with these parties and sometimes develop attitudes about them.

Once you know something about your judge, his experiences, and his likes and dislikes, you will be better able to present a case that the judge will find engaging and persuasive.

12.4 Bench Trials Versus Jury Trials

Why do trial judges conduct bench trials differently from jury trials? Three overriding judicial concerns are involved.

First, the most valuable commodity a trial judge has is time. Judges usually prefer settlements to trials and usually prefer bench trials to jury trials. If a case must be tried, judges want to try it as efficiently as possible, and a bench trial is an opportunity to save time. This means that the judge will want the lawyers to stipulate to as many facts and legal issues as possible. The judge will want to minimize evidentiary objections and limit them to important relevance and hear-say issues. The judge will focus quickly on the key disputed facts and issues, will want witnesses ready to testify about those key facts, and will actively discourage unnecessary repetition and proof on collateral matters. Remember that judges are professional observers who usually take extensive notes during a bench trial. Whatever they hear or see, they usually grasp quickly. They will want you to move on to something else just as quickly.

Second, the judge's notion of what he wants to hear and see trumps the law-yers' notions of what he should hear and see. In jury trials, everything you do should be focused on the jury's point of view. In bench trials, everything should be focused on the judge's perspective. Trial judges are concerned about the elements of claims, damages, and defenses, and about how the disputed issues will be proved. Some judges will tell you how they view the issues in the trial, what they see as the key factual and legal disputes, and what they want to hear and see to resolve those disputes. During the trial, the judge will indicate through his questions to lawyers and witnesses where his concerns and interests lie. Heed these suggestions.

Third, in trying to achieve justice, judges often find ways to get around tech-nical legal requirements to achieve what they believe is a just result. For example, in a civil case, the judge will know if an affirmative defense is a complete bar to any recovery by the plaintiff and may look for ways to avoid the affirmative defense. In a criminal case, the judge will know what the result of a finding of guilty on each count of the indictment will be under mandatory sentencing laws and may look for ways to avoid a lenient or harsh outcome. Judges (like jurors) will often be receptive to results that are compromises between an all-or-nothing outcome for the parties.

What does this mean for trial lawyers? Again, three overriding concerns are involved.

First, prepare thoroughly before trial so that you present your case clearly and efficiently to the judge. If you want the judge to treat your case seriously, you must treat it seriously, and that begins with preparation. Follow time limitations. Keep your witnesses informed of the trial schedule and have them available and ready to testify. When you make important substantive evidentiary objections, do so in a timely and forceful way that shows the judge you are well prepared on the facts and know the law of evidence.

Get to the heart of the dispute as quickly as possible, both in presenting your case and in cross-examining the other side's witnesses. Have your exhibits and visual aids organized intelligently and give your lists of witnesses and exhibits to the court clerk and opposing counsel. Focus on your best theory of the case and avoid alternative theories. Stick to the key facts, keep your presentation clear, and be ready to answer the judge's concerns and interests. Be flexible. A judge who is actively involved in the trial may want the lawyers to change direction and focus as the trial progresses. Communicating with the judge is an active process that involves verbal and nonverbal feedback. In short, watch the judge during a bench trial in much the same way as you watch jurors during a jury trial, and take heed of his messages.

Second, project a positive attitude. Judges are experienced, and they quickly sense who is ready and eager to be on trial and who would have preferred to delay or avoid the trial. The lawyer who projects the attitude that she's wanted this case to get to trial for a long time and expects to win it has an advantage. Show you care about your client and your case by treating all phases of the trial seriously.

This includes acting seriously in the judge's presence and having your game face on during the trial. Lawyers learn to look nonchalant when something bad happens during a jury trial; the same attitude helps in a bench trial.

Projecting a positive attitude includes being candid and reasonable. Judges value candor. Be precise and accurate in stating facts and applicable statutory and case law. If your case has a weakness or a problem, address it quickly and openly. If the other side's evidentiary objection has merit, concede the point. Fight only the battles you have to and the ones you can win. If the judge is about to make a mistake, protect the judge (and the record) by tactfully pointing out and correcting the mistake. Lawyers who try to confuse, mislead, or deceive soon lose the respect and trust of the trial judge. When trust leaves, your influence vanishes. This always proves costly.

Judges in bench trials are trying to reach fair and reasonable decisions, and they value lawyers who want the same outcome. Overly aggressive lawyers who appear willing to win at any cost and who value winning big more than being fair and reasonable quickly lose influence. This also proves costly.

Third, keep in mind that an experienced judge is still a human being who reacts to evidence much like jurors do. Impressions, especially first impressions, are important. This means you need to develop a clear theory of the case. Select appropriate themes and labels and use them consistently during the trial. Keep your presentation interesting and moving forward. Focus on the people and show why your people are the good guys, the ones wearing the white hats. Use interesting storytelling techniques. Keep the human, emotional core of the case, discarding the theatrics and embellishments that might be appropriate in a jury trial. Keep your witness testimony focused and vivid. Use visual aids such as blowups, diagrams, charts, and summaries liberally. Judges spend all day listening to lawyers, witnesses, and court personnel talk, so they appreciate exhibits and visual aids that highlight and summarize key information. These visuals provide an important break from the usual routine.

In short, a bench trial should never be "just a bench trial" during which lawyers present evidence in a disorganized, unfocused, boring way, under the belief that it makes no difference because the judge "will sort it all out." A bench trial offers opportunities for strong advocacy by competent trial lawyers at each stage of the trial.

12.5 Stages of a Bench Trial

Judicial concerns are important. They influence what trial lawyers do in each stage of a bench trial.

1. Opening Statements

An opening statement is an opportunity to persuade. Seize the opportunity whenever possible. What kind of opening statement should you make? How should it differ from an opening statement in a jury trial?

Judicial attitudes about opening statements range from "Please proceed with your opening statement" to "Counsel, I'm familiar with the facts and issues in the case and don't need any openings. Call your first witness." What accounts for the difference? Three factors are central: your jurisdiction's rules, your judge's attitude about opening statements in bench trials, and your judge's knowledge about the case from any previous contact with it.

Opening statements are largely discretionary. The federal system has no procedural or evidentiary rule governing them. State rules are largely silent as well. In states that do have a rule, it is usually general, permitting an opening statement that contains a concise and brief statement of the facts the lawyers intend to prove during the trial.

Some judges consider opening statements in bench trials a waste of time and bar them. At the other extreme, some judges want full opening statements. Most judges are probably somewhere in the middle. Find out your judge's preference. The final pretrial conference is a good time to ask.

Some judges vary their procedures depending on their previous contact with the case. The trial judge who has had the case since it was filed will be familiar with the facts and issues. In such cases, judges often either bar opening statements or permit only brief ones. In state jurisdictions using the assignment system, the judge will know little about the case and is more likely to permit full opening statements.

If your judge's practice is to bar or severely restrict opening statements, the final pretrial statement becomes all the more important. If the parties file a joint pretrial statement and can agree on the statement of uncontested and contested facts, there is no problem. If the parties cannot agree, each side will draft its own version. Regardless of how the statement is created, make sure it clearly reflects your positions on the uncontested and contested facts and issues in the case.

If the judge does not want to hear opening statements, try to change the judge's mind by asking to make a "brief" opening statement that will focus on the key factual and legal issues. Many judges will relent if the lawyers ask to make short openings. If the judge relents, make sure you are brief and that your opening focuses her thinking. If you do not push the judge to let you make at least a short opening statement, the judge may well conclude that any opening statement you would have made would not have been important anyway. At worst, the judge may think you have a weak case.

If the judge permits an opening statement, what should it contain? How should it be delivered?

An opening statement in a bench trial should help the judge understand how you intend to prove your case. This necessarily involves both law and facts. The judge will be focusing on the elements of the claims, damages, and defenses and how the evidence correlates to those elements. After all, the judge probably will make written findings of fact and conclusions of law at the end of the trial. There is no problem talking about the law during a bench trial, so spell out the required elements of your case, point out which ones will be contested, and show how you intend to prove those contested elements. That's what the judge will focus on during the trial. A good opening statement provides the judge with an organization of the facts and how they relate to the legal issues, a chronology of events if appropriate, and a general understanding of what happened and who is involved. If visual aids will help the judge—and they almost always will—use them.

Do not assume the judge is an expert on the applicable law. While any judge knows the elements of a common negligence or contract claim and the usual burdens of proof in civil and criminal cases, he may not know the elements of less commonly tried civil claims, criminal charges, or affirmative defenses. He may not know the burdens of proof applicable to particular claims and defenses or the existence of certain presumptions. Now is the time to gently educate the judge on what needs to be proved. If the judge is up to speed on the law, he will let you know. A good procedure is to have a copy of the pattern jury instructions for the elements of every claim, defense, and permissible damages that would be given if the case were tried to a jury. If there are any disputes over what needs to be proved to make a *prima facie* case on a claim or defense, or over what the proper measure of damages is, give the judge a copy of the appropriate instruction.

Second, tell the judge about the key facts you will present that will prove what you legally need to prove. In a bench trial, the judge is not moved by overly emotional storytelling, blatant appeals to sympathy, or repetitions of your strongest points, but this does not mean that you should sterilize your facts either. Keep the jury trial basics—vivid people stories told in a chronological or other clear way—but avoid the histrionics that will turn a judge off. Keep the drama, but avoid the theatrics. Remember that judges form impressions quickly based on their previous case experiences. If your case is different from the usual case, make that clear. And always tell the judge what specific damages and other relief you are seeking at the conclusion of the trial. The judge cannot read your mind and should not have to.

Project a positive attitude when you give your opening statement, no matter how short. Judges quickly sense whether you believe in your case and whether you expect to win. An opening statement in a bench trial can incorporate more law, and although the factual narration may not have the drama and theatrics appropriate to a jury trial, it should never be dull. Address the judge directly, maintain eye contact, and use your voice and body language assertively. Your attitude sends important signals—about you, your client, and your case—at a time when the judge is sensitive to such signals.

If the judge asks questions during your opening statement, address them immediately, much as you would in an appellate oral argument. Nothing irritates a judge more than to have a lawyer ignore one of his questions. If you do not know the answer, admit that and tell the judge you will have an answer shortly. Too many lawyers think they should always know the answer, and, if they don't, they make one up on the spot. Tell the judge, "I don't know, your honor, but I'll research it and file a brief on that point first thing in the morning."

Finally, evidentiary objections during opening statements are generally a waste of time in a bench trial. They accomplish little other than annoying the judge.

2. Direct Examinations

The core of most cases is the direct examinations of your witnesses in your case-in-chief. In what order should you call them? How should you organize the individual direct examinations? How should you present the deposition testimony of absent witnesses? Should you call the opposing party as an adverse witness? These are key decisions in both jury and bench trials.

First, try to call witnesses in the same order you would in a jury trial: Start strong, end strong, and avoid weak witnesses whenever possible. In bench trials, starting strong is just as important since judges also form impressions quickly. Try to call a witness who can tell the whole story at the beginning of your case, particularly if the judge is trying the case with breaks. The reason is the same as in jury trials: Making an initial strong impression is key. Call the witnesses in the order that tells the story of your case most effectively. It usually is a mistake to call witnesses out of order on the theory that it makes no difference to the judge in a bench trial. It does.

Avoid calling unnecessary corroboration witnesses. Unless the case hinges on disputed versions of events, transactions, or conversations (in which case you will want to call additional witnesses to buttress your side's version), judges are seldom influenced by witnesses who only corroborate what the judge has already learned from other witnesses or exhibits. In fact, a judge may cut the testimony short once she sees the witness is contributing nothing new.

Be sure to make a timely request to exclude witnesses from the courtroom during the trial, something lawyers frequently forget in the more informal atmosphere of a bench trial. (Under FRE 615, the exclusion order does not apply to parties, their representatives, or other essential witnesses, and some judges permit expert witnesses to remain in the courtroom and listen to each other's testimony.)

Direct examinations must be focused, and this is particularly true in bench trials. The judge wants you to get to the core of the testimony quickly. Therefore, keep the background information short and get to the point. Remember that most of any witness's testimony will be undisputed, so a reasonable amount of leading to elicit undisputed but necessary testimony will be permitted. However, when you elicit core testimony, make sure the witness does the testifying.

You can streamline the direct examination by incorporating stipulations and pretrial statements. For example, if the witness is testifying about a particular business meeting, you might say: "Your honor, Stipulation No. 6 covers when and where the meeting took place and who was present," and then immediately examine the witness about the conversations during that meeting. You might say: "Your honor, in the final pretrial statement the parties agreed that the defendant had authority to enter into binding contracts," and then go directly into the terms of the oral contract. The judge will appreciate efforts to cut through the preliminary and uncontested information quickly to get to the heart of the matter.

Efficiency and focus, however, should not come at the price of diluting the impact of the direct examination. Witnesses need to be prepared so that they testify forcefully and persuasively. Avoid the common mistake of thinking that since it is "just a bench trial," the judge wants only the facts and cannot be influenced by effective testimony. Judges appreciate well-prepared witnesses who communicate effectively as much as jurors do, and they hate lengthy, boring testimony as much as anyone else does. Keep the testimony vivid and visceral, leaving out only the theatrics. This is particularly true when the case hinges on the credibility of witnesses who testify to differing versions of disputed events or transactions. Think of ways to present the testimony creatively, remembering to incorporate exhibits and visual aids into the examinations whenever appropriate. Judges, like jurors, often would rather see it than just hear it.

Direct examinations in bench trials differ from jury trials in one important way. The judge may participate actively in the examinations. This can take two forms. Some judges will tell you where they want the direct examination to go. For example, the judge may say, "Counsel, I think I understand the background to this dispute now. I'm particularly interested in this witness' memory of the conversation between the presidents of the two companies." Some judges will tell you where they do not want the direct examination to go. For example, the judge may say, "I think I've heard enough about how the company generates and creates its records from other witnesses. Let's move on to something else." Heed the advice.

The other way judges participate is by directly questioning the witnesses. The questions may be to get additional information. For example, the judge may ask, "Ms. Williams, why didn't you write your memo about this meeting until three days later?" The questions may be to get clarifications, for example, "Mr. Johnson, I didn't follow you there. Exactly where were you when you had this conversation?" Some judges will ask questions during the examination, while others will try not to interrupt the examination and ask questions only at the end of the direct or cross-examination. Expect these interruptions, prepare your witnesses for them, and make sure that they answer the judge's questions immediately and candidly.

How should you present the deposition testimony of unavailable witnesses? Ask the judge. Most judges want the lawyers to mark up the deposition transcript to highlight what they believe is admissible and important. Some judges want the lawyers to make summaries of the relevant portions and to excerpt the actual questions and answers on key points. If the deposition was videotaped, most judges want to watch only the parts the lawyers designate as important. Whatever the method, you can be sure that the judge does not want you to read, with a "witness" on the stand, the questions and answers from the entire deposition transcript. Nor does the judge want to read extensive portions of any transcript. Make sure that the transcript or videotape is marked as an exhibit and is formally admitted in evidence.

Finally, should you call an adverse party as a witness in your case-in-chief? Lawyers, particularly for plaintiffs, often call the adverse party early in their case-in-chief, either hoping to catch the party unprepared or expecting that the party will make a bad impression and damage his own case. Calling the adverse party, of course, involves the risk that the strategy will fail. Is the risk different in a bench trial?

Remember that the judge is an experienced and sophisticated observer who understands the underlying strategic considerations. As such, your decision to call an adverse witness is less likely to surprise him and perhaps less likely to influence him. If you must call an adverse witness to establish a necessary element of a claim or defense, the judge will understand why you are calling that witness and assess the situation appropriately. On the other hand, if the only reason you are calling the adverse party is to badger him—all you have is showmanship, not substance—the judge will quickly understand that as well. Always ask yourself: What impact will this have on the judge?

3. Cross-Examinations

Should you cross-examine a particular witness? In jury trials, jurors expect cross-examination to follow every direct. Therefore, some lawyers ordinarily conduct some cross-examination of almost every witness in a jury trial. Bench trials, however, are different. The judge understands cross-examination and neither expects nor wants you to cross-examine unless you have something important to bring out. Put another way, judges have little patience with long-winded, rambling, unfocused cross-examinations, especially on collateral points that will not change the outcome of the case. This is not a good idea in a jury trial, and it is a terrible idea in a bench trial. When judges see these things happening, they usually will not hesitate to tell you. Do not let your cross-examinations reach that point.

Avoid trivial impeachment. In the heat of battle, lawyers sometimes feel that any inconsistency, no matter how minor, must be forcefully brought out. Remember, however, that judges understand impeachment, and they know what is meaningful and what is not. They know that witnesses, being human, rarely say exactly the same thing when repeatedly describing events and transactions. Minor differences, such as "the car was going about 25 mph," and "I think the car was going 25 to 30 mph," are not worth bringing out. The judge will quickly assess trivial impeachment for what it is: The lawyer has nothing significant to bring out during cross-examination of this witness.

Judges, being experienced, want you to do two things when you cross-examine: Get to the point and avoid the theatrics.

First, get to the point. Judges usually get the point of the cross-examination much more quickly than the average juror. For example, if you wish to show that a witness is biased in favor of the opposing party, simply bring out the fact showing the basis for bias—"The plaintiff owes you $100,000, doesn't she?"—and leave it alone. The judge will immediately understand the point; nothing more is necessary.

Second, avoid the theatrics. Judges are relatively immune to the atmosphere lawyers generate during cross-examination, particularly when it comes to impeachment. Before a jury, impeachment should progress step by step—the commit, credit, and confront method—and be accompanied with an attitude that signals to the jury how it should view the impeachment. Judges, on the other hand, know the impeachment technique and the reason for it but differ in their reactions to it.

Some judges just want the bottom line—the actual impeachment—without the customary build-up. For example, if a witness testifies that he saw the crash, on cross-examination you can simply ask him about making a prior inconsistent statement—"You told Officer Smith right after the crash that you only saw the cars after they had already collided, right?"—and leave it alone. The judge will immediately understand the point. Some judges like to see the impeaching document. If that is the case, have an extra copy available for the judge.

Other judges (often the ones who were experienced trial lawyers themselves) enjoy seeing good lawyers employ good impeachment technique. With such judges, the impeachment technique can approximate what you would do in front of a jury. How do you know what your judge likes and wants? Look and listen for the judge's verbal and nonverbal cues. If the judge looks resistant or put upon, adjust appropriately.

In some situations, judges may have more patience than jurors. Although they want you to get to the point, judges may let you go on longer during cross-examination than jurors might, so long as you continue to establish important points. This is particularly so if the cross-examination involves financial, technical, or scientific information and the witness is an expert. Jurors quickly get bored or confused; judges are more likely to understand that you are scoring points.

4. Exhibits

Should you use exhibits and visual aids during bench trials? If so, how will the judge rule on admissibility issues? How should you select the exhibits and visual aids? And how should you present them during the trial?

Some lawyers mistakenly think that since the case is "just a bench trial," it is not worth the time and expense to make serious courtroom exhibits because the judge likely will not be influenced by them. Talk to judges and you hear a different message: "I spend almost all my time listening to people talk. Why wouldn't I appreciate visual aids in a bench trial?" Judges, just like jurors, appreciate effective courtroom exhibits, find them influential, and want you to use them during bench trials.

Second, how will the judge rule on admissibility issues? Judges dislike dealing with technical foundation issues during trial. It is time-consuming and rarely accomplishes anything. Hence, they usually pressure the parties to stipulate to the admissibility of, or at least the foundation for, each side's exhibits before trial. (This means you must decide, before trial, which of your and your opponent's exhibits you are willing to admit in evidence by stipulation.) If that does not work, many judges deal with foundations informally at trial, rather than requiring a technically precise foundation, and pay attention only to serious relevancy or hearsay objections. When it comes to admitting exhibits, the "I'll let it in for what it's worth" approach is common.

In bench trials, judges do not want to be bothered with technical foundation issues. They want to focus on the big picture. Save your evidentiary objections for key exhibits and make only serious and well-founded relevancy and hearsay objections.

Third, how should you select exhibits and visual aids for a bench trial? The short answer is: exactly the way you would if it were a jury trial. Judges are human. They enjoy seeing exhibits and learn and remember better by seeing rather than by hearing. It is a big mistake to assume that judges will not be influenced by exhibits and visual aids. Courtroom exhibits send a positive message to the judge: This lawyer believes in his case and believes it is important, so he spent time and money to ensure that his exhibits make his case clear.

Consider using blowups of photographs, diagrams, records, documents, and other visual aids. Mount them on poster board or make them part of a computer presentation. Make them colorful and attractive. Judges, like jurors, particularly appreciate charts, diagrams, and summaries that show chronologies of events, steps in processes, and compilations of technical or detailed information. You might use exhibits in conjunction with witness testimony, the same way you would in a jury trial. Consider using computer animations and simulations that visualize and explain your expert witness's testimony.

Use FRE 1006 to condense the presentation of voluminous records. FRE 1006 permits making summaries of voluminous writings, recordings, and photographs that cannot be conveniently examined in court. Even though a summary is admissible without having the documents on which the summary is based first admitted in evidence, good practice dictates that the underlying documents be available in case the judge asks for them. If appropriate, cross-index the summary to the underlying documents. Judges love FRE 1006. It is a great rule to streamline the presentation of documentary evidence, and judges expect you to use it.

In bench trials involving more than a handful of documents, prepare a tabbed and indexed exhibit book or ring binder of your exhibits for the judge (and extra copies for opposing counsel and witnesses). Number the exhibits and tab them chronologically, by count, or in another logical way so that judge, lawyers, and witnesses can quickly find the appropriate exhibit. This kind of preparation again sends positive signals to the judge. Many judges have their own preferred ways of identifying, marking, and organizing documents for trials. Find out if your judge has preferences. If she does, follow them.

If the judge does not want her own set of exhibits, have a courtesy copy of each exhibit available as it is being discussed by the witness. For example, if the witness is testifying while using a blowup of an intersection diagram, give the judge a letter-sized copy of the exhibit. Many judges like to annotate their copy of the exhibit with notes as the witness testifies.

Finally, do not just give the judge a pile of preadmitted exhibits, thinking that the judge can, or will want to, "figure out" what the exhibits show. Not all exhibits are self-explanatory. Complicated records, such as financial and accounting records, need explanations and interpretations from witnesses, often experts, who can make sense of them and point out their significance. In these situations, the witness is the guide that takes the judge through the exhibits, explaining what they show and how they tie in to the other exhibits.

5. Experts

Expert witness testimony in bench trials often differs substantially from jury trials. The reason is FRE 611(a), which gives the trial judge power to control the "mode . . . of examining witnesses." Many judges use that power here, and it affects three areas of expert testimony: the expert's qualifications, the way the expert's testimony is presented, and questioning by the judge.

First, the judge is likely to short-circuit the expert qualifications and other background information to save time. Many judges ask the parties to stipulate to the qualifications of all the experts as meeting the minimum standards of FRE 702. Since almost all experts meet those standards, most lawyers will stipulate. Many judges then ask for the expert's résumé or CV (curriculum vitae) in lieu of actual testimony about the expert's education, training, and experience. The CV is commonly regarded as either a business record or otherwise reliable hearsay. The CV is marked as an exhibit and admitted. Since this happens so frequently, make sure you have a clean copy of the expert's CV available and that the CV details the expert's background appropriately, so that the judge can make an accurate credibility assessment. Remember that most experts write their CV to impress other experts in their field or potential clients. For courtroom purposes, make sure their CV will impress the judge.

Second, judges vary their procedures in taking testimony from experts, particularly on direct examination. Many judges treat experts like any other witnesses, with the usual direct, cross, and redirect examinations conducted by the lawyers. However, some judges like to get the expert's direct examination in written statement form, sometimes called a "written direct." Only the cross- and redirect examinations are done by actual questioning in court. (This is a common procedure in bankruptcy courts, where direct examinations are usually presented in affidavit form.) The idea is that having the direct examination in written form, rather than live testimony, saves time. Some judges ask for the expert's written report and use it in lieu of live testimony. If the judge wants some form of written direct, find out before trial and prepare the expert accordingly. If the judge wants to use the expert's report in lieu of live testimony, make sure the expert prepares her written report so that it clearly spells out her opinions and the reasoning she used to reach her opinions.

Third, judges often become actively involved in questioning the experts, both on direct and on cross. After all, if the judge is going to decide the case, the judge will want his questions answered. Welcome this as an opportunity. If the judge signals through his questions where his interests and concerns are, this is valuable information. Some judges ask questions whenever they want, while others try to wait until the direct or cross is completed before asking questions. Prepare your experts for this and make sure they immediately and directly answer the judge's questions.

Judges generally relax the technical requirements for expert testimony and permit latitude on both direct and cross to get to core issues quickly. For example, form objections such as leading or compound questions routinely are overruled, because judges want to get to the heart of the testimony quickly. Save your objections for important matters.

Trial judges are the last generalists. They have substantial knowledge in many areas but are experts in few. Do not assume that your judge is an expert on medicine, financial and accounting procedures, technology, or whatever else is involved in your case. Find out before trial. Make your expert the teacher and guide who explains what she did and why she did it. Do it without the expert sounding or acting condescending. Use visual aids to illustrate the expert's explanations. If the expert is being too basic or is moving too fast, the judge will probably let you know by telling you directly, through his questions to the expert, or through his nonverbal responses. Heed the signals and modify the expert's presentation accordingly.

On cross-examination, remember that experienced judges have seen all the routine cross-examinations that are done of common types of experts. For example, every civil trial judge has seen economists cross-examined on the discount rate they used to determine the present cash value of lost future income. In a bench trial, this kind of information can be covered very quickly on cross-examination.

Finally, keep in mind that trial judges become familiar with the experts who frequently appear in court. These include doctors, economists, engineers, and malpractice experts who are the daily fare in commonly tried cases. Trial judges soon know, from their own experience and from talking to other judges, who usually testifies for plaintiffs, who usually testifies for defendants, and who are the experts of last resort. Over time, trial judges may have formed attitudes about some of those experts, and their attitudes come into play when those experts testify. Learn about your expert's experiences with your judge early, preferably when you first consider retaining the expert.

6. Closing Arguments

The closing argument is your last opportunity to persuade. In a bench trial, what kind of closing argument is effective, and how does it differ from a jury trial? How should you deliver it? What kind of involvement does the judge have?

For judges, the decision in most bench trials is primarily analytical, not emotional. This is not to say that emotion plays no part, because judges are hardly blind to the human consequences of their decisions. Rather, it means that as the judge is listening to the arguments, he is thinking of his decision, not just in general terms, but in terms of the elements of the claims, damages, and defenses raised in the pleadings. The judge is thinking: Has the plaintiff proved the elements of her claims and damages? Has the defendant proved the elements of any counterclaims and affirmative defenses? Have they been proved to the required level of proof? After that comes the emotional part: Is this a fair and just result, or does the case allow for compromise? In short, the judge is thinking: Can I rule for one side, and should I? Good lawyers understand this and make arguments that address both concerns.

First, show the judge that you have proved what you are required to prove (or disprove). A sound approach is to structure your argument around the elements instructions for the claims, damages, and defenses that would be given if you were arguing a jury trial. Some judges appreciate having a written outline of your argument with bullet points. (In fact, some judges ask that the lawyers submit their closing arguments in written form.) Refer explicitly to the particular witness testimony and exhibits that prove (or disprove) these elements. The judge will have to do this later anyway. Use visual aids, particularly those that summarize key facts, chronologies of events, and relationships of parties and witnesses. Be accurate. Avoid misstating or exaggerating facts. Most judges take detailed notes during bench trials; if they get the sense that your "proof" of any required element requires stretching the facts, you're in trouble — in the present case and in future cases as well.

Give the judge a precise computation of your suggested damages, including percentages of relative liability for each party, present cash value of lost future income, prejudgment interest to date, and other compensable damages. Show how each item of damages was calculated and the evidence on which it is based. Prepare visual aids that make your requested damages clear, much as you would in a jury trial. Do not expect the judge to make these technical computations on her own.

Second, show that this is the right and fair outcome. Remember that in a bench trial, a judge can usually find a reason to make the case come out the way he thinks it should come out and justify that outcome in his findings and conclusions. Just like jurors in a jury trial, the judge wants to feel good about the result. Avoid making exaggerated claims or taking untenable positions that an experienced judge (and an appellate court) will find implausible. This is particularly so when asking for damages. Judges know what is reasonable and what jurors and other judges are likely to do given the facts at hand. The lawyer who appears to want a fair and reasonable result will have more influence with the judge.

This means that you need to be sensitive to the judge's instinctive inclination to find a compromise outcome that is still supported by the facts. Always ask yourself: If the judge were to reach a compromise outcome, what would it likely be, and can I live with that result? If so, argue why such an outcome is fair and is the least that should be done. If not, show why the outcome is unfair and why another outcome is the right one.

Third, address the concerns the judge has expressed during the trial through his comments and questions to witnesses and lawyers. Every judge sends signals during the course of a trial. Now is the perfect (and last) time to address these concerns and incorporate them into your argument.

How should you deliver a closing argument in a bench trial? First, make it substantially shorter than it would be before a jury. Judges often impose time limits. Even if they do not, they expect your argument to be short and to the point. Second, avoid the theatrics that may be appropriate in a jury trial. Overly emotional arguments and "war stories" that may be appropriate to make a point before a jury usually turn judges off. Stick to the law and the facts.

This does not mean that the closing arguments should be boring. Avoid the theatrics, yet show you are serious about the case, committed to your client, and have the winning facts. This is largely a matter of tone. Address the judge directly, maintain eye contact, and use your voice and body language assertively. Never give the judge a reason to think that you are just going through the motions or just "making a record."

Finally, what does the judge do during the arguments? Again, judges differ. Some judges sit and listen quietly, take notes by hand or on a laptop computer, and never interrupt. When this happens, lawyers never know whether the judge is actually listening because she is undecided or whether she already has decided what to do and is just waiting for you to finish. Since you never know for sure what the judge is thinking, keep arguing! (An exception may be in criminal cases in which the defendant is going to trial only to preserve error to appeal the judge's dispositive pretrial ruling, usually on a motion to suppress evidence or a confession. In such cases, your closing should be short, since you know the judge will find your client guilty based substantially on the evidence or confession, and you will then appeal from the judgment.)

Most judges ask questions during the closing arguments in bench trials. The questions can be about the evidence, elements of claims, damages, and defenses, and applicable case law. When this happens, lawyers never know whether the judge has genuine questions because he is still undecided or whether the judge has already made up his mind and is merely making sure that his grasp of the facts and law is defensible. Since you never know for sure, answer the judge's questions immediately and directly. A closing argument in a bench trial can closely approximate an appellate oral argument, where the lawyer's prepared argument is frequently interrupted with questions from the bench. Answering the judge's questions is always more important than your planned argument. If you do not know the answer, be candid. Tell the judge that you do not know and offer to file a memorandum on the point quickly.

During the arguments, the judge may signal, or even flatly state, which way he is inclined to rule. Deal with that reality. Try to modify his thinking rather than clash directly with it, much the way you would handle a judge's tough questions in an appellate oral argument.

7. Findings of Fact and Conclusions of Law

In a bench trial, the judge may be required to make findings of fact and conclusions of law. In federal courts, Fed. R. Civ. P. 52(a) requires them in civil cases, and Fed. R. Crim. P. 23(c) permits them in criminal cases. Some states follow the federal approach, while others permit the trial judge to make general findings that dispose of the case.

How will the trial judge make his findings of fact and conclusions of law, if he is required to make them? The recurring advice applies here as well: Know your judge.

Some judges like to decide the case immediately after the closing arguments and rule from the bench. Some take a short recess, then come back on the bench to announce the decision. Other judges always take time before announcing a decision and often do it in conjunction with issuing written findings and conclusions.

Some judges prefer to make findings of fact and conclusions of law on the record by dictating them in open court or reciting them in a memorandum order. This is common when the facts are uncomplicated and the issues simple. Other judges want the lawyers to draft proposed findings and conclusions and submit them to the court. Still other judges want transcripts of witness testimony to incorporate into the findings of fact. If judges want submissions from the lawyers or transcripts of testimony, it will be some time before they will be able to hand down their findings and conclusions.

If the judge wants the lawyers to draft proposed findings of fact and conclusions of law, a common procedure in state courts, use the opportunity. Spell out the elements of the claims, damages, and defenses. Recite the testimony of the witnesses and admitted exhibits. Show how the elements have been proved (or not proved) by the evidence. While the judge will probably draft the final findings and conclusions herself, your proposed findings and conclusions will serve as a blueprint, and the judge may incorporate parts of your proposed findings and conclusions into her final decision.

Under Fed. R. Civ. P. 58, it is the entry of judgment (not the issuing of the findings and conclusions) that terminates the case and starts the clock running for purposes of appeal. The date final judgment is entered is critical, since the time for filing a notice of appeal cannot be extended.

12.6 Other Contested Hearings

Bench trials, of course, are not the only kind of contested nonjury hearings. Courts frequently hear pretrial motions in proceedings that include the presentation of witnesses and exhibits. Court-ordered mandatory arbitration of smaller cases and medical negligence cases is common in many jurisdictions. Commercial contracts, particularly in the banking, securities, insurance, construction, and employment areas, frequently provide for arbitration of disputes in lieu of recourse to the court system. Administrative hearings before federal, state, and local regulatory bodies are common. Such proceedings may be before one person or may use a panel of three or more persons.

Preparation for representing a party in such contested proceedings is essentially identical to preparation for a bench trial. Learn the procedures and rules of evidence that will be followed in that proceeding. Research each judge, hearing officer, or arbitrator who will be conducting the proceeding. This is particularly important, because frequently the person or persons conducting the hearing will already have expertise in the subject matter, and you need to know that and modify your presentation appropriately. Maintain your assertiveness and dedication to your client's cause, but avoid the dramatics that would be appropriate only in a jury trial. In short, remember that effective advocacy counts in other contested proceedings just as it does in bench trials.

> ◼️◀ For an overview of bench trials and other matters without juries, please watch Video A.6, "Wyo STI: Bench Trials, Motions, and Other Hearings."

12.7 Conclusion

What do you need to know to try bench trials (and other contested hearings) effectively? First, understand how bench trial procedures differ from jury trials. Second, understand how your assigned judge will conduct the bench trial in your case. Third, recognize that the judge is an experienced jury of one, and wants you to be efficient, wants you to present the evidence a certain way, and wants the decision to achieve justice. Finally, prepare as if the case were a jury trial, then modify it appropriately for a bench trial. Keep the drama and human interest, lose the melodrama and theatrics. If you know how to try a case persuasively to a jury, there's no reason you can't try one persuasively to a judge as well.

INDEX